Brazil, Portugal and the Netherlands (1595-1630)

Daniel Strum

Brazil, Portugal and the Netherlands (1595-1630)

RIO DE JANEIRO

STANFORD, CALIFORNIA

2013

The Sugar Trade: Brazil, Portugal and the Netherlands (1595~1630)

Odebrecht Group Cultural Committee
Márcio Polidoro (Chairman)
Karolina Gutiez (Executive Secretary)
Genésio Lemos Couto
Marcelo Lyra
Marcos Wilson Spyer Rezende
Roberto Dias

Search Committee for the Odebrecht Historical Research ~ Clarival do Prado Valladares Prize in 2010
Francisco Soares Senna
José Mário Pereira
Lilia Moritz Schwarcz
Márcio Polidoro
Otávio Soares Dulci
Sergius Marsicano Gonzaga

Research Project Coordinator and Book Author
Daniel Strum

English translation by
Colin Foulkes (Introduction and Chapter Two)
Roopanjali Roy
H. Sabrina Gledhill (front matter, back matter and captions)

Translation revised by
Daniel Strum
H. Sabrina Gledhill
Ana Margarida Santos Pereira (captions)

Copy-editing by
Shirley Zauer
Ana Elisa Camasmie

Research Assistance ~ Sources and Literature
Ana Margarida Santos Pereira (Portugal)
Bárbara Carolina Dias (Brazil)
Bruno Gobbi Dias (Brazil)
Helena Margarida Barros Rodrigues (Portugal)
João Tiago dos Santos Costa (Portugal)
Lodewijk A. H. Christiaan Hulsman (Netherlands)
Rosangela Ana Gobbi Dias (Brazil)
Victor Bertochi Ferreira (Brazil)

Iconographic Research
Ana Margarida Santos Pereira (Coordinator)
Helena Margarida Barros Rodrigues (Worldwide)
João Tiago dos Santos Costa (Worldwide)
Plural Comunicação e Memória (Support in Brazil)

Co-publisher
Versal Editores
Stanford University Press

Editor-in-Chief
José Enrique Barreiro

Editor
Maria Isabel Borja

Graphic Design
Eduardo Vilas Boas

Layout
Eduardo Vilas Boas
Pedro Frischeisen

Production Manager
Marcos Paulo Ferreira

Maps, Schematic Maps and Genealogies
Ana Margarida Santos Pereira (Genealogies and Maps)
José Ferrão Afonso (Schematic Map of Porto)
José Luiz Mota Menezes (Schematic Maps of Olinda, Recife and Salvador)
Lodewijk A. H. Christiaan Hulsman (Plan of Amsterdam)
Luciano de Paula Almeida (Design)
Victor Bertochi Ferreira (Revision of Tables, Histograms and Revision of Schematic Maps)

Cover illustration
6B Estúdio

Calligraphy
Andréa Branco

Copy-Editors (Portuguese Edition)
Karine Fajardo
Vitoria Davies

Image Processing
Daniel Silvany Tavares

CTP, Printing and Finishing
Pancrom Indústria Gráfica

CIP-BRAZIL. Cataloging-in-Publication Data
SINDICATO NACIONAL DOS EDITORES DE LIVROS, RJ

S918c

Strum, Daniel
[O comércio do açúcar : Brasil, Portugal e Países Baixos (1595–1630). English]
The Sugar Trade: Brazil, Portugal and the Netherlands (1595–1630) / Daniel Strum; translated by Roopanjali Roy et al. – Rio de Janeiro; Versal : São Paulo: Odebrecht, 2012.

il.

Winner of the Odebrecht Historical Research – Clarival do Prado Valladares Prize
Appendix
Includes bibliographical references.
ISBN 978-85-89309-46-2

1. Sugar – Trade – History. 2. Brazil – History 3. Portugal – History 4. Netherlands – History. I. Odebrecht S.A. II. Title.

12-6220. CDD: 981.03
CDU: 94(81) "1595/1630"

29.08.12 10.09.12 038611

Stanford University Press
Stanford, California

First English edition globally distributed by Stanford University Press except Brazil.
ISBN: 978-0-8047-8721-5 (cloth)

Portrait of the Merchant Daniel Bernard (1626–1714) of Amsterdam; *Bartholomeus van der Helst (1669).*

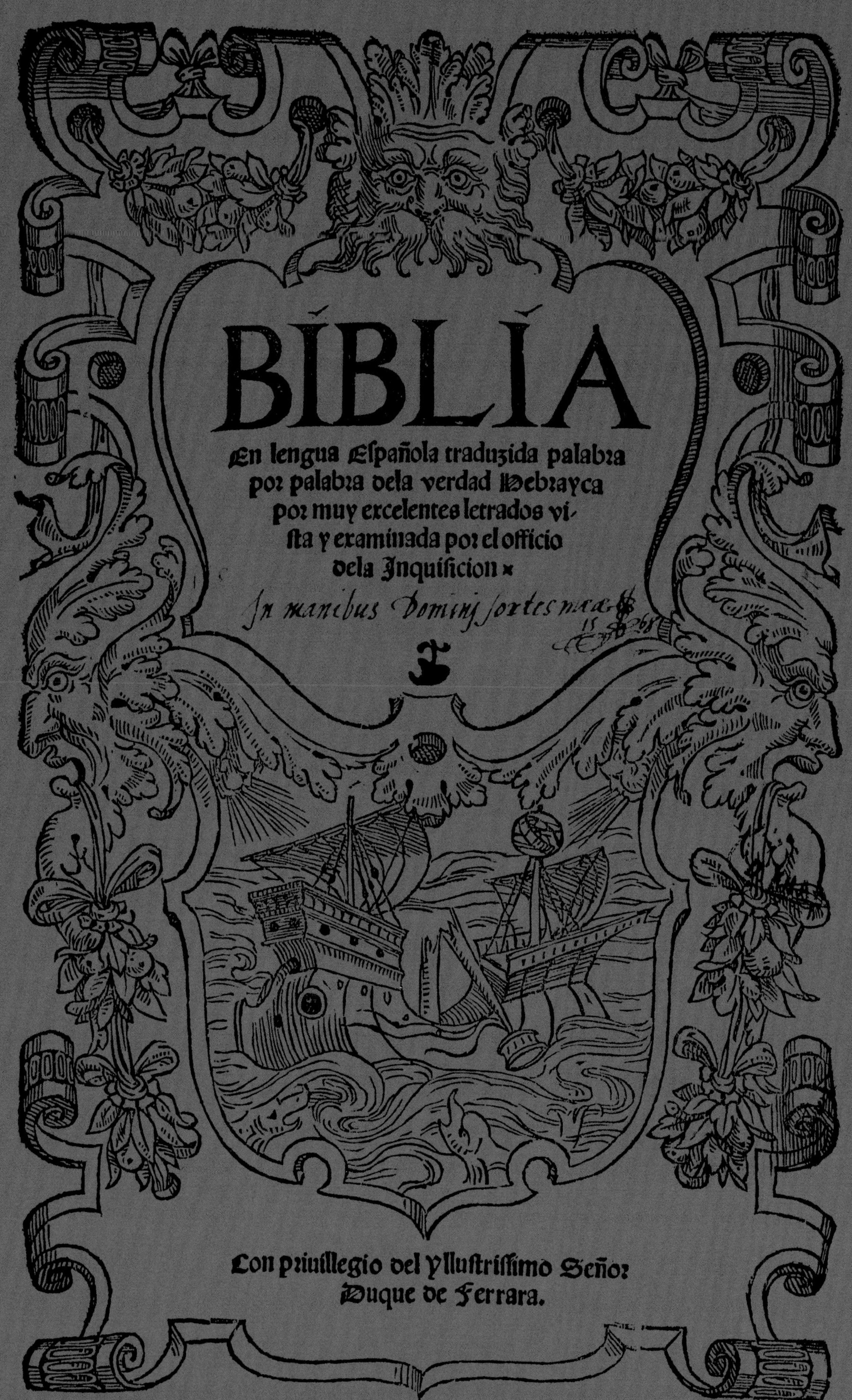

BIBLIA
En lengua Española traduzida palabra
por palabra dela verdad Hebrayca
por muy excelentes letrados vista y examinada por el officio
dela Inquisicion
Con privillegio del Yllustrissimo Señor
Duque de Ferrara.

Title page of the so-called Ferrara Bible, *a Spanish translation of the Hebrew Bible published in 1553.*

For the ones who inspired me - my grandparents:

Henia (Gênia) Beron Strum *Arnold Bernard (Tufa) Kleinberger*

Maria Lina (Má) de Oliveira

Irena (Ika) Silberberg Kleinberger *Adalbert (Dóliu) Strum*

לאלה שהשרו עליי מרוחם, סביי וסבותיי:

הניה בת יעקוב אריה ז"ל אברהם ברוך בן פנחס ז"ל

מריה לינה דה אוליבירה ז"ל

שולמית בת אליהו ז"ל דוד מאיר בן יצחק ז"ל

ת.נ.ב.צ.ה.

Terreiro do Paço in the Seventeenth Century; *Dirk Stoop (1662). The main backdrop of public life in Lisbon, the Terreiro do Paço was also a venue for commerce and conveyance of goods.*

Acknowledgements

Daniel Strum

I would like to thank the Odebrecht Group for the opportunity not only to bring this project to the light of day but also for the learning experience it has provided. I hope the initiative of the Odebrecht Historical Research Award – Clarival do Prado Valladares will set an example that will lead to a greater participation by the Brazilian private sector in the sponsorship of research in the humanities.

In particular, I would like to thank Marcio Polidoro, Maria Rossana C. Chiarella Souza, Aline Cristina Souza, Maria Helena Vieira Fraga and Helga Torres for being kind, considerate and helpful during the period when I was attempting to meet the challenge presented by the sponsor: writing, mainly from scratch and over a period of about a year and a half, a book intended for both specialists and non-specialists that examined the intricacies and overlapping spheres of the sugar trade between Brazil, Portugal and the Netherlands in the late 1500s and the following century with academic rigor and robust documentation.

Overcoming this bold and innovative challenge would have been impossible without the help of the research team that took part in this project: a transnational team, such as the subject of this book, based in Amsterdam, Lisbon, Setúbal, Recife, São Paulo and Itatiba, and sometimes in Funchal (Madeira), Juiz de Fora and Porto Velho. I have not met half of its members in person – an interesting case study for a researcher of overseas agency relations.

Going beyond the sponsor's challenge, we – the team – set ourselves a few more challenges when it came to the images for this book. We sought images that would not only illustrate it but rather add information. We selected a wide array of images of different types, formats and media, searching for original and little-known items and avoiding, whenever possible, the most obvious and celebrated items. The final result that we are presenting here is a selection of 376 images on a vast range of subjects sourced from more than 120 institutions and private collections from eighteen different countries.

I am especially grateful to Ana Margarida Pereira, who headed the Portuguese team and coordinated image research, which included contacting and negotiating with the institutions that own the rights to these images. Undertaking the job entailed not-insignificant personal sacrifice on her part. More than my right arm, she was my alter ego on this project, a constant adviser. The reader will clearly notice her efficiency in ensuring the acquisition of all these treasures to illustrate this work, including images found in unknown or unlikely places, some of which were last-minute requests.

When I mentioned the learning experience this project provided, I was primarily referring to that which came from working in collaboration with the extraordinary team of researchers I had the good fortune and honor to lead. I would like to thank Lodewijk Hulsman for his enthusiasm and curiosity; Victor Bertocchi Ferreira for his commitment and diligence; Helena Margarida Barros Rodrigues for her special care and efforts; João Tiago dos Santos Costa for his initiative and presence of mind, and Barbara Carolina Dias, Rosangela Ana Gobbi Dias and Bruno Gobbi Dias for their perseverance and tenacity. This is the least I can say about their contributions.

I would also like to recognize the efforts of Versal Editores, with my warmest thanks to the editor, Maria Isabel Borja, who, like a sugar master, undertook the delicate task of overseeing the production process, ensuring that nothing went awry. I would like to stress the care and understanding consistently expressed by José Enrique Barreiro, the talent and composure of Eduardo Vilas Boas and Marcos Paulo Ferreira, and the cooperation of Fenisio Pires.

My Portuguese team and I are grateful to Bento Pedroso Construções for its support in Europe, particularly Joaquim Simão, Lisete Nogueira, Luís Santos and the accounting and IT departments (José Cunha). All their contributions were key to the smooth running of our project, and I cannot fail to mention their enthusiastic hospitality. Similarly, I would like to thank the entire staff at the Regus Business Centre, in which our office in Lisbon was located.

We owe a great deal to the patient scholarship of José Ferrão Afonso, José Luiz Mota Menezes, and to our Lodewijk Hulsman for the maps and cartograms included herein. Our thanks also go to the photographers Lia Lubambo (in Pernambuco) and Isabel and Pedro Dantas dos Reis (in Portugal) for their superb work, which in some cases was extremely moving, and to Sónia Nobre for reproducing images from the Arquivo Histórico Municipal de Coimbra. We appreciate the efforts of Ileana Pradilla and Mariana Burlamaqui in identifying and acquiring images from the Brazilian archives.

Within the scope of this English language edition, I am deeply thankful for the enthusiasm, support and patience of those who helped bring this project to fruition: Norris Pope, Alan Harvey and Ariane de Pree-Kajfez (Stanford University Press); Márcio Polidoro (Odebrecht Group); and José Enrique Barreiro and Mariana Libman (Versal Editores). I am also sincerely grateful for the painstaking revisions undertaken by Shirley Zauer, Ana Elisa Camasmie, Ana Margarida Santos Pereira, Thereza Baumgarten and Luiza Vilela, as well as for the continued efforts of Eduardo Vilas Boas, Marcos Paulo Ferreira and Victor Bertochi Ferreira.

Some of the staff members of the institutions that own the images shown herein were truly outstanding, but if it would take too much space to list them all, and it would also be unfair to mention just a few. On behalf of the research team, I would like to thank the Alte Pinakothek, represented by Klaus Schrenk, for its help in sending the images produced especially for this book, and according to our instructions, of the reverse of Rembrandt's painting "The Descent from the Cross" or "Deposition of Christ," and Ana Margarida Araújo Camacho, the director of the Casa-Museu Frederico de Freitas, for reproductions of furniture made from sugar crates.

We owe the free release of images to Élvio de Sousa (Centro de Estudos de Arqueologia Moderna e Contemporânea, Santa Cruz – Madeira), Emile Schrijver (in charge of the René Braginsky Collection), Pancras van der Vlist and Onno Boers (Vereniging Vrienden van Amsterdamse Gevelstenen), Till Westermayer and

William B. Jordan. Other institutions have also provided images without charge: Museo Casa de la Moneda, the Mercers' Company, Castello di Issogne, Fries Scheepvaart Museum, Museum Meermanno-Westreenianum, the Arquivo Municipal de Viana do Castelo, Biblioteca Pública Municipal do Porto, the Gabinete de Arqueologia e Restauro da Câmara Municipal do Funchal, the Biblioteca Reale di Torino and the Museu-Biblioteca Condes de Castro Guimarães.

For allowing photography and facilitating our access to artworks and objects, and suggesting other images of interest, we are grateful to Father Armando Rodrigues (São Domingos Convent, Nossa Senhora de Monserrate Parish, Viana do Castelo), João Correia and Zélia Correia (the owners of the Jundiá sugar mill) and Maria Clara Ramos (Gabinete de Arqueologia e Restauro da Câmara Municipal do Funchal). For the assistance given to our photographers, we would also like to thank the Museu do Homem do Nordeste, the Arquivo Histórico Municipal de Coimbra, the Academia das Ciências de Lisboa, the Museu Arqueológico do Carmo, the Museu Militar de Lisboa, Imprensa Nacional - Casa da Moeda, the Archeological, the Instituto Arqueológico, Histórico e Geográfico Pernambucano and the Museu do Banco de Portugal.

For the precious information kindly provided, we are grateful to Arent Pol (Geldmuseum Utrecht), Glenn Murray (Asociación Amigos de la Casa de la Moneda de Segovia) and Julie Berger Hochstrasser (University of Iowa). We appreciate the suggestions and advice of Ana Isabel Ribeiro (Universidade de Coimbra), Emma Lefley (National Army Museum), Fredau Metselaar (Fries Museum), Carijn Oomkens (Waanders Publishers), Onésimo Santos (IPHAN-Rio Grande do Norte), Pedro Pinto (Universidade Nova de Lisboa), Lois Bailey and Daniel Blanchard (Yale University Press), as well as the Meadows Museum, the publishers of the Aufbau Journal and the Fundação Joaquim Nabuco (Fundaj).

I am personally indebted to many friends, colleagues and informal consultants for information, suggestions, comments and support of various kinds provided during different stages of this project. I would like to mention a few: Maurício Abadi, Márcio Svartman, Raquel Grisotto, Beni Lew, Íris Kantor, Cátia Antunes, Márcia Moisés Ribeiro, Rodrigo Ricupero, Antonio Marcos Furco, Leonardo Dantas, Daniel Breda, Clé Lesger, Leonor Freire Costa, Eddy Stols, Benjamin Robert, Odette Vlessing, Mark Henry Lazerson, Israel Rojtman, André Stern and Paula Zemel. When applicable, their specific contributions are credited in the text.

I would like to thank the entire staff that provided me with a functional working environment and pleasant home at First Full within the few square meters I occupied.

Finally, my thanks go out to my mentors and colleagues for everything they have taught me; to my parents, Ana Ruth Kleinberger Grozdea and Alexander Strum, for supporting me, in their own way, on the long and winding road that brought me to this project, and to my partner, Andreia dos Santos Menezes, a safe haven from storms and a fresh breeze in the doldrums.

Although I have dedicated this book to them, I would like to acknowledge my grandparents again for encouraging me to read, investigate and, particularly, to think for myself, a wisdom that they may have learned from their own life experience through the misfortunes of totalitarianism in the previous century, and which drove me to enter into the study of History.

Stanford, December 6, 2011.

Still Life with Dried
Fruits and Nuts,
Pretzels and Alfenim;
Clara Peeters (1611).

Table of Contents

Publisher's note:

To make the text more readable, we took the liberty of modernizing the archaic language of some of the documents quoted in this volume. For the same reason, abbreviations used in the original documents were transcribed in full. In other cases in which, despite the archaic spelling, the quotations did not contain terms or syntax that hindered its understanding by a contemporary reader, the sections were only italicized. Italics were meant to highlight the intentional maintenance of the original spelling.

To enrich the reader's experience without making it demanding to a non-specialist, the author's notes were divided into side notes and the endnotes. Side notes appear on the odd pages and are meant to clarify the body of the text. Endnotes are at the end of each chapter, and refer to the literature and the sources, and compare and delve further into the data and the opinions of the different scholars.

A Spanish Ship Explodes during the Battle of Gibraltar on April 25, 1607; *Cornelis Claesz. van Wieringen (ca. 1621). The Dutch painter portrays one of the many bloody episodes in the long war for the independence of that area of the Low Countries that is now called the Netherlands. The conflict between the Catholic Habsburg Empire and the Dutch Protestants had a strong impact on the shipment of and trade in Brazilian sugar.*

Foreword

Odebrecht Group

Sugar production was undoubtedly the most important economic enterprise undertaken during the first two centuries of Portugal's presence in Brazil. In the late sixteenth and early seventeenth centuries, this colony became the world's leading producer of what was one of the most coveted commodities during that period.

While recognizing the crucial role of sugar production in the development of Brazil in its early centuries, academic studies have largely overlooked the international trade in that commodity. According to Professor Stuart Schwartz, in his preface to this book, this is due to "the multinational nature of this trade, involving not only Brazil and Portugal, but London, Amsterdam, Antwerp, and Hamburg as well."

The scholar Daniel Strum has taken on this gargantuan task and devoted himself to researching and understanding the complex system of exchanges that ensured the export of Brazilian sugar to Portugal and its re-export from there to other regions, mainly the Low Countries.

The winner of the 2010 Odebrecht Historical Research Award – Clarival Prado Valladares, an Odebrecht initiative which annually selects an original scholarly proposal and gives it comprehensive support, from research to the publication of a richly illustrated book, Daniel Strum has delved into a vast collection of notarial, accounting, governmental and inquisitorial documents that reveal how, in the face of so many uncertainties of that period, it was possible to buy and receive shipments of sugar, which was produced in a far-off place such as Brazil, and transported across the Atlantic Ocean, which was plagued by adventurers and pirates.

The history of the multinational sugar trade comprises a broad mosaic of relations between the major European powers, not only during the timeframe established for this study (1595–1630), but throughout the preceding period, beginning with the Great Discoveries, allowing a better understanding of Brazil's place in this panorama. This book also shows us the preliminary structure of a system that laid the foundations of international trade and introduced economic, legal and financial procedures that are practiced to this day. In this sense, this is a work that helps us understand the society in which we live.

The Sugar Trade: Brazil, Portugal and the Netherlands (1595–1630) is the first book dedicated to economic history among the eight studies published with the imprint of the Odebrecht Historical Research Award – Clarival Prado Valladares. Its relevant and consistent content restates Odebrecht's aims in investing in this initiative: contributing to Brazilian historiography by sponsoring projects that help fill in gaps in our knowledge about the formation of our country.

View of Engenho Real in Brazil
(detail); Frans Post (ca. 1650–1655)

Sugar created Brazil and marked its character in ways that persisted long after sugar was no longer the predominant economic activity in the country. It was sugar that lay at the heart of the transformation of the relations with the indigenous peoples of Brazil from barter to slavery; sugar that generated the origins of the African slave trade with all its demographic, cultural and social impacts; and sugar that eventually attracted the Dutch rivals of Portugal who seized Pernambuco and the Northeast in the seventeenth century. But it was also sugar that provoked the colony's uprising against the Dutch occupation, and sugar that paid for the war that expelled the Dutch and then financed Portugal's war for independence against Habsburg Spain. "Without Angola, no slaves, without slaves no sugar, without sugar, no Brazil," was a saying with many variations that was often repeated in the Portuguese Atlantic world.

Modern historiography has long recognized the central importance of sugar in Brazil's development. Valuable studies have been done on the sugar economies of Pernambuco, Bahia and Rio de Janeiro; on the structure of the *engenhos* (sugar mills) and the role of the *lavradores de cana* (cane farmers); and on the functioning of slavery and the lives, work and resistance of the slaves. While there has been a well-developed parallel historiography on the slave trade and its importance in Brazil, the equally important sugar trade has never received the attention it has deserved and, in truth, it was on the docks of European ports that the success of sugar and the Brazilian colony was determined. The reason for this lacuna is in large part caused by the multinational nature of this trade, involving not only Brazil and Portugal, but London, Amsterdam, Antwerp and Hamburg as well. This was a truly multi-dimensional Atlantic commerce that crossed national and imperial boundaries and linked mercantile circuits that included Catholics, Protestants and Jews. To understand and analyze this trade has challenged the linguistic abilities and archival skills of many scholars. While there were a number of pioneering studies prior to the 1980s such as those of Frederic Mauro, Hermann Kellenbenz and Vitorino Magalhães Godinho which dealt mainly with the volume of the sugar trade and the changing market and profitability of sugar, only in the last two decades have important articles and monographs begun to give us a solid basis for understanding the structure of the trade, how it was organized and financed, what role the national states played in it, who its principal participants were and what their political and social goals were.

In this story of the birth of the sugar economy, the crucial years were the end of the sixteenth and beginning of the seventeenth centuries when the number of sugar mills grew rapidly from about sixty in 1570 to 350 in 1630. Portugal did not have a merchant marine large enough to handle the growing volume of this trade and it came to depend on the shipping of the Low Countries where the Portuguese had carried on an active commerce since the Middle Ages. By 1612, an annual production of close to 700,000 *arrobas* (about 10,500,000 kg) was being carried by 150 to 200 ships. This expanding commerce became more complicated after 1580 when a dynastic crisis brought Philip II of Spain to the throne of Portugal. With this dynastic change, Portugal's Brazilian sugar trade was subject to the policy decisions made by the Habsburg kings and was threatened by the enemies of their empire, particularly their English rivals and their Dutch opponents who were struggling to free themselves from Habsburg rule. Eventually, the Dutch attacks on Bahia in 1624 and their occupation of the Northeast after 1630 were a direct result of these policies.

In the 1980s, when I was writing the large study of the Brazilian sugar economy, *Sugar Plantations in the Formation of Brazilian Society: Bahia, 1550–1835*, I considered including a chapter on the sugar trade, but I decided not to do so because the documentation was so abundant and the themes — economic, political, social and religious — were so complex that to have written it would have distracted me from my main objective. Still, I realized that this was an essential part of the story of Brazil's history that needed more attention. In the last thirty years, a number of scholars have begun to write that story. Much of their work has been integrated into this book.

Daniel Strum now joins this new wave of scholarship and brings to Brazilian readers a thoroughly researched and carefully constructed description and analysis of the early sugar trade that gives attention to its social, economic, political and religious dimensions. His own dissertation on Portuguese Jews and New Christians in the sugar trade completed at The Hebrew University in Jerusalem has prepared him well for this broader topic. His command of languages, his work in Portuguese, Dutch, English and Spanish archives, the breadth of his erudition and his ability to synthesize a wide range of sources make this book a vital starting point for understanding the commerce that supported the growth of the colony in the period when Brazil became the world's leading producer of sugar and the first great plantation colony. This book is not just a study of the sugar trade, but an excellent introduction to a history of the Atlantic world, and to an essential aspect of the global economy and Brazil's role as a colony within it.

Stuart B. Schwartz, PhD
Professor of History at Yale University; specializes in the history of colonial Latin America

Purging house at the Jundiá Sugar-Mill. Nineteenth-century building in Vicência, Pernambuco, Brazil.

Acronyms and Abbreviations

ACL_CU Administração Central, Conselho Ultramarino

ADL Arquivo Distrital de Lisboa

ADP Arquivo Distrital do Porto

AGS Archivo General de Simancas

AHMP Arquivo Histórico Municipal do Porto

AMVCT Arquivo Municipal de Viana do Castelo

ant. Before

ANTT Arquivo Nacional da Torre do Tombo

attrib. Attributed to

BA Biblioteca da Ajuda

BNC Biblioteca Nazionale Centrale

BND Biblioteca Nacional Digital

BNP Biblioteca Nacional de Portugal

bpk Bildarchiv Preussischer Kulturbesitz

CA California

ca. *Circa*

cart. Cards

CC Corpo Cronológico

CEAM Centro de Estudos de Arqueologia Moderna e Contemporânea

COD Codex

coord. Coordinator

Cx. Box

D. Document

DC District of Columbia

dep. Department

des. Design/Drawing (by)

dig. Digital

dir. Direction

dr. Doctor

DRAC Direcção Regional dos Assuntos Culturais

ed. Editor

et al. Et alii (and other authors)

f. and fol.	Folio
fig.	Figure/Image
GAR	Gemeentearchief Rotterdam
grav.	Engraving (by)
IANTT	Arquivos Nacionais – Torre do Tombo *
IC	Inquisition of Coimbra *When followed by a number, indicates a file for proceedings.*
IL	Inquisition of Lisbon *When followed by a number, indicates a file for proceedings.*
IMC/MC	Instituto dos Museus e da Conservação/Ministério da Cultura
Impr.	Printer
inv. no.	Inventory number
IP	Instituto Público
JCB	John Carter Brown (Library)
Jr.	Junior
JUD	Judicial
l. and liv.	Book
LACMA	Los Angeles County Museum of Art
MA	Massachusetts
mç.	Pack
MO	Missouri
n./nn.	Note/Notes
n.d.	No Date
n.l.	No Location
n.n.	No Number
no.	Number
NA	Nationaal Archief (Den Haag/The Hague)
NEHA	Nederlandsch Economisch-Historisch Archief
Not.	Notary Public/Notarial Record/Fundo Notarial
NY	New York
OED	Oxford English Dictionary. Oxford: Oxford University Press, 2011.
ONA	Oud Notarieel Archief
ÖNB	Österreichische Nationalbibliothek
p./pp.	Page/pages
PA	Pennsylvania
pe.	Father (Priest)
PO1	Porto, Primeiro Cartório, 3ª série
PO2	Porto, Segundo Cartório, série única
PO4	Porto, Quarto Cartório, série única
post.	After
PRO	The National Archives, Public Record Office
RES	Reservados (Limited Access Collection)
RI	Rhode Island
RKD	Rijksbureau voor Kunsthistorische Documentatie
RMN	Reunion des Musées Nationaux
s.l.	no place
s/d or s.d.	no date
s/n	no number or no name
SAA	Stadsarchief Amsterdam
SJ	Society of Jesus
SLUB	Sächsische Landesbibliothek – Staats und Universitätsbibliothek (Dresden)
SMB	Staatliche Museen zu Berlin
SMK	Statens Museum for Kunst
SP	State Papers Office
SPSG	Stiftung Preußische Schlösser und Gärten (Berlin-Brandenburg)
SR Nr.	Document number attributed by the editors of the series of notarial records published in: W. C. Pieterse and E. M. Koen (eds.), "Notarial records [deeds] in Amsterdam relating to the Portuguese Jews in that town up to 1639." In: *Studia Rosenthaliana*, from 1967 onward. (See Appendix I.)
SSP	Secretarías Provinciales, Consejo de Portugal
STO	Santo Ofício (Holy Inquisition)
t.	Tome/Volume
TCPRT	Tribunal da Comarca do Porto
TRPRT	Tribunal da Relação do Porto
v.	verso
VVAG	Vereniging Vrienden van Amsterdamse Gevelstenen

* The acronym IANTT is used here because, during the early stages of the research that resulted in this book, that institution's official name was Instituto dos Arquivos Nacionais – Torre o Tombo.

The Two Bulls; *tapestry by Alexandre François Desportes (1661–1743), based on a Brazilian scene portrayed by Albert Eckhout, a member of the Dutch Mission to Brazil.*

Introduction

Daniel Strum

Sugar production in the sixteenth and seventeenth centuries transformed Brazil in a dramatic and permanent fashion. The planting of sugarcane and manufacture of sugar required vast tracts of fertile land, large quantities of firewood, protection against indigenous and foreign attacks, a substantial workforce and massive amounts of capital. As a result, sugar led to the disappearance of a large part of the Amerindian population and swathes of Atlantic forest in the colonized areas. It gave rise to the mass transfer of African slaves to work on its production, alongside or in the place of the indigenous peoples who had been enslaved or compelled to work for the Portuguese. The metropolis also induced, encouraged, and even forced European immigrants to try their luck in the colony, with greater or lesser success. Capital from different sources contributed to this process, which resulted in the emergence of a colonial society based on slavery in Portuguese America.

Map of the Brazilian Northeastern coast, from the captaincy of Rio Grande to that of Sergipe, produced by the Dutch cartographer Joan Blaeu in 1647, entitled "The part of Brazil that fell to the Belgians [Dutch]."

ASILIA
a parte paret
BELGIS.
PERNAMBUCO
TAMARICA
PARA YBA
RIO GRANDE
A CAPITANIA DE RIO
PARA
NAMBUCA
ACAPITANIA
DE ITA
MA
RACA
CAPITA
IA DE PA
RAIB
GRAN
DE
PRÆFECTURÆ
DE PARAIBA, ET
RIO GRANDE.

If it was the manufacture of sugar that transformed this region, such production was driven by extensive and extremely successful sales of that commodity. By the turn of the sixteenth century, Brazil stood out as the world's main sugar production center. The sugar produced in its coastal regions was generally channeled through Portugal, in southwestern Europe, and was distributed, to a large extent, from the Low Countries on the northeastern shores of the Atlantic, where sugar was often refined and then forwarded to its final markets. The sugar trade therefore encompassed an Atlantic supply chain,[1] if not a global one, since conserved fruits and marmalade made in Brazil traveled up the Río de la Plata, crossed the Andes, and arrived on the Pacific coast, in Chile.[2] Other sugar products crossed the Atlantic and Indian oceans, sailing from Lisbon to India.[3] These destinations, however, represented recognizably smaller markets.

By linking the emerging production center with consumers eager for the commodity, trade changed consumption patterns for sugar and the social habits that the use of that condiment entailed. The sugar trade contributed significantly to the vitality of the economies of Brazil, Portugal and the Netherlands, despite the numerous dangers and uncertainties involved. In fact, a twenty-first century observer might think, at first glance, that such a trade would only have appealed to adventurers and explorers. However, these difficulties were overcome, wherever possible, through various techniques and conventions, organizations and institutions – mercantile, legal and social – some of which had only recently emerged. This book offers the reader a panoramic view of the sugar trade encompassing Amsterdam, Porto (Oporto), Pernambuco, and Bahia during its golden age, between 1595 and 1630. It also seeks to place the trade within the context of that period, describe its operations and explore the challenges and risks it confronted and the means used to mitigate those risks.

The Boom

The Brazilian sugar boom began in the mid-sixteenth century, several decades before the period covered here (1595–1630). Nevertheless, it was only during the period under review that Brazil became the main supplier of the commodity to the European market.[4] It was also during this period that Brazilian sugar eclipsed, if not outshone, exotic goods from the East – such as spices, textiles, crockery, furniture, etc. – as the driving force behind the Portuguese economy in general and the north of the country in particular, where it would become vital. Brazil soon became the Portuguese crown's most important possession.[5]

Until the mid-sixteenth century, sugar production in that South American colony had been largely experimental. From that point on it grew extraordinarily, to a large extent due to the efforts of the Crown to safeguard and promote it. The number of sugar mills[6] increased almost without stopping until the end of the period covered here. Brazil came to satisfy what appeared to be an inexhaustible European demand for sugar-based goods. Some of its competitors, particularly Madeira, produced superior products, but Brazil's geographic and climatic conditions made its sugar cheaper.

To be sure, by the first decade of the seventeenth century the profitability of sugar production was showing signs of decline. This was due to increased costs arising from the intensive use of African

slave labor, which was more expensive than the Amerindian workforce, and the occupation of land and depletion of the soil in regions with easiest access to the main ports. This last factor forced a choice between lower productivity and higher transportation costs. Sugar-mill owners found it harder to pay their debts and strove to avoid seizure of their properties. From 1618 onwards, an economic crisis in Europe reduced the demand for sugar. In the following decade, renewed harassment of Portuguese shipping and the Dutch occupation of Salvador (1624–1625) made it even more difficult to market the commodity. Nevertheless, the overall situation of Brazil's sugar production remained positive during the entire examined period.

During the years covered in this book, Amsterdam grew from an average-sized trading center into Europe's main mercantile and financial hub, even if occasionally eclipsed by Hamburg, London and other centers. A significant part of the first stage of the economic expansion of the United Provinces of the Netherlands (currently the Kingdom of the Netherlands, often referred to as Holland, its main province) towards primacy in world trade took place during this period – at least until 1618–1621. After that, renewed European conflicts would damage Dutch trade and shipping.[7]

Sugar certainly did not play a vital role in the economy of the Dutch Republic, as it did in Brazil and Portugal, although the commodity brought vigor and prosperity. The importance of sugar to the

Sugar Mill in Brazil;
Frans Post (1640).

Dutch (and Iberian) economy is clearly demonstrated by the mobilization of troops and capital to conquer the areas that produced it. The aim was to appropriate the profits from the entire supply chain and take them away from the House of Habsburg, the Republic's enemy, with which Portugal was dynastically united from 1580 to 1640.

Throughout this period, the use of sugar in the West was gradually changing.[8] Originally an expensive condiment and a component of sumptuous decorations in displays of pomp and glory, it was becoming an increasingly commonplace ingredient in the cuisine of the middle and even lower classes. More and more, sweets, jam, compotes, candied fruit, cakes and other sugar-related products were reaching ever-humbler segments of society in growing quantities and at lower prices.

As a result of this increased availability, sugar migrated progressively from meat, fish and vegetable dishes, to those involving fruit, flour, milk and eggs. As the old warnings about the feeling of satiety that sugar provided gained strength, it moved to the final course of the meal and to snacks. In addition to being an active ingredient in medicine and pharmacology, sugar came to be used as a vehicle for other elements. At the same time, the first criticisms of over-consumption of sugar materialized. These warnings were based on a different view of physiology and chemistry.

The production and sale of comfits and gourmet sweets created an entirely new profession, that of confectioners. Likewise, the refining of sugar firmly established the profession of refiners. Both professions were composed of men from the middle to upper classes of the urban population. Meanwhile, the more down-market sweet making helped supplement and even generate the incomes of less fortunate families, while allowing them to consume some of the vast array of goods that the growing international trade offered. Women predominated among the more popular sweet-makers. Increasing production and consumption of sugar resulted in the growth of the economic and social importance attached to these activities.

Comfits were seen as a gift, a treat, and as such played a major role in the strengthening of interpersonal and family relationships. It also affected relationships of subordination and patronage, such as those between master and slave, nobleman and servant, employer and employee, and the powerful and the dependent. It gave rise to new spaces for conviviality, became part of the old ones, and was associated with multiple rituals, both public and private, of all kinds of lay and religious institutions. Certain sweet tidbits became associated with specific dates in the sacred and secular calendars.

Table with Sweets; *Tomás Hiepes (1624). Still lifes including sweets were a common theme in European art in the sixteenth and seventeenth centuries. However, the composition shown here is quite rare because of the presence of sugarcane.*

Published in 1624 in the Netherlands, the Book on Travels to the Kingdom of Brazil... *contains a print entitled "Pernambuco" which portrays the preparation of cassava flour and sugar on plantations.*

However, all these processes were slow, irregular and geographically varied. They began before the period covered here, and would only be concluded long afterwards. Nevertheless, the changes that took place in the course of those processes were clear, as was the impact of these new habits on social practices.

The Brazilian economy at the turn of the sixteenth to seventeenth century revolved around the sugar industry – the cultivation of sugarcane, and the production and sale of sugar. Brazil also exported comfits, conserves, compotes and marmalades made from sugar and molasses (which were cheap and abundant), and tropical and acclimatized temperate fruits. Cachaça, a distilled liquor made from sugarcane, was still being produced in relatively small quantities.[9]

Brazil's second main export to Europe was brazilwood. However, its export was a royal monopoly that was usually leased out to consortia of businessmen.[10] Tobacco was still in its infancy and would grow steadily until it entirely eclipsed brazilwood.[11] Furthermore, the colony's exports included cotton,[12] ginger (also used to make conserves),[13] leather[14] and a range of non-timber forest products, such as medicinal plants, tropical animals, hides and feathers.[15] However, exports of these other goods were comparatively small.

Trade not only provided an outlet for sugar and brought in the profits from its sale but also gave the colony's small European (and Europeanized) population access to a number of articles produced abroad. The main import – at least in terms of volume, and with the possible exception of enslaved Africans, who are not dealt with here – was wine. Some wines came from Portugal,[16] but most were from the Atlantic Islands – Madeira, and especially the Canaries. Their strong and sweet properties were better suited to voyages beyond the Equator, and as we will see, most ships bound for Brazil made stops in those islands to take on wine.[17]

Another important product was olive oil, which was generally produced in Portugal. Grain, Portugal's largest import, was less popular in Brazil, where the diet was based on cassava (manioc). Freight costs made grain far too expensive for consumption as a staple food. However, this does not mean that it was not imported and consumed on a smaller scale, particularly by the middle and upper classes. A large extent of Brazil's wheat imports came from the Azores. The consumption of imported grain, as well as wine, derived from cultural and religious customs. Culinary tradition can more justifiably account for imports of cod caught near far-off Newfoundland (in what is now Canada), and at times brought directly to Brazil.[18] This is

Above, the weathervane that identified the celebrated penitentiary in Amsterdam, founded in 1596 and known as the Rasphuis *(Rasp House). The prisoners' work included sawing and scraping or rasping wood to extract dye, and brazilwood was one of the materials used for that purpose.*

The tobacco carved into this decorated identification tablet (gable stone) stood out as an important export product of colonial Brazil.

Domestic scene with two women next to a cabinet filled with linen; Pieter de Hooch (1663). Linen and wool textiles were the Dutch Republic's main exports to Portugal, the Atlantic Islands and Brazil.

Olive oil may have been Portugal's most important export to Portuguese America.

Right, an engraving dating from the early eighteenth century shows cod fishing and drying. The fishing industry, local cuisine and periods of abstinence from meat for Catholics made cod from the northern seas an important article of consumption in both Portugal and Brazil.

because the Portuguese-Brazilian population lived almost entirely on the coast, or on the riverbanks, where there was plenty of fish. Otherwise, to a greater or lesser extent, Brazil sought the same Old World products as Portugal, with the exception of timber, which was abundant in its tropical forests.

The Dutch economy in general and Amsterdam's in particular were growing rapidly, and the sugar trade made them even more dynamic.[19] The importation, re-exportation and refining of the product impacted several sectors.[A] The number of sugar refineries and refiners increased sharply.[20] In addition to the refineries, Dutch linen and wool textile manufacturers also benefited from exports to Brazil and Portugal, which were purchased with sugar. Sugar was also imported in exchange for imports from the Baltic and Scandinavia such as grain, timber, copper, tar, lead, hemp and flax. Dutch ships took cod and other salted fish from English and French ports to Portugal. In the opposite direction, the Dutch Republic re-exported sugar to northern Europe, and even as far as the Mediterranean. Consequently, sugar boosted maritime transportation and shipbuilding, as well as the production of nautical equipment such as cooperage (the craft of making barrels and casks) to store cargo and provisions for the crew, among other industries. Indirectly, sugar gave a boost to the entire supply chain for these sectors.[21]

A. In 1622, some merchants based in the Dutch Republic pointed to this – with good reason, although overstated – in their defense of the freedom of trade with Brazil via Portugal, despite the resumption of war with Spain, and, as a consequence, with Portugal and its colonies in the previous year. The refineries and re-exports were the sectors that benefited most directly from the Brazilian sugar trade.

Three decorated identification plates carved in stone in the seventeenth century that adorned the façades of houses in Amsterdam (gable stones): the first shows the retail sale of sugar; the second, a sewing shop selling notions; and the third, manufacturing paper.

Imports to the City of Porto

The city of Porto was the largest regional trading hub in northern Portugal. Along with grain, its imports from the Old World, particularly northern Europe, also included raw and processed metals, timber, components for shipbuilding and civil construction, instruments for carpentry and cooperage, and materials for caulkers, rope-makers, goldsmiths and silversmiths, and so forth. All the inhabitants of Porto consumed imported textiles and clothing, bedclothes, tablecloths and towels in varying quantities and quality. Textile products were joined by other manufactured goods such as furniture, cutlery, crockery, paintings and paper.

Like the rest of Portugal, and to a lesser extent Brazil, Porto's residents systematically imported fish, particularly cod and sardines.[B] The sources consulted do not provide sufficient information to determine to what extent the products from northern Europe sold in Porto originated from the Dutch Republic – and even less the proportion imported from Amsterdam.[23] They do, however, allow that even if they did not export them, the Republic in general and Amsterdam in particular played a leading role in the transportation of these goods.[24]

The sugar trade was even more important to Portugal, the entryway for most of the sugar destined for northern Europe and the Mediterranean. This impact was even stronger on the north coast of the country, its most populous region, where the mountainous terrain and rocky soil resulted in poor grain production. Foreign trade was essential there, not only for the supply of cereal grains, particularly in years of bad harvests, but also for the acquisition of a wide range of goods from abroad: textiles, raw materials and tools for several trades, and even items for household use. International trade also stimulated internal commerce, handicrafts, agriculture and fishing, which were attracted to the main ports by foreign goods.[22]

However, because northern Portugal's exportable production was limited, the expansion of its imports depended on the re-export of colonial goods. Since Asia was Lisbon's prerogative, the South Atlantic offered new opportunities.[25] Consequently, during the fifteenth and sixteenth centuries, the re-export of products exchanged, harvested and cultivated in Madeira, the Azores, West Africa, the Spanish Americas and Brazil, predominantly sugar, guaranteed the region's subsistence without serious crises and met a large part of the local demand for both imported and domestic goods.

As in the Netherlands, sugar gave a boost to shipbuilding and shipping in the ports of northern Portugal, including the rope-making, sail-making and cooperage industries. Most of the wine exported from the islands was barreled in containers made in Portugal. Sugar, in turn, fueled the manufacture of the cauldrons and kettles in which those delicacies were prepared.[34]

B. The Dutch, however, were certainly not the only exporters to Porto. Most cod was caught by the English and the French, although Dutch ships stopped at these ports to take on cod bound for Portugal. Large quantities of textiles came from England and Germany, although most were probably transported on Dutch vessels. Leather also came from England, and a considerable amount of paper arrived from France. Spain, particularly the northern part of the Peninsula, and northern Europe were equally responsible for the supply of iron and steel, tar for caulking – which also came from the Canary Islands – and timber. Textiles also arrived from Spain, Italy and India. Germany, Italy and Spain are used here to designate regions that comprised a number of political units at the time, but which contemporaries broadly identified as single regions due to their linguistic and geographical commonalities, as much as German, Italian and Spanish.

Prints from the Book of Trades *published in Amsterdam in 1694: above, the production of casks, vats and barrels, one of the main export manufacturing activities in Porto; right, making copper cauldrons and kettles essential to the sugar mills, confectioners and sweet makers.*

Exports from the City of Porto

The main export product of the Douro region was sumac (*summāq*, in Arabic and Syriac), a plant that is now used as a herb or spice, but was then utilized by tanneries. It grew naturally in the Upper Douro region, from where it was taken to Porto, at the mouth of the River Douro.[26] The merchants of that city were also responsible for exporting part of the salt produced by Portugal's second-largest salt marsh near the Aveiro estuary, something between a lake and an inlet, less than 100 kilometers south of Porto.[27] In addition to sumac and salt, Porto probably exported some of the wine and olive oil produced in the north of the country.[28] It also shipped other farm products, some processed and others re-exported from the southern parts of the Kingdom. These included fish, Mediterranean fruits and nuts, such as almonds, dried figs and raisins,[29] and citrus fruit. It also re-exported all other Brazilian products,[30] with the possible exception of brazilwood, which should in principle have passed through Lisbon.[31] One of the most important exports from Portugal's other Atlantic colonies during the period covered here was woad from the Azores, which was an important textile dye.[32] Porto also supplied comfits, jellies, jams and marmalade made with fruits from the Mediterranean and sugar from Madeira and Brazil, exported along with other sugar comfits from the same colonies.[33]

Verwen by ℔.	en 100 ℔.	
Coucenilje Mestique	70 a 72 ß	
dito commune ——	55 a 56 ß	
Indigo Guatimalo ——	12 a 13 ß	tyt
dito Laure —— ——	61 a 62 stu	tyt
dito Karkees en Tripoli	67 st	cont
Spaens Groen ——	17 a 18 st	tyt
Ferneboucq —— ——	34 a 35 gl	cont
Sint Martens Hout ——	12 gl	cont
Ficet hout —— ——	7 gl	tyt
West-Indisch Hout ——		
Campets hout ——	24 gl	cont
Geel-hout ——	2,15 a 3 gl	cōt
Crappen —— nieuw	34 gl	cont
Ghemeyne —— ——	24 gl	tyt
Breslause —— nieuw	23 gl	
Wijnsteē van Duytsland	32 gl	cont
Italiaensen Wijnsteen -	14 gul	tyt
Groote Gal-noten ——	32 a 33 gl	cont
Grove Gomme ——	23 gl	cont
Pastel vā S.Michiel, bael	16 gl	
dito Thoulouse, de bael	gl	tyt
Smack de Port a Port —	28 ß	tyt
dito de Mallega ——		tyt
Engels Coper-root ——	gl	con
dito Luyckx ——	4,10 a 5 gl	con
Roomsen Aluyn ——	39 a 40 ß	cont
dito Luycksen Aluyn --	28 ß	cont
dito Engelschen Aluyn.	ß	cont

Official price-list for products on the Amsterdam Bourse in March 1636, including brazilwood (Fernemboucq), woad from the Azores (Pastel van S. Michiel) and sumac from Porto (Smack de Port a Port).

Risks and Challenges

The sugar trade was not all smooth sailing, however. A soluble product, sugar was transported in sailing ships built from wood and steered according to the stars and landmarks. Other goods, as well as passengers, means of payment and mail, traveled in the same manner. The dangers included bad weather, human error and, chiefly, piracy and privateering.

This period was marked by the conflict between the United Provinces of the Netherlands and the dual monarchy that linked Spain and Portugal. With the exception of the Twelve Years' Truce (1609–1621), the sugar route was the backdrop for warlike maneuvers, reciprocal privateering, trade embargoes and the confiscation of ships and merchandise. The expansion of this conflict to the overseas possessions of both powers in Africa, Asia and the Americas would result in the first war on a global scale. The dual monarchy was also at war with France and England until 1598 and 1604, respectively. Moreover, piracy perpetrated under the banner of Islam from North Africa harassed vessels departing or arriving in the Iberian Peninsula and the islands of Macaronesia – the Azores, Madeira, Canaries and Cape Verde. These attacks gained particular momentum from the second decade of the seventeenth century.

Experience, training, special routines and precautions, dispersion of cargo, large, well-armed vessels, sailing in groups of ships and convoys escorted by warships were all used to prevent losses and mitigate risks. These measures also entailed additional costs, however, just as insurance, which was ever more widely used and increasingly improved, meant paying premiums. Maritime transportation also required choosing between different strategies to balance the business opportunities available, the itineraries, the

Stichting W. van der Vorm

coordination of voyages, the availability and types of ships, freight charges and the other costs involved, as well as legal and political restrictions on maritime shipping.

In addition to managing the logistics and risks of transportation, merchants also had to administer their finances. Payments in advance, in installments or a lump sum due on a specific date, involved costs and benefits that had to be carefully managed. Currency consisted of precious metals minted into coins, which resulted in an infinite number of complications due to counterfeiting and debasement. Sugar was a commodity and therefore could replace coins as a medium of exchange, but this did not always make transactions less complex, quite the contrary. Coins and merchandise coexisted with several credit instruments, whose development was stimulated by the current expansion of trade and vice versa. The more the negotiability of these instruments was consolidated, the more liquidity the merchants had at their disposal to increase the volume and speed of their transactions. Alongside their own commercial and financial activities, they also made and received payments on behalf of their correspondents and third parties, giving rise to a proto-banking system.

During this period, when ever-increasing capital converged on Amsterdam, along with their investment returns, a number of organizations were established in that city, based on their predecessors in Venice, Brussels, Antwerp and London. They increased security and efficiency for its financial market. The Exchange Bank, a rather embryonic sort of central bank, increased the market's solvency and contained the money supply. The Bourse reduced the cost of information and gave rise to the development of derivatives. The Insurance Chamber regulated that sector, reducing risks and costs for both insurers and the insured. Finally, shares in the East India Company, which prospered under the protection of the central government, would later result in the emergence of the stock market. Those shares served as a guarantee for the evolving secondary market of securities issued by traders. To a certain extent, these advances would result in reduced interest rates and insurance premiums throughout the sugar route.

Merchants depended on their agents to avoid having to travel to other marketplaces themselves to buy and sell merchandise, receive and make payments, collect debts and settle accounts, and hire transport and other services. However, by employing an agent, the merchant also ran the risk of incurring losses resulting from the agent's actions. The advantages and dangers of employing agents were handled through different types of agency arrangements.

The risks due to misconduct not only stemmed from agents but also from debtors, transporters, suppliers, insurers and so on. However, the considerable ability of the courts from different jurisdictions and voluntary arbitration to enforce norms and obligations generally dissuaded opportunistic behavior. Furthermore, standard mercantile practices and customs became universalized throughout the Western marketplaces and formed a common code that, albeit frequently informal, was held and recognized as binding. It was even used in judicial sentences and arbitrations. Furthermore, it served as a criterion for the social and economic punishments imposed by peers in response to impropriety or bad reputation. As commercial routines were standardized and universalized, informal sanctions based on professional reputation became more effective and helped markets to integrate and expand. It is possible that a mercantile morality became so deeply internalized by merchants that it inhibited opportunistic behavior to some extent.

Courtyard of the Amsterdam Bourse; *Emanuel de Witte (1653).*

Merchants depended on information to ensure that obligations and rules were being complied with, as well as to manage their businesses. Different practices and strategies of correspondence, navigation and mercantile associations sought to guarantee an intense exchange of information between one marketplace and another. In each location, news circulated quickly and extensively because cities were small, their populations reduced, their social fabric relatively close-knit, and institutions and habits brought their residents into close contact. This was especially true regarding trade-related sites, professionals and interactions.

Perspectives

Sugar production during this period has been the subject of countless studies precisely because it was largely responsible for laying the foundations for the formation of contemporary Brazil. The consumption of sugar has attracted growing interest among scholars from various fields, such as gastronomy, medicine, gender studies and everyday life.[35] However, the sugar trade itself has been the subject of significantly less research.[36] Studies on the Brazilian,[37] Portuguese[38] and Dutch[39] economies mention it, but the most important contributions to the understanding of the intricacies of this trade may come from monographs on local and regional history,[40] and studies on maritime transport, port activities,[41] finance[42] and mercantile arithmetic.[43] The same can be said for studies on groups of merchants sharing common origins – those born in certain Portuguese harbor towns,[44] those from the Low Countries[45] and those of Jewish descent.[46]

In the last fifty years, few studies have dealt with the topic covered here, namely the sugar trade between Brazil, Portugal and the Netherlands during the decades that preceded the Dutch invasion of Pernambuco. Even fewer combine the examination of Brazilian, Portuguese and Dutch sources and literature. Among the rare integrative studies of this subject, based on documents relating to at least two of the regions, the works of Eddy Stols, Frédéric Mauro, David Grant Smith, Leonor Freire Costa and José Antônio Gonsalves de Mello stand out.[47] In more recent years, Christopher Ebert's and my own studies have attempted to take up where the pioneering efforts of scholars such as Stols and Mello left off by examining the sugar trade on the basis of the sources and literature on the three centers in question. Ebert's doctoral dissertation, later published as a book, analyzes various aspects of the sugar trade between Brazil, Portugal and northern Europe from 1550 to 1630. I have reexamined the importance of kinship and common ethnicity in relations among merchants of Jewish origin based in Amsterdam, Porto, Pernambuco and Bahia, and their overseas mercantile agents, focusing on the period between 1595 and 1618.[48]

Salvador, with Todos os Santos Bay in the foreground (1625).

Urbs
SALVADOR

Amplissimis Prudentissimisque
Dominis, D.D. Consulibus, Scabinis,
Totique Senatui Reipub:
Amstelredamenis,
Dominis suis Clementissimis Hanc suam
Amstelredami delineationem submisse dedicabāt
Harmanus Allardi Coster, et
Nicolaus Johannis Visscher

Amsterdam was, by far, the main commercial hub in the Dutch Republic.

Profile of Amsterdam; *Claes Jansz. Visscher and Hermanus Allardi Coster (1611).*

This book is a continuation of my first integrative study. However, it covers a broader perspective, adding new themes, sources and literature. Furthermore, it includes significant research into imagery, which is informative rather than illustrative. It is essentially based on the notarial records of Porto and Amsterdam, and documents resulting from the Inquisition's visitations in to Porto, Bahia and Pernambuco,[49] to which I have added Portuguese (better yet, Iberian) and Dutch government documents, some notarized deeds from Rotterdam and the only remaining book of accounts from a merchant of the period, Miguel Dias Santiago. These documents are housed in several archives and libraries in Portugal, Spain, the Netherlands and the United Kingdom.

With respect to Brazil, I have particularly examined the captaincies of Bahia and Pernambuco; in the Netherlands, the focus is on Amsterdam; and in Portugal, it is on Porto. Pernambuco and Bahia were the regions with the largest populations and sugar production,[50] and Amsterdam was, by far, the main commercial center in the Dutch Republic. Apparently, most of the Brazilian sugar that arrived in that city passed through the ports of northern Portugal, in the Entre-Douro-e-Minho region, of which Porto was the most important.[51]

Furthermore, the choice of Porto gives us a valuable glimpse of the mercantile activities in that city which was the backdrop for an extensive wave of arrests by the Inquisition between 1618 and 1621 that carefully targeted merchants of Jewish origin, most of whom were imprisoned and put on trial.[52] Their case records provide information that is unique in the wealth of details about trading practices. Cross-referencing it with other data obtained from notarized deeds in which the same merchants are mentioned provides a more complete picture of their operations and methods. Therefore, I have chosen Porto in order to scrutinize its notarial records as a case study. To a lesser degree, the same could be said of Bahia and Pernambuco, whose inhabitants (particularly those of Jewish origin) were also harassed by the Inquisition during this period and shortly before.[53]

The period examined in this book begins in 1595, when Amsterdam was beginning to replace Antwerp as the main sugar distributor in northern Europe. In the last decade of that century, merchants who were involved in imports of that tropical commodity began arriving in ever-increasing numbers. They were immigrants from Portugal, Brazil, the rest of the Iberian world and the provinces of the Low Countries that remained under Spanish rule, such as Flanders and Brabant, where Antwerp was located.[54] The study continues until 1630, when the Dutch conquest of Pernambuco would radically transform the structure of the sugar trade.

This book is divided into four sections. The first three chapters focus on the factors that preceded, succeeded and enfolded the sugar trade: the political-military context, sugar production and consumption of sweets. Chapter 1 presents an overview of the geopolitical context in which the European powers, among others, positioned themselves around the globe. Chapter 2 describes the trajectory of sugarcane until it took root in Brazil, the semi-industrial method of its conversion into sugar and the development of Brazilian production. Chapter 3 deals with the social and cultural transformations and impacts resulting from the dissemination of sugar consumption for various purposes.

The three chapters that follow form a second section, which covers navigation, maritime transport and linkage between ports. Chapter 4 focuses on the risks encountered at sea and the measures taken to miti-

Porto and mouth of the River Douro in a nautical chart dated 1634 made by Pedro Teixeira Albernaz, member of a celebrated family of Portuguese cartographers.

gate its effects. The strategies developed to make itineraries more efficient in relation to trade, to the costs of transportation and to the integration of the markets are the subject of Chapter 5. Chapter 6 describes cargo transportation procedures and the various fees charged for shipping.

The third section focuses on the financial aspect of the sugar trade: Chapter 7 describes forms and real means of payment, and Chapter 8 discusses fiduciary media and credit. The fourth and last section deals with bonds of trust, with overseas agents and their relationships with merchants in Chapter 9, and the transmission of and access to information, and mechanisms to ensure compliance with norms and agreements in the final chapter.

Introduction

1. The profound transformations resulting from the production of sugar in the Atlantic basin (and not only there) are highlighted, among many others, in E. O. Von Lippmann, *História do açúcar*, V. 2 (Rio de Janeiro: Instituto do Açúcar e do Álcool, 1942); N. Deerr, *The History of Sugar* (London: Chapman and Hall, 1949); G. Freyre, *Açúcar: uma sociologia do doce* (São Paulo: Global, 2007); V. L. A. Ferlini, *Açúcar e colonização* (São Paulo: Alameda, 2010); S. W. Mintz, *Sweetness and Power: The Place of Sugar in Modern History* (New York: Viking Penguin, 1985); J. H. Galloway, *The Sugar Cane Industry* (Cambridge: Cambridge University Press, 1989); S. Schwartz (ed.), *Tropical Babylons: Sugar and the Making of the Atlantic World, 1450–1680* (Chapel Hill: University of North Carolina Press, 2003).

2. A. P. Canabrava, *O comércio português no Rio da Prata (1580–1640)* (Belo Horizonte: Editora Itatiaia, 1984), p. 143.

3. J. Brandão, *Grandeza e abastança de Lisboa em 1552* (Lisbon: Livros Horizonte, 1990), p. 214; D. F. Gouveia, *Açúcar confeitado na Madeira*, Funchal, Direcção Regional dos Assuntos Culturais n. 11, p. 35; E. Stols, "The Expansion of the Sugar Market in Western Europe," in Schwartz, *Tropical Babylons*, p. 243.

4. See Chapter 2.

5. J. L. de Azevedo, *Épocas de Portugal económico* (Lisbon: Clássica Editora 1988), pp. 233–269; F. Mauro, *Portugal, o Brasil e o Atlântico, 1570–1670* (Lisbon: Editorial Estampa, 1989), v. 1, p. 243; J. R. Magalhães, "A estrutura das trocas," in José Mattoso, *História de Portugal*, V. 3 (Lisbon: Editorial Estampa, 1997), pp. 314–316. Focusing exclusively on revenues the Crown obtained directly from India and Brazil, Francisco Bethencourt concludes that Asia surpassed Brazil. However, his comparison does not account for the tax farming system, or the other sectors driven by the trade in both regions; see: F. Bethencourt and K. Chaudhuri, *História da Expansão Portuguesa* (Lisbon: Círculo de Leitores, 1998), v. 2, pp. 315–318. See also: J. M. Pedreira, "Costs and Financial Trends in the Portuguese Empire, 1415–1822," in F. Bethencourt and D. R. Curto (eds.), *Portuguese Oceanic Expansion, 1400–1800* (Cambridge: Cambridge University Press, 2007), p. 56.

6. *Engenho de açúcar* is translated here as "sugar mill" and *senhor de engenho* as "sugar-mill owner." *Engenho* referred then both to the mill itself, in the strict sense, and to the other manufacturing facilities, cane fields, slaves, livestock, etc., that such enterprises comprised. Both "plantation" and "planter" are avoided because "plantation" might refer to purely agricultural estates, failing to convey the semi-industrial activities of these enterprises, which, in fact, were far more important than farming. Moreover, the term "plantation" in British America often designated entire colonies or settlements, which might be ambiguous. Finally, "owner" alludes to the status of quasi-nobility, or lordship, which the word "*senhor*" within the title *senhor de engenho* dearly aspired to.

7. J. I. Israel, *Dutch Primacy in World Trade, 1585–1740* (Oxford: Clarendon Press, 1989), pp. 30–42, 404–415; J. de Vries, and A. van der Woude, *The First Modern Economy* (Cambridge: Cambridge University Press, 1997), pp. 368, 412–414, 425, 669–671; C. Lesger, *The Rise of the Amsterdam Market and Information Exchange* (Aldershot: Ashgate, 2006), pp. 85–92, 133–138, 258. These four authors establish the beginning of this period between the fall of Antwerp to forces loyal to the King of Spain, in 1585, and both the consolidation of the military power of the Dutch Republic and the clear emergence of Amsterdam as a major international trading center up to the end of the following decade. They also agree on the negative impact of the end of the Twelve Years' Truce on trade in Amsterdam. However, De Vries and Van der Woude suggest that the turning point came earlier, with the start of the Thirty Years' War in 1618.

8. See Chapter 3.

9. F. P. Laval, *Viagem de Francisco Pyrard de Laval* (Porto: Livraria Civilização, 1944), pp. 229–231; J. A. G. de Mello, *Gente da nação* (Recife: Editora Massangana, 1996), p. 44; L. M. Hutter, *Navegação nos séculos XVII e XVIII* (São Paulo: Edusp, 2005), pp. 141, 145; S. B. Schwartz, *Sugar Plantations in the Formation of Brazilian Society* (Cambridge: Cambridge University Press, 1985), pp. 162–163.

10. B. J. Souza, *O pau-brasil na história nacional* (São Paulo: Companhia Editora Nacional, 1939), pp. 106–153; Mauro, *Portugal, o Brasil e o Atlântico*, v. 1, pp. 176–180.

11. J. B. Nardi, *O fumo brasileiro no período colonial* (São Paulo: Editora Brasiliense, 1996), pp. 34–36.

12. Mauro, *Portugal, o Brasil e o Atlântico*, v. 2, p. 104; P. de Magalhães Gândavo, *Tractado da terra do Brasil*, fols. 6–7v.; D. de Campos Moreno, *Livro que dá razão do Estado do Brasil* (Recife: Arquivo Público Estadual, 1955), p. 140; G. S. de Sousa, *Tratado descritivo do Brasil* (Recife: Editora Massangana, 2000), p. 102; A. F.

Brandão, *Diálogos das grandezas do Brasil* (Recife: Editora Massangana, 1997), pp. 85–127.

13. Mauro, *Portugal, o Brasil e o Atlântico*, v. 2, p. 105.

14. ADP, Cabido, l. 110, fol. 10v.; l. 134, fols. 26v., 41v.–42; Mauro, *Portugal, o Brasil e o Atlântico*, v. 1, pp. 99–100.

15. M. L. Oliveira, *A história do Brazil de Frei Vicente do Salvador* (Rio de Janeiro: Odebrecht, Versal, 2008); R. C. Simonsen, *História econômica do Brasil, 1500–1820* (São Paulo: Editora Nacional, 1978), p. 52.

16. F. R. da Silva, *O Porto e o seu termo* (Porto: Arquivo Histórico – Câmara Municipal do Porto, 1988), v. 2, p. 891.

17. Sousa, *Tratado descritivo do Brasil*, p. 101. Father Fernão Cardim emphasized the trade and the consumption of wine in Brazil, including by the Amerindians; see: F. Cardim, *Tratados da terra e gente do Brasil* (Lisbon: CNCDP, 2000), pp. 220 (with respect to the Amerindians), 223, 244, 256. See also: E. d'Oliveira França and S. A. Siqueira, "Introduction and Notes," in *Segunda visitação do Santo Ofício às partes do Brasil pelo inquisidor e visitador Marcos Teixeira: Livro das Confissões e Ratificações da Bahia: 1618–1620* (São Paulo, Museu Paulista, Universidade de São Paulo, 1963), t. 17, pp. 277–278.

18. For details on Brazilian imports, see: ADP, NOT, PO2, l. 4, fol. 11 (1595-7-5), l. 35, fols. 191v.–192v. (1612-8-25), l. 37, fols. 154v.–155 (1613-8-17); SR no. 593; Mauro, *Portugal, o Brasil e o Atlântico*, v. 1, pp. 379–380; v. 2, pp. 18–20, 24–25, 84–90, 95–97; Mello, *Gente da nação,* pp. 44–46; L. F. Costa, *O transporte no Atlântico e a Companhia Geral do Comércio do Brasil (1580–1663)* (Lisbon: CNCDP, 2002), v. 1, pp. 284–290; Cardim, *Tratados da terra e gente do Brasil*, pp. 250–251.

19. On the plea for freedom of trade with Brazil via Portugal made by merchants based in the Dutch Republic, and the benefits of the sugar trade for the refineries and the Dutch re-exports, see: J. W. Ijzerman, *Journael van de reis naar Zuid-Amerika* (The Hague: Martinus Nijhoff, 1918), pp. 98–106; O. Vlessing, "New Light on the Earliest History of Amsterdam Portuguese Jews," in J. Michman (ed.), *Dutch Jewish History*, V. 3 (Jerusalem: The Institute for Research on Dutch Jewry, 1993), pp. 54–57; idem, "The Portuguese-Jewish Merchant Community in Seventeenth-Century Amsterdam," in C. Lesger and L. Noordegraaf (eds.), *Entrepreneurs and Entrepreneurship in Early Modern Times* (The Hague: Stichting Hollandse Historische Reeks, 1996), p. 233. On the linkage effect, see: A. O. Hirschman, "A Generalized Linkage Approach to Development with Special Reference to Staples," in A. O. Hirschman, *Essays in Trespassing: Economics to Politics and Beyond* (Cambridge: Cambridge University Press, 1981), pp. 59–97.

20. A. Poelwijk, *In dienste vant suyckerbacken* (Hilversum: Verloren, 2003), pp. 39–40, 55–57; J. Israel, *Dutch Primacy in World Trade*, p. 34; Ijzerman, *Journael van de reis naar Zuid-Amerika*, p. 103; Israel, *Dutch Primacy in World Trade*, p. 116; De Vries and Van der Woude, *The First Modern Economy*, p. 326.

21. Israel, *Dutch Primacy in World Trade*, pp. 35–36, 53–60, 80–101, 114–120, 190–196; D. M. Swetschinski, "The Portuguese Jewish Merchants of Seventeenth-Century Amsterdam: A Social Profile," PhD dissertation, Brandeis University, 1979, p. 150.

22. IAHMP, *Organização Antiga,* A-PUB-350, fols. 23v.–25v; Silva, *O Porto e o seu termo*, v. 1, pp. 119–120; Mauro, *Portugal, o Brasil e o Atlântico*, v. 2, pp. 13–17. See also for southern Portugal: J. R. Magalhães, *O Algarve econômico, 1600–1773* (Lisbon: Editorial Estampa, 1993), pp. 276–277.

23. Northern Portugal had a better supply of wood than the central and southern regions; see: Costa, *O transporte no Atlântico*, v. 1, pp. 465–466. Even so, the northern region imported it. For the imports of Porto, in particular, and of Portugal, in general, see: ADP, Cabido, books 110, 113, 134, passim; Mauro, *Portugal, o Brasil e o Atlântico*, v. 1, 137–141, 378–380; Silva, *O Porto e o seu termo*, v. 1, pp. 112, 117–130, 163, 187–188, 226, 231–232, 335, 539–543; v. 2, pp. 627, 639, 673–674, 696–698, 708, 746–757, 801–804, 839, 879–881, 1078–1079; Costa, *O transporte no Atlântico*, v. 1, pp. 88–89.

24. Costa, *O transporte no Atlântico*, v. 1, pp. 116–118; D. Strum, "The Portuguese Jews and New Christians in the Sugar Trade," PhD dissertation, The Hebrew University of Jerusalem, 2009, pp. 25–27; Silva, *O Porto e o seu termo*, v. 1, pp. 120–125, 328–345; M. A. F. Moreira, *Os mercadores de Viana e o comércio do açúcar brasileiro no século XVII* (Viana do Castelo: Câmara Municipal de Viana do Castelo, 1990), p. 185.

25. A. J. M. Barros, *Vinhos de escala e negócios das ilhas* (Porto: GEHVID, 2004), passim; Costa, *O transporte no Atlântico*, v. 1, pp. 81–111, 457–462.

26. SR no. 362, 379; Silva, *O Porto e o seu termo*, v. 1, pp. 124, 136, 180–183, 231–232, 331, 334, 462; v. 2, pp. 701, 1078–1079.

27. ADP, NOT, PO2, l. 40, fols. 195–195v. (1615-7-28); V. Rau, *Estudos sobre a história do sal português* (Lisbon: Editorial Presença, 1984), pp. 60–61.

28. Silva, *O Porto e o seu termo*, v. 1, pp. 124, 146–162; v. 2, pp. 696–702, 1078–1079.

29. ADP, NOT, PO2, l. 29, fols. 139–141 (1609-10-13).

30. ADP, NOT, PO1, l. 143, no number (1621-7-12).

31. Souza, *O pau-brasil na história nacional,* pp. 134–135; Mauro, *Portugal, o Brasil e o Atlântico*, v. 1, pp. 178–180.

32. ADP, NOT, PO2, l. 23, fols. 82v.–85v. (1605-4-2). PO2, l. 25, fols. 19–20v. (1606-3-3); ibid., fols. 64v.–65v. (1606-4-1); ADP, NOT, PO2, l. 26, fols. 238–239v. (1607-6-19).

33. IANTT, STO, IC 2736, fol: 24v. The same was true in Viana: Moreira, *Os mercadores de Viana*, pp. 31–32.

34. SR no. 1959; S. Lacerda, *A tanoaria: a arte e a técnica* (Porto: Universidade do Porto, 1998), passim; Silva, *O Porto e o seu termo*, v. 1, pp. 189–224; Costa, *O transporte no Atlântico*, v. 1, pp. 454–472; A. Polónia, "Vila do Conde: um porto nortenho na expansão ultramarina quinhentista," PhD dissertation, University of Porto, 1999, passim; A. J. M. Barros, "Porto: a construção de um espaço marítimo nos alvores dos tempos modernos," PhD dissertation, University of Porto, 2004, passim.

35. See the studies mentioned in Chapters 2 and 3, respectively.

36. Here, I am limiting myself to studies published in the last fifty years that deal with both the period and the geographic areas (Brazil, Portugal and the Netherlands) examined in this volume. This should not be regarded as overlooking the major contributions of studies whose focus falls outside these parameters. Solely to avoid excessive length, I have set them aside. The most pioneering studies include the contributions of the following authors, among many others: João Lúcio de Azevedo, Virgínia Rau, Roberto Cochrane Simonsen, Cáio Prado Júnior, Herbert I. Bloom, Hermann Kellenbenz, Hans Pohl and Johannes Gerard van Dillen, Engel Sluiter, Violet Barbour and António Sérgio. Major recent studies deal with the periods immediately before and after those discussed here, such as those by Amélia Polónia, Amândio Jorge Morais Barros, Cátia Antunes and Denise Helena Monteiro de Barros Carollo. These studies are mentioned in the bibliography. All the authors mentioned in this section ("Perspectives") have produced more than one study on the subject. However, for the sake of brevity, I am only mentioning their most relevant works.

37. For the studies on Brazil, see those cited in Chapter 2.

38. Among the studies on the Portuguese economy for the period that deal more specifically with sugar, we can highlight those by the following authors. (It is important to emphasize that the period in which the Habsburgs held the Portuguese throne have traditionally aroused less interest among the Portuguese historians, resulting in fewer studies.) The French historian Frédéric Mauro adopted a Braudelian approach, in which he analyzed processes of short and long duration to provide a detailed description of the Portuguese Atlantic economy; see: Mauro, *Portugal, o Brasil e o Atlântico*. Like Fernand Braudel and Mauro, Vitorino Magalhães Godinho also followed the historiographical approach known as the Analles School, which sought to apply the methodology of the social sciences (such as economics and sociology) to history. Godinho aimed to investigate Portuguese history in great detail and its impact on the world in the fifteenth and sixteenth centuries; see: V. M. Godinho, *Os descobrimentos e a economia mundial* (Lisbon: Editorial Presença, 1982–1983). Charles Ralph Boxer, a British military career officer, analyzed the interwoven history of the Portuguese and Dutch overseas empires; see: C. R. Boxer, *The Portuguese Seaborne Empire, 1415–1825* (London: Hutchinson, 1969). António Henrique Rodrigo de Oliveira Marques, originally a medievalist, has produced an excellent summary of the history of Portugal and its dominions, with special emphasis on its economic aspects, his focus of interest; see: A. H. de Oliveira Marques, *História de Portugal* (Lisbon: Palas Editores, 1983). Two collective studies should be highlighted on the history of Portugal and the Portuguese expansion overseas that give more prominence to the subject of sugar; see: J. Mattoso (ed.), *História*

de Portugal (Lisbon: Editorial Estampa, 1992–1993), and Bethencourt and Chaudhuri, *História da expansão portuguesa.*

39. De Vries and Van der Woude have produced a comprehensive overview of the economic development of the United Provinces, and Jonathan I. Israel surveyed the Dutch trade in the early modern period; see: J. de Vries and A. van der Woude, *The First Modern Economy* (Cambridge: Cambridge University Press, 1997) and Israel, *Dutch Primacy in World Trade.* Through the lens of spatial economics, Clé Lesger analyzed the rise of Amsterdam as the main European marketplace at the beginning of the seventeenth century; see: Lesger, *The Rise of the Amsterdam Market and Information Exchange.* Some collective works are also worthy of note; see: K. Davids and L. Noordegraaf (eds.), *The Dutch Economy in the Golden Age* (Amsterdam: NEHA, 1993); Lesger and Noordegraaf, *Entrepreneurs and Entrepreneurship in Early Modern Times* and F. S. Gaastra and L. Blussé (eds.), *Companies and Trade* (Leiden: University of Leiden Press, 1981).

40. Francisco Ribeiro da Silva examines the structures of the city of Porto during the Dynastic Union with Spain, providing important insights into the city's mercantile activities; see: Silva, *O Porto e o seu termo.* Joaquim Romero Magalhães explores the economy of the Algarve over a more extensive length of time, 1600–1773, with an emphasis on the later period; see: Magalhães, *O Algarve econômico.* We could also include in this category the important study by Oscar Gelderblom which focuses on the role of immigrants from the Southern Low Countries to Amsterdam's rise to becoming the main European marketplace; see: O. Gelderblom, *Zuid-Nederlandse kooplieden en de opkomst van de Amsterdamse stapelmarkt* (Hilversum: Verloren, 2000). José Antônio Gonsalves de Mello published a copy of a 1607 document that lists the ships that had embarked from Pernambuco since 1595 without complying with tax laws. Mello presents a fascinating introduction to the document, with details on the interested parties and the modus operandi of the underlying transactions; see: J. A. G. de Mello, "Os livros das saídas das urcas do porto do Recife," *Revista do IAHGP* (1993).

41. The economy of maritime transport between Portugal and Brazil was the basis of a study by Leonor Freire Costa, who ended up scrutinizing the structures and the vicissitudes of the trade. Costa achieves an excellent balance between an exhaustive archival research and a refined theoretical analysis: Costa, *O transporte no Atlântico*.

42. M. 'T Hart, J. Jonker, and J. L. van Zanden (eds.), *A Financial History of the Netherlands* (Cambridge: Cambridge University Press, 1997); M. Aymard (ed.), *Dutch Capitalism and World Capitalism* (Cambridge: Cambridge University Press, 1982).

43. Analyzing works on arithmetic from that period, António Augusto Marques de Almeida demonstrated how theoretical advances were responses to the demands engendered by the development of trading operations; see: A. A. Marques de Almeida, *Aritmética como descrição do real* (Lisbon: CNCDP, 1994).

44. Manuel António Fernandes Moreira has written about the role of Viana (do Castelo) in the Brazilian sugar trade and the impact of this trade on that town's economy and society; see: Moreira, *Os mercadores de Viana*.

45. Stols has studied the merchants and seafarers from the Low Countries engaged in the trade with Brazil, Portugal and the Iberian world; see: E. Stols, *De Spaanse Brabanders of de Handelsbetrekkingen der Zuidelijke Nederlanden met de Iberische Wereld* (Brussels: Paleis der Academién, 1971); idem, "Os mercadores flamengos em Portugal e no Brasil antes das conquistas holandesas," offprint of *Anais de História* (Assis: Unesp, 1973); idem, "The Southern Netherlands and the Foundation of the Dutch East and West Indies Companies," in *Acta Historiae Neerlandicae, Studies on the History of the Netherlands* (The Hague: Martinus Nijhoff, 1976); idem, "Dutch and Flemish Victims of the Inquisition in Brazil," in J. Lechner (ed.), *Essays on Cultural Identity in Colonial Latin America* (Leiden: TBC, 1988).

46. Among the studies on the role of the Portuguese Jews in the Amsterdam sugar trade, see those by Jonathan I. Israel, Swetschinski, E. M. Koen and Odette Vlessing. Koen (E. M. Koen, "Duarte Fernandes, koopman van de Portugese natie te Amsterdam," *Studia Rosenthaliana* 2:2 [1968]) and Vlessing (O. Vlessing, "Thomas Nunes Pina," in J. Bethlehem, F. Hiegentlich, and F. J. Hoogewoud (eds.), *Gids voor onderzoek naar de geshiedenis van de joden in Nederland* [Amsterdam: Schiphouwer en Brinkman, 2000]) produced micro-historical studies on the activities of two important New Christian/Jewish merchants and their families, Duarte Fernandes (Josua Habilio) and Tomas Nunes Pina (Josua Sarfati). In his comprehensive dissertation on the several aspects of the lives of the Portuguese Jews of Amsterdam in the seventeenth century, Swetschinski also explores their commercial activities; see: Swetschinski, "The Portuguese Jewish Merchants of Seventeenth-Century Amsterdam." Israel examines the

role of these Jews in the economic life of the Dutch Republic, Western Europe and the New World; see: J. I. Israel, "The Sephardi Contribution to Economic Life and Colonization in Europe and the New World," in Haim Beinart (ed.), *The Sephardi Legacy*, V. 2 (Jerusalem: Magnes, 1992). Vlessing has contributed to previous studies by examining new sources and performing a more profound analysis of other sources; see: Vlessing, "New Light on the Earliest History of Amsterdam Portuguese Jews" and "The Portuguese-Jewish Merchant Community in Seventeenth-Century Amsterdam." With respect to Brazil and Portugal, David G. Smith's doctoral dissertation explores the dynamics of what he calls the "mercantile class" of Lisbon and Bahia in the seventeenth century. Although Smith's dissertation does not solely examine the New Christians, he explores their New Christian question in depth and makes significant use of the Inquisition's sources; see: D. G. Smith, "The Mercantile Class of Portugal and Brazil in the Seventeenth Century," PhD dissertation, University of Texas, 1979. Smith deals with Portuguese merchants of non-Jewish origin in D. G. Smith, "Old Christian Merchants and the Foundation of the Brazil Company, 1649," *The Hispanic American Historical Review* 54:2 (1974). While studying the first activities of the Holy Office in Brazil, Sônia Siqueira da Silva concentrates largely on the economic aspects of life in the colony, particularly the trading activities of those mentioned in the inquisitorial documents; see: S. A. Siqueira, "A Inquisição portuguesa e a sociedade colonial – Ação do Santo Ofício na Bahia e Pernambuco na época das visitações," Professorial dissertation, University of São Paulo, 1994. José António Gonçalves de Mello analyzes several aspects of the presence of the New Christians in Pernambuco and later the Jews in Dutch-occupied Brazil. He emphasizes their economic activities and makes use of a wide range of sources; see: Mello, *Gente da nação.* More recently, the historical dictionary of the Portuguese Sephardic traders and businessmen, a collective study directed by António Augusto Marques de Almeida, presents short biographies of hundreds of Jewish and New Christian traders in Portugal and its colonies, and Jews of Portuguese origin abroad; see: A. A. Marques de Almeida (ed.), *Dicionário histórico dos sefarditas portugueses* (Lisbon: Campo da Comunicação, 2009), which contains references to several other micro-historical studies on New Christian traders. See also the study by this author: Strum, "The Portuguese Jews and New Christians in the Sugar Trade."

47. These authors have all made use of Portuguese sources that refer to both Brazil and Portugal. Mauro goes further and combines sources on both, preserved in French, Spanish, English and other libraries and archives. Mello uses English and Dutch documents, while Stols uses Dutch, Belgian and sources from other origins. See: Costa, *O transporte no Atlântico*; H. Johnson, "Das feitorias às capitanias," in H. Johnson and M. Silva (eds.), *Nova história da expansão portuguesa, V. 6: O Império luso-brasileiro, 1500–1620* (Lisbon: Editorial Estampa, 1992), pp. 207–239; idem, "A indústria do açúcar, 1570–1630," in ibid., pp. 240–302; Mauro, *Portugal, o Brasil e o Atlântico*; Mello, *Gente da nação*; idem, "Os livros das saídas das urcas do porto do Recife"; Smith, *The Mercantile Class of Portugal and Brazil*; Stols, *De Spaanse Brabanders*; idem, "Os mercadores flamengos"; idem, "The Southern Netherlands and the Foundation of the Dutch East and West Indies Companies"; idem, "Dutch and Flemish Victims of the Inquisition in Brazil." More recently, Cátia Antunes offers an innovative approach in an integrative study on the phenomenon of globalization in the early modern period, based on the economic ties between Amsterdam and Lisbon and the connections that developed further from both the locations. However, her study only refers to the second half of the 1600s; see: C. Antunes, *Globalisation in the Early Modern Period* (Amsterdam: Aksant, 2004).

48. C. Ebert, "The Trade in Brazilian Sugar," PhD dissertation, Columbia University, New York, 2004; idem, *Between Empires: Brazilian Sugar in the Early Atlantic Economy, 1550–1630* (Leiden: Brill, 2008); Strum, "The Portuguese Jews and New Christians in the Sugar Trade." Having consulted many of the same sources and dealt with similar questions, it is not surprising that both authors reached similar conclusions. Ebert's dissertation, however, covers a longer period (1550 to 1630) and a wider geographical scope (all the ports in Brazil, Portugal, the northern and southern Netherlands, Germany and England). He focuses on the different factors relating to trade and referred to the merchants from all the backgrounds involved in the sugar trade: Dutch, Flemish, German, and Portuguese, of Jewish origin or otherwise. Due to the broader scope of his study, Ebert had to rely more on the literature and secondary sources, mainly notarial records from Amsterdam, as well as some inquisitorial and administrative documents, both Portuguese and Dutch. My dissertation analyzes the relations between merchants of Jewish origin based in Amsterdam, Porto, Pernambuco and Bahia and their overseas trading agents in the same areas between 1595 and 1618. In addition to examining most of the sources Ebert consulted that were relevant to the scope of my dissertation, I have relied on extensive research of primary Portuguese sources, focusing on notarial records from Porto, which Ebert did not consult, and going into greater depth in the inquisitorial documents.

49. With respect to the notarial records from Amsterdam: to cover a larger number of records, I have used the series published by Wilhelmina Christina Pieterse and E. M. Koen in the periodical *Studia Rosenthaliana*, which contains an English summary of the notarial records between 1595 and 1627. These authors scrutinized the city's notarial registers and published the records featuring the names of Portuguese nationals, residing in the city or elsewhere, generally individuals of Jewish origin; see: W. C. Pieterse and E. M. Koen (eds.), "Notarial Records [Deeds] in Amsterdam Relating to the Portuguese Jews in That Town up to 1639," *Studia Rosenthaliana* (1967). I have quoted the records published in this series according to the numbers allocated to them by the editors. Appendix I contains a table of correspondence between the numbers of the records and the volumes, the number and pages of the periodical in which they were published. In addition to these English summaries, we used the index cards with a summary in Dutch organized by keywords, most of which are the work of Simon Hart: SAA, 30452. In some cases, I have consulted original documents from the Municipal Archive of Amsterdam, SAA, 5075: Archief van de Notarissen ter Standplaats Amsterdam. With respect to the notarial records from Porto, I have mainly used the deeds that referred to traders of Jewish origin, to which I have added others referring to foreigners operating in the city. Finally, due to the focus of the tribunal, the inquisitorial documents referred particularly to individuals of Jewish extraction. For more information about these sources, see: Strum, "The Portuguese Jews and New Christians in the Sugar Trade," pp. 58–63.

50. Mauro, *Portugal, o Brasil e o Atlântico*, v. 1, pp. 254–265; Schwartz, *Sugar Plantations in the Formation of Brazilian Society*, pp. 15–22; Johnson, "A indústria do açúcar, 1570–1630," pp. 240–251.

51. According to the charter contracts registered in Amsterdam's notarial records (at least with respect to the Portuguese Jews), most of their voyages were bound for that region; see: Swetschinski, "The Portuguese Jewish Merchants of Seventeenth-Century Amsterdam," pp. 142–144. A plea sent to the Dutch authorities in 1622 alleged that three-quarters of the sugar and other Brazilian products arrived in the Dutch Republic via Viana (do Castelo) and Porto, both of which are in Entre-Douro-e-Minho Province; see: Vlessing, "New Light on the Earliest History of Amsterdam Portuguese Jews," p. 55. Costa presents a different scenario. Based on a variety of Portuguese documents, she maintains that Lisbon dominated the sugar trade with Brazil, at least until the end of 1630s. Part of the cargo unloaded in the northern ports of Portugal, particularly in Viana, represented the final stop of voyages begun in Lisbon, directly or indirectly at the expense and direction of traders who resided there. However, the northern ports, particularly Porto and Viana, retained a substantial portion, and their share would grow from the 1620s onwards. This was when Madrid imposed stricter controls on Lisbon against the entry of ships and products from the Dutch Republic, camouflaged as if they were from allied or neutral countries. According to the author, it is possible that during that period, at a time of crisis for the trade, the northern ports may have outstripped Lisbon; see: Costa, *O transporte no Atlântico*, v. 1, pp. 91–111, 205, 333, 452–472. However, Costa does not believe that there was a significant amount of Dutch shipping between Portugal and Brazil, whether or not Dutch vessels passed themselves off as Portuguese, coordinated by merchants based in both Portugal and the Republic. This method may also have found a better reception in the northern ports and would have left few traces in the Portuguese documentation.

52. E. C. de Azevedo Mea, "A rotura das comunidades cristãs novas do litoral – Século XVII," in *O litoral em perspectiva histórica (sécs. XVI–XVIII): actas* (Porto: Centro Leonardo Coimbra, 2002), passim; idem, "Os portuenses perante o Santo Ofício, século XVI," in *I Congresso sobre a Diocese do Porto. Tempos e Lugares de Memória* (Porto: Faculdade de Letras da Universidade do Porto, 2002), passim.

53. *Primeira visitação do Santo Officio às partes do Brasil: confissões da Bahia: 1591–1592*; *Primeira visitação do Santo Officio às partes do Brasil: denunciações da Bahia: 1591–1593*; *Primeira Visitação do Santo Ofício às Partes do Brasil, Denunciações e Confissões de Pernambuco: 1593–1595*; *Segunda Visitação do Santo Ofício às Partes do Brasil pelo Inquisidor e Visitador Marcos Teixeira, Livro das Confissões e Ratificações da Bahia: 1618–1620*. See S. A. Siqueira, *A Inquisição portuguesa e a sociedade colonial* (São Paulo: Editora Ática, 1978).

54. Gelderblom, *Zuid-Nederlandse kooplieden en de opkomst van de Amsterdamse stapelmarkt*, pp. 114–122; Israel, *Dutch Primacy in World Trade*, pp. 30–42; De Vries and Van der Woude, *The First Modern Economy*, p. 368; Lesger, *The Rise of the Amsterdam Market and Information Exchange*, pp. 85–92, 133–138, 258; Pieterse and Koen, "Notarial Records [Deeds] in Amsterdam Relating to the Portuguese Jews in That Town up to 1639."

Chapter One

The Astronomer, *or* The Astrologer;
Johannes Vermeer (1668).

The Planisphere

Empires on the Move

It is impossible to understand the importance of sugar and the vicissitudes the sugar trade experienced without understanding the surrounding geopolitical context. The European overseas expansion began in the Middle Ages, but only matured in the sixteenth and seventeenth centuries. Seabound empires gradually formed and battled for overseas riches and control over territories and maritime spheres. The first real world war took place in precisely the period examined here. Theaters of war extended from the Far East to Brazil, encompassing Africa and Europe. The supremacy of the Habsburgs, whose dominions included Portugal and its overseas territories, appeared to be fading. Meanwhile, a new political entity, the Dutch Republic, was rapidly emerging as a major power.[1]

Taking the Cape

Portugal was the first European country to embark on an overseas expansion. This process began within the context of the Iberian Peninsula and the Maghreb towards the end of the Middle Ages. The expansion began almost as an extension of the "Reconquest," which, over the course of more than four centuries, progressively "liberated" Iberian territory from the Moors. Three of the main Iberian monarchies were consolidated during this process: Aragon, Castile and Portugal; alongside the kingdoms of Navarre, in the extreme northeast, and Granada, which was still under Muslim rule in the far south. This process later extended to the other side of the Mediterranean. Historically, the Iberian Peninsula, or *Al-Andalus*, was for the Muslims a logical continuation of Northwest Africa, or *Al-Maghrib*. For Christians, conquering North Africa was, perhaps – at least at first – a natural extension of the Reconquest within the peninsula.

The process of territorial expansion was of interest to many strata of society. The Crown mobilized the nobility and society in general to participate in a common project headed by the monarch, which later received the Pope's broad authorization and blessing as a holy crusade. From the Crown's perspective, conquest was a preferable occupation for the nobility compared to internecine quarrels or conspiracies to seize the throne. The conquered lands, with their natural resources and populations, provided fresh sources of revenue which then became part of the stock of grants which the Crown could distribute to anyone it wished to reward.

Nobles, gentlemen and knights from military orders, as well as commoners, had an opportunity to strengthen their power and rise socially and economically. The symbolic aspect of heroism and feats of arms, greatly esteemed during the period, cannot be overlooked. The Church, in turn, had a new flock of heathens or "infidels" to "save." These interests and values proliferated in the course of the overseas expansion, with different roles, nuances and contours.

During the centuries when the Reconquest was advancing on the Iberian Peninsula, urbanization and trade intensified in western Europe. Trade between the Mediterranean and northern Europe now began to take place increasingly by sea instead of over land and river routes. Sea transport enabled a greater flow of bulky products such as grain, timber, metal, wine and olive oil. The peninsula was situated right in the middle of this route and benefited from this process. The presence of Flemish, English, German, French, Italian and Iberian vessels intensified in Portuguese ports, and Portuguese vessels also sailed to northern Europe.

This process fueled the quest for products that could be exchanged for imported goods. Portugal exported honey, wax, dry and fresh fruit, wine, olive oil, leather and hides, cork, dried fish and, primarily, salt. The Crown promoted shipping and established commercial treaties with other kingdoms – mainly England – granted privileges to foreign merchants, especially Italians and Germans and established representative delegations abroad, particularly in Flanders. Foreigners also established agencies in Portugal.

The Maghreb and Granada, flanking the Strait of Gibraltar, were also on the route between the Christian Mediterranean and the northern Atlantic coast of Europe. The Muslim presence threatened

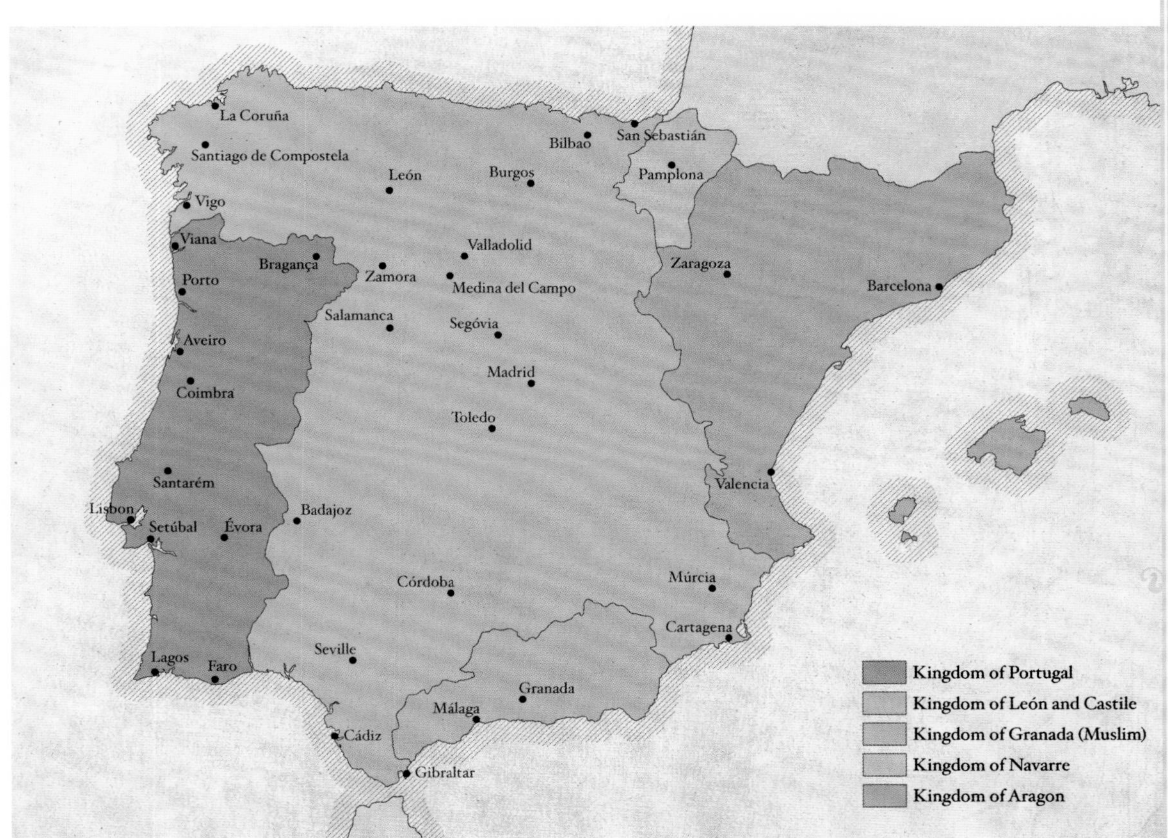

The Crowns of the Iberian Peninsula and the 'Reconquest'

The Crown of Aragon, which came to include Catalonia, part of the southern territory of what is now France and the Balearic Islands, expanded towards the south of the Iberian Peninsula to Valencia until the Castilians curtailed its expansion in Murcia. Aragon, then proceeded its expansion towards the central and eastern Mediterranean, where the Crown competed with Italian states in commercial and colonial enterprises and brought part of Greece, Sicily, Sardinia, and the southern regions of the Italian Peninsula under its influence. Even though the kingdom of Portugal was founded relatively late, it completed the process of recapturing its territory from the Moors quite quickly and staved off Castilian ambitions with regard to the Algarve. The Castilian "Reconquest" was the most protracted of all, gradually expanding the Crown of Castile's borders through Islamic territories towards the south until the conquest of Granada in 1492. These Iberian crowns did not coexist peacefully, and their internal political stability was often precarious as well.

Christian shipping, and conquests to be achieved in these regions could be interpreted as crusades to recapture lands that had been Christian seven hundred years earlier, as well as an effort to defend the economic interests of Christendom against the infidels. Hence, Portugal's overseas expansion began in Morocco with the expedition that conquered Ceuta in 1415.

The Portuguese victories in the Maghreb enhanced that kingdom's prestige among the Iberian monarchies. Furthermore, Portugal's campaigns in North Africa and its designs against Muslims elsewhere received steady support from the Holy See, which urged Christians to join in the effort and promised them shares in ecclesiastical revenues and indulgences, common means of compensation in the medieval political and ecclesiastical world.

While campaigns were organized against the Moors on both sides of the Strait, Portugal and Castile turned their attention to the Atlantic Islands. The Canaries and Madeira were already known to Europeans, at least

Large Fish Market; *Jan Brueghel, the Elder (1603). The large number of ships and people suggests that the ports were very busy and important in the lives of cities.*

Monastic military orders

Europeans in the Holy Land created monastic military orders in the Middle Ages. Their initial objective was to protect and take care of pilgrims and "liberate" the region from the Muslims. These orders established a presence in much of Western Europe from where new members and part of their resources were drawn, and were also involved in the Reconquest of the Iberian Peninsula, a process in which they played an important and active role. New orders whose activities were limited to the Iberian kingdoms emerged alongside the international orders such as the Knights Hospitaller and Templar. These newer orders included the Calatrava and Santiago orders – the latter was established in order to protect pilgrims traveling to Santiago de Compostela – and the Portuguese Order of Aviz (1175–1176), an offshoot of the Calatrava Order. The activities of these orders in Portuguese territory proved to be fundamental in shaping and consolidating the kingdom's frontiers, apart from defending, fortifying, repopulating and developing the conquered regions.

The military orders became powerful and influential institutions. Towards the end of the Middle Ages they possessed vast wealth and extensive lands, obtained as reward for the services they provided to several monarchs and popes.

After the Reconquest of the Algarve was concluded in the south, it was necessary to redefine the role of the orders established in Portugal and their power within the kingdom. The monarchs tried to make them hierarchically autonomous from bodies outside Portuguese territory, while drawing closer to them and subordinating them to the Crown, which would benefit from their capacity to mobilize human and material resources. The process began when the Order of Aviz became independent from the Calatrava Order. Shortly thereafter, after the Pope banned the Knights Templar, the Order of Christ was founded in Portugal in 1319, and inherited the Templars' assets. This process continued with the appointment of successive members of the royal family to high offices in these orders and reached its climax when the orders and their assets were incorporated into the Crown in the mid-sixteenth century.

from approximately 1380, but scouting expeditions aimed at occupation only took place in the early decades of the fifteenth century. Portugal and Castile vied for control over the Canary Islands throughout the fifteenth century, sending successive expeditions there and, seeking the support of the Holy See, which vacillated and even suggested dividing the island chain between the two powers.

It would take time to amass sufficient human, financial and managerial resources for a systematic occupation of the Atlantic Islands, which also entailed overcoming the difficult terrain and water conditions in Madeira, and the indigenous population in the Canaries. Europeans only effectively settled in Madeira around the middle of the century. Madeira was followed by the Canary Islands and the Azores, where reconnaissance and settlement took place later, but generally in a similar manner. Thus, at the outset, the economic exploitation of these territories concentrated on collecting local products: fish, dyes and enslaved indigenous people in the Canary Islands, and timber and dyes, such as dragon's blood and indigo, in Madeira.

As we will see, sugar manufacture thrived in Madeira and the Canary Islands, but was later replaced by wine. In the Azores, the colder climate prevented a sugar economy from flourishing, and its greater distance and lack of products with economic potential made it difficult to attract immigrants. Those islands' main exports were orchil and woad dyes and wheat.

Portuguese expeditions in Africa

In the thirty years after rounding Cape Bojador in 1434, the Portuguese explored twenty degrees off the African coast, from Cape Verde (the westernmost point of Africa), through Senegambia, Guinea and Sierra Leone, as far as what is now Liberia, including the Cape Verde islands (situated northwest of the eponymous cape). They built forts and trading posts (factories) along the African coast, such as Arguim, now in Mauritania. A new wave of southward expeditions began in the 1470s, exploring the islands of the Gulf of Guinea: Fernando Pó, São Tomé, Príncipe and Annobón, as well as part of the Gold Coast (also known as Mina Coast, present day Ghana), Cape Lopez and Cape St. Catherine (in modern-day Gabon).

The Portuguese expansion continued through expeditions along the African coast, where explorers hoped to find the source of the gold that supplied the trans-Saharan routes to the Maghreb. Portugal sought to control the flow of African gold, dominating entrepôts in the Maghreb and reaching sub-Saharan Africa.[A] The Portuguese also hoped to find a Christian kingdom governed by the powerful "Prester John," an idealized destination blending together elements of Abyssinians encountered during pilgrimages to Jerusalem or in Alexandria, Nestorian Christians scattered around Asia, and other vague notions and legends. They believed that Prester John would aid European crusading forces in an attack against Islam on two fronts, until the (re)liberation of Jerusalem.

The gold the Portuguese acquired on the African coast had a considerable impact on the economy of the realm at a time when urbanization and mercantilization increased the demand for coins in Portugal and Europe. The Portuguese also brought slaves from Africa, purchased in exchange for textiles and products from Morocco, among other items, without having to capture them, as was the case in both North Africa and the Canary Islands. They were put to work in Portugal and in Madeira, as well as re-exported from Portugal to other peninsular monarchies, the Canary Islands and other European kingdoms, so the slave trade could therefore be more lucrative than gold. Moreover, the Portuguese also imported various products from Africa such as gum arabic, civets (to extract musk), malagueta pepper, cotton, ivory, sea mammals, and so forth.

A. Europeans were already familiar with the African coast up to Cape Bojador, now in Western Sahara, where currents, winds and shoals hindered coastal sailing towards the south and whose long promontory in the middle of a desert coast appeared to signal the end of the world. They acquired from the Arabs some geographic notions of the coast of West Africa up to the Gulf of Guinea, including routes across the Sahara bringing gold from the interior of the continent and sea routes along the eastern African coast as far as to the Cape of Good Hope.

The fifteenth century was marked by fierce conflicts between Portugal and Castile, particularly during the reign of Alphonse V of Portugal. In 1474, the demise of Henry IV of Castile resulted in a civil war between the supporters of his half-sister Isabella, married to Ferdinand of Aragon, and the faction backing the late monarch's daughter, Joanna of Castile, La Beltraneja, whose mother was King Alphonse V of Portugal's sister. Alphonse V backed his niece, married her without papal dispensation, and declared himself and his wife to be the monarchs of Castile, going so far as minting coins.

Alphonse V's Castilian adventure drained Portugal of men and resources without enabling the monarch to impose his will either militarily or through diplomatic attempts to forge alliances with other European monarchies. Now Castile not only sparred with Portugal over the sovereignty of the Canary Islands but also laid claim to Guinea, meaning the coast of West Africa. The Treaty of Alcáçovas-Toledo (1479) ended the war, and Alphonse V and Joanna had to relinquish their ambitions. To maintain the peace, the treaty advocated the marriage of Alphonse V's grandson to one of Isabella's daughters, which might potentially unite the three main kingdoms on the Iberian Peninsula after Ferdinand II of Aragon and Isabella I of Castile had united both of their realms.

The Treaty of Alcáçovas-Toledo also resolved the dispute over territories outside the Iberian Peninsula, assigning to Portugal Guinea (as Africa south of Cape Bojador was termed), Madeira, the Azores and Cape Verde, as well as the kingdom of Fez to be conquered. Castile was given the right to conquer Granada and control over the Canary Islands, whose latitude was to serve as the dividing line for new lands to be explored – Castilian to the north and Portuguese to the south.

Until the late fifteenth century, the expansion was not a national, systematic or continuous undertaking, but rather the result of a set of individual initiatives derived from the diverse interests of local powers in the Algarve, military and religious orders,[B] nobles, the king and members of the royal family, such as Prince Henry the Navigator, and domestic and foreign merchants and seafarers. The Italians were an especially prominent element of the latter, particularly the Genoese, whose interests in Europe and in the Muslim Mediterranean benefited from the expansion.

After Alphonse V's death in 1481, John II intensified the Portuguese presence in Africa,[C] and, during his reign, the expansion eventually became a Crown enterprise, crystallizing the desire to reach Asia by sailing around Africa. Between 1487 and 1488, while Bartolomeu Dias was rounding the Cape of Good Hope, now in South Africa, an intelligence mission was organized to investigate the spice route east of the Mediterranean and to contact the mystical Prester John. Information collected by Pêro da Covilhã, the leading figure in this intelligence-gathering effort, provided Vasco da Gama's expedition, begun in 1497, with data about the sources and flow of spices, and on the feasibility of reaching India after rounding the southern tip of Africa. In Ethiopia, however, instead of a powerful ally, Covilhã found an impoverished kingdom in need of assistance.

Shortly after Dias rounded the Cape, another voyage made an even more decisive impact on history: under the aegis of Castile, Christopher Columbus reached the West Indies in 1492. In that same year, Ferdinand and Isabella completed the "Reconquest" by subduing Granada, the last Muslim kingdom on the Iberian Peninsula, expelling the Jews from Castile and Aragon and incorporating Granada into Castile. They were granted the title of "the Catholic Monarchs" for these feats.

The voyages of Dias and Christopher Columbus, as well as the information that the Portuguese Crown compiled about Asia, reignited the overseas controversy between Portugal and Castile, which argued that jurisdiction over new territories should be based on the right of discovery. After lengthy negotiations undertaken directly, as well as through the intercession of the Church, the Treaty of Tordesillas was signed in 1494, replacing the Treaty of Alçácovas-Toledo. The new treaty divided the globe into two spheres of influence: the western side, to be explored by the Castilians, and the eastern side, which was entrusted to the Portuguese. The line was the meridian that ran 370 leagues west of Cape Verde, thus safeguarding Portuguese shipping to India. Rome endorsed the treaty, making it illegitimate for other European nations to participate in the overseas expansion.

King John II did not live to see his dream of the Portuguese reaching India, as Vasco da Gama's expedition set out almost two years after his death, during the reign of Emmanuel I. In 1498, da Gama finally discovered the sea route to India, sailing around Africa. Shortly thereafter, in 1500, during another voyage to India, ships commanded by Pedro Álvares Cabral landed in Brazil. Yet the Portuguese Crown still focused on Asia at the time and paid scant attention to this new territory.

When they arrived in India, the Portuguese found a politically disparate region made up of fragmented units, often rivals. By exploiting the divisions between these political entities, either through diplomacy, by establishing peaceful trade relations or by force, the Portuguese, backed by their military fleets, gradually began to make inroads into the pre-existing trade networks. This process led to the emergence of the Carreira da Índia, the annual sea fleet between Portugal and Goa that provided access to Asian spices and made it possible to distribute them in European markets through Lisbon without the mediation of Muslim merchants in the Indian Ocean and Italian traders (especially Venetians) in the Mediterranean. Heavy investments were required in terms of outfitting ships, arms, munitions, soldiers, provisions for long voyages, and so on. Yet the Crown and private investors – direct and indirect alike – were eager to make huge profits from these ventures. Thus, Portugal sought to control this trade and to restrict competition as it had attempted to do with gold in Africa. To this end, during the initial years of their presence in India, the Portuguese focused on obtaining spices – black pepper, cinnamon, cloves, ginger, nutmeg, mace (the aril of nutmeg), and others – in the Malabar region, and on blocking the traditional Muslim routes for

B. In the mid-fifteenth century, the pope granted the Order of Christ spiritual jurisdiction over newly discovered lands and lands which were yet to be discovered by the Portuguese, thus rewarding the efforts of Prince Henry, who, as the master of the order, used its resources for exploratory maritime voyages.

C. King John II ordered that a castle be built in São Jorge da Mina (now Elmina, Ghana) to control access to the gold in the Gulf of Guinea. He also began settling São Tomé and sought to establish a Christian kingdom and ally in the Congo.

Above, a St. Vincent: Portuguese gold coin from the time of King Sebastian (1557–1578), initially valued at one thousand réis. There were also half-St. Vincent's worth 500 réis.

The "Portuguese": Portuguese gold coin from the reign of John III (1521–1557). In the sixteenth century, it was minted and used to either store of (metallic) value or make payments in Asia. Originally worth ten cruzados.

these products, seeking to dominate strategic strongholds, trading posts and – no less important – maritime straits.

However, over time, the Portuguese Crown eventually realized that in order to control and profit from this trade, it would also be necessary to take part in the pre-existing regional trade circuits in order to reach the sources of spice production and offer them attractive wares in exchange. Apart from precious metals, western products had few takers in Asian markets, thus it was imperative to obtain Asian goods directly from where they were produced and exchange them in other parts of that continent for items to be shipped to Europe via the Cape route.

The Portuguese sent numerous expeditions and diplomatic missions to other Asian regions – the Bay of Bengal, Ceylon, Southeast Asia, Insulindia,[D] China and Japan – where they later sought to establish permanent bases. Given the importance of the eastern coast of Africa for controlling the spice trade, they also strove to gain a foothold there. From Africa to the Far East, a system of trading posts and fortresses scattered over the areas that were of greatest commercial interest would provide a support network for the Portuguese State of India. Rather than focusing on the creation of a territorial empire, Portugal was more interested in controlling areas whose geographic, economic or logistical characteristics could bolster its trade network.

The first European kingdom to challenge Portuguese supremacy in the Far East was Portugal's old rival, Castile. Ferdinand Magellan's circumnavigation of the globe raised doubts about the limits of the Treaty of Tordesillas to the east, and the two mon-

Portuguese bases in the Indian Ocean

The conquest of Goa on the west coast of the Indian subcontinent in 1510 provided the Portuguese with an important and easily defensible strategic base with one of the best ports in the region, which enjoyed access to the central plateau and South India, the west coast and all the associated trade routes. For these reasons, Goa was also chosen to become the administrative capital of the Portuguese State of India, a role it played for four and a half centuries. Portugal sought to control the eastern Indian Ocean with the conquest of the city of Malacca, now in Malaysia, in 1511. The city dominated the Strait of Malacca, which separated Southeast Asia and Sumatra (in Insulindia) and constituted a main channel between the Pacific and Indian oceans. The city was a leading commercial hub in the trade between India and the Pacific markets, including China, eastern Southeast Asia and Insulindia. Moreover, it could serve as a strategic outpost for more systematic explorations of the eastern Indian Ocean, the South Seas and the Far East. The Portuguese also tried to control the Indian Ocean to the west. The conquest of Hormuz, at the entrance to the Persian Gulf, made it easier to block, or at least control, the access of Muslim merchants to the Indian Ocean, while facilitating contact with wealthy Persian merchants. This was also the case with the attempts to dominate Muscat, in what is now Oman. However, the Portuguese were unable to repeat their feats in the Red Sea, and failed to either maintain a fortress on the island of Socotra or to conquer Aden (Yemen).

D. The archipelago between Southeast Asia and Australia encompassing the modern-day territories of Indonesia, Singapore, East Timor, the Philippines, Brunei and Eastern Malaysia.

THEATR
SEPT
POLVS AR
Hec insula optima est et Saluberri
totus Septentrionis.
FRIGIDA ZONA.
MARE CONGELATVM.
ESTREITO DARIAN
AMERICA
AGANA.
CHIVGIGVA.
COGIBEL.
SAGVENA.
CANADAA.
ARATORIS.
BERGIREGIO.
ANIAN
CANAOGA.
ZVBGARA.
ALBARDOS.
AVANARES.
NORVBERGA.
CAPASCHI.
TOLM.
APALCHE.
SETE CIDA DES
FLORIDA.
TAGIL
COSSA.
NOVA GRANADA.
CALIFORNIA
NOVA SPANHA
Canal de Bahama.
TROPICVS CANCRI.
ANTILHAS.
TORRIDA.
CIRCVLVS ÆQVINOCTIALIS.
ACAMANI.
GVIANA
CARIBANA
ILHAS DE SALAMÃO.
NOVA GVINEA.
OMAGVA.
ZONA.
MARE
MOCOS.
SERRO.
OCCIDENS.
TROPICVS CAPRICORNI.
AVSTRALIS.
CHILE.
TOLTIN
TEMPERATA ZONA.
Hanc continentem Australem, no nulli Magallanicam regionem abeius inventore nuncupant.
PACIFICVM MARE.
TERRA DE GIGANTES.
CIRCVLVS ANTARCTICVS.
TERRA DO FOGO.
FRIGIDA
POLVS A
ME

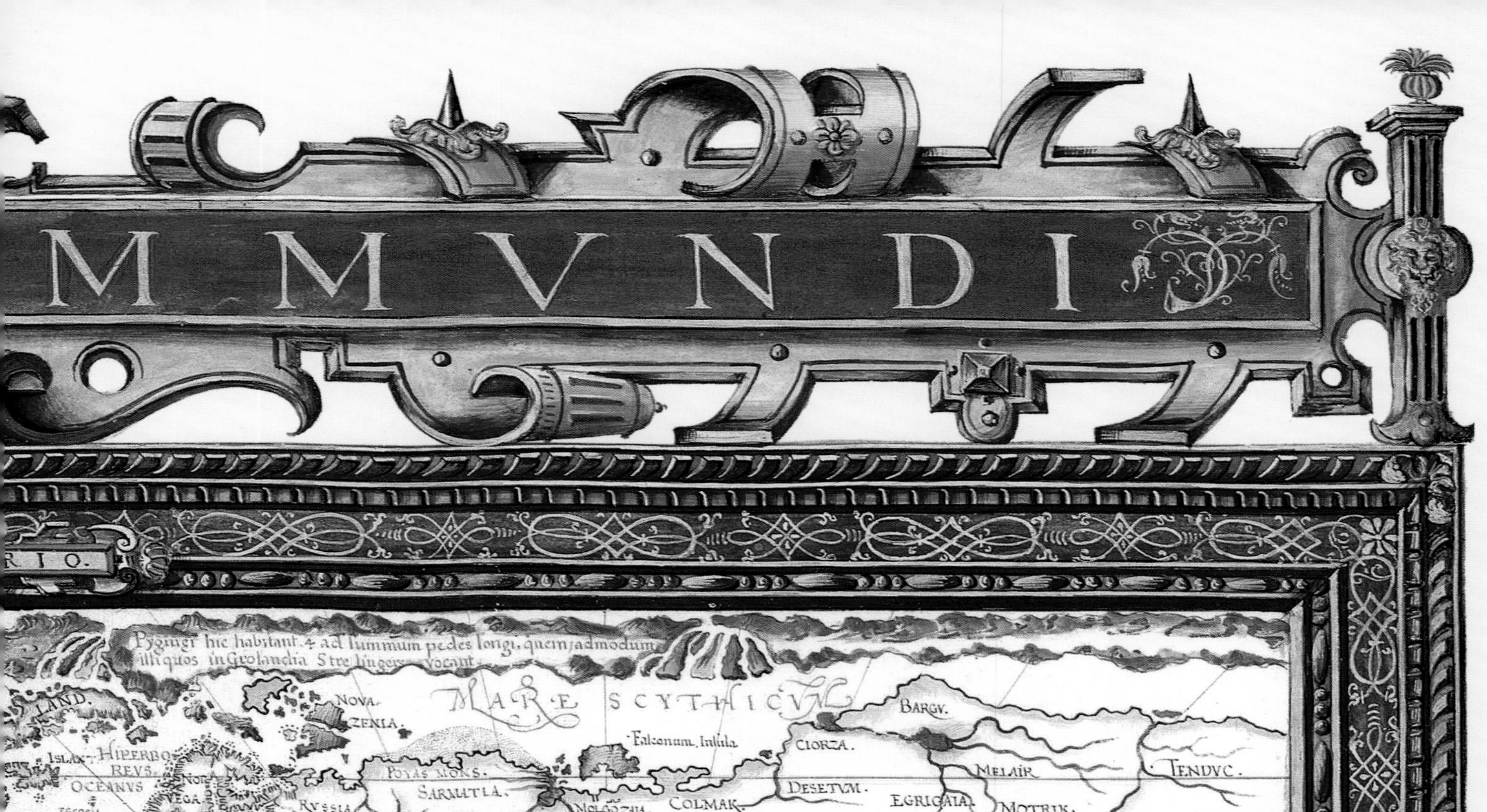

World map by João Baptista Lavanha and Luís Teixeira, published in the Atlas cosmografia *(1597 and 1612).*

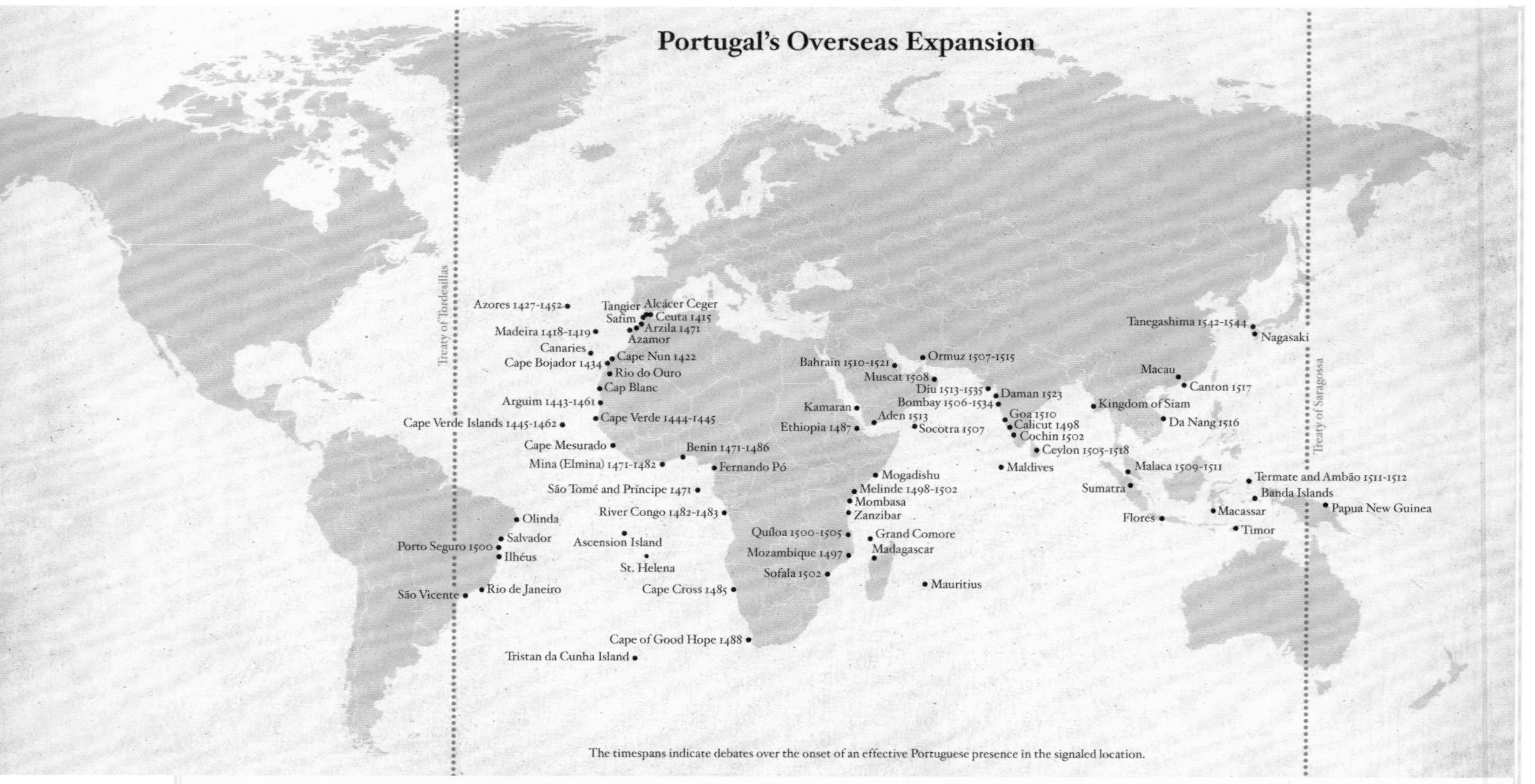

Portugal's inroads into Asia and Africa

After the conquest of Malacca in 1511, the Portuguese established commercial contacts with the Bay of Bengal, Siam (modern-day Thailand) and Pegu, now Myanmar or Burma. At the same time, they explored Insulindia in search of the Spice Islands, reaching Banda and Ambon, the islands of Sunda, Makassar, Ternate, Tidore and Timor, now divided between Indonesia and East Timor.

Portuguese expeditions continued towards the Far East, reaching China still in the second decade of the sixteenth century. Although their initial contacts with the Heavenly Kingdom were successful, subsequent attempts went awry. Ignorance of Chinese ways and customs led to a breakdown in diplomatic relations. Nevertheless, unofficial relations continued and enabled the Portuguese merchants to gain experience in trade and shipping in the China Sea.

Later, in 1543, three Portuguese merchants reached Japan for the first time. In the next few years, several others followed in their footsteps. From 1570 onwards, with the foundation of the port of Nagasaki, Portuguese traders had a fixed base in the country, and Nagasaki became the terminus for Portugal's overseas trade. As in India, the Portuguese were able to make the most of local circumstances, and began to serve as intermediaries in the trade between Japan and China, which had severed relations several years before. The establishment of a permanent base in Macao, on the Chinese coast, in 1557 facilitated this task. China was a source of silk, which was exchanged for Japanese silver, and both products were traded widely as part of Portugal's Asian commerce.

In Africa, the Portuguese in 1505 settled in Sofala, at the center of modern-day Mozambique, an important exporter of gold, and, in 1507, on the island of Mozambique, a strategic port on the India route. In the west, contacts with the kingdom of Congo developed further, and the Portuguese gained a foothold in Angola, founding Luanda in the 1570s. As we will see, the sugar economy flourished in São Tomé, reaching its height in the middle of the century, then declining in the last quarter.

archies began a dispute over the sovereignty of the Maluku Islands, which produced cloves, sandalwood, nutmeg and mace. Portugal acted militarily in the Far East and diplomatically on the Iberian Peninsula. Lacking the means to calculate the eastern meridian envisaged in the Treaty of Tordesillas, any solution would have to be based on compromise. In 1529, the Treaty of Zaragoza completed the process of delimiting the areas of influence of each kingdom by establishing a meridian at 297.5 leagues west of the islands, coupled with the Portuguese Crown's purchase of the archipelago. The same treaty also raised questions about the legitimacy of the Portuguese presence in the River Plate region and spurred the settlement of Brazil, leading to the creation of the system of hereditary captaincies, which we will see in the next chapter.

Building an Empire

Over the course of the sixteenth century, while Portugal concentrated its efforts on Asia, Castile converged on the Americas, where it had access to gold and, more importantly, silver. Aragon continued to focus on the Mediterranean, where it had possessions and dependencies. Castile and Aragon were united under the reign of Ferdinand and Isabella, during which the Americas were "discovered," and the precious metals mined there helped transform the Hispanic Monarchy into the foremost European power in the sixteenth century.

The offspring of the Catholic kings had a long-lasting impact on the continent's politics. The marriages of two of their daughters were negotiated with a view to achieving the final unification of the Iberian crowns under a great Catholic monarchy. The union of Castile and Aragon had upset the balance of power in the region, where, until then, Portugal and Aragon had provided a counterweight to Castilian might. With the conquest of Granada and the annexation of Navarre to the Hispanic Monarchy in 1512, Portugal became the only independent kingdom on the peninsula. If this merger was inevitable, it was better if the heir to the united throne came from within the family, a more honorable solution than a forced unification, as occurred in Navarre. Thus, Castile's eldest daughter, Princess Isabella of Aragon, married the heir to the Portuguese throne, Prince Alphonse, son of King John II. When the prince died prematurely, Isabella married the successor to the Portuguese throne, King Emmanuel I, the Fortunate. Isabella, however, died giving birth to the couple's only child, and the monarch went on to wed one of her younger sisters, Princess Mary.

The Catholic Monarchs' youngest daughter, Catherine, had a similar experience to that of her sister Isabella: widowed early after her marriage to the Prince of Wales, the heir to the English Crown, she married her first husband's brother and successor to the throne, Henry VIII. Catherine did not have any male children and Henry fell for her maid of honor, Anne Boleyn. Because he was unable to convince the Pope to annul his marriage to Catherine (among other reasons), Henry VIII broke with Catholicism and created the Church of England. Catherine's only child to survive infancy would rule England as Mary I, and was succeeded by Anne Boleyn's daughter, Elizabeth I.

Ferdinand and Isabella's alliance with the Tudors of England sought to establish a counterweight to France, the main rival of both nations on the European stage. The Catholic Monarchs disputed the

The Low Countries and their provinces

The Low Countries were formed by seventeen provinces. Nine were Dutch-speaking and were located on the Rhine, Waal and Meuse delta and north of these rivers – the counties of Holland (1) and Zeeland (2) and the lordships of Utrecht (3), Frisia (4), Drenthe (5), Overijssel (6), Groningen (7) and Ommelanden (8), the duchy of Guelderland and the county of Zutphen (9). Eight provinces were located south of the delta – the county of Flanders (10), the lordship of Mechelen (11), the duchies of Brabant (12), which included the Margraviate of Antwerp, and Limburg (13), still predominantly spoke Dutch. In the area of Wallonia, even further south, the French language predominated in the counties of Artois (14), Namur (15) and Hainaut (16), apart from the heterogeneous duchy of Luxembourg (17).

The first twelve roughly correspond to the region that adopted Calvinism during the Dutch Revolt and became part of the Republic of the United Provinces, later becoming the modern-day Kingdom of the Netherlands. The last five corresponded approximately to the region that remained Catholic and loyal to the Habsburgs, known as the Southern Low Countries, which would later become Belgium and Luxembourg.

The dukes of Burgundy and, subsequently, the Habsburgs ruled the Low Countries by means of governors appointed to areas that could encompass one or more provinces; these were the so-called *stadhouders*, literally "holders of the state." The Habsburgs also appointed a governor-general for the entire Low Countries. Governors-general were usually relatives of the sovereign, who acted as his substitute, at least officially. Moreover, each province had its own parliament, the so-called States, with representation for the nobility and the main cities. In their turn, these provincial States were represented at a joint parliament, the States-General, which had the privilege to limit the rulers' power to levy taxes and raise troops. Brussels became the administrative capital of the Low Countries.

border in the Pyrenees with France, as well as Aragon's possessions in Italy. With the same objective in mind, their only son, Prince Juan, and their second daughter, Joanna the Mad, wed the children of Maximilian I, the Holy Roman Emperor, and Mary of Burgundy, the sole descendant of the dukes of Burgundy.

The first real king of the unified Hispanic Monarchy was Charles (1500–1558). A grandson of the Catholic Monarchs, raised in Flanders, he assumed the throne upon the deaths of his uncles due to the declared incapacity to rule of his mother Joanna the Mad. He inherited the Crown of Castile from his maternal grandmother, whose dominions included Castile and León, Galicia and the Asturias, Granada and Navarre, as well as the American colonies. From his maternal grandfather he inherited the Crown of Aragon, alongside the kingdoms of Aragon, Catalonia, Valencia, Naples, Sicily and Sardinia. From his paternal grandmother he inherited the territories of the dukes of Burgundy, including the Low Countries and the Free County of Burgundy. Finally, he inherited the various Habsburg possessions in Central Europe from his paternal grandfather, Maximilian I (1459–1519), and succeeded him as emperor of the Holy Roman Empire, with the title of Charles V.[E]

Charles V spent a good part of his life clashing with the kings of France, mainly for hegemony in Italy, where he added the Duchy of Milan to his dominions. It was during his reign that Castile established its control over the Inca and Aztec empires. He also solved, in large measure, the question of the identity and sovereignty of the Low Countries, the region around the estuary of the Rhine, Waal, Ijssel, Meuse and Scheldt rivers, corresponding approximately to the modern-day Benelux territories and areas that are now part of northern France, such as Lille, Dunkirk, Arras and Cambrai, and western Germany. By the end of the fourteenth century, the Low Countries and northern Italy were the most urbanized areas of Europe. Even though, nominally, the ultimate sovereign of all the provinces that comprised the Low Countries was the Holy Roman Emperor or the king of France, the majority of these provinces – and the most important ones – belonged to the domains of the dukes of Burgundy, which Charlemagne inherited from his paternal grandmother.

As Charles V, he subjugated and seized control of the provinces which were still autonomous from Bourbon-Habsburg control in the north-eastern Low Countries,[F] forced the king of France to give him suzerainty over Flanders and Artois, and, since the other provinces were vassals of the Holy Roman Empire, he decided in 1548 and 1549 to separate them from the

E. Charles I of Spain and V of the Holy Roman Empire. He will be called "Charles V" here since this is how he was most commonly known. This is also the case with Philip II, who was also Philip I of Portugal.

F. Primarily Guelderland and Zutphen, the lords of the duke of Guelderland. Firmly opposed to the Burgundians-Habsburgs, the duke garnered the support of the city of Groningen, some nobles from Ommelanden and part of the provinces subordinated to the prince-bishopric of Utrecht – Utrecht, Overijssel and Drenthe. He supported the revolt in Frisia, which resisted submitting to the Burgundian-Habsburgs as well as to the hegemony of Holland among the provinces north of the rivers. It was largely due to the efforts of the States (parliament) of Holland that the revolt in Frisia was crushed. The prince-bishop of Utrecht abdicated his secular lordships to Charles V – authorized by the pope – and the duke of Guelderland renounced his claims to suzerainty over Groningen, Ommelanden and Drenthe. The duke died without leaving any direct legitimate heirs. His successor was also forced to cede the lordship to the emperor.

The Holy Roman Empire and the Habsburgs

The Holy Roman Empire had already encompassed a vast area in Central Europe for centuries, corresponding approximately to the modern-day territories of Germany, Austria, the Czech Republic, Slovakia, Switzerland and parts of other adjoining countries. The title of emperor was more symbolic than real, since the central powers and institutions were very weak. The region was a patchwork of numerous semi-independent states: principalities, archduchies, duchies and counties, prince-bishoprics, city-states, and so forth. The overlords of these units were all vassals of the emperor, but generally had more power in their territories than the sovereign had. Emperors were not succeeded hereditarily but rather chosen by seven electors – the Count Palatine of the Rhine, the king of Bohemia, the duke of Saxony, the margrave of Brandenburg and the archbishops of Cologne, Mainz and Trier – and confirmed by the pope. Candidates enticed the electors and the Holy See with economic advantages and political concessions, and even pressured them militarily.

The House of Habsburgs ruled the Archduchy of Austria, the most densely populated territory of the empire, rich in silver and copper from the Tyrol region, which ensured that it had enough troops and resources to guarantee its position within the empire, in particular, and Europe, in general. The dukes of Burgundy formed a secondary branch of the French royal family aiming to become the royal family. The Burgundian territories encompassed most of the Low Countries, among other territories on both sides of the border between France and the Holy Roman Empire.

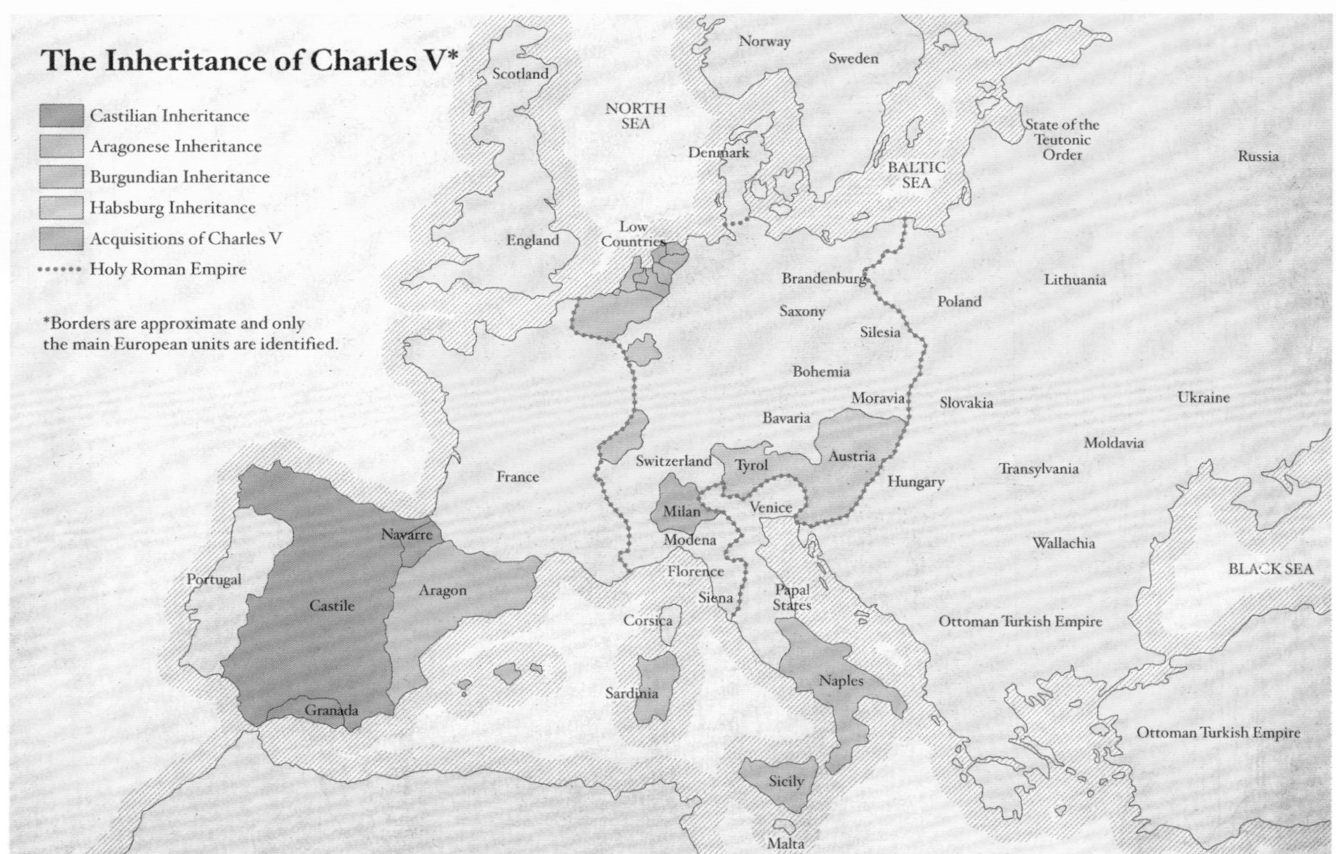

A musketeer holding his musket; *illustration by Jacob de Gheyn, for the military manual The Exercise of Armes (1607).*

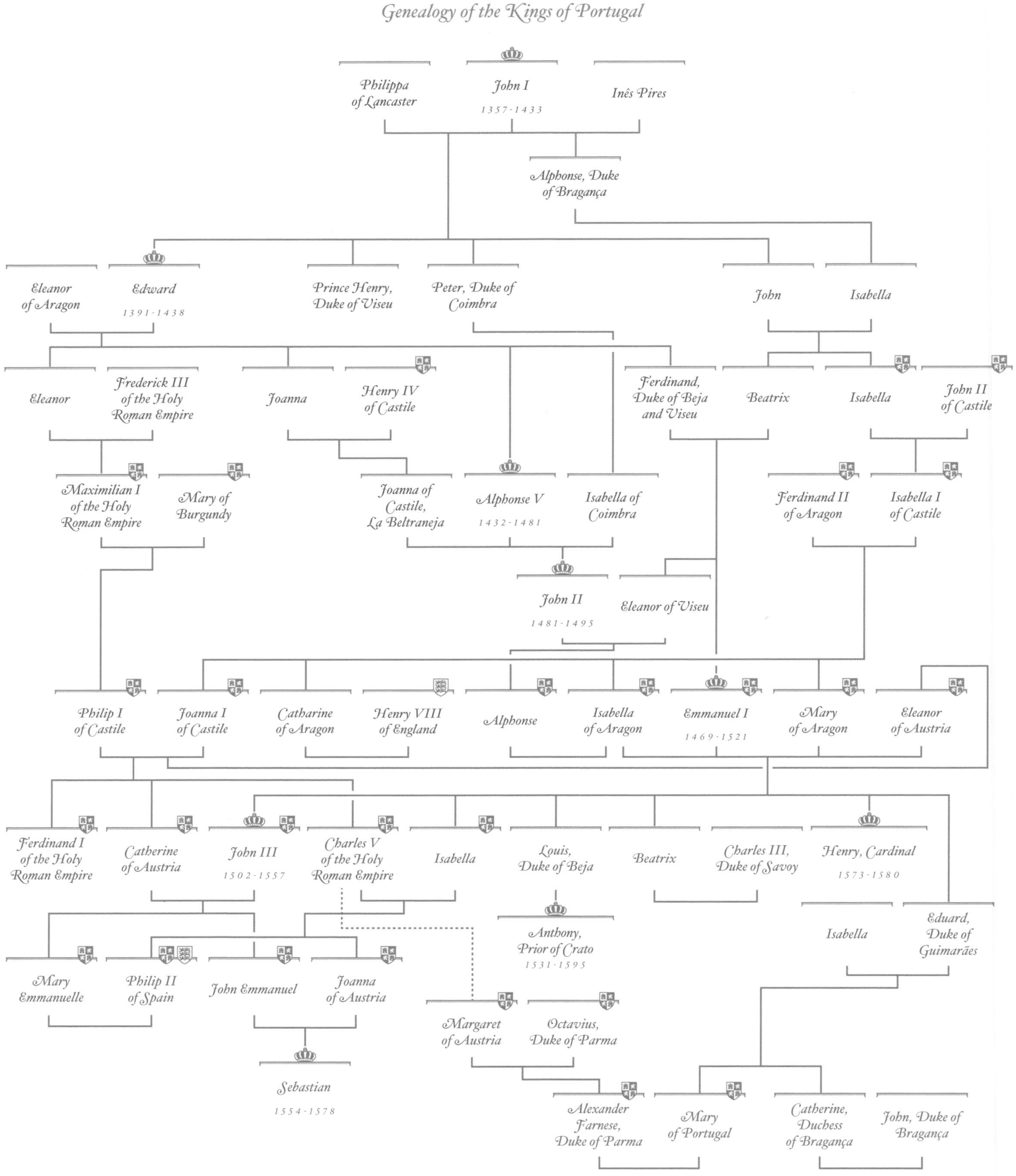

Indicates that the individual was a ruler of this monarchy. The years shown under their names are of birth and death.

Indicates that the same individual appears in the genealogy of the kings of Castile.

Indicates that the same individual appears in the genealogy of the kings of England.

Castilian and Portuguese disputes in the Far East

Closer ties between Portugal and Castile did not entirely prevent conflict, especially in the remote areas of the Pacific. Charles V's expeditions to the Maluku Islands showed that a trade route to the Pacific that required a return through the Strait of Magellan was not very lucrative, and that it was preferable to find a compromise with the Portuguese with regard to this archipelago. This was achieved with the Treaty of Zaragoza. These expeditions also resulted in the exploration of the Philippines which the treaty had left within the Castilian hemisphere. A more attractive route to the Philippines from Mexico was later established during the reign of Philip II. The islands were named after that monarch and began to be occupied by the Castilians. Fearing that their trade with the Maluku Islands, China and Japan would be undermined by competition with silver shipped from Acapulco (Mexico) to Manila, the Portuguese retaliated and the area became the setting for several clashes with Castilian fleets. However, after failing to establish a fixed base in China, the Castilians were obliged to trade with the Chinese in secret or through the Portuguese base in Macao.}

Empire and forge them into a single entity.[G] The Seventeen Provinces were to remain united under the dominion of Charles's descendants, who would hold the titles of lords, dukes, earls and counts of all of them.

Charles V used force to suppress revolts in Spain and the Low Countries, and managed to prevent the Ottoman Turks from advancing into Eastern Europe by land, but was unable to stop them from the Mediterranean. His worst defeats, however, were failing to put an end to the Protestant Reformation in the Holy Roman Empire and to thwart the insubordination of the German princes. He was eventually obliged to allow each German state to adopt the religion of its governor as the sole recognized faith – the principle of *cuius regio, eius religio*. He also maintained his alliance with Henry VIII of Protestant England.

As the successor to the Catholic Monarchs, Charles V insisted on strengthening ties with Portugal through matrimonial alliances and negotiated the marriage of his elder sister, Leonor, to King Emmanuel I, already the widower of his aunts Isabel and Mary, and gave the hand of his younger sister, Catherine of Austria, to his cousin John III (1502–1557), the son of King Emmanuel I and Queen Mary. If that were not enough, Charles V himself ended up marrying the John III's sister, Isabel of Portugal. A daughter of this marriage, Joanna of Austria, wed Prince John Emmanuel, the son of King John III, and bore the successor to the Portuguese throne, King Sebastian, the offspring of successive consanguineous marriages. Sebastian was born shortly after his father's death.

From the Portuguese point of view, these continuous matrimonial alliances could also prove beneficial. It was worthwhile to join forces against

G. This was the so-called Pragmatic Sanction, ratified by the States-General of the Low Countries, their provincial States and the Diet, the parliament of the Holy Roman Empire. It is necessary to note, however, that due to the complex ties of vassalage and jurisdiction within the Ancién Regime, even after the territorial consolidation implemented by Charles V, some enclaves, outside the monarch's jurisdiction and suzerainty, stayed within the territories of the Low Countries. After the Revolt, these enclaves also fell outside the purview of either the Republic of the United Provinces or the Southern Low Countries, and remained vassals of the Holy Empire or France for many centuries. The main such enclave was the prince-bishopric of Liège, which remained an autonomous pocket and a vassal of France. Similarly, some small enclaves within the Holy Roman Empire were part of the Low Countries and, after the Revolt, became part of the Republic or the Southern Low Countries.

Genealogy of the Kings of Castile

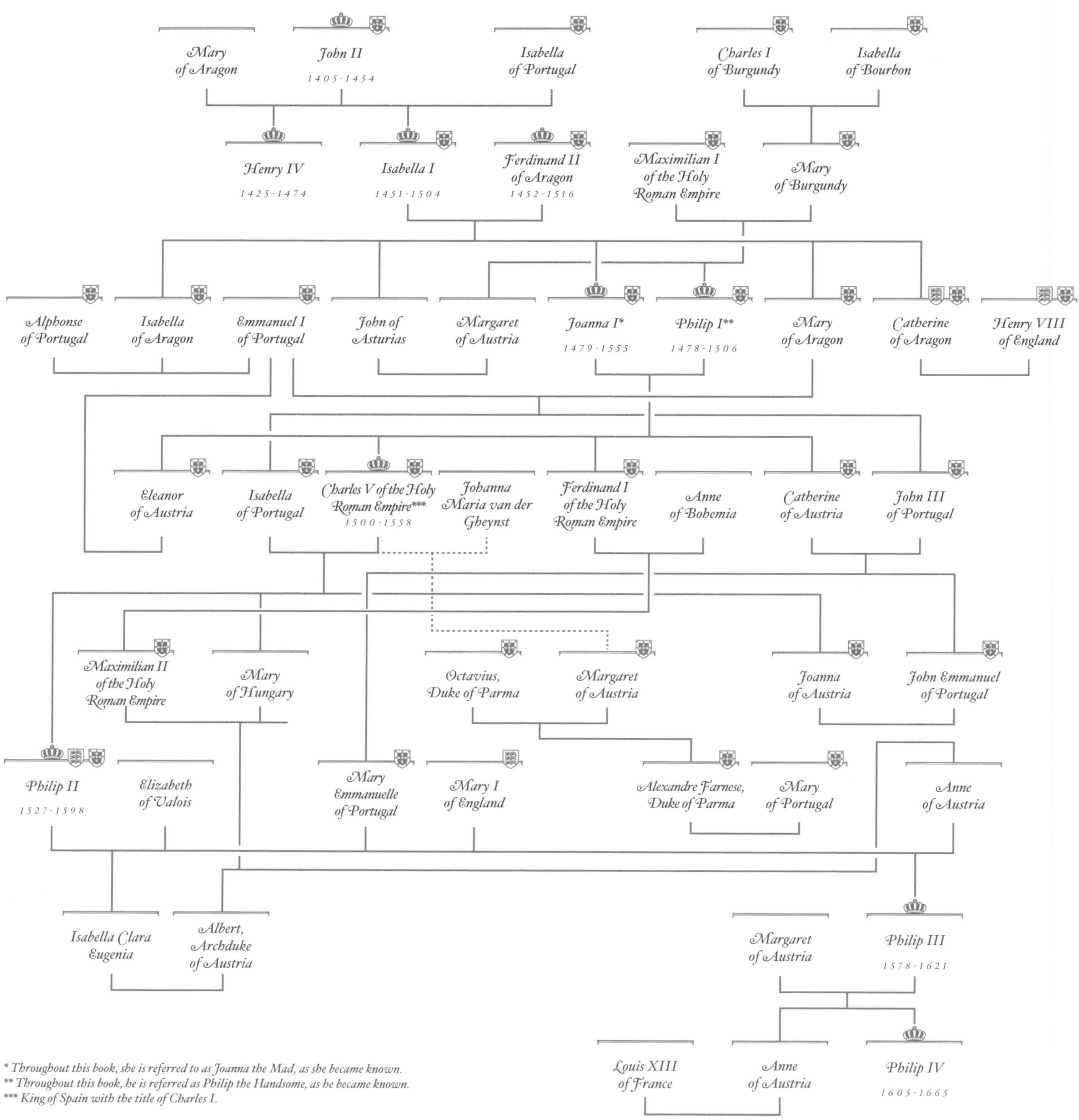

* Throughout this book, she is referred to as Joanna the Mad, as she became known.
** Throughout this book, he is referred as Philip the Handsome, as he became known.
*** King of Spain with the title of Charles I.

Indicates that the individual was a ruler of this monarchy. The years shown under their names are of birth and death.

Indicates that the same individual appears in the genealogy of the kings of Portugal.

Indicates that the same individual appears in the genealogy of the kings of England.

common enemies, as the Turks were advancing along the Mediterranean and in the Far East, endangering Portuguese commercial and geopolitical interests, while the Berbers threatened Portuguese strongholds in Morocco. Both of these enemies, the Ottomans and Moroccans, formed alliances with European powers such as England and France. Cooperation between Portugal and the Habsburgs facilitated assistance to Portuguese strongholds in North Africa, and shipping between the various Habsburg domains benefited from free passage along the Portuguese coast. Moreover, Portugal was a small and relatively weak kingdom, and its success abroad had already begun to attract the covetous attention of other European monarchies. The Habsburgs could provide support in those circumstances, if only to protect the reputation of their house.

However, these alliances hindered the neutral stance that Portugal tried to maintain in the conflict between the Habsburgs and the Valois of France. By becoming involved in the dynastic interests of the Habsburgs, Portugal implicitly chose a side, and attacks against Portuguese targets began to serve as a provocation – albeit indirectly – against Charles V and Philip II. The numerous agreements and treaties that Portugal established with France proved ineffective, and French corsairs attacked Portuguese vessels with growing intensity, especially in the English Channel, along the Portuguese coast and near the Atlantic archipelagos. France also contested Portugal's exclusive right, sanctioned by the Holy See, to trade with and colonize Brazil and Africa. French monarchs used Portugal's armed retaliation against privateers, colonial trade and colonizing initiatives as a pretext to issue letters of marque.[H] In the North Atlantic, the Gulf of Guinea and the Atlantic Islands, Portuguese merchants would also face attacks and attempts to conquer territory by English subjects, which also involved diplomatic efforts and reprisals.

Suppressing Sedition

The reign of Charles V did not end with his death, but rather ended with his abdication. He transferred the Holy Roman Empire to his brother Ferdinand and the rest of his dominions to his son, Philip II, between 1554 and 1558. The Hispanic Monarchy reached the height of its power and influence during the reign of Philip II (b. 1527, d. 1598). Although he was not the emperor in Central Europe, he inherited the Crown of Castile and its overseas possessions, the Crown of Aragon and its territories in Italy, the Low

H. A licence granted by a state to a private citizen to arm a ship and seize goods and vessels of another nation. The seized property would be considered as legitimate prizes of war.

Philip II at the Banquet of the Monarchs; *Alonso Sánchez Coello (1596). From right to left, seated at the table: Emperor Charles V; his wife Empress Isabella of Portugal; Philip II of Spain; Queen Anne of Austria, his fourth wife; Archduke Albert of Austria; Princess Isabella Clara Eugenia, his wife; and, with their backs turned, the Duke of Savoy and his wife Princess Catherine Michelle.*

Countries and other areas belonging to the dukes of Burgundy. He later added Portugal and its overseas dependencies in the Americas, Africa and Asia to his dominions.

Even more than his father, Philip II fought battles on several fronts: in the Mediterranean, Portugal, France, England, Ireland, the Americas and, above all, the Low Countries. He had ambitious imperial plans for the rest of Europe and beyond, viewing himself as the champion of Catholic orthodoxy against threats from Islam and the Reformation, and even from other heterodoxies. Naturally, his plans encompassed defending the dynastic interests of his house. Philip II was less diplomatic and pragmatic than his father, and could rely on much more silver from the Americas than Charles V did. Nevertheless, he repeatedly defaulted on payments to his bankers. In effect, his father's imperial policy, funded by German and Genoese bankers in exchange for present and future revenues from his territories, had already proved to be a heavy burden on his coffers. Therefore, shortly after Philip II ascended the throne, he declared a moratorium on debts to those bankers.

After his first wife, Princess Mary Emmanuelle (Maria Manuela) of Portugal, the daughter of King John III and Catherine of Austria, died giving birth to their first child, Philip II remarried in 1554. This time his wife was the Queen of England, Mary Tudor, Henry VIII's Catholic daughter with Catherine of Aragon. Mary Tudor and Philip II were co-regents of England and Ireland and, two years later, when Charles V abdicated, they also became co-regents of the Hispanic Monarchy. The objective was to counterbalance France's power, transforming the Hispanic Monarchy, England and the Low Countries into a single unit, which would also include Spanish territories in Italy and on the Franco-German border. However, the marriage contract stipulated that they could only bequeath both their crowns to their descendants, and not to each other, but the couple was childless. Mary Tudor (called "Bloody Mary" by the Protestants she persecuted) died in 1558. As a result, Philip II lost the English throne to Elizabeth I, the Virgin Queen, the daughter of Anne Boleyn and a Protestant to boot. Their relations were marked by mutual distrust, although the balance of power in Europe, particularly with regard to France, ensured that they maintained peaceful relations for almost three decades.

Philip II spent the early years of his reign in the Low Countries, from where he oversaw a war against France. His victory and peace with that kingdom (1559) enabled him not only to return to Spain but also to turn his gaze to the Mediterranean, where the Turks continued to increase their might. Alongside their Muslim allies, they spread terror among Christian sailors and threatened the northern coast of the Mediterranean basin.

Portugal's links with Castile became even closer during the reign of King Sebastian, particularly the period when Queen Catherine – Philip II's aunt – ruled as regent while Sebastian was a minor (1557–1562). The regency of Prince Henry, Sebastian's great-uncle (from 1562 to 1568), as well as his reign after his nephew's death, was marked by an ineffective attempt at maintaining independent and distant relations with Castile while establishing closer ties with France. After King Sebastian became an adult, clashes with the English resulted in an embargo being imposed on their ships and products. Attempts to achieve a peaceful solution to the conflict dragged on for several years, and an agreement signed in 1576 made slight progress. The context of the conflict with the Turks in the Mediterranean and the expan-

Half-vintém: *a silver coin from the reign of King Sebastian (1557–1578).*

sionist and crusading ventures of the youthful Portuguese monarch in Morocco reinforced Sebastian's ties with Philip II.

While Philip II was combating the Turks south of the Peninsula, to the north Protestantism threatened to take over France, which had entered into a period of civil war. Even worse, the Reformation was gaining ground in Philip II's own domains in the Low Countries. His administration there was insensitive to local traditions and rigorously instituted a policy of political centralization, increasing the power of the educated bureaucracy to the detriment of the nobility, which created dissent among aristocrats and urban oligarchies. Heavy taxation caused resentment all around, even more so because the funds appeared to be earmarked for imperial plans that had little to do with local interests. This was exacerbated by Philip II's intransigence in suppressing Protestantism, which was spreading widely, often with the

Iconoclasts in a church; *Dirck van Delen (1630). This painting recalls the destruction of sacred art works and church property in the Low Countries by Protestants in 1566.*

Medal used as an insignia by the Sea Beggars, the name given to the Dutch rebels who organized a naval guerrilla war using small vessels against the powerful pro-Hispanic forces.

acquiescence of the local nobility. To avoid unrest, an initiative that mobilized a large part of the nobility in 1566 presented a petition to the governor-general, an illegitimate half-sister of Philip II, Margaret of Parma, to suspend religious persecution and respect the privileges and liberties of the provinces. The petitioners were dubbed "beggars." The governor-general forwarded the petition to the sovereign.

The nobles' bold move in asking for greater tolerance encouraged the Protestants, who began to preach openly and worship in public. This resulted in renewed conflict, sparking an iconoclastic movement that swept through cities, destroying images and adornments in churches, as well as ecclesiastical properties. This was particularly evident in 1566 in Antwerp, which was then the main financial market and trading hub in northern Europe. With the help of leading Walloon nobles, the governor-general managed to re-establish order and suppress public Protestant worship.

Not satisfied, Philip II sent an enormous army to stamp out any sign of rebellion or heresy. He wanted to pacify the region once and for all so he could continue to focus his resources and attention on the struggle against the Turks in the Mediterranean. The commander of the newly arrived army, the Duke of Alba, set up an ad hoc tribunal to organize an investigation and execute all those linked to the revolts. He went even further and ordered the beheading of two of the highest nobles in the land, both of whom had been loyal to the king and Catholic, for tolerating the waves of Protestantism and dissidence. Many fled into exile.

Instead of pacifying the Low Countries, Alba added more fuel to the fire. The exiles included William I, Prince of Orange, known as William the Silent (1533–1584), who had maintained an attitude of conciliation and tolerance, and still sought to do so for some more time, with regard to both Philip II and the militant Calvinists. William raised funds from several sources, including France, and mustered troops among the Protestant princes and exiles with a view to removing Alba from power. He portrayed his struggle as a legalist act aimed at both restoring legitimacy and reconciling with the true sovereign, Philip II.

Unable to confront Alba on land, the rebels organized a guerrilla war at sea, mounted from German, English and French ports. Associated with the erstwhile petitioners, they became known as the "sea beggars." Their symbol was the Islamic crescent, with the slogan: "Better Turkish than Papist, despite the Mass," meaning that although they were Christians and took communion, they showed their solidarity with Philip II's other enemies while retaining their Christian identity. Philip II had achieved a major feat with the help of some Italian states by winning the Battle of Lepanto in 1571, thus pushing back Turkish expansion in the Mediterranean. The Turks were far from entirely vanquished, but presented a diminishing threat.

In order to maintain his troops, the Duke of Alba levied a new tax without abiding by the procedures required for doing so legitimately in the Low Countries. This only served to garner support for the rebel cause, which, in 1572, managed to capture and hold Brielle, a small port town in Holland surrounded by water. That victory encouraged the Protestants to rebel, and most of the cities in Holland and Zeeland, both maritime provinces, joined forces with the rebels and adopted Calvinism. There were some exceptions, such as Amsterdam, which remained Catholic and loyal for several years. Attempts to reconcile the political and religious camps, including the replacement of Alba, failed to overcome the two main challenges: demands for freedom of conscience and administrative autonomy.

Battle of Haarlemmermeer, *a naval engagement between the Hispanic forces and the Dutch rebels on May 26, 1573; Hendrick-Cornelisz. Vroom (ca. 1621).*

William I (1533–1584), Prince of Orange, Known as William the Silent; *Adriaen Thomasz. Key* (ca. 1570–1584).

The Dynastic Union: Philip II versus Anthony

Philip II negotiated the succession of the Portuguese throne throughout the reign of Cardinal Henry, who, wishing neither Philip nor Anthony to be his successor, planned to marry a noblewoman from Portugal or France, Castile's rival. Philip strove to neutralize these plans and the pope, who was linked to the Habsburgs, did not release the Portuguese monarch from his religious vows. The Spanish monarch then won over part of the Portuguese nobility, clergy and lettered classes, and avoided committing to other plans that could endanger his future sovereignty over Portugal.

The Dynastic Union was no surprise, since the policy of matrimonial alliances and the Iberian crowns' intentions with regard to each other's territories had remained consistent. This union was further facilitated by the fact that Portugal and the other Iberian kingdoms shared the same founding myth centered on the crusade, which the fight against the Muslims represented. In the second half of the sixteenth century, Philip II, King Sebastian and Cardinal Henry also shared an orthodox and intransigent Catholicism within a Europe where Humanism and Protestantism were gaining ground, Islam was still a threat, and in their view Judaism still appeared to be a latent danger.

However, Philip II faced resistance before he was able to ascend the Portuguese throne. In July 1580, the year Henry died, Anthony proclaimed himself king in Santarém, and was widely hailed in various locations which were against having a Castilian monarch. Anthony occupied Lisbon, but his troops were easily defeated by the forces commanded by the Duke of Alba, who had earlier suppressed the dissidents in the Low Countries, and Philip II was crowned Philip I of Portugal. (This volume uses only his Spanish title, as it is better known.)

Anthony sought refuge in northern Europe and later went to the Azores, which had not recognized Philip II's accession, and managed to repel Spanish attacks. He planned to counter-attack from the archipelago with the support of the Habsburgs' enemies.[J] Anthony eventually left the Azores to seek allies in Europe, and the islands were captured in 1583. Until his death he lived in France and England, where he tried to garner support for his cause. To this end he sold off the royal diamonds, proposed ceding sovereignty over Brazil and promised to muster Portuguese support against Philip II, without achieving any significant practical results. The main outcome was perhaps that, as the pretender to the throne of Portugal, Anthony issued privateering charters to adventurers of several nationalities who attacked Iberian vessels on his authority. In 1582, for example, at least eleven English ships sailed with his letters of marque. In 1589, Anthony returned to Portugal with Francis Drake's fleet, seeking to encourage the Portuguese to rise up against Philip II, but to no avail. He died in Paris in 1595.

The heavy expenditures incurred on these two battlefronts induced Philip II to declare bankruptcy in 1575, as he had done on two previous occasions in 1557 and 1560. Unpaid troops serving in the Spanish army mutinied, and the hordes sacked Antwerp for several days. The chaos of the so-called Spanish Fury, coupled with a power vacuum caused by the death of the governor-general, Luis de Requesens y Zúñiga,[I] led most of the provinces that had not taken part in the Revolt to strike a deal with the rebels: they would join forces to ward off the mutinous troops. Thus, they set aside prickly issues concerning religion and administrative autonomy to be resolved later through a subsequent reconciliation with the monarch. For the time being, the religious and political status quo would more or less be maintained, and persecution for reasons of conscience was suspended. This solution was called the Pacification of Ghent.

I. Luis de Requesens y Zúñiga took office after the removal of the Duke of Alba, who had replaced the monarch's half-sister, Margaret of Parma.

J. The conquest of the Portuguese throne from the Azores would be achieved centuries later by Peter (Pedro) I of Brazil and Peter IV of Portugal.

PATENTE
DAS MERCES, GRAÇAS,
E PRIVILEGIOS, DE QVE ELREI DOM PHILIPPE
nosso senhor fez merce a estes seus Regnos.

E a diante vai outra Patente das respostas das Cortes de Tomar.

¶ Estas Patentes mandou Sua Majestade que se posessem na Camara desta Cidade de Lisboa, & outras taes do mesmo teor na torre do Tombo, onde stão.

EM LISBOA,

PER ANTONIO RIBEIRO IMPRESSOR DEL REY
NOSSO SENHOR.
M.D.LXXXIII.

Title page of the charter containing the mercies, grace and favors granted by Philip II to Portugal and his dominions (1583).

However, no real pacification had taken place. In fact, a new conflict began to surface among three groups. The first group, headed by the new Spanish governors-general, were reactionaries who defended the restoration of Catholicism and royal authority. The second group comprised moderates, nobles and members of the urban aristocracy in the southern provinces, who, protective of their privileges and fearful of the damage the radicals could cause them, defended Catholicism and the king as long as the monarch signalled political concessions and kept foreign soldiers far away from the Low Countries. Finally, there were the radicals, not necessarily from the northern provinces, who wished to ensure autonomy and Protestantism for all the Low Countries. The latter were led by William the Silent, who, by force of circumstance, had joined their cause and adopted Calvinism.

The radicals managed to gain control in the other northern provinces, in addition to Holland and Zeeland: Frisia, Groningen, Gelderland, Utrecht and Overijssel, in which Protestantism became entrenched as the new religion. In 1578, a coup in the city of Amsterdam replaced the ruling class with returning exiles, and all Catholic churches were closed. This was called the Alteration. Meanwhile, the royalists entrenched themselves in the French-speaking south, while Brabant and Flanders turned into the setting for the conflicts between Protestants and Catholics. In 1579, the southern and French-speaking Walloon provinces aligned in support of the king and the Catholic church, signing the Union of Arras, while the northern provinces signed the Union of Utrecht to organize the defense along the border with the Holy Roman Empire.

Meanwhile, on the Iberian Peninsula, the long-envisaged union of the Portuguese Crown with the Hispanic Monarchy was coming about, but not as the Portuguese had hoped for, with a Portuguese king ruling Iberia. The disastrous campaign in Morocco in 1578 weakened Portugal militarily and caused a dynastic crisis when the young Portuguese monarch, King Sebastian, disappeared suddenly without leaving a direct successor. Cardinal Henry, his great-uncle, succeeded him but died two years later. He, too, left no heirs.

Philip II was the most powerful pretender to the throne and prevailed over the other contenders, particularly Anthony, the former prior[K] of the Knights Hospitaller Order in Portugal, which controlled vast lands and rights and was headquartered in Crato. He was the illegitimate son of Prince Luís, the son of King Emmanuel (Manuel).

Philip II was recognized as the king of Portugal in 1581 at the Cortes (parliament) of Tomar, which established the governing statutes for

Disputes between Portugal and Castile in the Far East after the Dynastic Union

Portugal and Castile still competed for markets in the Pacific despite legislation decreeing that the interests of each kingdom would continue to be separate in the Far East and forbidding trade outside their respective spheres of influence. Trade between the Castilian territory of the Philippines on the one hand, and China and Japan on the other, remained infrequent until the last decade of the sixteenth century, when more systematic efforts to promote it began to take effect. In the early seventeenth century, the Castilians began making more regular contact with the Japanese, which worried the Portuguese. Competition in trade was accompanied by an even more bitter rivalry over primacy in missionary activities in Japan, pitting the Jesuits, supported by the Portuguese, against the mendicant orders – Franciscans, Dominicans and Augustinians – favored by the government in Manila.

K. Anthony had been suspended from the priory in 1565 for behaving like a layman; he later served as the governor of Tangier and participated in the battle of Alcácer Quibir (Ksar el Kebir), where he was taken prisoner.

Portugal under the Dynastic Union. Portugal's autonomy, identity and symbols of sovereignty were to be preserved, as were the freedoms and ancient privileges, procedures and customs of the Portuguese Monarchy. Portugal would also maintain its administrative, financial, jurisdictional and military autonomy. Offices in the justice system and the central administration would be held exclusively by Portuguese nationals. To compensate for the monarch's absence from Portuguese territory during most of this period, the institutions of viceroy and the Council of Portugal were added to the institutional structure inherited from the previous dynasty. The viceroy was to be of royal blood and would embody the government in Portugal, while the Council of Portugal would represent the Portuguese administrative, judicial and ecclesiastical bodies before the monarch at court. In the absence of a viceroy, a board (junta) of Portuguese governors would carry out that role. The Portuguese and Castilian colonial empires would also stay separated, and, in theory, the Castilians were banned from Portuguese possessions and vice versa.

Between 1580 and 1640, the crowns of Spain and Portugal were united under the same ruler, but this did not imply unification, and in principle they would be maintained as distinct entities. In practice, this did not work out quite as planned. Once its sovereign was a Habsburg, Portugal would also suffer the consequences of the Habsburg's diplomatic and military policies. Thus, the French, the English and the Dutch targeted Portuguese possessions, as well as routes controlled by Portugal more frequently. However, the Castilian troops stationed in Portuguese coastal cities helped defend them against attacks by pirates and privateers without burdening the Portuguese coffers, which was particularly important at a time when Portugal's military was in disarray after King Sebastian's disastrous Moroccan campaign.

Forces from several Habsburg-controlled areas also participated in expeditions to assist Portugal's colonies, although the Portuguese often considered this support to be negligible in light of Philip's military might and the serious damage being inflicted on Portuguese possessions. Portuguese officials were not swayed by diplomatic compromises over Portugal's overseas interests, and sought definitive military solutions, which proved to be prejudicial. Furthermore, Portuguese troops also participated in expeditions organized against the monarch's enemies.

The cooperation between Portugal and Castile in North Africa was mutually beneficial, both for maintaining their respective local strongholds and the struggle against Muslim piracy, which was based in that region. In the Atlantic Islands, one kingdom provided the other with strategic bases of support, such as the Portuguese Azores and the Castilian Canary Islands, on the sea routes linking each to their respective colonies.

The two crowns also complemented each other in commercial terms. The Portuguese needed silver, which abounded in the Castilian Indies, while the Castilians increasingly needed labor, which Portuguese strongholds in Africa could provide in the form of slaves. The slave trade to Castilian colonies in the Americas, in turn, boosted Portugal's shipbuilding and transport sectors, generating employment in coastal towns.

Whether via the slave trade or through other means, the Portuguese penetrated Castilian possessions far more than the reverse. This was not always viewed favorably in Seville and Madrid, as, in effect, the Portuguese ended up breaking the system of controlled trade that Castile had sought to impose on its American colonies. Moreover, Castilian fleets bound for India often used Portuguese ports, which not only stimulated legal economic activities in those settlements but also gave rise to smuggling. After the Dynastic Union, trade in the Atlantic Islands was reinforced and the Portuguese gained more access to Castilian financial markets and farmed out further Castilian leasing contracts.

From the financial and administrative point of view, many decades would go by before consistent projects for greater coordination between the Iberian Habsburg crowns took shape, leading to quicker decision-making processes and greater administrative efficacy aimed at both reducing bureaucratic costs and effecting a more balanced distribution of the military expenditures burdening the Crown of Castile. Feelings of estrangement and resistance to the Dynastic Union emerged in different sections of Portuguese society, which felt that Portuguese interests were being undermined in geopolitical clashes and plans for internal reforms – political, administrative, financial and social – conceived at the Castilian court.

Deploying the Armada

While Philip II seized the Portuguese throne, his troops were advancing in the Low Countries. In an attempt to contain them, the rebels sought greater support and commitment from among the Hispanic Monarchy's potential rivals. In exchange, they offered the sovereignty of the United Provinces, linked by the 1579 Union of Utrecht. In order to pave the way for this proposal, in 1581 the States-General proclaimed the Act of Abjuration, in which they rejected the sovereignty of Philip II and his descendants. They first made overtures to the younger brother of the French monarch and his heir, the Duke of Anjou, who failed to either provide sufficient reinforcements to the south or to obtain domestic support, and ended up leaving the Low Countries in 1583. Meanwhile, with public finances and the Portuguese under control, and the French and Turks at bay, the Habsburg armies grew stronger and rapidly gained ground in Flanders and Brabant under the command of the Duke of Parma. William the Silent was assassinated while the Duke of Parma besieged Antwerp. The city fell after almost a year, in August 1585.

In general, during the Revolt, the majority of religious and political persecution and struggle took place precisely in the two provinces that had been the center of the mercantile

Two thousand réis with goshawk: *gold coin from the time of António, Prior of Crato (1580–1583).*

Sphere *or* two réis: *copper coin from the period of António, Prior of Crato (1580–1583).*

Twintigste Philipsdaalder: *silver coin from the reign of Philip II (1555–1598).*

and manufacturing sectors in the Low Countries – Flanders and Brabant. It was here that, from the outset, the clashes and pillaging had the most devastating and enduring effect. Until then, these two provinces had contained the region's most populous cities, responsible for most specialized and luxury products. These included Antwerp, which was once a leading commercial and financial centre in Europe, at least in the northern part of the continent. However, the waves of violence disrupted their economic activities, and the United Provinces' blockade preventing access to the sea and the maritime ports along the Flemish coast hindered the recovery of the southern provinces in general and Antwerp in particular.

During the course of the Revolt, many artisans sought shelter and sustenance in the rebellious northern provinces, where, in general and in the long term, the conflicts had a lesser impact. In the years after the fall of Antwerp, part of the population, including rich merchants, emigrated to other centers within and outside the Low Countries in order to avoid political and religious persecution, or were spurred on by the city's economic decline due to the upheaval, which continued to have a severe impact on the two neighboring provinces, Brabant and Flanders.

Until then, relations between the Hispanic Monarchy and England had been tense. Many Catholics, English and foreign alike, did not recognize Elizabeth I, a Protestant and the daughter of a marriage deemed to be invalid, as the legitimate heir to the English throne. The measures the queen implemented to reinforce the Church of England as the only legitimate church in the land only irked Spain, which supported British Catholics. England and the Hispanic Monarchy intervened actively in the religious wars in France, and the English supported the Dutch Revolt, albeit timidly and reluctantly. Elizabeth I also gave shelter to Anthony, the Prior of Crato, and stoked his pretensions to the Portuguese throne.

The Iberian Union and Philip II's advances, both in the Mediterranean as well as in the Low Countries, caused Elizabeth serious concern. The Spanish monarch would now be in a better position to support Catholic sedition in England and Ireland and to thwart English naval power. Thus, in 1585, the English queen decided to help the rebels in the Low Countries openly, with troops, horses and money, in exchange for the appointment of an English governor-general and influence in the administration of the Provinces. However, she declined the offer of sovereignty, since she saw questioning royal authority as a bad precedent and an option that would rule out any future understanding with Philip II. She sent the Earl of Leicester to govern the rebel provinces and command her troops, but like the Duke of Anjou, Leicester was unable to garner internal support to govern, and departed in humiliating circumstances in 1587. England's open support for the rebel provinces unleashed an all-out war between Elizabeth I and Philip II, which now extended to the economic arena through bans and embargoes on English and Dutch shipping and trade in the Habsburg domains. These measures sought to weaken the economies of the rebel provinces and England which were excluded from trade and shipping of colonial and Iberian products. Apart from this, their mercantile fleets became the object of systematic attacks by Habsburg fleets and privateers in their service.

As early as 1585, Philip II seized enemy ships anchored in the Hispanic Monarchy's ports and banned enemy vessels and goods in his domains. The Earl of Leicester, as the governor-general of the United Provinces, adopted similar measures and decreed an embargo on trade with Spain, Portugal and the Southern Low Countries which remained in force until the end of his brief administration (1586–1587).

Leeuwendaalder: *silver coin (1589). Minting coins was a sign of sovereignty.*

ORDIN·HOL·MO·NO·
15 89

Leeuwendaalder: *reverse of the coin shown on the previous page.*

Although they were frequently thwarted, circumvented or disregarded, these restrictions did have an impact on commerce by increasing the complexity, risks and costs of trade, as we will see in the following chapters. The recurrent embargoes imposed by the Hispanic Monarchy to weaken its enemies, particularly the Dutch, were also detrimental to Portugal. The prohibitions hindered the exports of salt – a prime Portuguese export product, traditionally purchased by the Dutch fishing industry, for which it was essential – as well as the re-export of colonial wares. Moreover, it hampered Portuguese supplies of grain and other items. The Dutch played a leading role in the distribution of these products, which now became prohibitively expensive as a result of the embargoes.

Meanwhile, Philip II was expending vast resources and a great deal of energy on preparations for his Invincible Armada. The fleet was intended to transport troops stationed in pacified Flanders to conquer England and thus, with papal support, put an end to, or at least retaliate against, insolence and heresy on both sides of the English Channel. Philip had intended to replace Elizabeth I with her cousin Mary Stuart, whom the English monarch had held prisoner for decades. However his plans were frustrated when Elizabeth authorized Mary's execution while this undertaking was still underway.

The preparations of the Armada were well known in England. To try to thwart Philip's plans, or at least minimize their impact, and avenge the seizure of English ships in 1585, a fleet under the command of Sir Francis Drake set sail in 1587. Drake inflicted considerable damage on the Iberian and Azorean coasts, but this did not stop the Armada venture from going forward.[L]

The Invincible Armada set sail from Lisbon the following year (1588). However, before it could take soldiers on board in Flanders, an Anglo-Dutch force attacked it and caused heavy casualties, aggravated by a storm that struck as the fleet was retreating. England and the Dutch rebels then launched, in 1589, a joint retaliatory expedition financed by private investors, under Drake's command. They tried to destroy remnants of the Armada being repaired in peninsular ports; intercept fleets returning with silver from the Americas, using the Azores as a base; and help incite a revolt in favor of Anthony, Prior of Crato, in Portugal. They did even more damage, but failed to bring about the intended strategic consequences.[M]

Apart from these squadrons, various minor fleets of English and, progressively, Dutch privateers began operating in the Atlantic, hindering the flow of troops and funds from the Iberian Peninsula to the strife-riven Low Countries. They sought to seize vessels coming from India and the Ameri-

Attacks by English privateers along the Brazilian coast

In 1587, English privateers seized or co-opted a Dutch hulk in Todos os Santos Bay and spent various weeks plundering the sugar plantations in the Recôncavo region, the city of Salvador's bay area. However, their raids did not garner them major profits. In 1591 and 1592, another fleet, commanded by Thomas Cavendish, who was attempting his second circumnavigation of the Earth, attacked the southern coast of Brazil, capturing ships. He raided the towns of Santos (twice) and São Vicente, looting and burning five sugar mills in the region, as well as Vitória, in the captaincy of Espírito Santo, where he suffered a heavy defeat.

In 1595, it was Pernambuco's turn to be attacked by James Lancaster, whose objective was to capture a carrack from India that had called in at Recife. The privateers occupied the port for about a month and attacked the warehouses where the cargo brought from India was stored, capturing a far more valuable prize than their usual booty. It is possible that the success of this attack resulted in another expedition being prepared to plunder Pernambuco, which was later diverted due to rumors that the Iberians were aware of these plans.

L. The fleet caused significant damage to the Spanish after arriving in Cadiz. It then continued on to the Algarve, where the English also attacked settlements on land and remained in the area between Cape St. Vincent and the Tagus estuary, capturing ships and destroying materials sent to supply the Spanish Armada in Lisbon. The English fleet did not attack Lisbon but instead headed for the Azores, probably with a view to intercepting a Castilian fleet coming from the Americas. Instead, it captured a carrack from India laden with valuable cargo.

M. The squadron inflicted some damage on the Spanish in La Coruña in Galicia, and blockaded Lisbon's harbor, seizing French and German ships that tried to break the siege. Their troops disembarked in Peniche, with Anthony, and reached the outskirts of Lisbon, but were unable to incite an uprising or mount a siege on the city, where the Iberian forces were well prepared. They re-embarked for the Atlantic Islands and engaged in pillaging.

Genealogy of the Kings of England

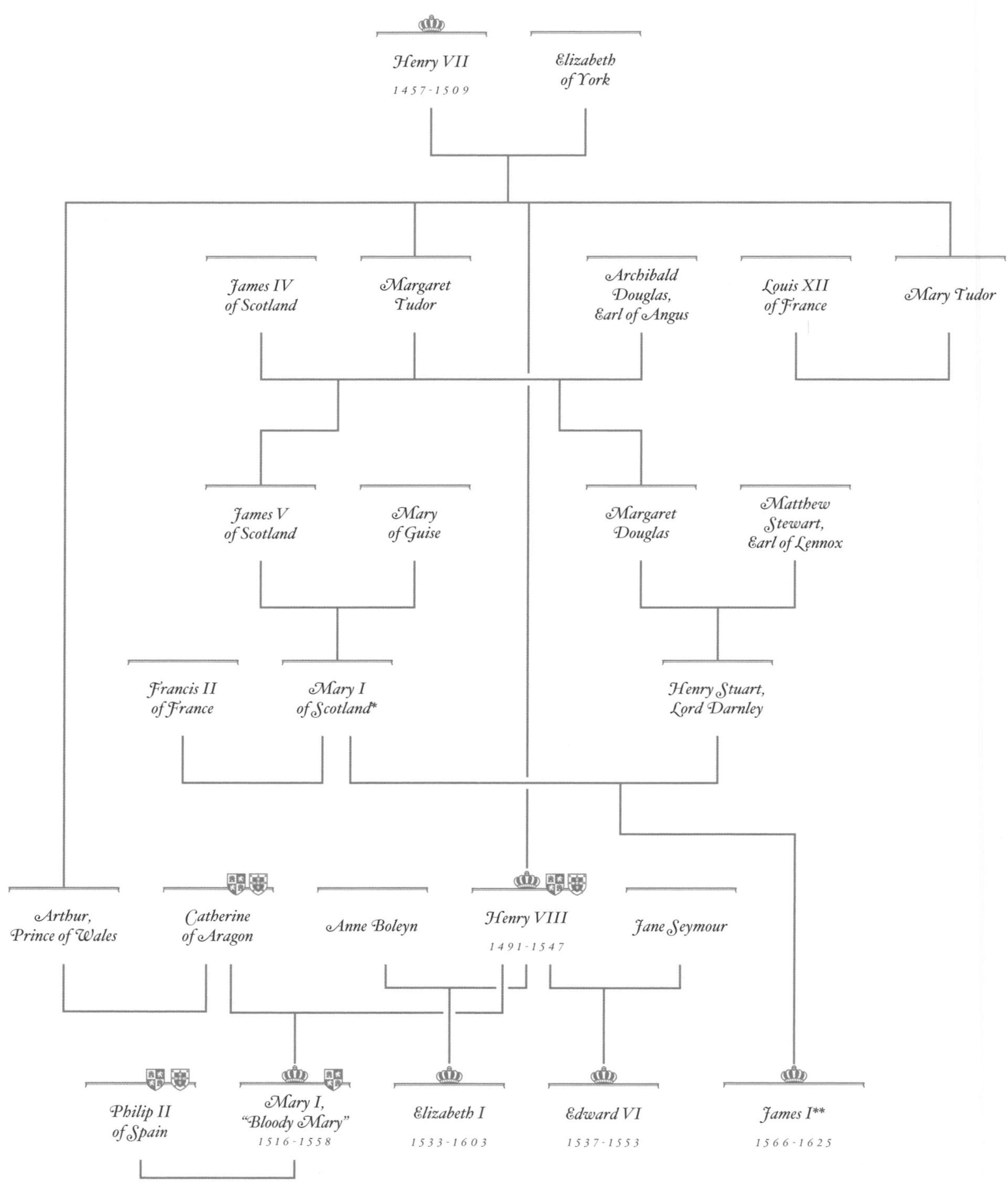

*Referred to in this book as Mary Stuart.
**James VI of Scotland.

Indicates that the individual was a ruler of this monarchy. The years shown under their names are of birth and death.

Indicates that the same individual appears in the genealogy of the kings of Portugal.

Indicates that the same individual appears in the genealogy of the kings of Castile.

cas to Iberia, and engaged in more daring incursions in the New World and the Atlantic Ocean. The most affected regions were the peninsular coast between Lisbon and Cadiz, the Canary Islands, the Azores and Cape Verde archipelagos, the coasts of Guinea (West Africa) and the Caribbean, and the Pacific coast of the Americas. Apart from attacks on the high seas, English privateers often threatened coastal communities on the Iberian Peninsula, spreading panic.

However, they were unable to either seize or obstruct the large, well-armed and heavily escorted silver fleets between the Americas and Spain, the most critical route line for the Habsburgs. They were more successful, however, with ships transporting sugar. In effect, the main prizes for English privateers were ships transporting sugar from Brazil, São Tomé, the Atlantic Islands and Morocco. In the three years after the Invincible Armada set sail, from 1588 to 1591, English privateers captured more than thirty-four ships laden with Brazilian sugar. In their transatlantic ventures, the English also attacked targets in Brazil: ships in transit, ports and plantations, among others.

The losses caused by privateers contributed towards the creation of the Mercantile Consulate in Portugal between 1592 and 1594. Its objectives included the creation of a coast guard fleet funded by a 3% tax on imports and exports. Efforts were made to improve intelligence and transmit information about English plans, in order to prepare defenses, avoid attacks or mount assaults against the enemy. Even though they were patently insufficient, these efforts to improve fortifications along the coast resulted in an increased capacity to dissuade privateers from disembarking in Portuguese territories, while counter-offensives by Iberian fleets did achieve a number of noteworthy victories. Nevertheless, the English continued to attack the Portuguese along the coast, on the high seas and on land. In 1596, English fleets repeated their attacks on Andalucía and the Algarve and, two years later, blockaded Lisbon again.

At the same time, in northern Europe, the Spanish defeated English forces supporting Protestants in France. Corsairs based in Dunkirk, which was then Flemish and loyal to the Habsburgs, began inflicting heavy casualties on Dutch and English merchant ships. The conflict between the Hispanic Monarchy and England took on greater proportions in 1595 with the onset of a revolt in Ireland supported by Spain. In the following year, Philip II made two attempts to send fleets against England, both of which were thwarted by weather conditions.

Spain became more deeply involved in the religious wars in France after the assassination of Henry III in 1589. It was no longer a question of containing the influence of and freedom afforded to the Calvinists, but rather of preventing the Protestant Henry of Navarre, an avowed Calvinist, from ascending the French throne. Philip II ordered the Duke of Parma to direct his troops in the Low Countries to assist Paris. Despite his military victories, Henry of Navarre was unable to capture Paris, which was reluctant to accept a Protestant king. He pragmatically decided to convert to Catholicism, convinced Paris to capitulate and obtained the pope's recognition of his title as Henry IV. Nevertheless, he failed to either placate Spain's opposition or obtain its recognition. War between the two kingdoms continued.

Henry IV calmed religious conflicts with the Edict of Nantes in 1598, in which he recognized the Catholic Church as the sole and official religion of France, but protected the Calvinists' freedom of conscience, and in certain cases also guaranteed tolerance for public worship. This ensured that France

NOT LONGE TIME SINCE I SAWE A COWE.
DID FLAUNDERS REPRESENTE
VPON WHOSE BACKE KINGE PHILLIP RODE
AS BEING MALECONTNT.

The Milch Cow (*ca.*1580–1595). *Satire of the Dutch revolt between 1581 and 1585: the milch cow personified the Low Countries (Flanders) and the figures around it represent the main characters involved in the conflict around its sovereignty. The fearful men stroking the cow apparently represent the States-General, which rejected Philip II's sovereignty in 1581. They seem perplexed at the difficulties the country is facing. In the center, Philip himself tries to ride the animal. On the left, Elizabeth I's discreet support for the Revolt is portrayed by the gesture of feeding the cow with a bundle of hay. On the right, a nobleman holds the animal's tail and shows the public his hand, on which the cow has apparently defecated. He is almost certainly the Duke of Anjou, who failed to garner internal support and beat a humiliating retreat from the Low Countries. The figure beneath the cow, drinking directly from its teats, is probably William the Silent, who, according to the caricature, made "a bucket of his pocket."*

THE QVEENE OF ENGLAND GIVING HAY
WHEARE ON THE COW DID FEEDE
AS ONE THAT WAS HER GREATEST HELPE
IN HER DISTRESSE AND NEEDE.
THE PRINCE OF ORANGE MILKT THE CO
AND MADE HIS PVRSE THE PAYLE,
THE COW DID SHYT IN MONSIEVRS HAND
WHILE HE DID HOLD HER TAYLE.

continued to be Catholic. Shortly thereafter he signed a peace treaty with Philip II, whose coffers were already depleted, but this did not prevent French pirates, especially Protestants (Huguenots), particularly those from the city of La Rochelle, from continuing sporadic predatory actions against Iberian vessels throughout the period covered in this volume. Nor did it put an end to continued French trade with Amerindians and colonial ventures along the Brazilian coast.

Spanish imperial military efforts could rely on stable supplies of silver from the Americas. However, Castilian revenues were committed to specific expenditures, the payment of debts and Philip II's multiple adventures. In 1596, the monarch was obliged to declare a fourth bankruptcy. The last decade of the century was also marked by surges of epidemics on the Iberian Peninsula and by poor harvests, increasing dependence on imports. This was a poor omen. It was clear that the king would not be able to achieve all his ambitions by means of force.

The Dutch Republic

The Hispanic Monarchy's war against France and England in the last fifteen years of the century afforded some relief to the United Provinces and enabled them to undergo rapid economic and military growth. They recovered territories to the east and south, and now controlled the Rhine, Waal and Ijssel rivers, and resumed trade with Germany. At the same time, northern (Dutch) naval forces imposed an efficient blockade on the Flemish coast and impeded Antwerp's access to the sea through the Scheldt River. The war was not yet over, but the existence of the United Provinces as a sovereign entity was no longer under threat, and their main mercantile centers were not exposed to attacks or pillaging.

Even before the Dutch Revolt, the maritime provinces of the Low Countries – particularly Holland and Zeeland – boasted a flourishing shipbuilding and maritime transport industry, which continued to grow despite the struggles and upheaval. Ships from Dutch port cities transported cheap and bulky products such as grain, timber, pitch, cordage, metals, dry fish, wine, olive oil and salt from the Baltic and Scandinavia to France, the Iberian Peninsula and, to a lesser extent, the Mediterranean, and vice versa.

The migration of many artisans from Flanders, Brabant and other southern provinces to the northern provinces meant that the traditional naval center now co-existed with an emerging manufacturing center. Wealthy merchants from the south took longer to arrive. They either sought refuge in Germany, France and England, or remained in the south despite the unrest. However, as soon as the United Provinces managed to keep the military front away from their main urban centers, around 1590, they began to arrive in growing numbers, and businessmen from other parts of Europe followed.

In 1590, five years after it began, the Spanish embargo was lifted. Philip II needed the Dutch, whom he still considered his subjects, to bring him grain from the Baltic and raw materials for shipbuilding. Thus, between 1590 and 1598, exchange between the rebel provinces and the Iberian Peninsula were once again feasible with just a few interruptions (such as in 1595), while Anglo-Iberian trade continued to be banned until 1603. The absence of English competition bolstered the prosperity of the United Provinces, particularly of Amsterdam.

Thanks to their vast mercantile fleet and thriving naval industry, the United Provinces could count on a flexible supply of vessels that made it possible to quickly direct shipping and re-exports to diverse destinations. A growing number of merchants with more capital and contacts began to trade with other regions and import and re-export goods that were not traditionally traded in the northern provinces. These goods included products from the Portuguese and Castilian overseas territories, especially sugar. The growing manufacturing sector in the United Provinces offered more commodities, some with high value added, which, exported along with traditional bulk goods, attracted luxury products brought in from new markets, such as spices, silks and other fine textiles, which were re-exported. Some of these re-export products, such as sugar, were processed in the United Provinces, and the growing manufacturing sector's demand for foreign raw materials fueled the Dutch shipping industry.

Beurtschip (1602): *a Dutch vessel used to transport people and small cargoes. Thanks to its thriving shipbuilding industry, a flexible supply of vessels facilitated the shipment and re-export of goods from the United Provinces to a variety of destinations.*

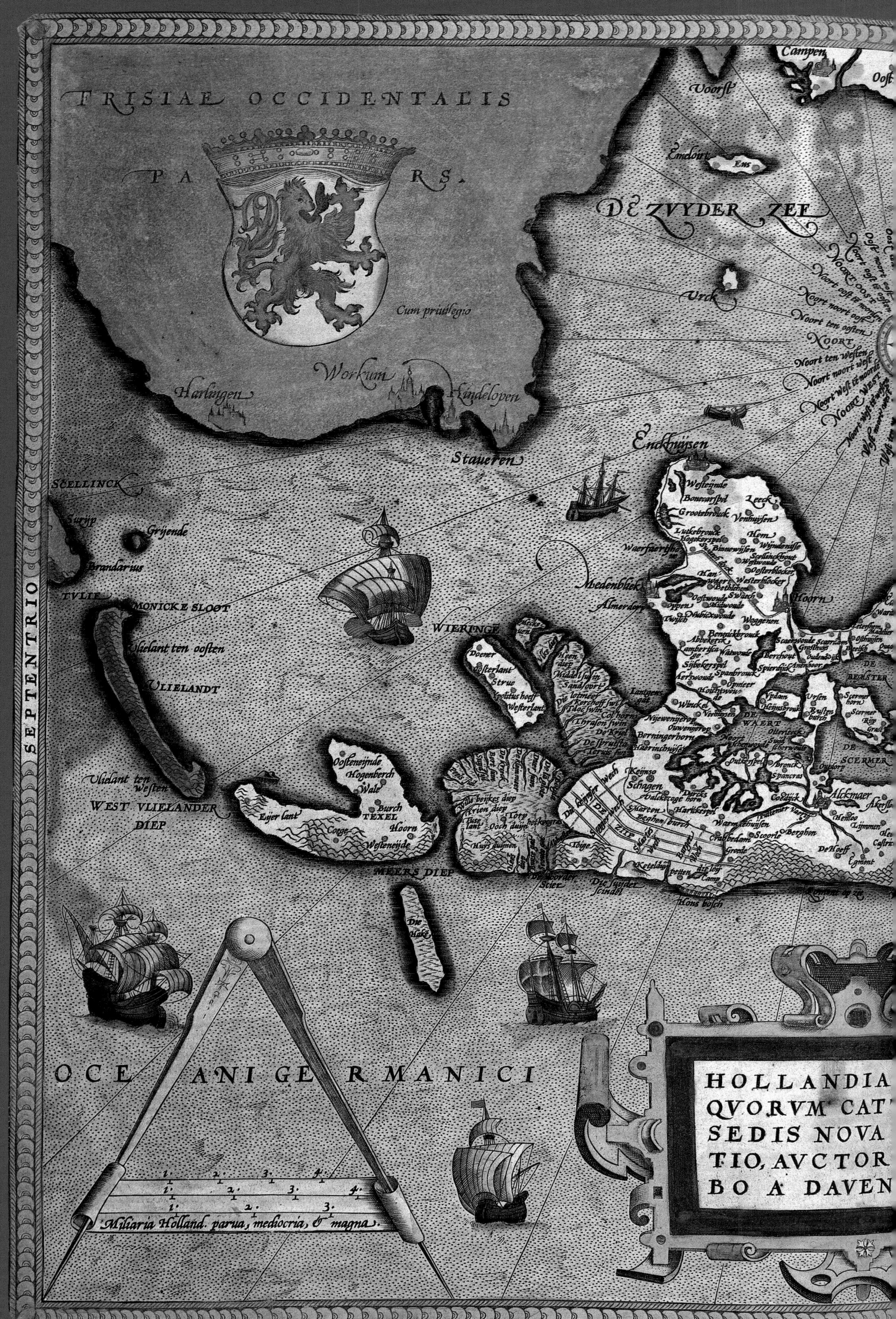

Depiction of the United Provinces (1602).

DVCATVS GELDRIÆ PARS.
DVCATVS BRABANT PARS.
MERIDIES
PARS.
Wolfheeſſom
Heeſſom
Reijncom
Wageningen
Rhenen
Garderen
Lunteren
Eede
Harder wijck
Putte
Voorthuijſen
Berreuelt
Emichuijſen
Tſherenloo
Terſchuer
Scarpezeel
Nijekerck
Amerſuoert
Eem fl.
Wouwenberg
Hulkeſteijn
Bunſchoten
Embrugghe
Lueſden
Soenſt
Barent
Vuerſen
Ooſtbrouck
Naerden
GOEY LANDT
Vtrecht
Vreeſwijck
Jutfaes
Yſelſteijn
Montfoort
Weeſp
Amſtelredam
Amſterveen
Sloten
Rietwijck
HAERLEMER MEER
LEYDER MEER
BRASEMEER
Haerlem
Hillegom
Liſſe
Leijde
Noortwijck
Catwijck
Valkenburg
Waſſenaer
Haghe
Delft
Schiedam
Vlaerdingen
Rotterdam
Goude
Oudewater
Scoonhouen
Cappelle
Graueſade
Staelduynen
DIE MAESE
Wijck te duer Stede
Culenburg
Vianen
Leerdam
Asperen
Heukelem
Gorichom
Worcum
Dordrecht
Sluijdrecht
Heeſden
Graue
Rauenſten
Megham
TIAE
Niulandt
Tſhertogenboſch
BOMMELER WEERT
Bommel
S. Geetruden berghe
Seuen bergen
Briele
VOORN
Goeree
Ouddorp
Browers hauen
SCOWEN
DVVELANT
Dirckxlant
Herkinge
Middelharniſ
Ouwetonge
Nieuwetonge
VOORN Stadt
Oolkens plaet
TIACEE
Bommende
DLANT VAN
PARS

Dutch participation in the Brazilian sugar trade in the sixteenth century

Flemish merchants had taken an active role in establishing the sugar industry in Madeira, the Canary Islands, Hispaniola and Brazil. With a greater or lesser participation of Portuguese ports as stopovers, from the mid-sixteenth century onwards traffic developed between the Low Countries and Brazil, frequently commanded from Antwerp. However, most of the trade between Brazil and the Low Countries entailed Portuguese intermediation until the last two decades of the sixteenth century, when the Dutch played a prominent role in shipping sugar from Brazilian ports, even compensating (along with Germans and Scandinavians) for the losses that English privateers inflicted on the Portuguese fleet. The flexible Dutch fleet helped export the colony's production, which was growing exponentially, and the larger and better-armed ships from northern Europe were safer, at least at first. This increased inroads made by Dutch shipping in Brazil was followed by the emergence of Amsterdam as a center for distributing and refining sugar in northern Europe, eclipsing Antwerp, and the growing migration of merchants involved in Iberian trade and refiners from the old center to the new one. The participation of foreigners in general in shipping to Brazil was restricted from 1591 onwards.

Former coat of arms of the city of Amsterdam showing a koggeschip, *a merchant vessel used in the North Sea and the Baltic.*

Apart from this, the concentration of transport facilities, capital and manufactured goods stimulated an active quest for new end markets. In effect, newly arrived merchants got involved in trading directly with the Levant – the eastern coast of the Mediterranean, then part of the Ottoman Empire – Russia, West Africa and even Brazil.

Largely due to its privileged location, even before the Revolt, Amsterdam was already the main port in the northern provinces. Since the city was linked to the sea through a deep estuary, the Zuiderzee, its port was sheltered from natural disasters such as floods, as well as from naval attacks. At the same time, consumers and producers in the interior of the Low Countries, Germany and northern France could easily reach the city by river and road.

The city gradually became an intermediary in the circulation of goods from various sources and financial credits between different centers. No less important, it also began to transmit information between mercantile centers. Ever since the so-called Alteration,*N* when it sided with the rebels and Calvinists in 1578, Amsterdam had been governed by a pro-commerce oligarchy, which, as we will see, developed municipal institutions to increase the security and efficiency of trade, such as the Bourse, the Exchange Bank and the Insurance Chamber.

Near death and seeing no end to the war in the Low Countries, Philip II conceived a plan that could lead to the pacification and even reunification of the region without making concessions that would undermine his prestige in terms of religion, autonomy or even the sovereignty of the northern provinces. He decided to make the Low Countries sovereign and independent, *de jure*, and bequeath them to his daughter, Isabella Clara Eugenia, who was to marry her cousin, Archduke Albert of Austria. Albert had previously governed Portugal and had been the governor-general of the Low Countries since 1596. At least officially, it would be Albert and Isabella who would make concessions that would return the rebel provinces to the Habsburg fold. Philip also astutely stipulated that if the couple was childless, which was likely since Isabella was thirty-two years old, the Low Countries would revert to the Hispanic Monarchy. Also, although they were the titular sovereigns, in practice Albert and Isabella would continue to depend on funds from Castile to maintain their troops.

Philip II died in 1598, and the archdukes assumed sovereignty of the Southern Low Countries. Peace negotiations ensued between Brussels, the capital of the Low Countries since the Burgundian period, and The Hague, the capital of the United Provinces. However, these attempts were eventually frustrated, since the rebels would not consent to either the sovereignty of the Habsburgs or reintroducing Catholicism. Taking advantage of a mutiny by Spanish troops after the end of the war with France, the rebels brought the battlefront to the southern provinces. They also attacked the Flemish coast to maintain a bridgehead for future incursions.

Sovereignty of the United Provinces was not transmitted to any monarch, and they gradually became organized as the Dutch Republic, governed by the States-General, which had gone from being an advisory and temporary body to becoming a deliberative and permanent entity. Within the politics of the States-General, Holland was the most prominent province, and within Holland, Amsterdam was the most influential city. Even though the balance of power was not stable, the city's mercantile interests played an important role in the decisions of the new Dutch Republic, which even intervened militarily to defend those interests.

The provinces that remained Catholic and loyal to the Habsburgs were progressively amalgamated into a single political entity, the Southern Low Countries, also known as the Spanish Low Countries. They remained under Spanish control or influence until the beginning of the eighteenth century and maintained Brussels as their capital. This division between the north and south later gave rise, more or less, to Belgium and Luxembourg in the south, and the Kingdom of the Netherlands in the north.

N. The name given to the change of power in Amsterdam on May 26, 1578, when the pro-Habsburg and Catholic city-government was deposed in favor of a rebel and Protestant one.

The exodus of Catholic magistrates and clergy from Amsterdam, shown here leaving Dam Square on May 26, 1578 after the great Alteration, when Amsterdam sided with the "rebels" and Protestants. Then, public Catholicism was proscribed, and the ruling class in the city was deposed and replaced with former exiles. Illustration by Jan Luyken, for Origin, Beginning, and Continuation of the Dutch Wars, *by Pieter Christiaensz. Bor (1679).*

Leo Belgicus: Portrayal of the Seventeen Provinces of the Low Countries; *Jan van Doetecum Jr. (1598). The provinces form a lion framed by the portraits of their governors-general appointed by the Habsburgs and stadhouders of the United Provinces, from Philip II to Archduke Albert and Prince Maurice of Nassau.*

Conflict Intensifies Overseas

Immediately after he was crowned in 1598, Philip III tried to use a combination of military and economic pressure in tandem with diplomacy to ensure the dynastic rights of the Habsburgs, tolerance of Catholicism where Protestantism held sway, the exclusion of foreigners from his colonies, and an honorable solution in the Low Countries. In the economic sphere, he not only resumed the policy of embargoes but also ordered the confiscation of all Dutch ships and goods in Iberian ports and sent their crews to row his galleys.

In response, on April 2, 1599, the States-General of the United Provinces declared that ships and goods belonging to Habsburg subjects were legitimate prizes of war. However, based on privileges previously granted by the Dutch authorities to Portuguese traders and the Republic's economic interests, merchants resident in the country, whether originally from Portugal or not, managed to ensure that this decree was relatively ineffective in the case of trade with Portugal and Brazil. The Dutch Republic also organized a fleet to retaliate for the seizure of ships and the mistreatment of its citizens. The period between 1598 and 1609 was marked by daring Dutch privateering raids along the Flemish and Iberian coasts, in the Atlantic Islands, the Caribbean, the Pacific and Brazil. However, while following the English model, they were not as intense as the incursions of the latter, nor as significant as Dutch privateering would become after 1621.

Apart from intensifying Dutch privateering and emboldening its corsairs, these embargoes encouraged Dutch ventures outside Europe. They mainly sought to reduce their subordination to Iberian caprices, avoid the premiums charged for Iberian intermediation and, perhaps, even establish fixed bases overseas. In some cases, their activities were an extension of prior attempts. This was the case with ventures to profit from salt extraction and trade in a variety of products in the Caribbean, the Amazon Basin and West Africa, albeit with limited results, with the exception of the profits made from the salt pans in the Caribbean.[9]

The Dutch had better luck in the Far East. In the last decade of the sixteenth century, companies were organized to trade with that region, particularly Insulindia, where the Portuguese presence was weaker. The Dutch authorities promoted these enterprises by granting them tax exemptions and by supplying them with arms and munitions. Their activities gained impetus after the 1598 embargo hindered Dutch access to spices brought by the annual fleet from India to Portugal. Their initial profits were meager, and competition between them resulted in a reduction of the arbitrage premium, making it difficult to join forces to ensure safety against attacks by Portuguese or Asian powers. These difficulties in imposing a monopoly on trade with the Far East were overcome through careful diplomatic efforts that balanced the objectives of the pioneering companies and the different Dutch regions involved in this trade, and eventually the Dutch East India Company (Verenigde Oost-Indische Compagnie), commonly known as the VOC, was chartered in 1602.

In Europe, the demise of two old rivals, Philip II and Elizabeth I, in a short span of time – in 1598 and 1603, respectively – and the detrimental impact the long conflict had inflicted on both their countries smoothed the path to peace. From the beginning of his reign, James I took a more conciliatory stance with regard to the Hispanic Monarchy. Despite Philip III's initial attempts to demonstrate his crusading spirit, his debacles in Algiers and Ireland, the impasse in the Low Countries and the subsequent deterioration of his financial situation forced him to adopt a more pragmatic approach. He signed a peace treaty with England in 1604.

Despite his tremendous financial investment and commitment to uphold the reputation of the Hispanic Monarchy, Philip III did not make progress against the Dutch by military means, and decided to use economic warfare to impel them to accept a truce. He believed that a peace with France and England and a truce with the rebel provinces would enable him to recoup his forces, and reorganize resources to finally engage in a decisive combat in which he would achieve his objectives. Thus, he strove to keep foreigners, particularly the rebels, out of the overseas colonies whose wealth supported his military might. He took energetic measures to prevent salt extraction and smuggling in the Caribbean,[Q] and ended the system of permits for foreign

The Dutch East India Company

The Dutch East India Company was given a monopoly for the Dutch trade east of the Cape of Good Hope.[P] The company also had political objectives. It was hoped that, apart from trading, it could undermine the Iberian presence and profits in the Far East, establishing some fortified strongholds in the region.

Managed by a board of seventeen directors – eight from Amsterdam, four from Zeeland, two from the south and two from the north of Holland, with a revolving vacancy occupied by one of the three minority regions — the company was based on open stock and merchants who were indigenous to the northern provinces, as well as immigrants from the southern provinces, participated in its funding.

The company's first major success occurred in 1605 when it seized Portuguese bases in the Maluku Islands, an important source of spices. Attempts to ensure a monopoly on the trade in these spices failed during those early years, but the VOC used its naval might to block its main competitors' access to these products and to deploy against Portuguese, Castilian and Chinese shipping. VOC fleets intercepted ships along the Goa-Macao and Macao-Nagasaki routes, taking a heavy toll on the finances of the Portuguese State of India. They also seized ships in transit in the Atlantic and in 1606 went so far as blockading the port of Lisbon, the final destination of the annual fleet from India to Europe.

O. In the last decade of the sixteenth century, the Caribbean was the focus of ventures by merchants based in the Republic interested in engaging in smuggling with the Spanish colonies. The Dutch also organized some expeditions to source salt on Sal Island in Cape Verde. However, when the 1598 Spanish embargo threatened to cut off supplies of this product, which was critical for one of the main industries of the Dutch economy, salted herrings, traditionally supplied by salt pans on the Iberian Peninsula, this resulted in fleets setting out from Dutch fishing ports to load salt in Punta de Araya, now in Venezuela. Others traded illegally with settlers in Venezuela, the more remote regions of the Greater Antilles, the part of Hispaniola that is now Haiti, Cuba and Puerto Rico, exchanging European wares for tobacco, pearls, hides and silver. They also traded in forest products, including brazilwood, with Amerindians along the Guyana coast, the Amazon Basin and regions where the Portuguese presence in Brazil was still tenuous, such as Paraíba and Espírito Santo. The Dutch continued to visit sugar exporting centers in Brazil in ships purporting to be from neutral countries, Scandinavia and German cities, as we will see later on. The Dutch had already traded directly with West Africa since the early 1590s, buying sugar in São Tomé and acquiring gold, ivory, gum, malagueta peppers and other spices in Senegal, Gambia and the Gulf of Guinea. Their main challenge was Portuguese military and diplomatic power in the region. Aimed at reducing Portuguese influence, in 1596 a merchant based in the Republic funded an attack on the fortress of São Jorge da Mina (now in Ghana), to no avail. The 1598 embargo encouraged more Dutch armed expeditions to Africa. Dutch attempts to form a cartel to avoid competition among themselves were eventually thwarted. Despite their failure to seize the islands of Príncipe and São Tomé in 1598 and 1599, and the fact that access to the sugar produced in these islands had been limited by the Hispanic authorities, the Dutch did manage to make some inroads in West Africa.

P. The charter issued to the VOC followed a model very similar to the monopoly granted by Queen Elizabeth I of England to the English East India Company (Governor and Company of Merchants of London Trading into the East Indies) two years earlier, with the same purposes and objectives. The English, however, had even less experience and would take longer to penetrate the Far East.

Q. Between 1603 and 1606, Philip III ordered the depopulation of the cattle-raising region in what is now Haiti – a move that later facilitated France's penetration of the region – put an end to tobacco growing in Venezuela and attacked the Dutch salt fleets anchored there.

240

Dutch attacks on Iberian overseas territories

As early as 1598, a Dutch fleet had attempted to capture the island of Príncipe, in the Gulf of Guinea. The following year, Dutch vessels attacked Portuguese and Amerindian settlements in Rio de Janeiro and other sites along the Brazilian coast, before sailing to the Strait of Magellan. In 1599, an enormous fleet commanded by Pieter van der Does sought revenge for the confiscation of Dutch ships in Iberian ports and mobilized the first large-scale Dutch naval fleet for a long-distance attack. Incorporating private ships recruited in exchange for a share of the booty, the fleet tried to seize the Castilian India Fleet near La Coruña. The Spanish, however, were aware of their plans and managed to elude them. The fleet then redirected its attacks to the Canary Islands and São Tomé, where it suffered heavy losses due to tropical disease. A squadron commanded by Hartmann and Broer was sent to Brazil, capturing the port of Salvador, Bahia, and the vessels moored there, and harassing the Recôncavo region for almost two months. Even though they seized cargo in Bahia, the results were rather disappointing for the Dutch.

A few years later, in December 1603, a smaller fleet commanded by Paulus van Caerden was officially organized against Brazil. Once again, it attacked Bahia, without capturing the city, but seized vessels and swept through the Recôncavo region. The fleet returned with a large amount of sugar, as well as some gold and silver, but failed to establish a fortress on the Brazilian coast as it had intended to.

Philip III on Horseback; *Diego Velazquez (1634–1635).*

The four-masted ship *De Hollandse Tuyn*, from Amsterdam, and others returning from Brazil under the command of Paulus van Caerden (1569–1615 or 1616) in 1605; *Hendrik-Cornelisz Vroom. For the third time since 1598, the Dutch attacked the Brazilian coast without establishing bases in its territory.*

Milling and transporting grain; an illustration from the Book of Trades*; Jan Luyken and Caspar Luyken (1694). The Dutch merchant fleet transported the grain required to supply the Iberian Peninsula.*

ships in Brazil, which had been in effect since 1591. In 1605, foreign vessels were entirely banned from Brazil, although some continued to visit the colony pretending to be Portuguese, as will be seen in greater detail. Furthermore, Philip sought to obstruct Dutch traffic through the Strait of Gibraltar and at their access to the Baltic.

In the meantime, he tried to favor Dutch loyalists and draw them closer to the Habsburg government of Archdukes Albert and Isabella in the Southern Low Countries. Without easing the economic pressure on his adversaries, he also sought to facilitate Dutch access to colonial products, as long as this trade was channelled through Iberian ports, while permitting Dutch merchants to supply grain to the Peninsula. Thus, on February 23, 1603, Philip III resumed trade with the enemy, but under fairly restrictive conditions, including prohibiting certain items, and requiring official permits, bonds and extraordinary taxes. The pressure on the Dutch increased when, in 1604, the monarch signed the peace with England and a trade agreement with France, and exempted these two kingdoms from the limitations imposed in 1603, as long as they did not transport products from the rebel provinces.

However, the system of restricted trade with the rebels did not bring the expected results and was revoked in 1605. The embargo resumed. In Portugal, the Dutch were given one year to sell their wares and leave the realm. From then on, entry would be punishable by death and the confiscation of their assets. The decree also prohibited Philip III's Portuguese subjects from protecting Dutchmen or acting as their commercial agents. In late 1607, an agreement with the German Hanseatic cities sought to reduce the role of the Dutch, their competitors, as intermediaries between the Iberian Peninsula on one side, and northern Europe and the Baltic on the other.

Since the turn of the century, there had been discussions in the Republic about the creation of a West India Company, which would concentrate efforts to confront Iberian power in the Americas and West Africa. The restrictions Philip III imposed on Dutch trade with his colonies and even with Iberia helped these ideas take shape, and in 1606, the authorities of the Republic and its provinces began to study models for organizing such a company.

The Twelve Years' Truce

An impasse prevailed in the military theater of the Low Countries between 1601 and 1604. Some Spanish conquests were achieved in subsequent years, until a ceasefire was signed in 1607, while the Dutch destroyed a Spanish fleet in the Bay of Gibraltar.

Both the Republic and the provinces under Spanish control were tired of endless warfare. The Hispanic Monarchy's insistence on defending the Catholic faith, its dynastic interests and its reputation in such widespread areas obliged it to constantly react to crises that broke out around the globe, and prevented the Crown from maintaining a consistent and prioritized foreign policy. This stance proved to be untenable. In effect, in 1606, Spanish finances no longer allowed the monarch to continue with his military ventures. The troops rebelled and the Crown declared yet another bankruptcy the following year. The Habsburgs were resigned to the fact that the United Provinces would not return to their control, even if symbolically, much less to the Catholic fold. They lowered their expectations: they now wanted to see Catholicism tolerated and to safeguard Habsburg colonial territories, with the VOC dissolved and plans to create a West India Company nipped in the bud. In exchange, they would recognize the Republic's sovereignty and give it access to peninsular ports.

The United Provinces, in their turn, resented the feeling of being besieged and the heavy tax burden that this constant state of alert imposed. Moreover, they feared the impact of a continued embargo, considering that England, France and the German maritime cities, no longer subject to these restrictions, could definitively divert the trade with Iberian kingdoms and colonies to their ports. Nevertheless, the Dutch Republic could not afford the political cost of dismantling the VOC in which part of the urban elite had invested, and was even less capable of managing the serious upheaval that tolerance of Catholicism would have caused in that country.

A temporary solution was found: the Republic promised to drop its plans to form a West India Company and cease attacks on areas controlled by the Portuguese in the Far East. In return, instead of a *de jure* recognition of its sovereignty and an enduring peace, it would only receive tacit recognition and a temporary truce – in a way an extension of the ceasefire in effect at the time. It became known as the Twelve Years' Truce, which began in 1609 and actually ended in 1621. The clauses of the agreement were negotiated in Brussels by Albert's administration, which was eager to maintain the peace and prosperity that the ceasefire had afforded its territories. When Madrid and Lisbon learned of the agreement, they were scandalized and outraged. They felt that unacceptable concessions had been made with regard to the Far East and Catholicism, which, above all else, was deemed a serious affront to the Hispanic Monarchy's reputation. However, the prevailing situation left no room for questioning and the agreement was ratified.

The truce provided international recognition for the Republic, whose foreign representatives were acknowledged as ambassadors. Freed from the burden of an ongoing war, the United Provinces were able to defend their commercial interests against England and Denmark. In this context, the division of the

Siege of Ostend (1601–1604);
Pieter Snayers (seventeenth century).
After a long siege, Hispanic troops recaptured the Flemish city of Ostend, which had been under Dutch rule.

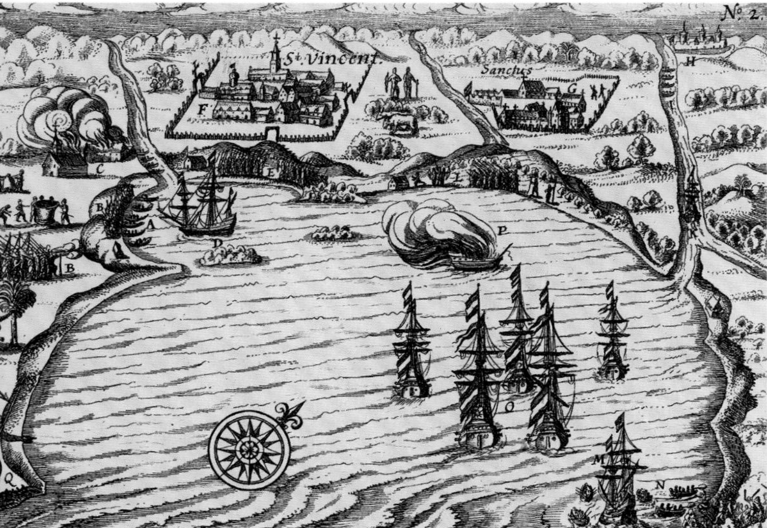

A VOC attack on the Brazilian coast during the Truce

During the truce, the southern coast of Brazil suffered another Dutch attack, this time by a VOC fleet commanded by Admiral Joris van Spilbergen, who sought to reach the East Indies through the Strait of Magellan. The fleet was attacked by the Portuguese while it tried to take on fresh water at Ilha Grande. It attempted to obtain supplies in the captaincy of São Vicente, but the settlers' reluctance to give them provisions and fears of a trap led the Dutch to attack the coast. To their surprise, they came across a sugar plantation, the first founded in Brazil, whose owners lived in the (Southern) Low Countries – the Schetz family of Antwerp. However, this attack was a sporadic incident and no longer part of a consistent policy.

Low Countries into two distinct political entities took permanent form: the Dutch Republic to the north and the Southern Low Countries to the south.

The embargo was lifted with the signing of the truce, and the Dutch were openly readmitted into Portugal and Spain.[R] They were also tacitly allowed into the Atlantic Islands, but not into Brazil. This situation continued until the truce ended in 1621. The agreement resulted in a significant reduction in conflicts in the Atlantic. Dutch privateering against Iberian targets became sporadic and privateering from Dunkirk targeting Dutch vessels on behalf of the Hispanic Monarchy diminished, as did clashes with Dutch ships in the southern Atlantic and the Mediterranean. However, as we will see, this relative peace was disturbed by Muslim piracy, which intensified during the truce.

For the Dutch Republic, the result was the consolidation of its position in shipping and re-exports between northern Europe (the North Sea, Baltic and Russia) and southern Europe (France, Spain, Portugal and Italy), extending as far as the Levant. However, the Iberian position strengthened in the West Indies. The creation of the West India Company had to wait, while the overt Dutch presence along Caribbean coasts and in the Amazon Basin diminished significantly. The Republic's plans to become an overseas power faded, at least for the time being. Nonetheless, it is also true that Amsterdam (and not Antwerp) increasingly became the main hub of distribution for spices and gems shipped annually from India to Portugal.[S]

Without the embargoes, Portugal could step up its exports and import products from the Republic or ship them aboard Dutch vessels at a lower cost. Without wars or a naval blockade, the truce also permitted an economic recovery in the Southern Low Countries. Competition from this quarter undermined the thriving manufacturing industry in the north, and deprived Zeeland of its role as an intermediary between Antwerp and the Atlantic.

On the same day the truce was signed in the north, Spain began to expel the Moriscos[T] – descendants of Muslims who had converted to Christianity and remained within the territories of Castile and Aragon. The expulsion was meant to both reinforce the Hispanic Monarchy's reputation as a champion

Admiral Joris van Spilbergen's fleet attacks São Vicente (1615). *The engraving illustrates the admiral's report on his campaign on the Brazilian coast, published in the book* Miroir Oost & West-Indical (Mirror of the East and West Indies), *1621.*

of the Catholic faith and thwart potential alliances between Moriscos on the one hand, and Turks, Berbers and the Dutch on the other. By 1614, hundreds of thousands of Moriscos had left the Iberian Peninsula, most of them going to North Africa, where they were not always warmly received. There, they joined forces with pirates and privateers using the Maghreb ports as bases for raiding Iberian ships. North African piracy and privateering plagued the waters of the triangle between that coast, the Iberian Peninsula and the Atlantic Islands, even going so far as to sack settlements in the Azores and Madeira.

Rapacious activities carried out under the aegis of the Ottomans or Moroccans were not just the work of Berbers, Turks and Arabs. They were joined by English, Dutch and French freebooters who found North African ports and flags to be an interesting source of revenue, particularly when their own states prevented them from engaging in such activities under their home flag. They brought their ships and arms from northern Europe and often embraced Islam. Their crews comprised converted former prisoners, including Iberians. They also ended up attacking European vessels flying other flags and capturing their crews, which made these pirates targets for Protestant corsairs and warships – thieves who robbed thieves.

Nevertheless, the Ottoman Empire and Morocco maintained cordial diplomatic relations with England, the Dutch Republic and France during the Twelve Years' Truce, making the most of the access to goods plundered from the Iberians, to whom the pacification of the waters afforded by the truce with the Dutch was relatively limited due to this intensification of Muslim piracy. Spanish and even Dutch attacks against these pirates' bases were unable to curb their activities.

During the truce, the Republic was engulfed in political and religious conflicts, which resulted in a radicalization in 1617 and 1618. By the end of this process, the hard-line Calvinist group advocating a single Reformed Church throughout the territory had prevailed. A more federative system was introduced, with the States-General circumscribing the sovereignty of the provinces, while the power of the stadhouder (governor) over provinces and cities was reinforced. Limiting the individual autonomy of provinces was especially important in the case of Holland, the wealthiest and most densely populated of them all. The group that prevailed viewed the truce as being a reversal in the Dutch colonial expansion, allowing pernicious foreign competition. Johan van Oldenbarnevelt, the architect of the truce, was imprisoned and subsequently beheaded in 1619 for high treason.

R. It is possible that, as a goodwill gesture, the Spanish embargo was occasionally relaxed from the summer of 1608 onwards, during the negotiations that preceded the truce.

S. In 1609, Portuguese warships began to patrol the waters of the Gulf of Guinea, capturing Dutch mercantile ships and threatening their local allies until the first Dutch fortress was built on the Gold Coast near São Jorge da Mina. During this period, the Dutch also began to trade hides in Manhattan, in North America. In the Far East, the VOC would have to respect the areas under Portuguese and Spanish control, which implied being resigned to not participating in most Asian trade. The company and its investors suffered with the consolidation and renewed impetus of the Portuguese State of India and growing English competition, with which they were forced to reach an agreement. The VOC's actions waned considerably. However, the VOC established a base on the Coromandel Coast in south-west India to import cotton textiles for their bases in Indonesia and, as the friction with the Portuguese increased, it captured the island of Solor, a source of sandalwood, a product coveted in other Asian regions. The situation intensified in the Maluku Islands, where the Dutch and Iberians had their closest fortresses. The conflicts there provided a pretext for the States-General to declare the termination of the truce in the Far East in 1614, and guarantee financial and naval support for the VOC.

T. Philip II suppressed a Morisco revolt in the region of the erstwhile Kingdom of Granada between 1568 and 1571, while the Duke of Alba tried to pacify the Low Countries. It was feared that the Moriscos could become a fifth column in the event of a Turkish invasion. The suppression resulted in a massacre, and the Granada Moriscos were scattered throughout Castile. The revolt ended the year the Turks were defeated at Lepanto but conquered Cyprus.

Johan van Oldenbarnevelt and Maurice of Nassau

Born into a patrician urban family, Johan van Oldenbarnevelt held several administrative posts until he was appointed the advocate, or spokesman, for the States of Holland in the States-General in 1586, and influenced the political decisions of the new Republic until 1619. The second most influential figure during this period was the son of William the Silent, Maurice of Nassau – a relative of Johan Maurits of Nassau-Siegen, who would later govern the territories the Dutch conquered in Brazil. Maurice was appointed stadhouder and captain-general (military commander) of most of the provinces. While Oldenbarnevelt was more tolerant and conciliatory, Maurice was a hardliner in both political and religious matters.

Jan van Oldenbarnevelt, Ridder, Heer van Berkel Rodenrys.

Hugo Grotius Pencionaris der Stat Rotterdam

Rombout Van Hoogerbeets Raets-heer Pensionaris der Stat Leyden:

Beheading of Johan van Oldenbarnevelt (1547–1619) on May 13, 1619; *Claes Jansz. Visscher II (1619). The main architect of the Truce, Oldenbarnevelt fell victim to the rise of more radical Calvinists.*

Johannes uyt den Boogaardt, gewesen Predikant van syn Excel.

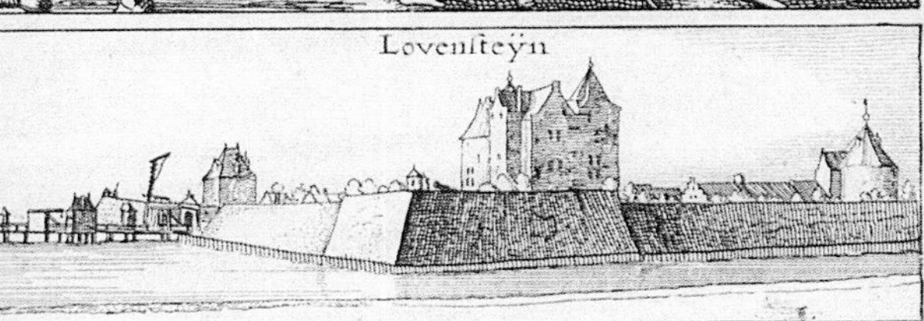

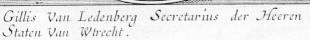

Gillis Van Ledenberg Secretarius der Heeren Staten Van Wtrecht.

Adolff van Wael, Heer van Moersberghen.

GERMANIA INFERIOR.
Gallia Belgica dicta, continens Hispaniarum Regis Provincias Septentrionales.
Formis Hæredum Gerardi de Iode.
Septe trio.
Meri dies
occidens.
ANGLIÆ
PARS
GALLIÆ
PARS
Zeelandia
Zuyder Zee.
Milliaria Germanica parua, Mediocria, & Magna.

War Resumes

In 1618, speculation was rife as to whether the truce would be renewed in 1621. At this point, a conflict broke out in the heart of Europe and dragged the continent into thirty years of war. Protestants in Bohemia, now in the Czech Republic, rebelled against Ferdinand (the future Ferdinand II), the Habsburg pretender to the Crown of the Holy Roman Empire and Philip III's uncle. The rebels offered the Crown of Bohemia to the most powerful Protestant prince in Germany, Frederick V, Elector Palatine of the Rhine, brother-in-law of James of England and nephew of Prince Maurice of Nassau.

Wracked by the Thirty Years War, Europe entered a period of crisis due to the extensive devastation and disruption caused by the fighting, a reduced influx of precious metals from Spanish America, the exaggerated use of monetary debasement, especially in Spain and Central Europe, largely to finance war efforts, and the growing difficulties in some areas of the Mediterranean to sustain themselves.

Even though the French and English monarchs, as well as the Scandinavians, were not inclined to participate in the conflict, Maurice of Nassau viewed this new theater of war as a way of reducing Spanish pressure on the Republic. The truce would lapse in three short years and nobody knew whether it would be renewed. He promised the Germanic rebels money and troops. Philip III, in turn, and subsequently Albert, sent troops to Central Europe to safeguard the interests of their dynasty and protect the lines of communication through which troops and resources moved from Italy to Austria, and to the Southern Low Countries, which were threatened by the conflagration. Shortly thereafter, Philip III deposed his chief minister until then, the Duke of Lerma, whose foreign policy had favored diplomatic efforts.

While the Protestants suffered successive defeats in Central Europe, negotiations to renew the Truce began. Maurice obtained the prerogative to act as negotiator and, in the hope that the truce would be extended, kept plans for the establishment of a Dutch West India Company on hold for a while longer. However, the Hispanic Monarchy considered that the prevailing terms of the truce and its implementation by the Republic had not been satisfactory, a notion that must have echoed in the monarch's ears during his visit to Portugal in 1619. A continued truce threatened to undermine his relations with his Portuguese subjects. It was hoped that the organization of a powerful campaign against the Dutch could sway them and make them capitulate to Spanish demands. Portuguese officials held that, in case of war, instead of costly efforts on land in Europe, the authorities should give priority to sending a powerful Iberian maritime force to attack Dutch positions in Asia, which they believed were still vulnerable.

Map of the Spanish Low Countries (1593).

Prince Maurice of Orange (1567–1625) during the battle of Nieuwpoort, on the Flemish coast, in 1600; *Hendrick Ambrosius Packx (1620–1625): a tactical victory without strategic consequence.*

The hardening of the Spanish position was also derived from a number of favorable events. The Habsburgs achieved significant victories in Central Europe in the first half of 1620. The Hispanic Monarchy demanded that the Dutch leave the East and West Indies, put an end to any restrictions on shipping in the Scheldt and tolerate Catholicism. However, it was prepared to offer the Dutch good conditions for importing colonial products on the Iberian Peninsula. It was not enough. The Republic peremptorily rejected those three demands.

Although the truce had expired, negotiations continued but to no avail. Hostilities resumed. Spain recalled the troops that had been sent to Germany, and disrupted river traffic between the Republic and the Southern Low Countries, Germany and France. Dunkirk and Ostend corsairs engaged in privateering on an unprecedented scale, causing immense damage to Dutch merchant and fishing ships, which were forced to avoid the English Channel. Dutch corsairs, in turn, became increasingly emboldened. The Republic once again blockaded the Flemish coast and imposed protectionist measures against imports from the Southern Low Countries.

Three weeks after Oldenbarnevelt was imprisoned, the States of Holland revived the plan to create the Dutch West India Company, aborted during negotiations for the truce in 1607. Initially, Prince Maurice had used internal discussions regarding the future company to exert pressure during the negotiations with Spain to extend the truce between 1618 and 1621. However, by 1621, the internal obstacles had already been overcome,[U] and the States-General issued the charter to create the West India Company (West-Indische Compagnie; WIC) on June 3, 1621.

The main difficulty in establishing the new company was ensuring that its capital was subscribed. As businessmen and seafarers did not believe the venture had a promising future, relatively few of them invested. The majority of the early investors lived in inland manufacturing towns, and they were often motivated by religious reasons. This delay in attracting capital meant that the company only began operating by the end of 1623 and continued to suffer from a chronic shortfall of working capital. To overcome these deficiencies, it was forced to raise capital again on different occasions, increasing its financial resources four-fold between 1623 and 1629.

Once the company's capital had been subscribed, the directors opted for an ambitious plan: conquering part of the coasts of Brazil and Africa. Sugar was already a valuable commodity in Dutch trade, and seizing it from the Iberians would be highly profitable. Unlike the gold and silver mines of

U. The domestic obstacles to the establishment of the WIC concerned the exclusion of salt from the monopoly to be granted to the company, and the presence of the provinces from the Dutch northeast, excluded from the VOC chambers, on the board of the new company.

Philip IV ascends the throne

The resumption of hostilities coincided with two successions in the Habsburg camp. Nineteen days before the truce elapsed, Philip IV succeeded his father, Philip III (1578–1621). The young monarch's court further accentuated the increasingly bellicose tendency, which had been evident since the Duke of Lerma was removed from office. Archduke Albert, who had always favored diplomacy and pragmatism, died just before the war resumed. The Southern Low Countries returned to nominal Spanish sovereignty, although they continued to be governed by Archduchess Isabella.

Portrait of Philip IV; *Diego Velazquez (1626–1629). The young king stiffened the embargo against the rebel provinces.*

Coach of Philip III; *Spanish school (sixteenth or seventeenth century).*

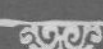

Spanish America, the wealth of Brazil – its sugar mills – was located on the coast, thus dispensing with long, complex military operations. Different from the Caribbean salt pans, the sugar plantations were more dispersed and could not be easily defended. In general, the Dutch felt that Portuguese America was less fortified than Spanish America and believed it could provide support for privateering against shipping in the Caribbean, the India-Portugal route, and perhaps even raids on the mines of Peru.

The plan envisaged capturing the captaincy of Bahia. The Dutch believed that, having achieved this foothold, they could easily overrun the other captaincies. At the same time, they tried to conquer Angola and secure supplies of slaves. While it was true that Brazil had Portuguese settlers, they were a minority. The directors of the WIC felt that slaves and Amerindians would have no say in this change in the region's sovereignty. With regard to the Portuguese, some of them descended from Jews who had been forced to convert over a century ago and would presumably be happy to be free from the Inquisitorial persecution to which they were subjected. In keeping with their rebellious, anti-Catholic way of thinking, the directors believed that the rest of the population would be happy to be rid of Spanish tyranny. Reality proved to be far more complex.

The fleet arrived in Salvador on May 8, 1624, and though the Brazil's governor-general was aware of its approach, Bahia was unable to mount suitable defenses. The governor was unable to keep enough troops mobilized for a long period while waiting for the Dutch to arrive. Upon seeing the naval might of the invaders, and being heavily bombarded continuously for two days, the local residents fled inland and the city fell without a fight. In July, a good part of the fleet that had conquered Bahia returned home with rich booty, and the following month, another fleet set sail for Angola.

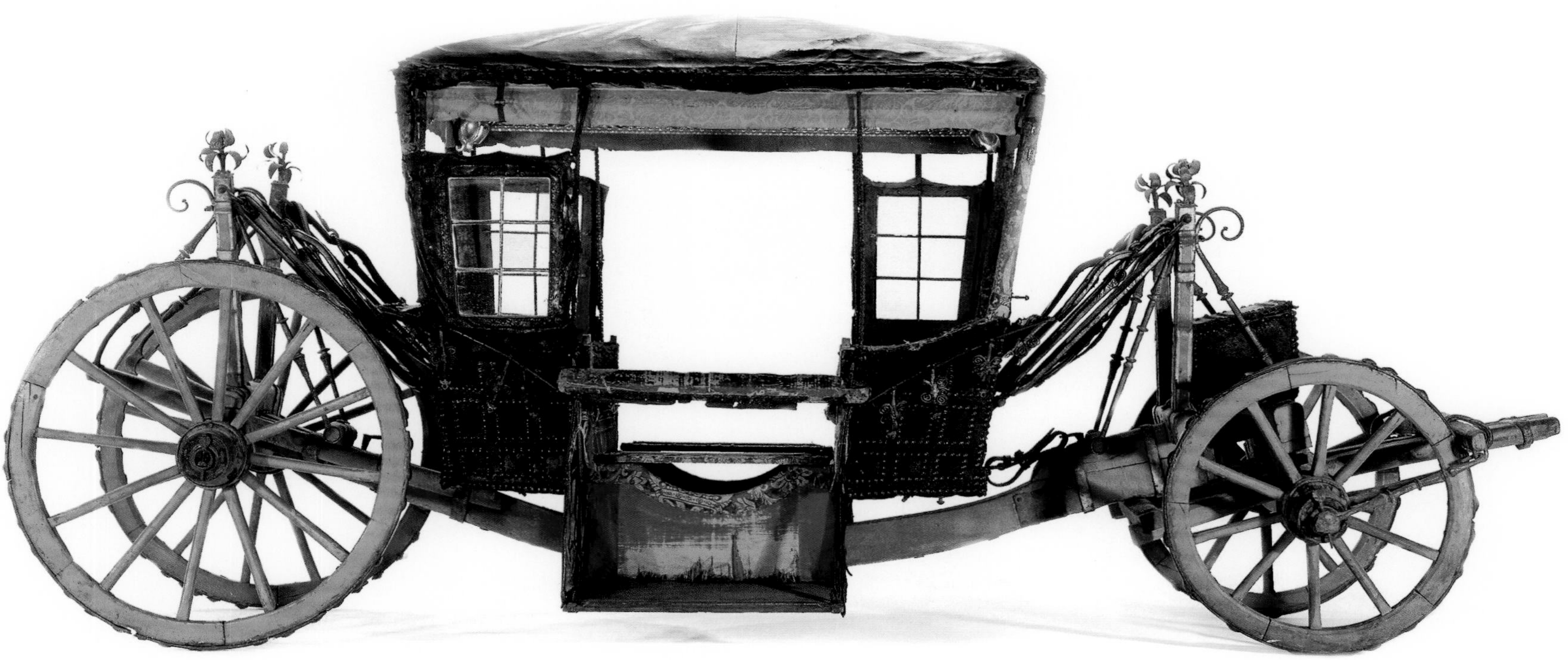

However, the tide soon turned against the Dutch. The inhabitants of Salvador refused to return to the city, and the Portuguese organized a guerrilla resistance. Some assistance arrived from Pernambuco and, later, from Portugal, while a powerful fleet was prepared to help Bahia. At the end of March 1625, a fleet consisting of Spanish, Portuguese and Neapolitan forces arrived in Brazil and recaptured Bahia after a month of fighting. The Dutch fleet that was to assist the invaders was unable to set sail from the Republic due to adverse winter weather, and by the time it finally reached Brazil the city had been recaptured. Believing that it would be of no avail, the Dutch fleet headed towards the Caribbean to engage in piracy.[v]

The WIC's main activities in the initial years of its existence involved the capture of Portuguese and Spanish shipping, as it viewed intensive privateering as the most efficient way of undermining Iberian power in the New World. Piracy during the WIC's early years was centered in the Caribbean, where the company tried to seize the powerful fleets transporting gold and silver to Spain, and those returning from Spain to the Indies, laden with merchandise. The Brazil route was the second theater of operations, while the Iberian Peninsula and the Atlantic Islands also suffered from Dutch attacks.

Charter granted by the States-General of the Republic of the Seven United Provinces of the Low Countries to the Dutch West India Company, creating the monopoly on shipping to the Western Hemisphere from the Cape of Good Hope to Manila in the Philippines (1621).

This world map by Petrus Plancius and Baptista van Doetecum, dated 1590, contains new information that improved the contours of the continents.

The Dutch West India Company

The mission of the Dutch West India Company (West-Indische Compagnie; WIC) included colonization, trade and privateering in the Americas, West Africa and the Atlantic Islands, objectives which sometimes conflicted and often alternated, depending on the circumstances. It was entitled to establish colonies, maintain armed troops and sign alliances, and had jurisdiction over the areas it conquered.

Like the Dutch East India Company (VOC), the new company had open capital. It was governed by a board of directors with nineteen representatives from its five regional councils: eight from Amsterdam, four from Zeeland, two from the Meuse River region (where Rotterdam is located), two from Groningen, two from the North Quarter (Noorderkwartier, part of Holland and West Frisia on the isthmus between the Zuiderzee and the sea) and a representative from the States-General.

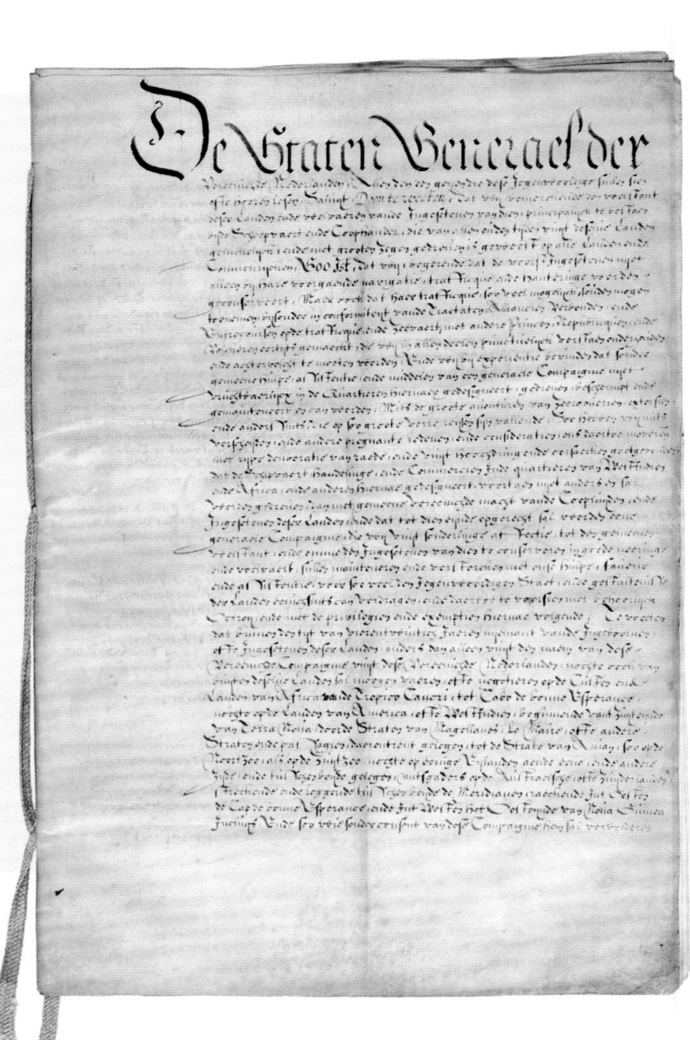

De Staten Generael der

Apart from the large fleets of ships planned to attack the coast or capture the Silver Fleet, small flotillas and even single vessels would be outfitted exclusively with a view to privateering. The famous WIC captain Piet Hein attacked Bahia twice in 1627 seizing a large quantity of sugar in the port. WIC ships continued to capture numerous vessels returning from Brazil over the following years.

While this was happening, over the course of the 1620s, the Dutch Republic's trade and shipping felt the effects of the embargoes and Dunkirk privateers. In 1625, Philip IV created institutions to oversee the effectiveness of the sanctions, the most important being the Junta del Almirantazgo, which stationed its *veedores del contrabando* (smuggling inspectors) in wet and dry ports on the Iberian Peninsula and the Atlantic Islands. The inspectors examined all incoming and outgoing ships and goods, as well as wares stored in shops, and confiscated any goods from enemy countries.

v. The WIC's efforts in Angola and São Jorge da Mina were also frustrated at the time. In 1624, the company was also defeated in Puerto Rico, and the Dutch were expelled from the Amazon. Its base in the Guianas was not of much use. The company was slightly more successful in trading hides in North America and gold in West Africa. However, this was not enough to cover its costs, let alone generate dividends for investors.

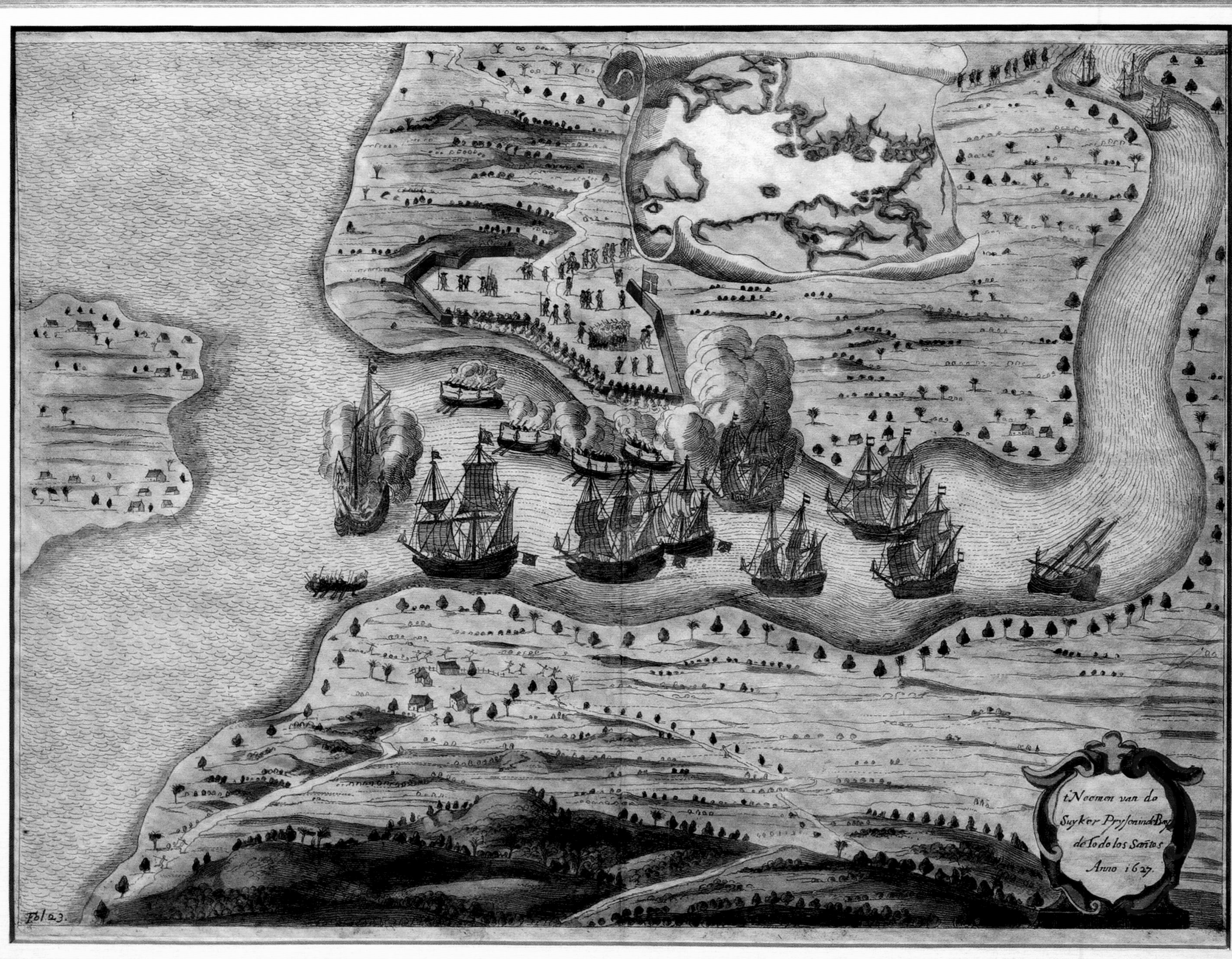

Todos os Santos Bay: the fleet commanded by Dutch Admiral Pieter Pietersz. Heyn captures ships laden with sugar (1627/1656).

It is clear that smugglers were not physically punished, and that confiscated wares were often released after paying fines. On other occasions, these goods were sold to third parties, some of them front men, below their market value. Moreover, the authorities issued special permits so that vital products such as grain, codfish and shipbuilding materials could be imported from enemy countries. Nevertheless, the institution served to keep foreign trade under control, channelling exports and keeping the domestic market's needs in mind, while reducing the volume of imports from enemy countries and raising the price of their products, consequently undermining their competitiveness in the Iberian market.

In Portuguese ports, the embargoes had a detrimental effect on trade and supplies, increasing tension with the court. Likewise, the more rigorous implementation of the embargoes harmed the Dutch manufacturing and fishing industries,[w] their trade and shipping in the Mediterranean, the Baltic and Asia, where products from the Iberian Peninsula were in great demand. An even more important factor was increased taxation in the Republic due to military expenditures. The stipend that England and France had allocated to the United Provinces since the beginning of the Revolt had been suspended when the truce began, and neither of the two countries was inclined to renew it now.

England only decided to enter the Thirty Years' War on the Protestant side in 1624, but its participation had negligible impact. The Hispanic Monarchy's troops advanced on the Low Countries and, in 1625, after a long siege, they captured the strategic city of Breda, whose lord was Maurice of Nassau, Prince of Orange, who had died in the meantime. Jolted by these Spanish victories, France resumed its subsidies to the Republic. Maurice was succeeded by his more pragmatic and tolerant younger brother, Frederick Henry. The Spanish offensive eventually lost steam, and Madrid halted it due to lack of funds.

However, the risk of a Hispanic-Imperial invasion continued to hover over the Republic and became a concrete threat in 1628. That same year, however, events in Italy brought some relief. France and the Hispanic Monarchy clashed over the succession in Mantua, a conflict that lasted until 1631, and the Habsburg troops and resources earmarked for the Low Countries were diverted to Italy. The tide turned in favor of the Dutch, and, in 1629, after a five-month siege, they captured the city of 's-Hertogenbosch, threatening Brussels, the capital of the Southern Low Countries.

W. The Dutch were unable to obtain salt to preserve fish in either the Iberian salt producing regions or along the Caribbean coast, which was well guarded and fortified by the Spain.

Four generations of the Princes of Orange: William I, Maurice and Frederick Henry, William II and William III; *attributed to Willem van Honthorst (1662–1666)*

Olivares and the Hispanic Monarchy

In 1622, the Count-Duke of Olivares emerged as Philip IV's favorite minister, and became the intermediary between the monarch and the numerous councils, boards and tribunals of the Hispanic Monarchy. Against the backdrop of the war and the fragmented Hispanic Monarchy, Olivares sought to implement a plan for reforms that would make it a more consistent unit with a streamlined administration, ensuring that the financial and military burden was more evenly distributed among its territorial entities instead of overburdening Castile. However, through these reforms, Castile would come to play an even more centralizing role. The victories of 1625 – against the Anglo-Dutch attack in Cadiz, the capture of Breda and the recovery of Salvador, which aligned leading Portuguese noble families – further enhanced the minister's prestige. He now sought to create a "union of arms" by which, if one of the Monarchy's entities was threatened, all the others would automatically come to its aid. In practice, this required the maintenance of standing troops throughout the realm.

Olivares created new administrative institutions whose members were loyal to him. They functioned in parallel to traditional bodies, which resulted in less resistance while implementing his reforms. However, as the war dragged on, with fewer Spanish victories and increased military costs, Olivares imposed new taxes on the entities that comprised the Monarchy. Apart from increasing the tax burden on various social groups, these innovations were not implemented in a manner traditionally considered legitimate. The result, in Portugal, was heightened antipathy towards the Dynastic Union, which was further aggravated as the Dutch made deeper inroads in the Atlantic and Indian oceans.

The Dutch Republic rejected Spain's proposals for a new truce, as the terms were not favorable towards various interests in important sectors in the Republic. The manufacturing cities feared competition from the Southern Low Countries. Keen to retain the benefits it had obtained as a result of the Dutch blockade of Flemish ports, that is, by serving as an intermediary between the Southern Low Countries and the Atlantic, the province of Zeeland opposed the agreement. Furthermore, neither of the two India companies nor their investors wished to see their overseas ventures interrupted again. Finally, the Republic believed it had a brighter economic and political future outside Europe, where it would be less subject to the threats and caprices of the continent's leading powers. This was the same position that Portugal had maintained ever since it embarked on its ventures in the Maghreb about two centuries earlier, when it sought to enhance its remote geographic position on the continent to distance itself from European conflicts, in which it had more to lose than gain.

In effect, the overseas situation now appeared to be positive for the Dutch. The VOC had made important inroads in Asia, to the detriment of the Portuguese and Castilians, mainly after it established a base of operations in Batavia (now Jakarta), in 1619. In 1628, the WIC achieved its first great feat: Piet Hein captured the Spanish Silver Fleet which had set sail from Mexico, off the coast of Cuba. This blow to the Spanish treasury probably led to the hasty dispatch of French troops to Italy. Three-quarters of the booty plundered from Spain was distributed as dividends to WIC shareholders to maintain investor confidence. The remainder was used to finance the company's most ambitious venture: the invasion of Pernambuco in 1630. On February 14, 1630, a fleet commanded by Hendrick Cornelisz. Loncq anchored off the coast of Olinda. The following morning marked the beginning of the period known as Dutch Brazil, which lasted until 1654.

The Surrender of Breda *or* The Lances; *Diego Velazquez (1634). The capture of Breda marked the height of the Hispanic advance at the beginning of the reign of Philip IV.*

The Planisphere

Chapter One

1. Much has been written about the subjects examined in this chapter, and, apart from making little sense, it would be impractical to provide an exhaustive list of all relevant studies, given space constraints. The following books are thus simply a suggested basic bibliography, containing some fundamental studies for readers wishing to delve deeper into these subjects or to find references for additional sources and literature. The suggested bibliography has been divided into four broad topics: 1) the Portuguese "Reconquest," overseas expansion and geopolitics; 2) the Spanish Monarchy, its geopolitics and Portugal during the Dynastic Union; 3) the Dutch Revolt, the development of the Republic and its overseas expansion; 4) privateering and piracy.

The Portuguese "Reconquest," Overseas Expansion and Geopolitics (for full bibliographic details, see Bibliography)
Albuquerque, L. de, *O tratado de Tordesilhas e as dificuldades técnicas da sua aplicação rigorosa.*
Albuquerque, L. de, *Portugal no mundo.*
Albuquerque, L. de, *Dicionário de história dos descobrimentos portugueses.*
Andrade, A. A., "Novos espaços, antigas estratégias: o enquadramento dos espaços orientais."
Baião, A., Cidade, H. and Múrias, M., *História da expansão portuguesa no mundo.*
Barbosa, P. G., *Reconquista cristã: séculos IX–XII.*
Bethencourt, F. and Chaudhuri, K., *História da expansão portuguesa.*
Boxer, C. R., *The Portuguese Seaborne Empire.*
Boyajian, J. C., *Portuguese Trade in Asia under the Habsburgs, 1580–1626.*
Cortesão, J., *História dos descobrimentos portugueses.*
Cortesão, J., *História da expansão portuguesa.*
Costa, J. P. Oliveira e, *Portugal e o Japão: o século namban.*
Costa, P. M. de. C. Pinto, "Ordens militares e fronteira: um desempenho militar, jurisdicional e político em tempos medievais."
Couto, J., *A construção do Brasil.*
Cruz, M. A. L., *D. Sebastião.*
Cunha, M. S. da, *Os espaços de um império: estudos e catálogo.*
Diffie, B. W., *Foundations of the Portuguese Empire, 1415–1580.*
Disney, A. R., *Twilight of the Pepper Empire: Portuguese Trade in Southwest India in the Early Seventeenth Century.*
Donkin, R. A., *Between East and West: The Moluccas and the Traffic in Spices up to the Arrival of Europeans.*
Fonseca, L. A. da, "O papel de Granada no horizonte da política peninsular portuguesa em meados do século XV."
Garcia, J. C., *O espaço medieval da reconquista no sudoeste da Península Ibérica.*
Gil, J., *Hidalgos y samurais. España y Japón en los siglos XVI y XVII.*
Godinho, V. M., "A evolução dos complexos histórico-geográficos."
Godinho, V. M., *Os descobrimentos e a economia mundial.*
Lach, D. F. and Kley, E. J. van, *Asia in the Making of Europe.*
Macedo, J. B. de, "História diplomática portuguesa: constantes e linhas de força."
Marques, A. H. de Oliveira, *História de Portugal.*
Marques, A. H. de Oliveira, *História dos portugueses no Extremo Oriente.*
Marques, A. H. de Oliveira and Dias, J. J. Alves, *Atlas histórico de Portugal e do ultramar português.*
Mattoso, J., *História de Portugal.*
Mattoso, J., *Identificação de um país: ensaios sobre as origens de Portugal: 1096–1325.*
Newitt, M. D. D., *A History of Portuguese Overseas Expansion, 1400–1668.*
Polónia, A., *D. Henrique.*
Serrão, J. and Marques, A. H. de Oliveira, *Nova história da expansão portuguesa.*
Serrão, J. and Marques, A. H. de Oliveira, *Nova história de Portugal.*
Stols, E., "Os mercadores flamengos em Portugal e no Brasil antes das conquistas holandesas."
Stols, E., "Convivências e conivências luso-flamengas na rota do açúcar brasileiro."
Subrahmanyam, S., *O império asiático português, 1500–1700. Uma história política e económica.*
Thomaz, L. F. and Alves, J. S., "Da cruzada ao Quinto Império."
Thomaz, L. F. *De Ceuta a Timor.*
Velez, M. S. B., "As linhas marítimo-comerciais portuguesas no Oriente (séc. XVI—meados do séc. XVII)."

The Spanish Monarchy, its Geopolitics and Portugal during the Dynastic Union
AHMP, Câmara Municipal, A-PUB-36, fols. 54–55.
BA, 44-XIII-50, fols. 24v.–25v.
Allen, P. C., *Felipe III y la Pax Hispanica, 1598–1621. El fracasso de la gran estrategia.*
Alloza Aparicio, A., "La Junta de Almirantazgo y la lucha contra el contrabando, 1625–1643."
Barata, M. R. T., "A União Ibérica e o mundo atlântico: 1580 e o processo político português."
Barros, A. J. M. "Porto: a construção de um espaço marítimo nos alvores dos tempos modernos."
Bouza Álvarez, F., "Portugal en la política internacional de Felipe II: por el suelo el mundo en pedazos."

Bouza Álvarez, F., *Portugal no tempo dos Filipes: política, cultura, representações (1580–1668)*.
Bouza Álvarez, F., *Filipe I*.
Costa, L. F., *O transporte no Atlântico e a Companhia Geral do Comércio do Brasil*, V. 1.
Cruz, M. A. L., *D. Sebastião*.
Domínguez Ortiz, A. and Vincent, B., *Historia de los moriscos*.
Ebert, C. "The Trade in Brazilian Sugar: Brazil, Portugal and Northwestern Europe, 1550–1630."
Elliott, J. H., *El conde-duque de Olivares, el político en una época de decadencia*.
Elliott, J. H., *Imperial Spain, 1496–1716*.
Emmer, P. C., "The First Global War: The Dutch versus Iberia in Asia, Africa and the New World, 1590–1609."
França, E. de Oliveira, *Portugal na época da Restauração*.
Heijer, H. den, *De geschiedenis van de WIC*.
Hespanha, A. M., "Os áustrias em Portugal – Balanço historiográfico."
IANTT, CC, 1-115-107.
IANTT, CC, 1-114-70.
Israel, J. I., "Spain, the Spanish Embargo and the Struggle for the Mastery of World Trade, 1585–1660."
Israel, J. I., *La República holandesa y el mundo hispânico, 1606–1661*.
Kamen, H., *Philip of Spain*.
Marques, A. H. de Oliveira, *História de Portugal*.
Mattoso, J., *História de Portugal*, V. 3.
Mauro, F., *Portugal, o Brasil e o Atlântico*, V. 1.
Mello, J. A. G. de, "Os livros das saídas das urcas do porto do Recife."
Monteiro, N. G., "As conjunturas políticas: Olivares e a Guerra dos Trinta Anos (1618–1648)."
Olival, F., *D. Filipe II*.
Oliveira, A. de, *Poder e oposição política em Portugal no período filipino, 1580–1640*.
Oliveira, A. de, *D. Filipe III*.
Parker, G., *The Grand Strategy of Philip II*.
Polónia, A., *D. Henrique*.
Ramos, R., *História de Portugal*.
Schaub, J. F., *Portugal au temps du comte-duc d'Olivares (1621– 1640)*.
Schaub, J. F., *Portugal na Monarquia Hispânica (1580–1640)*.
Segunda visitação do Santo Ofício às partes do Brasil pelo Inquisidor e Visitador Marcos Teixeira. Livro das Confissões e Ratificações da Bahia: 1618–1620.
Serrão, J. V., *História de Portugal*.
Serrão, J. V., *O tempo dos Filipes em Portugal e no Brasil: 1580–1668: estudos históricos*.
Sluiter, E., "Dutch-Spanish Rivalry in the Caribbean Area, 1594–1609."
Sluiter, E., "Os holandeses no Brasil antes de 1621."
Stols, E., "Os mercadores flamengos em Portugal e no Brasil antes das conquistas holandesas."
Stols, E., "Convivências e conivências luso-flamengas na rota do açúcar brasileiro."
Valladares, R., *A conquista de Lisboa: violência militar e comunidade política em Portugal,1578–1583*.
Yun Casalilla, B., *Marte contra Minerva: el precio del Imperio Español, c. 1450–1600*.

The Dutch Revolt, the Development of the Republic and its Overseas Expansion

Boxer, C. R., *The Dutch in Brazil, 1624–1654*.
Boxer, C. R., *The Dutch Seaborne Empire, 1600–1800*.
Ebert, C., "The Trade in Brazilian Sugar."
Emmer, P. C., "The First Global War."
Gaastra, F., *The Dutch East India Company: Expansion and Decline*.
Geyl, P., *The Revolt of the Netherlands, 1555–1609*.
Heijer, H. den, *De geschiedenis van de WIC*.
Israel, J. I., *Dutch Primacy in World Trade*.
Israel, J. I., "Spain, the Spanish Embargo and the Struggle for the Mastery of World Trade, 1585–1660."
Israel, J. I., *The Dutch Republic. Its Rise, Greatness and Fall, 1477–1806*.
Israel, J. I., *La República holandesa y el mundo hispânico, 1606–1661*.
Lesger, C., *The Rise of the Amsterdam Market and Information Exchange*.
Mello, E. C. de, *O Brasil holandês (1630–1654)*.
Parker, G., *The Dutch Revolt*.
Prak, M., *The Dutch Republic in the Seventeenth Century. The Golden Age*.
Sluiter, E., "Os holandeses no Brasil antes de 1621."
Sluiter, E., "Dutch-Spanish Rivalry in the Caribbean Area, 1594–1609."
Stols, E., "Os mercadores flamengos em Portugal e no Brasil antes das conquistas holandesas."
Stols, E., "Convivências e conivências luso-flamengas na rota do açúcar brasileiro."
Veen, E. van, "VOC Strategies in the Far East (1605–1640)."
Vries, J. de. and Woude, A. van der, *The First Modern Economy*.

Privateering and Piracy

Alberto, E. M. C. M., "As instituições de resgate de cativos em Portugal: sua estruturação e evolução no século XV."
Andrews, K. R., *Elizabethan Privateering. English Privateering during the Spanish War, 1585–160*.
Barros, A. J. M., "Porto: a construção de um espaço marítimo nos alvores dos tempos modernos."
Berger, P., Winz A. P. and Guedes, M. J., "Incursões de corsários e piratas na costa do Brasil."
Braga, I. M. R. M. D., *Entre a cristandade e o islão (séculos XV–XVII): cativos e renegados nas franjas de duas sociedades em confronto*.
Bruijn, J. R., "Scheepvaart en overheid omstreeks 1600."
Coindreau, R., *Les corsaires de Salé*.
Costa, L. F., *O transporte no Atlântico e a Companhia Geral do Comércio do Brasil*, V. 1.
Ebert, C., "The Trade in Brazilian Sugar."
Emmer, P. C., "The First Global War."
Grotius, H., *Commentary on the Law of Prize and Booty*.
Heijer, H. den, *De geschiedenis van de WIC*.
Israel, J. I., *Dutch Primacy in World Trade*.
Israel, J. I., "Spain, the Spanish Embargo and the Struggle for the Mastery of World Trade, 1585–1660."
Israel, J. I., *La República holandesa y el mundo hispânico, 1606–1661*.
IJzerman, J. W., *Journael van de reis naar Zuid-Amerika*.
Koen, E. M., "Duarte Fernandes, koopman van de Portugese natie te Amsterdam."
Lunsford, V. W., *Piracy and Privateering in the Golden Age Netherlands*.
Mauro, F., *Portugal, o Brasil e o Atlântico*, V. 1.
Silva, F. R. da, "Pirataria e corso sobre o Porto."
Silva, F. R., "O corso inglês e as populações do litoral lusitano (1580–1640)."
Sluiter, E., "Dutch-Spanish Rivalry in the Caribbean Area, 1594–1609."
Sluiter, E. "Os holandeses no Brasil antes de 1621."
SR nos. 87 n. 4; 170 n. 22.
Stols, E., "Os mercadores flamengos em Portugal e no Brasil antes das conquistas holandesas."
Stols, E., "Convivências e conivências luso-flamengas na rota do açúcar brasileiro."

Chapter Two

Canne d'Inde

Cane from India;
Charles Plumier (1688).

Cane and Sugar

From Asia to the Americas

Cane cultivation and sugar production followed a lengthy trajectory from Southeast Asia in antiquity to the Mediterranean in the Middle Ages, and on to the Atlantic in early modern times. It followed the sun around the globe until Portuguese America became the European market's main sugar supplier, even supplanting some of its competitors during the period in question. Sugar, in turn, gave rise to European colonization, consolidated Portugal's sovereignty over Brazil's coast, and shut out other European competitors. It also led to the deaths and enslavement of most of the Amerindians in the colonized areas, and resulted in the massive transatlantic traffic in African slaves to work in its production. A new colonial and slaveholding society would arise.

* *I am grateful to Rodrigo Ricupero for his valuable comments on this chapter.*

Early History

It is believed sugarcane originated in the Pacific Islands or Southeast Asia.[1] It is known for certain that some type of rudimentary crystallization of its juice was already being produced in northern India in antiquity. The first indications are linguistic, suggested by the change in the meaning of words in the ancient Indian languages of Sanskrit and Pali. The dating of these changes is difficult and involves a margin of error spanning several centuries. Between the seventh and fourth centuries B.C., the word *guḋa* came to signify not only the formation of balls and conglomeration, but also referred to sugar "coagulates," which were formed by boiling cane juice. Before the middle of the last millennium B.C., the Sanskrit word for granular particles, *śarkarã*, had come to designate crystalline sugar and, in different variations, entered the lexicon of civilizations west of India as sugar began to spread.

By the end of the fourth century B.C., there were references to the cultivation of sugarcane, the mills used to extract the juice and the production of sugar with different grades of purity, ranging between *guḋa* and *śarkarã.* Alexander the Great's generals may well have sampled these gradations of sugar in India. Still, in the classical world, it is likely that Indian sugar arrived in Rome in very small quantities, for medical purposes, via Arabia. By the third century B.C., sugar was also produced in Vietnam, from where it was sent to China. After the eighth century A.D., China also imported sugar from Persia through the Silk Road until it finally produced its own.

Like northern India, southwest Persia and Mesopotamia were located in regions drained by abundant perennial rivers. Even before the Arab invasion, sugar was produced in Persia and Sassanid Mesopotamia. (Predominantly Persian-speaking and Zoroastrian, the Sassanid Empire dominated the region between eastern Syria and the Indus Valley from the third century until the Muslim conquest in the seventh century A.D.) After India, Persia was the next main stop for sugar on its way to the New World.

After the Islamic conquest, some agricultural methods were developed enabling sugarcane to be grown in regions with less natural irrigation such as Syria, Palestine and Egypt, which was dependent on the flooding of the Nile. This is how sugar planting became established in these former Byzantine territories. It is reasonable to assume that cane may have already been cultivated in these regions while still part of that highly developed Christian Empire, although little is known about that period. The Muslims took sugar further afield, and between the ninth and eleventh centuries they introduced flourishing sugar crops into Cyprus, Sicily, North Africa, and the Iberian Peninsula. Sugarcane was already being planted in the tenth century, perhaps even earlier, in Al-Andaluz, the region of Iberia under Islamic control. Sugar production there began in the twelfth century, at the very latest. Hence, sugar was edging closer to Christian Europe. Although the Venetians had been importing this product from Egypt since before the Crusades, it was only after these campaigns that sugar irreversibly made its way into Western Europe. From then on, the Europeans themselves manufactured it in the Middle East, and its export provided an important source of income for the Crusader lords. Knights, pilgrims and merchants disseminated the product throughout the Christian West.

Gradually expelled from the Middle East, the Latin (Western) Christians intensified sugar production in the Mediterranean islands captured from the Muslims and Byzantines, such as Cyprus, Crete and Sicily. Although Sicilian production fell after the Normans conquered the island in the eleventh century, it made major strides in the early thirteenth century, and Sicily eventually became Europe's main sugar supplier. Nevertheless, Catholic Europe continued to import that commodity from the Muslim world to the east and west, and from what remained of the Byzantine Empire. In the thirteenth and fourteenth centuries, Muslim Granada exported sugar to Genoese and Florentine merchants, who distributed it throughout Europe.

In the fourteenth century, sugar production on the Muslim east coast of the Mediterranean basin declined for a number of reasons, including the Black Death and the Mongol and Turkish invasions. At the same time, production intensified in the Christian areas. By the end of the thirteenth century, when Sicily became part of the expanding sphere of influence of the Crown of Aragon in the Mediterranean, methods for the cultivation and the production of sugar had been assimilated in Valencia, a kingdom belonging to the same crown. Valencia's production, however, only gained strength in the early fifteenth century. It continued to grow over the course of the 1400s, fueled by investments from German bankers.

In the fifteenth and sixteenth centuries, the main Italian cities invested in sugar production and manufacture outside their home territory: Venice in Crete and Genoa in Granada, Sicily and Portuguese dominions. Portugal appears to have exported or re-exported sugar as far back as the twelfth century, as the manifest of a Portuguese ship that sank off the Flemish coast seems to suggest. This sugar may have come from the Algarve, which was still under Muslim rule. Nevertheless, at the turn of the fourteenth to the fifteenth century, the Algarve, by then part of Portugal, was certainly a cane growing and sugar manufacturing area. Genoa also had interests in southern Portugal. By the mid-1400s, sugarcane was being planted much further north, near Coimbra. Iberian sugar was not only exported to Italy and the Low Countries but also to the south of Germany and England.

Overseas expansion took sugar to the Atlantic Islands in the fifteenth century.[2] Madeira took the lead and sugar cultivation and production grew rapidly on that archipelago at the turn of the fifteenth to the sixteenth century, gaining pace in the last quarter of the 1400s. Genoese and Jews, some of whom were recent immigrants from other Iberian kingdoms and who were later forced to convert to Christianity (becoming New Christians), also played an active role in the distribution of sugar from Madeira, as did the Flemish, French, English and Germans.

Because the island was uninhabited, the Portuguese easily colonized Madeira. Nevertheless, the mountainous terrain and lack of natural irrigation in its hottest area, which was best suited for sugarcane cultivation, forced the settlers to build a system of irrigation channels called "*levadas*," which carried water from the mountains to the cane fields. Land ownership was fragmented in Madeira, and sugar-mill owners were not necessarily the largest landholders. Growing cane and manufacturing sugar were often two distinct activities. The milling techniques used in Madeira resulted in very low productivity compared to the results later obtained in São Tomé, the Canaries and the Americas. Indigenous slaves from the Canary Islands, the Barbary Coast and Guinea were used in a much lower proportion than they would be in São Tomé and the Americas.

Sugarloaf mold dating from the late fifteenth or early sixteenth century, found in an archeological site in Mata da Machada (Barreiro, Portugal).

Stages of sugar production from sugarcane. Print from the series in the catalogue Nova reperta, *by Jan van der Straet (ca. 1620–1630). Center, foreground, chopping cane, and in the background, from left, milling, pressing and boiling.*

Ioan . Galle excud .

Sugarloaf; part of a set recovered from archeological excavations in Jardim do Mar, in southwestern Madeira, and the Palace of the Consuls in Funchal.

From the early sixteenth century onward, several factors caused Madeira's sugar industry to drop sharply. These factors included soil depletion, lack of fertilizers and climate change. By the 1530s, the sugar industry was in crisis and cane fields were giving way to vineyards. Even so, sugar production continued in Madeira because its products were superior to those of São Tomé, and even those of Brazil.[3] Madeira saw a resurgence of its sugar industry during the Dutch occupation of the Brazilian northeast. However, aside from that brief upturn, the island's production remained modest, and was primarily focused on confectionery.

When Madeira began to reach its production capacity, sugar sought out new frontiers and found them on other Atlantic islands. Although the Europeans had been present in the Canary Islands well before the settlement of Madeira, the resistance of the island's indigenous people, known as Guanchos, delayed the effective occupation of their most fertile areas. It was only in the 1480s that sugar emerged in the Canaries with the assistance of technicians from Madeira and capital investments from Catalonia, Castile, Portugal, and, once again, Genoa. The use of slave labor, from the same sources as those employed in Madeira, was also limited, and was more prevalent in the sugar mills than in the cane fields.

Production in the Canary Islands peaked in the second quarter of the sixteenth century. Continuous deforestation not only reduced the stocks of fuel required for the manufacturing process but had an adverse effect on irrigation. In the last quarter of the century, the archipelago would also replace its cane fields with vineyards.

The Portuguese did not make any significant advances in the Azores, which had a colder climate, or in Cape Verde, which was too dry. They had better luck in São Tomé and, to a lesser degree, Príncipe. This island chain in the Gulf of Guinea was initially settled in the late fifteenth century with a view to manufacturing sugar there. However, production only became significant in the second quarter of the sixteenth century. The humid climate did not restrict cultivation to a few irrigated areas, yet planting depended on imported slave labor because those islands offered little appeal to Portuguese immigrants. São Tomé's production peaked in the mid-sixteenth century and fell in the last quarter due to the difficulties of controlling the enslaved workforce whose frequent uprisings disrupted production. Other factors that contributed to its drop were the Dutch attempts to conquer the islands and São Tomé's small territory, in comparison with the amount of land available for cultivation in Brazil, its new competitor. By the end of the first decade of the seventeenth century, production on the island had become marginal.

Finally, Spain and Portugal introduced sugar in the tropical Americas. Initially, it made the most progress on the island of Hispaniola, in what are now the Dominican Republic and Haiti.[4] As with São Tomé, irrigation was not difficult there, and, unlike

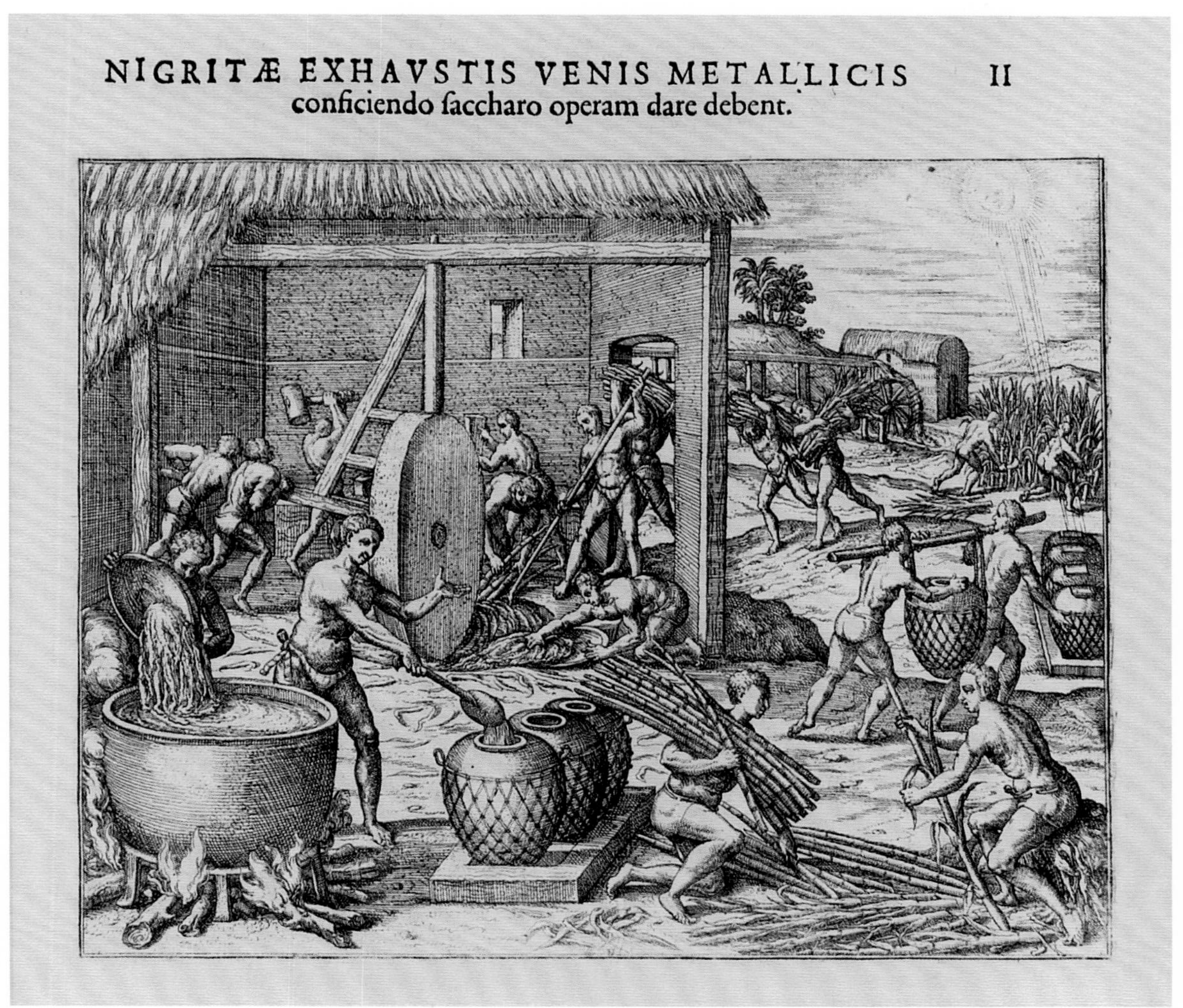

Madeira, there was no need for major investment in irrigation channels and terraces. It was easier and cheaper to plant new cane fields than to fertilize old ones. Specialists from Portugal, the Canary Islands and Italy transferred the sugar manufacturing technology there. Introduced in the 1520s, Hispaniola's sugar production made significant progress in the second quarter of the sixteenth century. However, a shortage of labor and transportation difficulties continued to hamper productivity. The island's output began to decline in the 1580s, due to the deviation of the route of the Spanish fleets to the Americas, followed by the forced depopulation of part of the island to prevent foreign contraband, as well as slave uprisings and the activities of privateers and pirates. Production in Jamaica, Puerto Rico and Cuba remained insignificant until the Dutch invasion of Pernambuco in Brazil.

NIGRITÆ EXHAVSTIS VENIS METALLICIS II
conficiendo ſaccharo operam dare debent.

In the Mediterranean, production remained steady and even grew in some places throughout the fifteenth and sixteenth centuries, despite the competition from the Atlantic Islands and Hispaniola. The same applied to Atlantic Morocco, mainly in the fertile basin of the Sous River. The Medicis and Valoises even attempted to take advantage of the expansionist trend and introduce production in Tuscany,

Here, an engraving by Theodore de Bry, after another stylized drawing by Jan van der Straet of the stages of sugar production on a Spanish-American sugar mill based on African slave labor. (1595).

Mulatto Man, *by Albert Eckhout (ca. 1610–ca. 1666). This work portrays a mulatto man beside a cane field. In the background, on the skyline, three ships represent the Atlantic trade.*

Languedoc and Provence, without success. However, the cultivation and manufacture of sugar in the Greater Mediterranean, including the adjacent Atlantic areas on the Iberian Peninsula and Morocco, succumbed to the effects of the lower price of Brazilian sugar in the last quarter of the sixteenth century. The region had few well-irrigated areas and its climate did not allow sugarcane to reach maximum maturity. This caused its sucrose content to be lower than that produced in tropical climes. Last, the increasing deforestation of the Mediterranean basin drove up the price of the firewood required for sugar production. Nevertheless, European demand kept up the price of the commodity until Brazil entered the market. Later, the coveted irrigated lands of the Mediterranean were used for other crops which were more profitable in the new economic conditions. Even so, sparse pockets of cane fields persisted there until the eighteenth century.[5]

None of these problems existed in Brazil, quite the contrary. In Brazil, as in Hispaniola and perhaps São Tomé, sugarcane found a climate that allowed it to mature fully, producing high sucrose content, with no risk of frost or difficulties in finding easily cultivatable terrain or water with which to irrigate the crops. In normal years, the forested coastal plain was blessed with abundant natural irrigation. Covered with native forest, the fertile soil known as *massapé* (a term already used in the Azores and Madeira[6]) was ideally suited to cultivation.[7] Unlike the Atlantic Islands (Macaronesia and São Tomé) and the Caribbean, Brazil contained extensive lowlands that lost fewer nutrients to leaching. Consequently, it was possible to either expand cultivation, thus affording scalability of production, or move from depleted soil to virgin land when necessary. Additionally, the many existing watercourses could be harnessed to generate mechanical energy.[8]

Thanks to these favorable conditions, Brazil could offer the market a product of satisfactory quality at a reasonable price. In the last quarter of the sixteenth century, Brazil's sugar was much cheaper than Madeira's but much more expensive than São Tomé's. However, in terms of quality, it was much closer to Madeira sugar, which continued to enjoy the best reputation. Throughout the last decade of the sixteenth century and the first three decades of the seventeenth century, this resulted in the export of Brazilian sugar to Madeira, where it was resold at a higher price and passed off as locally produced.[9]

In addition to less than premium quality, Brazilian production faced other constraints. With the exception of São Tomé and Príncipe, all the production areas that had preceded Brazil were closer to Europe, including those in the Caribbean. The greater distance to Portugal's South American colony resulted in higher transport costs. The low frequency of shipping had formerly harmed production in Hispaniola and São Tomé, so a new sea route was required to prevent a similar situation. Like

Sugarloaf made in Morocco using the same process known in the Atlantic in the fifteenth and sixteenth centuries.

alto que es. B. y a la parte de arriva asentar la linter
na. C. la qual mueva la Rueda. D. que tiene los caxa
les a la Redondo y su arbol tiene el ruello. E. el qual
muele la caña cortada y en la parte baxa del arbol
del Ruello ay un yerro. F. el qual es corvado para que
vaya abaxando la caña debaxo del Ruello para
que se muelga y en la Rueda. A. se le ha de asetar
unos caxales los quales muevan la linterna. G.
la qual tiene un manil doblado que es. H. el qual
tiene una Argolla encaxada en el con un bano
la qual levanta un cuchillo. I. haze que otra
bana. L. la qual tiene al cavo una orquilla
que va empuxando para riva la caño para que se
corte y quando abaxa esa bana. L. se retrae un
poco para empuxar un poco mas adelante las
caños que estan libadas en faxos o en manojos
y de aqui la toman y la ponen debaxo del Ruello
y despues de molido la van poniendo de unos va
sos y de aqui la ponen en unas capaças de esparto
casi como las que acostumbran poner las olivas

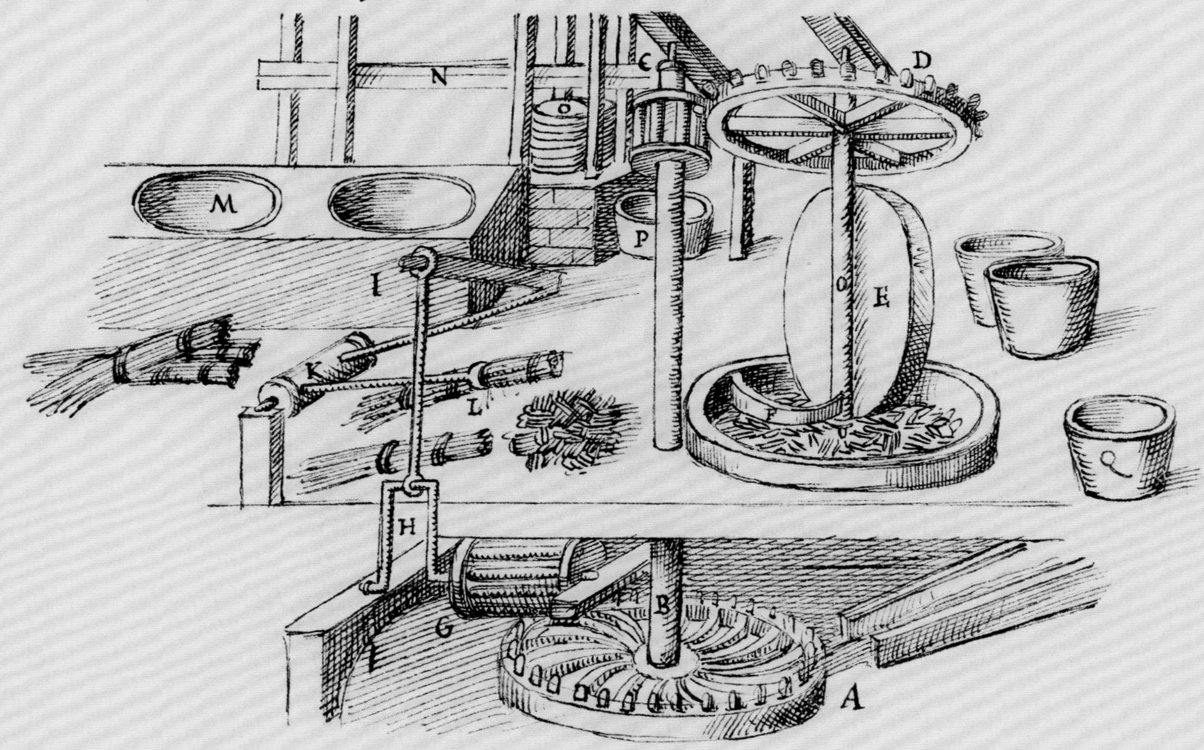

Molidas 1

those islands, Brazil required both specialists and unskilled workers. It needed to attract the former and compel the latter to work because the small Portuguese population was more inclined to seek its fortune in the Far East. As with the Canary Islands and the Caribbean, and unlike Madeira, Brazil was inhabited by an indigenous population. This had both advantages and disadvantages: the recurrent opposition and resistance of the Amerindians on the one hand, and the possibility of using them as a workforce through varying degrees of coercion on the other. Finally, significant investment was required to plant sugarcane and particularly to set up sugar mills, which required funds to buy slaves, livestock, copper instruments and other items, as well as to construct mills and other facilities, build carts and boats, divert rivers, prepare cane fields and pay for skilled labor, among others.[10]

The Manufacturing Process

Before examining the development of sugar production in Brazil, we will look at how the colony produced the commodity. As the quality of wine depends on the characteristics of the grape and its preparation, the quality of sugar depends on the climate, soil and altitude of the area where the cane is planted, the plant's background, favorable and unfavorable weather and other adverse conditions that might affect that particular harvest, and, last, the skill and care taken in its preparation. Physical conditions were determining factors. As with wine, they gave the product a geographical reputation, associating certain qualities with specific regions by virtue of their soil, climate and tradition.

Although more detailed information on this process dates to the early eighteenth century,[11] it is remarkably consistent and very similar to less detailed accounts from the beginning of the previous century.[12] Sugar manufacturing was divided into five stages: milling, boiling, purging, drying and packaging.

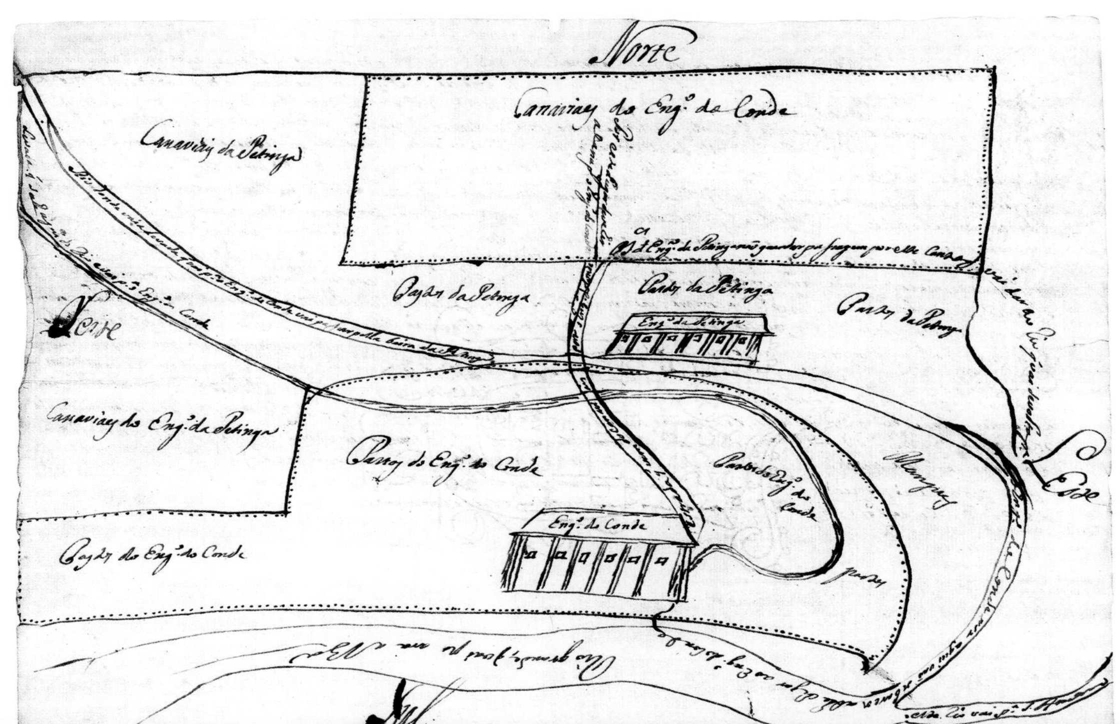

Late sixteenth-century Spanish sugar mill; *Pedro Juan de Lastanosa (prior to 1576). Note, on the right, the grindstone that crushes the cane with the screw press in the center (letter "O"). It appears to be an invention that aimed to increase the mechanization and efficiency of sugar mills, particularly the chopping and milling of the cane.*

Sketch of the Petinga Sugar Mill in the Recôncavo which was acquired in 1742 for the Jesuit College of Santo Antão in Lisbon; Father Luís da Rocha, (ca. 1742).

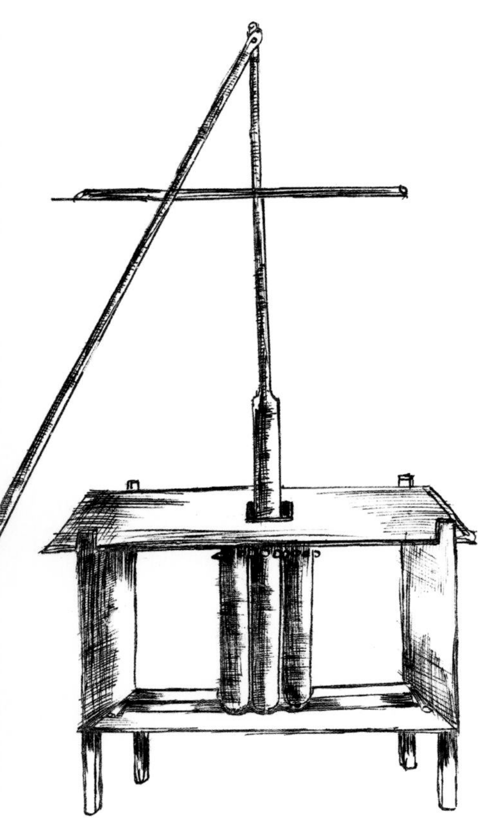

Three-roller mills (1613).

Sugar Mill and Mill; *Zacharias Wagener (1614–1668). Here we see the first cauldron set against the left wall, and above it, the pipe used to recycle scum. Right, the second cauldron. Between both cauldrons there is a receptacle to store the lye, with others beside it to hold water and the scum that will be reused. Against the other wall we see the teaches in decreasing sizes from left to right.*

The milling and boiling processes usually took place in different areas within the same building. Purging and packaging were usually done in another building, and drying took place in the open air.[13]

Initially, Brazil employed the same milling methods used in the Mediterranean and the Atlantic Islands.[14] The Mediterranean method used the same type of milling devices utilized to make olive oil: sugarcane was initially chopped prior to being crushed by a vertical grindstone rotating in a circular motion against another horizontal grindstone. Because all the juice was not entirely extracted at this stage, the bagasse (the dry, fibrous residue which remains after the juice is extracted from the crushed stalks of sugar cane) was taken to a crude screw press (*gangorra*), where it was placed at the end of a large beam, which generally had a ratcheting screw at the other end. The weight of the beam squeezed the bagasse, aided by the pressure produced by twisting the screw with human or animal traction. Another method involved using two horizontal cylinders to mill the cane, thereby avoiding the need to chop it, which saved time and effort. Even so, this method did not extract all the juice so it was also necessary to use the screw press.

Sometime between 1608 and 1613, a new type of mill was introduced. It also used cylinders, but now there were three, which were positioned vertically and juxtaposed. Using three-roller mills, one worker fed the cane through in one direction while another worker fed the bagasse back through the other, working non-stop. It was no longer necessary for someone to walk around the equipment to put the bagasse through again, as with the two-roller mills. The double action and juxtaposition of the cylinders made the stage involving the screw press unnecessary. This innovation was introduced gradually, and was utilized for some time along with the older methods.

All these mills could be driven by animal traction (horses or oxen) or water power. With its greater pressure and speed, the latter option was capable of processing a much larger amount of cane and avoided the need to replace tired or worn-out livestock. However, it was susceptible to drought and the more powerful overshot waterwheels depended on the availability of watercourses with vertical drops that could be diverted. It also required a more significant investment in equipment.[15]

Straw and mud were removed from the cane prior to placing it in the mill, where it was compressed to extract as much juice as possible. However, care had to be taken to prevent the bagasse from falling into the juice, which was taken to the kettle house, generally adjacent to the milling area and under the same roof. There it was purified, reduced and agglutinated, initially in two cauldrons or large kettles, and later in a series of teaches (small kettles), which were positioned side by side over their respective furnaces. This area was also known as the Copper House, named after the metal used to make the cauldrons, teaches, basins and tanks.

The first cauldron extracted the coarser impurities, removed along with the first scum produced by boiling. The rate of the boil was then reduced by adding water to the juice. To produce more scum, an alkaline solution was poured on the water, which helped flocculate the juice's impurities in the scum. This solution was lye (*decoada* in Portuguese), a mixture of hot ash from the furnaces and/or lime with boiling water. Lye contained potassium hydroxide and calcium hydroxide, substances that are used in whitening processes to this day.[16]

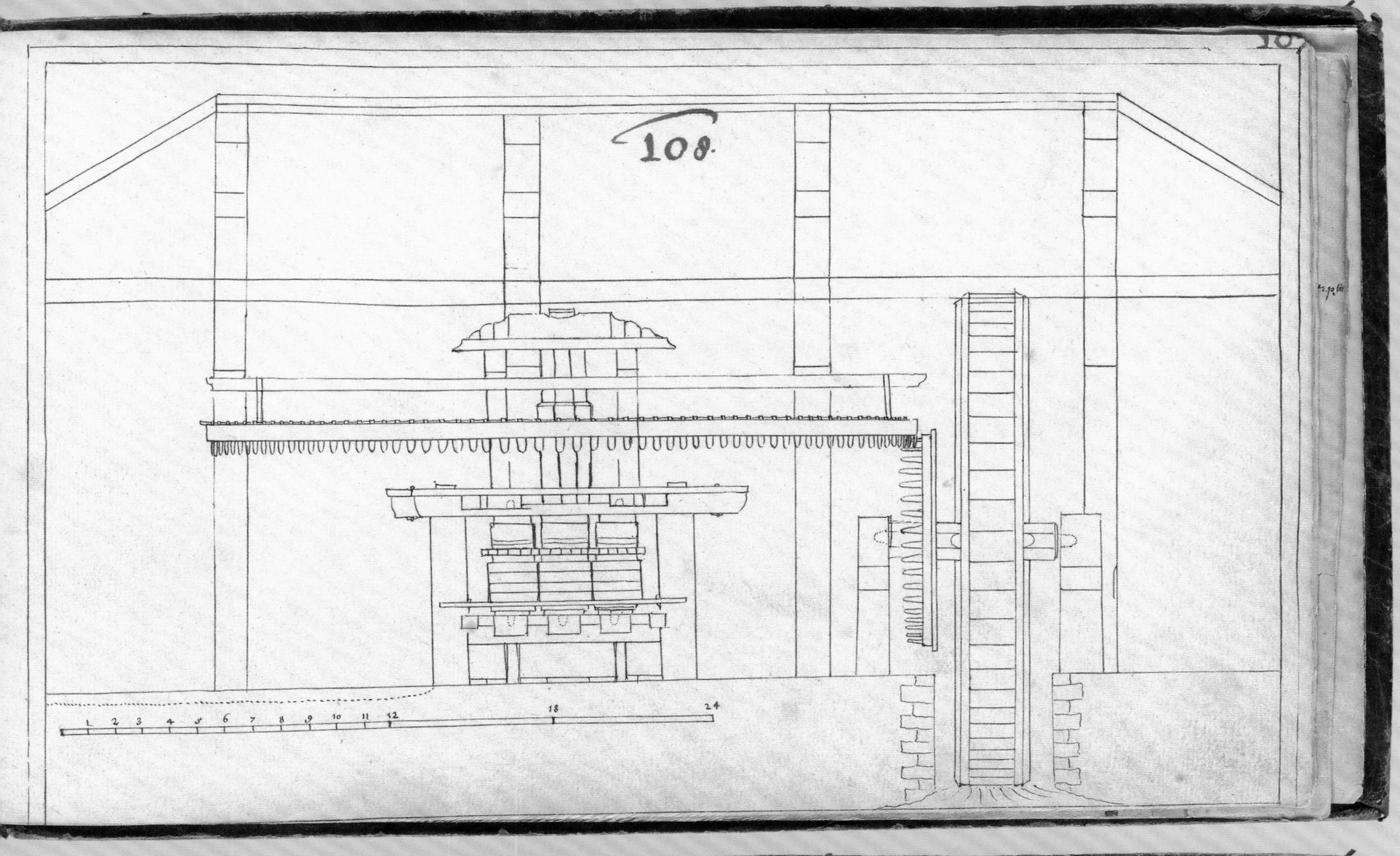
108
1 2 3 4 5 6 7 8 9 10 11 12 18 24

109

Clay sugarloaf mold from the Cordeiro Sugar Mill in Pernambuco (twentieth century).

The scum was not discarded, but was instead purified in a guitar-shaped pipe whose curves trapped bubbles containing impurities while allowing the condensed liquid to flow through. It was then returned to the same cauldron from which it had been removed. The procedure of alternately adding cold water and lye to reduce the boil and subsequently make the impurities flocculate, as well as skimming off the scum and carrying out the slow decanting process, was repeated several times. After half an hour, the juice was transferred to a second cauldron, where the procedure was repeated for a longer period until the juice thickened, having been reduced by evaporation, and was considered clean. It was then strained through pieces of cloth placed over a grille.

Afterwards, the juice was processed using more intense heat in teaches,[17] which were smaller and thicker than the cauldrons to cope with the high temperatures. The syrupy mixture (*melado*) was then boiled in those teaches until it reached saturation point. Each of the teaches held and produced an increasingly viscous and pure liquid, according to the stage of the process for which they were being used. The number of teaches and, consequently, the number of stages, could vary, depending on the mill. Animal fat was added to control the boil, and the process of skimming off impurities continued.

The final teache received a concentrated liquid that was beginning to crystallize naturally. The mixture was beaten in that teache, causing it to crystallize on the surface while a spoon known as a *batedeira* (beater), was used to stir and squeeze it to maintain its consistency until it came away from the teache. Using the same spoon, the mixture was scraped out and lifted from the teache to prevent it from burning. The process continued until the mixture had reached the right consistency for placing it into the mold.

The cone-shaped sugarloaf molds were made from clay, with a hole at the tip and an open base. Prior to placing the paste into the mold, the hole was blocked off and the sides were reinforced with fiber to prevent them from giving way. The molds were then inverted, and the paste introduced through the open base in three stages. At each stage, the paste was more crystallized than in the previous one, having been beaten longer. Therefore, these stages were referred to as tempering (*têmperas*), similar to the term used to describe incandescent metal fresh from the furnace. Before adding a new layer, the contents of the mold were stirred and squeezed with a large spatula or spoon to ensure that the recently inserted portion formed a single body along with the previous layer or layers.

The molds were then taken to the purging house, which was generally under a different roof. The plug was removed from the hole at the conical end of the mold and the paste was punctured with an iron tool. The molds were then placed in the circular openings of platforms assembled to hold them, with the conical end facing down. Beneath each platform, a trough collected the molasses that drained off through the punctured holes.

riet 2 Afgeſneden en Uitgeleeſen 3 Afvoering en ſamenbinding der rieten op braſiliſe wagens 4 Suijcker perſſe 5 Watermoolen om de perſſe te doen gaen 6 Bedeckte keetels en forneijſen
7 Pere met oſſen omgaende 8 Suijcker riet op de bergen en water landen waſſende 9 Suijvering van de ſappen 10 Kookink en verder ſuijveringh.
Pag: 7.8.9.
BRASILISE SUYKER WERKEN

Sugar production in a Brazilian sugar mill; *Romeyn de Hooghe, Utrecht (1682). Note the hard work involved in skimming off the scum. We can see a container of lye between the cauldrons, and a water vessel. Right, this depiction of the use of the molasses that runs out of the mold may also be intended to portray, in a stylized manner and possibly combining different processes: the reuse of scum and filtering of liquid from the cauldrons before it is transferred to the teaches. The pipe feeds a large tank beside the cauldrons, possibly transporting cane juice from the mill.*

The molds were then taken to the purging house, which was generally under a different roof. The plug was removed from the hole at the conical end of the mold and the paste was punctured with an iron tool. The molds were then placed in the circular openings of platforms assembled to hold them, with the conical end facing down. Beneath each platform, a trough collected the molasses that drained off through the punctured holes.

Purging house at the Jundiá Sugar Mill in Vicência, Pernambuco; nineteenth-century building.

Detail of View of Engenho Real in Brazil (ca. 1650–1655), by Frans Post. The sugar is dried and crushed on tarpaulins stretched out on a platform.

Then the claying process began. The cooled and dried sugar in the upper part of the mold was upturned, remolded, pounded and leveled. The mold was then covered with clay. Some days later, the clay was moistened and then left to dry for a few more days. The moisture released by the clay percolated the crystals, causing the molasses to flow between them.[A] The first clay seal was removed and the upper layer was stirred once again. It was then covered with a new layer of clay, which was moistened several times in a process that could take over a month. Both the introduction of the paste into the molds in portions with different levels of cooking and the revolving of the layers facilitated the absorption of the water in the clay and its decanting, without dissolving the crystals.

As the molasses continued to drip out, the clay layer descended. Finally, the clay was removed and the paste was left to purge for a few more days. The closer it was to the clay, the better the sugar. The sugar adjacent to the clay, known as *caras* (faces), due to its proximity to the *cara* (face) of the mold, was of the highest quality. The sugar nearest the funneled extremity of the cone was less pure and browner in color, as it contained more molasses and was less crystallized and dry. This was called muscovado or brown sugar.

Both the white and muscovado sugar obtained from the mold were referred to as *açúcar macho* (male sugar), due to its phallic shape.[B] The proportion of white to muscovado sugar varied, averaging two to one.[C] The white sugar could be divided into three types: the whitest and most crystallized, due to the contact with the clay; the sugar extracted from a point slightly deeper in the mold, which was darker, less crystallized and more granulated; and the third and final type, which was already slightly yellowed.[D] The lowest portion of the muscovado sugar, which was darkest and dampest due to its proximity to the conical end of the mold, was subjected to another purging process.

In addition to macho sugar, there was also *panela* sugar, comprising a higher proportion of molasses to crystals. This type of sugar was not subjected to the claying process, either because it had run out of the mold during purging or because it had never undergone the process.[E] It was either exported in this state or used for the production of *batido* (beaten) sugar in the sugar mill itself, or to distill spirits. To produce the batido sugar, the molasses was cooked, beaten again in the teaches and purged in the molds. The result was new white, muscovado and panela sugar, to which the adjective batido or *remel* was added, in the case of panela sugar. The process could be repeated several times,[F] and these types of sugar corresponded to approximately one-third of production.[18] The quality of the batido or *retame* sugar, another secondary processing method, was considered inferior. However, according to the sugar-mill owner and merchant Ambrósio Fernandes Brandão it all depended on the skill of the sugar master: "When you know how to process this sugar, one batch can be very good, another second-rate, and another extremely poor, depending on whether the sugar masters producing it are good or bad."[19]

It was also possible to produce sugar, albeit of inferior quality, by purging the scum from the teaches, which could not be done with the scum from the cauldrons. Throughout this entire process, other by-products that were of no use to the sugar production process were consumed by livestock, slaves and free workers as food supplements, sweets, drinks and used as a basic ingredient for preparing spirits and *rapadura* (raw brown sugar).

At the end of the purging process, the sugarloaf was removed from the mold. Only then could the positive outcome of all this work be confirmed. The muscovado sugar was sliced off with a machete. The white and muscovado sugar was taken to wooden platforms covered with tarpaulins. There, the blocks of sugar were broken up into ever smaller bits. Between one cracking and another, the bits were left to dry so that they would not pulverize. To ensure that they dried consistently, lumps were alternately piled in the center of the tarpaulin and then spread out over the ends. While they were stacked up, the ends of the tarpaulin and the platform absorbed the heat from the sun, which helped dry the bits when they were spread out again. Fearing the irreparable damage that moisture could cause to the sugar, this breaking process was only conducted on days when the sky was clear. If it threatened to rain at any time during the drying process, the workers would rush to make sure the sugar did not catch a single drop.

Once dry, the sugar was placed in previously prepared crates that were sealed on the inside with banana leaves and beaten clay to hold the sugar to-

A. The clay utilized was obtained from the loamy soil found near mangroves. Being porous, this type of clay permitted water to flow through easily and did not retain the molasses. The clay was left to dry on the trays where lye was prepared. This may have helped produce an alkaline lye solution that whitened the crystals; see: A. J. Antonil, *Cultura e opulência do Brasil por suas drogas e minas* (São Paulo: Editora da Universidade de São Paulo, 2007), pp. 95–96, 113, 157–159, 157–158, n. 37; J. M. Ucha, et al., "Apicum: gênese dos campos arenosos e degradação dos manguezais em dois municípios baianos," *Revista do Centro Federal de Educação Tecnológica da Bahia, 3*:2 (2004): passim.

B. The phallic associations that these molds and sugarloaves elicited, leading to the term "macho" being used to describe purged sugar, can be observed in a complaint made to the Holy Inquisition in Bahia in 1591. The accuser mentioned an episode in which "a sugar master molding sugar in the molds he said that if Our Lady were there he would also put her in that mold"; see: *Primeira visitação do Santo Offício às partes do Brasil: denunciações da Bahia, 1591–1593* (São Paulo: Editora Paulo Prado, 1925), pp. 331, 338.

C. In some cases, however, it seems that the ratio was reversed. We can assume that the clay sealing stage was sometimes cut short due to immediate trading opportunities or the availability of transport; see: R. C. Gonçalves, *Guerras e açúcares: política e economia na Capitania da Parayba – 1585–1630* (Bauru: Edusc, 2007), pp. 205–207.

D. By the end of the second half of the seventeenth century, these sub-types of white sugar were known as *finos* [fine] or *caras* [face], *redondo* [round] and *baixo* [low], respectively. The brown sugar obtained from the tip of the mold, which was moister and darker, was known as *cabucho* or *pé da forma* (Antonil, *Cultura e opulência do Brasil*, p. 167; Schwartz, *Sugar Plantations in the Formation of Brazilian Society*, pp. 122–125, 163).

E. Schwartz defines panela sugar as molasses that was not purged in the molds, not the molasses that flowed out of them (Ibid, pp. 120–121). However, Antonil, the main source for the sugar production process in Brazil, writes: "the product dripping from the macho molds is called *mel* (literally "honey"); while the run-off from the beaten white sugar is called *remel*. Some use the mel to produce cane spirit by distilling it; others cook it again to make *batidos*, and others sell them as panela sugar to those who distil or cook it. And the same applies to remel" (Antonil, *Cultura e opulência do Brasil*, p. 167).

F. According to Schwartz, up to six times, depending on the quality of the sugar (Schwartz, *Sugar Plantations in the Formation of Brazilian Society*, p. 119).

Once dry, the sugar was placed in previously prepared crates that were sealed on the inside with banana leaves and beaten clay to hold the sugar together and keep it consistent.

Brazilian landscape with a sugar mill *(detail)*; *Frans Post (1660)*.

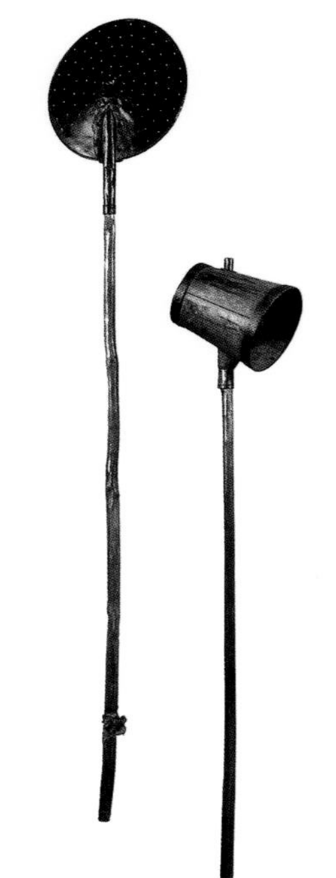

Wood and iron skimmer and mug used to transfer molasses from one pan to another.

Iron and copper teache from the Pau Amarelo sugar mill (Alagoas) (twentieth century).

gether and keep it consistent. The different types of white sugar would be separated prior to being broken up into bits and packaged in the wooden crates. We do not know whether it was standard practice to weigh and mark the crates before the second half of the seventeenth century,[G] as occurred later.[20] We only know that the crates were marked with the name of the person at whose expense and risk they were being shipped and the number that helped to identify the container on the bill of lading for a cargo dispatched in a single shipment. These indicators helped to track the crate along its route, detect fraud and identify where it had occurred. In fact, the fraud often began at the sugar mills, where batido sugar was sold as a higher-grade product by filling the crates with the inferior sugar and covering it with a layer of the finer kind. As we will see, the same thing could happen with muscovado and panela sugar at some point along the way.[21]

Instead of breaking up the sugarloaves into bits to make the so-called *açúcar abatido* (laying or crushed sugar), the loaves could also be packaged intact as *açúcar em pé* (standing sugar).[22] Sometimes, pieces of the white part of the loaves were cut off for sale as sweets. More valuable, the so-called caras, or the sugar at the base of the loaf, which represented less than half of the white mass, were cut, smoothed out and wrapped in straw or leather. The caras could also be broken up to fill small crates known as *fechos*. The white part of the loaf, preferably the whitest, could also be divided into sixths or eighths and sold in pieces (chips) with the corners trimmed to form cubes.

Crates, fechos or caras and barrels of molasses were then dispatched by boat or ox-cart to the ships that transported them to Europe or to warehouses – called *paços*[H] in Pernambuco and *trapiches* in Bahia – near the ports, where they awaited transatlantic shipment.[23] At the sugar mills, the crates were stored in areas sheltered from rain but exposed to the sun to protect the sugar from moisture, which was its greatest threat after packaging.[24]

This was almost an industrial process, which included machinery of some complexity, division of labor and a hierarchy among the individuals involved.[I] The workers were specialized in the different tasks that they carried out continuously, using specific tools. The production line required coordinating the different tasks. The amount of cane to be harvested on a day was determined by the sugar mill's milling capacity to prevent the cane from drying out while waiting for the mill. The milling, in turn, had to take into account the capacity and the pace of the kettles. These had to be coordinated with the teaches to prevent the juice from standing too long and turning sour. The kettleman, who stirred the juice and skimmed off the scum, and the stoker feeding the furnace, which was situated outside the building, had to coordinate their work to ensure that the juice and paste did not overflow or stop boiling. There could be no shortage of lye to purify the juice. When the paste was ready, there had to be enough molds ready to hold it, and there had to be enough tarpaulins to take full advantage of sunny days for drying purposes.[25]

The critical part of the process involved the smaller copper teaches, which determined the pace and amount of work that came before and after that stage. Consequently, every effort was made to maintain the cooking process at full capacity to maximize the sugar-mill owner's investments. However, pressure could also come from the fields. A hotter summer required an early harvest and overloaded the system.[26]

Sugar production involved critical and precise tasks, the results of which had a significant impact on the outcome of the process and return on investment. In the last teache for example, the paste could not be beaten too long because it would prevent it from purging in the mold. On the other hand, if it was not beaten long enough, it would leak out of the hole. During the purging stage, the quality of the crushed cane and the weather had to be taken into account. Sweeter, younger and less watery cane produced the best sugar. However, its paste took longer to be purged: it was distributed in a larger number of molds because it expanded as it crystallized. It produced a more crystallized sugar, although it was necessary to moisten the clay much more frequently. Conversely, a lower-quality sugar, if moistened more, ended up dissolving and being discharged along with the molasses. The heat also required wetting the molds more often.[27]

The head factor (*feitor-mor*) was at the top of the hierarchy. Except for cases where the sugar-mill owner was personally in charge, the factor took care of the financial and managerial aspects of the operation. He planned, coordinated and controlled the entire production process, assigning the tasks and supervising the work. He also coordinated the sugar mill's activities with those of the other sectors with which it was linked in the supply chain. Heading the technical side was the sugar master, whose skill depended on his experience.[28] It was he or his close subordinates who made the decisions on the most critical matters, generally between one stage and another in the process, for example, determining whether the juice in the second cauldron was clean and ready to be strained, whether the paste in the next to last copper teache was ready to be beaten in the last one, and how to insert the already beaten paste into the molds in the tempered layers. It was also necessary to take care of the equipment, which meant not overloading the mill with cane at any one time, and ensuring that the kettles always contained some liquid to prevent the fire from damaging the copper.

Naturally, the division, specialization and hierarchy of labor varied in accordance with the size of the sugar mill and the complexity of its equipment, which generally went hand-in-hand. A sugar mill could have more than one set of teaches, more than one mill or watermills, pipes and ducts instead of manual transport, cranes to lift the tank that held the juice from the mill and poured it into another tank in the area above the furnaces, and so forth. These tasks, in turn, could be spatially divided into a larger number of areas and buildings. Watermills crushed more cane, freeing up the bottleneck between the fields and the boiling house. However, the watermills' maximum output made it advisable to have two sets of copper teaches per mill.[29]

G. The weighing process helped calculate the share due to a cane farmer, whose cane was processed in the mill, whether or not he was a leaseholder of the mill owner, and the amount of tax owed. It also provided information for future buyers. Prior to packaging, the sugar was taken for weighing in the tarpaulins used to dry it. From the second half of the seventeenth century, the authorities attempted to make it obligatory for sugar mills to mark the cases with a branding iron to display the weight, quality and origin of the sugar and the name of the person at whose expense and risk it was transported. This information made it easier to evaluate the product because it listed the three main elements used in the calculation: mass, type and origin (Ibid., pp. 121–125).

H. The term *paço* was also used in Paraíba, but they apparently operated at a later date (Gonçalves, *Guerras e açúcares*, pp. 208–209).

I. Using a Marxist conceptual framework, Vera Ferlini describes the labor process in the sugar mills as being carried out by specific workers engaged in sequential and connected activities in a continuous process at a collective rather than individual pace. The division and specialization of labor and its spatial separation increased productivity to the point where it reduced the gaps in each individual's working day. Slaves performed most of the unskilled tasks. Free workers were assigned more complex technical posts and acted as supervisors and managers. Once the work was simplified by the sub-division of tasks, it was delegated to the slaves; see: V. L. A. Ferlini, *Terra, trabalho e poder: o mundo dos engenhos no Nordeste colonial* (Bauru: Edusc, 2003), pp. 135–213.

Launching in Brazil

In the first years after Pedro Álvares Cabral's fleet arrived on the east coast of South America, there were no significant results. Portugal continued focusing its efforts on its lucrative Asiatic venture, which was at its epic stage. The country had a sparse workforce and meager resources at its disposal. Between 1500 and 1530, Portuguese activity in the Americas was effectively limited to exploratory expeditions and coastal patrols, trade with the indigenous population to guarantee the supply of brazilwood and the establishment of some forts and trading posts. Even so, there are records of sales of Brazilian sugar in Antwerp in 1519, and of customs duties paid for it in Lisbon in 1526. Some sugar mills appear to have already been operating in Brazil in the second and third decades of the century, either on the initiative of the Crown or with its support, but their production was minimal.[30]

Guaranteeing Portuguese sovereignty over the territory that Portugal saw as its share of the Americas and countering the claims and assaults of France, and to a lesser degree, of Spain, required the effective presence of Portuguese settlements. To address this challenge without neglecting its interests in Asia, the Portuguese Crown delegated the undertaking to private enterprise through the hereditary captaincy system, which it had already done successfully in Madeira, albeit on a smaller scale. The Brazilian coast was divided into fifteen strips, each a captaincy, and distributed among twelve proprietors, who were chosen from among the royal functionaries, officers who had enjoyed the greatest success in the overseas enterprise in the Far East, amassing wealth that, it was hoped, could be invested in the colonization of Brazil.

1600/1650

These donations were made in the mid-1530s, but only eight of the fifteen strips were initially colonized. In those areas, the proprietors (donataries) established settlements and distributed land to those willing to cultivate it. Sugar production appeared to be a natural choice for the Crown, the proprietors, the settlers and the investors, due to the experience the Portuguese had gained in their other possessions and the large demand in the European market. Many of the proprietors built sugar mills with funds obtained from Portuguese and foreign merchants, some of whom lived in Portugal. Promising results were obtained in Porto Seguro, Ilhéus and Espírito Santo. Sugar mills were also established in Bahia and São Tomé (or Paraíba do Sul, in the northern part of the present-day Rio de Janeiro State).

The best results were obtained in São Vicente, on the coast of what is now São Paulo State, and further north in Pernambuco. This was possibly due to greater involvement on the part of the proprietors and their representatives, more significant fundraising efforts and better relations with the Amerindians. In São Vicente, the proprietor established a sugar mill in partnership with Flemish businessmen who later took over the venture, which was managed by its factors. A second sugar mill belonged to a Genoese. In Pernambuco, the proprietor took care of the security of the settlement, the town of Olinda. He found investors in Portugal, some of whom were representatives of major banking houses from southern Germany. He also brought farmers, technicians and craftsmen from the Iberian Peninsula and the Atlantic Islands at his own expense and assisted them in the cultivation of the land.

As in Madeira, the Canary Islands, São Tomé and the Caribbean, the main challenge was the significant manpower that sugarcane cultivation demanded. Farming virgin land in inhospitable areas for a venture

This drawing by Frans Post shows a two-wheeled, animal-driven mill (seventeenth century).

with a dubious outcome was hardly an inviting prospect. At the time, those Portuguese who were willing to settle overseas preferred to go to the Far East. The Amerindians could be won over through barter, albeit only temporarily, a situation which was incompatible with the continuous effort required to plant sugar-cane, and even more so to manufacture sugar. The native population met attempts to coerce them into working or to enslave them with aggression. The situation worsened when expeditions from one captaincy attempted to capture the native inhabitants of another, causing the Amerindians to vent their anger on innocent local settlers. By the end of the 1540s, the indigenous peoples were on the verge of driving the Portuguese from the entire coastline, and the settlers were indeed expelled from several areas, the most significant setback being the disastrous loss of Bahia and São Tomé. Across the rest of the territory, the Portuguese were confined to small enclaves within their settlements, and most of the investments were lost.

It became clear that the Brazilian enterprise could not last much longer without strong intervention from the Crown, which, in 1548, took the initiative through the creation of the General Government. Until then, the Crown had held the monopoly on the extraction of brazilwood, which it leased out to private individuals, while retaining some control over tax collection to ensure that it received its share of the captaincies' production. It now took the lead in the defense against both the resistant or insurgent Amerindians and foreigners, who were regarded as invaders. The Crown also tried to put an end to disputes among

French intervention and Portuguese settlements

Portugal began to change its attitude towards its New World possessions between 1520 and 1530. However, this was translated into political positioning rather than effective action on the ground. Doubts regarding the demarcation of the Treaty of Tordesillas threatened to exclude the River Plate (Río de la Plata) from Portuguese control, thus making it harder to gain access to the gold and silver that its upper reaches were known to contain. Even worse was the constant French presence on the Brazilian coast. France was at odds with Charles V, king of Castile, which gave it an additional reason to ignore the Iberian claims of sovereignty over the New World made by that treaty and to encourage overseas advances. In addition to trading with the Amerindians, the French also intended to establish permanent footholds in the Americas. Although Portugal attempted to remain neutral in the Franco-Habsburg conflict, French privateers seized Portuguese ships in the Atlantic and acquired brazilwood from along the Brazilian coast. John III of Portugal's diplomatic overtures to the King of France were fruitless, and Portugal's active repression of the French presence in "their" possessions gave France's monarchs a pretext to issue letters of marque.

It became urgent for Portugal to guarantee control of the Brazilian coastline to prevent its rivals from encroaching on the strategic route to and from India, extracting brazilwood, or tapping into the colony's immense agricultural potential, and seizing the mines that still might be found inland. The measures taken included capturing French ships, claiming Portuguese possession of the River Plate and founding Vila de São Vicente, halfway between the River Plate and Rio Grande (do Norte, on the northeastern tip of South America). However, they proved insufficient. If the Spanish conquest of Peru from the Pacific reduced Portugal's interest in the River Plate, the persistence of the French along the entire coastline, forming alliances with the indigenous peoples against the Portuguese and attacking their ships, increased Portugal's concern – an alarm that was only aggravated by the agreements reached among France, the Ottoman Empire and Morocco.

the settlers, and, moreover, sought to prevent unnecessary conflicts between the settlers and the indigenous population.

The General Government was expected to support the colonization efforts that had been associated with sugar production since the regulation that created it (*Regimento*), distributing land to those willing to build sugar mills and cultivate sugarcane. In return, it was to exercise greater influence over the administration of the captaincies and take over and govern some of them directly.

The greatest contribution of the General Government was the mobilization of its own available resources and those received from the metropolis to lead military incursions into the most strategic areas and defend the territory against the Amerindians and European rivals. During the first quarter of the century, it consolidated the Portuguese-controlled areas. Its capital Salvador served as a base for the expansion into the Recôncavo region (the area radiating from the Bay of All Saints), and the Portuguese took possession of the hinterland. They did the same in Pernambuco and Itamaracá: starting from the settlements Olinda and Igaraçu, they initially took control of the Capiberibe floodplain and the area between the two towns, later organizing two campaigns against the Amerindians, who were entrenched to the south in the area of Cabo de Santo Agostinho and the Serinhaém River. As soon as these areas became secure, they became occupied with sugar mills.

The Portuguese repelled indigenous raids on São Vicente from Guanabara Bay and in 1560 destroyed the fortress of the French, who had made their first attempt to gain a foothold on the coast and establish Antarctic France in 1555. Five years later, the fear that they might return and establish a base in the bay area resulted in the foundation of the city of Rio de Janeiro. This led to the repression of indigenous resistance with the help of residents of other captaincies and troops brought in from Portugal.

Nevertheless, the French continued to frequent the Brazilian coast and obtain brazilwood from the indigenous population in areas that were unpopulated or sparsely inhabited by the Portuguese. They assaulted Portuguese shipping and attacked settlements and fortifications such as Ilhéus, in what is now the state of Bahia, and Cabedelo, Paraíba. They even made some attempts to establish a colony – Equinoctial France – in Maranhão. This was a short-lived enterprise, which was overthrown by the Portuguese (1612–1615), but left the settlement of São Luís as a legacy.

If sugar production in Rio de Janeiro only became significant in the next century, probably due to harassment by the Amerindians, indigenous resis-

The establishment of the General Government in Brazil

Planning to establish Brazil's colonial capital there, the Crown purchased the captaincy of Bahia from the proprietor's heirs. The ownership of the captaincies that had not been colonized or had been lost to the Amerindians reverted to the king of Portugal. Only Pernambuco, Itamaracá, Ilhéus, Porto Seguro, Espírito Santo and São Vicente remained in private hands. In those areas, the General Government intervened in the judicial system, defense, and even in the administration. It would also assume the role of mediator in relations between the Christians and the "heathens."

The General Government transformed a collection of scattered colonial enclaves into an increasingly cohesive body. It created a representative of the Crown that was closer and more attentive to local matters, and which also sought to mediate in relations between the colonists and the metropolis. The city of Salvador was founded as the seat of this government. It was located near the middle of the coastal area designated to Portugal by the Treaty of Tordesillas, at the entrance of a bay with an excellent natural harbor that was easy to defend against seaborne attacks. Additionally, the soil in the Recôncavo region was ideal for cultivating sugarcane. In time, Salvador became the administrative, judicial and ecclesiastical capital of the State of Brazil.

tance in Ilhéus, Porto Seguro and Espírito Santo truly impeded its expansion in those areas. Production in São Vicente remained stagnant, possibly due to its narrow coastline and greater distance from Europe.

In the last quarter of the sixteenth century, the established colonies in Pernambuco and Bahia extended the boundaries of their settled territories to adjacent areas with the leadership or support of the General Government, and even with the help of troops deployed from Europe. From Bahia, they expanded northwards into the region between the Recôncavo and the São Francisco River, moving into the territory of the present-day state of Sergipe, which was more suitable for cattle raising. From Pernambuco, they also expanded northwards into the captaincies of Paraíba and Rio Grande (do Norte), with the former being quickly occupied by sugar mills. (The east-west coast that connects the Rio Grande to the Amazon will not be dealt with here, due to its irrelevance to the sugar economy industry at the beginning of the seventeenth century.)

The conquered territories were initially distributed to the settlers who stood out in these conflicts. The Regulation of Tomé de Souza, the first governor-general, contained specific guidelines on how the donations of land should be managed. Land and watercourses needed to run the mills were given to those who not only had an interest in operating sugar mills but also the means to establish them. However, land that exceeded the investor's means could not be donated, and a portion was set aside for the cane farmers (*lavradores*). The sugar-mill owner was obliged to process the sugarcane grown on the cane farmers' land in exchange for a share of the output. This allowed cane farmers with fewer available resources to share in production. At the same time, by retaining part of the sugar produced from the cane planted by the farmers, the sugar-mill owners were able to share the amortization and the risks of their investments.

Individuals who invested in new sugar mills or in the reconstruction of those that had been destroyed or abandoned were rewarded with a period of tax exemption. The Crown sought to encourage immigration to Brazil, initially providing free passage to residents of Madeira, the Azores and São Tomé, extending the tax exemptions, although for a shorter period, to immigrants who planted sugarcane. The Crown invested in the completion of the construction of a sugar mill in Bahia, which was to be managed by technicians sent from Madeira. Finally, it made an effort to ensure the effective occupation of the land and prevent owner absenteeism. The beneficiaries were to make use of the land within a certain period, under penalty of it being redistributed. While this rule was not always applied, the Crown's continued efforts to regulate settlement with a view to promoting sugar production demonstrated its support for the project.

In addition to the land, the settlers who had excelled in military campaigns were also rewarded with slaves. Amerindian rebels and insurgents could be legitimately enslaved, and many thousands were. No less important were the legal loopholes created by local authorities to permit the exploitation of this indigenous workforce, very often with the Crown's support, despite the clergy's efforts to exclude Amerindians from slavery, particularly those who had converted to Christianity.

While Portugal's colonial frontiers expanded, France's support bases, native allies and anchorages dwindled. Consequently, by the third quarter of the sixteenth century, the gradual increase of the area populated by the Portuguese, which was protected from both indigenous attacks and foreign incursions, created favorable conditions for the growth of sugar production in Brazil. All these efforts demonstrated

Celebration in the countryside; *Frans Post (1643 or 1645).*

The introduction of African slave labor to Brazil

The transition from indigenous to African slave labor was slow, non-linear and spatially varied. The potential number of indigenous inhabitants on the Bahian and northeastern coast that could be legitimately enslaved was reduced by wars, initial captures, the migration of some native groups and the diseases introduced by Europeans, who had also passed through Asia, and Africans. As the stock of indigenous who could be enslaved fell, their price increased. At the same time, the arduous and systematic work in the sugar mills caused high mortality rates among those already coerced to work.

African slaves were more expensive but possibly more resistant to disease. However, the main advantage was that their supply was more flexible and the legitimacy of their enslavement was not questioned. There were slaves waiting to be transported from African ports, brought there through a long-established network established within indigenous African societies. The demand from the Brazilian market stimulated this trade, which grew exponentially, resulting in the search for new "recruitment" areas. This was a dynamic process with repercussions on both sides of the Atlantic. Not only was the enslavement of Africans considered acceptable in more situations than Amerindian slavery, but the black people delivered to the Portuguese on the African coast were already enslaved. As there was no way of knowing the circumstances of their capture in the hinterland, both African slavery and the transatlantic slave trade were conveniently legitimized. Lastly, the trafficking of slaves was also a source of revenue for the Crown, through the leasing of export (and import) rights to Portuguese trading outposts in Africa.

Neither the Roman Catholic Church nor the Crown was interested in forming supply networks of indigenous slaves in the Brazilian hinterland, as they had developed in Africa. The Church saw the Amerindians as a flock to be converted and condemned their enslavement. The missionaries, particularly the Jesuits, attempted to bring them under their guardianship. The Crown wanted to keep peace and establish a steady alliance with the Amerindians to avoid any insurrections against its sovereignty. This presented a strategic threat to colonization, as did the African rebellions that occurred much later. At the same time, the Crown intended to gain more subjects through the conversion and acculturation of the indigenous inhabitants. The General Government promoted aldeamento, the process through which Amerindians of different origins were settled, by force if necessary, converted and encouraged to assimilate into the Portuguese culture. The government hoped to use these settlements to produce a source of paid labor. In general, the enslavement of Amerindians was only permitted when a slave was acquired from other indigenous groups, or in the case of "just wars" against the Amerindians. The definition of this concept became increasingly strict, but still allowed sufficient room for interpretation and negotiation.

At first, the presence of Africans was marginal. By the last quarter of the sixteenth century, they accounted for a quarter or a third of the slaves in Pernambuco and Bahia, and by the 1630s they were the vast majority. Just when a routine for the large-scale trafficking and use of African slave labor had been established, harassment by privateers reduced the supply and raised the price. To compensate for this supply drop, attempts to intensify the enslavement of Amerindians, mainly in the southern part of Brazil, resulted in acrimonious conflicts between the settlers and the Jesuits.[41]

the Crown's commitment to its establishment and expansion, and with the protection of the investments in sugarcane cultivation, mills and the sugar trade. As a result, those individuals who had an interest, capital and experience felt encouraged to get involved.

As we have seen, important foreign businessmen, mainly Flemish, Genoese and long-time German residents of Portugal, who were already connected with overseas Portuguese enterprises and the distribution of their products in Europe, made investments that were considered risky in Brazil and the Atlantic Islands. However, as the safety of these businesses increased and profits loomed, smaller investors, such as sugar-mill owners and cane farmers, began investing as well.

Estimates of Production

With lower costs than those of the competing regions due to the excellent topographical, geological, hydrological and climatic conditions, as well as the economies of scale thanks to the availability of extensive tracts of land, the number of sugar mills in Brazil grew continuously. The available information comes from the accounts of missionaries, Crown officers and entrepreneurs whose interests, incumbencies and focus were based there. It is therefore no surprise that they sometimes omitted data, overlooked captaincies and entire regions, and exaggerated certain figures. However, they demonstrate clear trends: the number of sugar mills grew steadily, increasing at a stronger pace between 1570 and 1585, and more slowly after that until the period between 1610 and 1612. This growth was initially concentrated in the captaincies of Bahia and Pernambuco.

Following is a table from Stuart B. Schwartz, who has gleaned the most representative and reliable statistics, although they are still not precise.[J]

Number of sugar mills in Brazil, 1570–1629[31]

	1570	1583	1612	1629
Pará, Ceará, Maranhão, Rio Grande	–	–	1	–
Paraíba	–	–	12	24
Itamaracá	1	–	10	18
Pernambuco	23	66	90	150
Sergipe	–	–	1	–
Bahia	18	36	50	80
Ilhéus	8	3	5	4
Porto Seguro	5	1	1	–
Espírito Santo	1	6	8	8
Rio de Janeiro	–	3	14	60
São Vicente and Santo Amaro	4	–	–	2
Total	**60**	**115**	**192**	**346**

Source: Schwartz, *Sugar Plantations in the Formation of Brazilian Society*, p. 165.

Since the nineteenth century, several authors have embarked on the arduous task of assessing Brazil's total sugar production.[32] The most recent attempts estimate the sugar mills' average production and multiply it by the number of mills. They then compare the results with those provided by contemporary chroniclers during the period in question.

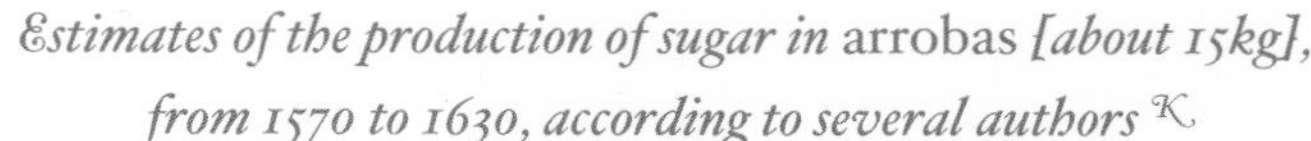

Estimates of the production of sugar in arrobas *[about 15kg], from 1570 to 1630, according to several authors* K.

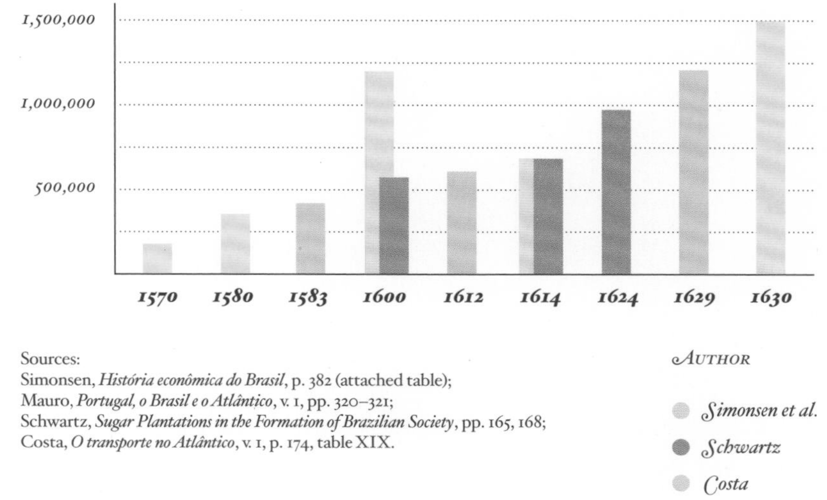

The above histogram shows three different approaches to the estimation of overall sugar production.[33] The actual amounts probably fall between the most conservative and optimistic projections, or around them.

The differences are due to the authors' varying appraisals of the sugar mills' size and average productivity, which depended on the frequency of the use of water power or animal traction. From the second decade of the seventeenth century, it was also determined by the percentage of sugar mills with two- or three-roller mills. Additionally, production could vary according to the amount of sunlight, heavy rain or drought, soil depletion, age of the plants, presence of pests, management quality, indigenous attacks and the expected demand.

Even in a good year, only a few large sugar mills powered by waterwheels produced an average of 6,000 arrobas (approximately 90,000 kg.). Even fewer managed to arrive at 10,000 arrobas (about 150,000 kg.), as some contemporary authors have estimated (see note 33). The vast majority produced between 2,000 and 6,000 arrobas, equivalent to 30,000 kg. and 90,000 kg.

J. Schwartz bases his figures on the following chroniclers for the respective years: Pero Magalhães Gândavo, for 1570; Father Fernão Cardim, for 1583; Sergeant-Major (*Sargento mor*); Digo de Campos Moreno, for 1612 (the data on the captaincies of Espírito Santo and Rio de Janeiro were reported by the Jesuit Jácome Monteiro in 1610); and, very probably, the head purveyor (*provedor-mor*), Pedro Cadena de Vilhasanti, for 1629. Others could be included, but they were even more incomplete and imprecise. (For the relevant bibliography, see n. 31 at the end of this chapter.) Frédéric Mauro selects what he considers to be the most reliable data and summarizes it with the following estimated figures: 1570 (60 sugar mills); 1585 (130); 1610 (230); 1629 (346) (Mauro, *Portugal, o Brasil e o Atlântico*, p. 257).

K. The histogram's first approach groups three authors who, in a certain way, complement each other – Roberto Cochrane Simonsen, Mircea Buescu and Mauro – while the other two estimates, by Schwartz and Costa, question the totals calculated by their predecessors. (For more details, see note 33 at the end of this chapter.)

The authors cited here are unanimous in confirming a boom in Brazil's sugar industry until the beginning of the 1610s, particularly between 1570 and 1585.[34] During this period, Brazil became the world's main supplier of the commodity. As we have seen, its competition exacerbated the inherent drawbacks of the Greater Mediterranean, Madeira, São Tomé and Hispaniola. In addition to the conditions already mentioned, this upsurge was also fueled by the international market or, more precisely, by the European market, which drove prices higher. This was particularly due to the influx of silver from the Americas, population growth, urbanization and idle capacity to supply this population in Europe, the progressive stability supported by institutional development, and the growing integration and expansion of the markets of the Old World (as well as the New), whose production was becoming increasingly more trade orientated.[35]

The data on prices is even more problematic than that concerning the number of sugar mills and their production. There are very few series of consistent prices and those in existence do not cover all the years. The figures usually do not differentiate the sub-types, the region of origin or the state of conservation, which are consequential factors in the pricing of sugar. The difficulties multiply when there are only a few observations available for a given year. This impedes the identification of both seasonal and short-term variations caused by changes or shifts in supply and demand for sugar and transport, and so forth. When the data has an institutional origin, the recorded prices have only slight movement or are tariffed. The main problem is that prices fluctuated frequently and very rapidly, sometimes even on the same day, which makes it difficult to estimate whether the data is representative.[36]

Yet again, despite their deficiencies, the statistics suggest certain trends. Here are presented the data collected by Christopher Ebert for Brazil, Portugal and northern Europe, as they are the most comprehensive set, including most of the previously published data, with a larger number of observations per year.[37]

Price of sugar in Brazil, in réis, per arroba[38]

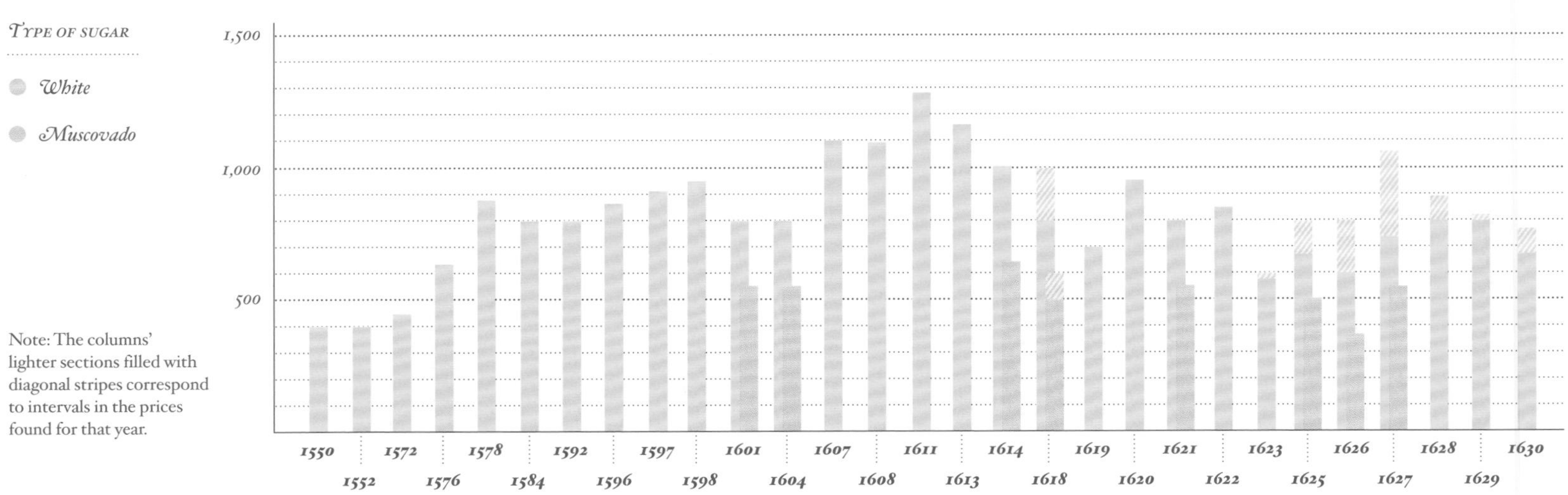

Source: Ebert, "The Trade in Brazilian Sugar," p. 189.

It can be seen that the price levels in the Brazil in the 1580s were already double what they had been mid-century. They continued to climb until 1611, but everything indicates that this was at a slower rate. In the second decade of the seventeenth century, they fell slightly before returning to the levels of the 1590s. This was possibly due to the stagnation of silver exports from Spanish America.[39]

Opinions are divided regarding the prosperity of the sugar industry in the second decade of the seventeenth century: costs were rising because the most desirable land near watercourses and close to trading centers had already been taken. The work was increasingly being done by African slaves, purchased on credit at high prices. With expenses on the rise, including the cost of capital, sugar-mill owners were more vulnerable to failed harvests, contractions in the demand for sugar and the losses caused by slave revolts, escapes and deaths.[40]

Losing Momentum?

However, there is no dispute that a downturn began between 1618 and 1623 and continued until the first years of the Dutch conquest of the Brazilian Northeast, although some considered it either circumstantial ("conjunctural") or cyclical.[42] In 1618, sugar prices began to fall in Europe and Brazil, reaching the levels of the previous century as demand for sugar contracted. The eruption of the Thirty Years' War among the European powers in 1618 brought about large-scale devastation and a disruption in the flow of merchandise and funds, while consuming vast resources. This period also witnessed a more pronounced reduction in the arrival of silver shipments to Europe from the Americas. To cover their costs, European governments drastically reduced the metal content of their coins. They later revalued them, creating even more uncertainty in the markets.[43]

Meanwhile, the supply of sugar increased,[44] and Brazil felt its impact. In 1618, Crown officers reported on the difficulty of finding bidders for farming of the collection of the *dízimos* (a ten-percent tax on the value of production). This was due to droughts, the death of slaves in epidemics and, possibly, as a result of the tax exemptions and immunities against seizure of property granted to sugar-mill owners by the Crown. The depletion of the soil in areas that had been cultivated for a longer period was apparently the reason a royal sugar mill in Bahia was unable to find a buyer or leaseholder, and other mills in the vicinity were abandoned. In Portugal, the lack of bidders in other tax farming auctions reflected these difficulties.[45]

While supply and demand diverged, trade suffered from religious-social repression and warfare. Between 1618 and 1621, a strong and premeditated wave of inquisitorial persecution in the Portuguese city of Porto (Oporto), a key re-exporting hub for sugar, and in Brazil, resulted in the imprisonment of dozens of merchants of Jewish descent, mainly in Portugal. The imprisonments and confiscation of the assets of prisoners and fugitives jolted the sugar trade.[46] Worse was to follow at the end of the Twelve Years' Truce in 1621. The resumption of hostilities restored the embargo on Dutch shipping and trade in Portugal, making the re-export of sugar even more costly in a shrinking market. Dutch privateers joined the Barbary pirates in attacking shipping in the triangle between the Iberian Peninsula, Morocco and the Atlantic Islands. To top it all off, the Dutch created the West India Company (WIC), which in 1623 and

Maciape Plantation; *Zacharias Wagener (1614–1668). Despite wartime transportation and labor problems, the number of plantations in Colonial Brazil continued to grow.*

1624 carried out audacious attacks on both sides of the Atlantic and attempted to conquer at least part of the region where the sugar industry had been established in Brazil. Indeed, for one year, between 1624 and 1625, the Company dominated the city of Salvador and terrorized the Recôncavo, destabilizing the region's production and trade.[47]

The war made shipping and slaves more costly.[48] With the reduction in the supply of transport, sugar inventories accumulated, and some sugar mills either shut down, reduced their production or were sold off or seized by creditors. As a result, in 1623 and 1624, the bids offered for tax farming revenues were significantly lower than in the previous decade.[49] Despite the reduced demand, the increased cost of slaves and the lack of transport, the number of sugar mills continued to grow in the colony, expanding particularly into virgin areas, and reached 346 in 1629.

Estimated total of dízimo revenue from Brazil[53]

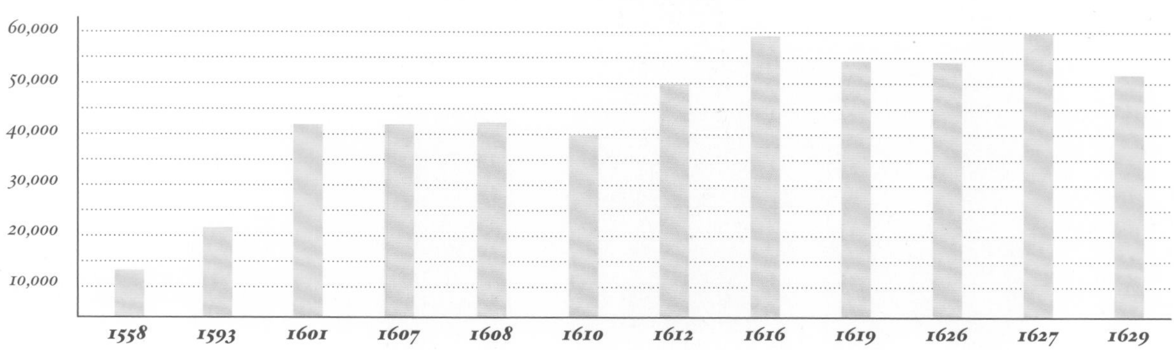

Sources: (1) Johnson, "A indústria do açúcar, 1570–1630"; (2) Mauro, *Portugal, Brasil e o Atlântico*, v. 1, pp. 335–337.

Dízimos and sugar export values

Instead of being collected directly – in this case by the Crown – the rights to collect dízimos (meaning a tenth; a ten-percent tax on the value of production) were sold off to third parties at a public auction. The figures available to us are not the values of the dízimos actually collected, but rather those of the winning bids for the right to collect them. Naturally, this indicates the winning bidders' expectations regarding the amounts they could collect. Their estimates were based on their assessment of the harvest and the economic circumstances. The tax was imposed on other products, but sugar constituted the majority.

As an indicator of the value of the sugar exports, the amounts collected as dízimo payments draw attention more for the omissions than the inclusions. The tax was not applied to second--grade types of sugar – the panela, mel, batido and retame varieties – and many producers were exempt from payment, such as the owners of recently built or rebuilt sugar mills, members of the military and ecclesiastical orders, and so forth. Consequently, neither the amount collected nor its estimated return reflected the total value of sugar exports. Furthermore, collection of the dízimos was subject to tax evasion. Even the tax farmers themselves tended to undervalue taxable production to reduce the amount payable to the Crown.

Dízimo collections from some captaincies were often grouped together – Pernambuco with Itamaracá and Paraíba, and Bahia with Sergipe, Ilhéus and Porto Seguro, for example — or listed individually. The data from all the captaincies was not always available, and the totals shown above may be incomplete. Additionally, payments could be made partly in merchandise and partly in currency, which further complicated the calculations. Last, the documents in which the figures are mentioned came from a variety of sources: official reports, petitions and complaints from tax farmers, proposals for the improvement of public accounts, among others. Even if the amounts of the winning bids for the dízimos were easily verifiable, some data could have been skewed by the authors of these documents, who were often interested parties in the transaction, including tax farmers who were unhappy with the amounts collected or projectors who hoped to receive benefits from the Crown upon reporting on the large discrepancies between the amounts the tax farmers offered and the actual taxable amounts.[52]

Sugar prices in Lisbon, Amsterdam, Antwerp and Hamburg[55]

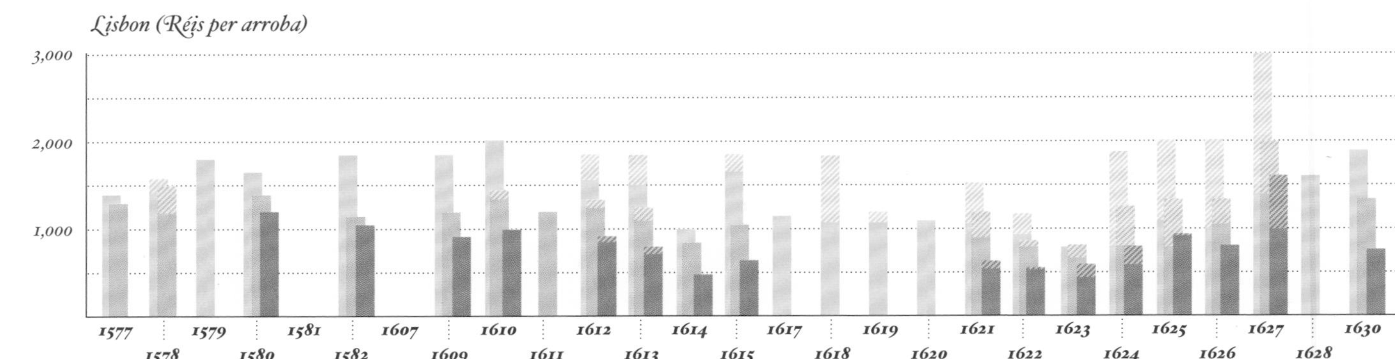

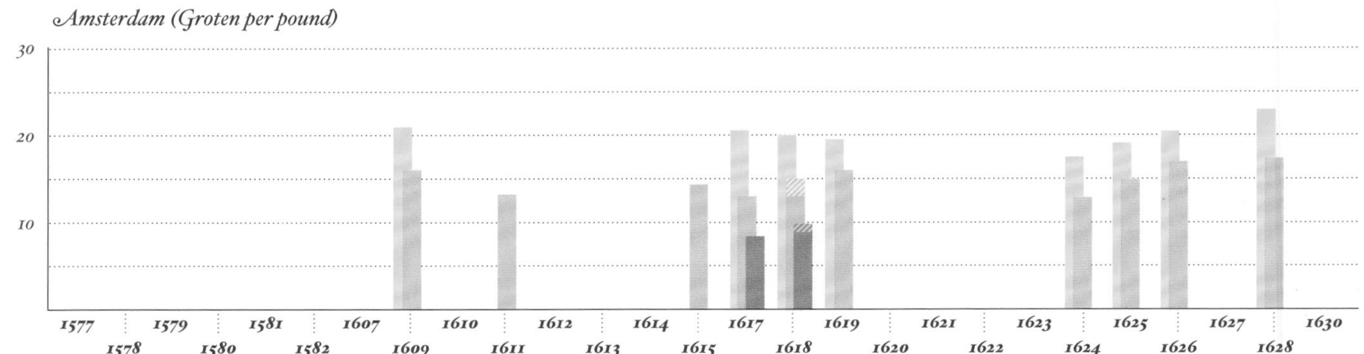

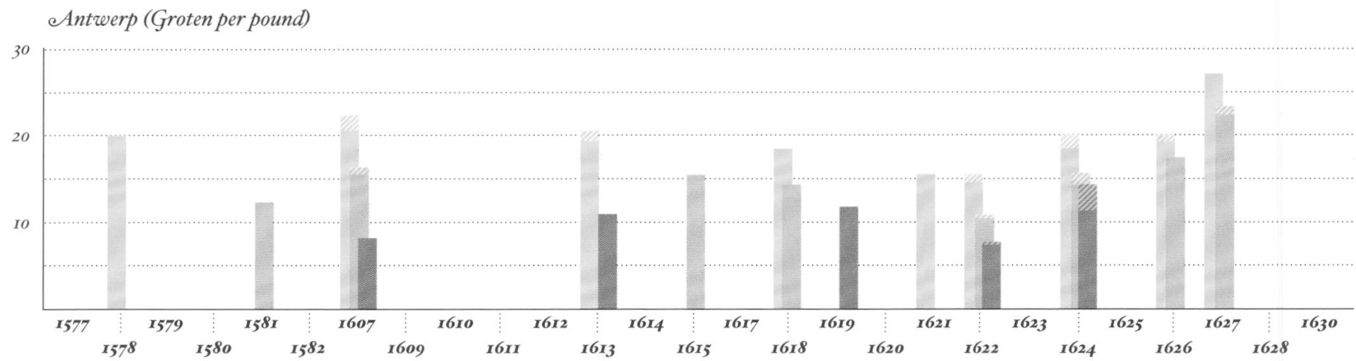

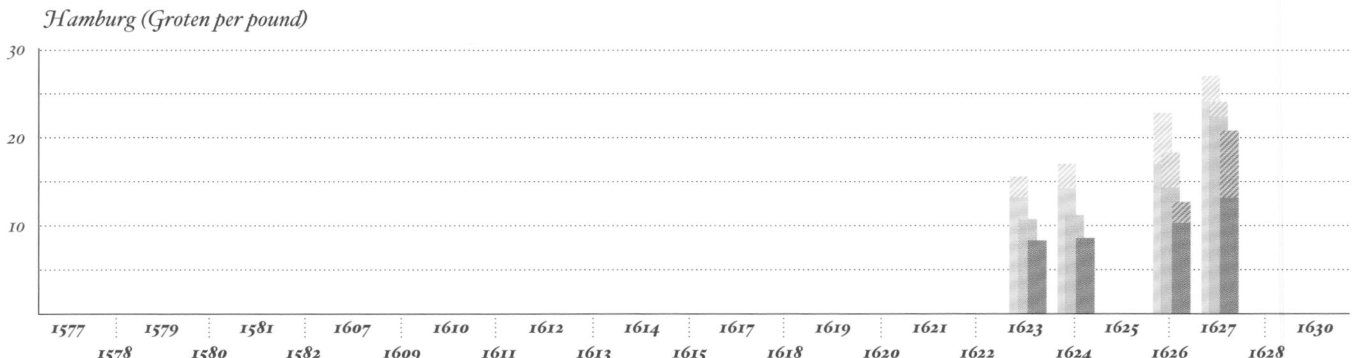

Note: The columns' lighter sections filled with diagonal stripes correspond to intervals in the prices found for that year.

Source: Ebert, "The Trade in Brazilian Sugar," pp. 193, 197, 198.

It is safe to say that, multiplying the output by the price, the revenues from the colony's sugar exports showed an upward trend during the period in question, from 1595 to 1630, with some highs and lows, at a faster or slower pace. This perception is reinforced by the values at which the dízimos taxes on the colony's production were leased. Despite some problems (see table) and falls between 1618 and 1626, the bids for collecting dízimos peaked around 1627, despite complaints from producers and tax farmers.[50] I interpret this as being due to increased production, even at the cost of lower profitability, and also possibly the expectation of years blessed with better weather and fewer epidemics. Ferlini's criticism of scholars' pessimistic outlook about the sugar industry at the turn of the third decade is valid. She observes that not only did the pace of production continue to increase but the price fluctuations were only circumstantial and temporary.[L] According to Ferlini, the crisis and economic reorganization in Europe would only definitively affect the colony's production in the second half of the century.[51]

The figures for sugar prices in Lisbon show a trend similar to those in Brazil: high until 1610, a slight downturn until 1618–1619, followed by strong depreciation, then recovery after 1625. Although scanter and relatively sparse, the data for northern Europe – Amsterdam, Antwerp, and Hamburg – indicates similar trends to Brazil and Lisbon.[54]

The main difference between the behavior of the prices in Brazil and Europe was that, in wartime, the disruption of transport resulted in highs for European prices and lows for colonial prices. The prices in Brazil had been climbing very gradually since 1625 – or rather, following the recapture of Bahia and the larger supply of transport – whereas, in Lisbon, prices followed the opposite trend: high after the Dutch conquest of Bahia and low after its recapture.[56] However, the available data does not allow for more significant inferences. It is too scanty and very often too unreliable to reach conclusive estimates about the profitability of the sugar trade, all the more so because it does not consider other aspects that influenced costs, besides transport. These included expenses with agents, port and cartage services, warehouse rentals and, mainly, taxation, including the local variations[M] – the northern Portuguese ports sought to encourage trade and shipping[57] – tax exemptions[58] and the impact of the systems for leasing tax revenue and methods of tax avoidance, evasion and fraud. All of these factors varied in the short term and from case to case.[59]

L. Regina Célia Gonçalves, in turn, emphasizes that the sugar business continued to be extremely advantageous in Rio de Janeiro (Gonçalves, *Guerras e açúcares*, pp. 183–184).

M. This book does not delve into the tax aspects of the sugar trade, as they merit an in-depth study.

Cane and Sugar

Chapter Two

1. For the spread of sugar production from Southeast Asia to the Mediterranean, between Antiquity and the early modern period, see: Deerr, *The History of Sugar*, v. 1, pp. 69–87; Galloway, *The Sugar Cane Industry*, pp. 19–47; W. D. Phillips Jr., "Sugar in Iberia," in Schwartz, *Tropical Babylons*, pp. 28–34; Godinho, *Os descobrimentos e a economia mundial*, v. 4, pp. 71–73.

2. On the Atlantic Islands, see: Mauro, *Portugal, o Brasil e o Atlântico*, v. 1, pp. 243–253; V. Rau, *O açúcar de S. Tomé no segundo quartel do século XVI* (Lisbon: Centro de Estudos de Marinha, 1971), pp. 3–6; Schwartz, *Sugar Plantations in the Formation of Brazilian Society*, pp. 7–15; A. Vieira, "Sugar Islands: The Sugar Economy of Madeira and the Canaries, 1450–1650," in Schwartz, *Tropical Babylons*, pp. 42–84; Galloway, *The Sugar Cane Industry*, pp. 48–61; M. J. P. F. Tavares, *Os judeus em Portugal no século XV*, V. 1 (Lisbon: Universidade Nova de Lisboa, 1982–1984), pp. 283 and 289–290.

3. Rau, *O Açúcar de S. Tomé no segundo quartel do século XVI*, p. 6.

4. On Hispaniola and Cuba, see: Galloway, *The Sugar Cane Industry,* pp. 61–70; G. Rodriguez Morel, "The Sugar Economy of Española in the Sixteenth Century," in Schwartz, *Tropical Babylons*, pp. 85–114; A. de la Fuente, "Sugar and Slavery in Early Colonial Cuba," in Schwartz, *Tropical Babylons*, pp. 114–157.

5. Galloway, *The Sugar Cane Industry*, pp. 33–34, 61; Phillips, "Sugar in Iberia," p. 27; Deerr, *The History of Sugar*, pp. 78–9, 81, 87, 95.

6. For the origin of the term *massapé* in Madeira, see the note by Andrée Mansuy in Antonil, *Cultura e opulência do Brasil*, p. 111, n. 1.

7. Schwartz, "A Commonwealth within Itself. The Early Brazilian Sugar Industry, 1550–1670," in Schwartz, *Tropical Babylons*, p. 159: "The Recôncavo of Bahia and the *várzea* (riverside lowlands) of Pernambuco had both the appropriate soils with large areas of massapé and the advantage of rivers [...] that supplied water to power the mills and provided for easy transport to the port"; Ferlini, *Terra, trabalho e poder*, pp. 221–222.

8. Mauro, *O Brasil, Portugal e o Atlântico*, v. 1, p. 254; Galloway, *The Sugar Cane Industry*, pp. 45–6. For the impact of these constraints on Madeira and the Canary Islands, see: Vieira, *Sugar Islands*, pp. 44–45, 48.

9. Mauro, *O Brasil, Portugal e o Atlântico*, v. 1, pp. 248–251; Ebert, "The Trade in Brazilian Sugar," p. 187; Vieira, *Sugar Islands*, p. 71.

10. See, among others: Simonsen, *História econômica do Brasil,* p. 98; Mauro, *O Brasil, Portugal e o Atlântico*, v. 1, pp. 279–298; Schwartz, *Sugar Plantations in the Formation of Brazilian Society*, pp. 202–241; Ferlini, *Terra, trabalho e poder*, pp. 215–285; C. Furtado, *Formação econômica do Brasil* (São Paulo: Editora Nacional, 1989), pp. 43–45.

11. Antonil, *Cultura e opulência do Brasil*, pp. 111–170.

12. Brandão, *Diálogos das grandezas do Brasil*, pp. 98–99; Oliveira, *A História do Brazil de Frei Vicente do Salvador*, v. 2, fols. 155–156. See also: R. Gama, *Engenho e tecnologia* (São Paulo: Livraria Duas Cidades, 1983), pp. 72–79, 163–164, 171; Mauro, *O Brasil, Portugal e o Atlântico*, v. 1, pp. 265–277; Schwartz, *Sugar Plantations in the Formation of Brazilian Society*, pp. 116–121; Galloway, *The Sugar Cane Industry*, pp. 37–40; Ferlini, *Terra, trabalho e poder*, pp. 135-213; 215-285

13. G. Gomes, *Engenho e arquitetura* (Recife: Editora Massangana, 2007), pp. 92–104, 182–185.

14. Vieira, *Sugar Islands*, p. 50; Schwartz, *Sugar Plantations in the Formation of Brazilian Society*, pp. 122–123, 126.

15. Specifically with respect to mills used for cane milling, see: Gândavo, *Tractado da terra do Brasil*, fol. 5v.; Cardim, *Tratados da terra e gente do Brasil,* pp. 244–245; Brandão, *Diálogos das grandezas do Brasil*, pp. 97–98; Oliveira, *A história do Brazil de Frei Vicente do Salvador*, v. 2, fols. 155–156; Antonil, *Cultura e opulência do Brasil*, pp. 121–136; Gama, *Engenho e tecnologia*, pp. 91, 97, 105, 107, 119, 123, 125–127, 130, 133; Mauro, *Portugal, o Brasil e o Atlântico*, v. 1, pp. 268–271; Schwartz, *Sugar Plantations in the Formation of Brazilian Society*, pp. 3–4, 22–23, 125–129; Ferlini, *Terra, trabalho e poder*, pp. 151–153.

16. I am grateful to Antonio Marcos Furco, chemical engineer and director of Industrial Technology at ETH Odebrecht Agroindustrial S.A., for providing the technical information, including the terminology.

17. Called *tachas* by Antonil.

18. Gonçalves, *Guerras e açúcares*, p. 207.

19. Brandão, *Diálogos das grandezas do Brasil*, pp. 99–100.

20. Schwartz, *Sugar Plantations in the Formation of Brazilian Society*, pp. 121–125.

21. Antonil, *Cultura e opulência do Brasil*, p. 166; PRO, SP, 9/104, fol. 126.

22. ADP, NOT, PO1, l. 132, fols. 18v.–20v. (1611-8-2).

23. Mauro, *Portugal, o Brasil e o Atlântico*, v. 1, pp. 306–307; Costa, *O transporte no Atlântico*, v. 1, pp. 330–331, 332–333; Gonçalves, *Guerras e açúcares*, pp. 208–209.

24. "...if the sugar becomes damp, even if it is again placed under the sun, it will never become as perfect as it once was: it is similar to how sugar that remains [has been allowed to stand] from one year to the next loses its vigor and whiteness, which it never recovers": Antonil, *Cultura e opulência do Brasil*, pp. 155, 163–165.

25. Brandão, *Diálogos das grandezas do Brasil*, pp. 100–101; Antonil, *Cultura e opulência do Brasil*, pp. 163–165.

26. Antonil, *Cultura e opulência do Brasil*, pp. 128–129; Gama, *Engenho e tecnologia*, pp. 74, 77–79; Schwartz, *Sugar Plantations in the Formation of Brazilian Society*, pp. 109–110

27. Antonil, *Cultura e opulência do Brasil*, pp. 159–162.

28. Ferlini, *Terra, trabalho e poder*, pp. 180–200.

29. Antonil, *Cultura e opulência do Brasil*, pp. 128–129; Gama, *Engenho e tecnologia*, pp. 74, 77–79; Schwartz, *Sugar Plantations in the Formation of Brazilian Society*, pp. 109–110

30. For the beginning of colonization and sugar production in Brazil, see: Sousa, *Tratado descritivo do Brasil*, passim; Oliveira, *A História do Brazil de Frei Vicente do Salvador*, v. 2, passim; "Regulation dated December 17, 1548, of the Governor-General of Brazil (Regimento de 17 de dezembro de 1548 do Governador Geral do Brasil)," in *Documentos para a história do açúcar*, V. 1 (Rio de Janeiro: Instituto do Açúcar e do Álcool, 1954), pp. 45–62; "Charter dated July 23, 1554, for Tax Exemption on Sugar (Alvará de 23 de Julho de 1554 de Isenção dos Tributos sobre Açúcar)," in ibid, pp. 111–113; "Charter dated October 5, 1555, for the Construction of a Sugar Mill by the Royal Treasury (Alvará de 5 de Outubro de 1555 sobre Construção de Engenho de Açúcar pela Fazenda Real)," in ibid., pp. 121–123; F. Varnhagen, *História geral do Brasil*, T. 1(São Paulo: Edições Melhoramentos, 1956), pp. 106, 168, 175–181, 198–202; Mauro, *Portugal, o Brasil e o Atlântico*, v. 1, pp. 202–206, 254–264; P. Berger, A. P. Winz, and M. J. Guedes, "Incursões de corsários e piratas na costa do Brasil," pp. 480–481, 486-487; P. Bonnichon and G. Ferrez, "A França Antártica," in *História naval brasileira*, v. 1, t. 2 (Rio de Janeiro: Serviço de Documentação Geral da Marinha, 1975), pp. 404–441, 447–470; P. Bonnichon and M. J. Guedes, "A França Equinocial," in *História naval brasileira*, pp. 525–541; Schwartz, *Sugar Plantations in the Formation of Brazilian Society*, pp. 15–22, 165–166; Ferlini, *Terra, trabalho e poder*, pp. 22, 84–85; Johnson, "Das feitorias às capitanias," pp. 237–238; Johnson, "A indústria do açúcar," pp. 259–260; M. B. Nizza da Silva, "A sociedade," in Johnson and Silva, *Nova história da expansão portuguesa*, 422–428; L. F. Alencastro, *O trato dos viventes: formação do Brasil no Atlântico Sul* (São Paulo: Companhia das Letras, 2000), pp. 117–120, 122, 125–127, 129; R. Ricupero, *A formação da elite colonial: Brasil, c.1530–c.1630* (São Paulo: Alameda, 2009), pp. 93–125, 243–322; Gonçalves, *Guerras e açúcares*, passim; Stols, "Os mercadores flamengos," passim; A. M. Ferreira, *Problemas marítimos entre Portugal e a França na primeira metade do século XVI* (Cascais: Patrimónia, 1995), passim; J. Couto, "O conflito luso-francês pelo domínio do Brasil até 1580," offprint of *Actas dos Segundos Cursos Internacionais de Verão de Cascais 1* (1996): 114–117; P. Merêa, "A solução tradicional da colonização do Brasil," in C. M. Dias (ed.), *História da Colonização Portuguesa do Brasil*, V. 3 (Porto: Litografia Nacional, 1924), p. 167; F. N. Carvalho, "Da instituição das capitanias-donatárias ao estabelecimento do Governo-Geral," in Johnson and Silva, *Nova História da Expansão Portuguesa*, p. 115; A. V. de Saldanha, *As capitanias do Brasil. Antecedentes, desenvolvimento e extinção de um fenómeno atlântico* (Lisbon: CNCDP, 2001), pp. 21–22.

31. M. Buescu, *História econômica do Brasil: pesquisas e análises* (Rio de Janeiro: Apec Editora S.A., 1970), p. 66; Mauro, *Portugal, o Brasil e o Atlântico*, v. 1, pp. 254–265; Schwartz, *Sugar Plantations in the Formation of Brazilian Society*, pp. 164–167; Costa, *O transporte no Atlântico*, v. 1, pp. 166–167; Ferlini, *Açúcar e colonização*, pp. 75–76. Gonçalves, *Guerras e açúcares*, pp. 186–194.

32. F. A. Varnhagen, *História geral do Brasil*, T. 2 (São Paulo: Edições Melhoramentos, 1948), pp. 21–22.

33. Simonsen estimates the total production of Brazilian sugar from the figures presented by several sources, some prima facie, some by interpolation and some by projections that are not made clear to the reader. Simonsen refers to data that he considers to be the most reliable and representative. However, he neither justifies his choices nor compares the totals for the number of mills and the overall production with the mills' production capacity: Simonsen, *História econômica do Brasil*, pp. 112–113, table from the text, p. 382. Celso Furtado considers the figures Simonsen chose to be too conservative and refers to earlier estimates to state categorically that: "By the end of the sixteenth century, sugar production very probably exceeded two million arrobas": Furtado, *Formação econômica do Brasil*, pp. 42–43. Buescu has produced the first study that offers a more critical consideration of sugar production and productivity. He calls attention to the incongruence of the data: either the number of sugar mills was larger or the total production was lower. This is because the average productivity could not have been 10,000 arrobas, and much less the amounts extrapolated by Furtado and others. Interpolating the data provided by chroniclers, he estimates that in 1600 there were between 160 and 200 sugar mills, rather than the 120 that Simonsen suggests. However, Buescu estimates that these mills produced between 6,000 and 7,000 arrobas each, giving a total annual production of between 960,000 and 1.4 million arrobas, i.e., with the same average of 1.2 million arrobas as presented by Simonsen. The average productivity that Buescu calculates represents nothing more than a simple average between 3,000 and 4,000 arrobas, for the smaller sugar mills and 10,000 arrobas, as suggested by the same chroniclers, for the larger sugar mills. Unlike his successors, the author does not consider the changes in the size of these units or their productivity and/or underuse: Buescu, *História econômica do Brasil*, pp. 83–84, 92–93. Mauro uses the numbers Simonsen provided, to which he adds others from new sources that he has gathered, which indicate a much higher productivity from the number of sugar mills listed: Mauro, *Portugal, o Brasil e o Atlântico*, v. 1, pp. 320–321. See also Costa's criticism of Simonsen, Mauro and Buescu in Costa, *O transporte no Atlântico*, v. 1, pp. 168–169. Based on some of Buescu's procedures, Schwartz stipulates that there were between 190 and 200 sugar mills in Brazil in 1600, positing that their average annual productivity was closer to 4,700 arrobas per sugar mill prior to 1612, and 3,700 arrobas with the introduction of three-roller mills. According to him, these were cheaper and encouraged the construction of small units, which produced less sugar each. Annual production of 10,000 to 12,000 arrobas was the privilege of only a few sugar mills in good years. In addition to the revaluation of the average production per sugar mill, Schwartz presented other estimates of overall production, based on a reexamination of the sources used by the previous studies and the analysis of additional documents: Schwartz, *Sugar Plantations in the Formation of Brazilian Society*, pp. 167–168, 176; Moreno, *Livro que dá razão do Estado do Brasil*, pp. 116, 212; AHU_ACL_CU_005-02, Cx. 2, D. 100 – [Bahia, after August 6, 1614]. Costa has reviewed and discussed these authors' arguments, pointing out discrepancies and inconsistencies. Her viewpoint is closer to Schwartz's, albeit even more conservative. Based on chronicles, reports, and information from the Dutch period for the captaincies of Pernambuco, Itamaracá, Paraíba and Rio Grande, she arrived at an average amount of annual production per sugar mill of 3,500 arrobas. However, her emphasis on the captaincies to the north of Bahia, where, on average, the sugar mills were probably smaller than those in the Recôncavo – or at least appear to have been so in the second half of the seventeenth century – may have resulted in an average that is slightly over-conservative. It is true that Costa highlights that the large sugar mills with hydropower were not unknown in Pernambuco. However, she points out that even the largest sugar mills in Bahia had a significant margin of under-use. Therefore, she recommends discretion when estimating their real productivity, and takes the average of 3,500 arrobas/sugar mill/year as a constant at the turn of the sixteenth to the seventeenth century. Costa then multiplies this by the number of sugar mills indicated by Schwartz for the period and accordingly arrives at her estimates of total production: Costa, *O transporte no Atlântico*, v. 1, pp. 166–174; Schwartz, *Sugar Plantations in the Formation of Brazilian Society*, p. 167. It is interesting to note that in a more recent study, Schwartz adopts more optimistic estimates for the production of the Brazilian sugar mills. These are based on a memorandum containing information that was sent to the West India Company and suggested a figure of 4,800 arrobas per sugar mill in 1623. In a previous calculation by Schwartz, the average was close to 3,700 arrobas. However, this new evaluation did not cause Schwartz significantly to alter his estimate for Brazil's total production. According to him, this was approximately 680,000 arrobas, up to 1610, and between 1 million and 1.5 million arrobas in the 1620s: S. B. Schwartz, "A Commonwealth within Itself," in Schwartz, *Tropical Babylons*, pp. 162–164.

Quite reasonably, Gonçalves emphasizes that the data in this memorandum could well have been inflated to impress the company's directors: Gonçalves, *Guerras e açúcares*, p. 213.

34. Schwartz, "A Commonwealth within Itself," p. 162; Gonçalves, *Guerras e açúcares*, pp. 202, 212–213.

35. This subject is highly controversial. See, for example, the overviews by E. J. Hamilton, *American Treasure and the Price Revolution in Spain, 1501–1650* (New York: Octagon Books, 1965), passim; F. Braudel, *O Mediterrâneo e o mundo mediterrânico na época de Filipe II* (São Paulo: Martins Fontes, 1983), v. 1, pp. 564–585; v. 2, pp. 262–265; J. de Vries, *A economia da Europa numa época de crise, 1600 –1750* (Lisbon: Publicações Dom Quixote, 1983), pp. 30–40; R. Cameron, *Concise Economic History of the World, from Paleolithic Times to the Present* (New York: Oxford University Press, 1997), pp. 95–129.

36. SR no. 1600; Schwartz, *Sugar Plantations in the Formation of Brazilian Society*, pp. 167–169; Ebert, "The Trade in Brazilian Sugar," pp. 183–185, 187–189.

37. Ibid., pp. 189–199.

38. Based on: Schwartz, *Sugar Plantations in the Formation of Brazilian Society*, 498–499 and Mauro, *Portugal, o Brasil e o Atlântico*, v. 1, Apêndice, Preço do açúcar no Brasil. For 1621–1624, inclusive, Ferlini gives different figures, despite basing them on the same sources as Schwartz, which Ebert also used:
1621 955
1622 556
1623 518
1624 518
Ferlini, *Terra, trabalho e poder*, p. 89.

39. Hamilton, *American Treasure and the Price Revolution in Spain*, pp. 34–35.

40. For Mauro, the profitability of the colonial sugar industry stabilized between 1600 and 1625. Nevertheless, Mauro speculates that the introduction of the three-roller mill reduced the production cost of the sugar in Brazil and, accordingly, its price in Brazil: Mauro, *Portugal, o Brasil e o Atlântico*, v. 1, pp. 314–317. A specialist on the economics of the Bahian sugar mills, Schwartz does not deviate very far from this evaluation. For him, there was a period of deceleration from 1585 and a new surge of growth after 1612. The intensity of this second upturn was less than that of the first (1570–1585) and was not due to the prices but to the technological innovation of the vertical three-roller mill. This accelerated the amortization of invested capital, increased efficiency and provided economies of scale. During this phase, growth was lower in the traditional productive captaincies of Pernambuco and Bahia, and more intense in Rio de Janeiro and to the north of Pernambuco in Itamaracá and Paraíba. Prosperity benefited from the Twelve Years' Truce, from 1609 to 1621, which restrained the hostilities between the Dutch Republic and Spain with which Portugal (and Brazil) were united at the time: Schwartz, *Sugar Plantations in the Formation of Brazilian Society* pp. 166–172. Evaldo Cabral de Mello, a researcher who focused on the recovery of Pernambuco from the Dutch, takes a different view. He believes that there were already signs of a crisis in the second decade of the seventeenth century, when the indigenous workforce was replaced by the more expensive African labor. This increased the indebtedness of the sugar-mill owners, who purchased slaves on credit. They were more susceptible to the reduction in the demand for sugar and to the adversities affecting their slaves or emanating from them. In 1614, an epidemic had a devastating impact. In that decade, the sugar-mill owners requested a moratorium on their debts, and the trade felt the effects of pirates based on the North African coast: E. C. de Mello, *Olinda Restaurada: guerra e açúcar no Nordeste, 1630–1654* (Rio de Janeiro: Topbooks, 1998), pp. 88–89. Leonor Freire Costa, a specialist on the transportation of sugar, goes further. She emphasizes the difficulties alleged by the producers on requesting the Crown for the moratorium on their debts to merchants. She also refers to the ongoing clashes between the sugar-mill owners and the cane farmers on the one hand, and the merchants and the tax leaseholders on the other. By 1612, the Crown had determined that seizure of indebted sugar-mill owners' properties should be limited to two-thirds of their revenues, and those of the cane farmers to an amount equivalent to half their harvests. Despite the complaints by the merchants and the tax farmers, the Crown extended the period of protection for defaulters. If, initially, it was the merchants who invested in production, now production and shipment were sectors independent from trade: Costa, *O transporte no Atlântico*, v. 1, pp. 59–61, 218–219. See also: IANTT, CC 1-115-107; Correspondência do Governador Dom Diogo de Meneses – 1608–1612, pp. 67–68; AHU_ACL_CU_005-02, Cx. 1, D. 52 – [Lisbon, prior to November 28, 1613]; C. M. M. Mendes, "A coroa portuguesa e a colonização do Brasil. Aspectos da atuação do Estado na constituição da colônia," *História: Revista do Departamento de História da Unesp 16* (1997), passim. Ferlini, also a specialist in the economics of the sugar mills, notes the complaints by the producers, merchants and tax farmers. Nevertheless, by observing the long-term development of the total production, the prices of sugar and slaves, and the global situation (conjuncture), she emphasizes: "Even if, from 1611, we note a decline in the prices of white sugar in Bahia, the general trend continued upwards [...] However, until 1650, the general outlook was positive": Ferlini, *Terra, trabalho e poder*, pp. 86–87. See also: Ferlini, *Açúcar e colonização*, pp. 76–77. Finally, Gonçalves, a researcher on the sugar industry in Paraíba, emphasizes the surge of growth experienced in this still peripheral region, but qualifies it. The growth in the number of sugar mills in Paraíba had been particularly strong in the 1610s, and generally involved the installation of hydro-powered mills, which were more expensive but more productive. Additionally, this was on virgin land that produced much more sugar. Nevertheless, with respect to its higher productivity, the author emphasizes that Paraíba's production was insignificant within Brazil's total. She calls attention to the fact that, even before the Dutch invasion, there were inactive sugar mills in the northern captaincies, with more in some and fewer in others: Gonçalves, *Guerras e açúcares*, pp. 192–203, 213–214, 230.

41. Mauro, *Portugal, o Brasil e o Atlântico*, v. 1, pp. 202–206, 213–241; Schwartz, *Sugar Plantations in the Formation of Brazilian Society*, pp. 55–72; Johnson, "Das feitorias às capitanias," pp. 237–238; Johnson, "A indústria do açúcar," pp. 259–260; Alencastro, *O trato dos viventes*, pp. 117–120, 122, 125–127, 129.

42. Schwartz, *Sugar Plantations in the Formation of Brazilian Society*, pp. 171–176; Ferlini, *Terra, trabalho e poder*, pp. 88, 90–95, 98.

43. Hamilton, *American Treasure and the Price Revolution in Spain*, pp. 93–103, 211–221.

44. Ferlini, *Terra, trabalho e poder*, pp. 90–92.

45. AHU_ACL_CU_005-02, Cx. 1, D. 71 – Bahia, [prior to June 26, 1614]; Cx. 2, D. 172 – Bahia, August 6, 1618; D. 173 – Bahia, August 4, 1618; D. 205 – 207 – [Lisbon, July 3, 1619]; Costa, *O transporte no Atlântico*, v. 1, pp. 61–62, 215–216; Ferlini, *Açúcar e colonização*, pp. 76–77.

46. Strum, "The Portuguese Jews and New Christians in the Sugar Trade," passim; Costa, *O Transporte no Atlântico*, v. 1, pp. 61–62; Mea, "A rotura das comunidades cristãs novas do litoral", passim; idem., "Os portuenses perante o Santo Ofício – século XVI," passim; *Primeira visitação do Santo Officio às partes do Brasil: confissões da Bahia 1591–1592*; *Primeira visitação do Santo Officio às partes do Brasil: denunciações da Bahia, 1591–1593*; *Primeira visitação do Santo Ofício às partes do Brasil, denunciações e confissões de Pernambuco: 1593–1595*; *Segunda visitação do Santo Ofício às partes do Brasil pelo inquisidor e visitador Marcos Teixeira*; Siqueira, "A inquisição portuguesa e a sociedade colonial."

47. Schwartz, *Sugar Plantations in the Formation of Brazilian Society*, p. 173; Mello, *Olinda Restaurada*, pp. 91–92.

48. Ferlini, *Terra, trabalho e poder*, pp. 92–94.

49. AHU_ACL_CU_005-02, Cx. 3, D.283, 371, 372 and 373; Schwartz, *Sugar Plantations in the Formation of Brazilian Society*, pp. 173–175; Costa, *O Transporte no Atlântico*, v. 1, p. 220; Mello, *Olinda Restaurada*, pp. 92–94, 220–221.

50. Mauro, *Portugal, o Brasil e o Atlântico*, v. 1, pp. 316–317, 323–325; Schwartz, *Sugar Plantations in the Formation of Brazilian Society*, pp. 173–177; Costa, *O transporte no Atlântico*, v. 1, pp. 59–60; Gonçalves, *Guerras e açúcares*, pp. 212–213; Ferlini, *Terra, trabalho e poder*, p. 86; idem, *Açúcar e colonização*, pp. 76–77; Mello, *Olinda restaurada*, p. 90.

51. Ferlini, *Terra, trabalho e poder*, pp. 87–88, 98; idem, *Açúcar e colonização*, pp. 76–77. For the development of Brazilian sugar production, see also: Mello, "Os livros das saídas das urcas do porto do Recife," pp. 24–25; Moreira, *Os mercadores de Viana*, pp. 24–29, 135–140.

52. Schwartz, *Sugar Plantations in the Formation of Brazilian Society*, pp. 173–177.

53. The data Schwarz provides in his graph on the dízimos of the captaincies of Bahia, Ilhéus, Sergipe and Porto Seguro do not coincide with the data presented by Mauro in some cases. This is possibly due to the manner in which the graph was plotted: Schwartz, *Sugar Plantations in the Formation of Brazilian Society*, p. 175.

54. Here Ebert's data are also used: Ebert, "The Trade in Brazilian Sugar," pp. 192–198.

55. Ebert's data on Lisbon is mainly based on the amounts from the Lisbon customs published by Costa. They are also based on the information mentioned in the correspondence of Pedro Clarisse, a merchant from the Low Countries based in Lisbon, published by the Belgian historian Eddy Stols, a specialist in the trade between the Southern Netherlands and the Iberian World. Ebert adds some observations published by Mauro and others published by J. Nanninga Uitterdijk for the years 1570–1580 to the data from Costa and Stols, as well as the two primary sources that he researched himself: J. N. Uitterdijk, *Een Kamper handelshuis te Lissabon, 1572–1594, handelscorrespondentie, rekeningen en bescheiden* (Zwolle: De erven J. J. Tijl, 1904), pp. 40, 49, 57, 72, 94, 130, 250, 262, 310, 323, 374; Mauro, *Portugal, o Brasil e o Atlântico*, v. 1, Apêndice, Preço do açúcar em Lisboa; Stols, *De Spaanse Brabanders*, pp. 203–207; Costa, *O transporte no Atlântico*, v. 1, p. 241; IANTT, STO, IL, 3148. Ebert also adds a Dutch source for the year 1610, which quotes 1,850 réis for white sugar and 1,200 réis for muscovado sugar in Porto. This sugar may have arrived in the previous year: SR no. 396; SAA, 30452; Archief van S. Hart, 873, l. 258, fol. 5v. For Antwerp, Ebert uses the data published by Stols based on the same correspondence, to which he adds another source that he consulted and two observations from the sixteenth century published by Hans Pohl and Uitterdijk. However, Ebert states that he is convinced that Stols was mistaken in the currency for Antwerp, using stuivers instead of groten, which produced much more inflated figures. Ebert also calculates the arroba at 28 pounds Flemish, in place of the 32 pounds used by Stols: H. Pohl, "Die Zuckereinfuhr nach Antwerpen durch Portugiesische Kaufleute während des 80 jährigen Krieges." *Jahrbuch für Geschichte von Staat, Wirtschaft und Gesellschaft Lateinamerikas* 4 (1967): 348–373; Uitterdijk, *Een Kamper handelshuis*, p. 348; Stols, *De Spaanse Brabanders*, v. 2, Bijlagen, pp. 203–207; SR no. 954. Ebert also used Stols' data for Hamburg: ibid., v. 2, Bijlagen, pp. 203–207. For Amsterdam, Ebert used the price lists of the Amsterdam guild of brokers, published by Nicolaas Wilhelmus Posthumus, and another five sources that he collected. However, Ebert converts Posthumus's data of gulden into groten (one groot = 0.025 gulden): N. W. Posthumus, *Nederlandsche prijsgeschiedenis*, v. 1 (Leiden: Brill, 1943), pp. 119, 122 and SR nos. 387, 456, 1150, 1259, 1417.

56. Ebert, "The Trade in Brazilian Sugar," pp. 186, 190.

57. Regarding tax incentives in the northern ports, see: Moreira, *Os mercadores de Viana*, pp. 181–188; Silva, *O Porto e o seu termo*, v. 1, p. 331; v. 2, p. 867.

58. Regarding some exemptions, see: Schwartz, *Sugar Plantations in the Formation of Brazilian Society*, pp. 173–177.

59. Costa and Ebert have sought to calculate the profitability of the sugar trade. Costa contrasts her estimates for the difference of prices between the colony and the metropolis with her data on the variation of freight rates. She believes that the arbitrage – the difference between the value of the sugar in Brazil and in Portugal – began to shrink progressively from 1605, and at a faster rate from 1610 to 1614. She suggests that the period of the Twelve Years' Truce increased the integration of the markets, thus reducing the disparity of prices, and that the war produced the opposite effect. She concluded that from 1613 until 1625 there were only small gains because freight charges – "one of the highest costs in trading sugar" – did not decrease and even tended to rise. This was due to the reduction in the supply of shipping and the increase of the costs of protection from Barbary pirates and, later, Dutch privateers, followed by attacks from the WIC. From 1618, with the contraction of demand, merchants not only experienced lower profitability but also traded in smaller volumes. If there were profits to be accrued, they were only from the re-export of sugar from Portugal to northern Europe. Costa implies that the major merchants were losing interest in the sugar trade. In order to confront these challenges and to find a solution for the output of their sugar mills, sugar-mill owners became new entrepreneurs and sought to distribute their products in Portugal on their own account. Hence, they vertically reintegrated production with trade. If, on the one hand, they profited as middlemen, on the other hand, they took the risks, which were increasing at the time. As a result, they brought pressure for an escorted fleet to be organized. Following the capture of Bahia in 1624, profit margins began to expand, with ups and downs due to the Dutch presence on colonial soil and close to its ports. Shipping disruption increased the price differences between Brazil and Europe, which were exacerbated by attacks on vessels and warehouses, which reduced the supply of the product sufficiently to compensate for the high freight rates: Costa, *O transporte no Atlântico*, v. 1, pp. 61, 89, 179, 204–206, 220–221, 239–248, 370–372, 379–380. See also: AHU_ACL_CU_Consultas Serviço Real, COD. 35, fols. 187–188 – [October 14, 1623]; Mello, "Os livros das saídas das urcas do porto do Recife," pp. 92–94, 220–221; Ebert, "The Trade in Brazilian Sugar," pp. 201–202; Moreira, *Os mercadores de Viana*, p. 64. Ebert reviews Costa's analysis and emphasizes that the figures supplied from the correspondence of Pedro Clarisse, a Flemish merchant operating in Lisbon (see note 65), published by Stols, are higher than those of the customs figures that Costa uses. Ebert believes that the amounts from the customs were underestimated and indicates a profitability margin for the trade on the passage between Brazil and Portugal that is higher than that calculated by Costa. The merchant's figures also suggest a slightly later turning point, in 1619 rather than 1618. Ebert laments the lack of data for muscovado and panela sugar in Brazil and speculates that the margin for these could be even larger. By adding the taxes and omitting the insurance, which he believes was rarely used, Ebert estimates more favorable results for the merchants. This applies both to shipments between Brazil and Portugal and between Portugal and northern Europe, where profitability was relatively proportional to the distance. He concludes by saying that the merchants would not have been involved in this trade if there were no expectations of significant gains, even during the Truce, when the risks and the margins were lower: Ebert, "The Trade in Brazilian Sugar," pp. 188–189, 198, 205–208, 213.

Chapter Three

Still Life with Parrot;
Georg Flegel (1566–1638).

Into the Mouth

From Remedy to Repast

The consumption of sugar depended on its availability and the consumer's means of acquiring it, whereas the manner in which it was consumed varied according to its price, scarcity or abundance, current medicinal and culinary concepts, gastronomic preferences and the social meanings attributed to it. Over the centuries, sugar was used as medicine, seasoning, decorative material, sweetener and food preservative. These uses were not mutually exclusive and often coexisted or overlapped. Over time, some of these uses faded away while others became more predominant, albeit not in a linear process.[1]

The period covered here comprises an epoch when sugar became increasingly popular in Western Europe, during which its use as a sweetener overshadowed that of honey, and sugar reached the height of its popularity as a condiment in a varied range of dishes, both for culinary and medicinal purposes. Confectionery emerged as a specialized field, and sweets became ingrained in social and recreational practices. Sweet preparations were prized as gifts and were incorporated into the rituals of religious and lay institutions, as well as into interpersonal, family and superior-subordinate relationships. At the same time, its medicinal use began to be criticized, and its presence as a seasoning in meat, fish and vegetable dishes gradually diminished. Sugar was now increasingly reserved for the sweets and cakes served at the end of meals, as well as in snacks and breakfast dishes. Thanks to its increasing supply, sugar could be consumed more frequently, in larger quantities and by many more people, which resulted in a reconsideration of its effects in terms of appetite, palate and health.

Available information about the consumption of sugar and sweets in the Middle Ages, and even in early modern times, mostly referencing the upper echelons of society, is scarce and fragmentary. This chapter seeks to provide a chronological description while focusing on certain topics in greater detail, and sometimes going back in time in order to introduce the precursors for phenomena that only fully developed much later.

Man attacked by bees swarming from a hive; illustration from the Bestiary and other texts (ca. 1450). Thirteenth- and fourteenth-century cookbooks show that honey was beginning to be replaced with sugar. By 1630, sugar had become the most popular sweetener in Western Europe.

Universal Remedy

Honey and dried fruit were the main sweeteners in the Roman world. It is not clear whether sugar from sugarcane was known to the Romans, but if it was, it would have come from India via the Arabian Peninsula, and Roman citizens would have used it in minute quantities for medicinal purposes.[2] Even less is known about the consumption of sugar between the end of the Western Roman Empire and the early medieval period. As has been seen, cane sugar reached Latin Catholic Europe through the Muslim world via three means: Christian regions in contact with Muslim areas, such as the Iberian Peninsula, southern Italy and the Mediterranean Islands; areas conquered from Muslims during the Crusades and the "Reconquest"; and trade conducted by Italian cities and later by their Catalan and French counterparts.

In twelfth-century England, ledgers of the Royal Household record purchases of sugar that was to be used at court as a condiment. In the following century, the Royal Household and wealthy families, even those resident in remote parts of England, purchased sugar from Egypt, Cyprus, Sicily and the Maghreb. The amount of sugar the royal court acquired grew exponentially, and it was often used in England's aristocratic and episcopal manors as well. Sugar was bought in loaves and slabs, and in the form of rose and violet sugar, mixed with the essence extracted from the petals of those flowers, as they are used in Asian cuisine to this day.[3] Similarly, in Portugal, different types of sugar were listed alongside spices and fruit in the Inventory and Accounts of the household of King Dinis between 1278 and 1282. They include rose sugar and different types of sugar imported from Egypt and other Saracen lands.[4]

Hence, Muslims introduced into Europe not only sugar but also a wide range of culinary habits. During the Middle Ages in general, the Islamic world was significantly more urbanized, with cities far larger than was the average in predominantly rural Christian Europe. Furthermore, Muslim courtly and intellectual life was far more refined, evolving from deep-rooted traditions. Islamic cuisine was influenced by the different ingredients, habits and scientific traditions of the regions that were brought under the banner of Islam. It is important to bear in mind that, apart from the Arabian Peninsula, where Islam originated, Muslims had conquered Palestine, Syria, Egypt and the Maghreb from the Byzantines. In these regions, the traditions, from their Hellenistic, Roman and Byzantine past and various local influences mingled. Further east, Muslims conquered Mesopotamia and Persia from the Sassanids, a predominantly Persian-speaking and Zoroastrian empire, with highly evolved court ceremonies, and which had mastered sugar production techniques. The Muslim sphere of influence also encompassed part of western India, which had a long history of sugar production, alongside Malaysia and Insulindia, Central Asia, northern sub-Saharan Africa and East Africa.

At a time when there were few other resources, diet was one of the main forms of medical treatment. It was believed that diet had effects on the spirit, since cuisine, which not only involved the palate but also the senses of sight, smell and touch, could activate the transcendental powers of the ingredients being used, emulating paradise and elevating the diner. Within this rationale, in the Muslim world the combination of sugar with spices was considered beneficial, since the former nourished the body while the latter nourished the spirit.[5]

Xylo Aloes

aturę mis. calidę et sicę melius ex eo nigrꝝ ponderosum et amarꝝ Iuuam si retinet confortat splen & stomachu. Nocum ęgtudib; cerebri calidis. Remotio t nocumenti conseruatur in Camphora.

Zuchar

aturæ calidę et humidę in 1°. melius ex eo. album clarum. Iu. mudificat corp' et pdest renib; et uesicę. Nocum siti efficit et comouet cholerã. Remotio nocumenti cum granatis acetosis.

Cana mellis

aturæ calidę et humidę in 1°. melius ex ea. multę succositatis et dulcedinis Iuuamentu. pectori et tussi. Nocumentu generat uentositates Remotio nocum. cum lauatr aqua calida.

Candi

aturæ calidæ in 1°. humidę in 1° melius ex eo purę transparens et leue. Iuuamentum cannæ pulmonis Nocumentum stomachis cholericis Remotio nocumenti cu mu sis fructibus.

60

30v

Harvesting sugarcane and the sale of sugarloaves and candy sugar in Tables of Health, *a treatise by the Christian Arab physician Ibn Butlan, shown in a Latin manuscript version from Venice dated 1490.*

Man purging sugar, drinking the molasses dripping from the mold and displaying white sugarloaves in an illustration from the fifteenth-century version of the Book of Herbs, *by the Greco-Roman pharmacologist Pedanius Dioscorides (40–90 AD).*

Becharia ca. est in tercio gradu sic in quarto radix eius ... herbe per decem annos seruatur. Vinum decoctionis eius contra siccam tussim valet. Contra dolores ventris et intestinorum ex ventositate uel ex frigore. Suppositorium ex eo et trifera magna factum matricem calefacit et mundificat. Salsamentum ex eo factum uel trifera magna et ... marino et pisce asso et aceto appetitum incitat

Zizania herba est nascitur inter triticum siccis corrumpit ... habet acutam et venenosam. Ideo mentem turbat et inebriat si farine uel pani miscentur ... mulieres ex ea suffumigentur et vulua ... conceptio ... eciam ... aceto et ad ... valent cocta cum vino et stercore columbino et lini semine cataplasmate facto apostema dissoluit et scrofulas cocto eciam cum radice ... vulneribus ... putrefactis apposita sanat ea et mundificat

Bibulle tressus est cibus ex duabus causis ... nocet ... una ... viscositatem olei. altera per viscositatem farine ... et venarum via oppilant ... cum melle manducet ... precipue ... et splenetice

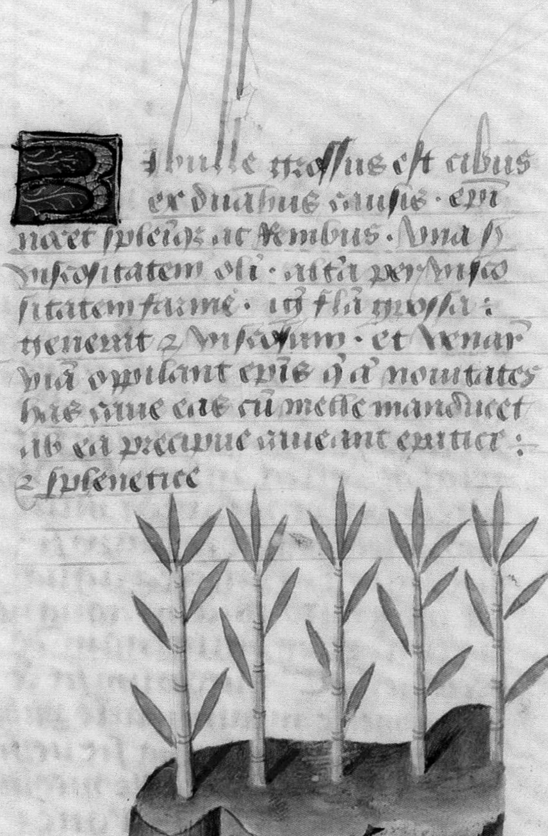

Zuccarum

Zuccara ca. est et hu... temperate ... grossa ... est ... in medio ... dissoluitur

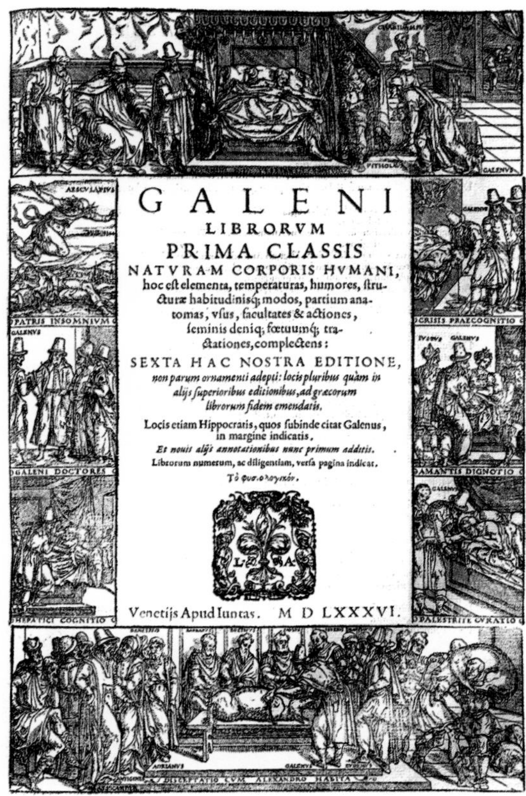

GALENI
LIBRORVM
PRIMA CLASSIS
NATVRAM CORPORIS HVMANI,
hoc est elementa, temperaturas, humores, structuræ habitudinisq; modos, partium anatomas, vsus, facultates & actiones, seminis deniq; fœtuumq; tractationes, complectens:
SEXTA HAC NOSTRA EDITIONE,
non parum ornamenti adepti: locis pluribus quàm in alijs superioribus editionibus, ad græcorum librorum fidem emendatis.
Locis etiam Hippocratis, quos subinde citat Galenus, in margine indicatis.
Et nouis alijs annotationibus nunc primum additis.
Librorum numerum, ac diligentiam, versa pagina indicat.
Τὸ φυσιολογικόν.
L A
Venetijs Apud Iuntas. M D LXXXVI.

Thirteenth- and fourteenth-century recipe books provide a glimpse of medieval European court cuisine, which was apparently equally concerned about the presentation of dishes as well as their taste, dominated by the strong flavors of spices, alternating between sour and sweet. Sugar gradually replaced traditional sweeteners, especially honey, as well as dates and raisins. Such as in Arab cuisine, sugar was mixed with rose water, almond milk and citrus juices. The use of colorants such as saffron, as well as spices, was also a common practice, and dishes consequently acquired a golden hue. Sugar was also used to temper the heat of spices, enhance the flavor of rose water and almond milk, and counteract the acidity of citrus. It was also common to sprinkle dishes with sugar, cinnamon and other spices to obtain a golden color, and add fragrance and sweet flavor. Sugar and spices were prime ingredients when added to pastry and wine, even more so if it was drunk hot.[6]

This penchant for sweet flavors was not uniform in geographic terms throughout medieval Europe. It was more evident in Italy, Languedoc (southern France) and England, and less so in northern France, near Paris. According to Bruno Laurioux, who has conducted extensive research on medieval diet, it was a matter of taste, as France was no farther from sugar producing areas than England, where the anthropologist Sidney Mintz has noted that a combination of sugar and honey was used to sweeten dishes.[7] However, the French would continue to have less of a sweet tooth, although sweet and sour dishes were widespread in French society.

This golden, spiced and sweetened cuisine did not emerge on account of taste, tradition or status alone, but was highly influenced by medicine. Medieval European medical traditions were based on concepts that had developed by the fifth century B.C. and had been included in the Hippocratic Collection. They were supplemented by the pharmacopeia of Dioscorides and the science of Aristotle, subsequently being systemized by the Roman physician Galen in the second century A.D., and undergoing other influences, especially from India. All this knowledge was once again reorganized by physicians from an Arab cultural background, such as the renowned Central Asian doctor Abū `Alī al-Ḥusayn ibn `Abd Allāh ibn Sīnā (known in Europe as Avicenna).

These works were later translated from the Arabic, either directly or via Hebrew, and studied and adapted by Europeans in the twelfth century. Subsequently, with the advent of Humanism in the fifteenth century, the Classical tradition began to be retrieved directly from "recovered" Greek and Latin texts, and in the following century. It was only then that this long tradition began to be refuted on the basis of chemical knowledge derived from experiments in alchemy.[8]

Thus, in Christian Europe, sugar and spices would have appeared simultaneously as remedies and condiments. It is possible that they were initially more used as medicines than as seasonings. Cane sugar which, if it was in fact prescribed by doctors in

Title page of the 1586 edition of On the Nature of the Human Body *by the Roman physician Claudius Galenus (Galen; ca.129–216 AD), which systemized the pharmacopeia of Dioscorides and the science of Aristotle. For Galen, the heat and moisture of food could be calculated, an idea that was developed further in the Middle Ages. Although most of his teachings have since been refuted, until the nineteenth century Galen was widely considered one of the greatest authorities in Medicine.*

Thirteenth- or fourteenth-century illustration portraying the commercial life of a medieval city. Right, the apothecary's shop sells sugarloaves and advertises the sale of hippocras, or mulled wine.

Pharmacy; *Master Colin (fifteenth/sixteenth century). In Christian Europe, sugar was originally used for both medical and culinary purposes and may have been disseminated more rapidly as a remedy than a condiment.*

Antiquity, was only employed marginally and obscurely now began to play a significant role in pharmacology.[9] At the end of the thirteenth century, a professor at the University of Bologna[10] developed the formulations Avicenna prescribed to cure melancholy. These remedies to soothe the heart, which included precious metals and stones, corals and pearls, silk, and the like, should now contain sugar and be ingested with wine. The importance of sugar as a pharmaceutical ingredient is reflected in the medieval French expression "apothicaire sans sucre" (apothecary out of sugar), used to denote absolute despair and helplessness.[11]

Doctors also advised their patients about their diet, physical activities, rest, emotional state, climate, healthy air, and so forth. Their clients came from the well-heeled sections of society for whom such recipe books were written. Dietetic and culinary literature soon merged into one. The physiological concept popular during the Middle Ages and much of the Modern Age was that digestion, as well as life in general, was a form of cooking. Through "baking," Nature produced raw ingredients which, in their turn, became edible by means of cooking and, once ingested, were digested by body heat. Excrement was the non-digestible part which was returned to the cycle of life. All foodstuffs were hence slightly hot, as sweetness was also believed to be. It was advisable to sweeten the basic ingredients that were not naturally sweet in order to make them edible. Condiments facilitated the process of digestive "cooking," helping to heat the food.

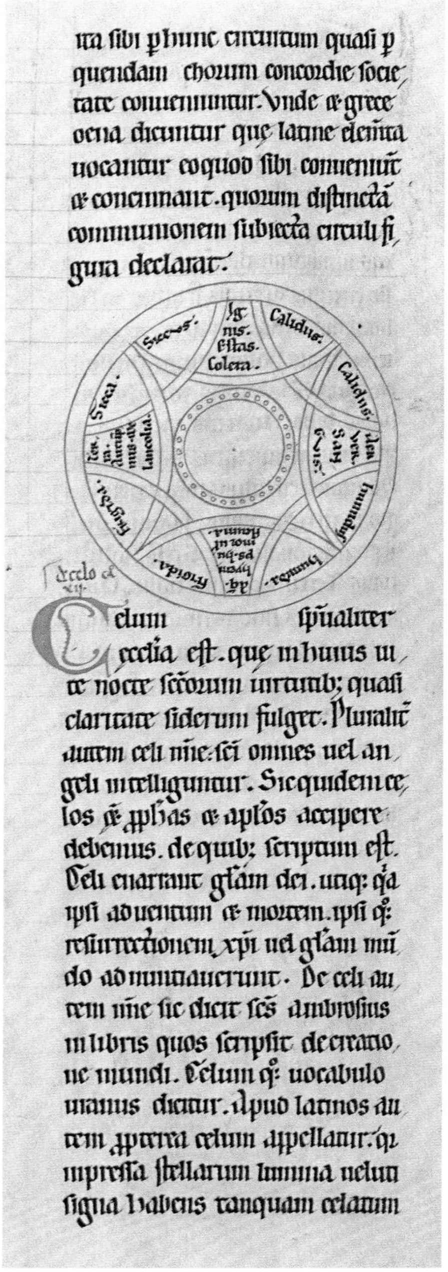

Individuals were classified into four categories of temperament – sanguine, choleric, phlegmatic and melancholic – determined by a greater or lesser presence of body fluids known as humors. Blood predominated in sanguine individuals, phlegm (mucus) in phlegmatic individuals, yellow bile in choleric individuals and black bile in melancholic ones. Humors were classified according to their temperature (cold or hot) and moisture (dry or wet), and were also linked to Aristotelian elements: earth, water, fire and air.[12]

Temperament	*Humor*	*Heat*	*Moisture*	*Element*
Sanguine	*Blood*	*Hot*	*Wet*	*Air*
Choleric	*Yellow bile*	*Hot*	*Dry*	*Fire*
Melancholic	*Black bile*	*Cold*	*Wet*	*Earth*
Phlegmatic	*Phlegm*	*Cold*	*Dry*	*Water*

Foodstuffs were classified in the same way: hot or cold, dry or wet. When they could barely be felt, the intensity of these qualities was low. If they were too strong, they could be toxic.[13] According to culinary historian Jean-Louis Flandrin, it was believed that individuals should eat according to their desires, which reflected what was suited to their temperament. Foods were either compatible or incompatible. Temperaments were immutable, and hence should not be disturbed. Thus, banquets should cater to the temperaments of all diners.

Condiments and sauces, which altered the nature (degree of moisture and heat) of basic ingredients such as meat, fowl, fish, vegetables and fruit, should be used to prepare basic foods that were far-removed from the eater's temperament. Thus, dishes would be more palatable for those individuals, hence the Portuguese term *tempero* for seasonings. The correction wrought by condiments also reduced the risk of ingesting foodstuffs deemed to be dangerous due to excess heat or moisture. Spices and acidic ingredients were very hot or cold and consequently had a far greater corrective effect than sugar and honey, which were just slightly hot.[A] On the other hand, this excess of heat or cold of spices and acidic ingredients was often tempered with sugar. Many recipes that included sugar were, in effect, aimed at treating patients or tempering the effects of spices without eliminating their good qualities. Imbalances in humors caused by climate, age and, above all, ailments, were also to be restored to the proper balance through corrective ingredients.[14]

"Elementary diagram" from Etymologiae De natura rerum ad Sisebutum; *Isidore of Seville (560–636 AD), showing variations of heat, cold, dryness and moisture in a thirteenth-century manuscript.*

Increased Use in Cooking

In the late Middle Ages and the early Modern Age, the cuisine served to the elite strata of Christian and Muslim society between northwest India and northwest Europe was, to a large extent, quite similar. According to historian Rachel Laudan, it included thick purées, numerous spices, sweet-and-sour sauces, cooked vegetables and mulled wine, which was imbibed on a far lesser scale in the Muslim world. Sugar could be found in virtually all dishes in a meal, not just in cakes and fruit recipes but also in meat, fowl, fish and vegetable dishes. It was believed that sugar could not spoil any dish, and recipes sought to combine its taste with the dietetic value of the ingredients and make them more digestible.[15]

The quantity and proportion of sugar used in court cuisine intensified, as demonstrated by culinary historian T. Sarah Peterson. Although the measurements are not exact, they do provide some idea of scale: a recipe for medieval blancmange for twelve people in a fourteenth-century Italian book recommended 1.5 pounds (approximately 680.3 g)[B] of sugar for every four chickens. In the next century, a French book suggests one pound of sugar for a suckling pig. In the late 1500s, two pounds of sugar were used for every ten pounds of meat. These proportions were similar to those utilized in thirteenth-century Muslim cuisine in the West, where one chicken was cooked with three pounds of sugar.[16] This growing consumption was fueled by the expansion of sugar-producing areas, some new, in the Mediterranean and the Atlantic, especially Madeira.

It is true that there were regional differences, with sugar having taken deeper roots on the Iberian and Italian peninsulas and in England at the dawn of the Modern Age.[17] Sugar even began to be appreciated in France, which had used this condiment more sparingly in the Middle Ages. By the late sixteenth century, the French court was using it in vast quantities.[18]

Basic dietary knowledge about humors was increasingly incorporated into elite circles and shared by cooks, doctors and diners. Because medical resources were limited, therapeutic methods emphasized preventive measures. The principle of achieving balance by using ingredients with opposite properties was reinforced in the mid-sixteenth century. Ideally, the human body should be slightly warm and slightly moist; that is, moderately sanguine. Instead of respecting individual temperaments, dictated by desire, to prevent illness, individuals should be balanced according to the standard of the sanguine temperament. Doctors thus began to prescribe

A. According to Alfredo Saramago, a historian specializing in Portuguese cuisine, honey and sugar were both hot, but, unlike sugar, honey was dry and hence required greater care in its use; see: A. Saramago, *Para a história da doçaria conventual portuguesa* (Lisbon: CTT Correios, 2000), p. 23.

B. These measures varied significantly in different regions and changed over the course of time. The figures shown here only serve to suggest the scale involved.

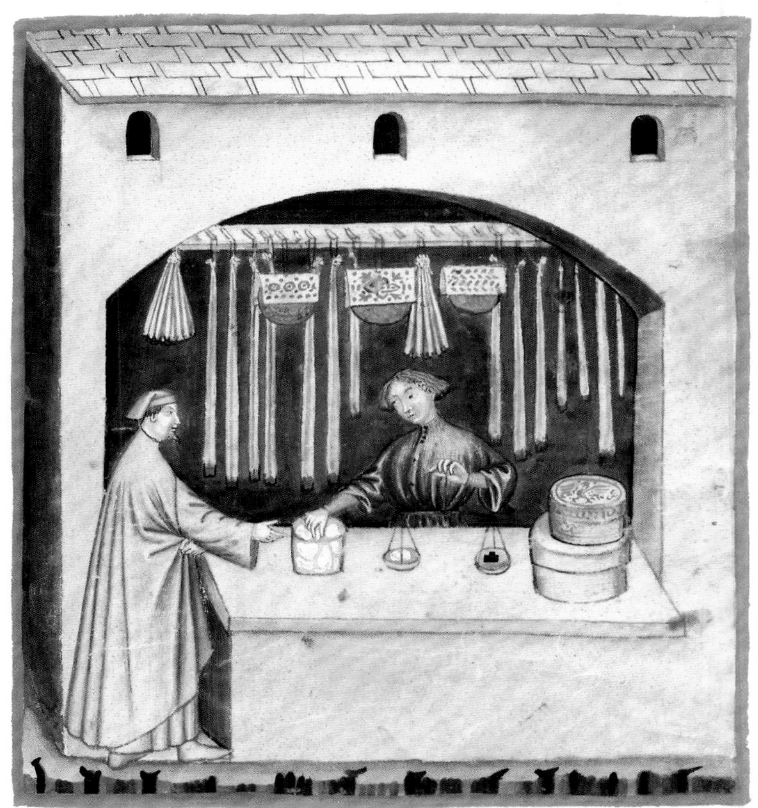

individual preventive diets, going beyond variations according to age, gender, climate, and so forth, as in the past.[19]

Hence, ideal repasts should also be slightly moist and hot. In this sense, the perfect sixteenth-century dish was blancmange, a kind of gruel made with rice or rice flour, chicken and almond milk, with a sprinkling of sugar. All the ingredients were slightly moist and hot, and this was how the dish was supposed to be served. The consistency of the gruel made it more digestible.[20] The disciplined Philip II is known to have eaten this dish three times a week.[21] On the other hand, fruit and vegetables were very cold and moist, and hence spoiled easily. Therefore it was advisable to eat dry or cooked fruit, preferably with the addition of sugar, including marmalade, unless the eater wanted to make use of their coldness and wetness for medicinal purposes.[22]

Over the course of the sixteenth century, sugar continued to be used for pharmacological purposes, although by the late fifteenth century its increasing availability and use meant that its sale was no longer the privilege of apothecaries in the Low Countries.[23] Emperor Charles V's surgeon prescribed sugar pills in moderation for fever or choleric temperaments, both of which were hot.[24] Gil Vicente mentions the use of rose sugar for lovesickness. A sugar-based remedy known as "*mezinha*" was applied as a poultice in Portugal and Portuguese colonies. In Brazil, the Jesuits recommended sprinkling the eyes with white sugar to treat corneal ulcers.[25] As we will see, in Portugal the sugar confectioners sold was subject to supervision by apothecaries, and some of the sugar and sweets in their stores was to be set aside for sale in small quantities to people of lesser means.[26]

Sugarloaf mold (fifteenth/sixteenth century) from archeological excavations in the Monastery of Jesus in Aveiro, Portugal.

Selling Sugar by Weight. *Illustration from the fourteenth-century version of the treatise* Theatrum sanitatis *by Ibn Butlân, showing the retail sale of sugar;* Giovannino De' Grassi.

After studying ancient texts, the Humanists found fault with Arab-inspired culinary traditions but did not break with them, nor did they reject the medical traditions inherited from or via the Arab world; quite the contrary.[27] The salad was created in Italy, and was originally viewed as a dish like any other, including meat dishes, but was seasoned with salt and acidic ingredients, such as vinegar, citrus juices, wine, verjuice, mustard, and so on. Salads followed the recommendations of the ancients who advocated that the first course be very salty, so as to whet the appetite. Salads were not supposed to be sweetened, since, according to other ancient authors, honey could weaken other flavors, including salt. As sugar was even stronger than honey, it would undermine the capacity of the salt and vinegar to stimulate the appetite.[28] The perception of sugar as a moderator of appetite and the scruples of the Renaissance in regard to its use may not have been due simply to the study of the classics, but mainly to the increasing popularization of the product during early modern times.[C]

In practice, however, salads were served as sweetened dishes, and some contained significant amounts of sugar. This cuisine would continue to be quite eclectic for some time. From the courts of Italian principalities, these new Renaissance trends would make their way to France, the center of European courtly life, where the Tuscan Catherine of Medici reigned supreme for almost half a century. From Paris, they spread out to the rest of the continent.[29]

This sixteenth-century eclecticism is clearly evident in a manuscript of Portuguese recipes ostensibly prepared for Princess Mary of Portugal. While analyzing it, Antonieta Buriti de Souza Hosokawa pointed out its inclination towards sweet-and-sour flavors, since the manuscript included sugar in 42.3 percent of its meat recipes, along with sour flavors such as vinegar and lemon, salt and pepper. Spices like cloves, saffron, pepper and ginger also appear relatively frequently. Sugar and salt are used in the same proportions in the section on meat dishes, which calls for pieces of meat to be served on slices of sugar-coated bread. Sugar is also the most common ingredient in egg dishes, which range from scrambled eggs to pies. The third section of the manuscript covers milk dishes. Almost all of them, including the omnipresent blancmange, comprise sugar, apart from different types of flour, eggs and milk, of course. Finally, sugar is king in the "section on conserves," which refers, above all, to fruit preserves and some cakes and sweets. A pie (pasty) stuffed with kid liver is sprinkled with sugar and cinnamon, while another, stuffed with cooked lamb or pork, is made with butter and sugar.[30]

C. See the opinion of Felipe Fernández Armesto: "Most of the new recipes of the Renaissance were not particularly salty, although they represented a repudiation of the nauseating sweetness so in vogue in the Middle Ages. I think that this had little to do with Roman inspiration and more to do with a fact that will be examined further in the next chapter that sugar, previously an exotic luxury, had become an everyday product, available in abundance during this period": F. Fernández-Armesto, *Comida: uma história* (Rio de Janeiro: Record, 2004), p. 186.

According to recent studies, as of the sixteenth century, sweets were present on the tables of members of all strata of society in Portugal, the Atlantic islands and Brazil, at least as delicacies reserved for special occasions.

Breakfast Table with Fruit Pie; *Willem Claesz. Heda (1631).*

Decorative Use

Sugar was also used in diverse ways for decorations: it was mixed with gum, such as tragacanth (*Astragalus gummifer*) and gum arabic, nuts, especially almonds to make marzipan or starches particularly rice. Sugar was also crystallized in molds and sugar syrup was cooked to hardening point, producing a malleable paste that could be molded into figures that could then be painted and displayed. These figures were often crafted into sophisticated compositions. It was also possible to acquire sugar that had already been colored with roses or violets. These practices were known in Europe at least since the late twelfth century. However, according to Sidney Mintz, in the Middle Ages the cost of the large quantities of sugar required meant that its use for decoration was restricted to royalty and the aristocracy, the clergy and the lesser nobility. These dainty figures were a symbol of social distinction, objects of desire, and were used in ostentatious ceremonies, which charmed onlookers.[31] In effect, until the second half of the seventeenth century, grand banquets sought to impress more by means of the ingeniousness of their decorations than the flavor of their dishes.[32]

Table decorated with animals and plants molded in sugar paste for the wedding banquet of the Duke of Jülich-Cleves-Berg and the Margravine of Baden in 1585; Franz Hogenberg.

The decorative use of sugar reached its peak in the late fifteenth century[D] and early sixteenth century when grand historic, mythological and religious scenes were composed. These scenes were comprised of sculptures of humans and animals, plants and mythological figures, and first decorated the nuptial tables of princely Italian families, as described by Eddy Stols. In the 1530s, this trend was imported into the Low Countries and the Burgundian court banquets, which until then had been decorated with figures and tableaux made from non-edible materials such as wax or tallow, and now included scenes made from sugar-based paste.[33]

The most spectacular displays were perhaps those arranged by Portuguese representatives or members of the Portuguese royal family in the Low Countries to flaunt the abundance of this expensive ingredient. It is possible that this phenomenon reached its height in Brussels in 1565 during the marriage of the Princess Mary of Portugal (the same royal for whom the book of recipes analyzed by Hosokawa had been purportedly prepared), when she wed Alexander Farnese, the future Duke of Parma, who would reclaim the Southern Low Countries and Antwerp for the Habsburgs. Even the candelabra and table service used at the wedding festivities were made of sugar. A huge tableau was also crafted, theatrically depicting the route the princess had taken on her way to Brussels. Among many marvels, it included miniatures of buildings and city scenes, with exotic animals from Portuguese dominions in Africa and Asia. The largest pieces were so big that it took several men to carry them.

Even the mother of the groom, Margaret of Parma, the governor-general of the Low Countries and illegitimate daughter of Charles V, had seen a flamboyant sugar sculpture displayed at her own nuptials twenty years earlier in Naples. This fashion soon reached the English court of Henry VIII, and *pièces montées* were prominently displayed during the receptions for Elizabeth I and James I. In the late sixteenth century, similar sumptuous creations are mentioned in France on different festive occasions. Renowned artists were hired to sculpt them.[34]

According to Sidney Mintz, in the sixteenth century the use of sugar in decorative compositions was no longer restricted to the nobility but also extended to wealthier segments of urban society. They were described in recipe books that were probably aimed at wider audiences.[E] Mintz observes that the social status attributed to sugar waned as its economic and culinary importance increased. The growth of its supply sapped its symbolic capital,

D. At the end of the fifteenth century, in Évora, sugar and preserves had already been served at the wedding of the ill-fated Prince Alphonse, King João II's heir, who was expected to become the first monarch of the entire Iberian Peninsula. However, it is not known if they were accompanied by this theatrical splendor; see: S. D. Arnaut, *A arte de comer em Portugal na Idade Média* (Sintra: Colares Editora, 2000), p. 103; G. de Resende, *Crónica de D. João II e miscelânea* (Lisbon: Imprensa Nacional-Casa da Moeda, 1973), ch. 117, pp. 156, 160.

E. Mintz may have been referring to books that taught the art of preparing sugar gum and not fondant which could be sculpted, or *alfenim*, which contained far more sugar and, being brittle, had to be wrapped in cotton wool before being transported (Mintz, *Sweetness and Power*, pp. 87, 90–91, 95).

while its economic weight grew with its increased production, trade, transport, refining and taxation. Nevertheless, although in the second half of the seventeenth century these compositions were already flaunted by individuals of lesser stature, such as merchants, it was precisely at this time that sugar sculptures reached their apogee in European courts, particularly in Rome.[35] Apart from miniatures, figures and statues, these compositions also included sweet delicacies such as candied (crystallized) fruit or fruit prepared in preserves, compotes, ground to a paste or sun dried, generically called comfits.

In the absence of more sophisticated means of preserving foodstuffs, sugar was added to the stock of known methods for conserving food, such as drying food in the sun, salting, vinegar preserves and preserving food with lard. In high concentrations, sugar reduces the metabolism of microbes, hindering their reproduction and even killing them. When covered or cooked with sugar until reaching crystallization point, or when soaked in a highly concentrated syrup, fruit loses its internal moisture and is covered by a protective layer which is combined with the fruit's own pectin. This is also the case with fruit kept and served in syrup or as a paste, such as marmalade, jam and jelly. Drying fruit in the sun likewise reduces internal moisture and increases the concentration of sugar, while boiling kills or weakens micro-organisms. However, making comfits was a laborious process that required fruit to be carefully cleaned and often necessitated several rounds of cooking, always keeping a watchful eye on the setting points.[36]

Sugar comfits were known to exist in Persia as far back as the ninth century, and they had gained popularity in Europe since the Middle Ages. The English court had consumed sweets at least since the fifteenth century,[37] and by the middle of that century, the Madeira Islands archipelago had already mastered confectionery techniques. From the sixteenth century onwards, the Madeira confectionery industry developed even further. Competition with other producing areas caused the islanders to seek out new niche markets. Madeira's sweets were made from the Mediterranean fruit grown there, such as lemons, citron, pears, peaches, oranges and squash, and locally produced sugar, whose quality was considered to be the best, or among the best, in the world. Madeira's confectioners were particularly known for their candied citron rinds, first pickled in brine and then sweetened, dried in the sun and cut into the human and animal figures which so delighted their aristocratic consumers.

The Portuguese Crown purchased sweets, preserves and dried fruit from the islands in massive quantities.[38] Meanwhile, in the early 1500s, King Emmanuel (Manuel) used these delicacies as a diplomatic tool, offering them as gifts which he often presented to foreign authorities, including the Pope and the Sheikh of Mozambique. In the first quarter of the sixteenth century, Madeira candies and blocks of solid brown

Still life with pottery, candied fruit, biscuits and other comfits; *Juan van der Hamen y León (1627)*.

sugar (*rapadura*) packed in barrels, boxes, chests, trunks, gift boxes, pallets and baskets were exported to Flanders and Italy, from where they were probably re-exported to the rest of Europe and the Levant.

During the early seventeenth century, Madeira also exported preserves made from exotic fruits such as coconuts, tamarinds and pineapples.[39] Candied fruit from different parts of the Mediterranean, Africa and India were served at Princess Mary's wedding. More than three decades earlier, sweets from Madeira had been served at a feast the Portuguese ambassador prepared for Emperor Charles V and his sister Mary of Austria, Queen of Hungary, then governor-general of the Netherlands, in honor of the birth of Prince Emmanuel, the future Portuguese monarch. Years later, Mary of Austria would present her nephew, the future Philip II, with an "enchanted chamber" richly decorated with comfits.[F] Stols mentions other examples of similar sugary excesses in the Low Countries, Catalonia and Milan in the mid-sixteenth century.

Still Life with Fruit (dried and candied) and Comfits; *Georg Flegel (1566–1638)*.

Confectionery and the nobility

It seems that, at least during the fifteenth and sixteenth centuries, queens and princesses and influential nobles such as Beatrice, Duchess of Viseu, the sister-in-law, aunt and mother of several monarchs, brought confectioners with them as part of their dowry and entourage.[40] Catherine of Austria, the wife of King João III, brought a Flemish confectioner to Portugal, and he was supplied with vast quantities of sugar. Years later, she interceded on behalf of another of her confectioners, this time a Portuguese, with Lisbon authorities who wanted him to operate, together with the other confectioners, from the Rua do Saco. Queen Mary Emmanuelle (Maria Manuela), the first wife of the future Philip II, brought her confectioner with her from Portugal. This was also the case with Princess Joanna of Austria, sister of Philip II and mother of King Sebastian, when she returned to Castile as a widow to assume the regency until her brother arrived from Flanders.[41]

The Portuguese kings also had their confectioners.[G] King Afonso V employed one as far back as 1478, a tradition maintained during the reigns of other Portuguese monarchs. Although we do not know whether it carried on continuously, the tradition lasted at least until the reign of Philip II.

The growing consumption of sugar in the 1500s resulted in specialization within cookbooks.[42] Even though specialized books pertaining to confectionery had circulated in Catalonia and in Italy from the fourteenth century onwards, it was only in the mid-sixteenth century that cookbooks dedicated to confectionery became established as a specific genre, especially in France. Publications in this genre included a work written by the mystic, Michel de Nostredame, better known as Nostradamus, who was influenced by alchemy.

Given the medicinal nature of the culinary arts, recipes for comfits not only included compotes, syrups and preserves made with vinegar, mustard and other preservatives, but also encompassed cosmetics such as soaps, pomades and perfumes. These recipes were followed by recommendations for their use, the directions for each product and the care that should be taken with them. According to Philip and Mary Hyman, historians specializing in French cuisine, the link between sweets and cosmetics was perfectly logical: since sugar facilitated digestion, sweets, whether made from fruit or other ingredients, should be reserved for the final stage of a meal, right before the diners cleansed themselves, when cosmetics would be used.[43]

This same trend of specialized works on confectionery can be seen in Castile, where four volumes on this subject were published at the end of the century. Books produced in Italy, France and the Netherlands on agronomy, pharmacy and chemistry, which included alchemy, also covered confectionery, in view of its medicinal importance.[44]

The Street Vendor's Tray

The available sources do not indicate precisely how or when more plebeian segments of society began to consume sweets, much less sweets made from sugar. It would not be surprising if this consumption began in regions where there was a more plentiful supply of sweeteners, such as Italy, Spain and Portugal.[45]

On the Iberian Peninsula, sweets derived from Arab traditions had been eaten by the lower classes since the Middle Ages. These were known as *alféloas*, an initially generic term derived from the Arab word for "sweet," *halwā*, which later came to specifically designate a paste made of honey or sugar cooked to setting point, which, after being cooled, could be molded and turned white, ending up with the consistency of caramel.[46] Even before the mid-fourteenth century, King Alphonse IV prohibited gambling with

F. Comfits were also given as gifts to members of royal families (Stols, "The Expansion of the Sugar Market in Western Europe," pp. 237–238, 243–244).

G. Grand aristocratic houses also adhered to these practices, such as the dukes of Braganza, in their palace at Vila Viçosa; see: G. M. Sequeira, *Depois do terramoto. Subsídios para a história dos bairros ocidentais de Lisboa*, V. 3 (Lisbon: Academia das Ciências de Lisboa, 1967), p. 415.

Sweet sellers in Lisbon and Brazil

Gilberto Freyre offers an interesting comparison between Lisbon in the sixteen hundreds and major Brazilian cities in the early twentieth century: "A custom deriving from sixteenth-century Lisbon was that of black women with pans, baskets and trays of sweets who would walk the streets of Rio, Bahia and Recife hawking their alféloas, their *alfenims* and their sweets. Women also hawked sweet couscous and rice pudding in Brazil, under the canopy of a leafy fig tree, on trays propped on X-shaped wooden frames. A sixteenth-century Portuguese manuscript [*Grandeza e Abastança de Lisboa em 1552*, attributed to João Brandão] describes women selling sweets who would wake the children of Lisbon while calling out their wares: "As soon as the children hear their calls, they hop out of bed and beg their parents to give them some money." Exactly the same thing would happen in Brazil, generation after generation, until modern times. Black women calling out: 'Eh! Alfenim' or 'Eh! Cakes,' while children cried and cajoled their parents to give them money to buy alfenim and cake."[53]

Still Life with Oysters, Comfits and Fruit; *Osias Beert (1610). A broken piece of alfenim appears at the edge of the table.*

dice[47] in which bets were paid in foodstuffs meat, fish, grain, nuts, salt, water, vinegar and alféloas. [48]

Going by the chronicler Fernão Lopes, it would appear that these delicacies were neither expensive nor all that rare. He observed that by the end of that century it was possible to buy alféloas with one of the smallest denomination coins in circulation.[H] He further recorded that, during the siege of Lisbon by Queen Leonor and the Castilians, in the course of the Aviz Revolution in 1384, some residents of the city ate alféloas when they could not find bread.[I] On the side of the besiegers, their doctors, surgeons and apothecaries also used candies, sugars and preserves to treat their troops.[J/49] In all likelihood, these first references to the low price and easy availability of these delicacies are exaggerated, at least if they were made from sugar instead of honey, because in the first half of the century the tax on sugar was the same as that levied for pepper, saffron and other spices or metals, reflecting its scarcity. This is corroborated by sources listing the expenditures of various institutions.[50]

A century later, the sovereign once again dealt with the question of alféloas. During the Cortes (a kind of extraordinary parliament) that met in 1490, the people complained about certain Castilians who roamed the kingdom selling alféloas. First, they claimed that this drove up the price of honey, and second that it "made children cry and caused them to ask their parents for money to buy the said alféloas, while some even stole money to pay for them."[51] Apparently, the tidbits had strong links with games of chance, since alféloa sellers were accused of teaching young people card and dice games. It is possible that the sweets were the prize. The commoners (*povos*) asked the monarch to ban the sale of these alféloas in the kingdom. However, he refused, only agreeing to prohibit games of dice. It is clear that honey continued to be used along with sugar. However, it appears that the latter was now more readily available to the masses, undoubtedly due to sugar production in the Algarve and Madeira.[52]

At the beginning of the following century, the law codex known as the *Ordenações Manuelinas* once again dealt with this temptation. Men were forbidden to sell sweets, since it was believed they could be scoundrels who would take children down a treacherous path. However, the regulations allowed women "who wished to sell alféloas in the streets or squares as well as in their own homes or inns could do so without penalties."[54] As Arnaut aptly observes, perhaps these sweets were not the same type of caramel candy that would later become popular in the northeast of Brazil. This author also highlighted how a profession for women was thus established: that of the female sweet seller or *alfeloeira*.[55]

Sweets from Madeira were important for the livelihoods of many families on the island, especially for women, and not just the poor. In addition to preserves and comfits, they also made alfenims and alféloas. The social importance of this activity was

Alfenim: From Persia to Pernambuco

Known as alfenim from the Persian, through Arabic, al-fānid was a delicacy that was especially amenable to being molded. It was made by blending egg whites and sugar beaten until stiffening point to produce a dry white sugar paste. In Iberia these sweets were eaten at the Alhambra in Granada to commemorate the birth of the prophet Mohammed in 1362, and contained almond oil. They were also found among of delicacies that the Portuguese Crown presented to the Holy See. Gilberto Freyre sang effusive praises about this candy, saying, "it cannot be touched with the fingers like this," since it was quite brittle. Hence, he compared it to the dainty young women of his home state, Pernambuco.[56]

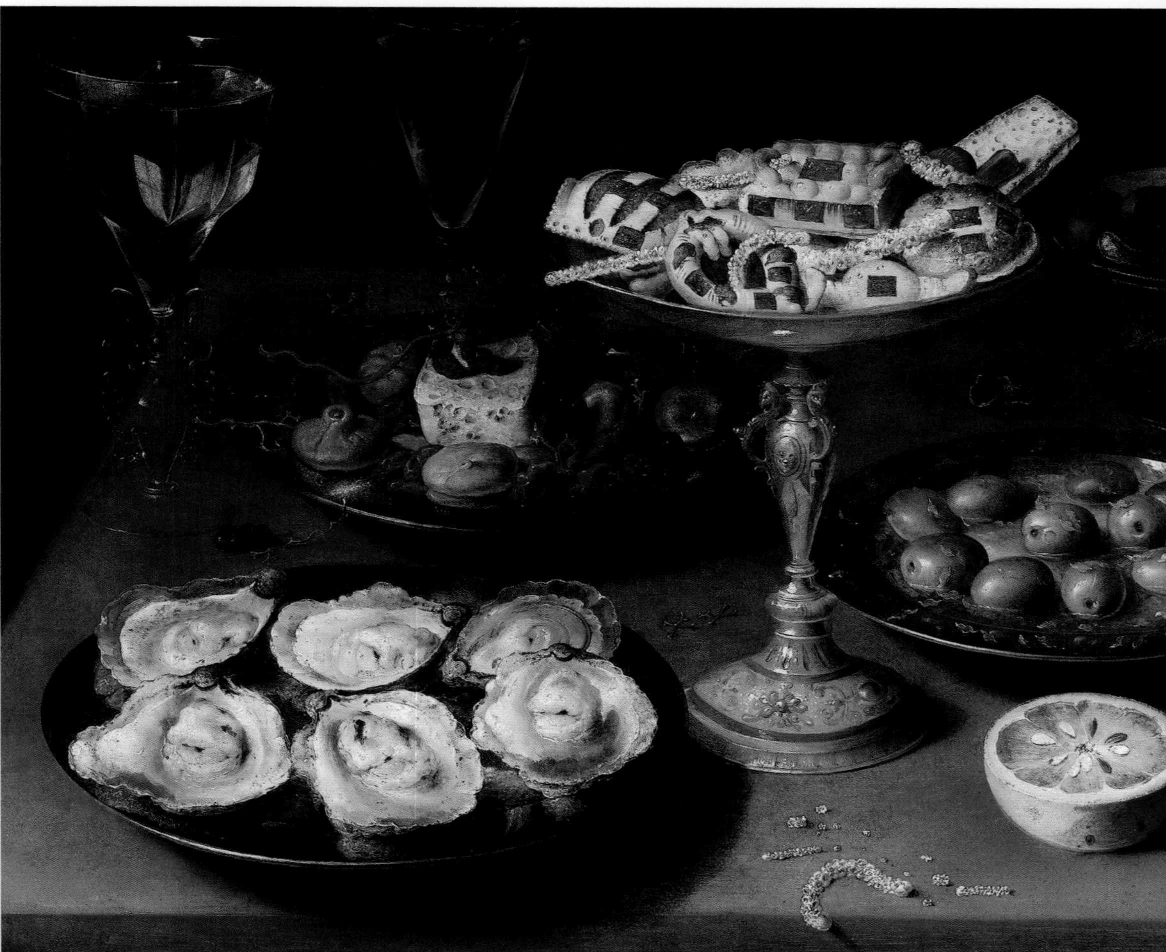

already abundantly clear as early as 1469. For its protection, the production of preserves, alfenims, comfits and crystallized fruit was reserved exclusively for people born in the islands until the end fifteenth century. Sugar masters were also banned from working in this industry. Most of Madeira's production, especially the best-quality items, was earmarked for export and consumed outside Portuguese territories. As we have seen, sugar from Madeira and the Canary Islands was considered to be the best for confectionery throughout Europe. Part of these sweets was sent to Portugal's overseas dominions and consumed during ocean voyages. The crisis that wracked Madeira's sugar industry did not undermine the local confectionery sector, but rather resulted in the archipelago specializing in manufacturing sweets. A significant amount of the sugar that was still produced locally was used for that purpose, and in the seventeenth century not insignificant quantities of sugar were imported from Brazil.[57]

H. "And anyone who wanted to make smaller coins from these old coins would cut a coin in half with a scissors, or would bite it with their teeth, and half of that coin was called a "mealha" or "pogeja" and it could buy a smidgeon of mustard, or alféloas, or some lupini beans, and the like....": F. Lopes, *Crónica de D. Fernando* (Porto: Livraria Civilização-Editora, 1966), ch. 55, p. 146.

I. "There was no wheat in the city to be sold, and if there was any, it was very scarce and so expensive that the poor could not afford it; here, an alqueire of wheat was worth four pounds; and an alqueire of corn was worth forty soldos; and a canada of wine cost three and four pounds; and there was such a shortage with each passing day that even if people were willing to pay a doubloon for some bread; it was impossible to find bread for sale; and they began to eat bread made from olive bagasse, and cheeses made from roots and mallows; and there were some who survived by eating alféloas"; see F. Lopes, *Crónica de D. João I* (Porto: Livraria Civilização-Editora, 1983), v. 1, ch. 148, p. 306.

J. "Many boats and skiffs came from Seville with provisions and weapons and whatever other things were necessary; and not only provisions but many varied and abundant spices were also for sale. There were physicians and surgeons and apothecaries who not only had the things necessary to preserve the body at the ready but also various types of comfits and sugar and preserves, which they had in abundance" (Ibid., v. 1, ch. 114, p. 220).

In Lisbon, too, the abundance of sugar enabled a "popular" sweet-making sector to expand and develop. Once again, women would play an important role. While lauding the city, the chronicler João Brandão, believed to be the author of the manuscript entitled *Grandeza e abastança de Lisboa em 1552* (*Lisbon's Greatness and Wealth in 1552*), provides important economic and social information. He describes the women of different hues and backgrounds who sold morsels along the waterfront, the bustling area where sailors, stevedores, caulkers, soldiers and traders came and went:

> *In this city there are fifty women, white and black, freed and enslaved, who go out onto the waterfront every morning bearing large pots filled with rice, couscousK and peas, calling out their wares. Since the children hear them in their beds, they wake up and cry for their fathers and mothers to give them money. In truth, it is not too bad, because the children eat this food for lunch [i.e., breakfast]. This is also the case with young working lads, both whites as well as blacks, who make a meal of these tidbits and fill their bellies. In this manner their pots and pans get worn out very quickly; they can even make 200 réis each, and even more. Assuming that each makes 150 réis, that amounts to 7,500 réis per day, and that should be multiplied by 300 days a year, because the only day on which they do not sell their wares is Sunday, thus amounting to 5,660 cruzados.*[58]

One again finds these treats, even those from the pots and pans of female street vendors, inducing working youths and children, *filius familiae*, to splurge. The sale of delicacies picked up especially near the holiday seasons, primarily around Christmas. Brandão observes:

> *In this city, fifteen days prior to Christmas until Epiphany, 30 women sit along the waterfront and near the Old Pillory with their tables covered with sparkling white tablecloths and mantles, and arrayed on them are sweets made from sesame seeds and pine nuts, nougat, marmalade, candied orange and citron peel, and farteis [sugar and almond cakes], and all sorts of preserves.*[59]

Here, Brandão underscores the difference between popular sweet-making and aristocratic confectionery, the latter being made with expensive ingredients and prepared with great care. However, at the end of the day, all this simply proved that Lisbon was a city of abundance:

> *Extravagant people spend a great deal on these treats, which is the case with most noble families, in whose houses vast sums of money are spent on costly fruit and preserves of all kinds. Judging by the many different kinds of fruit, I would think they could easily spend more than 20,000 cruzados. And this lavish expenditure enhances the greatness and wealth of the land.*[60]

The Pastry Vendor; *Abraham Bosse (ca. 1638). In a free translation of the French caption: "This fine and pleasantly humored confectioner is ripping off a young boy who, for his part, willingly eats the cakes that are presented into his hand."*

According to this chronicler, those thirty women would sell "honey sweets" throughout the year, or most of it. This term included sweets made from sesame and pine nuts, alféloas and "other honeyed things."[61] Despite their name, could these "honey sweets" have also included tidbits made with sugar? If so, in what proportion?

If the sale of sweets employed thirty women, honey sales employed another twenty.[62] About fifty more would have been employed in making jams, rose sugar and orange delights probably made from orange rinds "which they sell to people going to India and Guinea."[63]/[L] In his enthusiastic inventory, Brandão attempts to calculate how many round boxes would have been produced just to store marmalade, and arrived at an estimated figure of 500 round boxes per year. He also mentions rose sugar, which would have brought in a good deal of money.[64]

At the same time that Brandão wrote his manuscript, the archdiocese of Lisbon commissioned an inventory listing the revenues of all the religious institutions in the city, as well as the number of houses, inhabitants and their professions and occupations. This "Summary," prepared by Cristóvão Rodrigues de Oliveira, shows an even larger number of female sweet-makers. Oliveira classified them according to the types of sweets they prepared.[65]

Women who make candied fruit 60
Women who make alféloa 23
Women who make zezevinhos 24
Women who make vermicelli sweets 28
Women who make fried sweets 26
Women who make [sweet?] couscous 23
Women who make [sweet?] rice[M] *27*

Ce Pastissier est fin et d'vne humeur plaisante
Pour escroquer l'argent de ce petit garçon ;
Mais luy de son costé sçait de bonne façon
Engloutir les pastez que sa main luy presante.

Candied oranges and similar confections not only served to preserve the fruit during long voyages to India and Africa, but, apparently, travellers even made money selling these treats in the Far East.[N] During the same period, the humanist Damião de Góis also highlighted the presence of comfits among the products sold in the busy Terreiro do Paço square in Lisbon, next to the ships on the Tagus River, the shipyards and Ribeira Palace.[66]

The popular art of making conserves was not limited to Portugal and Madeira. It was also prevalent in other sugar-producing areas such as Valencia and Sicily, and even in regions where sugarcane was not cultivated, such as Lorraine, where women began to play a more prominent role in these professional pursuits from the fourteenth century onwards. While sales required women to be exposed to the outside world, preparing food products did not. This activity could also be done modestly at home, just like spinning and weaving. Sweet-making supplemented a family's income,[O] or even supported it (especially in a society where men often set out for overseas territories). In addition to keeping women busy with a modest but productive activity, preparing foodstuffs allowed daughters and wives to delight visitors, welcome relatives, enchant their spouses and pamper their parents.[67]

K. Even though the author did not specify that the rice and couscous were sweet, some researchers believe they were, such as José da Felicidade Alves, who organized the edition we used and titled this excerpt: Title 166, "About Women Selling Sweetened Rice [or rather, Rice Pudding]": Brandão, *Grandeza e abastança de Lisboa em 1552*, p. 13.

L. Although sweets were also made in Bengal, Luso-Indian confectionery had developed significantly in Goa by late 1530s (Godinho, *Os descobrimentos e a economia mundial*, v. 4, p. 357).

M. We do not know for certain whether the rice and couscous were sweet.

N. Vasco da Gama had already taken comfits to Africa and India. Sweets were later sold in Japan and, even if they were made in the Far East, they followed or were influenced by Portuguese recipes (Gouveia, "Açúcar confeitado na Madeira," p. 35).

O. This was a predominantly female market-oriented domestic occupation aimed at earning extra income for consumption, particularly of exotic and luxury goods, which became accessible to broader sections of society. Jan de Vries called this process the "Industrious Revolution," and, according to him, it only occurred consistently, profoundly and enduringly in the "long eighteenth century," that is, between 1650 and 1850, and paved the way for the Industrial Revolution. To be sure, De Vries has found precedents of this "Industrious Revolution" in the eighteenth-century Dutch Republic. Nevertheless, he does not include foodstuffs in his list of proto-industrial sectors; see: J. de Vries, *The Industrious Revolution: Consumer Behavior and the Household Economy, 1650 to the Present* (New York: Cambridge University Press, 2008), pp. 10, 44, 52, 71–72, 78, 92, 96–97, 104, 140–141, 177.

Religious Applications

Bearing in mind the role that women played in making sweets, particularly for general consumption, it is no surprise that convents also helped popularize sweets among the masses and perfected confectionery techniques. This was the case in Portugal, Spain and their overseas territories. Nuns had a considerable amount of free time, and sweets could be prepared inside the cloisters with no harm done to their modesty.[68] Sweet-making provided the convents and the nuns themselves with an additional source of income. Moreover, they could match their cuisine with the religious calendar, selling or distributing certain sweets on specific holidays. Sensual delights combined with holy occasions, skills with sweets, sugary treats with religious rituals.

Nuns in Madeira spent their spare time making sweets during the sixteenth century, when account books from convents show frequent purchases of fruit and sugar from Madeira and Brazil, apart from donations of sugar. Some of their delicacies were earmarked for sale and distribution during different religious festivals, particularly processions. According to Alberto Vieira there were also sweets specifically associated with holidays: "candied potatoes for Christmas, sweet fritters during Shrovetide (Carnival), candied fruit (*talhadas*) at Easter and on the day of Our Lady of the Incarnation."[69]

In continental Portugal, however, it was only after the seventeenth century that the production of comfits and conserves would develop in convents and the retreats where widows, unmarried women and those whose husbands were absent could live without necessarily taking religious vows. The subsequent advances of Portuguese confectionery owed a great deal to these convent traditions.[P] Since monastic life at that time had less to do with a vocation than planning for matrimonial alliances and investments in dowries, sweets also allowed nuns to pamper and allure loved ones who lived outside the cloisters.[70]

Nuns played an important role in sweet-making outside the Iberian world as well. Stols emphasizes this fact in the context of France and the region of the Low Countries under Spanish rule, where the Counter-Reformation increased the number of convents in Catholic areas, while others were shut down in Protestant areas. Many Spanish nuns were taken to new and old monasteries in the loyal Catholic provinces, and Stols believes that they might have at least enriched the production of Flemish convent sweets. The Low Countries had an even stronger tradition of urban retreats, further reinforced by the Counter-Reformation. Known as *begijntjes*, the women living there also associated their sweets with the religious calendar.[71]

Portuguese hospitals and Santas Casas in Portugal and the Atlantic Islands also received donations in sugar and sweets, and either fed them to their patients or sold them to increase their revenues.[73] Women staying at retreats in the Low Countries also donated their sweets to the sick and to children.

In the Low Countries, sweets also played a significant role during public social occasions. They were eaten during gatherings at chambers of rhetoric, literary societies that held plays and poetry recitals, among other activities, and were very popular in those parts. Expenditure on sweets would have comprised prominent entries in the account books of these associations. Sweets were also sold outdoors in Antwerp towards the end of the year, when the Scheldt River froze over, although probably on a far smaller scale than in Lisbon.[74]

Santas Casas de Misericórdia

The institutions known as *Santas Casas de Misericórdia* ["Holy Houses of Mercy"] were voluntary charitable associations that played an important role in Portuguese social assistance during the Modern Age. Their secular mission was to redeem captives, treat the sick and mentally ill, provide dowries for female orphans whether for marriage or to enter a convent shelter the poor, help prisoners and free individuals imprisoned for debts. Over the course of the sixteenth and seventeenth centuries, many Santas Casas were established in Portuguese cities, towns and colonies. Being a member of a Misericórdia brotherhood was a status symbol, demonstrating membership in the urban patrician class.[72]

Sweets were ideally suited for distribution rituals, according to Stols. Thus, Spanish soldiers, whose presence was not always welcome, distributed sweets and fruits during the carnival period in the Southern Low Countries.[75] Such treats were very popular with children, who cajoled their parents and even filched money from them to buy such delicacies, and received them as gifts during family, social and religious events. This established positive ties with the institutions hosting those occasions. Associated with specific local or regional, periodic and special occasions, these treats came to symbolize such celebrations.

In Brazil too, sweets played an important role in religious and distribution rituals from very early on. During the Holy Inquisition's first visitation to Brazil, in 1591, the Jesuit Luiz da Grã denounced a sugar master from the captaincy of São Vicente, a New Christian who was no longer alive, on the basis of a witness's account. A procession was customarily held on Maundy Thursday to celebrate the Passion of Christ, with images of Jesus carrying a cross on his back, and Pharisees. The sugar master carried a box of sweets provided by the local Santa Casa da Misericórdia to console the penitent.[Q] However, the individual in question "always gave solace and sweets to the Pharisees and nothing to the statue of Christ."[76]

Stols also observes the sacred-secular connections of sweets, highlighting a type of sweet known both as "nun farts" and "whore farts" in France and Flanders. Both Stols and Freyre have pointed out the seraphic and celestial names bestowed upon sweets within and outside convent confectionery traditions.[77]

P. Portuguese poetry from the second half of the fifteenth century and early sixteenth century also mentions sweets such as "trutas" made by nuns, and sweet cheese buns (fartalejos) (Arnaut, *A arte de comer*, pp. 103–104). The following verse was compiled into the *Cancioneiro geral*: "Dom Henrique de Sá to Diogo Brandão, sending him some "trutas" made by nuns: These "trutas" are the kind / I was telling you about perfection! / They are made from eggs and cinnamon, / You will not be able / To get enough of them. / I learned this from a story / That a lady once told me, / Which did not flatter you much: G. de Resende, *Cancioneiro geral* (Coimbra: Centro de Estudos Românicos, 1973), p. 355 (no. 426).

Q. In Lisbon, it was customary to distribute candied fruit in Maundy Thursday processions, at least from 1562 onwards (Sequeira, *Depois do terramoto*, v. 3, pp. 413–414).

Glasgow Shopkeeper.
Sugarloaves for sale in a late eighteenth-century shop in Scotland.

Confectionery in Shops

Apart from lowly sweet makers, there were also well-established confectioners who made more costly comfits and preserves and had their own shops. João Brandão lists thirty confectionery stores active in mid-sixteenth century Lisbon, and about four or five people would have worked in each one.[78] Attempts were made to concentrate these shops into a single street, due to complaints by residents. The latter wished to keep away the flies and bees attracted by the sugar being processed near their houses in the better parts of town. During that period, there was a "Confectioners' Street," which survived the Marquis de Pombal's reforms in the aftermath of the 1755 Lisbon earthquake.[R] However, sweets were undoubtedly made elsewhere as well.[79]

The expansion of this activity, both among the middle-class and male section of the urban population as well as lower-class females, resulted in the early regulation of this profession by means of rules drawn up in 1575.[S] The Crown and the municipalities often regulated professions, by limiting entry through exams and other selection procedures, establishing a hierarchy within the profession and stipulating codes of conduct and quality standards.[80] In Porto, it was only during the period covered here that confectioners were recognized as an individual profession, with their own magistrate and clerk, and were represented at the Corpus Christi procession in which they were to intone six chants accompanied by lutes and tambourines. There were four foreigners among the confectioners from Porto, demonstrating the profession's association with exports.[81]

In 1610, the Lisbon Senate sought to control the profession even further. It banned the sale of sweets on the streets, and limited its merchandise to confectioners who had established stores. These were also the only ones authorized to sell alfenims, pastries, and so forth, "since they are not necessary foods and spoil our youth." The penalties were lower for illegal sales of such treats (1,000 réis) and higher (8,000 réis) for sweets made from fruit, which were consumed for medicinal purposes and more expensive.

This regulation of the profession did not result in the exclusion of humble sweet makers who sold their treats in the streets and public plazas. It is possible, however, that once the sector's regulations were reinforced, the number of confectionery stores could have increased while the number of itinerant female sweet sellers may have fallen. In 1620, Friar Nicolau de Oliveira, in yet another book that extolled Lisbon's virtues, now with a view

R. Confectioners were originally concentrated in the parish of Our Lady of Martyrs, and subsequently in the parish of St. Nicholas, which had an eponymous street. In 1580, Venetian travellers mentioned the sale of sweets and dried and candied fruits in shops on Rua Nova, in one of the finer districts of Lisbon, which reinforces the view that confectionery was at least sold in wealthier areas rather than just in the zones reserved for production (for references, see note 79 in this chapter).

S. In fact, even prior to this, in 1539, confectioners were already recognized as a specialized profession, using the banner of the Archangel St. Michael. They marched in processions under this standard, especially during the Corpus Christi parade, in which each profession had its own place in the event. In 1563, they formed a brotherhood under the patronage of Our Lady of the Olive Tree. Brotherhoods were voluntary organizations, not necessarily linked to a profession, established for social, religious and/or assistance purposes, involving mutual aid among its members. They were defined by a set of regulations or commitments, stipulating their regular operations, prerequisites for joining the brotherhood, and both the individual and the collective rights and duties of its members; see: E. F. Oliveira, *Elementos para a história do município de Lisboa* (Lisbon: Tipographia Universal, 1882–1911), v. 5, p. 581, note.

Regulations governing the confectioner's profession

The regulations that governed the profession of confectioner stipulated that in order to be entitled to practice their craft publicly, confectioners would have to pass an exam to prove their skills by preparing delicacies with roses, Madeira island specialties, citron skins and tubers and coating them with sugar. They also had to prepare sugared almonds, preserved pears and peaches, rose sugar, marmalade and jam, marzipan and alfenims, among others. To prevent speculation in sugar, confectioners were allowed to neither purchase it directly from ships nor take it directly to their shops. They were obliged to declare the crates they had bought to the magistrate appointed for the profession, who would split the sugar among all the confectioners.

The regulations also stipulated best practices, with only fixed weighing scales being allowed. Part of the sugar, alfenims and preserves were to be reserved to be sold in small quantities to those who could not afford buy them in bulk and needed them for medicinal purposes. Only superior-quality sugar could be used to produce cold sweets used as a fever remedy. The city government, magistrate and apothecaries were to inspect confectioners' shops.

The scarcity of almonds meant that confectioners could not sell them cooked in honey. Sweets made from sesame seeds and pine nuts, prepared with honey, could only be sold in December. In other words, this confirms the practice described by Brandão that safeguarded against excessive gluttony and wasted honey. According to Consiglieri and Abel, the tradition of making sweets with honey continued. The production and sale of marmalade and jam made with honey or sugar, however, were open to all.[82]

Par vn excez de friandise
Icy lon donne du ragoust;
Et lon y vend, pour plaire au goust,
Toute sorte de marchandise.
A Paris, Chez Mel.or Tauernier, Grauer

The Pastry Shop; *Abraham Bosse (ca. 1638). The popularization of sugar is reflected in the arts and literature, particularly in re-exporting regions, but also in Italy, Germany and France. In these portrayals, sweets are often associated with childhood and innocence, abundance and exoticism, love and consolation, as Eddy Stols has observed.*

Bosse in. et fe.
rauaille à son tour,
met la main à la paste;
it des pastez à la haste,
re les met dans le four.
Pour de l'argent on donne à tous
Des maccarrons, des darioles,
Des gasteaux diuers des rissoles
Du biscuit, et de. petits chous.
Cette boutique à des delices,
Qui charment en mille façons
Les filles les petits garçons,
Les seruantes et les Nourrices.
ur du Roy pour les Tailles-douces, demeurant en l'Isle du Palais, sur le Quay qui regarde la Megisserie, à l'Assphere auec Priuilege du Roy.

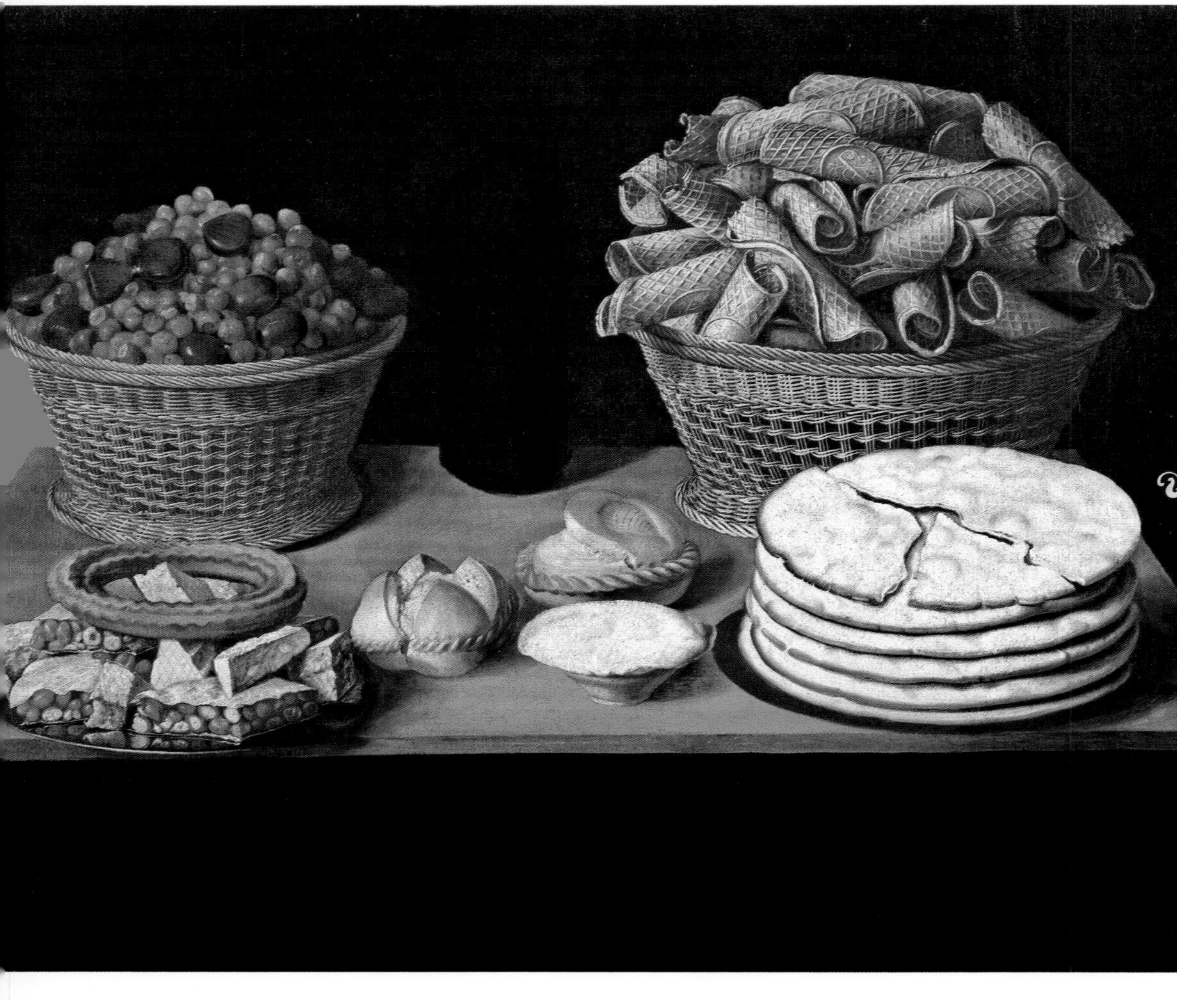

Attempts to regulate the sale of sweets

Castile also sought to regulate the public sale of sweets. In 1573, a petition submitted to the Cortes (parliament) called sweet vendors "vagabonds and idlers." The petition specifically complained about the sale of *canutillos de suplicaciones*, a type of biscuit or wafer rolled like a drinking straw or boat, which Cervantes mentions in *Don Quixote* as being good for digestion along with bits of marmalade. In 1585, their sale was banned in Madrid. Over the course of the Middle Ages, the authorities tried in vain to limit the sale of these rolls in Paris during the Christmas period and other festivals celebrated with processions. This treat was so popular that its production became specialized as an independent profession from that of bakers until it was incorporated into another specialized profession in 1566, that of pastry makers, who made cakes and pies.[86]

Still Life with Sweets and Dried Fruit and Nuts; *Tomás Hiepes (1610–1674).*

to persuading the Hispanic monarchs to transfer the capital to the mouth of the Tagus, stated that at the time there were fifty-four confectioners. On the other hand, he mentioned sixty "women who make sweets for sale, sold from their houses as well as on the streets, aside from the confectionery stores." There were also fifteen "girls who sell sweets from door to door,"[84] and forty pastry makers.[85]

Competition must also have been intense among confectioners in Lisbon. In 1626, a clause was added to the regulations stipulating that almonds could not be purchased without a permit from the profession's magistrate, who was to ensure the equitable distribution of this ingredient. In the 1640s, complaints were once again made against itinerant women selling sweets and the bans were reiterated.[87]

The twofold process of professionalization of the confectioner's trade, including pastry and cake shops, and making it an all-male activity, alongside the female and plebeian occupations of sweetmakers and sellers was not an exclusively Portuguese phenomenon. It also occurred in the Low Countries without the creation of a professional guild, as Stols has aptly observed.[88] Nevertheless, it is worth noting that men had always figured among the lowlier sweet makers.[89] Whether catering to the masses or professional, the specialization of sweet-making in the sixteenth century resulted in the emergence of regional sweets in several parts of Europe,[T] which became symbols of local identity.[90]

Another activity that became specialized and came to be an essentially male profession at the beginning of early modern times was sugar refining. In order to be transported and traded, sugarcane juice first had to be converted into crystals, even in its crudest form. These crystals could be refined later to further remove impurities. Refining sugar was a process that was akin to sugar production, as it basically consisted of dissolving the sugar, cooking it again and purifying it. Impurities were removed by flocculating foreign substances with the help of potash, agglutination with egg whites or ox blood, the crystallization of sugar by means of saturation, and the percolation of crystals with a new round of purging.

Refining added value to the browner types of sugar, such as the muscovado and panela varieties. White Brazilian sugar did not need to be refined to be consumed or used in confectionery,[91] even though refining could make it purer, whiter and drier. In any case, refining provided a wider assortment of sugar, which catered to consumers of various tastes and means.

Refining sugar was a costly proposition just like sugar production. Refining required investments in equipment such as copper pots and ceramic molds, among others. It also necessitated facilities, including storage space, apart from the high cost of fuel and intensive, specialized labor. To be sure, some small-scale and even home-based refining workshops did exist, and even final consumers often refined sugar domestically by themselves.[92] It was advisable for refineries to be located in areas that had access to cheap fuel, and it was best if they were close to consumer markets.[U] Such heavy investments were often not worth the risk if the product had to be shipped over long distances as sugar crystals could end up clumped together due to humidity, become salty, or even worse, washed away because they were poorly packaged or a ship had taken on water. There was also the risk of capture by pirates or privateers and even the danger of shipwreck.[93] Furthermore, if sugar was refined close to the end markets, the damage suffered during transport, such as water infiltration, could be rectified.[94] Finally, if refined close to consumer markets, it would be easier to adjust the quality of the

T. T. Sarah Peterson mentions that merchants also sold comfits, cakes, tarts, jams and jellies in England at the end of the sixteenth century; see: T. S. Peterson, *Acquired Taste: The French Origins of Modern Cooking* (New York: Cornell University Press, 1994), p. 5.

U. For Stuart B. Schwartz, the absence of refineries in Brazil and Portugal was due to a lack of competition between Portuguese confectioners, who operated in a less sophisticated marketplace (Schwartz, *Sugar Plantation in the Formation of Brazilian Society*, p. 162; Stols, "The Expansion of the Sugar Market in Western Europe," pp. 260, 270).

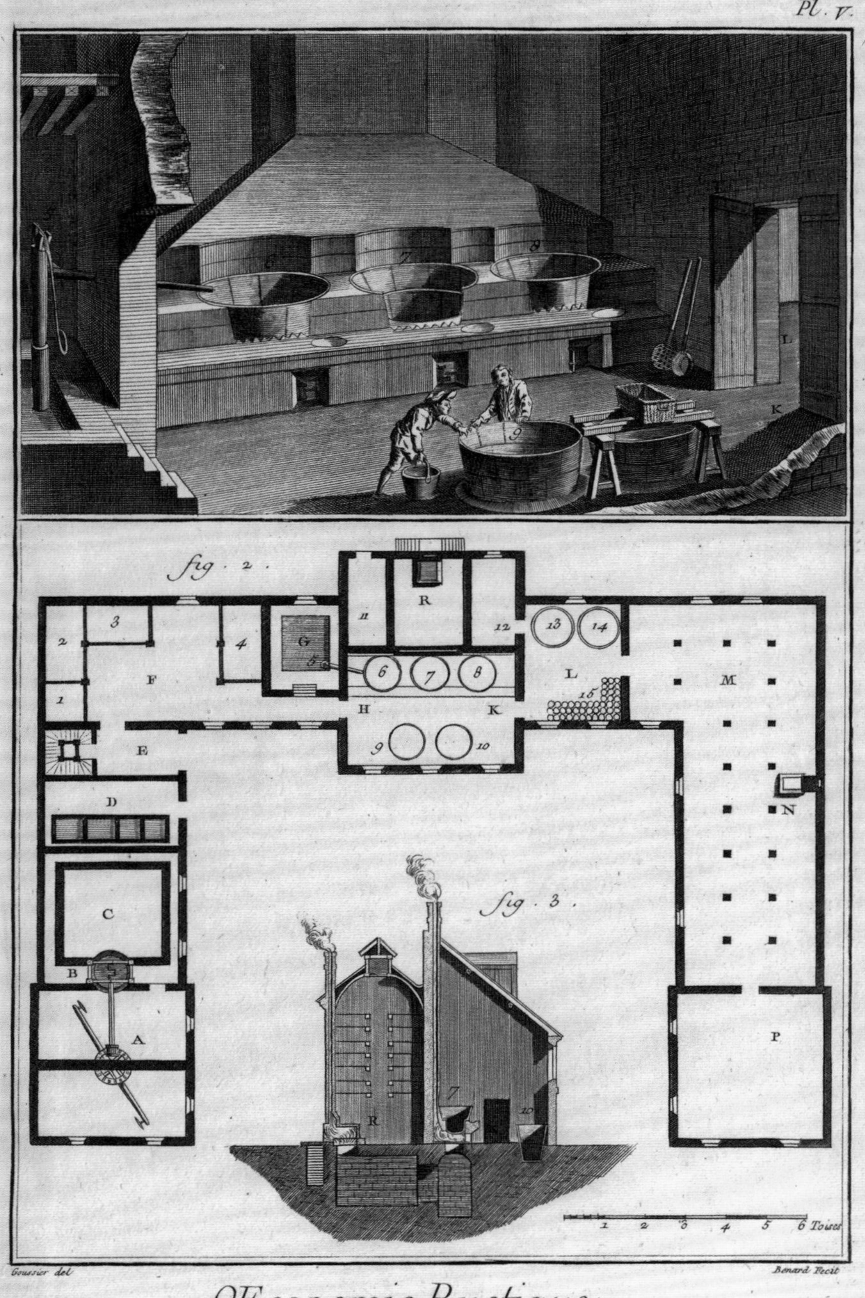

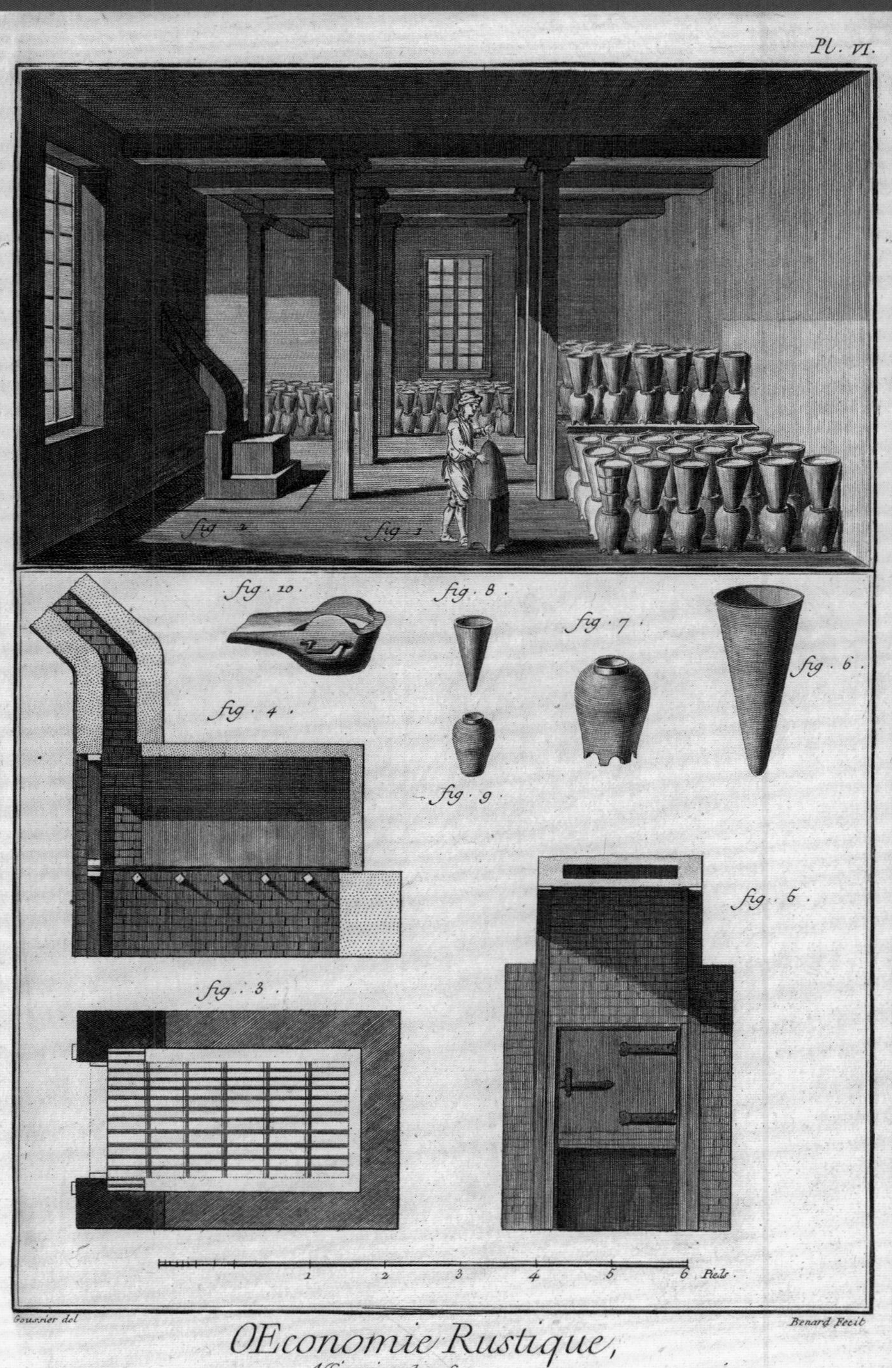

These illustrations from the famous Encyclopedia *compiled by Denis Diderot and Jean Le Rond d'Alembert show the interior of a sugar refinery, its plan and details of its equipment (1762).*

sugar to local demand and avoid incurring high costs that might not have been absorbed if the market was more inclined towards products of lower quality and price.

Thus, from the last quarter of the fifteenth century onwards, sugar refining became an emerging sector in some leading Italian and Flemish centers such as Venice, Bologna and Antwerp.[v] Northern Italy and northwestern Europe were the most densely populated, rich and urbanized areas of the continent.[w] They also had access to cheaper fuel compared to the southern Mediterranean or the Atlantic Islands, areas to which the sugar industry expanded.[95] Italian masters may have introduced refining techniques into Antwerp, which by the mid-sixteenth century stood out as a leading mercantile hub, a key locale for the distribution of luxury goods and a prime sugar refining center in northern Europe, if not all of Europe. Then, the city already had a significant number of refiners, about twenty-five. In 1575, there were twenty-eight.[96]

Even so, around the middle of the sixteenth century, a sugar refinery also operated in Lisbon for some time. Run by Italians,[97] it employed between eight[98] and twenty[99] sugar masters.[100] Refining did not develop in Lisbon purportedly because the high fuel consumption it required would have strained the city's resources. In 1620, Friar Nicolau de Oliveira reported that eight sugar refiners were active in Lisbon.[101] However, the existence of refining in Portugal is a subject that merits further research. At any rate, the refining industry in Lisbon was probably aimed at supplying the Portuguese or Iberian market for the aforesaid reasons.

With the expansion of production and consumption, the refining industry spread to various other major European trading centers. By the turn of the sixteenth century, refining briefly surged in London, fuelled by Elizabethan privateering against Iberian ships, mainly vessels laden with sugar from Brazil.[102] Between the 1590s and the second decade of the seventeenth century, refineries were also established in leading French Atlantic ports, such as La Rochelle and Rouen. The expansion of the refining industry reached Leghorn (Livorno), a Tuscan port that emerged in the 1620s. More refineries were created in leading mercantile hubs in Germany, such as Augsburg, Nuremberg and Leipzig, from the mid-sixteenth century.[103]

Along with all the other misfortunes Antwerp suffered owing to the religious, political and military turmoil of the late sixteenth century, it saw the mounting emergence of competitors in sugar refining and distribution, until Amsterdam and Hamburg finally achieved superiority in the 1630s.[104]

v. Given the scope of this study, I have taken a more qualitative approach. Quantitative data pertaining to the consumption of sugar, especially with regard to the Southern Low Countries and Germany, even if fragmentary, can be found in the sources listed in note 95 to this chapter.

w. It is worth noting that regions associated with a high level of consumption and production were connected from the outset: Flemish, Italian and German merchants, apart from other nationalities, and Iberians, of course, actively participated in establishing sugar production in the Atlantic Madeira, the Canary Islands, Hispaniola and Brazil. They participated even more intensely in the distribution of sugar in Europe, which occurred alongside the trade in other exotic and luxury products: spices, fine fabrics, gems, jewelry, etc. Refined or not, from the second half of the sixteenth century, sugar was re-exported from Amsterdam, Antwerp and Hamburg to the Baltic, to the hinterland of Germany and France, as well as to Italy and the Mediterranean. It also reached these markets directly from the Iberian Peninsula, which was often part of shipping, if not trade, between northwest Europe and the Mediterranean. The integration of these markets and their agents makes it difficult to establish a hierarchy among them (Ibid., pp. 265–266, 273; Costa, *O transporte no Atlântico*, v. 1, pp. 98–100).

Sugar Refiner and Refinery in an illustration from the Book of Trades *by Jan and Caspar Luyken (1694).*

The number of active refineries in Amsterdam reflected the increasing importance of the sugar trade to the city's economy. The authors of a 1622 petition to lift the ban on trade with Brazil via Portugal, despite the resumption of the war with Spain (and, consequently, with Portugal and its colonies) in the previous year, stressed this consequence. They stated that at the end of the sixteenth century there had been only three or four refineries in the city, but that number had climbed to twenty-five. There were two other refineries in Middelburg and Zeeland, another in Delft and a fourth in the village of Wormer, both in Holland.[105] If we included the sugar refiners active in Amsterdam, studied by Arjan Pelwijk, the numbers would be even higher—and the industry's growth would have been more robust than the petition stated.[106]

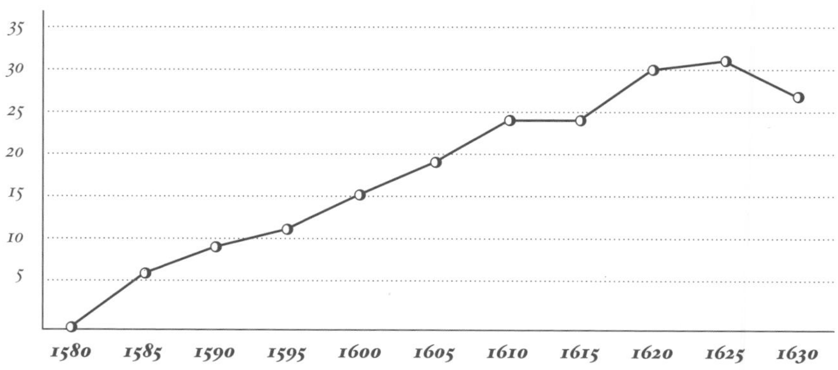

Source: A. Poelwijk, *In dienste vant suyckerbacken:De Amsterdamse uikernijverheid en haar ondernemers, 1580–1630* (Hilversum: Verloren, 2003), p. 56.

Domestic Consumption

The popularization of sugar was not just evident in goodies purchased or received outside the home but was also visible within the household. Yet historians disagree as to the time when sugar consumption became a mass and popular phenomenon, and sugar emerged as a basic and everyday ingredient among the middle and lower classes.

The traditional view of culinary history, greatly focused on France and England, states that sugar only became a popular product in the eighteenth century or, at best, towards the end of the seventeenth century. That was when hot, stimulating and exotic beverages such as tea, coffee and chocolate became all the rage, served with cakes and other sweets. Sidney Mintz may have summed up this debate best by observing that sugar began to be used by a growing number of people, who consumed it more frequently until it became a daily habit. Sugar thus lost its aristocratic aura and became part of commoners' rituals as well.[107]

More recent studies, however, particularly those on regions that began to export or re-export sugar at an early stage, have revised this narrative. While examining the social impact of Portuguese-Brazilian sweets, historian Leila Mezan Algranti observes that sweets were already present on the tables of members of all strata of sixteenth-century society in Portugal, the Atlantic islands and Brazil. Sugar, however, was not yet a basic staple. It was a dispensable and exceptional product that played a role in commemorations, and was associated with public events (religious holidays and secular festivities) and private celebrations (weddings and christenings). On a more personal level, sweets played a social role as treats and gifts, comfort and support, hospitality and entertainment. Algranti concludes by saying: "Thus, as a symbol of status, love, festivities and sociability, sugar took on many meanings without losing its original medicinal and nutritional value."[108] Hence, the role of sweets in the home was not far removed from treats bought from confectioners, sweet sellers and nuns or those distributed during public events.

Stols[109] has gone even further, arguing that sugar was popularized even earlier, and became an important commodity from the late Middle Ages onwards. By the mid-sixteenth century, it was already commonplace throughout Western Europe, and had carved a prominent niche for itself as a culinary ingredient. It played as great a role in the expansion of capitalist trade as did pepper, grain, wool and textiles, products highlighted by classic theoreticians.[Y] Stols demonstrates how sweets became popular in the Low Countries, a region that emerged as a center for the distribution of sugar in the sixteenth century. Sweets were a prominent part of the budgets of merchants' households, and the wealthier ones introduced new utensils made of porcelain, copper and silver to accommodate and handle sugar, sweets and cakes: pots, skimmers, molds and baking kettles, graters, spoons and sugar bowls. It is no surprise that the oldest known sugar bowl belonged to a Portuguese New Christian woman who lived in Antwerp in 1617, and also owned several other sets of utensils related to sweets.

As Antwerp became a leading sugar refining center in the sixteenth century, there are indications that the lower classes used the molasses that were

X. Poelwijk attributes the difference to small entrepreneurs who served as their own refiners, who were overlooked by the surveys of more industrialized refineries (Poelwijk, *In dienste vant suyckerbacken*, pp. 55–56).

Y. Immanuel Wallerstein, however, refers to other basic foodstuffs, such as fish and meat, apart from fuels, and even mentions sugar as a drive behind colonization. For Fernand Braudel, sugar was a luxury product that was disseminated quite late, along with exotic beverages (for references, see note 109 of this chapter).

Banquet at the Home of Burgomaster Rockox; *Frans Francken, the Younger* (ca. 1630–1635).

discarded during the refining process as a sweetener. There are also signs that some of the common folk used inferior-quality sugar at home, perhaps in the form of sugar loaves, which they consumed sparingly. In Flanders, as in the Portuguese world, sweets played an important role in interpersonal and family relations. They appeared on lists of donations to religious orders, and were presented by wealthier individuals to dependents and retainers, reinforcing hierarchical relationships. Stols carefully observes that these relationships also figured in the depiction of wealthy visitors to their estates portrayed in paintings and engravings by masters from the Brueghel family.[7]

According to Stols, this widespread popularization went beyond the sugar distribution hubs. Prescriptions for preserves, sugar and syrups in a medical volume dedicated to the poor (*Les oeuvres charitables*, by Philbert Guybert, published in 1630) indicate that. The recommendation by another French author, Pierre Belon, that large marine animals be seasoned with sugar, also suggest that this product was used by the lower classes.[110] However, during the early seventeenth century, a French agronomist named Olivier de Serres still discerned an indication of social distinction in the use of honey and sugar, the former being used by individuals of humbler means and the latter by more distinguished members of society.[111] Alain Huetz de Lemps also points out that the use of sugar took longer to trickle down to the lower classes in France.[112]

Silver sugar bowl with "Chinoiserie" decorative motifs and latch (*London, 1683–1684*).

Three sugarloaves, identification plaque of sugar refinery in *Amsterdam* (*eighteenth century*).

As for Portugal, judging by contemporary accounts, sugar was still a treat reserved for the wealthier classes in the last quarter of the sixteenth century. The Archbishop of Goa, Friar Gaspar de Leão, complained that it was precisely greed and the inventions of confectioners, sweet makers and wealthier homes that made the demand exceed the supply. As a result, the price of sugar rose, hindering its access to people who only needed it for medicinal purposes:

> *And so these women arrived on the scene, but with inventions detrimental to the common good. The price of sugar has risen so much that poor sick people cannot buy even an ounce to alleviate their fevers. I can recount an incident that will astound you. I remember that when I was a lad, there was no sugar in Hispania [i.e., the Iberian Peninsula], but in Valencia and that which came from a small island of ours called Madeira. Although that was all the sugar there was, its price never exceeded five hundred réis per arroba. Nowadays, notwithstanding the abundance of sugar incoming from India, and the carracks laden with it arriving from Brazil, it sells for two thousand réis per arroba: this is because of gluttony, the carnal sister of greed, of egg sweets, "trutas" and pastries, and infinite inventions that this greedy lass has invented, going from table to table: so there is no time to appreciate flavors, while stomachs continue to be sacrificed, another extravagance much-loved by these people.*[113]

Z First, by Pieter Brueghel, the elder, and then by Jan Brueghel, the elder, and Pieter Brueghel, the younger, between 1597 and 1625 (Stols, "The Expansion of the Sugar Market in Western Europe," pp. 249–251).

Sweets played an important role in interpersonal and family relations. They appeared on lists of donations to religious orders and were presented by wealthier individuals to dependents and servants, reinforcing hierarchical relationships.

Visit to the Farm; *Jan Brueghel, the Elder (ca. 1597).*

While sugar was still a luxury at the end of the sixteenth century, this situation changed quickly, so much so that in the first decade of the following century, the jurist, linguist and historian Duarte Nunes de Leão observed that what had once been a symbol of social distinction for the upper classes was now a sign of distinction flaunted among the humble artisans who toiled for a living. He may have been exaggerating when he wrote that the quality of marmalade, jams and fruit pastes made with sugar, ambergris and musk was a cause for envy among them:

> *But because in Portugal people were so enamored with the inventions from the islands of Madeira, Cape Verde, São Tomé, and Brazil, from whence shiploads of sugar come every year, that they no longer use honey, unless the foodstuff prepared necessitates it. Because marmalade, which once was made with honey in noble houses, now an artisan will not eat it but if it is made from sugar with hints of ambergris and musk: which are nowadays also much sought after and a matter of honor...*[114]

In the Dutch Republic, during the war to gain control of the Brazilian northeast, a poet sang, with some embellishment:

> *What hangs from a bough or grows in the fields*
> *Comes here and falls into people's mouths.*
> *How many blows are suffered today in torrid Brazil*
> *To bring its fruits to this faraway land!*
> *No sugarcane grows here in the valleys,*
> *But even so, our youths are gorged with sugar.*[115]

In Brazil, confectionery traditions from Iberia and Madeira came together with tropical fruit and acclimatized European plants, and an abundance of sugar.[116] Moreover, attempts were made to reconcile tropical botanical discoveries with the current humoral medicine. At the end of the sixteenth century, Gabriel Soares de Sousa described plants and trees along the coast and in the hinterland at length, comparing them to European plant life and listing their properties, particularly their medicinal uses. For instance, with regard to cashew fruit, he wrote: "They make a preserve with these cashew fruits, which is very mild, and they are peerless when eaten immediately after being cooked in sugar and sprinkled with cinnamon"; about a certain variety of banana he observed: "they are delicious when cooked in sugar with cinnamon, and when dried in the sun they taste like dried peaches"; as for mangabas (*Hancornia speciosa*): "when they are swollen they are perfect to be preserved in sugar, being very medicinal and tasty"; while cajá (*Spondias mombin*), "which is cold and healthy by nature": "is fed to feverish patients, since it is cooling and tasty, and the fruit has the same name as the tree, which grows far from the coast."[117]

During the second decade of the seventeenth century, Ambrósio Fernandes Brandão explained how to make marzipan with Brazilian pine nuts, harvested from araucaria trees (and hence different from the Portuguese variety), and how to use guavas or araçá, decidedly tropical fruits, to treat digestive problems.

Many people use them [pine nuts]. After shelling them they remove the thin skin around and in the middle of the kernel, for which reason they have to be split in half, and then they join them again and enclose them within a fruit known as guava, and, if no guavas are available then they use a fruit called araçá, and they leave them to roast along with the fruit on the embers, and when it is roasted they remove them, because with the heat of the fire the nuts release all their toxins into the fruit, and, once the fruit is discarded, they grind the nuts in a mortar with a little bit of white sugar, which the nuts incorporate, and once everything has been incorporated they make a small cake, which they once again roast on a clay pot resting on coals, it then becomes a dough like marzipan. It is necessary to keep in mind that only five nuts should be used for purging, which the patient should ingest an hour before dawn, and it is wonderfully effective, after which the patient should be fed chicken broth to control the bowels.[118]

Brandão also recommended replacing blancmange with a gruel of cassava (manioc) flour, chicken and fish broth and sugar, which was called "mingau" in Brazil. A few years later, Friar Vicente do Salvador also recommended giving patients a mixture of cassava flour and sugar.[119] Brandão also highlighted the qualities of a squash known as "guiné" in Portugal and "jerimu" in Brazil, which lasted a long time when preserved with sugar.[120]

Algranti emphasizes that sweets had an impact on social relations in the colony as well: for wealthier freepersons, it meant distinction; for slaves, social levelling, when they were given sweets as a gift or a food supplement (in the case of inferior sub-products derived from the sugar production process, which, as has been seen, were given to them).[121]

Re-evaluating the Properties of Sugar

The first divergences from age-old medical traditions began to surface in the sixteenth century. A mystic and alchemist Paracelsus questioned humoral medicine and stated that illnesses were not caused by internal imbalances of humors, but were instead intoxications due to external aggression, which could be cured with small doses of the same toxin. Cures could be effected with minerals. This medical philosophy was rooted in Arab and European alchemical traditions, knowledge of minerals dating back to Antiquity, neo-Platonic cosmology, Renaissance Hermeticism and, no less important, folk medicine. However, considering the weight of Classical authority, especially in European universities, and Paracelsus's pedantic personality and his unorthodox ideas with regard to cosmology, it is no surprise that he initially had few followers, and those remained on the fringes of the medical establishment. Some of them found employment as physicians in royal courts and in medical academies associated with universities. They laid great emphasis on laboratory experiments, which they viewed as a means of revealing the secrets of the cosmos.[122]

One of Paracelsus's followers was Joseph du Chesne, who became the physician of Henry IV of France towards the end of his career. It was precisely during a surge in sugar production in Brazil in 1606 that Du Chesne voiced the first "scientific" criticism of the consumption of sugar: "Under its whiteness, sugar hides a great blackness and under its sweetness a great acrimony, such that it equals aqua fortis [nitric or sulphuric acid]."[123] He was possibly alluding to the aftertaste and the blackened teeth and cavities found in individuals who ate sugar. Following in the footsteps of Paracelsus, he said that sugar could even prove to be a solvent capable of dissolving gold, and that traditional physicians did not understand this because they only had superficial knowledge of it. At the same time, a German botanist, Jakob Theodor, known as Tabernaemontanus, extolled the qualities of sugar from Madeira and the Canary Islands, but warned that sugar could rot the teeth, at least in individuals with a bilious temperament. Another follower of Paracelsus, an Italian named Leonardo Fioravanti, condemned the excessive consumption of marzipan and preserves. However, many more swallows would be needed to make a summer, as people paid little heed.[124]

According to Flandrin, the period when humoral medicine had the strongest influence on cuisine took place precisely during the second half of the sixteenth century and the first half of the seventeenth century.[125] From then on, gastronomy tended to distance itself from the principles that had guided it for centuries. This is clearly evident in French cookbooks. Although sugar consumption increased, the num-

Apothecary sugar containers, probably from the convent of Nossa Senhora do Vencimento do Monte do Carmo, in Lisbon (ca. 1755–1785).

ber of recipes containing sugar declined. There were fewer meat, fowl, fish and vegetables recipes that included sugar, which was now considered as being less compatible with them. This marked the beginning of the contrast between sweet and savory (salty) flavors.

Sweets were increasingly reserved for luncheon, more like modern breakfasts, as well as snacks and other light meals. For dinner and supper, the equivalent of our modern-day lunch and dinner, sweets were relegated to the end of the meal, along with almond milk and rosewater. Arab traditions began to give way. Most dishes were now meant to serve the purpose of a Renaissance salad, that is, to stimulate the appetite. Fruit went from being an appetizer to a dessert, and when it was served as an appetizer it was accompanied by salty ingredients, such as smoked ham. In more sophisticated meals, sweets were served not only at the end of the meal but also between each course, comprising several dishes. If hosts wanted their guests to linger after meals, a salad was served as dessert or after dessert. At the same time, the use of sugar increased in recipes involving grain, cereals, eggs and milk products, apart from fruit, lemonade and new colonial sweet drinks, coffee, tea and chocolate. Colonial beverages, fruit and some comfits were served as snacks and light repasts. confectionery was firmly associated with pastries.[126]

This trend took longer to take hold in other parts in Europe and even peripheral areas of France, as Flandrin noted when analyzing accounts by French travellers abroad in the late seventeenth century. They complained about the excessive use of sugar and ambergris in Biscay, and the sweet salads in Flanders and even Ireland.[127]

This trend was also evident in Portugal, but the transformation would not be completed until the end of the seventeenth century. The oldest printed cookbook in Portugal that has survived to modern times, *Arte de cozinha* (*Art of Cooking*) was published in 1680.[AA] The author, Domingos Rodrigues, served Queen Mary Frances of Savoy, whose parents had been served by the author (François Pierre de la Varenne, 1615–1678) of the classic *Le cuisinier françois*, a benchmark for the new trends. According to Alfredo Saramago, Rodrigues's book became a reference work for Portuguese haute cuisine, which had previously tended to equate sophistication with ostentation instead of pleasing the palate, so much so that excessive sugar and spices distorted the natural flavor of food.

Arte de cozinha also introduced vegetables and increased the use of spices (in 70 percent of the recipes), but curiously enough, it significantly reduced

AA. Apparently, another sixteenth-century manuscript existed, but it did not survive. Stols attributes the absence of printed cookbooks to the vitality of Portuguese practices, which involved the oral and handwritten transmission of recipes, and does not imply a lack of interest in cuisine (Ibid., p. 245).

their quantities in each. The ubiquitous blancmange was perforce present. However, there were discernibly fewer references to sugar, which was used in far smaller proportions in meat recipes than in the sixteenth-century manuscript ostensibly written for Princess Mary. In this volume, sugar is mentioned in just 14 percent of the recipes and tends to be placed towards the end of a meal. Sweets are divided into two categories, those eaten with a spoon, generally for dessert, and drier snacks. However, the process of transformation proved to be slow, and tradition and innovation coexisted peacefully. Coatings of sugar and cinnamon lingered on, as did acidic and sweet-sour flavors (50 percent of recipes). Folk traditions such as treats made with couscous and vermicelli, and convent sweets such as egg creams and pastries, blended with foreign innovations such as mille-feuille.[128]

In Flandrin's opinion, serving sugar at the end of meals was part of a process that freed gastronomy from medicine, at least in France. The French were more concerned about the taste of dishes than their dietary functions. Peterson emphasizes that it became increasingly evident that sugar inhibited the appetite and masked tastes, not just from a perusal of ancient texts but as a result of practical experience, towards which the growing supply and consumption of sugar undoubtedly contributed. Culinary historian Rachel Laudan observes that the change in European eating habits in the mid-seventeenth century was only made possible by the new theories that developed in medicine, since otherwise these changes would have been considered dangerous to human health. The new theories not only authorized these changes in diet but took a less favorable view of sugar.[129]

Medicine based on chemistry (or alchemy), known as iatrochemistry, was developed over the course of the seventeenth century by researchers such as Jan Baptista van Helmont, Franz de la Boë (Franciscus Sylvius) and Thomas Willis in the Southern Low Countries, the Dutch Republic and England. Iatrochemists compared digestion, as well as the entire life cycle, to fermentation and distillation instead of cooking, as in humoral medicine. Sugar particularly came under fire towards the end of the century, when iatrochemistry was less controversial.[130] Analyzing the high sugar content of the urine of diabetic patients, Willis, a renowned British doctor, concluded that:

> *Sugar, distilled by itself, yields a liquor scarcely inferior to aqua fortis. Therefore it is very probable that mixing sugar with almost all our food, and taken to so great a degree, from its daily use, renders the blood and humours salt and acrid;*[AB] *and consequently scorbutic.*[131]

Scurvy caused people to lose their teeth. Sugar was no longer the panacea it had been in the past. Worse, excessive consumption of sugar was already perceived to be unhealthy. According to Laudan, these new views of sugar would have prevented cooks from sprinkling it liberally on dishes. Sugar became the subject of a new genre of books that focused on its decorative properties and not its medicinal uses.[132] Nevertheless, at least in the Portuguese world, sugar continued to be used, if not as an active ingredient then as a vehicle* in the preparation of medicines such as syrups or electuaries, consisting of powdered extracts contained in sugar syrup or honey.[133]

Still Life with Sweets; *Josefa de Ayala, known as Josefa de Óbidos (1676). In the mid-seventeenth century, the creations of convent confectionery and popular sweet making stood side by side with French innovations in desserts and snacks.*

* Thanks are due to Márcia Moisés Ribeiro for information regarding the use of sugar as a vehicle for medicines and for suggesting the book mentioned here.

For Mintz, this transformation was the result of a change in the social significance attributed to sugar, which was no longer a sumptuous luxury reserved for royalty. As its symbolic power waned, rich and poor alike came to shun its consumption. According to Mintz, the growing supply of sugar destroyed the mystique that had surrounded this condiment, and it was not surprising that the use of sugar as a spice tended to disappear as sugar itself became more abundant.[134]

In short, the growing supply and widespread consumption of sugar paradoxically resulted in a redefinition of its use. It was now employed more discerningly, although sugar itself was more available and abundant than ever before.

AB. Laudan suggests that the link between sugar and sourness could have been due to the use of egg whites in the refining process; see: R. Laudan, "A Kind of Chemistry," Petits Propos Culinaires 62 (1999): 17.

Blancmange: Portuguese and Brazilian recipes dating from the fifteenth, sixteenth and twentieth centuries:

Princess Mary's manuscript, 16th century

"Blancmange

Take the breast of a black chicken and boil it without salt, and it should not be cooked thoroughly but enough so that one can remove the meat intact and after the meat has been removed put it in a bowl of cold water and then shred the meat, the finer the better. And for one breast you will need one *arratel* of rice, cleaned and washed very well and then dried and cleaned with a cloth and the rice should be crushed and strained through a silken sieve and then put one *canada* of milk in the bowl along with seven ounces of sugar. Then take the chicken and pound it thrice in a mortar and put it into the milk in the bowl. Then add the rice flour and some salt and season it well. Once it is well mixed put it on a low flame and stir it constantly. When it begins to thicken, beat it till it becomes stiff, then remove it from the fire in time and keep beating it and when it is half cooked add the sugar and taste it and if it is not too sweet you can add some more sugar and when it is cooked remove it from the pan and fill it into bowls, dusting them with powdered sugar."

Source: A. B. S. Hosokawa, "O tratado da cozinha portuguesa – códice, *I.E.*, 33: aspectos culturais e linguísticos," PhD dissertation, Universidade of São Paulo, 2006, pp. 298–300.

Arte de Cozinha [Art of Cooking], by Domingos Rodrigues, 1680:

BLANCMANGE

"After semi-cooking a chicken breast, shred the meat into a bowl. With a spoon add 2 canadas of milk, 2 arratels of sugar and 1¼ arratels of rice flour, mix everything well and cook it together. While the mixture is cooking, gradually add ½ a canada of milk to refresh it and 1 arratels of sugar. When it is cooked (which can be ascertained by piercing it with a knife and seeing if it comes out clean), add some flower water, remove it from the flame and cut it into pieces. A fish or lobster blancmange can be made in the same manner instead of using chicken."

Source: C. Couto, *Arte de cozinha: alimentação e dietética em Portugal e no Brasil (séculos XVII–XIX)* (São Paulo: Editora Senac São Paulo, 2007), p. 61.

Açúcar [Sugar], by Gilberto Freyre, 1939:

HEAVENLY PERNAMBUCO BLANCMANGE

"The milk of 1 coconut, 3 teaspoons (60 g) of cornstarch. Sugar to taste. 1 small spoon of salt. Heat all the ingredients in a pan until the mixture is well cooked. Moisten a mold and put the mixture into it, cooling it until it can be removed without breaking."

Source: Freyre, *Açúcar: uma sociologia do doce*, p. 143.

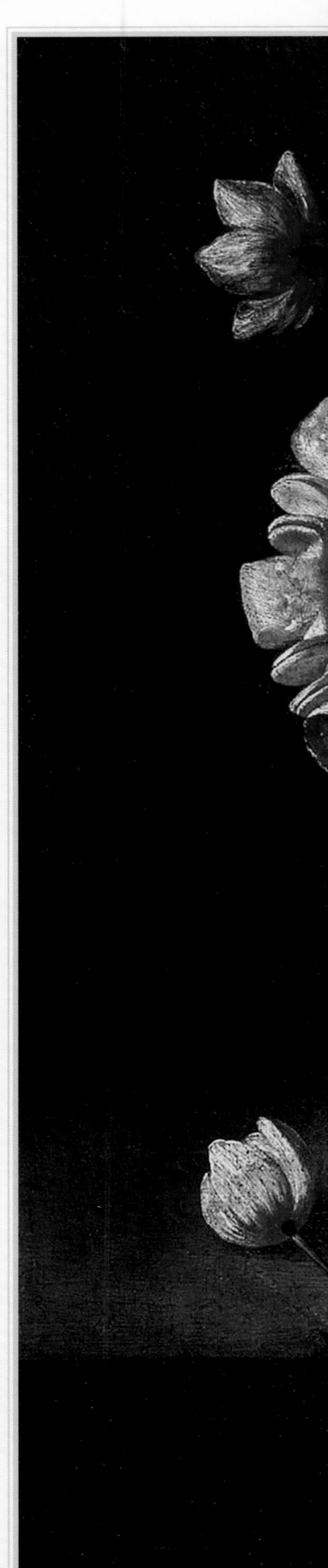

Still Life: Basket with Flowers and Various Types of Sweets; *Josefa de Ayala, known as Josefa de Óbidos (1630–1684).*

Into the Mouth

Chapter Three

1. See the discussion about the uses of sugar in Mintz, *Sweetness and Power*, p. 78.

2. Peterson, *Acquired Taste*, pp. 1–3; Mintz, *Sweetness and Power*, pp. 96–97; Galloway, *The Sugar Cane Industry*, p. 23.

3. Mintz, *Sweetness and Power*, pp. 82–83; R. L Barbieri and E. R. T. Stumpf, "Origem, evolução e história das rosas cultivadas," *Revista Brasileira de Agrociência 11*:3 (2005): 267–271.

4. *Inventários e Contas da Casa de D. Denis (1278–1282)*, *Arquivo Histórico Português 10* (1916): 48–51; Arnaut, *A arte de comer em Portugal na Idade Média*, pp. 44–45.

5. Peterson, *Acquired Taste*, pp. 15–18; R. Laudan, "Birth of the Modern Diet," *Scientific American 11* (exclusive online issue, 2004): 11.

6. Peterson, *Acquired Taste*, pp. 1–3; Mintz, *Sweetness and Power*, pp. 85–86.

7. B. Larioux, "Cozinhas medievais (séculos XIV e XV)," in J. L. Flandrin and M. Montanari (eds.), *História da Alimentação* (São Paulo: Estação Liberdade, 1998), pp. 454–456, 458; Mintz, *Sweetness and Power*, pp. 84–85.

8. A. G. Debus, *Man and Nature in the Renaissance* (London: Cambridge University Press, 1978), pp. 16–17; Laudan, "A Kind of Chemistry," pp. 9–10; Laudan, "Birth of the Modern Diet," pp. 11–13; Couto, *Arte de cozinha*, p. 52.

9. J. L. Flandrin, "Tempero, cozinha e dietética nos séculos XIV, XV e XVI," in Flandrin and Montanari, *História da Alimentação*, p. 481; Mintz, *Sweetness and Power*, pp. 96–97.

10. Peterson, *Acquired Taste*, pp. 24–25.

11. J. L. Flandrin, "Da dietética à gastronomia, ou a liberação da gula," in Flandrin and Montanari, *História da Alimentação*, p. 675; Mintz, *Sweetness and Power*, p. 101.

12. Laudan, "Birth of the Modern Diet," pp. 11, 13; Flandrin, "Tempero, cozinha e dietética," pp. 481–482, 487–488.

13. Laudan, "A Kind of Chemistry," p. 11.

14. Flandrin, "Tempero, cozinha e dietética," pp. 486–488, 493; Flandrin, "Da dietética à gastronomia," pp. 668–669, 675–677; Couto, *Arte de cozinha*, pp. 52–53; Saramago, *Para a história da doçaria conventual portuguesa*, p. 23.

15. Laudan, "Birth of the Modern Diet," p. 11; J. L. Flandrin, "Preferências alimentares e arte culinária (séculos XVI–XVIII)," in Flandrin and Montanari, *História da Alimentação*, p. 654; Flandrin, "Tempero, cozinha e dietética," p. 495.

16. Peterson, *Acquired Taste*, pp. 4–5.

17. Larioux, "Cozinhas medievais," pp. 455–456.

18. Peterson, *Acquired Taste*, p. 4; Flandrin, "Preferências alimentares e arte culinária," p. 655.

19. Laudan, "A Kind of Chemistry," pp. 9–11; Laudan, "Birth of the Modern Diet," pp. 11–13; Flandrin, "Tempero, cozinha e dietética," p. 486; Flandrin, "Da dietética à gastronomia," pp. 668–669, 676; Couto, *Arte de cozinha*, p. 53.

20. Laudan, "Birth of the Modern Diet," p. 14; idem, "A Kind of Chemistry," p. 11.

21. Stols, "The Expansion of the Sugar Market in Western Europe," p. 244.

22. Laudan, "A Kind of Chemistry," pp. 11–12; Mintz, *Sweetness and Power*, p. 103.

23. H. J. Cook, *Matters of Exchange: Commerce, Medicine, and Science in the Dutch Golden Age* (New Haven: Yale University Press, 2007), p. 420, no. 91.

24. Stols, "The Expansion of the Sugar Market in Western Europe," pp. 239–240, 244–245; A. H. Lemps, "As bebidas coloniais e a rápida expansão do açúcar," in Flandrin and Montanari, *História da Alimentação*, p. 612.

25. Godinho, *Os descobrimentos e a economia mundial*, v. 4, pp. 69–70; L. C. Santos Filho, *História geral da medicina brasileira*, V. 1 (São Paulo: Editora da Universidade de São Paulo, 1991), p. 123.

26. Oliveira, *Elementos para a história do município de Lisboa*, v. 15, pp. 379–385, note.

27. Peterson, *Acquired Taste*, p. 53.

28. Ibid., pp. 184–187.

29. Flandrin, "Preferências alimentares e arte culinária," pp. 654, 656, 666; A. Saramago, "Prefácio," in D. Rodrigues, *Arte de cozinha* (Sintra: Colares Editora, 1995), p. 11; Stols, "The Expansion of the Sugar Market in Western Europe," pp. 247–248, 250.

30. Hosokawa, "O tratado da cozinha portuguesa," pp. 79, 82, 87–89, 93; Couto, *Arte de cozinha*, pp. 41–42, 44.

31. Mintz, *Sweetness and Power*, pp. 79, 87–91.

32. H. Coutts and I. Day, "Sugar Sculpture, Porcelain and Table Layout 1530–1830," *Taking Shape* (*online papers and proceedings*, 2008): 2.

33. Stols, "The Expansion of the Sugar Market in Western Europe," p. 238.

34. Ibid., pp. 237–240; Coutts and Day, "Sugar Sculpture, Porcelain and Table Layout," pp. 1, 5; Lemps, "As bebidas coloniais e a rápida expansão do açúcar," p. 612.

35. Coutts and Day, "Sugar Sculpture, Porcelain and Table Layout," pp. 3–5; Gouveia, "Açúcar confeitado na Madeira," pp. 40–41; Stols, "The Expansion of the Sugar Market in Western Europe," p. 252.

36. L. M. Algranti, "Alimentação, saúde e sociabilidade: a arte de conservar e confeitar os frutos (XVth–XVIIIth centuries)," *História: Questões & Debates: Revista do Departamento de História da UFPR* (2005): 47; idem, "Os doces na culinária luso-brasileira: da cozinha dos conventos à cozinha da casa 'brasileira,' séculos XVII a XIX." *Anais de História de Além-Mar: Revista da Faculdade de Ciências Sociais e Humanas da Universidade Nova de Lisboa 6* (2005): 149; A. Vieira, *Açúcares, meles e aguardente no quotidiano madeirense* (Funchal: CEHA Biblioteca Digital, 2004), p. 3.

37. Mintz, *Sweetness and Power*, p. 123.

38. F. M. S. Viterbo, "Artes industriaes e industrias portuguezas. A industria sacharina," offprint of *O Instituto: Revista Científica e Literária 55* (1908): 11–12.

39. Gouveia, "Açúcar confeitado na Madeira," pp. 35–37, 39–40, 45; Stols, "The Expansion of the Sugar Market in Western Europe," p. 241; Arnaut, *A arte de comer em Portugal na Idade Média*, p. 48; Vieira, *Açúcares, meles e aguardente no quotidiano madeirense*, pp. 2, 6–7; Godinho, *Os descobrimentos e a economia mundial*, v. 4, p. 80.

40. The duchess also introduced a variety of sweets as part of her repertoire: Arnaut, *A arte de comer em Portugal na Idade Média*, pp. 50, 104.

41. Stols, "The Expansion of the Sugar Market in Western Europe," pp. 243–244; C. Consiglieri and M. Abel, *A tradição conventual na doçaria de Lisboa* (Sintra: Colares Editora, 1999), pp. 20–21.

42. Stols, "The Expansion of the Sugar Market in Western Europe," pp. 244–245, 247; Algranti, "Alimentação, saúde e sociabilidade," pp. 39–43; Flandrin, "Preferências alimentares e arte culinária," pp. 654–655; P. Hyman and M. Hyman, "Os livros de cozinha na França entre os séculos XV e XIX," in Flandrin and Montanari, *História da Alimentação*, p. 629.

43. Ibid., p. 630.

44. Stols, "The Expansion of the Sugar Market in Western Europe," pp. 244–246, 249.

45. Lemps, "As bebidas coloniais e a rápida expansão do açúcar," p. 613; Laudan, "Birth of the Modern Diet," pp. 11, 16; Couto, *Arte de cozinha*, p. 23.

46. Gouveia, "Açúcar confeitado na Madeira," p. 45; Algranti, "Alimentação, saúde e sociabilidade," p. 37.

47. *Ordenações do Senhor Rei D. Afonso V*, V. 5 (Coimbra: Real Imprensa da Universidade), 1792, Title 41.

48. However, Consiglieri and Abel viewed this ban as a protectionist measure against Castilian confectioners, which does not appear to have been the case (Consiglieri and Abel, *A tradição conventual na doçaria de Lisboa*, pp. 31–32).

49. See also: Arnaut, *A arte de comer em Portugal na Idade Média*, pp. 101, 103.

50. Ibid., pp. 22, 44–45.

51. Library of the University of Coimbra, Ms. 696, pp. 270–271, in Arnaut, *A arte de comer em Portugal na Idade Média*, pp. 101–102. See also: Stols, "The Expansion of the Sugar Market in Western Europe," pp. 239–240.

52. Arnaut, *A arte de comer em Portugal na Idade Média*, pp. 101–102; Consiglieri and Abel, *A tradição conventual na doçaria de Lisboa*, pp. 31–32.

53. Freyre, *Açúcar: uma sociologia do doce*, p. 93.

54. *Ordenações Manuelinas*, V. 5 (Lisbon: Fundação Calouste Gulbenkian, 1984), title CI.

55. Arnaut, *A arte de comer em Portugal na Idade Média*, pp. 32, 104.

56. C. Trillo San José, "Los aranceles de la ciudad de Granada al final de la Edad Media," *Arqueología y Territorio Medieval: Revista de Arqueología del Área de Historia Medieval 3* (1996): 256; Gouveia, "Açúcar confeitado na Madeira," pp. 37, 39, 45; Freyre, *Açúcar: uma sociologia do doce*, p. 49.

57. Gouveia, "Açúcar confeitado na Madeira," pp. 39, 42; Vieira, *Açúcares, meles e aguardente no quotidiano madeirense*, pp. 2–5.

58. Brandão, *Grandeza e abastança de Lisboa em 1552*, p. 72. See also: Stols, "The Expansion of the Sugar Market in Western Europe," pp. 242–243; Freyre, *Açúcar: uma sociologia do doce*, p. 93.

59. Brandão, *Grandeza e abastança de Lisboa em 1552*, p. 87.

60. Ibid.

61. Ibid., p. 210.

62. Ibid., p. 212.

63. Ibid., p. 214.

64. Ibid., p. 71 (for Brandão's data). See also: Stols, "The Expansion of the Sugar Market in Western Europe," pp. 242–243.

65. C. R. Oliveira, *Lisboa em 1551* (Lisbon: Livros Horizonte, 1987), p. 99; Consiglieri and Abel, *A tradição conventual na doçaria de Lisboa*, p. 22.

66. Stols, "The Expansion of the Sugar Market in Western Europe," p. 243; F. Castelo-Branco, "A influência portuguesa na culinária japonesa," in R. Carneiro and A. T. Matos, *O século cristão do Japão. Actas do Colóquio Comemorativo dos 450 anos de Amizade Portugal-Japão* (Lisbon: Centro de Estudos dos Povos e Culturas de Expressão Portuguesa, 1994), pp. 617–627.

67. Algranti, "Alimentação, saúde e sociabilidade," p. 37; Stols, "The Expansion of the Sugar Market in Western Europe," pp. 240, 245; De Vries, *The Industrious Revolution*, pp. 10, 44, 52, 71–72, 78, 92, 96–97, 104, 140–141, 177.

68. Stols, "The Expansion of the Sugar Market in Western Europe," p. 242.

69. Vieira, *Açúcares, meles e aguardente no quotidiano madeirense*, pp. 5–6.

70. Although they mainly refer to later periods, see: Algranti, "Alimentação, saúde e sociabilidade," p. 37; Stols, "The Expansion of the Sugar Market in Western Europe," p. 242; S. C. de Almeida, "Noivas de Adão e noivas de Cristo. Sedução, casamento e dotação feminina no Pernambuco colonial," *Varia História: Revista do Departamento de História da UFMG 31* (2004): 231–235; I. M. D. Braga, "Vaidades nos conventos femininos ou das dificuldades em deixar a vida mundana (séculos XVII–XVIII)," *Revista de História da Sociedade e da Cultura 10*, t. 1 (2010): 306, 315–316; P. M. Tavares, *Mesa, doces e amores no séc. XVII português* (Sintra: Colares Editora, 1999), pp. 36–39.

71. Stols, "The Expansion of the Sugar Market in Western Europe," pp. 248–249.

72. E. C. de Azevedo Mea, "A Igreja em reforma," in J. Serrão and A. H. de Oliveira Marques, *Nova história de Portugal*, V. 5 (Lisbon: Editorial Presença, 1998), pp. 441–444; A. Ferrand de Almeida, "As misericórdias," in Mattoso, *História de Portugal*, v. 3, pp. 169–176.

73. Vieira, *Açúcares, meles e aguardente no quotidiano madeirense*, pp. 1, 5–6.

74. Stols, "The Expansion of the Sugar Market in Western Europe," pp. 248–251.

75. Ibid., p. 249.

76. *Primeira visitação do Santo Officio às partes do Brasil: denunciações da Bahia*, p. 331. See also: Freyre, *Açúcar: uma sociologia do doce*, p. 87; J. R. Tinhorão, *As festas no Brasil colonial* (São Paulo: Editora 34, 2000), p. 69; Sequeira, *Depois do terramoto*, v. 3, pp. 413–414.

77. Stols, "The Expansion of the Sugar Market in Western Europe," pp. 241, 248; Freyre, *Açúcar: uma sociologia do doce*, p. 72.

78. Brandão, *Grandeza e abastança de Lisboa em 1552*, p. 196.

79. Consiglieri and Abel, *A tradição conventual na doçaria de Lisboa*, pp. 16–18, 20–21; Brandão, *Grandeza e abastança de Lisboa em 1552*, p. 218; Sequeira, *Depois do terramoto*, v. 3, p. 415.

80. M. J. P. F. Tavares, *Pobreza e morte em Portugal na Idade Média* (Lisbon: Presença, 1989), p. 112; A. H. de Oliveira Marques, *A sociedade medieval portuguesa* (Lisbon: Livraria Sá da Costa, 1974), pp. 136–150; M. Costa, "Os ourives na Lisboa de Quatrocentos," in L. Krus, L. F. Oliveira and J. L. Fontes, *Lisboa Medieval – Os rostos da cidade* (Lisbon: Livros Horizonte, 2007), pp. 288–314; F. Pereira, *Ofícios do couro na Lisboa medieval* (Lisbon: Prefácio, 2008), passim.

81. Silva, *O Porto e o seu termo*, v. 1, pp. 199, 207, 345; A. Cruz, *Os mesteres do Porto. Subsídios para a história das antigas corporações dos ofícios mecânicos*, V. 1 (Porto: Edição do Sub-Secretariado de Estado das Corporações e Previdência Social, 1943), p. 138.

82. Oliveira, *Elementos para a história do município de Lisboa*, v. 15, pp. 373–385, 379–385, note; Consiglieri and Abel, *A tradição conventual na doçaria de Lisboa*, pp. 18–19, 23.

83. Stols, "The Expansion of the Sugar Market in Western Europe," pp. 251–256.

84. N. d'Oliveyra, *Livro das grandezas de Lisboa* (Lisbon: Jorge Rodriguez, 1620), pp. 95, 97, 98.

85. Consiglieri and Abel, *A tradição conventual na doçaria de Lisboa*, pp. 23–25.

86. Miguel de Cervantes Saavedra, *El ingenioso hidalgo don Quijote de la Mancha*, part 2 (Madrid: Oficina de D. E. Aguado, 1836), t. 5, ch. 157, p. 436; F. Desportes, "Os ofícios da alimentação," in Flandrin and Montanari, *História da Alimentação*, pp. 429–430.

87. F. P. Langhans, *As corporações dos ofícios mecânicos. Subsídios para a sua história.* With an essay by Marcello Caetano. (Lisbon: Imprensa Nacional de Lisboa, 1943–1946.), pp. 566–567, 568–571.

88. Stols, "The Expansion of the Sugar Market in Western Europe," p. 249.

89. Algranti, "Alimentação, saúde e sociabilidade," p. 37; Gouveia, "Açúcar confeitado na Madeira," p. 38; Peterson, *Acquired Taste*, p. 5.

90. Stols, "The Expansion of the Sugar Market in Western Europe," pp. 256–257.

91. Schwartz, *Sugar Plantations in the Formation of Brazilian Society*, p. 162.

92. Stols, "The Expansion of the Sugar Market in Western Europe," pp. 268–269.

93. Poelwijk, *In dienste vant suyckerbacken*, pp. 63–64; Schwartz, *Sugar Plantations in the Formation of Brazilian Society*, p. 162; Stols, "The Expansion of the Sugar Market in Western Europe," pp. 260, 270.

94. Galloway, *The Sugar Cane Industry*, pp. 37–40; Stols, "The Expansion of the Sugar Market in Western Europe," p. 260.

95. For quantitative data about the consumption of sugar, see: Stols, "The Expansion of the Sugar Market in Western Europe," pp. 258–260; D. J. Harreld, "Atlantic Sugar and Antwerp's Trade with Germany in the Sixteenth Century," *Journal of Early Modern History* 7 (2003): 148–163; H. Pohl, "Die Zuckereinfuhr nach Antwerpen durch Portugiesische Kaufleute während des 80jährigen Krieges," pp. 348–373; Stols, "The Expansion of the Sugar Market in Western Europe," pp. 265–266, 273; Costa, *O transporte no Atlântico*, v. 1, pp. 98–100.

96. Stols, "The Expansion of the Sugar Market in Western Europe," pp. 260–265, 268–269.

97. Brandão, *Grandeza e abastança de Lisboa em 1552*, p. 215.

98. Oliveira, *Lisboa em 1551*, p. 98

99. Brandão, *Grandeza e abastança de Lisboa em 1552*, p. 215.

100. See also: Consiglieri and Abel, *A tradição conventual na doçaria de Lisboa*, p. 22.

101. Oliveira, *Elementos para a história do município de Lisboa*, v. 15, pp. 245–250, n. 3 (and note on p. 479 in v. 11).

102. Andrews, *Elizabethan Privateering*, pp. 208–209, 230–233.

103. Stols, "The Expansion of the Sugar Market in Western Europe," pp. 270–274.

104. Poelwijk, *In dienste vant suyckerbacken*, pp. 39–40; Israel, *Dutch Primacy in World Trade*, p. 34.

105. IJzerman, *Journael van de reis naar Zuid-Amerika*, p. 103; Israel, *Dutch Primacy in World Trade*, p. 116; De Vries and Van der Woude, *The First Modern Economy*, p. 326.

106. Poelwijk, *In dienste vant suyckerbacken*, pp. 55–56.

107. Mintz, *Sweetness and Power*, pp. 108, 121–123, 140.

108. Algranti, "Alimentação, saúde e sociabilidade," p. 36; idem, "Os doces na culinária luso-brasileira," p. 141.

109. Stols, "The Expansion of the Sugar Market in Western Europe," pp. 237–240, 249. Stols mentions Fernand Braudel and Immanuel Wallerstein: F. Braudel, *Civilização material, economia e capitalismo* (São Paulo: Martins Fontes, 1996). v. 1, pp. 89–160, 161–236, 237–301, v. 3, pp. 75–155, 157–254; I. Wallerstein, *El moderno sistema mundial. La agricultura capitalista y los Orígenes de la economía-mundo europea en el siglo XVI*, V. 1 (Madrid: Siglo XXI Editores, 1991), pp. 59–73.

110. Stols, "The Expansion of the Sugar Market in Western Europe," pp. 247, 250–251.

111. Peterson, *Acquired Taste*, p. 5.

112. Lemps, "As bebidas coloniais e a rápida expansão do açúcar," p. 613.

113. G. de Leão, *Desengano de perdidos* (Coimbra: University of Coimbra, 1958), ch. 7, p. 149. See also: Godinho, *Os descobrimentos e a economia mundial*, v. 4, pp. 69, 75.

114. D. N. Leão, *Descripção do Reino de Portugal* (Lisbon: Jorge Rodriguez, 1610), fol. 42v.; Gouveia, "Açúcar confeitado na Madeira," p. 35.

115. J. B. Hochstrasser, *Still Life and Trade in the Dutch Golden Age* (New Haven: Yale University Press, 2007), Appendix I, pp. 281–282. See also: Stols, "The Expansion of the Sugar Market in Western Europe," p. 253.

116. Algranti, "Alimentação, saúde e sociabilidade," p. 37; idem, "Os doces na culinária luso-brasileira," p. 150.

117. Sousa, *Tratado descritivo do Brasil*, pp. 147–163; Freyre, *Açúcar: uma sociologia do doce*, p. 70.

118. Brandão, *Diálogos das grandezas do Brasil*, p. 77.

119. Oliveira, *A história do Brazil de Frei Vicente do Salvador*, v. 2, fol. 15v.

120. Brandão, *Diálogos das grandezas do Brasil*, p. 135.

121. Algranti, "Os doces na culinária luso-brasileira," p. 156.

122. Debus, *Man and Nature in the Renaissance*, pp. 17–18, 20–21, 27, 29, 31–32; Laudan, "A Kind of Chemistry," pp. 13–14; Laudan, "Birth of the Modern Diet," pp. 14–15; Couto, *Arte de cozinha*, pp. 53–55.

123. Laudan, "Birth of the Modern Diet," p. 15.

124. Mintz, *Sweetness and Power*, p. 103; Stols, "The Expansion of the Sugar Market in Western Europe," pp. 257–258; Laudan, "A Kind of Chemistry," p. 13; Laudan, "Birth of the Modern Diet," p. 15; Flandrin, "Da dietética à gastronomia," pp. 678–679; Couto, *Arte de cozinha*, p. 55.

125. Flandrin, "Da dietética à gastronomia," pp. 667, 675–676.

126. Peterson, *Acquired Taste*, pp. 184–187, 189–190; Flandrin, "Preferências alimentares e arte culinária," pp. 654–655; idem, "Da dietética à gastronomia," pp. 675, 687; Hyman and Hyman, *Os livros de cozinha na França entre os séculos XV e XIX*, pp. 632–633.

127. Flandrin, "Preferências alimentares e arte culinária," pp. 656, 666; Stols, "The Expansion of the Sugar Market in Western Europe," pp. 250–251.

128. Saramago, "Prefácio," pp. 11–23, 26–27, 29; Couto, *Arte de cozinha*, pp. 31, 37–39, 45, 61–63; Consiglieri and Abel, *A tradição conventual na doçaria de Lisboa*, pp. 38–40; Stols, "The Expansion of the Sugar Market in Western Europe," p. 245.

129. Flandrin, "Preferências alimentares e arte culinária," pp. 654–655; idem, "Da dietética à gastronomia," pp. 675, 687; Peterson, *Acquired Taste*, pp. 184–187, 189–190; Laudan, "A Kind of Chemistry," pp. 12–13; idem, "Birth of the Modern Diet," p. 11.

130. Debus, *Man and Nature in the Renaissance*, p. 27; Laudan, "A Kind of Chemistry," pp. 13–14; idem, "Birth of the Modern Diet," pp. 14–15.

131. Ibid., p. 15 (original quote). For further information about the medical debate regarding sugar, see: Saramago, *Para a história da doçaria conventual portuguesa*, pp. 24–31.

132. Laudan, "A Kind of Chemistry," p. 17; idem, "Birth of the Modern Diet, p. 15.

133. Santos Filho, *História geral da medicina brasileira*, v. 1, pp. 332–333.

134. Mintz, *Sweetness and Power*, pp. 86, 96.

Chapter Four

Dutch Ships Attacking Spanish Galleys near the English Coast in October 1602; *Hendrik-Cornelisz. Vroom (1617).*

Into the Deep

Perils at Sea

The technology available for navigation and the geopolitical context of the age exposed ships and their cargoes to numerous risks. This chapter will examine the procedures, practices and strategies that sought to either prevent or mitigate the damage from such mishaps. In this book, subjects related to shipping are often based on a critical reading of the meticulous seminal study by Leonor Freire Costa on sugar transport between Brazil and Portugal, as well as Christopher Ebert's attempts to apply Costa's method to routes that involved the Dutch Republic.[1] *As the reader will see, I have sought to contribute to their work and to that of many other authors, with original data and insights based on my own research and analysis.*

Navigation schools and manuals proliferated in Amsterdam. Above, a navigation school is portrayed on the title page of the Dutch manual Column of Lightning *(1652).*

Opposite, the title page of a compendium on the use of sea charts, also published in Amsterdam (1602).

Since the late sixteenth century, the activities of shipmasters and pilots were regulated in Portugal and required practical experience and theoretical knowledge. Opposite, a page from Viana do Castelo's Sailors' Registry, *dated 1600.*

Rocking the Boat

Ships could run aground on sandbanks, or be swept off course by the tides, delayed by calms or buffeted by capricious winds. Ships were wrecked by storms and adverse winds, rough seas and collisions with a variety of objects, particularly rocks, reefs, shoals, floating ice, icebergs and other vessels. When crews lit fires that got out of hand, their ships could be engulfed in flames.[2]

In many cases, ships did not sink, but simply took in water, which could be enough to damage or spoil their cargo. In Amsterdam, for example, at the request of a Portuguese Jewish merchant, a notary visited the *Post*, a ship that had just arrived from Porto in July 1618, and attested to the delivery of a nearly empty crate of sugar. The merchant demanded compensation, either from the insurers or the shipmaster, who declared that he had indeed received a full crate from the merchant's counterpart in Porto, but that its contents had been dissolved by seawater — a case of force majeure.[3]

The truth is that most of these disasters were not the result of either natural or mechanical mishaps but rather of human fault. Dangerous geographical features, whether visible or not, could be skirted as long as shipowners hired experienced, skilled and careful crews and harbor pilots. Shipmasters, ship's pilots and sailors were expected to anticipate where to find nearby anchorages for repairs and supplies of fresh water, and also be aware of tides, storms, adverse winds, rocks, gravel, sandbanks, tides, frozen stretches and other hazards to be avoided, sailing around them if necessary.[4] As for fires, to prevent most incidents it was enough to have a careful crew that kept a watchful eye on stoves, lamps, pipes and gunpowder, particularly when the ship was rocking.[5]

T'ghebruyck vande Zeecaerte/
Gheschreuen in maniere van een T'samensprake/ meest ghemaeckt door Doctoor Thomas Hood, Professor inde Schole vande Zeevaert tot Londen in Enghelande.
TOT AMSTELREDAM.
By Cornelis Claesz. Boeckvercooper opt water int Schrijfboeck/ bijde oude Brugghe/ Anno 1602.

In actuality, seafarers had already built up nearly a century of experience. By the end of the sixteenth century, the sea routes – known as *carreiras* in Portuguese – were relatively well known. The Crown itself had commissioned exploratory expeditions. A good example of this is the name given to the reefs to the south of the modern-day state of Bahia: "Abrolhos," which in Portuguese means "keep your eyes open." This was a warning to pilots to be alert and skirt the reefs that wrecked many ships sailing to the southern regions of the continent or on their way to the Cape of Good Hope. An expedition sent by the governor-general, on the orders of the central authorities, surveyed these shoals in 1605.[6]

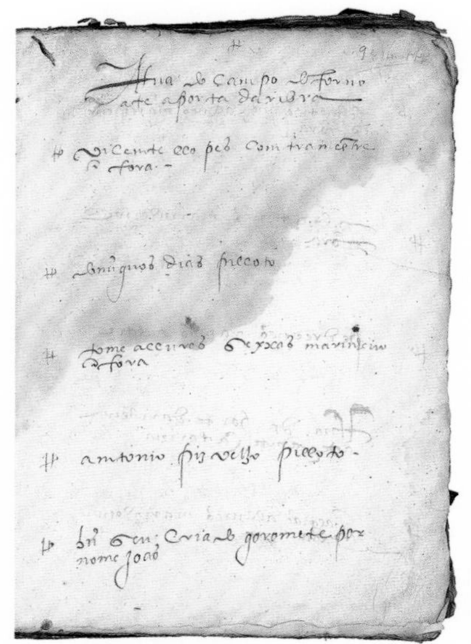

Nautical knowledge was taught by experienced sailors and at schools for pilots. In Amsterdam, there was a steady increase in the number of these courses available from the late sixteenth century onwards. One of them was taught by the famous cosmographer Petrus Plancius, who instructed his pupils from the pulpit of St. Olaf's Chapel (*Sint Olofskapel*), which also sometimes served as a bourse. Manuals for pilots and cartography compilations became a literary genre published in ever-larger print runs. This was how amassed experience was consolidated even further, disseminated abundantly and with increasing accuracy.[7]

It was the shipmaster who commanded its vessel, being responsible for its administration and life on board, while the pilot steered the ship. In theory, from 1592, in Portugal, shipmasters and pilots had to undertake exams, which required a minimum of six round trips, as well as theoretical studies overseen by the chief cosmographer. Apart from nautical expertise, qualifying to become a shipmaster entailed knowledge about shipbuilding, supplies, artillery, munitions, stowing cargo, and so forth. There were specific licenses for each route, hence, a license for the India route (*Carreira da Índia*) was not recognized on the Brazil route (*Carreira do Brasil*) and vice versa. Normally, candidates also made the most of their studies to acquire the necessary qualifications to sail on certain routes while sitting for professional exams for both shipmasters and pilots. However, it is likely that not all shipmasters and pilots were certified, since few obtained licenses and fewer still took care to ensure that their qualifications were noted in shipping contracts.[8]

It was customary to pay the crew at the end of a voyage. Payment consisted of shares in the profits to all, and wages to the senior officers only. This meant that they were all committed to ensuring that their ship arrived safely at its destination. The owners of vessels and cargoes could also hold them liable in civil courts, and the authorities who oversaw their activities could punish pilots for failures attributable to them.[9]

As many accidents occurred near the coast and at the entrance to ports, shipmasters used harbor pilots to guide their vessels into port if local laws or harbor conditions so required. In the city of Porto, it was obligatory,[13] and in Amsterdam, it was necessary. In 1617, merchants living in the Low Countries ascribed responsibility for their vessel being shipwrecked to a shipmaster because he had entered the harbor (through the Vlie passage, north of the island of Vlieland) without a qualified pilot.[14]

Responsibilities and virtues expected of a shipmaster

The importance of a shipmaster's prudence and diligence is evident in the following example: in December 1621, a French shipmaster set sail from Lisbon to Amsterdam with a cargo of sugar and salt. He arrived at the island of Texel, at the entrance to the Zuiderzee, on January 8, in the depths of winter. It is worth noting that Amsterdam is situated at the mouth of the Amstel River and on the waters of the River IJ, which, in turn, emptied into an enormous saltwater lake, the Zuiderzee, an inlet that penetrated deep into Dutch territory (encompassing an area of about 5,000 km^2) until its waters were dammed in the twentieth century. The Zuiderzee was separated from the North Sea by a wall of sandbanks and islands consisting of dunes, the West Frisian Islands, and its two main entrances were near the islands of Texel and Vlieland. This lake was also replete with shoals that hindered navigation.

The shipmaster arrived at the entrance to the lake during the frost. Being unable to enter, he sought shelter in a passage between an isthmus of the continent and the island of Texel, in Huisduinen, near Den Helder. However, floating ice and northwest winds forced the ship to leave this anchorage and seek a safer spot. While weighing anchor, the capstan and the anchor's stocks snapped and, after reaching the sea, the vessel collided with another ship, breaking the top of the main mast and the bowsprit (the mast that projects out almost horizontally from the prow), along with its main yard (the spar perpendicular to the mast, which secures the sails). The ship returned to Huisduinen and, to anchor safely in shallow waters, the shipmaster unloaded its entire cargo of sugar and the salt and hired small boats to take it to Amsterdam.[10]

The shipmaster also hired professionals to repair the vessel and a pilot to guide it to the island of Scholvershoek, in the Heligoland archipelago, off the Elbe estuary, a safe place to wait for the ice to thaw.[11] By the end of March, he was in Amsterdam, where he gave an account of his mishaps and the expenditure he had incurred to the owners of the vessel, who were Portuguese Jews. He was paid for the journey he had just concluded and given instructions for a new voyage.[12]

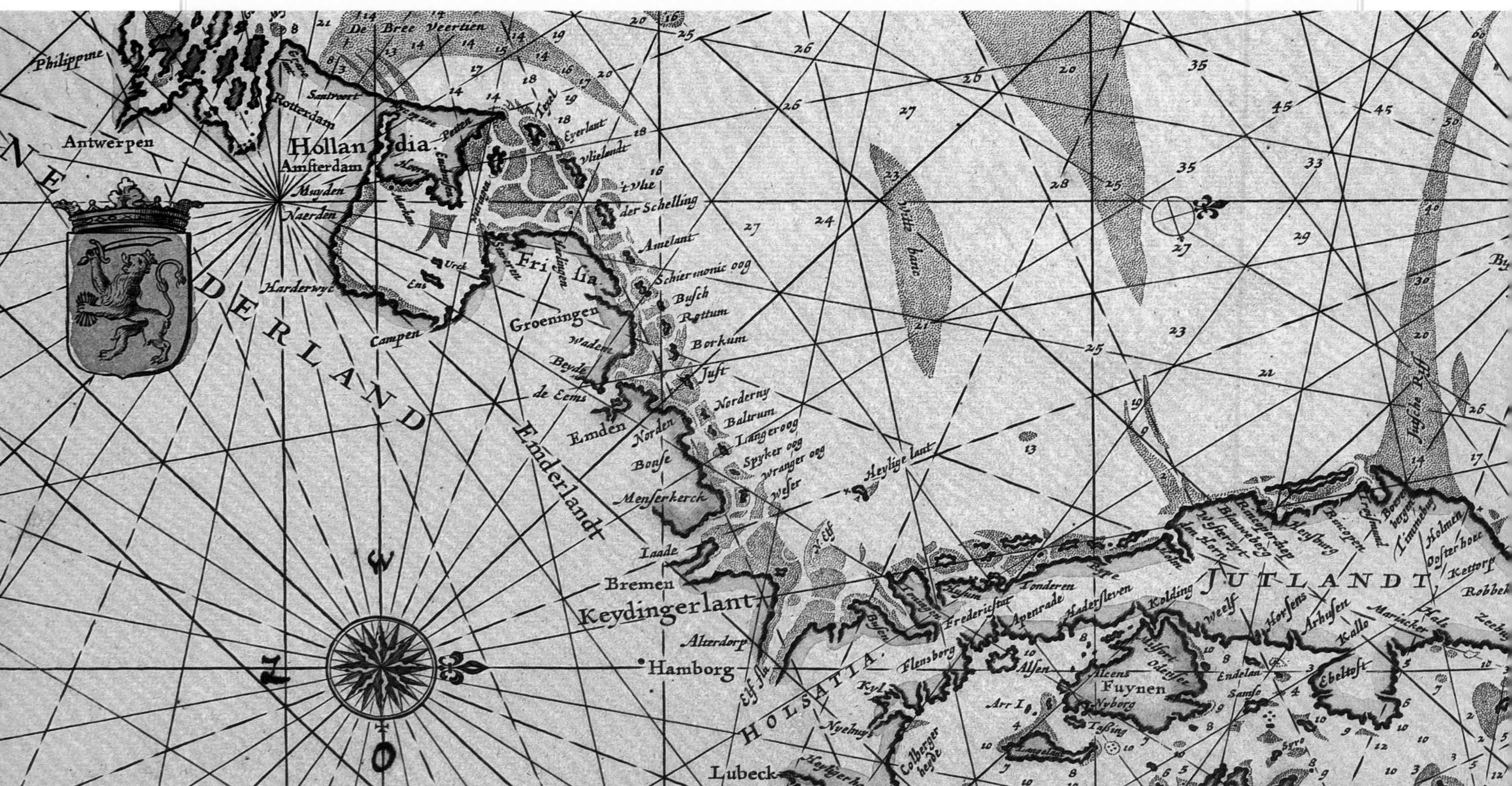

Along with the choice of the crew, the selection of a sound vessel in good condition and carefully maintained were factors that greatly contributed towards surviving mishaps and accidents.[15] Shipping contracts obliged shipmasters and pilots to ensure that the "ship's keel and sides were sealed, the vessel was well sailed and manned and outfitted with everything that was habitually necessary on such voyages so that nothing is lost owing to a lack of such measures."[16] A sealed keel and sides meant a watertight hull. The keel, on which the entire structure of the ship is built, runs along the centerline of the length of the ship at the bottom of the hull. Even though being watertight was an obvious prerequisite, some felt the need to explicitly include this requirement in contracts.[17] In case of accidents, it was recommended that the vessel be equipped with a cauldron to boil pitch in case emergency caulking was necessary.[18] A "well-sailed" ship would be equipped with the appropriate sails; "well-manned" meant that it would have sufficient and suitably skilled sailors; and "outfitted" meant that it would have the necessary sailing equipment, including the masts, rigging – the system of ropes that held up the masts and sails – anchors, spare canvas to repair sails, and so forth.[19] In some cases, the individuals chartering the vessel were even more specific about the equipment they thought necessary: one of the documents uncovered during this research stipulates that the ship must be "outfitted with two sets of sails, one of which is to be new, with the vessel's oars, mooring ropes and anchors."[20]

Apart from having a suitable hull and equipment, it was no less important to stow the merchandise safely below deck in order to keep it dry and safe from harm. It was common for shipping contracts to contain clauses such as this: "The said shipmaster will stow [the merchandise] inside the said ship below its decks in dry and suitable places, and well packed."[21] The shipmaster was also supposed to ensure that the cargo was well distributed,[22] make the vessel ready, and take on all necessary supplies for the voyage. Apart from being repeatedly stated in shipping contracts, these obligations were already widely recognized and incorporated into the mercantile customs of several countries at the time.[23]

Insurance Coverage

Despite every care and due diligence, after some time fate inexorably prevailed and a ship could sink, take on water, burn or be captured. In fact, privateering and piracy, deriving from the geopolitical context of that age, occasionally benefiting from the crew's mistakes, caused far more damage than misfortunes or adverse weather. In effect, around 1627, at a time when the Dutch West India Company (WIC) was harassing the Brazilian coast and trying to gain a foothold on land, the governor of Pernambuco, Matias de Albuquerque, stated:

> *Experience has shown that for many years now no ship in these parts has been lost at sea coming from that state, because it is already a very familiar voyage and seafarers have a great deal of experience on that route. All the vessels that are lost have been stolen by the enemies of this Crown, the Dutch, the English, Moors, Turks....*[24]

The most persistent human threat was that of Muslim piracy, which intensified after the Morisco population was expelled from Spain between 1609 and 1614. As we saw in Chapter 1, the Moriscos were

Chart of the North Sea, *showing the coasts of the surrounding countries; printed in Amsterdam in the mid-seventeenth century.*

descendants of Muslims who had converted to Christianity in previous centuries, under varying degrees of coercion. After the expulsion order, many of them emigrated to North Africa, openly embracing Islam, and they greatly contributed towards the acts of piracy perpetrated from that region. Muslim piracy – practiced by Berbers, Turks, re-Islamized Moriscos, former Christian captives, and others – was concentrated in the triangle between the Iberian coast, the Canary Islands and the Azores.

Furthermore, the Huguenots (French Calvinists) from La Rochelle, enemies of the papist Habsburgs, attacked Portuguese and Spanish vessels with renewed vigor in the Bay of Biscay (Basque country) and along the Iberian Peninsula's Atlantic coast. English privateering went even further, taking a heavy toll on Portuguese shipping along the coast of Portugal, in the Atlantic Islands and on the shores of Brazil. Peace with France, in 1598, and England, in 1604, reduced the frequency of these attacks, but did not put an end to them. (In fact, English privateering had already been officially suspended since 1603 as a goodwill gesture during the peace negotiations.)

Finally, the Dutch admiralty (navy) and privateers attacked Portuguese vessels, ports, fortresses and colonies from 1598 onwards. They were joined by the Dutch East India Company (VOC), officially created in 1602. The Twelve Years' Truce, the agreement that suspended the conflict between the ruler of Spain (and Portugal) and the Dutch Republic between 1609 and 1621, halted hostilities on a large scale but did not put a stop to occasional attacks across the Atlantic. Dutch onslaughts resumed with redoubled and growing intensity in 1621, and when the Dutch West India Company (WIC) went into action in 1623, it further expanded the impact of the Netherlands' predatory activities. In the opposite direction, Dutch ships were attacked in the English Channel by corsairs from Dunkirk and other ports along the Southern Low Countries in the service of the Habsburgs.[25]

An apparently simple way of reducing these risks was to spread a large consignment into smaller lots among several vessels. These were precisely the instructions a merchant in Porto gave his agent, who was setting out from Aveiro, Portugal, for Pernambuco, with a call at the Canary Islands. The agent was to buy sugar in Brazil with the proceeds of the sale of wine loaded in the Canary Islands and merchandise taken from Portugal on behalf of the said merchant from Porto and several other merchants whom this agent represented, totaling more than 1,500,000 réis. The agent was to send the sugar preferably to Porto or Viana in consignments of up to twenty crates per vessel,[A] mixing crates with higher value, in size and/or quality, with those with lower value: "You will load in each ship that sets sail for this city or Viana up to twenty assorted crates as you think fit, a few more of some than of others."[26]

On another occasion, an agent was instructed to use part of the proceeds of sales realized in Pernambuco to load three tons of sugar aboard the carrack on which he was sailing to the Captaincy (Pernambuco) and which had been chartered for that purpose. The agent was to try and send the remaining proceeds to Portugal by means of a bill of exchange. If he was unable to find a reliable means of transferring the money, he was to send the funds in the form of white sugar via another carrack or ship; only as a last resort was he to send coins, and if so they were to be sent in hulks,[B] which were safer vessels.[27]

Another way of mitigating risks (or rather potential losses) was to take out insurance policies, which obviously meant paying a premium and complying with all the indemnity procedures, which were often laborious. The underlying concept of insurance was essentially not very different from dividing cargo into various ships, that is, spreading the risk. However, in the case of insurance, the risk was transferred to and divided amongst the insurers.

The mechanism was quite simple: a consortium of individuals underwrote an insurance policy, which, at the time, was merely a handwritten private document. A policy specified the indemnity to be paid out in case of a loss, described the goods being insured, the vessel, the route and the premium being paid by the policyholder. In order to take out a policy, the prospective purchaser sought out potential underwriters and showed them the bill of lading. As we shall see in greater detail, the bill of lading was a document in which the shipmaster acknowledged having received a certain consignment, specifying its contents; who was sending the goods; the destination and route; the person who was to receive the goods and the party on whose account and risk it was laden.

On August 26, 1606, a merchant from Porto, a New Christian named Domingos Lopes Vitória, chartered a caravel, the *Nossa Senhora da Boa Nova*, from the shipmaster Baltasar Gonçalves, nicknamed "*o ponha*." The vessel was to transport eight tons of merchandise to Rio de Janeiro, with a stopover in Madeira, and would bring the proceeds from the sale of those goods back to Porto. These transactions were entrusted to an agent of Domingos.[C] On October 30 and 31 and November 1, a Portuguese Jew took out an insurance policy for this cargo in Amsterdam from three Dutchmen. The premium was quite high: 36% of the amount insured. After the ship had sailed, the purchaser of the policy informed the insurers that the cargo shipped had in fact weighed less than the expected eight tons, consisting of four double-sized barrels (one ton each), containing nails, other pieces of metal, 104 quintals of iron and four arrobas of weights and weighing scales.[28] In this case, we can also observe cargoes being distributed among several vessels and covered by insurance. At approximately the same time, Domingos Lopes Vitória sent a second consignment to Brazil on another ship via the Atlantic Islands. It was also of relatively small value, and insured in Amsterdam.[D/29]

In a study on the Amsterdam insurance market in the eighteenth century, Frank C. Spooner has identified war, blockades, piracy, privateering, embargoes and other political or military events as the main factors driving up insurance premiums. In peacetime, the main variables were the seasons of the year, the distance being traveled, the type of cargo and the dangers

A. Leonor Freire Costa also indicates about twenty crates being the number of units loaded into each hulk by Ambrósio Fernandes Brandão's agent in Brazil and by Gaspar Fernandes Anjo in Pernambuco. Costa emphasizes that after 1624, when Dutch attacks on Brazilian soil and in Brazilian waters became increasingly audacious, spreading out cargoes in this manner was less effective, since predatory activities reduced the supply of shipping, making insurance the primary means of safeguarding cargoes; Costa, *O transporte no Atlântico*, v. 1, pp. 188, 387).

B. "... and you will load and send what remains [of the proceeds] on any other carrack or ship coming to Portugal if you do not find a reliable bill [of exchange] through which to send the proceeds; and if you are unable to find a reliable bills or wares, send the proceeds in cash through whichever hulk you see fit coming to Lisbon or Viana" (ADP, NOT, PO2, l. 4, fols. 11–13 [1595-7-5]).

C. A New Christian named Jorge Esteves chartered freight space in the same contract and with the same conditions, for the same voyage (ADP, NOT, PO2, l. 25, fols. 183v.–187v. [1606-8-26]).

D. The consignment was loaded on a ship named *São Miguel*, commanded by a shipmaster named Pedro Álvares of Miragaia, and consisted of a double-sized barrel and another smaller barrel, containing scissors and iron tools, along with six pots of saffron and two barrels of wine (SR no. 249).

Informality and trust in the insurance market

In one curious case, the insurers knew virtually nothing about what they had insured. On a voyage from Brazil to Portugal – possibly from Espírito Santo to Lisbon – a caravel loaded with sugar belonging to several traders was captured by the East India Company fleet. At least three Dutch underwriters had insured the cargo, or part of it, through a policy taken out by a Portuguese Jew who was an agent of the cargo's owner. The insurers wanted to demand the return of the cargo from the Company, and notified the agent, asking him to send them the following details: the names of the shipmasters and the individuals to whom the merchandise was being sent, the amount of sugar insured, the items described in the bills of lading, the bills of lading themselves, and the marks of the merchants on whose risk and account the goods were being sent. The agent knew little more than the insurers: he replied that he did not have the bills of lading, and that he had not been informed of the number of crates or how they were marked. However, he had other crates in his warehouse that had been shipped on the account of the same people and which he could allow the insurers to check the marks on those crates. As to their other questions, the insurers were advised to seek out the caravel's shipmaster, whom the Company's fleet had taken to the city.[30]

specific to each route. There is no reason to assume that these parameters would have been any different during the period examined here. Winter had little influence on voyages to warmer climes such as Portugal and Brazil. However, the longer the distance was, the higher the premiums, but in a relatively low proportion. The premiums for outward voyages were lower than for homebound voyages, probably because there was more information available about the ship and the cargo being sent. There was always a minimum insurance premium, even for the shortest journeys, to cover the risks inherent to port maneuvers. Cargoes with a higher value per volume increased the risks and hence the premiums.

Until the eighteenth century, the main changes had to do with the specialization of shipping and the insurance market.[31] As Amsterdam became the main European emporium, its insurance industry developed further. Businessmen regarded insurance as a side activity in which they could invest part of their surplus capital.[32] Apparently some of them used to underwrite policies jointly, specializing in the routes they were most familiar with. In the case mentioned above, the same individuals underwrote the two policies purchased for the two shipments sent at the same time aboard different ships by Domingos Lopes Vitória.[33]

Taking out insurance meant that there had to be individuals who wanted to insure their goods and others inclined to invest in underwriting policies. Two institutions helped bring these parties together: the Bourse and brokers. Merchants from the most diverse sectors thronged the Bourse, and the role of brokers was to match complementary interests.[34] Sometimes brokers wrote out policies and then looked for underwriters. The brokerage fee ranged from 0.25 to 0.35% of the premium, half of which was paid by the insurer and the other half by the policyholder. Brokers were expected to assess the creditworthiness of the counterparties and not allow contracts between individuals who were unable to fulfil their commitments.[35]

Premiums of up to 7% were to be paid immediately, and higher percentages could be paid in installments, as in the case of the cargo sent by Domingos Lopes Vitória. In theory, insurance was subject to an obligatory deductible of 10% of the amount insured. In the event of a claim, the insurers were notified (*insinuatie*). If it was a total loss or if it the insured goods had not been heard of for a certain amount of time, the policyholder abandoned the goods on behalf of the underwriters; if a partial loss had occurred, the damages assessed were paid. In the latter situation, both the insurers and the insured tried to salvage whatever they could and settle their accounts.

Amsterdam's Former City Hall; *Pieter Jansz. Saenredam (1657). The Insurance Chamber functioned at this site.*

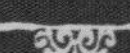

Record Book of the Amsterdam College of Commissioners of Insurance for 1598 to 1621. *Record of a request for restitution of an insurance premium on cargo that should have arrived from Brazil but was never shipped. The policy was underwritten in May 1598 for a voyage from Pernambuco to Lisbon or the Dutch Republic, for 300 Flemish pounds at 10 percent.*

The insured party could, however, authorize the insurers to take any measures necessary to recover any salvageable goods on their behalf, sell them, if possible, and then be repaid or indemnified.

It was not unusual for the broker to conduct these procedures or act as an intermediary. However, when problems were expected, the insured party could opt to use the services of a notary. Brokers also received premiums on behalf of underwriters and took care of financial settlements in case of indemnities.[36]

The payment of indemnities gave rise to fraud on the part of the insured, and malicious evasion on the part of insurers. Both were moderated by another institution, the Insurance Chamber (*Assurantiekamer*). This was a municipal body that adjudicated cases pertaining to insurance and obliged recalcitrant insurers to pay up or exempted them when they were found not to be liable. It also instructed policyholders to pay their debts when premiums purchased on credit had not been paid a timely fashion, and when parties tried to cancel their policies once they were sure that their goods were no longer at risk. This was what the policyholder attempted to do in the case of one of the policies in favor of Domingos Lopes Vitória four and a half months after the policy had been taken out.[8] The individuals summoned were obliged to appear before the chamber on pain of being fined and losing their right to appeal. The chamber's decisions were subject to appeal before the city's aldermen (*schepen*),[37] and fraud cases were sent to the common courts.[38]

The chamber obliged one of the members of the consortium that insured the carrack *Nossa Senhora da Luz*, mentioned in Chapter 6, to pay an indemnity[39] when, almost five years after it was built, the carrack was seized by French pirates on its way back to Porto from Bahia.[40] However, in order for the insured party to receive the 73 pounds Flemish and 12 *schellingen* due, along with an additional 12% interest awarded by the court, he had to present a leading Portuguese Jewish merchant in the city as a guarantor, who pledged to return this sum to the insurer if the insured party recovered the insured goods. This was because both the insurers and the insured were trying to recover them.[41]

The parties presented affidavits prepared by notaries from witnesses such as shipmasters, boatmen, trimmers, porters and assessors, as we have seen in the case of the crate of sugar which arrived almost empty, and which the shipmaster claimed was due to force majeure. The Insurance Chamber sought the assistance of the brokers, who not only knew the parties but also collected information about the routes in question. The fact that Amsterdam was a hub for various routes facilitated the flow of information and reduced the risk of fraud, as we will see in Chapter 10.

There were no insurers in Porto. However, some merchants in that city provided insurance services, which they contracted through their counterparts in larger cities such as Lisbon, Seville and Amsterdam.[42] Similarly, merchants in Brazil used their counterparts in European hubs to insure their merchandise and shares in ships.

Lisbon did not have such highly developed institutions in its insurance market. Policies were written and registered by a "merchandise insurance clerk," who operated in the Insurance House, which was situated on Rua Nova dos Mercadores, a street that also served as a bourse. Litigation involving insurance was judged by the customs house magistrate or the magistrate for India, Mina and Brazil, who had jurisdiction over cases pertaining to shipping and trade, a jurisdiction that was delegated to the Consulate, a short-lived mercantile court formed by merchants. (It was founded between 1592 and 1594 and dissolved in 1602.)[43]

In 1622, the States-General banned insurance coverage for cargoes and vessels belonging to enemy subjects, including the Portuguese and Spaniards. This measure sought to avoid conflicts between Dutch insurers and their fellow countrymen who seized the cargoes. The latter included the Dutch India Companies – first the East India Company, followed by the West India Company – the Admiralty and privateers. The ban had little effect, all the more so because it was difficult to establish if the cargoes belonged to enemies or not, since many consignments were shipped on behalf of merchants living in the city or their counterparts who were based elsewhere, or so they claimed.[44]

Insurance was expensive and possibly not always purchased. This was why a proposal mooted in 1628 came to nothing. It had sought to establish a chartered insurance company to which premiums were to be paid exclusively on pain of confiscation of uninsured ships and cargoes. The *Ghenerale Compagnie van Assurantie* was envisaged as a private organization, with a public charter to be granted to some of the most prominent businessmen in Amsterdam. Its jurisdiction would have encompassed the entire Republic. Merchants and shipowners from Amsterdam opposed the plan, stating that exclusion from competition and the opportunity to invest in insurance was worrisome, as was the prospect of disputing payments with such a powerful institution. Furthermore, they claimed that profit margins were too low to

& The last signature was added on November 1, 1606, and the request for cancellation was filed on March 14 (SR no. 249)

afford paying for insurance premiums as well, observing that, at that time, only those with large sums of money at stake took out insurance policies.[45]

Sugar undoubtedly had a higher absolute value than most of the commodities traditionally bought and sold in the Republic – grain, timber, metal, salt and wine – and, also in absolute terms the profit margins in the sugar trade were higher as well. The oldest known insurance policies purchased in Amsterdam covered a voyage to Portugal, Italy and the Levant, from where products with higher value per volume were also shipped.[46]

Due to the high cost of premiums sometimes only part of the cargo was insured. For example, notarial deeds from Amsterdam record the case of a consignment valued at 450 pounds Flemish shipped from Zeeland to the Canary Islands (where it might have been exchanged for wine subsequently shipped to Brazil) insured for just 350 pounds.[47] It is also possible that when other, equally costly methods of protection were used, such as artillery and convoys escorted by warships, insurance was dispensed with altogether or obtained for an even smaller fraction of the value of the cargo.[48]

Selecting a Vessel

The use of large vessels with enough artillery and men to handle it was an alternative or supplement to insurance. To better understand these methods of protection, we should know more about the types and sizes of the ships that plied the sugar route. A widow from Porto described how her husband and brother-in-law had often sent large numbers of sugar crates in carracks, ships, hulks, caravels and other vessels.[49] In effect, these are the main ships to figure amongst the typologies of Portuguese vessels, in addition to pataches. The types of Dutch ships used on the sugar route explicitly mentioned in the sources consulted include the *fluitschip*,[50] *boeijer*,[51] *vlieboot*,[52] patache and *spiegelschip*.[53]

According to Costa, size more than shape was the main difference among Portuguese vessels, which could be divided into large and small ships. A capacity of 130 tons may be used as the dividing line, above which vessels could be bought or sold tax-free. Some carracks plying the Brazil route even had a capacity of 350 tons.[54] (Tons were measures of volume or, rather, density, corresponding to 1.5 m^3, with up to fifteen quintals [900 kg] of mass.)[55]

The use of large vessels equipped with artillery was effective in dissuading Muslim pirates from attacking. These pirates operated out of northern Africa and, from the 1610s onwards, infested the triangle between Portugal, the Azores and Madeira, with official and unofficial support from the Dutch Republic. They had limited naval resources and their fleets consisted of small vessels, which rarely reached 200 tons. Their tactics were based on superior force and sudden attacks, preferably with the element of surprise (even resorting to the ruse of false flags). They preferred swift and easily maneuverable vessels (sailing ships that could also be rowed), typically xebecs and tartanes, using them to attack easy targets. Such targets comprised small merchant ships sailing unarmed or with limited firepower, traveling alone or separated from their fleets or convoys. When success was doubtful, they preferred to escape with their ships than risk even greater losses.[F/61]

View of the City of Lisbon. *Attributed to António de Holanda; illustrates Duarte Galvão's Chronicle of King Afonso Henriques (sixteenth century), showing two caravels in the foreground sailing toward the right.*

Caravels, "ships" and pataches

Caravels, the iconic vessels of the Iberian "Discoveries," were swift, agile, streamlined vessels without a forecastle. Rigged with three masts and triangular lateen sails, they used oars whenever necessary. The lateen rigging allowed the vessel to sail into the wind, in zigzag fashion. In the Atlantic, caravels were usually small vessels, generally with a capacity of 60 to 80 tons; whereas caravels sailing the Cape route to the Far East, rounding the Cape of Good Hope in the southernmost region of Africa, could reach a capacity of 180 tons.

Another type of relatively small vessel was the "ship" [navio in Portuguese], a generic name used to designate fully rigged vessels with at least one rear mast (mizzen) with a lateen sail for greater agility and two forward masts with square sails (rectangular sails which became rounded when full) to make the best use of the wind. The size of their decks tended to be smaller in order to make the ships more navigable. Although they varied in size, the "ships" that sailed the Atlantic were modest, with a capacity of roughly 40 to 100 tons.

Apart from the caravel, all the other vessels mentioned here had mixed rigging, in some cases more masts, with a larger number of sails per mast, were added. In reality, some larger caravels also had mixed rigging and were hence called "round caravels" (*caravelas redondas*), which are hardly distinguishable from ships. In any case, it seems that they were quite rare on the Brazil route.

Pataches could be converted into military vessels and had much in common with galleons: low and sleek hull lines and four masts, two square sails to the fore and two lateen sails aft. This design allowed for greater speed and maneuverability, which were vital in combat. Their low forecastles reduced their weight and provided a smaller target for enemy artillery. They had a prominent beakhead, which could perhaps be used to ram enemy ships, but this maneuver was costly, since it would break the bowsprit just above the beak-head. Unlike galleons, pataches were generally modest-sized vessels with an approximate capacity of 50 to 70 tons.[G]

F. The same system was used by Turkish and Berber pirates in the Mediterranean, according to Alberto Tenenti, who studied maritime insurance in Venice during the same period; see: A. Tenenti, *Naufrages, corsaires et assurances maritimes à Venise* (Paris: S.E.V.P.E.N, 1959), pp. 29–30.

G. Writing on Moroccan pirates, Roger Coindreau stated, however, that pataches were unsuited for high seas operations; see: Coindreau, *Les corsaires de Salé*, p. 97.

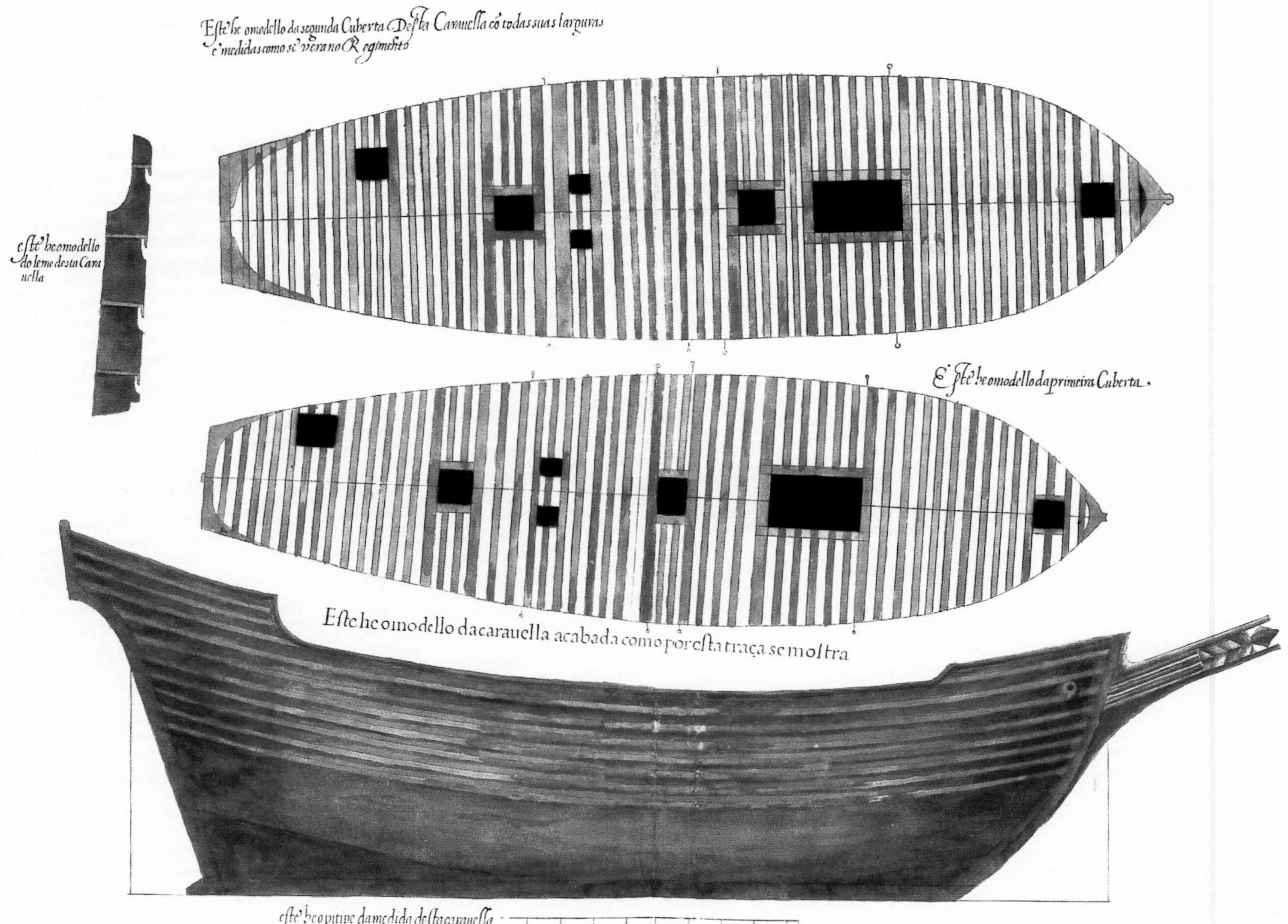

Illustration of a caravel from the Book of Carpentry Sketches, *a Portuguese shipbuilding treatise by Manuel Fernandes. Printed in 1616, this work is an invaluable source for the study of Iberian shipbuilding in early modern times. The headings at the top of the drawing describe the model for the second deck of the caravel; on the left margin, the model for the rudder; on the right, the first deck, and below, the completed vessel.*

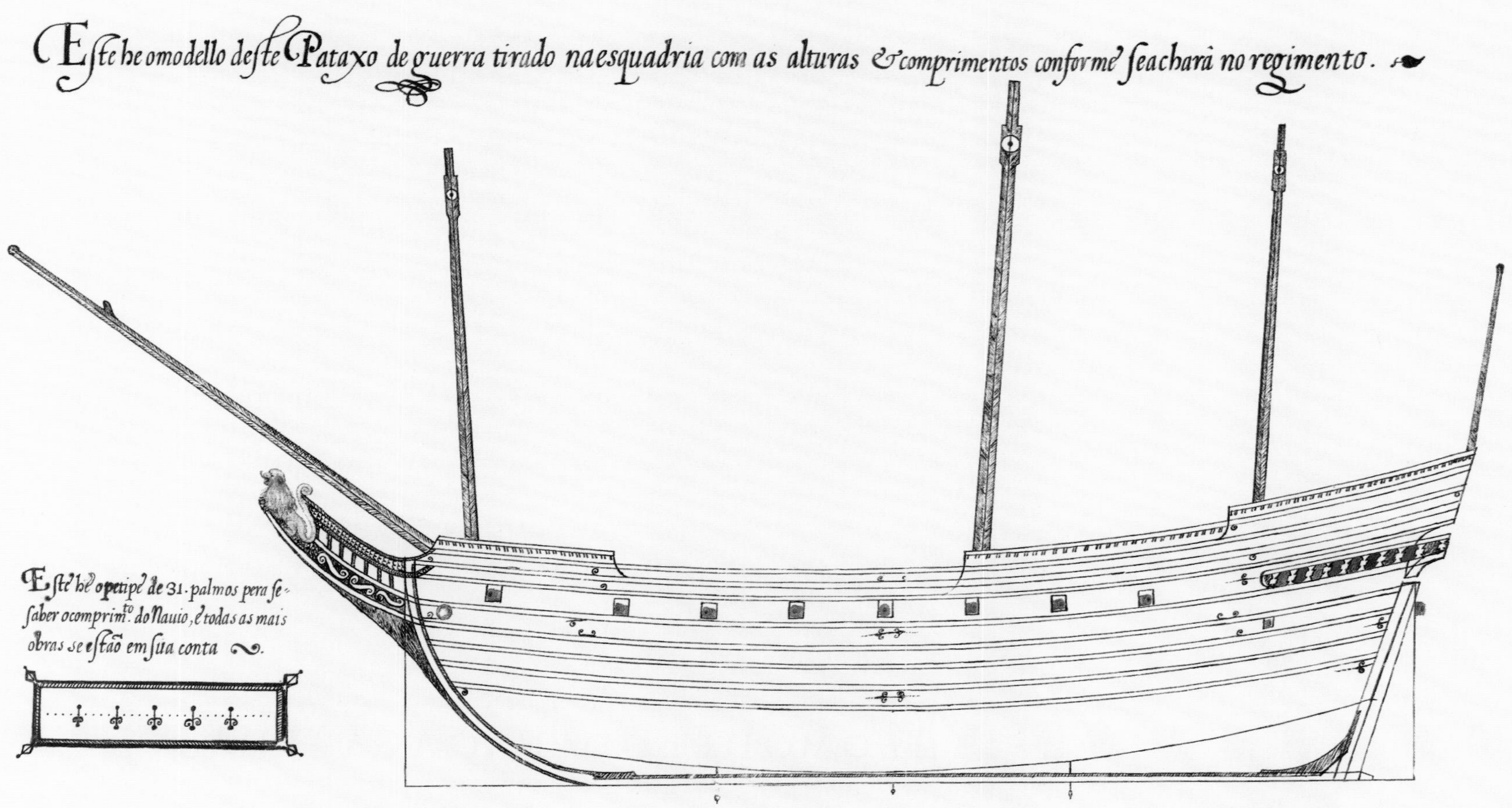
Este he omodello deste Pataxo de guerra tirado naesquadria com as alturas & comprimentos conforme seachara no regimento.
Este he opetipe de 31. palmos pera se-
saber ocomprimto. do Nauio, e todas as mais
obras se estão em sua conta

The same treatise shows a war patache.

Carracks and hulks

Carracks [*naus* in Portuguese] were the largest Portuguese vessels. Similar to the Mediterranean "carracas," they were tall ships with a low correlation between their length and width (about 3:1), and high forecastles and aftercastles, larger in the stern. In terms of their cross-section, carracks were vertically elongated and shaped like a shield. They were ideally suited for transporting cargo over long distances on well-known routes. Apparently, the main difference between ships and carracks was their size, and perhaps the former were more streamlined vessels while the latter were higher and bulkier.[56]

Other vessels with greater capacities plied the Brazil route alongside carracks, but those were foreign ships. In the Portuguese system of nomenclature, "hulk" was a generic designation for vessels built in northern Europe – the Low Countries, Germany or Scandinavia. "Hulks" were equipped with full (mixed) rigging and their size was comparable to carracks, but with more rounded hulls and flatter bottoms. They could also be adapted for war. Their round shape and flat bottom meant that hulks had better floatability, which had two important consequences: it enabled these vessels to enter shallow harbors, such as the port of Amsterdam, and meant that they could transport heavy cargoes. Indeed, since the Middle Ages, Dutch and Hanseatic (German) seafarers had transported grain and timber from northeast Europe, salt and wine from the southwest regions of the continent, and herrings from the North Sea.[57]

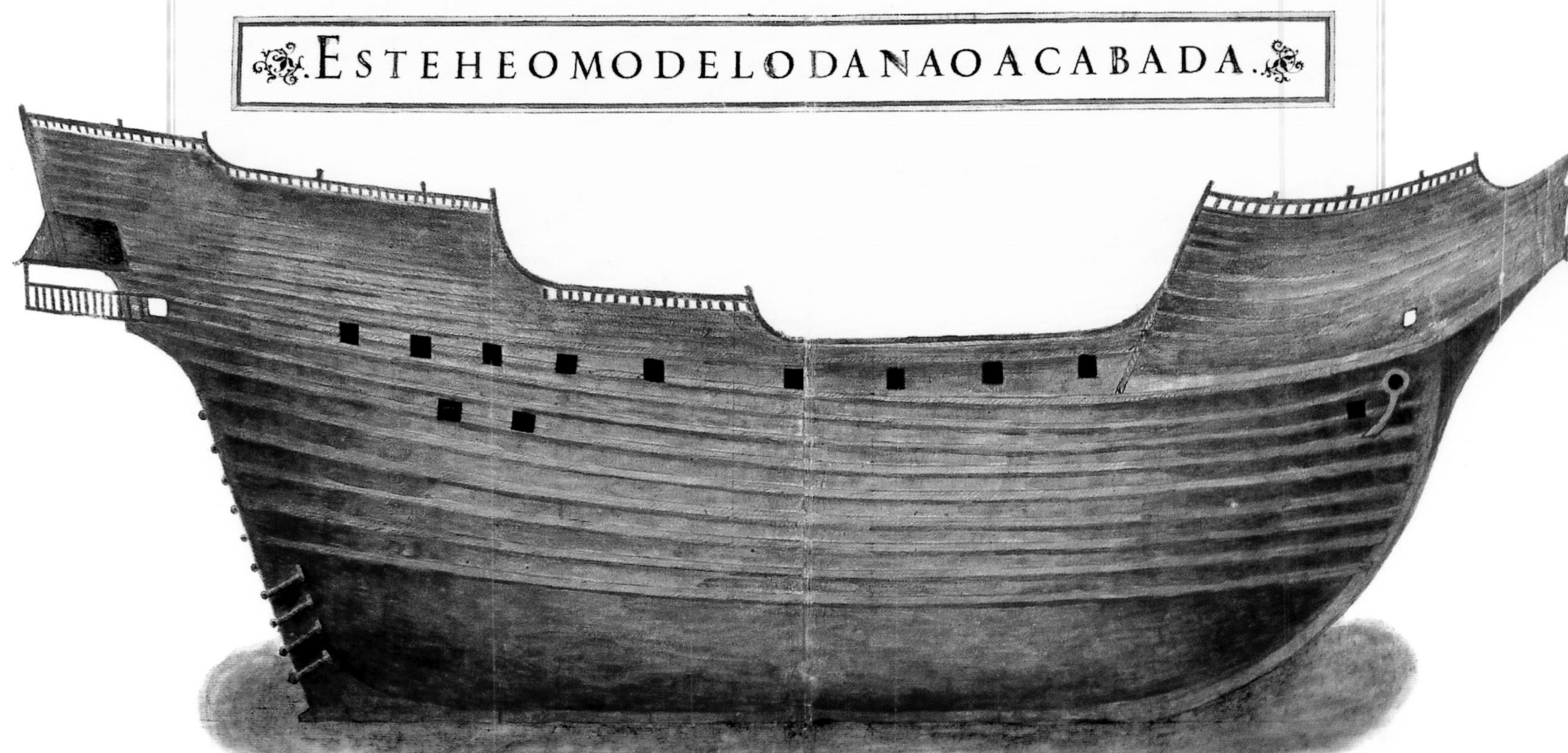
ESTEHEOMODELODANAOACABADA.

Model of a carrack. *Illustration from a Portuguese shipbuilding treatise (1616).*

Dutch hulk and boeijer *portrayed in an engraving based on a drawing by Pieter Bruegel, the Elder (1565).*

Portuguese carrack portrayed on the title page of the Book of the Consulate of the Sea, *printed in Barcelona in 1523.*

The *fluitschip*

The fluitschip or "flute ship" fell into the same category as hulks. Like the *caravela* in the Portuguese-speaking world, the fluitschip was legendary in Dutch narratives as a classic ship. Its design, which dated from the last decade of the sixteenth century, was intended to minimize the cost of transporting goods with small profit margins, low value per unit but large bulk. Its name (flute) was derived from its appearance. When viewed from above, it was very long. Over time, its length grew even further vis-à-vis its width. Its cross-section was pear-shaped, with an almost flat bottom. Overall, it resembled a rustic flute. The prow and stern bulged out, but with a short launch (the distance to the foremost floating point, in the case of the prow, or the rearmost, in the case of the stern), which made it almost perpendicular to the water. This increased the available space within the hold, which resembled a rounded box.

This design was particularly useful for trade in the Baltic, since it reduced the toll charged on ships in the Øresund strait in Denmark, between the North Sea and the Baltic. This toll was calculated according to the width of a vessel's deck, which in the case of the fluitschip was narrower, while its maximum width was close to the ship's bottom. Its volume was well distributed horizontally, along the entire length of its long hull.

It had a small aftercastle and no forecastle. After artillery was introduced to naval warfare, the military effectiveness of the fore- and aftercastles as posts for archers and a redoubt against invaders was greatly reduced. Eliminating or minimizing castles improved the ship's navigability. In southward voyages, which were riskier ventures, it was common for ships to have a lower prow and a beak-head, like galleons.

The fluitschip was known for requiring a small crew in relation to its capacity, due to the greater use of pulleys to handle the rigging. It also had fewer sails, since its masts were relatively short, and perhaps this was why these vessels were slower than Iberian ships, as hulks had been in the sixteenth century. However, speed was a less important factor for efficiency than the cost of the crew and the use of space. Topmasts rigged with another sail were sometimes attached to fixed masts. This increased a vessel's speed without entailing the cost of high fixed masts, which were hard to find and therefore expensive. In the early years, the tonnage of flutes would have been modest, possibly around 200 tons, but they reached their optimum tonnage towards the end of the seventeenth century, with capacities of 300 to 500 tons.[58]

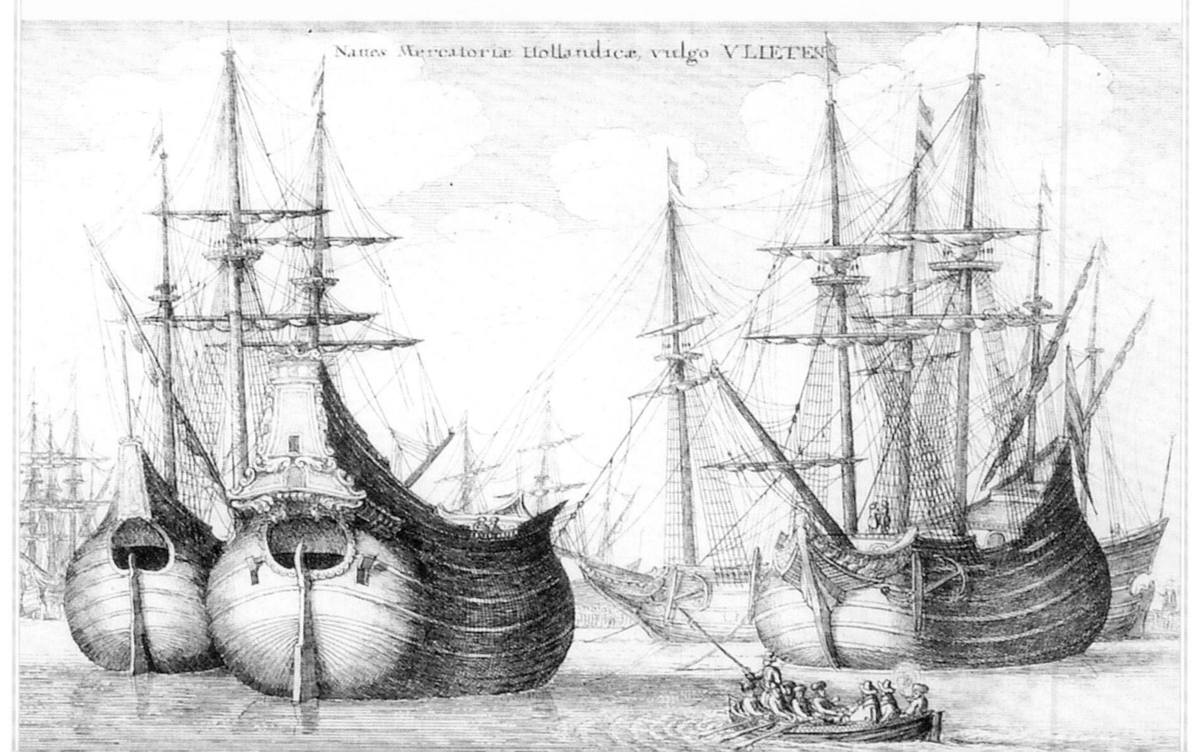

On this page, "Fluitschips" *bound for Asia, much larger than those that sailed the Atlantic.*

Opposite on the left, a pinnace, (the Golden Dolphin*), a vessel better suited for combat, and therefore used on voyages in the Mediterranean, is bound for the Strait of Gilbraltar, while a fluitschip (the* Cat*) is en route to France. Right, another fluitschip, armed and equipped with a beak-head to prepare it for the hostile environment of a voyage to the Iberian Peninsula, alongside a war frigate (*spiegelschip*) from Amsterdam's Admiralty.*

De Hasewint een Spaens Vaerder.
De Vryheyt een Oorloogs Schip

The *boeijer*, *vlieboot*, pinnace and *spiegelschip*

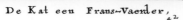

The *boeijer* (or *boyer*) was a vessel whose size was somewhere between those of a hulk and a fluitschip, ranging from 50 to 130 tons, and somewhat similar to caravels. The main mast had a square sail, but instead of being perpendicular to the keel, it followed the vessel's length, as did the rear lateen sail mast. The *vlieboot* was a smaller ship, which rarely reached 100 tons and dominated Dutch fleets in the last two decades of the sixteenth century, along with other smaller vessels.[59] The pinnace and the *spiegelschip* stood out due to their flat sterns, vertical to the water, contrary to the Dutch tradition of rounded sterns, albeit with a short launch. Both could be adapted for war and were more agile, since they had a larger sail area and higher masts. Richard W. Unger, a well-known scholar of Dutch shipbuilding, states that these vessels were more suitable for voyages to the Iberian Peninsula, the Mediterranean and the Indies, where more valuable cargoes could offset the greater expenditure in masts and sails, while their military capacity provided a solution for higher human risks. As can be seen when comparing the illustrations, it was hard to distinguish between a pinnace,[H] a patache and a *spiegelschip*, if there was any difference.[60]

H. The term "pinnace" would later be used to designate a small warship, used in operations requiring speed and agility, assisted by oars (Coindreau, *Les corsaires de Salé*, pp. 93–94; Andrews, *Elizabethan Privateering*, p. 35).

In this engraving by Jan Porcellis, dated 1627, a large boejer *of approximately 88 tons.*

View of the City of Paraíba; *Johannes Vingboons (1665). The Dutch artist's painting shows various types of vessels being used in shipping between Brazil and Europe during the Dutch occupation of the Brazilian Northeast.*

In the 1580s, English privateers also used small vessels, generally under 100 tons, with lighter artillery. This changed in the following decade due to the intensification of the Anglo-Spanish war and England's growing participation in the transportation of high-value Mediterranean and colonial goods, including the privateers' prizes. As many of the vessels used in privateering were originally merchant ships, this increase in their capacities was primarily a response to the need to protect their English owners and shippers.

Anonymous graffiti on a wall in the Church of the Visitation at Wied Quirda in Haz-Zebbug (Malta), portraying a ship, possibly a xebec or a Maltese tartane.

Hence, by the end of the sixteenth century, ships ranging from 200 to 300 tons already predominated in British privateering fleets.[62] These fleets included at least one large and well-armed ship, both to protect their vessels against enemies as well as to terrorize their prey. At the same times, privateering fleets included a small, quick and agile ship, commonly a pinnace or patache. Ideal for catching and boarding prizes, these smaller vessels used oars for swift maneuvers, often sailing against the wind. They could also enter shallow waters where their victims sought safe haven. Such were both the fleets operating along the

Iberian coasts and in the Atlantic Islands, on the one hand, and those that sailed to Brazil, generally during an expedition against Spanish ports in the Pacific, on the other.[63]

Between 1598 and 1609 and after 1621, Dutch fleets followed the pattern of their English counterparts. The Dutch West India Company (WIC) would also continue to use the same tactics to pillage the Iberian Atlantic between 1623 and the conquest of Pernambuco in 1630.[I/64]

Merchant ships, particularly if they were large and well-armed, could fight off these powerful corsair fleets, but were unable to intimidate them. Any skirmish would probably have entailed more losses instead of protecting the merchandise, since corsair crews were larger and better trained for combat, especially when it came to artillery. Hence, the most prudent solution was flight.[J/65]

As a result, the makeup of the set of vessel types used to transport sugar varied according to these martial considerations. The final decades of the sixteenth century were marked by English privateer attacks, and while hulks from the Low Countries, Scandinavia and Germany might not have been able to hold them off, they did at least make up for the losses the Portuguese fleet suffered during a period when sugar production was growing rapidly. In this regard, Brazilian sugar was the main victim of Elizabeth I's privateering against Philip II and III.[66]

Since they provided greater protection, hulks were frequently requisitioned for voyages to Brazil by governors-general and other authorities,[67] as well as to transport currency (see Chapter 8). It can be assumed that the fact that these hulks belonged to residents in neutral nations[K] (Germany or Scandinavia, for example) or were even Dutch vessels disguised as neutral ships, as will be seen shortly, helped protect them against English and Dutch privateering.[68] During this period,[L] foreign hulks and Portuguese carracks, which were both larger vessels, would have transported the bulk of Brazil's sugar production, while the smaller caravels were relegated to a secondary role.[69]

Caravels regained their predominance at the turn of the century since they were better suited to escaping privateers' attacks, whose fleets were growing more formidable. The intensification of Barbary piracy in the second decade of the century – at the height of the Twelve Years' Truce – would have encouraged a greater use of carracks. Finally, the WIC's operations in the Atlantic obliged merchants to use a mixed strategy of combining different kinds of vessels: caravels to flee from the Dutch and carracks to ward off the Moors.[70]

I. Even during the Twelve Years' Truce (1609–1621), a squadron of the Dutch East India Company (VOC), with ships ranging between 450 and 600 tons, stopped in Brazil on its way to the Strait of Magellan.

J. Venetian shipping also used the same defensive tactic. Most of Venice's ships had small crews and little artillery and ammunition. When facing ships from northern Europe, which were far bigger and better armed, they had no alternative but to try to escape as quickly as possible or surrender, which also seems to have been a common practice. In the meantime, the Venetians tried to encourage the construction of faster ships to flee from corsairs (Tenenti, *Naufrages, corsaires et assurances maritimes à Venise*, pp. 35–36, 39, 47–48). According to Violet Barbour, in the seventeenth century artillery was becoming a decisive factor in naval battles, replacing hand-to-hand combat. For this to happen, shipbuilding and artillery techniques had to undergo a process of specialization that ended up distinguishing warships from merchant ships. This process, however, continued beyond the end of that century; see: V. Barbour, "Dutch and English Merchant Shipping in the Seventeenth Century," *The Economic History Review* 2:2 (1930): 261–262.

K. However, neutrality could unravel through an alliance with aggressors, as was the case with the Dutch crew of a hulk who joined the English privateers who attacked Bahia in 1587; see: Berger, Winz, and Guedes, "Incursões de corsários e piratas na costa do Brasil," p. 494.

L. According to Costa, to a certain extent this period went on until 1605, when, in her view, foreign ships stopped visiting the colony in compliance with Portuguese laws. From the time when foreign shipping to Brazil was banned that year, caravels were hastily mobilized to make up for the absence of foreign vessels. Originally used for fishing, some of these caravels were redeployed on the Brazil route. Their smaller size meant that less capital was needed to build each vessel. This consequently entailed smaller consortia of owners and, hence, greater agility in terms of outfitting. Even between 1601 and 1614, a time Costa dubbed the "period of caravels," carracks and hulks continued to sail, as indicated by customs records in the city of Viana (Costa, *O transporte no Atlântico*, v. 1, pp. 190–198, 200–206.)

The Dutch Fleet Defeats Spain in the Battle of Gibraltar in 1607; *portrayed by Cornelis Claesz. van Wieringen (ca. 1619). In the center, a small, easily maneuverable vessel is used to board a slightly bigger ship. At the same time, large and well-armed ships around them give each other cover and protection. Left, the ship flying the Portuguese coat of arms seems to be firing on the sailboat that is preparing to board. When sailing in convoys, larger ships were responsible for engaging attackers in combat with heavy artillery.*

Ships of different tonnages were also used in the stretch between Portugal and the Low Countries.[M] Vessels with larger capacities were preferable when the voyage to Portugal was part of an itinerary that only ended in the Mediterranean and it was necessary to be prepared for a far longer voyage with many stopovers, lengthy sojourns and uncertain itineraries, which were determined along the way.[71] These vessels were also more susceptible to Muslim piracy and naval forces in the service of the Habsburgs. The size of Dutch vessels that carried not only sugar and other colonial products from Portugal, but also low-value, bulky commodities such as salt might well have been larger.[72]

Apart from the safety factor, the size of the vessels had an impact on the economics of shipping. Large vessels generally employed a proportionally smaller crew and the investment necessary for building and outfitting each ton of carrying capacity was also lower. Moreover, size was not overly detrimental to speed. Finally, in the case of Portugal, the Crown, wishing to encourage the use of larger ships to increase its naval might, exempted large vessels from paying a 10% transfer tax (*sisa*) on sales and purchases.[73]

However, the greater efficiency of large vessels was less critical on transatlantic voyages, since, unlike the long journeys to India, zigzag itineraries around Mediterranean ports and the triangular traffic between West Africa and the Americas, the sailing time between Portugal and Brazil was relatively short – about two months for the outward journey and three for the way back to Europe[74] – dispensing with the need for large amounts of supplies that took up carrying capacity. Moreover, bigger vessels required larger investments, not only to purchase them but also to maintain a larger crew. These investments in additional capacity paid off only if more efficient use of the vessel's space and time was made. Such efficiency gains required goods ready to be loaded on ports and, as we will see, a great deal of coordination among the vessel's loaders, who often were to be found on the other side of the Atlantic.

It was easier to optimize the capacities of smaller vessels, which in turn reduced the need for large stocks on land and the need to coordinate among parties or endure long waits in ports.[75] Furthermore, the construction and acquisition of these vessels was cheaper in absolute terms. Notary deeds from that period illustrate this: a quarter of a carrack was sold in 1617 for 340,000 réis, while a quarter of a caravel was purchased four years earlier for 60,000 réis, both purchases having been made in Porto.[76] Such com-

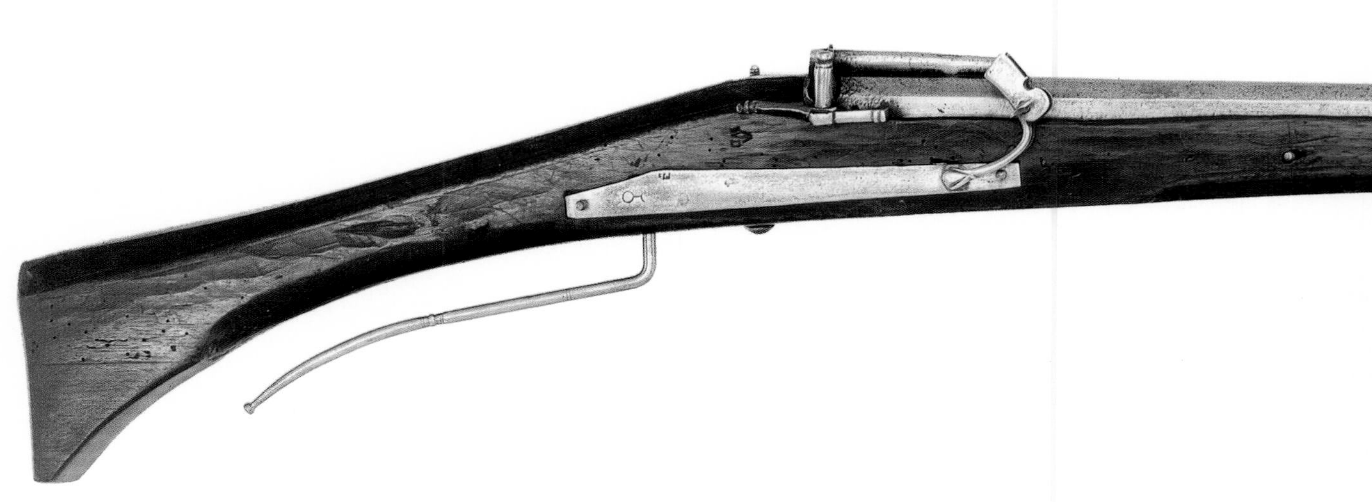

Matchlock musket (ca. 1560).

parison should also take into account the ships' capacities and age, as well as the supply/demand ratio and inflation; the figures nonetheless do indicate the order of magnitude in the price difference.[77]

Still, the sugar trade probably afforded profit margins that allowed some leeway for inefficiency in shipping, as well as higher freight rates to ensure cargo safety.[78]

Arming Ships

A large ship was of little use in terms of protection if the vessel was not equipped with artillery, and even smaller ships were sometimes heavily armed. Shipping contracts often obliged the shipmaster to take along "four pieces of heavy artillery and two stone guns with some muskets and pikes." This was what was required for a carrack that was to sail between Porto and Pernambuco, calling in at the Canary Islands, in 1615.[79] The previous year, another carrack,[N] which was to sail directly to Bahia, was required to have six pieces of heavy artillery and two stone guns, with sufficient gunpowder, ammunition and gunners.[80] "Heavy" artillery meant large cannons, while stone guns were smaller guns that fired rocks.[81]

Although artillery and the gunners to handle it could safeguard against losses caused by pirates, they also made the voyage more costly. In a shipping contract signed in 1615 for a voyage from Porto to Rio de Janeiro, the parties signed an addendum stating that, owing to extra expenditure of 100,000 réis on artillery, the charterer of the vessel was to pay an additional 500 réis per ton, adding up the freight rates to 10,000 réis, instead of the original 9,500 réis.[82]

M. According to Richard Unger, sixteenth-century Hanseatic hulks were large but Dutch hulks generally did not exceed 200 tons and usually had a capacity of 50 to 130 tons; see: R. W. Unger, *The Ship in the Medieval Economy* (Montreal: McGill-Queen's University Press, 1980), pp. 223, 262. Based on data pertaining to voyages between the Baltic and Portugal, Ebert emphasized the large capacities of ships plying the route between the Low Countries and Portugal, which ranged, on average, between 100 and 200 tons before the Twelve Years' Truce and between 200 and 300 tons during the Truce. However, Ebert did not distinguish between voyages to the Mediterranean that called in at Portugal from those whose final destination was Portugal. He also did not distinguish between different destination ports in Portugal and the cargoes they offered, particularly salt-exporting ports such as Setúbal and Aveiro. The author underscores the fact that this route was dominated by products with a low price-volume ratio, such as grain and salt, and that shipping contracts for these large vessels rarely mentioned the presence of sugar, even though he believed that it would undoubtedly have been shipped aboard many of them (Ebert, "The Trade in Brazilian Sugar," pp. 112–113). My research regarding ships chartered by Portuguese Jews in Amsterdam for voyages to Porto, a hub for sugar, shows that vessels generally had a capacity of 200 tons or under, slightly less than the norm for ships visiting Setúbal, the leading port for salt shipments. The ships that sailed to the Mediterranean via Portugal had far larger capacities, ranging from 240 to 400 tons (references can be found in note 72), apart from being far better armed. A plan to levy a tonnage tax on ships' capacities, submitted to the Dutch States-General in 1634, declared that ships which habitually sailed to Portugal, Spain and the Mediterranean had capacities of around 400 tons. Odette Vlessing observes that such capacities would also have been the norm for the sugar trade with Portugal until 1621. However, I believe that the large ships mentioned in the document would have referred to vessels sailing to the Mediterranean, which called in at Iberian ports (Vlessing, "New Light on the Earliest History of Amsterdam Portuguese Jews," p. 72, n. 87).

N. A third carrack, sailing to Bahia, was even more heavily armed, with eight pieces of heavy artillery, four stone guns, bombardiers for each man, pikes, muskets, gunpowder and the necessary ammunition; see: ADP, NOT, PO1, l. 137, fols. 131–133 (1616-3-11).

Portuguese crews' reluctance to fight privateers

With evident malice and exaggeration, the French traveler Francisco Pyrard de Laval stressed the reluctance of the Portuguese to engage in combat in the Atlantic, stating that they preferred to hand over their precious cargoes rather than risk their lives, even if they outnumbered their opponents. He was referring to his arrival on the Iberian coast in January 1611, when the crew immediately surrendered to an approaching ship suspected of being an enemy vessel: "We encountered a small ship which, like us, was also entering [the port of Baiona, Galicia, where they were bound, due to bad weather in Lisbon], at the sight of which all our Portuguese became extremely fearful, and we might as well have already been boarded by the enemy, even though in all we were close to one hundred men; because they are people who lack self--confidence and have no resolve at all, and are nothing but hollow words and vainglory. They are good traders and good sailors; and nothing else. I am certain that fifteen or twenty Frenchmen could have easily captured us; and the ship was worth more than 500,000 écus." Nevertheless, the fears of his Portuguese shipmates were not unfounded, as Laval himself observed: "The previous day, a corsair ship had seized a caravel in this exact spot; and when we entered, they were both anchored there in the said islands [Baiona (Cíes) Islands], where they unloaded the caravel; but they were on one shore and we sailed along the other, and we went quite close to the city...."[91]

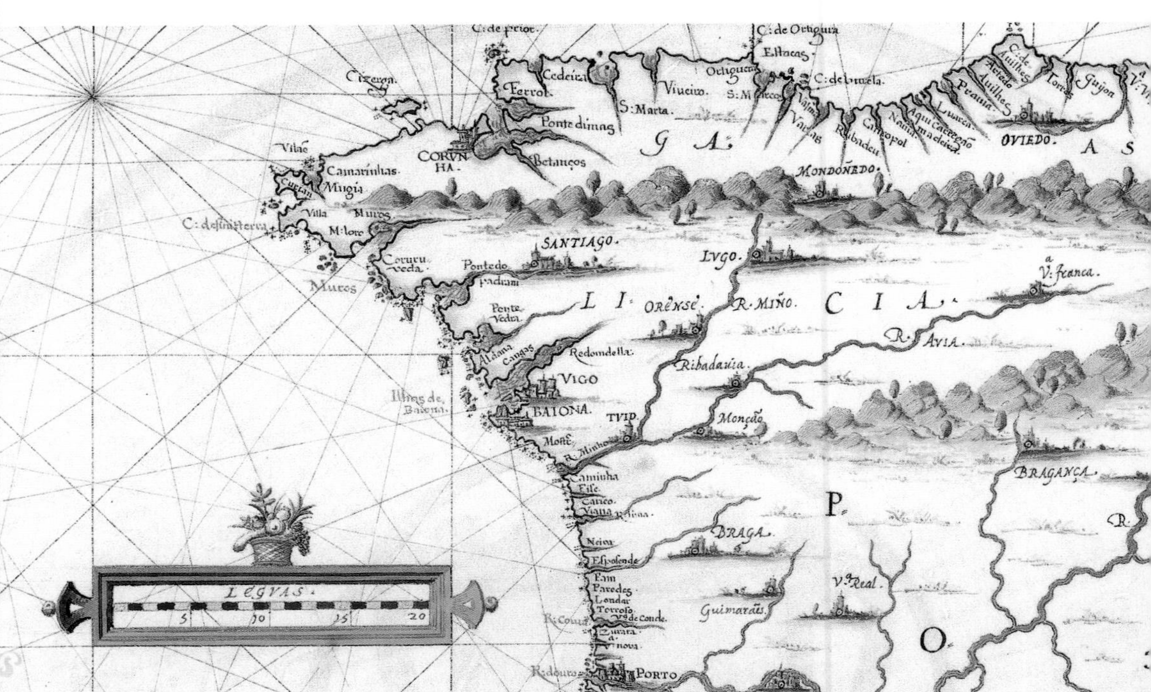

This chart of the western portion of the Iberian Peninsula in the Atlas Cosmografia *(1597 and 1612) shows the Cies or Baiona Islands near Vigo.*

Another addendum, which was even more explicit with regard to artillery costs, was included in a shipping contract signed in Amsterdam in 1609 for a round trip to Porto involving a 200-ton ship. The original freight charge for the entire cargo was 1,430 guldens, but the individuals chartering the vessel agreed to pay 1,550 guldens on condition that the ship was to be armed with eight iron cannons and four stone guns, and to carry a crew of twelve men and a cabin boy, so it would be able to use all its firepower if necessary.[83]

Artillery also entailed indirect costs, since weapons occupied space that could otherwise have been used to transport merchandise,[o] not just due to the additional size and weight of the guns, ammunition and gunners but also on account of the larger quantity of water and provisions necessary for a bigger crew.[84]

In theory, from the middle of the sixteenth century onwards, all Portuguese ships were supposed to carry artillery on board. However, this law was widely disregarded, as was subsequent legislation to this effect.[p] In 1571, King Sebastian reinforced these requirements, and went even further: he stipulated the type of weapons that ships were to carry, in accordance with their tonnage, and required vessels to have a suitable crew which could effectively use the weapons mounted on the ships. In 1622, Philip IV re-enacted King Sebastian's law, complaining that it was being ignored.[85]

Muslim pirates and their Portuguese captives

It is quite possible that seafarers had a more compelling reason to resist Muslim pirates than Christian privateers. In the case of Portugal, the struggle against the infidel was deeply ingrained in its symbolic universe. Portugal had, in effect, been born to this conflict.[92] However, both for the Portuguese as well as for other Christians, there were more immediate and concrete reasons to actively resist the Moors: the latter ordinarily held the surrendered crews as part of the prize. Crewmembers were either held for ransom, with money sent from Europe, or sold into slavery.

In Portugal, the Church granted indulgences to anyone who donated funds to ransom captives in North Africa. Sales of indulgences had helped raise funds for the crusades against the infidels since the Middle Ages, and in the late sixteenth century this was extended to efforts to free those who had fallen under the enemy's yoke. Religious orders and brotherhoods dedicated themselves to this mission.[93] Private individuals also strove to ransom their loved ones, as can be seen in the example of a pilot from Leça, a town near Porto, who pledged to return the money he had received from a "Flemish" merchant living in that city to ransom his cousin who was being held hostage in Algeria.[94]

Christians, on the other hand, could not hold other Christians captive, and generally left defeated crews in boats near the coast, or set them free in the ports to which they had taken the captured ships. Examples include the crew of a Portuguese ship on the Lisbon-Bahia route in 1622, which French corsairs left on the island of Madeira, close to where the vessel was seized. Two weeks after it had set out from Lisbon, the ship had been forced to make an emergency stopover on the island to caulk the hull, which was taking on water. It was taken four days after it resumed its journey.[95]

The following year, near the islands off the coast of Baiona (Cíes Islands), in Galicia, a vessel commanded by an English shipmaster was seized by Dutch corsairs, who left the crew there. They took the cargo of sugar that had been loaded in Viana and was being consigned to a Portuguese Jew in Hamburg.[96] Part of the crew of a Portuguese vessel seized by two VOC ships in March 1619, when the Twelve Years' Truce was still in effect, was taken even further afield. The attack took place between five and six degrees north, possibly in the Gulf of Guinea or between the African and Brazilian coasts. Some Portuguese died in combat and others were taken prisoner. They were transported to the East Indies. One of them was only released in November 1623, when a Company fleet returned to Amsterdam. In the meantime, he served a Company officer in Jakarta and on the Coromandel coast (in India).[97]

O. The use of the Dutch fluitschip to transport bulky and low value products on a large scale became widespread with the Twelve Years' Truce, when it was possible to dispense with artillery as a defense against Dunkirk corsairs (Barbour, "Dutch and English Merchant Shipping in the Seventeenth Century," p. 280).

P. The Venetian senate also tried, to no avail, to make it compulsory to sail in large and well-armed vessels. Some proposals in this regard were discussed but were eventually rejected (Tenenti, *Naufrages, corsaires et assurances maritimes à Venise*, pp. 48, 56).

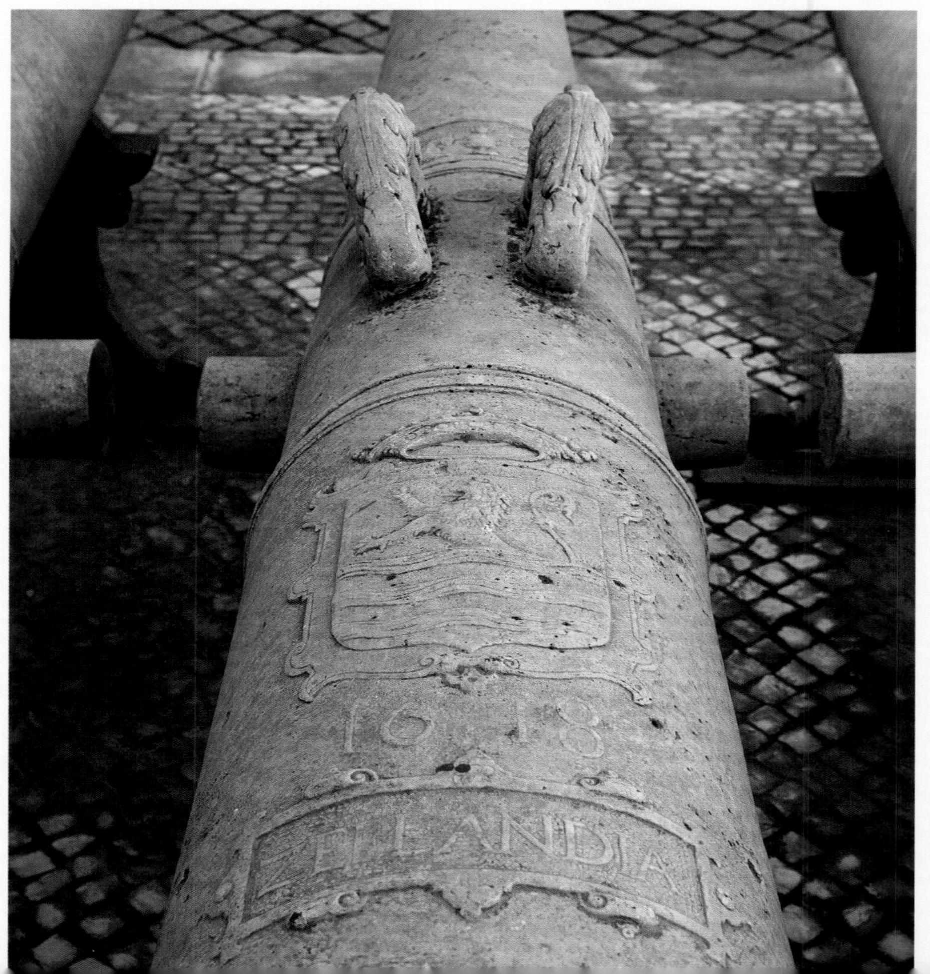

Early sixteenth-century stone gun (Breech-Loading Iron Swivel Gun).

The Book of Trades, *by Jan and Caspar Luyken, published in Amsterdam in 1694, depicts how cannons are made.*

Cannon; *manufactured in Zeeland (Dutch Republic), ended up in Portugal (1618).*

This defiance is not surprising. It did not derive just from the direct and indirect costs of using artillery but also from its effectiveness, or rather the lack thereof. All indications are that gunners were few and far between and not very skilled, as some Portuguese merchants trading in Brazilian sugar in Amsterdam declared to the Dutch authorities. In their view, the artillery aboard Portuguese ships was only used as a form of dissuasion, as well as a ruse to charge higher freight rates, since Portuguese gunners were inept: "Those [ships] which are equipped with artillery do so more to exploit charterers, resulting in higher fright rates, since there is not a single expert gunner in Viana and Porto who knows how to handle the artillery properly; and the king will not allow any Dutchman to travel aboard the vessels."[86]

The shortage of Portuguese gunners both in terms of quantity and quality appears to be corroborated by local sources, and is even acknowledged in government documents.[Q] In 1626, the Crown complained about a reduction in the number of gunners for all the kingdom's fleets, including those bound for India, as well as coastal fleets and those formed ad hoc to assist India and Brazil in times of need against the offensives of the Dutch East and West India companies. The fleets also suffered from intense competition for gunners from fortresses scattered along the coasts of the vast Portuguese empire.[87]

If the king himself found it hard to find gunners, when he could coerce individuals to serve aboard his ships, what hope did private shipowners and charterers have? Offering larger salaries would probably not have sufficed,[R] since the few skilled professionals in that field were already conscripted into royal service.[88] Furthermore, the small Portuguese population was constantly deprived of its youth, especially the most intrepid, who set out, never to return, in search of opportunities overseas or in the service of the Crown there. This weakness was aggravated by the negligible efforts made to train personnel, and to both increase and maintain the number of gunners along overstretched imperial borders in the four corners of the world. It was further compounded by the Hispanic Monarchy's growing reluctance to trust foreigners, even if they were subjects of allied or neutral nations, to serve in the colonies or even to visit them.[89]

Keeping in mind the low cost-benefit ratio of using artillery aboard Portuguese vessels, it is no surprise that shipmasters continued practicing the ruse of weighing anchor from Lisbon with artillery on board, only to sail down the Tagus and leave the guns in the town of Cascais at the mouth of the river. This practice was deplored in the abovementioned regula-

Q. In the sixteenth century, the Crown recruited gunners in northern Europe and, in 1605, a ship from Viana brought a gunner from the Low Countries to Brazil (Stols, "Os mercadores flamengos," pp. 16, 35)

R. In 1618, during the Twelve Years' Truce, the king appeared to consider a proposal suggested by a resident of the Algarve to include foreigners amongst the six gunners who he wished to send aboard each of his two vessels sailing to Brazil (AHU_ACL_CU_005-02, Cx. 2, D. 192 – [Lisbon 1618, December, 21]; D. 193 – [1619]). However, in 1634, when Dutch forces were already operating from South America, shipmasters from the Porto region requested that the artillery aboard their ships be manned by foreign experts, since, according to them, there was an acute shortage of Portuguese gunners and "without them [foreigners] the artillery is of no use." The Treasury Council (Board) advised the monarch to consent to the request, since "many ships are seized by pirates even though they are equipped with sufficient artillery to defend themselves, owing to a lack of gunners" (AHU_ACL_CU_CONSULTA DE PARTES, COD. 40, fols. 21v.–22 – [Lisbon, August 2, 1634]).

tions, which sought to regulate the use of artillery in 1571. As Costa astutely asked: "Of what use was an armed vessel if it was poorly equipped and manned by a crew that was completely unskilled in handling the artillery?"[90]

During periods when Muslim piracy or small Christian expeditions presented a greater threat, the most viable solution may have been to use larger vessels with clearly visible artillery to scare off pirates, as is suggested by the document submitted by the Portuguese sugar merchants in Amsterdam; that is, they had guns but no gunners, additional men or large stores of ammunition. This strategy had a smaller impact on shipping costs, while being somewhat effective in terms of dissuasion. In fact, artillery, gunners and additional men were costly, heavy and took up space, while producing negligible results.[S] Attackers were undoubtedly far more motivated to fight and capture the booty than unskilled seafarers with little incentive to risk their lives to defend other people's ships and merchandise, even if they did receive a share in the voyage's profits.

Travelling in Convoy

To avoid pirate attacks, it helped to group ships together in fleets protected by well-armed vessels. The best situation was for merchant ships, even if armed, to be flanked by warships. In this case, the system was called traveling in convoy. This concentrated naval might was generally sufficient to convince pirates and privateers to look for more vulnerable prey. This was the system used by Portugal on the India route, and by Castile on the *Flotas de Índias* sailing to Spanish America.

The law issued by King Sebastian ordering ships to carry weaponry also decreed that ships sailing to Brazil and São Tomé were to travel in two annual fleets, one in August and another in March. The ships that traveled outside these fleets were to sail with the India fleet as far as the Equator. That envisaged Brazil fleet would comprise just four ships, and the convoy would be only deployed for the outward journey. Nevertheless, when information came in about approaching corsair fleets, the governor-general of Brazil was instructed to ensure that ships returning to Portugal were to travel in groups. In practice, however, until the WIC established an active presence in the Atlantic, after 1623–1624, the term "fleet" continued to be vague and was used only sporadically, on an ad hoc basis and without any effective coercive force being applied by government institutions.

Sailing as a fleet was of little interest to private individuals, irrespective of whether they were shippers or shipmasters. According to Costa, without an escort of warships, fleets offered few advantages, while the disadvantages were clearly apparent. The costs of faster vessels were augmented by having to wait for slower ones, and the scant coordination and discipline among the ships meant that the fleet sometimes scattered midway. In ports, the vessels that were ready to leave had to wait until the other ships were loaded. This situation was aggravated by congestion in ports where ships were being loaded simultaneously, which made the stevedores' work go more slowly. Merchants were disadvantaged by simultaneous arrivals and departures of ships, which saturated markets, causing an excess supply at the time and increasing demand during the rest of the year.[98]

Nevertheless, in light of the growing losses inflicted by the WIC and the Crown's indecisiveness about providing escorts for ships plying the Brazil route, private merchants spontaneously decided to organize their vessels into a fleet in Pernambuco in 1626. They waited until September, so they would arrive in Portugal when the northern European squadrons stayed in port due to the winter ice.[99] Plans to sail in convoys had been considered since the late 1610s, even before the WIC was created. Yet all these proposals included taxes or fees to be paid by shippers to offset the costs of the escort provided by warships. Some suggested that private vessels should be coerced into being converted into warships.[T] Apart from all the aforesaid inherent drawbacks of sailing as a fleet, these additional costs deterred most of the parties involved – merchants, royal officials, sugar-mill owners and seafarers – or, at least, the more influential among them. The first consistent attempt to form a convoy was thwarted by the Dutch invasion of Pernambuco. Concrete measures were only taken when the Dutch had already established a firm presence on Brazilian soil.[100]

To justify the additional costs of the fleet and convoy, it was necessary for the arbitrage to be sufficient or for the value of the cargo to be large enough so that, in absolute terms, the profit margins could dilute these costs. As Ebert has aptly suggested, the absolute value of sugar cargoes probably did not justify the costs incurred on account of large ships as escorts,[U] unlike the precious metals transported by the Spanish *flota* or the spices, gems and Asian products shipped along the Portuguese India route.[101] Costa has emphasized that it was only an increased arbitrage premium caused by the numerous casualties inflicted by the WIC – which reduced the supply of sugar to Europe and European products in Brazil – that induced the players involved in the trade to consider the alternative of traveling together in convoy more seriously.[102]

Interestingly enough, a similar proposal was mooted at about the same time in the Low Countries. The mooted General Insurance Company was also to provide a fleet of warships to escort Dutch vessels.[V] The plan was proposed in 1628, in response to the activities of Dunkirk corsairs in the service of Spain in the Southern Low Countries, but was rejected in 1636. Convoys to the Mediterranean would only be adopted later, but the inherent problems of traveling in fleets also ensured that the obligation of joining such convoys was frequently evaded.[103]

To be sure, sailing in convoys was not an infallible tactic. Larger and well-organized corsair fleets could capture an entire convoy, as in the case

S. "In light of such a threat, Portuguese carracks or hulks bought in Portuguese ports pretended to be well-armed as a means of deterrent, even though it was rare to find weapons on deck that could defend these vessels. Stone guns and muskets, handled by inept crews, were of little use when faced with large and well-armed vessels, such as those that made the Dutch and English privateering seem terrifying. The Salé pirates lacked this power, and carracks gave the Portuguese fleet the impression of being a respectable adversary, unlike caravels, which attracted attention because of their lightweight appearance" (Costa, *O transporte no Atlântico*, v. 1, pp. 196–197).

T. The Venetians also experimented with the system of convoys, for the same reasons. Even though the Venetian authorities imposed convoys in a more stringent manner during this period, citizens still flouted the respective directives (Tenenti, *Naufrages, corsaires et assurances maritimes à Venise*, pp. 44, 48–49).

U. According to a report to the English Crown during the second half of the seventeenth century, the routes that were used to transport low value, bulky products, such as in the Baltic, would not compensate for the cost of artillery, unlike the routes that were used for expensive products, such as Mediterranean and Asian routes (Barbour, "Dutch and English Merchant Shipping in the Seventeenth Century," pp. 261–262).

V. In addition to insurance and convoys, the Company would have a monopoly on the trade with the Levant for a 24-year term; see: S. C. Go, "Marine Insurance in the Netherlands, 1600–1870," PhD dissertation, Vrije University Amsterdam, 2009, pp. 138–139; V. Barbour, *Capitalism in Amsterdam in the 17th Century* (Ann Arbor: University of Michigan Press, 1963), p. 34.

of the Spanish flota that succumbed to the Dutch West India Company fleet commanded by Piet Hein in 1628 (the silver it carried served to finance the company's invasion of Pernambuco). This was also the case with a gigantic Anglo-Dutch convoy which protected trade with the Levant. It was decimated by Louis XIV's navy off the coast of Lagos, Portugal, in 1693.[104] In fact, Lisbon merchants responded to one of the proposals for escorted shipping submitted to the Crown by observing that departures on fixed dates helped the enemy prepare predatory expeditions:

> *And it seemed even wiser to avoid sailing in fleets from Brazil to Portugal because experience has shown that when ships sail together they are at even greater risk because they have no defence against strong enemies and the knowledge that they will sail together allows pirates to be prepared and to lie in wait for them according to the monsoon seasons [fleet's sailing schedule] and stops which they know they will frequent, which can be avoided when ships travel individually, especially when they have cargoes, since they can escape more easily and it would deprive them [the pirates] of the opportunity to lie in wait for the ships in full force and in this manner one can ensure that the enemy does not come specifically to lie in wait for the fleets.*[105]

Finally, the use of insurance, even if it entailed high premiums, eliminated the incentive to use convoys. The premiums were linked to the probability of attacks, whereas armed escorts had to protect the fleet from attacks whether they occurred or not. When the threat emanated from the Dutch, and the parties involved lived in the Republic or passed their wares off as belonging to Dutch owners, the victims had a greater chance of recovering what had been seized.[106] Insurers in Amsterdam who had to indemnify clients trading with the Iberian world, and Portuguese vessels also had a greater chance of recovering vessels and merchandise seized by their compatriots.[107] Again, to avoid conflicts between insurers and privateers, in 1622 the States-General of the United Provinces prohibited insuring cargoes and vessels belonging to enemy subjects.[108]

Even so, insurance must have proved to be a sufficiently interesting proposition, both for the insurers and the insured, in order to justify its continued existence, so much so that, in 1626, a Portuguese businesswoman demanded that two Dutchmen pay for the insurance of a ship sailing from Pernambuco to Lisbon, which she alleged had been seized by pirates, a fact the insurers questioned, first demanding to know the name of the vessel.[109]

With or without insurance, until the WIC infested the waters of the Atlantic, and probably even afterwards, the best response at least to privateers was to use small vessels, which, traveling separately, could immediately flee at the first sight of trouble. It was not heroic[110] or patriotic or even pious (since corsairs were generally Protestants or Muslims), but it was undoubtedly more economical and less risky. Flight was easier in smaller vessels such as caravels, ships and pataches – small, agile and easily maneuverable, and even lighter without the additional weight of artillery, gunners and extra men.[111] Decades later, Father Vieira is said to have told King João IV: "Caravels, Sire, are schools of flight and make cowards of seafarers, handing over to the enemy, at first shot, the substance of Brazil."[112]

Lieutenant-Admiral Pieter Pietersz. Heyn (1577–1629); *Paulus Moreelse (1630).* *In addition to playing a leading role in the Company's activities on the coasts of Brazil and Africa, Heyn was the commander of the WIC's fleet which captured a Castilian silver fleet returning from Mexico. This feat helped finance the WIC's invasion of Pernambuco, and weaken Spain in its conflict with the Dutch in the Low Countries, and the French in Italy.*

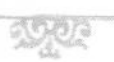

Into the Deep

Chapter Four

1. Costa, *O transporte no Atlântico*; Ebert, "The Trade in Brazilian Sugar."

2. Mauro, *Portugal, o Brasil e o Atlântico*, pp. 128–132; F. C. Spooner, *Risks at Sea: Amsterdam Insurance and Maritime Europe, 1766–1780* (Cambridge: Cambridge University Press, 1983), pp. 132–142; Moreira, *Os mercadores de Viana*, pp. 68–70, 79–86.

3. SR no. 1483. Two other Portuguese Jews had similar documents recorded by a notary public with regard to the same case: ibid., n. 29.

4. Polónia, "Mestres e pilotos das carreiras ultramarinas (1596–1648)," offprint of *História: Revista da Faculdade de Letras da Universidade do Porto 2nd series 12* (1995): 291.

5. Moreira, *Os mercadores de Viana*, p. 86. About the crew's actions, see also: Mauro, *Portugal, o Brasil e o Atlântico*, v. 1, p. 130.

6. "Correspondência do governador Dom Diogo de Meneses: 1608–1612," *Anais da Fundação Biblioteca Nacional 57* (1935): 50–51; Mauro, *Portugal, o Brasil e o Atlântico*, v. 1, pp. 145–146.

7. Lesger, *The Rise of the Amsterdam Market and Information Exchange*, pp. 226–229, 231–232.

8. Polónia, "Mestres e pilotos das carreiras ultramarinas," pp. 273–274, 291–293, 295; idem, "Os náuticos das carreiras ultramarinas," *Oceanos – Navios e navegações, Portugal e o mar 38* (1999): 122–125; Costa, *O transporte no Atlântico*, v. 1, pp. 450–452; Mauro, *Portugal, O Brasil e o Atlântico*, v. 1, pp. 105–106.

9. Costa, *O transporte no Atlântico*, v. 1, p. 360; Polónia, "Mestres e pilotos das carreiras ultramarinas," p. 292.

10. This was a common practice: Spooner, *Risks at Sea*, pp. 134–135.

11. SR no. 2605.

12. SR nos. 2603, 2604.

13. Silva, *O Porto e o seu termo*, v. 1, pp. 110–111; Barros, "Porto: a construção de um espaço marítimo," v. 1, pp. 118–127.

14. SR no. 1160, n. 34.

15. Mauro, *Portugal, o Brasil e o Atlântico*, v. 1, p. 130.

16. ADP, NOT, PO2, l. 40, fols. 11v.–12v. (1615-1-14).

17. "...watertight keel and sides so that nothing is lost due to neglect or oversights" – ADP, NOT, PO2, l. 36, fols. 121–123 (1612-11-29).

18. ADP, NOT, PO2, l. 36, fols. 293v.–295 (1613-4-12).

19. Costa, *O transporte no Atlântico*, v. 1, p. 365.

20. ADP, NOT, PO2, l. 36, fols. 121–123 (1612-11-29).

21. ADP, NOT, PO1, l. 133, fols. 70–72v. (1612-6-20).

22. Mauro, *Portugal, o Brasil e o Atlântico*, v. 1, p. 130.

23. G. Malynes, *Consuetudo: vel, lex mercatoria* (London: Adam Islip, 1622), pp. 134–144, 152–158, 174–182; Mauro, *Portugal, o Brasil e o Atlântico*, v. 1, pp. 85–109, 115–132; Hutter, *Navegação nos séculos XVII e XVIII*, pp. 167–213; Moreira, *Os mercadores de Viana*, pp. 49–51; Costa, *O transporte no Atlântico*, v. 1, pp. 344–345, 439–440.

24. *Livro primeiro do governo do Brasil, 1607–1633* (Lisbon: Comissão Nacional para as Comemorações dos Descobrimentos Portugueses, 2001), p. 50. See also: Costa, *O transporte no Atlântico*, v. 1, pp. 444–445.

25. Emmer, "The First Global War," passim; Israel, *Dutch Primacy in World Trade*, pp. 40–42, 62–73, 80–90, 101–112, 121–162; Sluiter, "Dutch-Spanish Rivalry in the Caribbean Area," passim; Mauro, *Portugal, o Brasil e o Atlântico*, v. 1, pp. 193–196, 200–201; Moreira, *Os mercadores de Viana*, pp. 70–79; Costa, *O transporte no Atlântico*, v. 1, pp. 8–9, 79–80, 192–201; Berger, Winz and Guedes, "Incursões de corsários e piratas na costa do Brasil," pp. 1–8; M. J. Guedes, "As guerras

holandesas no mar," in *História Naval Brasileira*, v. 2, t. 1 A, pp. 80–81, 85, 88–89; Boxer, *The Dutch in Brazil*, pp. 28–30; 33–34; H. den Heijer, *De geschiedenis van de WIC*,, pp. 55–59; Silva, "O corso inglês e as populações do litoral lusitano," pp. 311–336; idem, "Pirataria e corso sobre o Porto," pp. 1–27; Allen, *Felipe III y la Pax Hispanica*, pp. 75, 122; Ebert, "The Trade in Brazilian Sugar," pp. 161–167, 174–175. On Dutch piracy and privateering during the Twelve Years' Truce, see: SR nos. 657, 663, 664, 794. Eddy Stols has noted cases of attacks by privateers from one country against privateers from another on homebound journeys from Brazil: Stols, "Os mercadores flamengos," p. 45. With regard to pirates operating from North Africa, see: Coindreau, *Les corsaires de Salé*, passim; M. García-Arenal and G. Wiegers, *Un hombre en tres mundos. Samuel Pallache, un judío marroquí en la Europa protestante y en la católica* (Madrid: Siglo XXI de España Editores, 2006), pp. 79–94.

26. ADP, NOT, PO2, l. 37, fols. 48–50 (1613-6-10). For further information about this case, see also: Costa, *O transporte no Atlântico*, v. 1, p. 96. On risk spreading, see: ibid., v. 1, pp. 176, 180, 188, 192–195, 200, 202, 243–244, 262, 387, 426. See also: Barros, "Porto: a construção de um espaço marítimo," v. 1, p. 815.

27. See also: Costa, *O transporte no Atlântico*, v. 1, p. 189.

28. SR no. 249.

29. Ibid. With regard to this type of strategy, see also: Go, "Marine Insurance in the Netherlands," pp. 119–122.

30. SR nos. 657, 664, n. 47.

31. Spooner, *Risks at Sea*, pp. 120–150, 248–249.

32. Go, "Marine Insurance in the Netherlands," p. 68.

33. SR no. 249. See also: Barbour, *Capitalism in Amsterdam in the 17th Century*, pp. 33–34.

34. Spooner, *Risks at Sea*, p. 19.

35. Go, "Marine Insurance in the Netherlands," pp. 73–95; Spooner, *Risks at Sea*, pp. 22–23.

36. Go, "Marine Insurance in the Netherlands," pp. 84, 122, 154.

37. *Schepenen* (plural), also known as *échevins*.

38. Go, "Marine Insurance in the Netherlands," pp. 95–117, 123; Spooner, *Risks at Sea*, p. 18; M. Hell, "De oude geuzen en de Opstand: politiek en lokaal bestuur in tijd van oorlog en expansie 1578–1650," in W. Frijhoff and M. Prak, *Geschiedenis van Amsterdam, deel II-A: centrum van de wereld 1578–1650* (Amsterdam: SUN, 2004), pp. 290–295; Barbour, *Capitalism in Amsterdam in the 17th Century*, p. 33; Israel, *Dutch Primacy in World Trade*, p. 76.

39. ADP, NOT, PO2, l. 35 (1612-7-17), fols. 145–145v.

40. For further information about this case, see: SR no. 1031.

41. SR nos. 1614, 1662, 1746.

42. IANTT, STO, IC 5304, *Sessão de Inventário (02-08-1618)*. For further information about insurance purchased in Lisbon, see: ADP, NOT, PO1, l. 133, fols. 158v.–159v. (1612-9-22). With regard to Seville: ADP, NOT, PO1, l. 148, fols. 65–65v. (1624-6-14); l. 148, fols. 66–66v. (1624-6-14). With regard to individuals from outside the city who insured their goods and ships in Amsterdam, see: Go, "Marine Insurance in the Netherlands," p. 125.

43. Almeida, *Aritmética como descrição do real*, v. 2, pp. 364–365; Costa, *O transporte no Atlântico*, v. 1, pp. 228, 266–269; Moreira, *Os mercadores de Viana*, p. 126.

44. Ebert, "The Trade in Brazilian Sugar," pp. 149–151.

45. Go, "Marine Insurance in the Netherlands," pp. 138–139

46. Ibid., p. 147.

47. SR no. 1580; SAA, 30452, 381B, fols. 506–508.

48. Go, "Marine Insurance in the Netherlands," pp. 119–122. These do not include contracts in which one borrowed assets for a voyage, committing to repay the loan and a fixed interest rate if he arrived safely, while the lender undertook all risks caused by sea, fire and seizure during the voyage. These "bottomry contracts" or "sea loans" are detailed in Chapter 9, which deals with contractual arrangements used in overseas mercantile agency relations. Chapter 6 describes the "general averages," whereby losses were shared by all consignors. Neither "sea loans" nor "general averages" precluded insurance, quite to the contrary.

49. ADP, NOT, PO2, l. 16, fol. 124v. (1601-5-30).

50. SR nos. 1626, 3123.

51. With regard to the *boeijer* or *boyer*: SR no. 3230.

52. GAR, ONA, inv. no. 18, *Aktenummer/Blz*. 8/24.

53. SR no. 843.

54. Costa, *O transporte no Atlântico*, v. 1, p. 185; A. D. Hazlett, "The Nau of the Livro Nautico: Reconstructing a Sixteenth-Century Indiaman from Texts," PhD dissertation, Texas A&M University, 2007.

55. Costa, *O transporte no Atlântico*, v. 1, pp. 309–311.

56. F. Domingues, *Os navios do mar oceano: teoria e empiria na arquitetura naval portuguesa dos séculos XVI e XVII* (Lisbon: Centro de História da Universidade de Lisboa, 2004), pp. 252–258, 262–264, 266, 269; Costa, *O transporte no Atlântico*, v. 1, pp. 181–184. With regard to "ships," see also: Coindreau, *Les corsaires de Salé*, pp. 95–96.

57. Costa, *O transporte no Atlântico*, v. 1, pp. 183–185; Polónia, "Vila do Conde," v. 2, pp. 356–357; Barros, "Porto: a construção de um espaço marítimo," v. 1, pp. 808–818; Moreira, *Os mercadores de Viana*, pp. 39–41; R. W. Unger, *Dutch Shipbuilding before 1800: Ships and Guilds* (Amsterdam: Van Gorcum, 1978), pp. 33–35; Unger, *The Ship in the Medieval Economy*, pp. 220–223, 262. C. R. Phillips, *Six Galleons for the King of Spain: Imperial Defense in the Early Seventeenth Century* (Baltimore: Johns Hopkins University Press, 1986), pp. 34–40; Coindreau, *Les corsaires de Salé*, p. 97.

58. Unger, *Dutch Shipbuilding before 1800*, pp. 36–46; idem, *The Ship in the Medieval Economy*, pp. 223, 263; Barbour, "Dutch and English Merchant Shipping in the Seventeenth Century," pp. 280, 282; De Vries and Van der Woude, *The First Modern Economy*, pp. 296–297.

59. Unger, *Dutch Shipbuilding before 1800*, pp. 35–36, 49. With regard to the *vlieboot* and the *fluitschip*, see also: Coindreau, *Les corsaires de Salé*, p. 96.

60. Unger, *Dutch Shipbuilding before 1800*, pp. 27, 38, 46; idem, *The Ship in in the Medieval Economy*, pp. 261–264. On the term "pinnace" and the interchange between the terms "pinnace" and "patache," see: Coindreau, *Les corsaires de Salé*, pp. 93–94; Andrews, *Elizabethan Privateering*, p. 35; Domingues, *Os navios do mar oceano*, p. 266.

61. Coindreau, *Les corsaires de Salé*, pp. 87, 98, 103–111, 133–135; Mello, "Os livros das saídas das urcas do porto do Recife," pp. 24–25; Mauro, *Portugal, o Brasil e o Atlântico*, v. 1, pp. 193–195, v. 2, pp. 200–201; Costa, *O transporte no Atlântico*, v. 1, pp. 196–198; Tenenti, *Naufrages, corsaires et assurances maritimes à Venise*, pp. 29–30.

62. As far as Andrews has been able to ascertain: Andrews, *Elizabethan Privateering*, pp. 32–33.

63. Ibid., pp. 34–38, 211; Berger, Winz, and Guedes "Incursões de corsários e piratas na costa do Brasil," pp. 490–491, 493–494, 499–500.

64. Ibid., pp. 501–508; Guedes, "As guerras holandesas no mar," pp. 80–81, 85, 88–89; Boxer, *The Dutch in Brazil*, pp. 28–30; 33–34; Heijer, *De geschiedenis van de WIC*, pp. 55–59; Ebert, "The Trade in Brazilian Sugar," pp. 174–175.

65. Berger, Winz, and Guedes, "Incursões de corsários e piratas na costa do Brasil," p. 511; Costa, *O transporte no Atlântico*, v. 1, pp. 199–202; Tenenti, *Naufrages, corsaires et assurances maritimes à Venise*, pp. 35–36, 39, 47–48; Barbour, "Dutch and English Merchant Shipping in the Seventeenth Century," pp. 261–262.

66. Andrews, *Elizabethan Privateering*, pp. 133, 207.

67. Sluiter, "Os holandeses no Brasil antes de 1621," v. 46, p. 201; Mello, "Os livros das saídas das urcas do porto do Recife," p. 26.

68. See, for example, the case of the cargoes mentioned in Vlessing, "New Light on the Earliest History of Amsterdam Portuguese Jews," pp. 57–60; idem, "The Portuguese-Jewish Merchant Community in Seventeenth-Century Amsterdam," pp. 233–235.

69. See also: Stols, "Os mercadores flamengos," pp. 46–47; Ebert, "The Trade in Brazilian Sugar," pp. 110–111.

70. Costa, *O transporte no Atlântico*, v. 1, pp. 190–198, 200–206.

71. SR no. 880.

72. Israel, *Dutch Primacy in World Trade*, pp. 7–11, 18–26, 34–37, 48–60, 86–101; Unger, *The Ship in the Medieval Economy*, pp. 223, 262; Ebert, "The Trade in Brazilian Sugar," pp. 112–113. The data pertains, respectively, to the period between 1591 and 1602, and the year 1618, and has been published by: J. W. IJzerman, "Amsterdamsche bevrachtingscontracten 1591–1602, 1. de vaart op Spanje en Portugal," in *Economisch-Historisch Jaarboek 17* (1931): 163–291; P. H. Winkelman (ed.), *Bronnen voor de geschiedenis van de Nederlandse oostzeehandel in de zeventinde eeuw, Deel II, Amsterdamse bevrachtingscontracten van notaris Jan Franssen Bruyningh 1593–1600* (Leiden: Martinus Nijhoff, 1977), v. 6, p. 177. Sources pertaining to ships chartered by Portuguese Jews in Amsterdam for voyages to Porto, a sugar re-export hub: SR nos. 39, 40, 48, 49, 50, 89, 284, 291, 299, 379, 641, 1161, 1185, 1223, 1261, 1544. On the tonnage of ships chartered in Amsterdam by Portuguese Jews: Koen, "Duarte Fernandes," p. 189. Sources regarding ships which visited Setúbal: SR nos. 885, 896, 907, 909, 925, 927, 928, 930, 931, 932, 956, 958, 962, 990, 991, 997, 1003, 1004, 1005, 1006, 1007, 1011, 1034, 1051, 1066, 1076, 1083, 1090, 1098, 1101, 1102, 1104, 1109, 1118, 1119, 1120, 1122, 1123, 1137, 1138, 1143, 1146, 1147, 1151, 1152, 1153, 1154, 1155, 1156, 1159, 1160, 1162, 1169, 1186, 1187, 1188, 1189, 1192, 1210, 1215, 1226, 1229, 1230, 1234, 1238, 1239, 1240, 1245, 1247, 1253, 1282, 1285, 1472, 1475, 1476, 1496, 1546, 1552, 1559, 1563, 1727, 1737. Sources regarding ships traveling to the Mediterranean via Portugal: SR nos. 230, 250, 254, 266, 267, 292, 880, 968; Vlessing, *New Light on the Earliest History of Amsterdam Portuguese Jews*, p. 72, n. 87.

73. ADP, NOT, PO1, l. 138, fols. [missing]–194v (1617-4-30). See also: Costa, *O transporte no Atlântico*, v. 1, pp. 184–185, 200.

74. Ibid., v. 1, pp. 345–346.

75. Ibid., v. 1, pp. 176, 180, 185, 187–190, 308–309, 323, 342–343, 348–350.

76. ADP, NOT, PO2, l. 36, fols. 293v.–295 (1613-4-12); PO1, l. 138, fols. [missing]–194v. (1617-4-30).

77. For more systematic data about sales in Lisbon, see: Costa, *O transporte no Atlântico*, v. 1, pp. 361–369.

78. Barbour, "Dutch and English Merchant Shipping in the Seventeenth Century," p. 265. Costa believes that the profitability margin on sugar allowed less room for manoeuver than Ebert: Costa, *O transporte no Atlântico*, v. 1, pp. 179, 204–206, 370–372, 379–380. See also: Ebert, "The Trade in Brazilian Sugar," pp. 188–189, 198, 201–202, 205–208, 213; Moreira, *Os mercadores de Viana*, p. 64.

79. ADP, NOT, PO2, l. 40, fols. 78v.–79v. (1615-3-18).

80. ADP, NOT, PO1, l. 135a, fols. 66–68v. (1614-6-23). ADP, NOT, PO1, l. 137, fols. 131–133 (1616-3-11).

81. Oliveira, *A história do Brazil de Frei Vicente do Salvador*, v. 2, fol. 149v.

82. ADP, NOT, PO2, l. 40, fols. 24–25v. (1615-1-23).

83. SR no. 354.

84. Costa, *O transporte no Atlântico*, v. 1, p. 209.

85. Mauro, *Portugal, o Brasil e o Atlântico*, v. 1, p. 200; Costa, *O transporte no Atlântico*, v. 1, pp. 208–210, 344-369; Moreira, *Os mercadores de Viana*, p. 73.

86. IJzerman, *Journael van de reis naar Zuid-Amerika*, p. 103. Also published by:

O. Vlessing, "De Portugezen in de Gouden Eeuw II," *Habinjan/De opbouw*, Amsterdam, 1992, p. 21.

87. Costa, *O transporte no Atlântico*, v. 1, p. 199. See also: V. Rau and M. F. Gomes da Silva, *Os manuscritos do Arquivo da Casa de Cadaval respeitantes ao Brasil* (Coimbra: Imprensa da Universidade, 1956), v. 1, pp. 21–22.

88. See also: Costa, *O transporte no Atlântico*, v. 1, pp. 69, 212–213.

89. M. Severim de Faria, "Dos remédios para a falta de gente," in S. António, *Antologia dos Economistas Portugueses (século XVII)* (Lisbon: Livraria Sá da Costa Editora, 1974), pp. 127–128; D. do Couto, *Decadas da Asia, V. 3, década IX* (Lisbon: Na Officina de Domingos Gonsalves, 1736); idem, *O soldado prático* (Lisbon: Livraria Sá da Costa, 1954); D. Gomes Solis, *Discursos sobre los comercios de las dos Índias: donde se tratan matérias importantes de estado y guerra* (Lisbon: s.n., 1622); idem, *Alegación en favor de la Compañia de la India Oriental: comercios ultramarinos, que de nuevo se instituyó en el reyno de Portugal* (Lisbon: Editorial Império, 1955); Costa, *O transporte no Atlântico*, v. 1, pp. 201, 222–223

90. Ibid., pp. 199, 209.

91. Laval, *Viagem de Francisco Pyrard de Laval*, v. 2, p. 243.

92. Mattoso, *Identificação de um país,* v. 1, pp. 336–337.

93. Braga, *Entre a cristandade e o islão*, p. 164; S. Chahon, *Os convidados para a ceia do Senhor: as missas e a vivência leiga do catolicismo na cidade do Rio de Janeiro e arredores (1750–1820)* (São Paulo: Editora da Universidade de São Paulo, 2008), pp. 46–47; Coindreau, *Les corsaires de Salé*, pp. 50–51; García-Arenal and Wiegers, *Un hombre en tres mundos*, pp. 88–90; Mea, "A Igreja em reforma," pp. 441–444; Almeida, "As misericórdias," pp. 169–176.

94. ADP, NOT, PO1, l. 148, fols. 128v.–129v. (1624-8-2). For further information about operations to ransom captives, see: Moreira, *Os mercadores de Viana*, pp. 75–76.

95. SR no. 2693.

96. SR no. 2808.

97. SR nos. 3022 n. 56, 3024 n. 57.

98. Costa, *O transporte no Atlântico*, v. 1, pp. 208–212; Go, "Marine Insurance in the Netherlands," p. 119.

99. Costa, *O transporte no Atlântico*, Vv. 1, pp. 225–226.

100. Rau and Silva, *Os manuscritos do Arquivo da Casa de Cadaval respeitantes ao Brasil*, v. 1, pp. 21–22; Costa, *O transporte no Atlântico*, v. 1, pp. 196, 213–224; Smith, "The Mercantile Class of Portugal and Brazil," pp. 166–168.

101. Ebert, "The Trade in Brazilian Sugar," p. 109.

102. Costa, *O transporte no Atlântico*, v. 1, pp. 220–227, 240, 246–247.

103. Boxer, *The Dutch in Brazil*, pp. 29–30; Heijer, *De geschiedenis van de WIC*, pp. 59–64; Israel, *Dutch Primacy in World Trade*, pp. 229–230.

104. Ibid, pp. 310–311; Go, "Marine Insurance in the Netherlands," p. 133.

105. AHU_ACL_CU_Consultas Serviço Real, Cod. 35, fol. 189v. – [October 14, 1623]. See also: Costa, *O transporte no Atlântico*, v. 1, p. 221.

106. For an example of partial success in recovering seized assets, see: SR no. 3101. See also: Stols, "Os mercadores flamengos," pp. 46–47.

107. Costa, *O transporte no Atlântico*, v. 1, pp. 229–231.

108. Barbour, *Capitalism in Amsterdam in the 17th Century*, p. 34; J. I. Israel, "Spain and the Dutch Sephardim, 1609–1660," in idem, *Empires and Entrepots*, pp. 379–380.

109. SR no. 3385.

110. About the question of heroism at sea, see: Coindreau, *Les corsaires de Salé*, pp. 134–135.

111. Mauro, *Portugal, o Brasil e o Atlântico*, v. 1, p. 193; Costa, *O transporte no Atlântico*, v. 1, pp. 199–201, 213.

112. J. L. de. Azevedo (ed.), *Cartas do padre Antonio Vieira*, V. 3 (Coimbra: Imprensa da Universidade, 1928), p. 564.

Chapter Five

The North Sea coasts of England, France and the Low Countries (1597 and 1612) shown on a Portuguese sea chart.

Routes
Itineraries and Ports

This chapter will examine the itineraries or routes used to transport sugar from Brazilian ports to the Dutch entrepôt, as well as the geographic, legal and political constraints and economic variables that influenced these routes between 1595 and 1630.

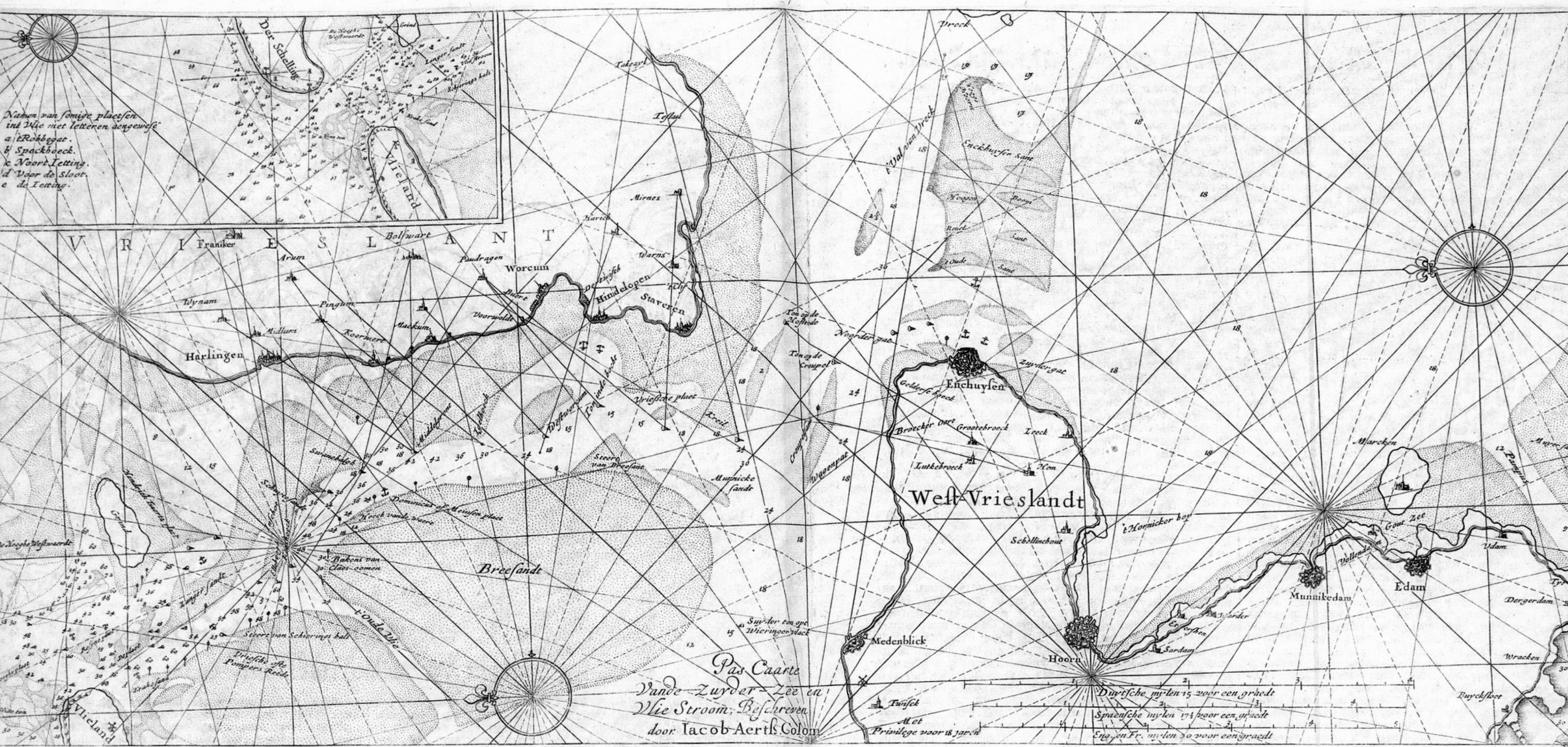

This 1652 map shows the Vliestroom, one of the seaways through the shallows of the Zuiderzee, the inlet that linked the North Sea to Amsterdam.

Intensity of Traffic

The Atlantic Ocean was navigable throughout the year with a greater or lesser degree of ease, unlike the Indian Ocean, where shipping depended on the monsoons.[1] The seasonal influence of the currents along the Brazilian coast apparently affected coastal shipping more than ocean voyages.[A] In northern Europe, when ice floated on the Zuiderzee, the inlet affording access to Amsterdam, goods were loaded and unloaded in ports further south such as Middelburg, Rotterdam and other ports in Zeeland, the Meuse and Rhine deltas[2] or one of the numerous outlets of the Zuiderzee, from where the goods were taken to the city in small boats.[3] (See the box in the previous chapter, on page 242, on the case of a shipmaster who, being unable to enter the lake, sent his cargo of sugar and salt to the city in boats and wintered in the Elbe delta.)

Apart from there being no natural or technological impediments restricting shipping, sugar was available for loading throughout the year, since the mills operated almost continuously. The Sergipe do Conde sugar mill, studied by Stuart B. Schwartz,[4] only stopped in May, June and July, due to heavy rains in the Recôncavo region, around the Bay of All Saints. The same sugar mill operated from June 25 to April 25 of the following year, according to a report penned by Father Estevão Pereira in 1635.[5] Another priest,

Father Antonil, stated that sugarcane was harvested from August to April inclusive, with an additional two months needed to produce the sugar. Two or three months of inactivity was relatively little downtime, and did not prevent the product from being stored for loading as long as it was for a short time and packed very carefully to avoid damage by moisture.[6]

It is worth noting that in adverse seasons there were always arbitrage profits that could outweigh the additional costs, time and risks,[7] as can be seen in the arguments of the Olinda City Council when rejecting a proposal to consolidate shipping into a single convoy in 1619:

> *...hence, with them [the convoy], we would eliminate the competition of merchant vessels, which frequent this captaincy and other captaincies in this State throughout the year, and we would have to depend on just one fleet per year, which would be very detrimental in terms of the provisions that these captaincies continuously need.*[B]

Merchants sought to disperse shipping and maintain a more intense, frequent and continuous maritime traffic in goods, means of payment and information. Apart from spreading the risk of each voyage, distributing cargo meant that merchants did not have to keep large stocks of imports or goods ready for export. Hence, they reduced their inventory costs and depreciation risks. They kept a few items on hand for sale or to be shipped in the near future, and ordered small quantities of goods through their agents in accordance with market trends.[8] This procedure also protected merchants against substantial fluctuations in price. One shipment could compensate for another, and the continuous flow of net assets and means of payment offered greater security for business activities in general. Finally, continuous shipments enabled the merchants to respond more quickly to changes in supply and demand in the markets from where they imported, and to which they exported goods. The importance of maintaining constant communication was emphasized by traders in Lisbon, who, in 1626, stated that the price of sugar in Brazil had dropped to very low levels owing to the disruption in its transport flow caused by the great loss of ships to Barbary pirates and Dutch privateers.[9]

In effect, there was frequent ship traffic. My study of Portuguese Jews and New Christians involved in the sugar trade shows that ships were chartered in Porto to sail to Brazil throughout the year, while the Brazilian historian Regina Célia Gonçalves notes that ships from Paraíba departed for

A. "Because it has already happened to me (not just once, but many times) that I have sent some papers to be adjudicated in Bahia [at the Court of Appeal] and, at the same time that I sent them there, I sent other similar papers to Portugal, and the documents which were sent to Portugal were returned well before the papers from Bahia; because sailing along this entire coast is conditioned by the monsoon winds, and if it happens that the winds are unfavorable, then matters get greatly delayed" (Brandão, *Diálogos das grandezas do Brasil*, p. 37). With regard to the opening of the road linking Pernambuco to Bahia, Friar Vicente do Salvador wrote, with some exaggeration: "... Nowadays one travels easily, and safely, by road and people come and go every day with their appeals [to the said court], and on other business, without having to wait six months for the monsoon, as was the case in the past, when very often a reply was received from Portugal before being received from here [Bahia] or from Pernambuco"; see: Oliveira, *A História do Brazil de Frei Vicente do Salvador*, v. 2, fol. 124. However, the same friar observed that the difficulties of coastal sailing could be overcome by using small caravels, which could also be rowed, instead of large carracks (Ibid, v. 2, fols. 118–118v.). Prior to 1579, Pedro de Magalhães Gândavo stated that coastal sailing was possible in adverse seasons, although, "When they sail against the weather, vessels run great risks and more often than not return to anchor in the port from which they set sail" (BNP, BND, Gândavo, *Tractado da terra do Brasil*, fols. 21–22).

B. *Livro primeiro do governo do Brasil*, p. 341. From their side, Lisbon businessmen stated: "Cargo from Brazil cannot come in a single fleet since it is comprised of sugar, which is produced nine months of the year, and considering how it is produced, sugar cannot possibly wait from the beginning to the end of the harvest without suffering great damages" (AHU_ACL_CU_Consultas Serviço Real, COD. 35, fols. 187–188 – [October 14, 1623]).

"... cargo from Brazil cannot come in a single fleet since it comprises sugar, wich is produced nine months of the Year."

Map of Brazil (ca. 1690).

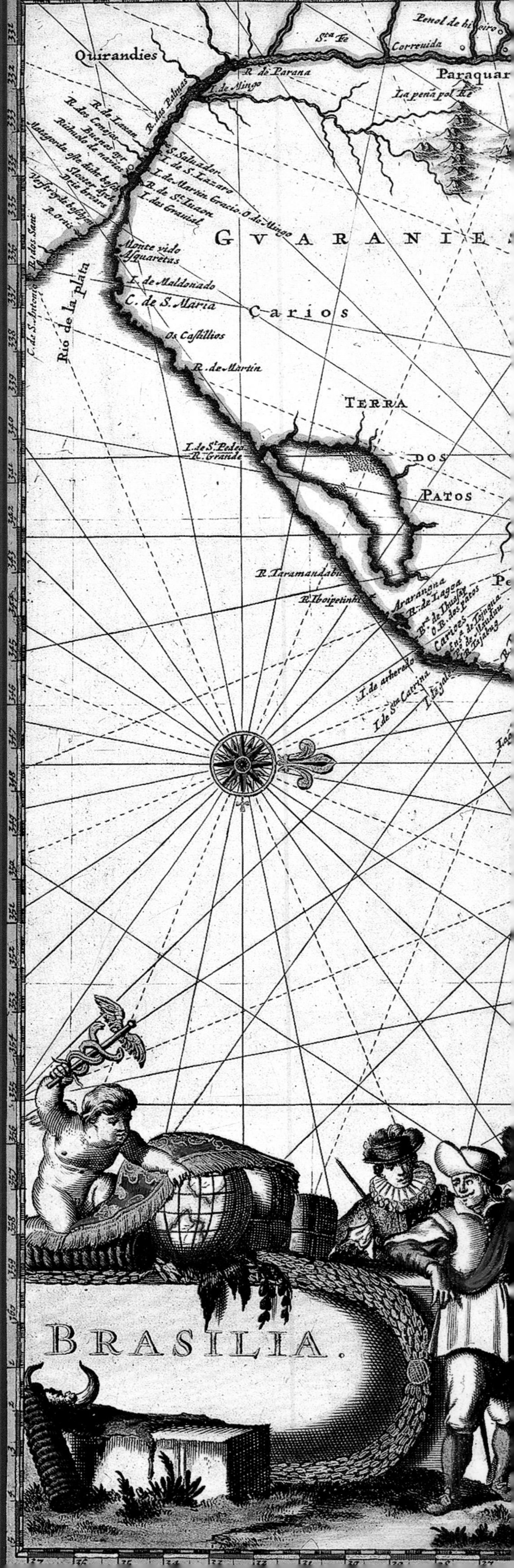

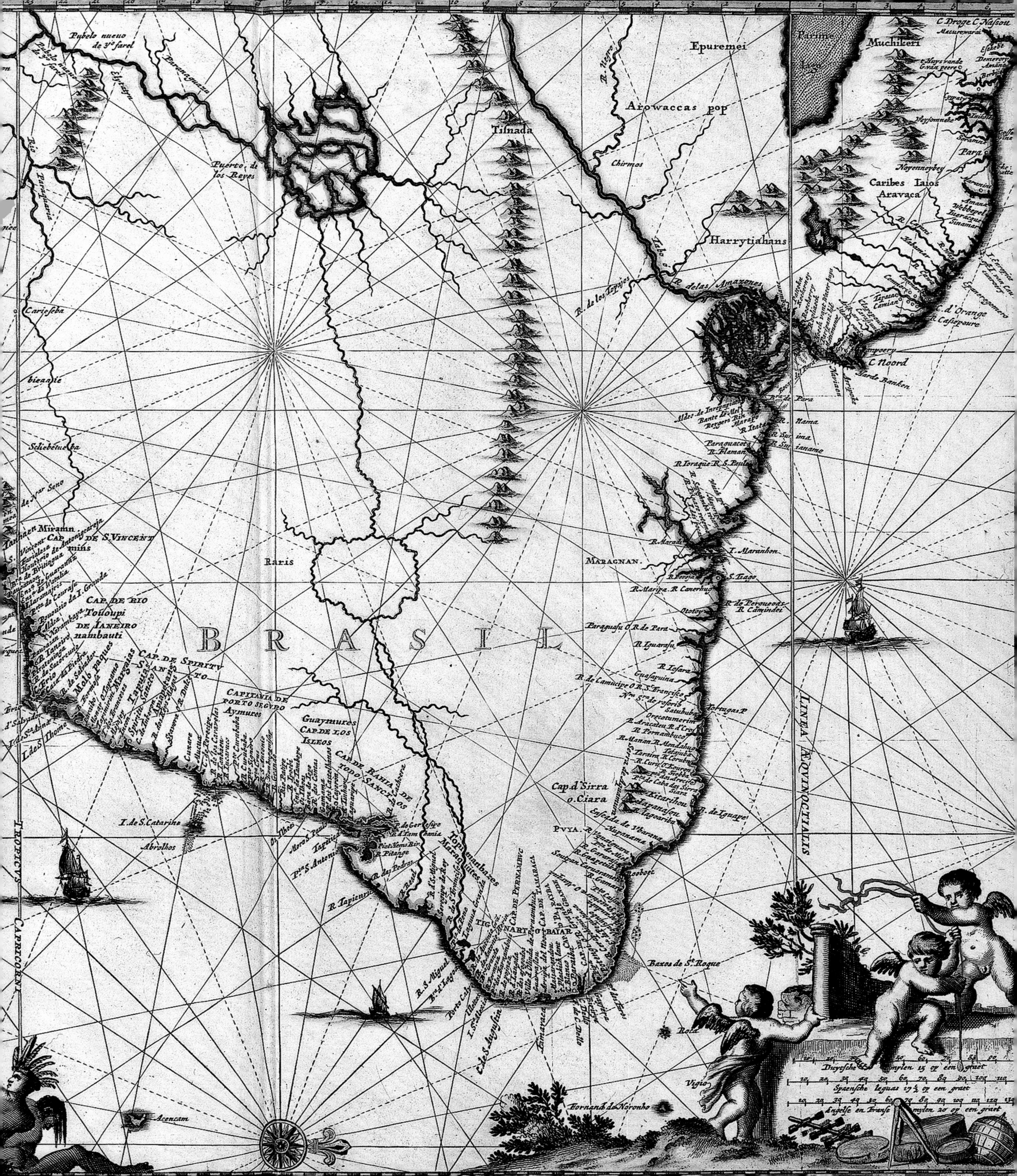

BRASIL
Epuremei
Arowaccas pop
Tilnada
Muchikeri
Caribes Iaios
Aravaca
Harrytiahans
Puerto de los Reyes
Chirmos
R. de los Topajos
R. delas Amazones
C. d'Orange
C. Noord
Raris
MARAGNAN.
I. Maranhon
CAP DE S. VINCENT
CAP. DE RIO DE IANEIRO
CAP. DE SPIRITV SANCTO
CAPITANIA DE PORTO SEGVRO
Guaymures
CAP. DE LOS ILEOS
CAP. DE BAHIA DE TODO SANCTOS
CAP. DE PERNAMBVC
Cap. d'Sirra o. Ciara
Baxos de S.t Roque
I. de S. Catarina
Abrolhos
Fornand de Noronho
TROPICVS CAPRICORNI
LINEA ÆQVINOCTIALIS
Duytsche mylen 15 op een graet
Spaensche leguas 17½ op een graet
Engelse en Franse mylen 20 op een graet

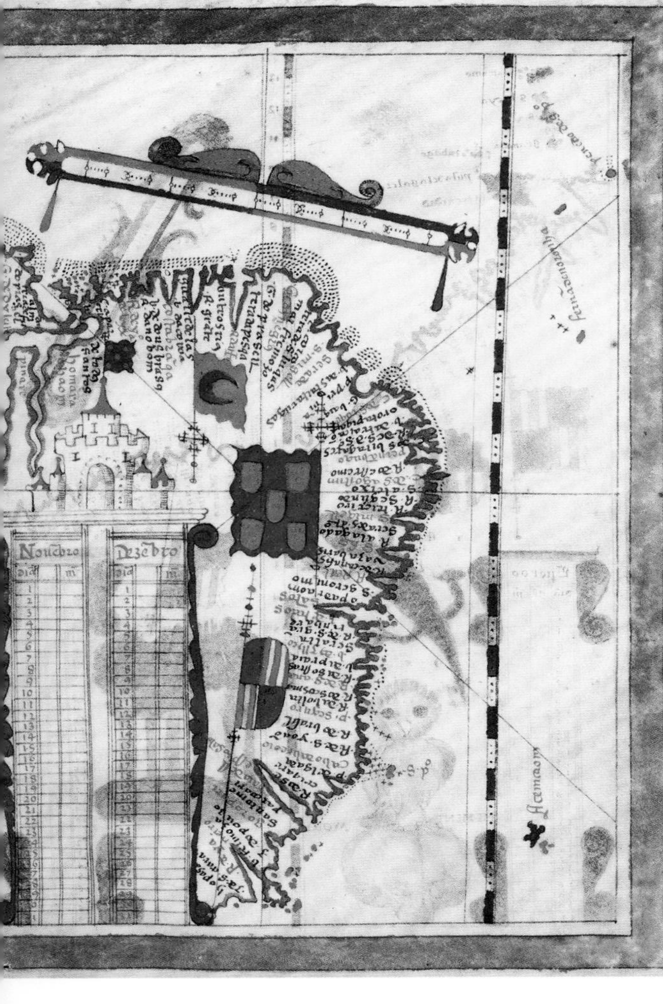

Map of the Brazilian coast, from the Amazon to Rio de Janeiro (1550–1560).

different Portuguese ports practically every month of the year, to a greater or lesser extent.[10] In 1580, Gabriel Soares de Sousa observed that, over the course of that year, more than twenty-three large ships remained anchored in Bahia and many seafarers from other lands stayed in that port.[11] Almost half a century later, Diogo de Campos Moreno stated that in the port of Recife, "more than two hundred mariners can be found at any time."[12] In approximately the same period, Ambrósio Fernandes Brandão declared that, at any time, it was always possible to see more than thirty ships anchored in that port in Pernambuco.[C]

None of this means that maritime traffic was not affected by seasonal factors. In Bahia, sugar mills halted their operations during the rainy season. Towards the end of the year, storms would occur in the area between the Azores and Portugal, where arrivals and departures were more hazardous in winter.[13] Ice was an even more serious problem, not only in the Zuiderzee but also in ports of the Baltic, Russia and Scandinavia, which were inaccessible between December and February and dangerous in March, October and November. Hence, re-exports to these areas closer to the Arctic had to set sail from Iberia at the end of winter or in time to arrive at their destination when the ice had already thawed.

Consequently, the ideal scenario was to leave Brazil during the Southern Hemisphere summer or autumn and arrive in Portugal between February and August,[14] so that it would be possible to reach northern European ports during the Northern Hemisphere summer or early autumn.[D] In the opposite direction, ships would leave Portugal in summer or autumn, after receiving cargoes from northern Europe, and would arrive in the Brazilian spring, when more sugar began to leave the molds, or in summer, to set sail again during the ideal period, in summer and autumn.[E]

However, the intensity of this traffic depended on whether there was a sufficient supply of ships. Leonor Freire Costa has estimated that the Brazilian production of sugar would have required between 150 and 300 vessels a year.[F] This figure would have increased as production expanded, and when shipping relied more on smaller vessels, which were safer from corsairs. The data available – from notary records, reports and proposals, chronicles and a few surviving customs records – only allow for conjecture. As we will see, notary records are more often than not full of gaps. Accounts by chroniclers, projectors and even officials tended to be unreliable and often exaggerated.

At the same time, charter records in Amsterdam and reports about Dutch ships seized by Iberian authorities while embargoes had been imposed show that there were over 100, perhaps even a few hundred, Dutch ships anchored in Portuguese ports in peacetime.[H] Many of these vessels came to load salt in Setúbal, Aveiro and smaller salt ports.[23] During the years when the Spanish embargo was enforced most

Sailing ships

Writing in 1583, Father Fernão Cardim stated that more than forty ships arrived in Pernambuco every year, and they were still not enough to transport all the available sugar.15 During the same decade, the enterprising settler Gabriel Soares de Sousa stated that between forty and fifty ships visited Pernambuco annually, and that more than twenty-three large vessels could be found in Bahia throughout the year.16 Friar Vicente do Salvador described how, in February 1585, there were no more than thirty ships in Pernambuco.[17] An English intelligence document produced for Elizabeth I's military campaign against Philip II sought to list all the vessels in Portuguese ports in 1586, including the fleets, galleys and carracks which plied the India route, known as the *Carreira da Índia*, arrived at a total of 269 vessels, most of which were caravels.[18]

Later, the merchant and sugar-mill owner Ambrósio Fernandes Brandão claimed that in 1618, the captaincies of Pernambuco, Itamaracá and Paraíba (the latter being virtual subsidiaries of Pernambuco) produced sufficient sugar to fill between 130 and 140 carracks. A subsequent note updated the figures cited in the text to 180 and 200. Elsewhere, Brandão assured his readers that more than 120 carracks went to Pernambuco alone every year and more than twenty visited Itamaracá and Paraíba. He observed that even twenty India carracks (Indiamen), which had a capacity of about 500 tons, would not be enough to carry the cargo of all the ships that visited the Brazilian Northeast.[19]

The Portuguese Treasury Council stated that in 1620, forty carracks from Bahia and another eighty from Pernambuco went to Lisbon, while about another eighty would have sailed from Brazil to other Portuguese ports.[20] In 1626, businessmen from Lisbon complained to the State Council that in that year, the depredations of the WIC and Berber corsairs had reduced the 120 ships that used to arrive in that city laden with sugar to a miserable twenty.[21] This data is clearly exaggerated. The governor of Pernambuco, Matias de Albuquerque, estimated that 300 ships plied the Brazilian route in 1627.[G] A proposal dating from 1629 stated that the colony's sugar production would require 279 ships, each with a capacity of 120 tons.[22]

strictly, such as in 1598 and 1609, the number of Dutch ships visiting Portugal would undoubtedly have been lower.[I] During the course of his attempts to convince the Spanish Habsburgs to make Lisbon their capital, Luis Mendes de Vasconcelos wrote, in 1608, in clear exaggeration, that the city had such an abundant supply of wheat, barley and rye, as well as cheese, butter and cured ham, because every year more than 3,000 ships from "Flanders," Germany and France called in there laden with merchandise, mainly wheat.[24] Be that as it may, there is no doubt that shipping sugar, even if accompanied by other commodities, would have mobilized several dozen Dutch ships during that period.

C. "This port has an excellent harbor, guarded by two fortresses well equipped with artillery and soldiers, who defend them; ships anchor on the inner shore... There are always more than thirty ships anchored in the port at any time of the year, because every year the port sends more than one hundred and twenty ships laden with sugar, brazilwood and cotton" (Brandão, *Diálogos das grandezas do Brasil*, p. 32).

D. In effect, a record of customs duties paid in Porto in 1591 indicates clearance of sugars during all months except for October, November and December (ADP, *Cabido*, l. 113).

E. Based on customs house sources in Paraíba in the period 1606–1614, Gonçalves reveals a higher flow of ship departures from Paraíba to ports in Portugal during the meridional autumn (between February and June), and fewer departures in the spring (August to November) (Gonçalves, *Guerras e açúcares*, pp. 256–261). Voyages from the Low Countries to the Baltic lasted one or two months and three or four months between Portugal and the Baltic. Spooner, while analyzing data from Rotterdam concerning insurance at the end of the eighteenth century, highlighted two peak periods for journeys from Holland to Iberia and the Mediterranean – April–May and October–November–December – and attributed them to the rhythm of fleets from Spanish America and the need to go south in the winter and in the spring when voyages extended to the Baltic or to other associated regions (Spooner, *Risks at Sea*, pp. 120–126). Looking at the currents along the Brazilian coast, which were called monsoons in the early modern times, Frédéric Mauro stated that ships should ideally set sail from Brazil between April and October, arriving in Portugal in October or November. In the other direction it was best to leave Portugal between September and February (Mauro, *Portugal, o Brasil e o Atlântico*, v. 1, p. 112). Currents, however, adversely affected coastal more than ocean sailing (see note b). Moreover, most of the ideal period for departures from Brazil indicated by Mauro would have coincided with the rainy interlude between sugarcane harvests in Bahia, whereas arrivals would have been too close to the Northern Hemisphere winter.

F. Costa has estimated between 118 and 141, in 1583, 196 to 236, in 1612, and 212 to 236, in 1629. She later adjusted these figures, taking into account the projected makeup of the fleet as well as the estimated average capacity utilization rate. Her calculation yielded the following figures: 145 and 179, in 1583, 271 and 345, in 1612, 181 and 246, in 1621, and 230 and 334, in 1629 (Costa, *O transporte no Atlântico*, v. 1, pp. 178, 203–204).

G. "... Every year more than 300 ships belonging to residents from all over Entre-Douro-e-Minho, Beira and the Tagus, through the ports of Viana, Porto and Lisbon, load cargoes for Brazil, including woollen fabrics, linen, olive oil, other fruits and handicrafts, which return with sugar that has been exchanged for the foreign provisions and textiles they need" (*Livro primeiro do governo do Brasil*, p. 381).

H. In 1544, more than one hundred ships set out for Portugal, from Middelburg in Zeeland, which served Antwerp as an advance port at the mouth of the Scheldt River (Stols, "Os mercadores flamengos," p. 29).

I. The Spanish embargo would have affected eighty-three vessels from Holland and Zeeland in Lisbon and Setúbal in 1595, and fifty-three hulks would have refrained from entering the port in Setúbal; see: J. Gentil da Silva, *Stratégie dês affaires à Lisbonne entre 1595 et 1607. Lettres marchandes dês Rodrigues d'Evora et Veiga* (Paris: Librarie Armand Colin, 1956), p. 36.

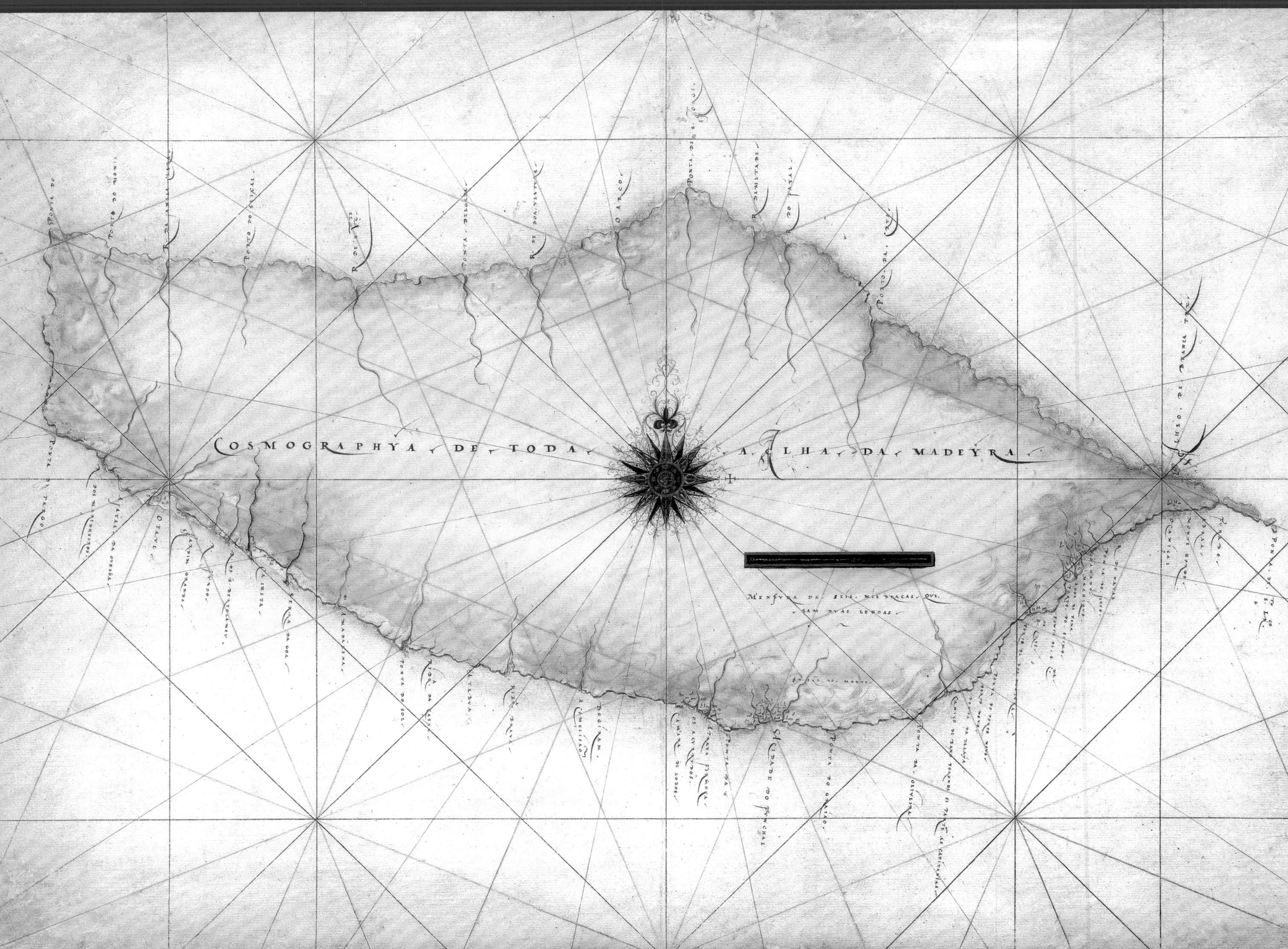

The Island of Madeira on a sea chart produced after 1650. The caption says: "Cosmography of the entire Island of Madeira."

The Canary Islands on a Dutch Map (1618). *The Madeira and the Canary Islands were frequent stopovers for ships bound for Brazil.*

Stopovers en Route

Direct voyages from Portugal to Pernambuco or to Bahia would take about two months, the homeward journey required around three months, while it took a month to sail from Amsterdam to Porto and another month to return. Voyages could require more or less time depending on seasonal or occasional changes in currents and winds.[25] Stopovers and idle spells before setting sail could extend the duration of voyages. When ships setting out from virtually anywhere sailed to Brazil, they almost always called in at the Atlantic Islands, especially Madeira and, even more frequently, at the Canary Islands. During these stopovers, ships were loaded with wine bound for Brazil.[26] The islands were on the way, and, at least in terms of volume, their wine was the main product imported into Brazil, only surpassed perhaps by slaves, mostly brought directly from Africa.

Calling in at the islands, therefore, allowed making better use of the leased space – since the other Brazilian imports were relatively less bulky – without increasing costs for merchants.[27] According to Costa, these stopovers at the islands did not have a significant impact on freight rates, despite the added costs to shipping.[28] Such costs included supplies for the crew during the laytime in Madeira and the Canary Islands, and the extended duration of the journey to Brazil of twenty days,[29] on average. Stopping at these islands on the homeward journey was less common, except when they substituted for Portugal in the trade between Brazil and northern Europe, but this will be examined later.[30]

Timeline of the legal framework for shipping and trade among the Low Countries, Portugal and Brazil

1580	*Dynastic union between Portugal and Spain, which was at war with the United Provinces*
1585	*Iberian embargo on enemy ships and products*
1586	*The Earl of Leicester, governor-general of the United Provinces, bans trade with the dominions of Philip II*
1587	*Dutch embargo lifted*
1590	*Iberian embargo against the Dutch suspended*
1591	*Direct shipping between Brazil and foreign nations is limited with the introduction of a system of bonds for trade with the colony*
1595	*Brief Iberian embargo against the Dutch*
1598	*Resumption of the Iberian embargo*
1603	*Replacement of the embargo with the system of controlled trade*
1605	*End of the system of controlled trade*
	Resumption of the embargo against the Dutch, with restrictions on their presence in Portugal
	End of the bond system for trading with Brazil
	Ban on foreign shipping to Brazil
	Decree expelling foreigners from the colony
1609	*Initiation of the Twelve Years' Truce and suspension of the embargo*
	All foreign ships continue to be banned from going to Brazil.
1621	*Expiration of the Twelve Years' Truce and resumption of the embargo*
1625	*Creation of the* Junta del Almirantazgo *and stricter enforcement of the embargo*

Taxation during the controlled trade system

The system in effect between 1603 and 1605 in Spain and Portugal decreed that neither exports nor imports could pay taxes to the Dutch authorities. Imported products would be subject to a 30% tax and numerous items were prohibited.[35] Exemption from this 30% tax would be granted only to those who obtained a passport (license) and seals for the products from the authorities of the Southern Low Countries, and provided guarantors to ensure that the cargo would be unloaded in either loyal or neutral ports. The surety would only be released after certificates issued in the port of discharge were produced.

Lay days in the ports of Bahia and Pernambuco generally lasted two months, being extended further when ships brought wine from the islands. Then, it was necessary to wait until the wine was sold, so that sugar could be bought with the proceeds of the sale. The intensification of predatory activities in the 1620s meant that ships stayed in ports for shorter periods, since the risk was greater in port than on the high seas.[31] On round voyages between Amsterdam and Porto laytime usually lasted two months,[32] while sometimes the need for a third month was also stipulated.[33]

Ships deviated from their habitual routes to avoid areas where pirate or corsair activity was expected. In 1602, the authorities in Brazil were alerted by the Hispanic Court that ships about to set sail should avoid Lisbon, whose harbor was being blockaded by a fleet from Holland and Zeeland, probably commanded by the Lord of Opdam. The activities of corsairs from Dunkirk – a city located in the part of the Low Countries under Habsburg control – against the Republic's ships caused merchants living there to instruct shipmasters coming from the south to avoid the English Channel, and sail around the British Isles instead.[34]

Circumventing Embargoes

Routes were also influenced by legal constraints resulting from the commercial warfare being waged by the Hispanic Monarchy on one side, and the United Provinces on the other. It is important to keep in mind that the Habsburgs prohibited trade with the Republic and Dutch shipping from 1598 to 1603, 1605 to 1609 and from 1621 onwards. In addition, between 1603 and 1605, a complex system of licenses, bonds and extraordinary taxes was in effect.

However, even while these embargoes were in effect, Dutch ships continued to sail to Portugal, to a greater or lesser extent, bearing the flags of neutral nations. They sometimes obtained passports (licenses) from Hispanic authorities in those countries, and even changed crews, partially or entirely. On other occasions, merchants based in the Netherlands chartered ships from neutral countries,[J] or traded through their ports.[36] In all likelihood, the enforcement of the embargo was less stringent in smaller Portuguese ports, and even in Porto and Viana, in northern Portugal. The local authorities in these port towns turned a blind eye to this type of subterfuge or even tacitly condoned it.[37]

The extent of these ploys is suggested in an agreement signed one year after the expiration of the Truce, between two Portuguese Jews in Amster-

J. Jonathan I. Israel, however, believes that the use of foreign flags would have ended after ninety-four camouflaged Dutch ships were seized by the Spanish authorities in Andalucía in 1587. From then on, foreign ships and crews were preferred, as well as intermediation by neutral countries. However, Israel admits that until 1598 the enforcement of the embargo in Portugal was less stringent than in Castile, particularly in ports smaller than Lisbon and Setúbal (Israel, "Spain, the Spanish Embargo and the Struggle for the Mastery of World Trade," pp. 192, 194–195, 197–199).

The Atlantic could be sailed throughout the entire year, which facilitated a continuous flow of trade.

Chart of the Atlantic (*ca. 1600*).

E V R O P A
BARBARIA.
AFRICA
Serra Lioa
MINA
ropico de Cancro.
Linha equinocial.
das Amazonas.
E R V.
Brasil.
Mundo nouo.
Serro de potosi.
Rio paragoay
RIO PA RA NA.
RIO DA PRATA
CHILI.
Terra de Gigantes.
TROPICO DE CAPRICORNIO.

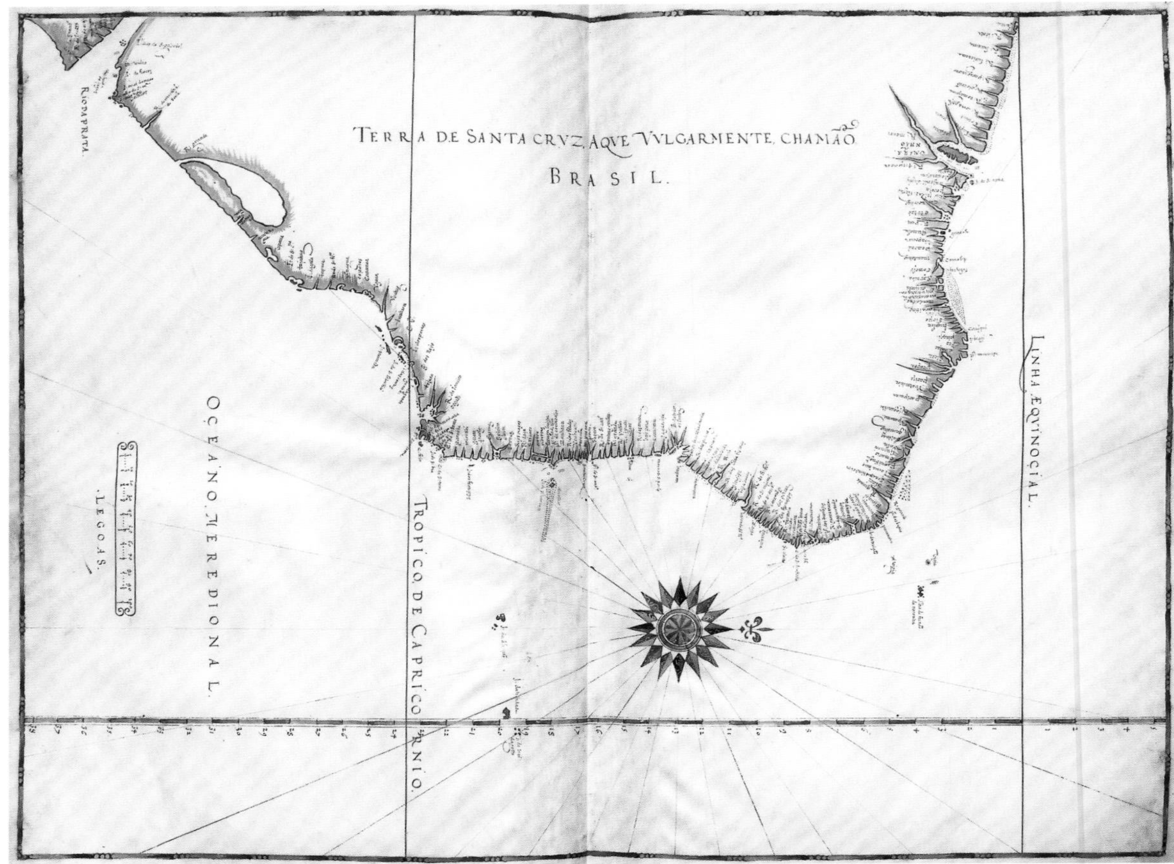

Portuguese nautical chart depicting Brazil from the Northern Amazon to River Plate *(ca. 1616)*.

dam, who owned a ship named *De Hope* (*The Hope*), and the shipmaster of the vessel, who lived in Vlissingen, in Zeeland. The agreement stipulated that the shipmaster was to make a round journey from Amsterdam to Viana, from where the ship would bring sugar and other goods. A visit to Aveiro to load salt was also included. The shipmaster was to hire a crew of eleven English sailors and sail via the Isle of Wight, in the English Channel, where he was to obtain a passport and other documents. Apart from this, in order to ensure that things went smoothly in Portugal, the shipmaster was to carry a pro forma bill of lading, stating that the merchandise on the outward voyage had been loaded by one Willem Crosse (William Cross), an Englishman, and that Crosse was also the owner of the ship.[38]

Dutch ships were also passed off as French[39] and German vessels.[40] It was not uncommon to insert a clause in freight contracts with express instructions for shipmasters to return to the Republic, even though bills of lading indicated other destinations.[41]

The more complex the camouflage, the greater was the expense. The costs and risks involved induced some merchants to shift to neutral trading centers. This was the case with many Portuguese Jews in Amsterdam, for whom trade with the Iberian world had great importance. Towards the expiration of the Truce, they migrated to Hamburg and Glückstadt, on the lower Elbe. This shift did not mean that embargoed trading centers were bypassed when the services and goods offered there were necessary.

Merchants simply reorganized their supply chain, which now became longer and more expensive.[42]

Legal constraints also affected shipping to Brazil. From 1591 onwards, foreigners who wished to sail legally to Portuguese colonies had to begin and end their journeys in Portuguese ports. A double bond system was created to ensure this. Foreign ships leaving from Portuguese ports for Brazil had to post a bond guaranteeing that if they did not return to Portugal, at least they would have paid the customs duties due in Portugal. Bonds were to be posted at the Board (*Juízo*) for India, Mina and Brazil, which managed the Crown's overseas monopolies.[43] In Brazil, shippers had to record the quantities and qualities of all the products exported before the Crown's purveyor (*provedor*) and treasurer (*almoxarife*). Shipmasters, in turn, had to provide guarantors resident in the colony who stood for the value of the consignments, as assessed by the Crown's officials. These guarantors would only be released from their security obligations when the applicable duties were paid in Portugal.[44]

At the end of the sixteenth century, a considerable part of the shipping between Brazil and Europe was carried out by foreign hulks.[K] Most of them purported to be "German" or Hanseatic, and many were, in fact, vessels from Holland or Zeeland pretending to be neutral Hanseatic ships or even loyal Flemish vessels, so as not to face problems in the Iberian domains. Irrespective of whether they were actually German or not,[L] there is no doubt that they transported merchandise on behalf of individuals living in the Dutch Republic.[45] In a way, the intense participation of northern European hulks in the sugar shipping was the result of common interests in deterring British privateers. The latter diverted the distribution and refining of sugar from both the Iberian Peninsula, on the one hand, and the Low Countries and Germany on the other, to England on an alarming scale.[46]

In 1594, the Hispanic monarch had supposedly acquiesced to requests by certain leaseholders of rights over the Brazilian trade to organize two annual fleets of twenty hulks, each of which would have a capacity of two hundred tons. The hulks, their crews and equipment had already been booked in cities of Holland. The objective was to counter the decimation of the Portuguese fleet by English privateers. The ships were to set sail from Lisbon with Portuguese shipmasters, and they would have to return there in accordance with the system of bonds in effect. The goods that would be sent from there to Holland and Zeeland would be given prefer-

K. Vessels from the Low Countries, some serving Flemish investors who had invested resources in sugar mills in Brazil, already transported sugar between Brazil and their ports, with or without calling in at Portugal, since the mid sixteenth century (Stols, "Os mercadores flamengos," pp. 24–25, 28).

L. Costa mentioned the case of the hulk Santa Maria, with a capacity of more than 260 tons, which purported to be a German vessel, from the city of Emden, in Eastern Frisia, and was exposed (Costa, *O transporte no Atlântico*, v. 1, pp. 188–189).

ence over other cargoes. The ships would not tarry very long in Lisbon, so as not to give corsairs enough time to organize an attack and capture the entire fleet. The English informant who described this arrangement stated that the hulks were already in Lisbon for this purpose.

This venture was seemingly short lived, probably because private merchants resisted the fleet system. The Crown was also reluctant to use it, as it exposed its colonies to the rebel Dutchmen, who were already planning attacks on the Hispanic dominions in Asia and elsewhere. In 1599, contractors for the customs duties in ports in Portugal alleged that they had the right to send twenty hulks every year, half the previous number, and asked for an exemption from the new tax charged in Brazil, of one cruzado per crate of sugar. They thus tried in vain to contain the influx of foreign hulks that ended up sailing from Brazil directly to northern Europe without paying the duties due in Portugal.[47]

The bond system was complex and left room for fraud. Foreign ships did not always comply with the obligation to call in at Portuguese ports on the homeward journey, and the shippers and their guarantors often preferred to pay the value of the merchandise if and when they were asked to do so. Hermann Kellenbenz observes that, in 1590, Hamburg alone received eleven ships arriving directly from Brazil. By 1602, this figure had risen to nineteen. That same year, a lengthy lawsuit was filed because three ships from Lübeck failed to call in to Lisbon.[48] There were also cases where ships wishing to sail to Brazil directly from Spain – without stopping and posting bonds in Portugal – were penalized.[49] Such flouters of the law were denounced by a Crown official, Domingos de Abreu e Brito, who urged that the taxes that were to be paid in Lisbon be settled immediately in the colony, either in cash or in sugar, since certificates ended up not being sent and bonds were never collected. Brito complained that regulations were not put into effect, not only due to the system's complexity but mainly owing to the corruption that was rampant amongst Crown officials, saying that: "Thence, your treasury officials enrich themselves and since they never collect [bonds] from guarantors, the royal treasury suffers losses."[50]

Nevertheless, it appears that the bonds were only monitored after the system ceased to operate. In 1607, a magistrate named Sebastião de Carvalho ordered the transcription of all records on exports from the port of Recife that had still not been regularized. Some cases dated back to 1595. These transcriptions recorded cases in which guarantors had not brought a certificate to Olinda confirming that the cargo had been cleared at a customs house in Portugal, or presented it after the stipulated deadline. In the latter situation, the certificates confirmed that the duties had been paid in Portugal, even if the respective hulk had sailed directly to northern Europe, but the clerk later annulled the validity of the certificates for having been submitted too late.

The document mentions thirty-four hulks, at least eight of which had failed to call in at Portugal on the homeward voyage. Perhaps there were many more than eight cases, since the document only refers to the vessels whose shippers broke the law and omits those who complied. When a ship sailed towards northern Europe, but the shippers' correspondents paid the duties in Portugal in time, it was perfectly legal.[M] In these eight or more cases, the parties believed that there was little to be gained by calling in at a Portuguese port and preferred not to risk sailing near the Iberian coast, which was plagued by English corsairs until 1603, and by Dutch privateers from 1598 onwards.[N]

Dodging Colonial Restrictions

Foreign trade and the presence of non-Portuguese nationals in Brazil ended up being banned in 1605 for political and economic reasons, apart from non-compliance with stopovers or payment of duties in Portugal. These bans sought to reinforce Portuguese control over the territory, prevent tax evasion associated with visits by foreigners, and prevent them from gathering information that might help plan future invasions. It was hoped that keeping Brazilian trade as an exclusively Portuguese prerogative would stimulate the Portuguese shipbuilding industry, as well as other sectors involved in producing and selling items linked to the Brazilian imports or exports. Furthermore, the compulsory channeling of trade through Portugal would increase customs revenues in metropolitan ports.[51]

This ban on foreign ships must have reduced their presence in Brazilian waters, but it did not eliminate it entirely. In January 1622, Portuguese Jews in Amsterdam submitted a petition they called a "deduction" (*deductie*, in Dutch), pleading the exemption of vessels sailing between Brazil and Portugal from attacks by Dutch privateers. The petitioners highlighted the contribution of the Brazilian sugar trade to the Dutch economy since 1580, and particularly during the Truce. Their objective was to convince the Dutch authorities of the strategic importance of this commerce:

> *During the said twelve years this shipping and trade have increased so vigorously that every year more than 10, 12 and 15 ships, here, in these lands, were built and outfitted, and annually about 40 or 50 brought wares from Brazil to here, via Portugal, laden with even thousands of crates of sugar, apart from brazilwood, ginger, cotton, hides and other products in large quantities.... We were so successful in this trade that during this twelve-year period we drove out of these routes all the Portuguese caravels which [earlier] infested [these waters], transporting sugar, given the capacity of our ships, and [thus] half, and even 2/3, of this traffic was taken over and incorporated by us, and this was due to the discretion of our factors in Portugal, under Portuguese names, who also play a part and a role in this trade jointly with us.*[52]

The authors of this petition distinguished between the Brazilian trade and the commerce along other Portuguese and Iberian routes, such as the India route known as the *Carreira da Índia* and the routes to West Africa.

M. The document notes that, for the same vessel, some guarantors produced certificates after the deadline, while others did not even submit any certificate at all. However, the document omits vessels that had complied. It is also possible that some vessels had gone to Portugal but the guarantors had not been diligent enough to bring the certificate (Mello, "Os livros das saídas das urcas do porto do Recife," pp. 26–30). Ebert considered all cases in which ships failed to call in to Portugal to be illegal, not taking into account the cases in which the duties had or could have been paid there (Ebert, "The Trade in Brazilian Sugar," pp. 169–170).

N. In much the same manner as after 1624, Portuguese ships reduced their stopovers in the islands and laytime in Brazilian ports in order to reduce their exposure to Dutch privateering (Costa, *O transporte no Atlântico*, v. 1, pp. 341–342).

Nautical chart of the Portuguese coast from the Lima River to the Mondego River (1586).

rtugal, aist drie mijlen van v is, en daer beneffens zeijlt.
iuxtague eam nauigas.
Als dit Swarte hoeuelken oost te zuijden van v leijt, soe issmen open voer die Riuier van Aueiro. Vbi ngellus monticubus vpcurum versus a te situs est, ex diametro es e regione fluuij aueirani.
Montego.
LIÆ PARS.
Port de Port.
Port de Marzagaij.
Muistrol.
Aleixo.
S. Iuan de Foz.
Duero Rio.
Closter.
Ville noua.
Grege.
S. Catelina.
Sout landt.
Aueiro.
Incasa.
Die Riuier van Aueiro.
Sout landt.
Outa.
Sout landt.
Lagos.
Mira.
Mondego R.
Capo de Montego.
Pasage.
ORIENS
MERIDIES Z.
OCCIDENS
WESTER ZEE.
Cum Priuilegio ad decennium.
Die Zee Caerte van Portugal, tusschen Camino en Montego, alsoe dat landt all daer in sijn ghedaente is, met alle sijne haeuen enn ondiepten, met groeter naerstichejt en vliedt ghecorrigeert
Ora maritima Portugalliæ inter Caminum et Montegum, quemadmodum Regio illa in sua stat figura cum omnibus suis portubus, atq vadis sũmo studio a Luca Ioannis aurigario descripta.

Mast-making *in an illustration from the* Book of Trades *(1694). One of the most important sectors of the Republic's economy, shipbuilding benefited from economies of scale.*

Shipyard *in an illustration from the* Book of Trades *(1694).*

The Dutch already traded directly on these other routes and did not wish to see their commercial and predatory interests affected. The merchants alleged that Dutch subjects did not have a stake either in the ships or in the wares being transported on these other routes, and hence were not affected by privateering. This, however, was not the case in the Brazilian trade: "While it is quite different in the case of the ships and the goods which are shipped to Brazil, in which trade we, as much as the Portuguese, and they with us, are inseparably intertwined, mixed and involved."[53]

The stratagem suggested in this petition is probably the same one indicated by some notary sources: a Portuguese Jew from Amsterdam, Tomas Nunes Pina, owned 5/6ths of a Dutch ship named *De Coninck David* ("King David"), which had a capacity of 140 tons. Pina appointed Huibert Pietersz. of Amsterdam as the shipmaster of the vessel in the last week of 1620. He was supposed to hand the ship over in Viana to an Old Christian merchant, who was a member of the local oligarchy, Gaspar Caminha Rego,[54] and another Viana merchant,[O] who would pay him half his salary, the other half having been paid in Amsterdam.[P/55]

The ship arrived at the beginning of the following year in the port of Viana, where it was renamed the *Nossa Senhora do Carmo*,[56] and was now entrusted to the command of a shipmaster and pilot from Viana. It departed from Viana headed for Bahia, calling in at the Canary Islands. On the homeward journey to Viana, it was captured by Dutch warships and taken to Rotterdam since the Truce had expired. Both the shipmaster and the pilot from Viana stated that the bills of lading for the homeward journey had been made out in the name of Gaspar Caminha Rego in Viana, even though in truth they were being shipped on behalf of the Jewish merchant in Amsterdam. The Dutch shipmaster did not testify about the case along with his peers from Viana. Apparently, he did not sail to Bahia but remained in Viana instead.[57]

The similarity between the subterfuge indicated in the petition and the case described here may not have been a coincidence. The leader of the group of Portuguese Jews who submitted the petition was none other than Tomas Nunes Pina, who tried to prove to the Dutch authorities that the *Nossa Senhora do Carmo* was not a Portuguese ship but rather a Dutch vessel, and that its cargo did not belong to Gaspar Caminha Rego but to himself, and should hence be returned.[58] It is possible, however, that, contrary to Pina's arguments, no fraud had been committed against the Iberian authorities. Instead, the vessel would have become Portuguese, and the first shipmaster would have merely been hired to deliver the ship to

O. This other merchant was Baltasar de Barros, who paid a transfer tax on sugar in Viana in 1629 (Moreira, *Os mercadores de Viana*, p. 171).

P. From the Republic, the ship took diverse merchandise and a letter of credit from the shipowner addressed to Gaspar Caminha Rego, so that the latter could instruct a merchant in the Canary Islands to load forty barrels of wine. A traveling agent handled the sale of the wares brought from the Republic, and, apparently, the wine too. The proceeds resulted in 125 crates of sugar and nine small containers of ginger. The voyage would also have generated revenue for the merchant, as the vessel's shipowner. Hence, the ship brought a further six crates of white sugar and two of muscovado sugar, which corresponded to the freight rates for the outward journey and averages for the homeward journey paid in Bahia. One of the individuals chartering the vessel was Floris den Otter, a Dutch merchant who lived in Viana. Den Otter ordered another Dutchman, based in the Canary Islands, to hand over ten barrels of wine to the agent who was traveling on board, who may have bought nine crates of white and muscovado sugar and half a crate of tobacco with the proceeds. It is possible that this "Flemish" Floris den Otter, the Old Christian Gaspar Caminha Rego, or the first shipmaster, from Amsterdam – all of them, two or just one of them – owned the remaining sixth share of the ship. It is also likely that there were more shippers, since the almost 143 crates of sugar on the homeward journey and the fifty barrels of wine on the outward journey – the cargo brought from Holland is unknown – would have represented something like one-third or one quarter of the ship's 140-ton capacity.

Jan Bicker

Jan Bicker actively participated in trade in the Eastern Mediterranean and shipbuilding. Born into a patrician Amsterdam family, years after commissioning the ship *Nossa Senhora do Rosário*, he became a magistrate in the city, as his brothers did. His son-in-law, Johan de Witt, would become the most influential politician in the Republic, holding the main office in the Province of Holland, that of Grand Pensionary, between 1653 and 1672. Jan Bicker's various properties included an island off the coast of the city, which still bears his name, Bickerseiland. One of his brothers was a director of the East India Company, while another was a member of the consortium that negotiated the purchase of all the mace (the aril of nutmeg, consumed as a spice) imported by the Company in 1621.[63]

Portrait of Jan Gerritsz. Bicker, *who would play a leading role in trade with Italy and the Levant and become a burgomaster of Amsterdam; attributed to Wallerant Vaillant.*

its new owners or managers in Viana, from where it would only sail on Portuguese routes.

In effect, there are cases of Dutch vessels purchased on behalf of merchants based in Portugal. In one such case, in 1616, four Jews from Amsterdam bought a share each in a ship on behalf of counterparts in Porto, declaring that they had done so to outfit the vessel and send it to its owners in Portugal.[59]

However, there were also Dutch vessels sailing between the Republic and Brazil via Portugal, even after the 1605 ban, which did not even change their names or shipmasters. In 1618, a shipmaster from Rotterdam committed to sailing from Holland to Brazil, with a stopover in Porto. He would sail on a ship that had recently been built in the Low Countries. The vessel had a capacity of 360 tons and had been named *Nossa Senhora do Rosário* from the outset. A 1/8th share of this ship belonged to a Portuguese Jew from Amsterdam, the brother of a New Christian merchant based in Porto.[60] It is possible that local crew was taken aboard in Porto, or at least a pilot who was familiar with the Brazil route, and who could pretend to be the shipmaster before the Portuguese authorities, although this was not explicitly stipulated in the contract.[61]

Another Dutch ship likewise named *Nossa Senhora do Rosário* may also have proceeded in this manner. In 1620, this ship, or carrack, as it is identified in some of the documents, with a capacity of 280 tons, had a shipmaster from Rotterdam and a captain from Porto. At the time, the title of captain denoted a military command. Yet this was a merchant vessel. Hence, it can be assumed that the title referred to a nautical rank, or better, that the nautical command of the vessel was shared or alternated between the Portuguese and the Dutchman, depending on who was asking. It is also possible that the Dutchman only sailed on the European legs of the voyage. A young merchant named Jan Bicker commissioned the construction of the ship, being responsible for its "administration and accounts." Bicker retained ownership of half the ship and sold 3/16ths to a Portuguese Jew. The other owners are unknown. The captain of the ship, who was ready to set sail for Porto, was to hand the vessel over in that port to the co-owners' proxies, who could sell their respective shares in the ship, either entirely or in part.[62]

It is clear how difficult, or well-nigh impossible, it is to estimate the percentage of Dutch vessels involved in trade with Brazil,[Q] especially because they were often rebaptized or even given Catholic names from the outset. Dutch ships often sailed with Portuguese crews, and their owner-

[Q] Christopher Ebert concedes that the number of ten to fifteen Dutch ships incorporated into the Brazilian fleet every year during the Truce might have been somewhat exaggerated, albeit well within the realm of possibility. He agrees that there is nothing to substantiate the statements in the "*deductie*," but calculated, multiplying the number of ships by 200 tons, that the Dutch vessels incorporated into the Brazilian fleet would have totaled at least 2,000 tons, corresponding to 16% of the annual production of sugar in 1612, which would have been 672,000 arrobas or 12,444 tons, at 54 arrobas to a ton (Ebert, "The Trade in Brazilian Sugar," pp. 127, 129–130).

Manuel Fernandes, *said to be a master carpenter at the Lisbon shipyards and the author of the* Book of Carpentry Sketches *(1616), a treatise on shipbuilding. It contains descriptions of several types of Portuguese vessels from the sixteenth and seventeenth centuries illustrated with scale drawings, including the oldest known technical sketches of caravels.*

Fluitschip *portrayed in an engraving dated 1629.*

ship was frequently shared among individuals living in the Iberian world and abroad, either foreigners or exiles.[64] Portuguese vessels generally had Marian, Christological, hagiological and angelic names, while the names of Dutch ships were usually heroic or exotic, derived from the Old Testament and Greco-Roman mythology.[65]

The identification of these vessels' origins is complicated even further because Dutch-built ships openly integrated into the Portuguese fleet, without being camouflaged as Catholic. These ships sailed in strictly Portuguese circuits, with exclusively Portuguese crews and owners, as was possibly the case with the vessel bought by the four Jews in Amsterdam on behalf of their counterparts in Porto. Dutch-built ships were sold in Portugal, and some could be identified due to their pagan names or to references indicating that they were constructed abroad.[66] Similar features were probably not recorded in the case of many other vessels.

Flute Vessels

The presence of Dutch vessels in shipping routes between Portugal and Brazil could be explained by the supposedly lower transport costs.[67] The Dutch had a long tradition of trading in products with a low price-volume ratio that yielded small profit margins, therefore requiring low transport costs. These bulky goods[68] encouraged the development of vessels such as the fluitschip, which needed a smaller crew and allowed a maximum use of the cargo space.[69] Ebert has sought to compare the efficiency of Dutch ships and Portuguese ships, based on their freight capacity and the size of their crews. He estimates the ton/man ratio (t/m) of four ships with a capacity ranging between 180 and 300 tons that sailed from Amsterdam to Brazil, in 1595–1596, whose freight contracts mentioned the capacity and the size of the crew. The result varied from 9 to 11.9 t/m, far above the 5 t/m estimated by Costa for Portuguese ships sailing between Portugal and Brazil; but nonetheless below the 20 t/m Richard W. Unger estimated for Dutch ships in general, and those in the Baltic in particular.[70]

Apart from being more economical, Dutch vessels would have had lower construction costs, since the premium on capital – that is, interest – in the Republic was lower than in other European markets. Furthermore, shipping attracted resources from individuals who, although not directly involved in trade and shipping, viewed ship ownership as a good investment.[71] Some authors have highlighted the limited durability of Dutch ships, offset by their low cost. It appears that in the context of the intense privateering and piracy which plagued the sugar route, durability would have been secondary.[72]

It is possible that the cost of Dutch-built ships was further reduced by the introduction of wind-powered saws in the shipyards. The extent to which this equipment was in widespread use in the period examined here has, however, been questioned by Unger, the very author who greatly emphasized the importance of mechanization. Unger believes that few shipyards actually used this technology and, at the end of the day, the main source of power continued to be from human or animal muscle.[73] In any case, massive stocks of raw materials and the organization and standardization of production accelerated shipbuilding.[74] Shipbuilding might also have become cheaper due to the extensive use of timber from Norway, a market in which the Dutch predominated thanks to their large volume of purchases and the Republic's trade policy.[75] At any rate, as one of the largest sectors of the Republic's economy, the shipping industry benefited from economies of scale.[76] Finally, it is possible that the sheer size of the trading hub and the wide range of routes linked to Amsterdam, as well as the number of voyages commissioned from there, helped reduce idle spells between one voyage and another, thus reducing the freight rates of the Dutch fleet, as Violet Barbour has suggested.[77]

Een Fluyt
De Vlagh en Seylen vlack voor uyt
Maeckt korte Reyse voor de Fluyt

R. As for Portugal, owners would generally have been individuals originally involved in shipping, trade or fishing. Costa argues that investments in shipping were independent from investment in trade, and often even conflicted with the latter, since shipowners sought the highest freight rates while traders sought the lowest ones (Costa, *O transporte no Atlântico*, v. 1, pp. 391–437).

Therefore, if Dutch ships were in fact cheaper and more economical,[78] their participation in the sugar route, whether disguised as Portuguese vessels or not, would have benefited the entire chain. During periods of sharp increase in production, the limitations of both the forest resources and the shipbuilding industry of Portugal obliged imports of raw material, even contemplating imports of masts from the Republic in times of war.[S] Portuguese officials raised the matter with the monarch but faced resistance from Madrid with regard to relaxing the trade warfare policy.[79] It nonetheless appears that the Portuguese shipbuilding industry had no other choice but to remain competitive since, as has been seen, there were no entry barriers to importing vessels.[T]

The rare instances of Portuguese shipping bound for northern Europe can be explained less by the lower competitiveness of Portuguese vessels than by competitive advantages.[U] In the last four decades of the sixteenth century, religious and political conflicts in the North Atlantic made this route less attractive and far more dangerous for Portuguese shipping, at a time when opportunities in the Portuguese Atlantic and Spanish Indies were expanding rapidly – the latter particularly due to the slave trade – in addition to the Cape Route. The scarcity of Portuguese gunners meant that Portuguese ships preferred to stay in safer waters; at that time, too, the colonial routes were much further away from the center of conflicts. On these routes, Portuguese investors and seamen might enjoy the backing of the Iberian crowns and even benefitted from protectionist measures. Moreover, the Portuguese population was small and constantly drained by emigration. Attempting to cover all routes would have entailed spreading their resources too thin. It was better to focus on an area that was not insubstantial in itself. The Dutch and Germans, on the other hand, were able to rely on the demographic potential of a vast German hinterland to serve their shipping industry.[80] Thus, foreigners began to dominate transport links between Portuguese ports and northern Europe.[81]

Finally, it is important to note that in case anyone decided to use foreign vessels in voyages to Brazil, it was recommended that at least part of the crew be Portuguese, not only because they had greater experience in the South Atlantic but hiring them would also prevent Portuguese seafarers from resenting foreign competition, which could have dire consequences given the Crown's sensitivity to this matter. This was possibly what happened in the case of the 280-ton ship that had a shipmaster from Rotterdam and a *captain* from Porto.

Channeling via Portugal

Since Brazil was the production center and the Low Countries the main distribution hub, it is reasonable to ask why Portuguese ports channeled this traffic instead of the product being taken directly to northern Europe. The question is even more pertinent if one considers that, to a greater or lesser degree, Dutch ships and individuals were present in Brazilian waters.

At least in the North-South direction, most of the traffic between the Netherlands and Brazil included a stopover in Portuguese ports or had Portuguese hubs acting as intermediaries between Brazil and other European gateways, even before it was legally required. It is possible that, the main reason for this channeling was the possibility of making better use of supply and demand along the route and to take advantage of

Wheatfield *depicted on a stone tablet in Amsterdam. The Iberian Peninsula imported large quantities of grain from Northern Europe.*

efficiency gains in transport. Considering that directing trade through Portuguese ports required only a slight change of route, the gains to be made on account of transport efficiency and enhanced imports and exports could outweigh the additional costs. The same rationale applying to stopovers in the Atlantic islands was equally applicable here. The holds of ships setting out from the Low Countries contained a mix of cargoes that sought to satisfy the demand for northern European products in Portugal, Brazil and Madeira, or the Canary Islands.[82] In Portugal, the composition of this basket would be modified by removing items that were sought after locally while other products were added, whether sourced from Portugal or available there, according to the expected demand in Brazil and the Atlantic isles the ship would visit.

Thus, timber and some of the grain, metal and manufactured products from northern Europe would remain in Portugal. At the same time, olive oil, dry fruits, empty wine barrels,[83] and miscellaneous Portuguese, Spanish, Asian and Mediterranean wares would be loaded into the hold in their stead. When ships reached the islands, some of these products would be unloaded, and the empty barrels were either filled with wine or replaced with full ones.[84] In this way, the merchants operating along the entire route derived profits from exports of northern European products to Portugal and from the sale of Portuguese and Atlantic island goods in Brazil.

Furthermore, the process also garnered efficiency gains in shipping, because ships that crossed the Atlantic directly from the Low Countries to Brazil would have carried a relatively small volume of merchandise. Brazil was self-sufficient in timber, imported only small quantities of grain – replaced there by cassava (manioc) – and, considering its smaller population, had a far lower demand for metal and manufactured goods than Portugal.

The combination of products with a high ratio of value to volume – such as manufactured goods – and low-value, high-volume commodities – such as timber, grain and wine – in the hold of the same ship enabled more ves-

S. Even before the Truce began, a projector, Luís Mendes de Vasconcelos, lamented the dependence on timber brought from the Low Countries, when Brazil was so rich in this resource (L. M. Vasconcelos, *Do sítio de Lisboa, diálogos (1608)* (Lisbon: Livros Horizonte, 1990), pp. 129–130).

T. Foreign competition was probably counterbalanced by a certain moderation of Portuguese buyers with regard to imported vessels, even more so from enemies. Moderation would have been recommendable so as to prevent Portuguese shipmasters, carpenters and other professionals directly or indirectly involved in naval construction, a sector which generated a great deal of employment, joining protectionist movements. Such movements would possibly have been backed by the local authorities, anxious to sustain their communities, and by the Crown, concerned about the expansion of its rivals' shipping. However, this is mere conjecture.

U. This does not mean that Portuguese vessels never traded with northern Europe. Manuel António Fernandes Moreira mentioned some voyages, but emphasized the limited participation of the Viana fleet in sugar exports to the Mediterranean and northern Europe (Moreira, *Os mercadores de Viana*, pp. 53, 61–63).

The Baker; *Job Adriaensz. Berckheyde (ca. 1681). Sugar exports ensured that Portugal met its demand for grain, which production in the north of the country could not always satisfy.*

sels to sail the route. As a result, the flow of information increased, and the chain of supply and demand improved. Moreover, shipping more expensive goods along with cheaper products in a larger number of vessels helped spread the risk.[85]

Finally, while the voyage from northern Europe to Brazil was not overly long, the stopovers in Portugal and the islands enabled travelers to walk on dry land. Meanwhile the vessel had its stocks of fresh water and provisions replenished, which freed up cargo space that would otherwise have had to be used to stow sufficient provisions for the entire journey.[86]

The same rationale was also applicable to the South-North direction, albeit to a lesser extent. Part of the sugar and other Brazilian products, such as comfits, ginger and cotton, remained in Porto, from where it was distributed to Iberian markets and the Mediterranean, especially Italy.[v] Brazilwood was not considered here because it was subject to a royal monopoly leased to private individuals, and apparently the entire trade in this timber was channeled through Lisbon.[87]

In Porto, sugar and other Brazilian products could be combined with sumac, an important product exported from the Douro region. Porto also exported traditional Mediterranean commodities such as olive oil, wine, dry fruit, fresh citrus, and so forth, apart from hides and merchandise from other parts of the Iberian world. Fruit was sourced primarily from the Algarve, in southern Portugal, and was very often processed in Porto in the form of comfits. In some cases, sugar was loaded along with salt, one of Portugal's main export products, which was also produced in the Aveiro lagoon, relatively close to Porto.[w] Some voyages included stops at both ports, Porto and Aveiro; sugar was loaded at one port and salt at the other.[88] Once again, cargoes combined products with a greater and lesser value by volume.

So far, the advantages of including Portuguese ports in general, and Porto in particular, in the trade in Brazilian sugar to be distributed via Amsterdam were applicable both to stopovers in Porto as well as for Portuguese intermediation. The latter case meant dividing shipping, if not trade, into two segments – between Brazil and Portugal, and between Portugal and the Netherlands.[x] A brief stopover in Porto avoided wasting time contracting a new voyage with the shipmaster and other shippers, since the vessel was already available. It also shortened waiting time until all the cargo for the onward journey was delivered, because at least part of the shipment had already been stowed below decks. This was applicable in the case of the open stopovers before 1605, with the ship being camou-

v. Eddy Stols aptly argues: "Direct trade between the Low Countries and Brazil did not offer as many advantages as the triangular trade between the Low Countries-Portugal-Brazil-Low Countries. Flemish ships and ships from northern Europe in general were unable to take sufficient cargoes of textiles and other industrial products for a Brazilian market that was still quite limited, with different consumption habits. Hence, it was imperative to call in at Portugal, Andalusia or the Azores, Madeira and the Canary Islands in order to load olive oil, wine and other farm produce exclusive to the Mediterranean region to supply the Brazilian market. Even on the homeward journey, the direct route from Brazil to northern Europe was not always the most suitable because large quantities of sugar and brazilwood could be sold in Iberian markets or through Iberia to Italian hubs, especially in Venice, which consumed vast amounts of Brazilian sugar" (Stols, "Os mercadores flamengos," pp. 42–43).

w. Even though voyages to Porto could be combined with stopovers in Aveiro, it is not evident whether this was a common practice. In any case, some freight contracts signed in Amsterdam stipulated that shipmasters were to proceed in this manner or were to follow the instructions they received before departure (SR nos. 47, 48, 49, 76, 89, 1223).

x. Even considering that the sugar trade was managed from northeast Europe, Costa states that Portuguese port cities were not mere stopovers, where ships made perfunctory stops on a route linking a production center and a distribution center, but that they were in fact real commercial hubs, where imported and exported products exchanged hands before being shipped out again and consumed. However, Costa added that until the 1620s, a good part of the sugar which passed through Portuguese ports was sent from Brazil on behalf of merchants based in northeast Europe (Costa, *O transporte no Atlântico*, v. 1, pp. 134–140).

This tile panel shows Lisbon's Ribeira Velha Market in the Early Eighteenth Century.

flaged or rebaptized, during embargoes or after foreign shipping to Brazil was banned. As in the case of camouflage for loyal vessels, it is possible that smaller Portuguese ports were also more amenable to the scheme of rebaptizing ships with Portuguese identities.[89]

Nonetheless, it was sometimes advantageous to separate the two legs of Atlantic voyages, using larger vessels for the first, which arrived in Porto with timber and grain and returned to northern Europe with salt and sugar; while smaller ships sailed between Porto and Brazil. Smaller vessels were better suited to the volume of the merchandise being transported on that southern leg. In this case, Portuguese intermediation for Brazilian products also enabled the voyage from the Low Countries to Portugal to be included as a stopover in journeys beyond the Strait of Gibraltar, in far larger vessels.[Y] As we have seen, being located one-third of the way from Amsterdam and two-thirds of the journey from Brazil, while enjoying excellent communications with both regions, Portuguese intermediation always facilitated matching supply and demand in both directions, thus obtaining better terms of trade.[90]

The costs incurred on account of intermediation in a Portuguese port could also be reduced by improved coordination of vessels plying the two segments, so as to minimize idle spells waiting for cargo in port. Perhaps this was the case with the sugar and other merchandise loaded in Bahia by a merchant named Custódio Nunes, sent to another merchant in Porto, who, in turn, loaded the cargo there onto a ship commanded by a Dutch shipmaster, consigned to a Portuguese Jew in Amsterdam, on whose account they had presumably been shipped from Bahia.[91] In the opposite direction, Paulo de Pina consigned two shipments in Amsterdam, each one in a Dutch ship, to another merchant in Porto, who then sent them in two caravels to a trader in Pernambuco.[92] This coordination was easier when the owners of the cargoes were on the same page with each other and with the ship's crew, which was more likely to take place when the former were also the owners of the vessel.

There was yet another and more compelling reason for Portuguese ports, particularly Porto, to be true intermediaries in the sugar trade and not just stopovers. As already pointed out, northern Portugal had a larger population than that of Brazil, and a far higher demand for northern European products than in the South American colony. However, that region had few products to offer in exchange, therefore some of the demand continued to be latent. To attract foreign products, Porto merchants and seafarers needed to ensure that it was more lucrative for foreigners to import sugar through Porto than to obtain it directly from the other side of the Atlantic. For this reason they might have accepted lower profit margins, so that the price of sugar in Porto was sufficiently similar to prices in Brazil, and the risks and costs involved in the process, not just with regard to transport but the entire transaction, meant that direct imports made little sense for other European nations.[Z]

Yet the costs and risks involved in Portuguese intermediation or stopovers were not negligible: to anchor off the walls of Porto, for example, ships had to enter through the sinuous Douro mouth, replete with sandbanks and submerged rocks, which made it necessary to hire harbor pilots to guide ships to the anchorage. In effect, accidents occurred most frequently while approaching the coast or entering the harbor, during maneuvers and during loading and unloading.[93] Furthermore, as with stopovers in the islands, these stops entailed higher transport costs due to expenditure for idle crews while

Nautical chart dated 1642, showing the Portuguese coast, from Leça to Aveiro, and the sinuous Douro outlet. Ships required a highly experienced harbor pilot to navigate the river mouth and reach the anchorage off the walls of the city of Porto.

Map of the entire Portuguese coast (1648).

waiting for goods to be loaded and unloaded, and during calms when ships waited for wind so they could set sail. Probably, at least in the case of intermediation, it was necessary to unload the cargo, take it to the customs house, and from there perhaps to a store or a warehouse to later reload the goods onto another ship, which meant repeating the entire operation in the reverse order. All this entailed duties, taxes, fees and emoluments, costs that sugar sourced from Pernambuco and Bahia, presumably bound for Amsterdam, would incur in Porto.[94]

The greater the number of products involved in the process, the longer it took. Handling costs were correspondingly higher and, worst of all, there was a greater risk of losses and damage caused by accidents in moving cargo on land or if goods were stored unsuitably in warehouses until they were re-exported. If someone was appointed to oversee the process, his services would naturally also have to be remunerated.

The ban on direct trade greatly favored Portugal's role as intermediary, or at least as a stopover. If an infringement was discovered, the risks to merchandise, ships, crews and counterparts, both in Brazil and in Portugal, would probably have exceeded the costs and dangers involved in channeling the trade through Portugal.[95] The tax incentives that sought to reduce the cost of intermediation in northern Portuguese ports also contributed towards ensuring that merchants from the rest of Europe preferred to procure sugar in Portugal.[96]

Nevertheless, direct and illegal trade with Brazil still continued, without resorting to the subterfuge of rebaptizing ships, when an operation had little or no interest in trading with mainland Portugal and the players involved in the venture were inclined to run the risk of being unmasked, so as to enhance their profits by avoiding intermediation costs.[97] However, there are very few documented cases of open infractions after 1605. Many of the cases recorded occurred in the year immediately after the ban was decreed. Perhaps they might even have already been planned when such voyages were legal. On the other hand, it appears that the central authorities took some time to impose the new rules on the colonial administration. This is suggested in the correspondence in which the monarch complained to authorities in Brazil about their lack of action in face of the French smuggling in Rio de Janeiro. However, a Dutch ship was seized in Recife.[98]

After 1605–1606, smuggling generally involved operations which sought to import brazilwood directly from indigenous people, who cut

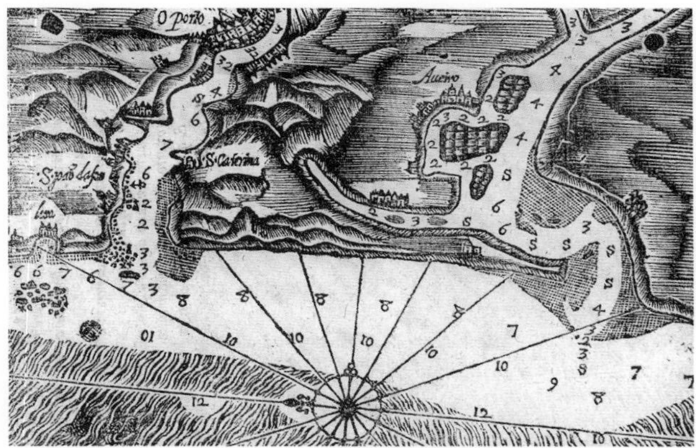

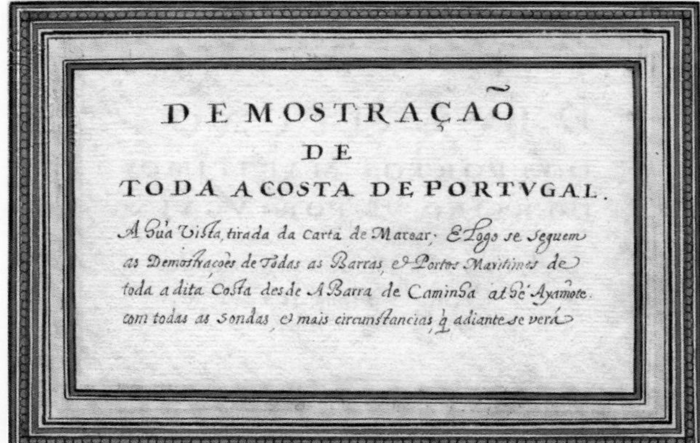

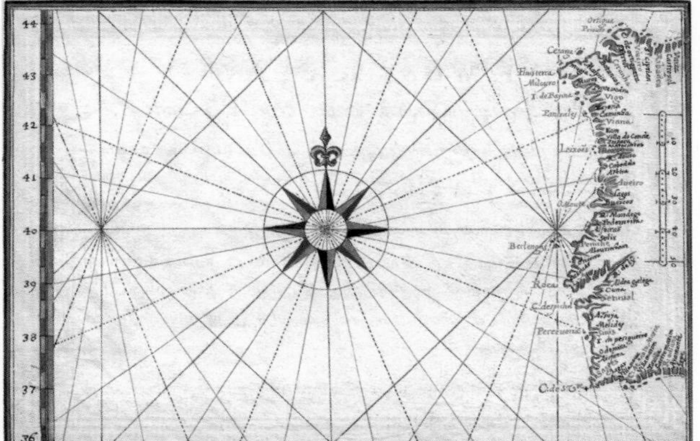

Y. According to Costa, after 1605, the sugar trade was divided into two complementary routes: the "primary" routes, which brought sugar from Brazil to Portugal, and the "secondary" routes, which distributed the sugar to the Mediterranean, the North Sea and the Baltic (Costa, *O transporte no Atlântico*, v. 1, pp. 115–116).

Z. A survey by Ebert of some quotations for sugar prices in Brazil, Lisbon and Amsterdam and freight rates between Brazil and Lisbon, in Portuguese vessels, and between Lisbon and Amsterdam, in Dutch vessels, suggests that there was a greater ratio of transport costs to arbitrage profits in the former route than the latter. However, these results should be viewed with care, since they are based on limited data about very volatile prices, namely, sugar prices, freight and exchange rates (Ebert, "The Trade in Brazilian Sugar," pp. 206–207).

Fragment of a world map drawn by the Ottoman admiral Hadji Muhammad, known in the West as Piri Reis, in 1513.

and processed the timber in regions where there was little colonization, or from Luso-Brazilians. The latter case took place in the more peripheral captaincies with small European populations and greater scarcity of imported products. In these captaincies, the administrative structure monitoring trade was not only less developed but also more amenable to the desires of the local population.[99] Other cases of smuggling involved fleeting and immediate exchanges between foreigners and Portuguese, residents or seafarers. The latter were often compelled to barter, and might have been even sacked by foreigners who participated in some of these incursions.[100]

What limited sugar from being smuggled was the risk to resident agents or frequent travelers, since, unlike brazilwood, sugar was produced in a complex manufacturing process which involved many European or Europeanized individuals. Therefore, such deals would not go unnoticed if they were conducted repeatedly. It was even more difficult when the sugar was purchased with the proceeds from the sale of imported products. In such cases, the ship would have to wait for a longer period. This was particularly true if goods were sold on credit, and it was necessary to wait until the transaction was completed, and the sugar was duly received. Delays meant a greater risk of being discovered. The other alternative was for the transaction to be arranged beforehand with local residents, who would already have stored significant quantities of sugar ready to be loaded.[101] In both cases, repeat transactions would have drawn attention, posing a risk for the settlers or frequent travelers involved in the process. It was therefore preferable to pay the costs of Portuguese intermediation and use condoned forms of subterfuge such as camouflaging or rebaptizing ships, rather than challenging the authorities with flagrant violations of the law.

Intermediation via the Atlantic Isles often replaced that of ports in mainland Portugal when the latter were of little interest to northern European merchants.[102] Traders and seafarers declared in Amsterdam that, with the implementation of the Truce, foreign ships were tacitly allowed in the islands.[103] Even after the Truce was over, commerce siphoned through the islands continued.[AA] This is suggested by freight contracts registered in Amsterdam,[104] which also indicated that the islands were stopovers for Dutch ships that were camouflaged or rebaptized to appear to be, respectively, neutral or Portuguese vessels.[105]

AA. Even though it was only very shortly after the 1605 ban was decreed, a Dutch shipmaster was arrested in Madeira (SR no. 200).

Routes

Chapter Five

1. Costa, *O transporte no Atlântico*, v. 1, p. 250.

2. SR nos. 75, 76, 77, 1102, 3117. On the impact of climatic and political conditions on shipping, see also: Ebert, "The Trade in Brazilian Sugar," p. 108.

3. SR. nos. 2603, 2604.

4. Schwartz, *Sugar Plantations in the Formation of Brazilian Society*, pp. 99–106.

5. Mauro, *Portugal, o Brasil e o Atlântico*, v. 1, p. 281.

6. Antonil, *Cultura e opulência do Brasil*, pp. 155, 118–119, 163–165.

7. On arbitrage profits compensating for the risks of sailing during adverse seasons, see: Spooner, *Risks at Sea*, p. 252.

8. Costa, *O transporte no Atlântico*, v. 1, pp. 188, 329–332.

9. Rau and Silva, *Os manuscritos do arquivo da Casa de Cadaval respeitantes ao Brasil*, v. 1, pp. 21–22. See also: Costa, *O transporte no Atlântico*, v. 1, pp. 222–223.

10. Strum, "The Portuguese Jews and New Christians in the Sugar Trade," pp. 202–203; Gonçalves, *Guerras e açúcares*, pp. 256–261.

11. Sousa, *Tratado descritivo do Brasil*, pp. 96, 102.

12. Moreno, *Livro que dá razão do Estado do Brasil*, p. 178.

13. Moreira, *Os mercadores de Viana*, pp. 83–85.

14. With regard to voyages between Portugal and Brazil, see: ibid., pp. 83–85.

15. Cardim, *Tratados da terra e gente do Brasil*, p. 255.

16. Sousa, *Tratado descritivo do Brasil*, pp. 21, 96, 102.

17. Oliveira, *A História do Brazil de Frei Vicente do Salvador*, v. 2, fols. 101v.–102.

18. This document's data are not very reliable, since the total sum does not match the sums for each port, a difference of thirty-five units. The author indicates a very large number (sixty caravels) for Tavira, a small port in the Algarve, and appears to confuse the East Indies with the West Indies: L. A. Rebello da Silva, *História de Portugal nos séculos XVII e XVIII*, V. 3 (Lisbon: Imprensa Nacional, 1867), pp. 536–537. On this document, see also: Costa, *O transporte no Atlântico*, v. 1, pp. 178–179.

19. Brandão, *Diálogos das grandezas do Brasil*, pp. 25, 30, 32, 89–90; Costa, *O transporte no Atlântico*, v. 1, p. 179.

20. AHU_ACL_CU_Consultas de Partes, COD. 33, fol. 5 – [Lisbon, January 13, 1621]. See also: Costa, *O transporte no Atlântico*, v. 1, p. 196.

21. Ibid., pp. 222–223.

22. F. Mauro, "Le Brésil au XVIIe siècle: documents inédits relatifs à l'Atlantique Portugais." offprint of *Brasília 11* (1961): 170 ff.

23. Rau, *Estudos sobre a história do sal português*, pp. 147–191; Stols, "Os mercadores flamengos," p. 29.

24. Vasconcelos, *Do sítio de Lisboa*, p. 128.

25. Costa, *O transporte no Atlântico*, v. 1, pp. 345–347; Mauro, *Portugal, o Brasil, e o Atlântico*, v. 1, 49–55, 111–115; Moreira, *Os mercadores de Viana*, pp. 67–70; Cardim, *Tratados da terra e gente do Brasil*, pp. 215, 281; Moreira, *Os mercadores de Viana*, pp. 68–69.

26. Costa, *O transporte no Atlântico*, v. 1, pp. 276–291.

27. Ibid., p. 78.

28. Ibid., pp. 272, 325–326.

29. Ibid., p. 340.

30. SR no. 807; Israel, "Spain and the Dutch Sephardim," p. 363; França and Siqueira,

"Introduction and Notes," pp. 167–168, 283–292; Sluiter, "Os holandeses no Brasil antes de 1621," pp. 205–206.

31. Costa, *O transporte no Atlântico*, v. 1, pp. 338–341.

32. SR nos. 50, 76, 89, 354, 641.

33. SR nos. 379, 426. In another case, however, a contract stipulated a laytime of one month in Portugal for a journey in which a shipmaster was instructed to call in to both Lisbon and Porto: SR no. 284.

34. SR no. 35; Costa, *O transporte no Atlântico*, v. 1, p. 210; Ebert, "The Trade in Brazilian Sugar," p. 69.

35. IANTT, STO, IC, 1-114-70, fols. 266–272; Israel, "Spain and the Dutch Sephardim," p. 195. For further information, see: Sluiter, "Os holandeses no Brasil antes de 1621," pp. 194–195; Ebert, "The Trade in Brazilian Sugar," pp. 68–71.

36. SR no. 283; IJzerman, *Journael van de reis naar Zuid-Amerika*, p. 99; Koen, "Duarte Fernandes," pp. 188, 191; D. M. Swetschinski, "From the Middle Ages to the Golden Age, 1516–1621," in J. C. H. Bloom, R. G. Fucks-Mansfeld and I. Schöffer (eds.), *The History of the Jews in the Netherlands* (Oxford: The Littman Library of Jewish Civilization, 2002), p. 77; D. M. Swetschinski, *Reluctant Cosmopolitans – The Portuguese Jews of Seventeenth-Century Amsterdam* (London: The Littman Library of Jewish Civilization, 2000), p. 107; Costa, *O transporte no Atlântico*, v. 1, p. 63; J. I. Israel, "The Economic Contribution of the Dutch Sephardic Jewry," in Israel, *Empires and Entrepots*, p. 421; Israel, *Dutch Primacy in World Trade*, p. 58; Sluiter, "Os holandeses no Brasil antes de 1621," pp. 191–199; Ebert, "The Trade in Brazilian Sugar," pp. 33, 77, 100, 177.

37. IJzerman, "Amsterdamsche bevrachtingscontracten 1591–1602," pp. 163–291; idem, *Journael van de reis naar Zuid-Amerika*, pp. 99–100; Israel, "Spain, the Spanish Embargo, and the Struggle for the Mastery of World Trade," pp. 191–192, 194–198; Israel, "The Economic Contribution of the Dutch Sephardic Jewry to Holland's Golden Age, 1595–1713," in idem, *Empires and Entrepots*, pp. 421, 423; idem, *Dutch Primacy in World Trade*, p. 58; Costa, *O transporte no Atlântico*, v. 1, p. 63; Vlessing, "The Portuguese-Jewish Merchant Community in Seventeenth-Century Amsterdam," pp. 238–239; Ebert, "The Trade in Brazilian Sugar," pp. 44–45, 241–244.

38. SR nos. 1521, 2622, 2706, 2707; a similar case can be seen in SR no. 2594.

39. SR no. 2596.

40. SR no. 2721.

41. See, for example: SR no. 2987.

42. Israel emphasized the higher costs and the need to migrate, while Vlessing downplayed their impact: Israel, "Spain, the Spanish Embargo and the Struggle for the Mastery of World Trade," p. 194; idem, "Spain and the Dutch Sephardim," pp. 371–373, 376–377; idem, *Dutch Primacy in World Trade*, pp. 125, 132, 137; Vlessing, "New Light on the Earliest History of Amsterdam Portuguese Jews," p. 53. On a migrant who possibly anticipated the end of the Twelve Years' Truce, see: Koen, "Duarte Fernandes," p. 193; Swetschinski, "The Portuguese Jewish Merchants of Seventeenth Century Amsterdam," pp. 165–166.

43. *Ordenações filipinas* (Lisbon: Fundação Calouste Gulbenkian, 1985), book 1, title LI; C. A. C. Geraldes, "Casa da Índia: um estudo de estrutura e funcionalidade (1509–1630)," Master's thesis, Universidade de Lisboa, 1997.

44. SAA, 30452: Archief van S. Hart, 875, l. 197, fols. 173–174; Mello, "Os livros das saídas das urcas do porto do Recife," pp. 29–30; Costa, *O transporte no Atlântico*, v. 1, p. 186; Stols, "Os mercadores flamengos," p. 33.

45. Ebert, "The Trade in Brazilian Sugar," pp. 125–126, 63, 169, 171–174.

46. Andrews, *Elizabethan Privateering*, pp. 133, 207–209, 232–233.

47. AHU_ACL_CU_005-02, Cx. 1, D. 1 – [October 13, 1599]; H. Livermore, "A marinha mercante holandesa no comércio do Brasil," *Revista Portuguesa de História 5* (1951): passim; Costa, *O transporte no Atlântico*, v. 1, p. 186.

48. Hermann Kellenbenz believes that the risks engendered by this process would have discouraged direct homeward journeys: H. Kellenbenz, "Der Brasilienhandel der Hamburger 'Portugiesen' zu Ende des 16. und in der ersten Hälfte des 17 Jahrhunderts," *Portugiesische Forschungen der Görres-Gesellschaft, Aufsätze zur Portugiesischen Kulturgeschichte 1* (1960): 317–318.

49. In 1597, two Dutch ships sought to set sail from Cadiz directly to Pernambuco: Ebert, "The Trade in Brazilian Sugar," p. 169; Sônia A. Siqueira and Eduardo d'Oliveira França suggested that between 1587 and 1605, a period when ships from neutral countries could legally call in at the colony, the inspection of neutral vessels in Portugal, as a result of more stringent embargoes, encouraged camouflaged Dutch ships to sail directly to Brazil, where the embargo was not implemented so strictly: França and Siqueira, "Introduction and Notes," p. 183. Both of these authors also presented a broad overview of Habsburg policies with regard to foreign shipping in Portugal, Brazil and the Atlantic Isles: ibid., pp. 173–198. Ebert also believes that the embargoes encouraged illegal trade, while the Truce discouraged such commerce by allowing legal trade intermediated in Portugal: Ebert, "The Trade in Brazilian Sugar," p. 173.

50. D. de Abreu e Brito, *Um inquérito à vida administrativa e econômica de Angola e do Brasil* (Coimbra: Imprensa da Universidade, 1931), pp. 73–74. See also: Ricupero, *A formação da elite colonial*, p. 199.

51. IANTT, STO, IC, 1-115-107.

52. NA, *Staten-Generaal*, 1.01.02, *Liassen Admiraliteyten, Ingekomen ordinaris brieven en stukken betreffende admiraliteits-en zeezaken*, 5486, published by IJzerman, *Journael van de reis naar Zuid-Amerika*, p. 100; Vlessing, "De Portuguezen in de Gouden Eeuw II," pp. 19–20. For an English translation of this passage, see: idem, "New Light on the Earliest History of Amsterdam Portuguese Jews," pp. 54–55; idem, "The Portuguese-Jewish Merchant Community in Seventeenth-Century Amsterdam," p. 231; Swetschinski, *Reluctant Cosmopolitans*, p. 110. See also: Sluiter, "Os holandeses no Brasil antes de 1621," p. 204.

53. NA, *Staten-Generaal*, 1.01.02, *Liassen Admiraliteyten, Ingekomen ordinaris brieven en stukken betreffende admiraliteits-en zeezaken*, 5486, published by IJzerman, *Journael van de reis naar Zuid-Amerika*, p. 101; Vlessing, "De Portuguezen in de Gouden Eeuw II," p. 20. See also: Ebert, "The Trade in Brazilian Sugar," pp. 128–129.

54. Moreira, *Os mercadores de Viana*, pp. 151–153; Costa, *O transporte no Atlântico*, v. 1, pp. 135–136; Vlessing, "Thomas Nunes Pina," p. 116.

55. SR no. 2288. With regard to this case, see also: Ebert, "The Trade in Brazilian Sugar," p. 128. Ebert, however, stated that the cargo of merchandise coming from the Netherlands was sold in Viana. He also confused the name of the agent in the Canary Islands, Teixeira, in this case João (Juan) Teixeira, with a toponym. Stols likewise mentioned the case to illustrate this phenomenon: E. Stols, "Convivências e conivências luso-flamengas na rota do açúcar brasileiro," p. 123. Moreira believed Floris den Otter to be English, whom he called "Flores da Nota." Floris liquidated his business in Viana in 1622: Moreira, *Os mercadores de Viana*, p. 202.

56. In the original source, the ship's name was abbreviated: *A Senhora do Carmo*: SR no. 2613.

57. SAA, 5075: Archief van de Notarissen ter Standplaats Amsterdam, l. 646A, fols. 39–41; SAA, 30452: Archief van S. Hart, 874; SR no. 2644.

58. Vlessing, "Thomas Nunes Pina"; idem, "New Light on the Earliest History of Amsterdam Portuguese Jews," pp. 54–57, 71–72, especially nn. 84 and 85; idem, "The Portuguese-Jewish Merchant Community in Seventeenth-Century Amsterdam," pp. 231, 233, n. 50. See also: Israel, "Spain and the Dutch Sephardim," pp. 379–380.

59. SR no. 1078.

60. SAA, 5075: Archief van de Notarissen ter Standplaats Amsterdam, l. 611B, fol. 430, SR no. 1456; Ebert, "The Trade in Brazilian Sugar," pp. 127–128.

61. Ebert believes that this was a case of illegal trade with Brazil, but does not take into account that the ship had left the Low Countries as a Portuguese vessel, as indicated by its Catholic name (*Our Lady of the Rosary*): Ebert, "The Trade in Brazilian Sugar," pp. 127–128.

62. SAA, 5075: Archief van de Notarissen ter Standplaats Amsterdam, l. 645b, fols. 992–993; SR nos. 2109, 2110.

63. B. Bakker, "De zichtbare stad 1578–1813," in: W. Frijhoff and M. Prak,

Geschiedenis van Amsterdam, deel II-A: centrum van de wereld 1578–1650 (Amsterdam: SUN, 2004), p. 36; Hell, "De oude geuzen en de Opstand," pp. 257, 275; Israel, *Dutch Primacy in World Trade*, p. 151; Lesger, *The Rise of the Amsterdam Market*, pp. 172, 178, 279.

64. Note one of these vessels, a 180-ton ship belonging to two Dutch merchants from Amsterdam, who sold its other half to a New Christian merchant in Porto, through the latter's Jewish counterpart in Amsterdam: SR no. 1573. For further information about this and another similar case, see: Ebert, "The Trade in Brazilian Sugar," pp. 126–127.

65. Moreira, *Os mercadores de Viana*, pp. 45–46.

66. Costa, *O transporte no Atlântico*, v. 1, pp. 362–364.

67. Ebert believed that there was a greater presence of Dutch ships during the Truce, which contributed towards the lower freight rates on voyages between Portugal and Brazil indicated by Costa. However, both authors agree that the main factor influencing freight rates was risk: Ebert, "The Trade in Brazilian Sugar," pp. 129–130, 204.

68. Israel, *Dutch Primacy in World Trade*, pp. 7–11, 18–26, 34–37, 48–60, 86–101; Barbour, "Dutch and English Merchant Shipping in the Seventeenth Century," pp. 264–266; De Vries and Van der Woude, *The First Modern Economy*, pp. 299–300.

69. Unger, *The Ship in the Medieval Economy*, pp. 223, 263. Violet Barbour highlighted the fact that the Dutch freight rates were lower than the rates charged by their competitors on the same routes: Barbour, "Dutch and English Merchant Shipping in the Seventeenth Century," p. 285. Kenneth R. Andrews emphasized that the limited English participation in the sugar trade was due to the technical inferiority of British vessels as compared to Dutch vessels, where the cheap and efficient fluitschip was "particularly suitable for the Brazil trade": Andrews, *Elizabethan Privateering*, p. 213. In 1619, a series of Dutch brokers, insurers and merchants declared that, "some 20 years ago ships were built in Hoorn and elsewhere that are called flutes, and that these are good ships that are often chartered to ship grain and other goods to Spain, Portugal or Italy and that these ships are quite as good as *spiegelschepen* [plural of *spiegelschip*]." This statement was made at the request of a Portuguese Jew in Amsterdam, who chartered ships on behalf of the contractors responsible for supplying grain to the almost isolated Portuguese strongholds in North Africa: SR no. 1626. Others stated that "rye and wheat are often shipped from here as well as from the Baltic to Portugal and Italy in ships that are called flutes and that these flutes are good ships." They emphasized that they themselves chartered them and that only the ship's name was mentioned in insurance policies, which did not specify the type of ship, but they had never heard of problems due to this: SR no. 1655. In effect, it was rare for the category of ship to be mentioned in notary records in Amsterdam, but in 1624 two Portuguese Jews bought five-eighths of a fluyt from a Dutch merchant, while the remaining three-eighths stayed in the possession of the vendor and the shipmaster: SR no. 3123. For information about the contractors' counterpart, see: SR no. 425, n. 34, 987; Swetschinski, "The Portuguese Jewish Merchants of Seventeenth-Century Amsterdam," p. 151; idem, "From the Middle Ages to the Golden Age," p. 79; idem, *Reluctant Cosmopolitans*, pp. 109–110; Mauro, *Portugal, o Brasil, e o Atlântico*, v. 1, pp. 176, 187; Israel, "Spain and the Dutch Sephardim," p. 359; idem, "The Economic Contribution of the Dutch Sephardic Jewry," p. 423.

70. Ebert, "The Trade in Brazilian Sugar," pp. 112–113; Costa, *O transporte no Atlântico*, v. 1, pp. 348–349, 356–357; Unger, *Dutch Shipbuilding before 1800*, pp. 44, 190, n. 24.

71. Barbour, "Dutch and English Merchant Shipping in the Seventeenth Century," pp. 270–271, 278; Costa, *O transporte no Atlântico*, v. 1, pp. 391–437.

72. Unger, *Dutch Shipbuilding before 1800*, p. 44. See also: Barbour, "Dutch and English Merchant Shipping in the Seventeenth Century," p. 276.

73. Unger, *Dutch Shipbuilding before 1800*, pp. 61–62.

74. Barbour, "Dutch and English Merchant Shipping in the Seventeenth Century," p. 277.

75. Ibid, p. 273.

76. Unger, *Dutch Shipbuilding before 1800*, pp. 4–11, 61–62; Ebert, "The Trade in Brazilian Sugar," pp. 123–124.

77. Barbour, *Capitalism in Amsterdam in the 17th Century*, p. 20.

78. Ebert's attempts to demonstrate that ships purchased in Amsterdam to sail to Brazil or to Portugal were cheaper than those purchased in Lisbon do not withstand scrutiny. The results derived from five examples are not very different from the cost of per ton freight capacities in Portugal estimated by Costa: between 5,783 and 10,048 réis. Apart from this, while developing his analysis, Ebert compared the price of the vessel *Nossa Senhora do Rosário*, sold in Amsterdam in 1618, with the prices of two other vessels sold in Portugal the previous year. However, the data on these two Portuguese vessels was published by Costa, who emphasized that their prices were relatively high, and that their pagan names, *Fénix* and *Broa*, indicated that they would almost certainly have been brought from northern Europe: Ebert, "The Trade in Brazilian Sugar," p. 125; Costa, *O transporte no Atlântico*, v. 1, pp. 362–364. Without considering tonnage, Moreira inferred that vessels built in Viana were not more expensive than Dutch vessels. Yet his calculations suggest that the cost would have been above 11,500 réis per ton. While looking at this seeming contradiction, one should bear in mind that his data are mostly from the second half of the seventeenth century: Moreira, *Os mercadores de Viana*, pp. 89–90, 90, n. 13. Barbour presents some sources that corroborate the argument that Dutch vessels were significantly cheaper than English vessels even at the end of the seventeenth century. However, she also stressed that Dutch ships were exported to other European nations, including the sale of ships seized by Dunkirk corsairs: Barbour, "Dutch and English Merchant Shipping in the Seventeenth Century," pp. 275, 286, 288. On the exports of Dutch ships, see also: De Vries and Van der Woude, *The First Modern Economy*, pp. 296–297.

79. On the discussions of the Treasury Council after the expiration of the Truce, see: AHU_ACL_CU_Consultas Serviço Real, COD. 35, fols. 13v.–14 – [Lisbon, January 14, 1623]; Ebert, "The Trade in Brazilian Sugar," pp. 122–123; Costa, *O transporte no Atlântico*, v. 1, p. 179.

80. Costa, *O transporte no Atlântico*, v. 1, pp. 448–450, 462; De Vries and Van der Woude, *The First Modern Economy*, pp. 642–646.

81. Costa, *O transporte no Atlântico*, v. 1, pp. 115–116.

82. Ebert developed the same reasoning: Ebert, "The Trade in Brazilian Sugar," pp. 169–170, 180.

83. SR no. 1959.

84. See this volume's introduction for the products that were imported and exported from Portugal and Brazil.

85. Costa, *O transporte no Atlântico*, v. 1, pp. 276–291.

86. Stols, "Os mercadores flamengos," p. 25.

87. Souza, *O pau-brasil na história nacional*, pp. 134–135; Mauro, *Portugal, o Brasil, e o Atlântico*, v. 1, pp. 178–180.

88. Ebert emphasized the combination of sugar and salt for enhancing shipping efficiency: Ebert, "The Trade in Brazilian Sugar," pp. 169–170.

89. IJzerman, "Amsterdamsche bevrachtingscontracten 1591–1602," pp. 163–291; idem, *Journael van de reis naar Zuid-Amerika*, pp. 99–100; Israel, "Spain, the Spanish Embargo and the Struggle for the Mastery of World Trade," pp. 191–192, 194–198; idem, "The Economic Contribution of the Dutch Sephardic Jewry," pp. 421, 423; idem, *Dutch Primacy in World Trade*, p. 58; Costa, *O transporte no Atlântico*, v. 1, p. 63; Vlessing, "The Portuguese-Jewish Merchant Community in Seventeenth-Century Amsterdam," pp. 238–239; Ebert, "The Trade in Brazilian Sugar," pp. 44–45, 241–244.

90. See the discussion about the concepts and functions of staples, gateways and hinterlands from the point of view of spatial economics in a historical context, prepared by Clé Lesger: *The Rise of the Amsterdam Market*, pp. 12–13, 56–57, 75–78, 98–99, 184–213. See also: Ebert, "The Trade in Brazilian Sugar," p. 180.

91. SR nos. 1548, 1647.

92. SR no. 1371.

93. Silva, *O Porto e o seu termo*, v. 1, pp. 110–111; Barros, "Porto: a construção de um espaço marítimo," v. 1, pp. 118–127; Moreira, *Os mercadores de Viana*, pp. 82–85.

94. ADP, NOT, PO2, l. 54, fols. 20v.–23v. (1619-6-10). On the impact of delays in ports and customs clearing see: Ebert, "The Trade in Brazilian Sugar," pp. 105–106; Costa, *O transporte no Atlântico*, v. 1, pp. 329–338.

95. Just like Israel, Costa is of the view that, from 1605 onwards, few foreign vessels sailed directly to Brazil, most of this commerce being channelled via Portugal, at least to comply with the law and pay customs duties: Israel, *Dutch Primacy in World Trade*, p. 107; idem, "Spain, the Spanish Embargo and the Struggle for the Mastery of World Trade," p. 194; Costa, *O transporte no Atlântico*, v. 1, pp. 116–119, 123, 156–158, 190. Ebert followed a similar train of thought, even though he mentioned an example of illegal direct trade after 1605: Ebert, "The Trade in Brazilian Sugar," pp. 173–174. França and Siqueira, however, are of the view that illegal direct trade was more frequent: França and Siqueira, "Introduction and Notes," pp. 157, 190–198. Engel Sluiter and Stols argue that the bans imposed by the Hispanic monarchs did not effectively succeed in deterring Flemish and Dutch trade and shipping to Brazil and Portugal. According to them, enforcement of bans would have consisted, more often than not, of bureaucratic and perfunctory measures: Sluiter, "Os holandeses no Brasil antes de 1621," pp. 204–205; Stols, "Os mercadores flamengos," p. 44.

96. Moreira emphasized the various strategies that the Town Council of Viana do Castelo, the second largest port in northern Portugal, used to attract foreign shipping and channel sugar exports: Moreira, *Os mercadores de Viana*, pp. 181–188. On similar means used by the municipal authorities in Porto, see: Silva, *O Porto e o seu termo*, v. 1, p. 331, v. 2, p. 867.

97. In this regard, I agree with the arguments propounded by Ebert to ensure that smuggling was prevented: Ebert, "The Trade in Brazilian Sugar," p. 161: "It is worth noting, however, that there were reasons to play by the rules. The trade in Brazilian sugar was relatively lightly regulated. And moreover, though sugar production was not as centralized as silver production in the New World, it did tend to group around a few major ports, so some controls were possible. Sugar production was usually riverine, and the bulk of production flowed along rivers through cities such as Salvador and Recife, where the taxing and regulating authority of the state was well represented. Once departed from Brazil, ships carrying sugar were required to return to Portugal, but this made economic sense as well. The nearest European ports were in Portugal, and Portugal was a centralized trans-shipment region for both northern European and Mediterranean markets. Additionally, in spite of the taxes (at least 20%) that accrued to sugar in the Portuguese metropolis, prices were always high enough before 1630 to guarantee profits after taxes. A moderately restrictive trade regimen characterized by high profits did not necessarily invite cheating."

98. BA, 51-V-71, fols. 84, 86v.–87, 100–100v.; Mauro, "Le Brésil au XVIIe siècle," pp. 225–226; Ebert, "The Trade in Brazilian Sugar," p. 170.

99. Ibid., pp. 160–161.

100. Israel, *Dutch Primacy in World Trade*, p. 107; Ebert, "The Trade in Brazilian Sugar," pp. 173–175; Stols, "Os mercadores flamengos," p. 46.

101. Costa, *O transporte no Atlântico*, v. 1, pp. 333–339.

102. SR no. 807; Israel, "Spain and the Dutch Sephardim," p. 363.

103. SR no. 1905 n. 58; Israel, *Dutch Primacy in World Trade*, p. 107.

104. Ebert, "The Trade in Brazilian Sugar," p. 177.

105. SR no. 2228.

Chapter Six

The Fall of Icarus (detail); *Pieter Bruegel, the Elder (1527/1528–1569). A large carrack sails across this Flemish master's canvas.*

On Board

Transporting cargo

This chapter examines the chartering of maritime transport services and the concerns that it entailed. It will touch upon the administration of ships, types of charter arrangements, transport costs and the variables that affected freight rates, as well as the options merchants had to consider while contracting services, which included making the most of the capacity available on their own ships.

Shipping Consortia

In early modern times, ships generally belonged to a consortium of investors. The ownership of cargo space was divided into multiples of two, three and five, generally in thirds, quarters, sixths or eighths, or even in twelfths or sixteenths. Shared ownership spread risks and reduced the outlay by each individual investor. Some co-owners had more shares than others, corresponding to a larger or smaller cargo space.[1]

The ownership of a carrack named the *Nossa Senhora da Luz* is an excellent example. The vessel was ready to sail in mid-July 1612, and was owned by its shipmaster and five New Christian merchants from Porto:[2]

Pantaleão Luis (mestre)	1/4
Gonçalo Lopes Vilaflor	1/4
Antonio da Costa	1/8
Diogo Cardoso Nunes	1/8
Antonio Mendes Ribeiro	1/8
Gaspar Marcos Mendes	1/8

Dutch pinnace sailing near a rocky shore; *Hendrik Cornelisz. Vroom (1628). Shipmasters were responsible for ensuring the safety of their vessel, crew, cargo and passengers.*

In Holland, there had been a longstanding tradition of extensive division of ship ownership, even reaching shares as small as 1/64ths. Such small shares required small outlays per capita, and enabled investors who did not belong to the world of shipping and trade to dabble in the sector. These investors even included rural folk, who thus risked only a small part of their capital. In this manner, more funds were driven into the transport sector. However, there are no indications that the Dutch ships operating in the trade with both Portugal and Brazil had such extensively divided ownership, with the possible exception of vessels that sailed from the Baltic to Portugal and from there to the Mediterranean.[3]

In Portugal, a more intense subdivision of ownership became an increasingly popular means of spreading risk after the intensification of privateering by the Dutch West Indies Company (WIC) in the Americas, which occurred around 1623 and 1624. As of 1630, following the capture of Pernambuco, the Dutch presence on Brazilian soil induced Portuguese shipowners to invest in shares as small as 1/50ths. The transport sector thus managed to mobilize more resources to replace lost vessels and mitigate the added risk.[4]

Shipowners entrusted the administration of their vessel to the shipmaster, who was often also one of the shareholders, as in the case of the *Nossa Senhora da Luz*. It was also quite common for shipmasters to commission master carpenters to build the vessel. Once the ship was ready, the master would divide the ownership shares among his partners, who would often have advanced him credit for building the vessel, and then appointed him as its master.

The shipmaster of the carrack *Nossa Senhora da Luz* submitted an acknowledgment to each of the five merchants who were his fellow shareholders. The acknowledgements handed over to two of them stated that one-eighth of the ship had been built on commission of the merchant in question, specifying that this one-eighth share, along with all the equipment, rigging and supplies for the journey, had cost 129,625 réis, which the merchant had already paid directly to the carpenter on the shipmaster's behalf. The acknowledgements presented to the other three partners referred to their contributions towards the ship's artillery, but made no mention of payments to the carpenter.[5]

Shipmasters were responsible for hiring the crew, receiving the ship's revenues, paying expenses, and distributing the ship's earnings. The expenses included supplies of water, firewood, and food, weapons and ammunition, as well as repairs and purchases of new equipment. Shipmasters were obliged to take care of the vessel and its cargo, and any passengers on board. They also had to keep records of their transactions and to periodically submit statements to the partners. In the acknowledgements handed over to the shareowners of the *Nossa Senhora da Luz*, the shipmaster committed to provide the merchant his share of the vessel's revenues and render accounts for all voyages, as well as to comply with his orders. To further reinforce the solidarity between the parties, two of the other owners appeared as witnesses in each report.[6]

In truth, the merchants and co-owners of the *Nossa Senhora da Luz* did not yet fully trust the shipmaster, Pantaleão Luís. They granted a power of attorney to an agent, another New Christian merchant from Porto, perhaps a brother of one of the owners. The agent was to sail aboard the ship on its maiden voyage from Porto to Pernambuco, with a stopover in the Canary Islands. In this power of attorney, the agent was described as a merchant and shareholder of the carrack, which would suggest that he might have purchased a small share from one of the other owners. Be that as it may, he was granted the necessary authority to take charge of all the vessel's revenues received by the shipmaster[7] In case the shipmaster did anything detrimental to the carrack, the company or its owners, he could replace him or appoint a substitute and sue the shipmaster in the colony's courts.[8] In the absence of the traveling agent, or in case he was unable to perform his duties, these powers would be transferred to prominent merchants in Pernambuco and Bahia, two in each captaincy. Hence, the grantors protected themselves against the possibility that any of these merchants in Brazil would be unable to shoulder the responsibility due to force majeure.[9]

Apart from being the administrator, the shipmaster was also the final authority with regard to any issues that arose while at sea. In the maritime hierarchy, the shipmaster's second in command was the pilot, who was responsible for the technical aspects pertaining to navigation, and could replace the shipmaster if necessary. Senior mariners could replace both the shipmaster and pilot in their absence, or if they were both unable to perform their duties.[10] In addition to the shipmaster, the pilot was also often one of the partners, and other mariners could also have a share in the vessel's ownership. In Portugal, only the shipmaster and the pilot received salaries, the so-called "advantages." Apart from this, they had a share in the dividends distributed among the crew, receiving the same as other officers, while junior sailors and cabin boys received smaller fractions. In truth, the profits from each voyage were divided in two: half or one third of the profits were distributed amongst the owners, and half or two-thirds were distributed amongst the crew. Hence, when the shipmaster and the pilot were co-owners of the vessel, they also received their share of the dividends distributed among the owners. When there were losses, the sailors had to content themselves with receiving enough for their subsistence during the voyage.[e4]

Chartering a Shipment

Generally, the shipmaster was the one who leased cargo space to third parties, but owners could do so as well. A ship's entire freight capacity could be leased to a single charterer, or several portions could be leased to different charterers. These chartering types are known as "voyage charter" and "space charter." In both cases, charterers often sub-let the hired space to third parties, or contracted freight on behalf of third parties.[11]This opened up a range of business activities around freight chartering.

Those who wished to book space for their goods were matched with the shipmasters, owners and sub-charterers who wished to make the space available aboard ships more profitable through various means. Such means included notices regarding the departure of vessels, brokers and private interaction in both meeting places with bourse-like functions and other sites regularly frequented by merchants[12] The Amsterdam bourse even had brokers specializing in freight, as will shortly be seen.[13]

In freight contracts, the parties agreed on the following items: the itinerary, the laytime in each port, the cargo to be transported on each stretch and the remuneration for the service.[14] Charterers' main concern was that merchandise reached its destination safely and on time. Therefore, charterers required that the freight capacity they leased was actually reserved for them. In cases of "voyage charters," shipmasters

Uriel da Costa

Jerônimo da Costa Brandão was the brother of Gabriel da Costa, who later became the famous Portuguese Jewish heretic Uriel da Costa. The latter was a New Christian who was raised in Porto as a Catholic in an environment in which many of his relatives and acquaintances were accused of secretly practicing Judaism. Gabriel migrated to Northern Europe in 1614, along with his mother and siblings, including Jerônimo. He was circumcised and adopted the name Uriel da Costa, becoming part of new Jewish communities formed essentially by émigrés from Iberia who settled in Hamburg and Amsterdam. However, he did not adapt well to the dictates of rabbinical Judaism. Moreover, he questioned the legitimacy of rules that contradicted or diverged from what he understood as being stipulated in the Bible. His ideas were considered heretical, and he ended up being excommunicated, first by the community in Hamburg, on instructions from Venice and, subsequently, by the community in Amsterdam. Nevertheless, his deep ties with the Portuguese-Jewish community, including close relatives, made it impossible for him to live on its margins. He claimed to repent and was twice readmitted. The second time, he was obliged to undergo a humiliating ceremony that sought to exprobate his heterodoxy. His difficulty in reconciling a great spiritual restlessness and aberrant ideas with his social ties gave him no respite, and Uriel eventually committed suicide. He became a symbol of the tremendous intellectual ferment of the Portuguese-Jewish community in Amsterdam, whose greatest exponent was Baruch Spinoza (Bento Espinosa).[16]

EXAME
Das tradicoẽs Phari-
ſeas conferidas com á lei
eſcrita
Por
URIEL JURISTA HEBREO,
Com repoſta a hum
SEMVEL DA SILVA
que faz officio de medico, ſeu
falſo calumniador.

AMSTERDAM,
Em caſa de Paulo à Raveſteyn anno da
criaçaõ do Mundo 5384.

Title page of Examination of Pharisaic Traditions *(1624), by Uriel da Costa, the most outstanding example of intellectual ferment of his time in Amsterdam's Portuguese Jewish community.*

were often expressly prohibited from transporting merchandise belonging to other parties. Yet such contracts sometimes allowed shipmasters and crewmembers to carry some personal cargo, while on other occasions this was expressly forbidden as well.

An enlightening example can be found in a freight contract signed by Jerônimo da Costa Brandão, who chartered the entire capacity of a carrack that was to sail from Porto to Pernambuco, calling in at the Canary Islands. The contract specified that the vessel was to load 80 tons of goods in Porto, and would take aboard as much cargo as Brandão wished in the Canary Islands, while the shipmaster and the pilot could utilize any remaining space. The contract was later amended, stating that all the cargo on the outward journey was to be delivered to Garachico, in the Canary Islands. The homebound voyage should be directly to Porto from Pernambuco, bringing the proceeds of the cargo sold, including the cargo transported from Porto as well the cargo from the Canary Islands. The remaining space, if there was any, would still be available to the shipmaster and the pilot, who were only forbidden to lease it to other parties.[15]

A. "Advantages" were deducted from the total amount to be divided among the owners and "folks," i.e., the crew. It was sometimes specified that the cost of artillery would be deducted from the total, and that crew would be responsible for part of the "supplies" (the cost of provisions and equipment), which was deducted from their share of the profits. Sailors could be rewarded for good service with "quintaladas," which were permits to take cargo on board (Costa, *O transporte no Atlântico*, v. 1, pp. 356–359, 429–430, 441; Moreira, Os mercadores de Viana, pp. 50–55, 93).

The concept of 'tons'

It would be opportune at this point to shed some light on the concept of "tons." Derived from the word "tun," used to denote a barrel of wine, the "ton" was a generic measure for maritime transport. It was equivalent to a volume of 1.5 m^3 and could not exceed fifteen quintals (900 kg) in terms of weight.[28] According to Costa, wine barrels had the ideal density for maritime transport, occupying half a ton, and, when full, weighed about 27.5 arrobas (412.5 kg, since an arroba was the equivalent of a little under 15 kg). As for sugar, tons were equivalent to 54 arrobas (810 kg), which was comparable to wine barrels. This was with regard to "crushed" (or rather "laying," *abatido*) sugar, that is, a sugar loaf broken up into small pieces or crystals. When the sugar was "standing," that is, when whole sugar loaves were wrapped and packed, as was customary in São Tomé and sometimes even in Brazil, the ton was only equivalent to 36 arrobas of weight, since whole loaves of sugar occupied more space.[29] In effect, merchants and sailors from Amsterdam – Portuguese and Dutch alike – declared, in 1617, that 54 arrobas of sugar was the standard measure used to calculate freight rates between Brazil and Portugal.[30] In the Netherlands, the standard unit for maritime transport was the "last," which was equivalent to two Portuguese tons, that is, 108 arrobas.

Each section of space equivalent to a ton in a ship's hold could generally accommodate four or five crates weighing ten to twelve arrobas (150 to 180 kg each), or three crates weighing eighteen to twenty arrobas (270 to 300 kg each). The ideal occupation of each ton was four crates weighing 13.5 arrobas each or three crates weighing eighteen arrobas each. Any deviation from this optimum arrangement hindered the ship's floatability and the use of the freight capacity.[31]

Nevertheless, there were major variations in the sizes and weight of crates. Sometimes even a single shipment had significant differences: a consignment shipped from Bahia, in 1616, consisted of five crates, which respectively weighed 14.5, 17.5, 18, 18.5 and 20 arrobas.[32] There were also regional variations: crates from Pernambuco paid higher freight charges than those from Bahia in a charter signed in Amsterdam in 1616.[33] The difference was probably due to the fact that crates from Pernambuco were larger in size. Indeed, charters recorded in the port town of Viana stated that a ton consisted of four crates from Pernambuco and five from Bahia.[34]

In reality, the correspondence between crates and tons was not consistent, as is clearly evident in a freight contract signed in Amsterdam in 1627. This contract stipulated that the freight charges would be calculated on the basis of lasts consisting of eight crates of sugar, four barrels of wine or 4,000 pounds of preserves. However, to leave no room for ambiguities, the parties included an addendum explaining that, instead of calculating the last as being equivalent to eight crates, the "habitual" measures of weight would be used, that is, 108 arrobas, at 32 pounds per arroba.[35]

A no less important clause of freight contracts was that the stipulated laytime of each stopover had to be long enough to conclude all the transactions required to load goods without tarrying too long in port. Contracts determined the maximum laytime. However, once all the cargo had been stowed on board, the shipmaster was to set sail immediately with the first favorable winds.[17] In the contract signed by Jerônimo da Costa Brandão, the shipmaster was allowed to stay in the Canary Islands for about two weeks, subsequently setting out for Pernambuco with the cargo loaded during that period.[18] Once in Pernambuco, the ship was to remain there for six months. This was a relatively long period, compared to the average laytime in that captaincy, namely a little less than two months, according to Leonor Freire Costa, in *O transporte no Atlântico e a Companhia Geral do Comércio do Brasil*. The unusual laytime was due to the fact that the homeward cargo would not be ready and waiting to be loaded by a counterpart, but would instead be purchased by the charterer and his retainer with the proceeds from the sale of the cargo transported on the outward voyage.[19] From the merchant's point of view, unnecessary stopovers, and even unloading in the wrong destination, were worse than delays in ports, as the contracts sometimes took care to emphasize.[20]

Delays in loading (demurrage) were also a prime concern of shipmasters, since they meant maintaining an idle crew and bearing the ship's opportunity cost. Thus, the charterer had to ensure that all the cargo was delivered, either personally or through agents, within the stipulated laytime. If this time elapsed without the cargo being received, the shipmaster would lodge official complaints and protests with the authorities against those responsible for loading the goods. If this produced no results, then, after registering the protests, the ship would leave. The charterer was obliged to pay for the transport costs of the homeward voyage, even if only a part of the cargo, or none at all, had been transported. This is known as a "dead-freight."[21]

This clause was quite prominent and lengthy in the contract Jerônimo da Costa Brandão signed, considering the large amount of cargo space being chartered. If six months elapsed without the cargo being loaded because the merchant was at fault, the shipmaster could lodge all the necessary protests and paperwork with the court in Pernambuco. He would then be free to set sail for any destination he wished, whether empty, or transporting third parties' cargo in the space originally chartered by Jerônimo. The latter would, nonetheless, have to pay the shipmaster the agreed sum, as if the ship had effectively brought back Jerônimo's freight.[22] On the other hand, if the charterer or his agent required the shipmaster to stay longer than originally stipulated in the contract, and the shipmaster was agreeable to this, the contracting party would pay a fine for every day of delay.[23]

From the shipmaster's point of view, the primary concern was to ensure that he was paid for his services. The charterer guaranteed that the shipmaster would receive, either from him or his agents, the agreed sums at the departure port, at stopovers, at the destination and return ports within the stipulated periods.[B] The main form of payment consisted of freight charges. In Portugal, this was calculated on the basis of tons loaded – a measure of density – and, normally, was paid some time after the merchandise was delivered. For voyages between Portugal and Brazil, in addition to the freight charges, charterers also paid "averages" [*avarias* in Portuguese], a kind of deposit paid to the shipmaster before departure. The "averages" sum was lower than the freight charges and was often calculated according to the number of containers transporting goods instead of by a uniform measure, such as tons. In the case of sugar, averages were calculated per crates. Such payments should not be confused with general averages or averages accustomed, related respectively to the distribution of losses due to force majeure and port expenses, as we will see.[24]

B. A contract signed in Viana stipulated that if the agent in Brazil did not comply with instructions, the shipmaster would be paid upon his return to Viana and would be paid interest for maritime risks as if he had taken a sea loan (or bottomry contract, an arrangement examined in further detail in chapter 9), at the rate of 50% (Moreira, *Os mercadores de Viana*, p. 65).

Thus, for the outbound leg of the journey, Jerônimo da Costa Brandão was to pay averages at 300 réis per ton in the Canaries[C] and freight at 3,000 réis per ton after the ship's arrival in Pernambuco. For the homeward journey, he would pay, in Pernambuco, averages at 400 réis per crate – that is, about 100 réis per ton – and freight at 9,000 réis per ton twenty days after the ship arrived in Porto. As for the charterer and his retainer, should he wish to take one, they would be allowed to travel out and back at no additional cost.

For journeys between Portugal and Brazil, freight charges and, to a lesser extent, averages were higher on the homeward leg than on the outward journey. Manuel António Fernandes Moreira and Costa have attributed this to the fact that the homeward journey took longer – and hence entailed greater costs. The latter emphasized that, from the shipmaster's point of view, even if it was possible to charge dead-freight for undelivered cargo, the greater remuneration for the homebound journey would be an additional compensation for the risk of insufficient cargo on that leg, whether due to the charterer's agents or because the shipmaster was unable to find demand for the remaining space which he was entitled to transact.[25]

Moreover, it is likewise possible that the higher remuneration for the homeward journey offered merchants greater security that the shipmaster would better comply with the stipulated obligations. An analogous rationale could explain why the averages, which represented a smaller amount, were paid before departure on each leg, while the freight charges, much higher sums, were paid on arrival. Similarly, one third of the "advantages," the salary which the consortium of shipowners paid to the shipmaster and the pilot, were handed over in Brazil and two thirds were paid after the vessel's return.[26]

In practice, it was common for the share of averages that should ordinarily have been paid in Brazil to be paid after returning to Portugal. This was a convenient solution for both the shipmaster as well as the merchants: the shipmaster received the funds he did not need to spend in the colony upon his return to Portugal, without incurring the risk of losing merchandise, money or instruments of credit. Merchants, in turn, gained time and money by postponing payment of the averages to the moment when the operation was concluded. In these arrangements, the averages were calculated according to the types of sugar shipped, and very likely on the basis of the proceeds they were expected to obtain. Sometimes, even the averages that were to have been paid in Portugal before the outward voyage were paid after the ship returned home.[27]

In Amsterdam, "voyage charters" were common.[36] Such charters were sometimes paid on the basis of a lump sum for the entire ship and voyage,[37] and sometimes per last, in much the same manner as was done in Portugal per ton.[38] References to the cargo capacity of ships are common in contracts from the Netherlands, but not in those from Portugal. Capacity figures indicate that very often it was not entirely occupied by these charterers. In other cases, more frequently on journeys that spanned the Mediterranean, the ship was chartered on a monthly basis, "time charter."[39] No averages were paid and generally the freight charges were only paid when the shipmaster returned successfully. This is what is indicated in contracts pertaining to trips to Porto by Portuguese Jews living in Amsterdam.[40] It was not uncommon for the shipmaster to receive sums before or during the voyage, at the destination port or during stopovers, to prepare and outfit the ship. However, these funds were provided as a loan, which was deducted from the total settlement at the end of the voyage.[41] Since the shipmaster risked not being able to conclude the homeward voyage due to force majeure, such as shipwreck or seizure by Iberian authorities, it was also customary to include clauses specifying that in such circumstances the shipmaster would be paid for the first leg of the voyage.[42]

In other cases, contracts were signed just for the outward journey, whereby the freight charges were paid at the destination, as stated in records pertaining to ships chartered to transport grain[43] and codfish loaded in England[44] to Porto. On the other hand there were voyages in which the charterers had little or no interest in the outward journey, allowing the shipmaster to use the cargo space as he liked, as long as it did not entail delays or risks to the vessel.[D]

When the entire capacity of ship was booked on a "voyage charter" basis, the remaining space could only be rented to third parties with the agreement of the charterers or their agents. Sometimes contracts even forbade cargo in the shipmaster's cabin.[45] The charterers would be the beneficiaries of the freight charges paid subsequently by third parties for transporting cargo.[E] In some cases, where the freight was charged on the basis of lasts, instead of being based on the entire ship and voyage, it was stipulated that if the shipmaster loaded sugar belonging to third parties in any remaining cargo space, the original charterers would pay the same charges contracted by subsequent charterers instead of the sums originally agreed upon.[46]

In Portugal, it was also common to find similar arrangements for the homeward voyage from Brazil, only stipulating whether the price paid by charterers would be equal to the higher, the lower or the average price paid by other users. In Portuguese contracts, such conditions were more common in periods of greater uncertainty due to the geopolitical situation, or in arrangements that combined the services of an overseas commercial agency with transport services.[47]

The costs of transport – freight charges and averages – varied in accordance with supply and demand, risk, the use of artillery, type of navigation (in fleets, escorted convoys or separately), the route, the type of ship and cargo and, perhaps, whether the merchandise belonged to the owners of the vessel. In the medium term, the demand for transport reflected the prosperity of the trade being conducted on the route in question. Supply reflected the capacity of the shipbuilding industries and losses to stock caused by corsairs and pirates, alongside the competing demand for shipping on other routes.

According to four brokers in Amsterdam specializing in freight, supply and demand could fluctuate quite rapidly and rates could vary significantly, depending on when contracts were signed and the destinations involved. Short-term variations were also evident, both in Portugal as well

C. The practice was for averages for the outward journey to be paid at the departure port – in this case in the city of Porto – however, since the charterer was traveling on board and the cargo would apparently be delivered entirely in the Canary Islands, the averages were to be paid in that archipelago; see: ADP, NOT, PO2, l. 35, fols. 120v.–122v. (1612-7-10).

D. This was the case with a voyage between Amsterdam and the Algarve, southern Portugal, with a stopover in Dieppe, France, during which the shipmaster would unload grain and other products which he was transporting on his own account, but with the permission of the charterer (SR no. 281). Similarly, on a voyage between Amsterdam and Viana, the shipmaster and owners allowed the charterer to load ten lasts without paying freight charges on the outward journey, but they could lease cargo space to other parties, as long as this did not entail a delay in the ship's departure. On the homeward voyage, however, leasing cargo space to third parties was prohibited, and the entire cargo brought by the charterer would be comprised of sugar (SR no. 349).

E. Proceeds from transporting letters, money and passengers generally went to the shipping consortium, and not to charterers, even though such transportation had to be approved by charterers or their agents. In some cases, the payment for such transport was divided between the shipping consortium and the charterers (SR nos. 50, 354).

In the Netherlands, the greater subdivision of ship ownership attracted investors to the shipping industry.

View of Amsterdam from the IJ River (1606).

as in Holland, in cases in which different charterers paid disparate amounts for freight on the same voyage, and when charterers agreed to pay a sum equal to the lower, the higher or the average of freight charges contracted by additional charterers.[48]

Predatory activities were the variable that caused the most discernible impact on freight charges. In addition to reducing available transport supply, they increased risks, inducing owners and crews to demand a greater premium for risking their lives, freedom and assets. The intensification of privateering and piracy also increased insurance premiums. Likewise, it often entailed expenditure on account of the purchase of artillery and ammunition and contracting additional crew, which also increased the opportunity costs of the cargo space, since it was partially occupied by ammunition and additional provisions. Furthermore, excessive dispersal of shipments also meant underutilizing the net tonnage of ships.[F] It is likely that deviating from standard routes to avoid areas with a higher incidence of corsairs and pirates also added to freight costs.

Costa has observed that freight rates were relatively stable between 1580 and 1623, when they were driven up by the WIC's activities. Until then, rates had been somewhat higher between 1580 and 1601 due to English and Dutch privateering. Rates then fell slightly until the beginning of the second decade of the 1600s, when Muslim piracy necessitated a small increase.[G] Christopher Ebert states that although the freight contracts signed in Amsterdam, which he has studied, do not permit a systematic analysis, they do indicate a steep rise in freight charges between the peaceful period of 1609–1611 and the turbulent year of 1627. Prices even tripled.[49]

As we have seen, in Amsterdam it was common for ships to be chartered for outward or homebound legs of journeys to Portugal. Shipmasters preferred the simultaneous charter of both legs and even offered discounts in order to guarantee that the ship would be chartered in both directions. This was what the aforementioned four specialized freight brokers in Amsterdam stated in 1618.[50] Voyages contracted in Portugal bound for Brazil typically encompassed both the outward and homeward journeys. Perhaps this was why variations in the itinerary had less of an impact on freight charges. The presence or absence of stopovers on the way to Brazil, as well as whether Pernambuco or Bahia was the final destination, had little or no impact on the prices charged for transport.[51] Freight contracts signed in Viana reveal that short distances were proportionally more expensive than longer distances, perhaps because chartering a long voyage ensured that a ship would be hired for a considerable period of time instead of risking several idle spells waiting for new contracts.[52]

The types and sizes of the ships also had less impact on freight charges. In general, all prices would fluctuate according to the same upward or downward trends, though caravels had slightly lower rates and carracks had slightly higher rates,[53] probably due to the varying levels of security each provided. Ebert estimated that, calculated in réis per ton, the average freight rates charged in the Netherlands for a voyage to Portugal were about half the values charged in Portugal for a voyage to Brazil for journeys of average duration in both segments. Ebert attributed this disparity to the greater efficiency found in Dutch shipping. Still, the Dutch flag may have helped make the difference by reducing the risks and costs of privateering and piracy. If the presence of ships built in the Republic on voyages between Portugal and

Brazil – whether lawful or not – provided efficiency gains, such gains should have spread across the entire shipping sector. As we saw in the previous chapter, shipping and trade in ships were relatively competitive markets, at least until the supply fell from 1623 onwards. On the leg between the Iberian Peninsula and Brazilian coasts, flying the Dutch flag for protection was constrained by the extent to which such an expedient could affect the sensibilities of both the competition and the Hispanic authorities.[54]

Finally, merchandise with different densities involved, in theory, different freight charges which compensated for the underutilization of the available cargo space. High-density shipments caused a loss of floatability, on the one hand, and on the other, containers' size did not optimally fit the layout of holds, wasting part of the cargo space.[55]

Below Deck

Freight contracts often had clauses pertaining to the costs and fees associated with port activities. In order to avoid differences, contracts stipulated which parties would be responsible for loading and unloading the merchandise. Such services and expenses involved the boats taking the goods in and out to the ship, the stowing of the cargo below deck, generally according to the custom in each port,[56] and customs clearances.[57]

Sometimes the parties established that a trimmer would be hired by the charterers or their agents to stow the cargo. In one of the cases examined, it was stipulated that the shipmaster and his crew would not be liable for anything that happened to the wine while the trimmer was stowing barrels in the Canary Islands.[58] There were contracts that also specified whether the charterer would pay for loading and unloading cargo, the entry and exit fees at ports, hiring pilots to guide the ship into and out of harbors,[59] and the launching at the port of departure.[60] In contracts signed in Amsterdam, it was customary for charterers to pay for piloting services.[61]

In Portugal, in addition to charterers often being responsible for loading cargo on board and paying the fees for entering and exiting harbors, there was also mention of a charge for "primage and petilodeminage" (*limão e petilimão*).[62] Apparently this fee was paid for hiring hands and ropes to assist with the moorage, as well as for rewarding the shipmaster for the use of his cordage while unloading merchandise, and to sailors for assisting in this task.[63]

In Amsterdam, charterers habitually paid the shipmaster but not the consortium that owned the ship,[H] a bonus known as *priemgeld* (also primage

F. It can also be noted that journeys as a fleet extended the average duration of voyages, and hence increased the costs of maintaining crews and stocking merchandise, apart from reducing the arbitrage between purchases and sales. However, during this period, fleet shipping was never a standard practice and hence its impact on costs was limited to the cases in which it was requested.

G. The 1% rise in freight rates between 1602 and 1623 proved to be quite irrelevant when there were short term variations of more than 10%. On the other hand, Costa identifies a correlation between higher freight rates, between 1622 and 1628, not just with the WIC's predatory actions but also with a rise in the price of sugar, which, in truth, she attributes to the same hostile activities, which would have hindered integration between Brazilian and European markets and increased arbitrage profits (Costa, *O transporte no Atlântico*, v. 1, pp. 179, 204–206, 379–380). Costa emphasizes that freight rates did not always dovetail with the diplomatic context. In effect, freight rates fell between 1601–1606, "far from any expectation of peace, while they even rose before the Twelve Years' Truce was over": ibid., pp. 370–372. Nevertheless, one may reasonably argue that the aforementioned fall in freight rates was perhaps due to the peace treaty with France in 1598 and the end of English privateering and, subsequently, the peace with England in 1603 and 1604 (Ibid., pp. 78–79; Allen, *Felipe III y la pax hispanica*, pp. 40, 160, 194). The rise in freight charges during the Twelve Years' Truce was in all likelihood attributable to Muslim piracy.

H. Although on some occasions both the shipmaster and the owners received a gift, as was the case on a voyage from Amsterdam to Vila Nova de Portimão, in the Algarve, for which the shipmaster received 35 guldens and each of the two owners received a crate of dried figs (SR no. 3352).

FAZENDO UIAGEM MEL. GOMES FERRAS, D LXA. IO
PA. PERNÃO BUQUO, NA CARAVELA POR NOME S. AN.
FOI POR CABO. VERDE E ESTANDO. SURTA NO PORTO
DA CIDADE. D S. TIAGO, EM O PRO. D OUTUBRO D ANNO D 16SS, E HŨA
SESTA FRA. A NOVE LHE DU HŨA TROMENTA. E SE VIRÃO PERDI=
DOS NA SADA D DITO PORTO E CHAMANDO POR NOSA SA. DOS REMEDIOS,
COM MTA. DVAÇÃO OS LIVRACE DO PERIGO, EM Q ESTAVÃO, E ASIMOS LI
VROU. PRA LEMBRANÇA DA MCE. Q LHE FES LHE MANDU FAZER ESTE PAINEL

in English). This bonus was generally paid at the end of the voyage,[64] sometimes at the beginning,[65] and on yet other occasions, both before and after the journey. It often consisted of a new hat, a cloak, a flag or wine, and was sometimes paid partly in cash and partly in goods.[66] A contract signed in 1610 guaranteed the shipmaster a flag before he weighed anchor from Amsterdam with grain, timber and other products for two of the following three ports: Pontevedra, in Galicia (Spain), Porto and Viana, from where the vessel was to bring sugar to either Amsterdam or Dunkirk (Southern Netherlands), while he was to get a new cloak on his return.[67]

Finally, along with the costs incurred when entering and exiting the harbor, contracts sometimes alluded to "petty averages" or "averages accustomed," which were different from the averages that, in a certain way, were an integral part of the freight charges. On a voyage from Olinda to Viana, the charterer paid freight charges at 8,500 réis per ton and averages at 500 réis per crate. Apart from this, the freight charges were rounded up, adding a sum equivalent to half an arroba (about 79 réis) per crate, on account of averages accustomed.[68]

It is possible that these extra fees and bonuses helped the shipmaster pay for some implicit costs, so to speak, such as port entry "gratuities." This is reflected in a document studied by Costa that describes the accounts of a ship on a voyage between Lisbon and Paraíba. Upon arriving at the Tagus River, the shipmaster would have to give gratuities to the captain of the Belém Tower, the registrar of discharges and health officials who strove to ensure that "pestilential" people did not set foot on shore. Apart from this, the shipmaster had to contend with the loss of two crates of sugar, which were habitually pilfered at the customs house in Lisbon.[69]

One of the main issues addressed in freight contracts was the onus for losses and damages caused by force majeure, that is, situations for which the shipmaster was not culpable. Generally, merchants ran the risk on the merchandise and the shipmaster the risk on the vessel. In some cases, it was established that damage to cargo, whether transported on the account of the charterers or the shipmaster and the crew, would be shared by all.[70] These were known as "general averages," a medieval term for losses incurred when vessels under threat were lightened by throwing cargo overboard (jettisoning). Such damages were to be shared by all shippers, since sacrificing the lost goods had saved the remaining cargo. Here, this concept extended to cases in which the merchandise was not necessarily cast into the sea, but was simply damaged. Hence it functioned as a sort of self-insurance amongst owners of the cargo on board.

According to Malynes' traders' manual, if the allocation of general averages or "contributions" was assessed before arriving at the destination port, the amount being divided would be calculated on the basis of the purchase price; if it was assessed after arriving at the port, the total would be calculated on the basis of the sale price. In any case, the shipmaster was to apportion the damages before unloading and was to withhold everyone's merchandise until they had all paid their share.[71]

In certain contracts recorded in Porto, it was stipulated that while apportioning damages as general averages, the shipmaster's share would include not only the merchandise he himself was taking but also the freight charges that he was to receive, as well as his share in the vessel if the former were not enough. The amount of the damages was to be assessed amicably by the parties or by two honest men who were

בא״י אמ״ה שעשה את הים
הגדול
יהי רצון מלפניך
שאלהינו ואלהי אבותינו שיה
עסק זה לרפואה כי רופא
חנם אתה · ברוך אתה ה׳
רופא חולים

Miracle of Our Lady of Remedies for Manuel Gomes Ferraz (*1656*). *In the caption, a traveler dedicates this work, commissioned from an anonymous painter, as an ex-voto for Our Lady of Remedies for sparing him from being shipwrecked.*

Prayer for ocean crossings in a Jewish book of blessings printed in Austria in 1751.

Seventeenth-century "sugar-crate" closet. According to scholars Alberto Vieira and Leonardo Dantas Silva, hardwood such as jequitibá (Cariniana), *tapinhoã* (Ocotea glaucina), *Brazilian walnut* (Ocotea porosa) *and vinhático* (Plathymenia reticulata) *were used to make shipping crates for Brazilian sugar and was reused to make furniture. Called "sugar crate" furniture to this day, several examples of these items can be found on the Island of Madeira. Gunther Joppig, who was once in charge of the musical instruments department of the Munich Municipal Museum, observes that wood from sugar crates could also be recycled in Europe to make musical instruments.*

Descent from the Cross; *Rembrandt van Rijn (1606–1669). According to microscopic examination by Peter Klein, of the University of Hamburg's Department of Wood Science, Rembrandt, who lived in a predominantly Portuguese-Jewish district of Amsterdam, painted this work on cedar, supposedly recycled from sugar crates. The artist is also believed to have used other types of South American wood, such as jequitibá, in his works, possibly obtained in the same manner.*

NIEMAT·EN·KENT·HE·SELVE
NEMO NON
ELCK
H·COCK·EXCVD·CVM·PRIVILEG
Nemo non quærit passim sua commoda, Nemo
Non quęrit sese cunctis in rebus agendis,
Nemo non inhiat priuatis vndique lucris,
Hic trahit, ille trahit, cunctis amor vnus habendi est.

Seven Deadly Sins: Avarice; *Pieter Brueghel, the Elder (1550/1570). In this drawing by the Flemish artist, several types of containers bear the marks of different merchants.*

A form for a bill of lading

The National Archives at The Hague contains a bill of lading for a fardel of baize to be transported from Amsterdam to Porto in 1617.[I] It is transcribed in full below. The words in boldface correspond to the text filled in by hand in the original. The rest of the text was printed.

*I, **Diricx Cornelisz. Claes** of **Enchuijsen*** [Enkhuizen], *shipmaster after God of my ship called **De Lieffde*** [the "Love"], *currently anchored off **Amsterdam** so as to be able with the first favorable winds (which God will grant) to sail for **Porto in Portugal** where I shall unload directly, declare and acknowledge that I have received under the decks of my ship from **Mr. Luis Pereira da Silva**, namely **a fardel with baize**, all dry and well stowed and marked with the aforesaid mark. I hereby undertake to deliver the entire consignment (if God grants me a safe voyage) aboard my ship to the said **Port-à-Port*** [i.e., the city of Porto, as it was called by the French], *to the Honorable **Mr. Jan de Leon*** [João de Leão] ***or his appointee**, or his factor or representative, as long as I am paid a sum of **one ducat*** [i.e., one Portuguese cruzado] for the freight of the aforementioned [cargo]. *And the* [general] *averages shall be determined according to maritime usage and customs. And so as to comply with this, I pledge my person, all my goods and my said ship with all its effects. In acknowledgement of the above, I have signed three bills of lading of the same tenor and content with my name and in my handwriting; if one [copy] is satisfied the others will no longer be valid. Written in **Amsterdam**, on the **10th of August 1617**."* *Below the printed text, the shipmaster inserted an erratum by hand: **"I mean one ducat and (a) half as freight charges Dirik Corneleije."*** On the left-hand side there is a drawing of the mark of the consignor, Luis Pereira da Silva, on whose behalf the goods were being shipped, and the number of the container, in this case, simply ***"No. 1."*** The following text was printed on the right-hand side: *"These good and true bills of lading are printed and were sold at the book of the Bourse with due care and honesty by Jan Tomasz.*[79]

Ick ... van ... Schipper naest Godt van mynen Schepe ghenaemt ... als nu ter tijt ghereet ligghende voor ... om metten eersten goeden winde (die Godt verleenen sal) te seylen na ... al waer mijn rechte ontladinge zijn sal, oorconde ẽn kenne, dat ick ontfange hebbe onder den overloop van mijn voorsz. Schip, van u ... te weten ...

al drooge ẽn wel geconditioneert, ẽn gemerct met dit voorstaende merck. Al het welcke ick beloove te leveren (indien my Godt behouden reyse verleent) met myn voorsz. Schip tot ... voorsz. aenden Eersamen ... ofte aen zynen Facteur ofte Gedeputeerden, mits my betalende voor myn vracht van dit voorsz. goet ... Ende de Averye na der Usantien vander Zee. Ẽn om dit te voldoen dat voorsz. is, soo verbinde ic my selven ẽn alle mijn goet, ẽn myn voorsz. Schip met alle zyn toebehooren. In kennisse der waerhz. so hebbe ic drie Cõnossementen hier af õderteeckent met mynen name, oft mynen Schryvent vã mynent wegen, al vã eender inhout, het eene voldaen, de ander van geender weerden. Geschreven in ... op den ... dach ... Anno ...

Dese goede op... Connossementẽ ... druct ende wer... cocht op den bo... de Beurs in't va... tich ende onno... by Ian Tomesz.

Original bill of lading produced by shipmaster Diricx Cornelisz. Claes of Enkhuizen for cargo to be delivered in Porto, received from Luis Pereira da Silva on August 10, 1617, in Amsterdam.

familiar with commerce and shipping, and who would act as arbiters.[72] In all likelihood, the idea was to avoid letting matters reach the customs house's magistrate,[73] which would only prolong the disputes. In Amsterdam, it was stipulated that damages would be apportioned according to usage and custom.[74] In theory, however, from 1606 onwards, the Insurance Chamber was responsible for resolving disputes about general averages. In fact, the full name of this court was expanded to Kamer van Assurantie en Avarij (Insurance and Averages Chamber).[75]

Various other clauses were included in freight contracts, either to protect parties or due to specific features of the voyage. As a guarantee for any obligation, the charterer generally pledged the merchandise being transported, whereas the transporter pledged his share in the ship. Both parties agreed upon a jurisdiction for legal disputes.[76] In Portugal, the shipmaster was discharged from his obligations after presenting a certificate from the customs officials confirming that the goods had been unloaded. Merchants were released upon paying the freight charges, along with any other applicable fees.[77]

Once the terms of the freight contract had been agreed upon, the merchants delivered their wares, whose containers – crates, barrels, tins, fardels, and so forth – were identified with a distinctive mark. Such a mark could indicate the person sending the merchandise (the consignor), the person receiving the wares (the consignee) or even a third party, who could be located anywhere, on whose account and risk this shipment was made. These marks were important for claiming restitution in cases of damage, salvage, fraud, theft and capture or seizure, as well as for insurance purposes. This was clear in a case in which the insurer, wishing to retrieve sugar taken by the East India Company, asked the insurance contractor to inform him of the identifying marks.[78]

While handing over the cargo, a bill of lading was signed, and in the case of shipping between Portugal and Brazil, averages were paid. A bill of lading was – and still is – a kind of receipt issued by the shipmaster to the consignor upon receiving the cargo. In a bill of lading, the shipmaster identified himself, along with his ship, and acknowledged the cargo being received, specifying its contents. The master declared that the cargo was loaded by the consignor and delivered on board – if this was the case – and that it had been suitably stowed under the decks. Bills of lading also specified the destination port and the itinerary to be followed, named the consignor and consignees, and stated on whose behalf the cargo was being

I. This bill of lading is almost identical to the models of other bills of lading, surviving copies of which are quite rare; one bill of lading was published by Moreira and signed in Bahia on 2 December 1651, and another was published by Costa and signed in São Luís do Maranhão on 8 May 1655, having later been transcribed by a notary in Porto, referring to a shipment of sugar to the latter city. The Bahia bill of lading has the singular feature of the consignees being two sailors who sailed aboard the caravel and were to sell the sugar on behalf of the consignor. The bill of lading was issued by these two sailors, since the shipmaster did not need to deliver the cargo to them at the destination, and the bill of lading included details about the remuneration for these services as mercantile agents (NA, 1.01.02, 12561.33.1; Moreira, *Os mercadores de Viana*, pp. 58–60; Costa, *O transporte no Atlântico*, v. 1, p. 443; v. 2, p. 13). Both these documents differ from the model for a bill of lading described by the Englishman Gerard Malynes in terms of the inclusion of the remuneration to be paid for the transportation, which the latter author could have omitted; see: Malynes, *Consuetudo*: vel, lex mercatoria, pp. 134–135.

shipped, and that the containers had been marked accordingly. Finally, the shipmaster promised, on behalf of the consignor, that if God brought him safe and sound to the destination, he would hand over the said cargo to the consignees, who would pay him the freight charges stipulated therein. The document also stated that three identical copies had been prepared, and that, when one of them was produced, the others would be null and void. The shipmaster would then sign it, mentioning the place and date.

Bills of lading followed nearly the same formula both in Portugal and in the Netherlands, as part of mercantile practices and customs used throughout Europe. Standardization allowed forms to be printed, leaving blanks to be filled in with information pertaining to that specific voyage. In Amsterdam, printed bills of lading were sold at the Bourse, where consignors often met masters and freight brokers.

The shipmaster left one of the three copies of the bill of lading with the consignor, kept another, and handed over the third copy to the consignee. It was common for a fourth copy to be sent aboard another ship, beforehand, to advise the consignee about the shipment, and to enable the merchandise to be insured before the voyage. A merchant wrote the following instructions to both the shipmaster and the trader who would serve as his agents on a voyage between Porto and Pernambuco via the Canary Islands:

> *...and you will inform him, António da Costa, aboard which ship you will be sending him the said goods, whether aboard your ship or on another vessel, so as to enable him to insure his goods, which sugar will come marked with his, António da Costa's, mark, and four bills of lading of the same tenor are to be issued, and you will take one with you and two [will be sent] through other ships and one will remain on land in the said Brazil.*[80]

In the absence of a bill of lading, a letter from the consignor providing information about the cargo could replace it. In Amsterdam, to resolve a dispute about the ownership of a crate of sugar brought from Porto to this city by a shipmaster named Jan Marts without the respective bill of lading, it was necessary for two Portuguese Jews to testify before the notary, stating that they knew that the said crate had been consigned to Belchior Lopes, since the consignor in Porto had written to one of them to confirm this.[81]

Original private freight contract for the transportation of goods between Lisbon and Salvador in 1591, attached to a notary's book (identified by Leonor Freire Costa). After the general conditions for the voyage were stipulated, written by one of the charterers and endorsed by the shipmaster, in the following two days, each of the new shippers specified the amounts for the outgoing and homebound journeys in their own handwriting, and named their agents in Bahia.

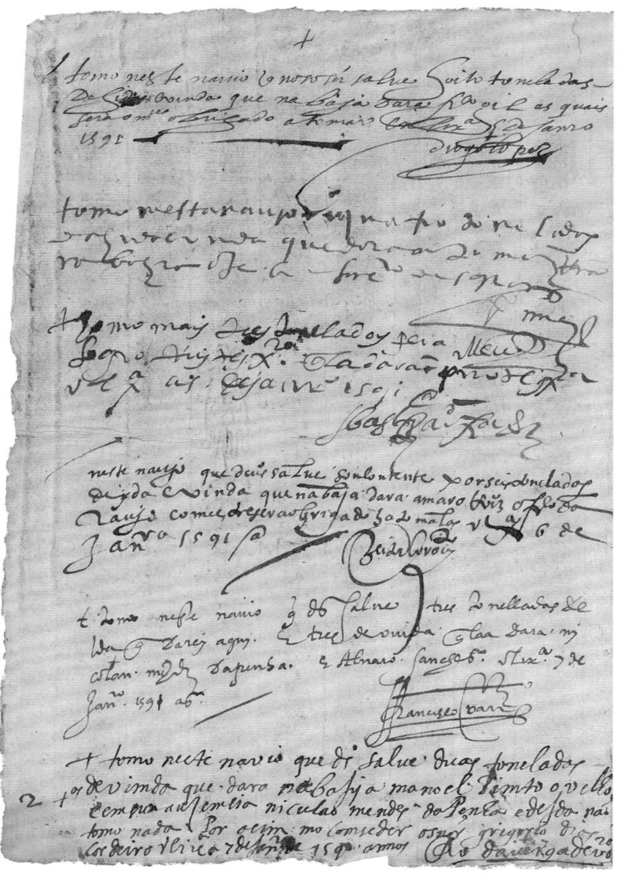

Registering Contracts

Not all freight contracts were notarized or even written, and there were almost always several consignors for the same voyage: as we have seen, the involvement of multiple shippers spread the risk. However, to speed up the process and reduce costs, it was common for only some or even just one of the charterers to settle the terms of the contract and sign for the others. The latter' names were not always mentioned, and were often referred to generically as "others."

In some cases, however, the existence of such "others" was not even mentioned. Nominal charterers could charter cargo space that their compatriots or counterparts abroad had requested or hired space that they later sublet. Hence, they acted as intermediaries between other shippers and the shipmasters. The larger the space hired by a single charterer, the greater the probability that it masked a larger number of interested parties. While such measures helped speed up the process for merchants, they hinder modern-day research by omitting many details.[82]

Sources indicate that the vast majority of transport agreements were never formalized before a notary. Costa has exhaustively scrutinized freight contracts notarized in Lisbon and Porto between 1580 and 1663. In her series, in only a few years, there were more than five contracts for voyages to Brazil registered, and many years in which there were none at all. Hence, notarial deeds reflect a fairly small share of the actual traffic.

To be sure, Costa has noted that only the books of five of the eighteen notary offices that ostensibly functioned in Lisbon at the time have survived. Furthermore, some notaries more than others specialized in commercial matters in general, and in freight contracts in particular. The small number of freight contracts that have been found, and the gaps in the series could therefore be partially explained by the disappearance of documentation. Moreover, notaries were allowed to discard documents fifty years after they were prepared.[83]

Such gaps are less evident in Porto, at least with regard to the years between 1595 and 1618. During this period, three notary offices operated uninterruptedly in this city, and another one, or rather two, functioned intermittently. Relatively complete series of documents have survived from two of the first three notaries, while haphazard and incomplete documentation exists from the third office, including records from the intermittently open offices, the bulk of whose primary archives have been lost.[84]

A perusal of contracts found in Amsterdam signed by Portuguese Jews for journeys to Portuguese ports between 1598 and 1616 also reveals several years in which there were only three, two or no contracts. Excluding ports in the Algarve and the salt ports (Setúbal and Aveiro), the number of contracts per year averaged less than four. Indeed, the exceptional number of fifty-one contracts registered in 1616 reflected the needs of Setúbal salt contractors, who, at the same time, were also leaseholders of the brazilwood monopoly and suppliers of grain to Portuguese strongholds in Morocco. The contractors booked the transportation of these bulky goods through their agents in Amsterdam. The contractors' factor in Amsterdam arranged the charter of about two hundred vessels between 1616 and 1618.[85]

The fact is that nothing prevented parties from agreeing upon freight terms without formalizing such agreements before a notary. Although Portuguese law stipulated that it was compulsory to register all contracts worth more than 60,000 réis before a notary if it were to serve as admissible evidence,[86] not all cargo space leased individually by merchants reached that figure.[J] Furthermore, Portuguese, as well as Dutch doctrine and jurisprudence,[87] admitted that "The promptness [haste] in contracts between merchants exempts registering them before a notary"; therefore, private documents and witnesses were admissible as evidence.[88]

Merchants tended to skip notaries not only because of the urgency inherent in their transactions but also to cut costs. In Portugal, the law called for a fee of 44 réis for deeds amounting to one and a half pages, and slightly less for a note (transcribed copy) if the party wished to keep one. The fees rose or fell according to the length of the document.[89] The impact of such formality depended on the length of the document, on the one hand, which extended when unusual conditions were stipulated, and on size of the shipment and freight rates, on the other. Hence, the bearing of the formality was negligible when the document concerned a substantial value to be paid for transport, but significant when these were slight.[90]

Apparently, merchants and shipmasters tended to be satisfied with private contracts written in their own hand or, in the case of Lisbon, scribbled by unofficial scribes, who acted as notaries and proved to be faster and cheaper. In other cases, the bills of lading received from shipmasters were sufficient, even if they did not consider all the legs of a voyage, questions related to port activities, and so forth.[91] Oral agreements were also used on occasion, albeit probably not dispensing with the bills of lading. This was the case with a Dutch shipmaster and a Portuguese Jewish merchant in Amsterdam, for a voyage to Porto transporting 81 lasts (162 tons) of grain to be delivered to a "Flemish merchant" and to another (presumably Portuguese) merchant.

However, oral agreements were fraught with peril precisely because they were not recorded on paper. In 1621, for example, consignees in Porto took delivery of cargo, but refused to pay the freight charges of four Castilian reales per last (two tons), since the grain was slightly damp. The shipmaster claimed that the damages were caused by storms and bad weather, and sought to recoup the freight charges from the charterer after returning to Amsterdam. The charterer, however, refused to pay, saying that he was not the actual shipper, but rather the consignees were, and that he had only engaged the shipmaster's services on their instructions. The shipmaster, therefore, should recover the charges at the destination port.

These were issues which could have been described at length in a written contract, but the absence of such an agreement did not mean that a shipmaster had no recourse: the court in Amsterdam backed his claim and obliged the charterer to pay him. A witness appearing on behalf of the plaintiff stated that he had been sailing for twenty-five years to Italy, Spain and other lands, and, to the best of his knowledge, it was customary on voyages to those lands for the charterer to ensure that the freight charges were paid at the port where the goods were unloaded; but if the charges were not paid there, the charterer would pay them at the port of origin.[92] As we have seen, freight contracted in Amsterdam for one-way journeys stipulated that payment would be made at the destination, while freight for homeward journeys was generally paid in full upon the vessel's return.

The increase or decrease in the number of notary records could be partially (but not entirely) explained by the expansion or shrinkage of trade or shipping.[93] Registering contracts before a notary probably derived, above all, from a lack of trust among the parties. This was often the case when the services of a new shipmaster were being engaged, when other interested parties were absent (identified or hidden), or when greater uncertainty prevailed at sea; for example, when privateers were particularly active. Wariness also originated from chartering *sui generis* voyages – protracted journeys, with large or precious consignments or variable itineraries, and so forth.[94] Costa has noted that it was unusual for shipmasters to repeatedly appear in notary contracts, which was not due to limited sailings. Costa believes that a shipmaster's reputation in mercantile circles, in general, and his familiarity with the charterers, in particular, dispensed with slow and costly formalities. She also emphasizes that in the few cases where shipmasters were mentioned in more than one contract, it was generally in the context of a new charterer.[95]

Shippers and Shipowners

Another reason for dispensing with registered freight contracts could be that not only was the charterer well acquainted with the shipmaster, but he even owned the vessel, wholly or in part.[96] Many merchants invested in ships. They acquired shares, and sometimes got together with other investors and commissioned entire vessels. A merchant from Porto paid his debts to his brother-in-law by transferring the shares he owned in three ships which were then in different locations. These shares corresponded to half of two carracks and five-sixths of a ship, which were respectively at anchor in the Guadalquivir River, near Seville, in Aveiro, ready to set sail for Brazil, and fishing off the island of Madeira.[97] These merchant-shipowners could make use of their shares of cargo space by either filling them with their own merchandise or leasing them to third parties.

There was a trade-off between using their own space on the one hand, and separating their investment in ships from trade in merchandise on the other. Loading their own wares in their share of space concentrated the risk. If a ship belonging to another owner was lost, "better lose the saddle than the horse." Moreover, when owners were consignors, they were not exempt from paying freight charges. The freight charges were due to the shipping consortium as a whole, and would be distributed as profits if there were any,

J. More than three tons out and back would be required for the freight charges and averages to be of sufficient value to legally necessitate public registration, considering freight charges at 5,000 and 10,000 réis per ton, for the outward and homeward journey, and averages at 500 réis per ton for the outward journey and at 2,000 for the homeward voyage (500 réis per crate times four crates per ton) (Costa, *O transporte no Atlântico*, v. 1, pp. 76–77, 243–244).

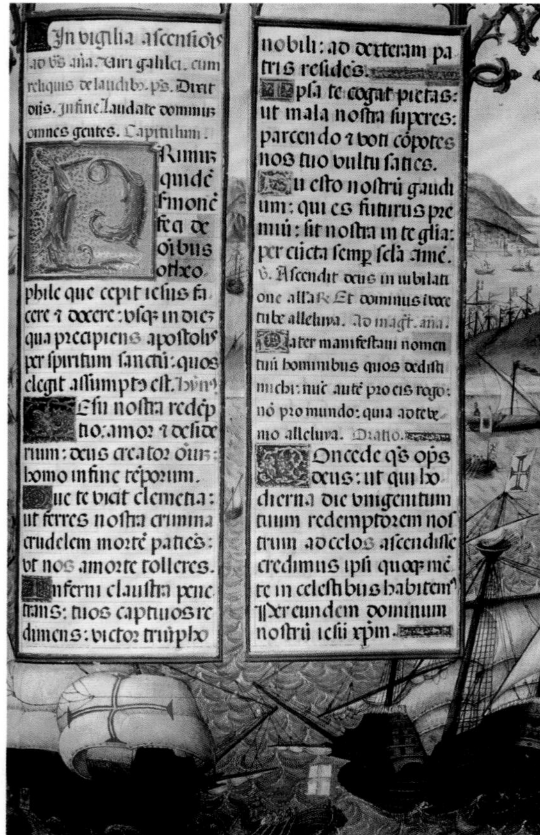

Page from a sixteenth-century breviary, illustrated with vessels carrying the cross of the Order of Christ, the symbol of Christian warriors, on their sails.

or would contribute towards compensating for damages. Thus, an owner's interests were diametrically opposed to those of the charterer: while owners strove to impose high freight charges, charterers sought to ensure that these charges were as low as possible.[98] Nonetheless, at the end of the day, any monies merchant-shipowners paid for transportation ended up as revenue. Of course, a voyage could result in losses in terms of shipping revenues, and merchant-shipowners could even end up paying more than other consignors to whom the shipmaster might have leased cargo space at lower rates in order to make the most of the ship's capacity. However, the same could also occur if merchants shipped their goods in spaces leased from other owners or if they leased out their space to strangers.

On the other hand, by using their own space, merchants could increase the speed of their transactions and make additional efficiency gains in transport. A group of merchants who routinely traded along certain routes could benefit from their shares in ships if they managed to optimize their capacity. That way, they could profit from the transport efficiency afforded by the use of larger ships and reduce laytime in ports through pre-arranged shipments.[99] In effect, it is highly unlikely that the owners of the newly built *Nossa Senhora do Rosário*, capable of transporting 360 tons, had commissioned the vessel to see it remain idle in its voyages between Holland and Brazil, via Portugal.[100] The ship's large capacity would probably have been used by the co-owners together with their associates and clients. Likewise, shipping in two autonomous segments could be synchronized better when using one's own ships. Finally, merchants were in a better position than shipmasters, assisted perhaps by brokers, to identify third parties interested in shipping cargo, and could thus streamline contracts and stowing.[101]

Trust in shipmasters and crews was another good reason to use one's own cargo space, primarily because a merchant's profits depended in large measure on the seafarers' loyalty and acumen. As masters' position depended on shareholders' endorsement, it was in the shipmasters' interests to please them.[102] This element of reliability was even more crucial in voyages involving illegal subterfuges such as camouflage and rebaptism. Such ruses necessitated collusion among the parties involved: shipmaster, charterers, consignors, consignees, owners and insurers.[103] Shipments aboard one's own vessels, such as on the *Nossa Senhora do Rosário*, serving associates with whom owners worked in close collaboration, contributed towards such integration, even if this might have entailed higher transport and agency costs, so as to reward the loyalty of the shipmaster and trading agents.[104]

During periods when cargo space was in short supply, having a guaranteed space aboard a vessel could make the difference between goods reaching a destination or not. In all likelihood, it also made merchant-owners more competitive as mercantile agents, offering transport along with agency services. Costa has observed that this was the case from 1623 onwards, when privateering and piracy decimated the stock of Portuguese vessels, and made seafarers reluctant to venture overseas. Merchants who could afford to do so bought diverse shares in various vessels, spreading the risk, and requisitioned their spaces with clauses that required shipmasters to "give them room," that is, to reserve their share of space for their own wares, and not allowing this space to be leased to third parties.[105] Controlling shipping was a strategic challenge to be resolved by vertical integration, which could not be left to the mercy of the market.[106]

Until then, merchants could choose to use cargo space in ships which they co-owned for themselves and for their counterparts and associates, as well as to privately sub-charter part of this cargo space. In addition, they could charter any space they still required from third parties; all this depending on the opportunities arising for both themselves and their network of associates. This is what is suggested by the case of the *Nossa Senhora da Conceição*, entrusted to the care of shipmaster Gaspar Luis.[107]

The ship was captured by French corsairs, and one of its shareholders, a New Christian from Porto named Diogo Lopes Pinto, appointed, in September 1617, a Portuguese Jew to recover or obtain compensation for the third share he owned in the ship and the cargo, which ended up reaching the city of Amsterdam.[108] The power of attorney listed a consignment of fifty-three crates of sugar loaded in Bahia, to be delivered to the said Diogo Lopes Pinto, not in Porto, where he lived, but in Viana.

Of this cargo, twenty crates were being shipped on behalf of the merchant and owner. Four of them corresponded to one-third of the value of the freight charges and averages collected by the master, and proportional to the merchant's share in the ship. The remaining sixteen crates were the result of ordinary commercial operations, and were due to the merchant-owner.[L] Even though the other thirty-three crates had been consigned to Diogo Lopes Pinto, they were being shipped on behalf of three parties living in the Canary Islands, associates of Diogo Lopes Pinto. With these fifty-three crates, Diogo Lopes Pinto was using between 40% and 100% of the space he owned in the vessel described as being a "ship." If there was any residual space he would have allowed it to be leased out to third parties or else remain underutilized. Approximately 30% of the cargo space that he made actual use of was for his own use, and 60% was for his associates, while the remaining 10% comprised cargo corresponding to his freight charges and averages.[M] Once again, sharing space with associates and strangers alike meant spreading the risk.[N]

K. Costa has conjectured that merchants who were also co-owners had a privileged relationship with the shipmasters and, when differentiated freight charges were practiced on a journey, they could access the more beneficial rates (Costa, *O transporte no Atlântico*, v. 1, pp. 378, 426).

L. Following the study by another specialist in ports and shipping, Amélia Polónia, on the professional distribution of co-owners from Vila do Conde between 1560 and 1620, Costa believes that until the 1620s, owners were, as a rule, seafarers, strictly speaking, and shipping consortiums involved a small number of partners. If there were merchants who ventured to invest in outfitting ships, they did so to profit from transportation and leasing out cargo space to third parties, but not with a view to their own trading activities. Resorting to their own shares was rather an occasional than a consistent practice (Polónia, "Vila do Conde," v. 2, p. 390; Costa, *O transporte no Atlântico*, v. 1, pp. 424–425, 435). Costa asserts that, during more peaceful periods, trade and shipping were two autonomous sectors, there being "a clear frontier between trade and shipping." She seeks to corroborate this thesis with the "abundance of freight contracts, visible amidst notary activities in Lisbon, Porto or Viana." However, as we have seen, the data compiled by Costa herself indicates a relative infrequency of such notarized contracts (Ibid., v. 1, pp. 391, 424–425).

M. A "ship" had a capacity of between 40 and 100 tons, and each ton could correspond to three or four crates. Hence, the third share belonging to Diogo Lopes Pinto would be capable of holding between forty and 133 crates. The section allocated for his own commercial operations would occupy from 4 to 5.3 tons. Such volumes are compatible with the distribution of cargoes observed by Costa for the years between 1580 and 1601, when most contracts mentioned five or more shippers, the majority of whom occupied less than 4.6 to 7.8 tons (Ibid., *O transporte no Atlântico*, v. 1, pp. 253–254).

N. Costa noted a similar strategy implemented between 1588 and 1594 by two merchants from Lisbon, Afonso Vaz d'Évora and Diogo Francês. Both used their own space for their own cargo and also leased it to third parties while, immediately thereafter, leasing space from third parties aboard other vessels. However, Costa did not consider here, as she did at another stage, that the leasing of the total capacity of ships belonging to third parties by these two merchants was partially or entirely commissioned by their associates. Apart from this, the leasing of others' spaces after leasing out one's own space perhaps resulted from the different new opportunities emerging: "They did not spurn the opportunity to develop privileged relationships with shipmasters, their partners [fellow co-owners], to ensure transportation, but they did not always entirely explore the cargo potential inherent to each part owned. In contracts for leasing out space aboard their own ships, they were accompanied by other merchants, and also intervened in situations [leasing] pertaining to ships in which they did not own any share. The spreading of risk, distributing cargo over different vessels, gave rise to similar actions. However, it must be noted that Afonso Vaz d'Évora did not overlook the opportunity to fill the entire capacity of a vessel he did not own, hiring it through a 'voyage charter.' There must have been other reasons for owners to risk more cargo in ships they did not own than on their own ships" (Ibid., v. 1, pp. 426–428).

1. Costa, *O transporte no Atlântico*, v. 1, pp. 396–413; Moreira, *Os mercadores de Viana*, pp. 47–48.

2. ADP, NOT, PO2, l. 35, fols. 144–147 (1612-7-17).

3. Israel, *Dutch Primacy in World Trade*, pp. 21–24, 75; Lesger, *The Rise of the Amsterdam Market*, pp. 59–60; De Vries and Van der Woude, *The First Modern Economy*, p. 338; Barbour, "Dutch and English Merchant Shipping in the Seventeenth Century," pp. 278–279.

4. Costa, *O transporte no Atlântico*, v. 1, pp. 399, 410–411.

5. ADP, NOT, PO2, l. 35, fols. 145–145v. (1612-7-17).

6. Ibid.

7. "...so that should God take the ship safely to Brazil, to the captaincy of Pernambuco or any other destination, the said shipmaster Pantalião Luís will settle accounts of all the freight charges and averages applicable to the said voyage and will charge and keep with him what is lawfully due to each of the parties": ibid.

8. "...and should he do something he should not do so as to defraud anything in terms of freight charges or averages and matters concerning the said carrack they said that they agreed to grant all their powers, as they effectively granted with unrestricted and general administration powers, to the said Manuel Ribeiro so that he himself could be the shipmaster of the said carrack or could appoint and select as shipmaster the individual he deemed fit": ibid.

9. ADP, NOT, PO2, l. 35 (1612-7-17), fols. 144–144v.

10. Malynes, *Consuetudo: vel, lex mercatoria*, pp. 144–146, 151–152; Moreira, *Os mercadores de Viana*, pp. 49–55; Polónia, "Mestres e pilotos das carreiras ultramarinas," pp. 291–293; Costa, *O transporte no Atlântico*, v. 1, pp. 345, 438–439, 450–451; Polónia, "Os náuticos das carreiras ultramarinas," pp. 124–125; Lesger, *The Rise of the Amsterdam Market*, pp. 231–232; Mauro, *Portugal, o Brasil e o Atlântico*, v. 1, pp. 103–104.

11. Costa, *O transporte no Atlântico*, v. 1, pp. 253, 262–263.

12. Ibid., pp. 250–251; Moreira, *Os mercadores de Viana*, p. 49.

13. SR no. 1596.

14. Costa, *O transporte no Atlântico*, v. 1, pp. 264–265; Moreira, *Os mercadores de Viana*, pp. 55–67.

15. ADP, NOT, PO2, l. 35, fols. 120v–122v (1612-7-10). See also: I. S. Révah, *Uriel da Costa et les marranes de Porto* (Paris: Centre Culturel Calouste Gulbenkian, 2004), pp. 414–415.

16. For bibliography on the topic, see: U. da Costa, *Exame das tradições farisaicas. Acrescentado com Samuel da Silva, Tratado da imortalidade da alma* (Braga: Editora APPACDM, 1995); Révah, *Uriel da Costa et les marranes de Porto*; Y. Kaplan, "The Intellectual Ferment in the Spanish-Portuguese Community of Seventeenth Century Amsterdam," in H. Beinart (ed.), *The Sephardi Legacy*, V. 2 (Jerusalem: Magnes, 1992).

17. Moreira, *Os mercadores de Viana*, pp. 69–70.

18. ADP, NOT, PO2, l. 35, fols. 120v.–122v. (1612-7-10).

19. Ibid.

20. ADP, NOT, PO1, l. 136, fols. 110–112 (1615-8-18); l. 138, fols. 133–135 (1617-4-12); PO2, l. 36, fols. 176–178 (1613-1-4).

21. Malynes, *Consuetudo: vel, lex mercatoria*, p. 117.

22. ADP, NOT, PO2, l. 35, fols. 120v.–122v. (1612-7-10).

23. Costa, *O transporte no Atlântico*, v. 1, pp. 353–354

24. "*Avarias grossas*" corresponded to what in English were known as "general averages," while "*avarias costumadas*" corresponded to "averages accustomed" or "petty averages." Costa suggests that the origin of the third and most

common type of averages, which were paid as remuneration for shipping prior to departure, was related to a similarly named fee charged by the Portuguese factory in Antwerp (the representation of Portuguese merchants in the city) to cover the corporation's expenses. However, Costa also considers that these averages, which, in practice, were part of the freight charges paid by consignors, were equivalent to averages accustomed, which, as shall be seen, were probably smaller sums, for minor costs associated with, for example, loading and unloading cargo and entering and exiting ports. The statistics compiled by Costa about freight contracts registered in the notary records in Lisbon and Porto between 1580 and 1640 indicate that averages amounted to about 10% of the shipping costs on the outward journey, and between 15% to 22% on the homebound voyage (Ibid., pp. 372–374). Moreira states that the freight charges for the homebound journey to Brazil were not calculated per ton but rather on the basis of crates of sugar as were the averages. Nevertheless, he also cites an example in which the freight charges were calculated on the basis of tons (Moreira, *Os mercadores de Viana*, pp. 62, 97).

25. Costa, *O transporte no Atlântico*, v. 1, pp. 374–376, 380; Moreira, *Os mercadores de Viana*, p. 65.

26. Ibid, pp. 50–52.

27. PRO, SP, 9/104, fols. 87v., 94v., 98v.

28. Costa, *O transporte no Atlântico*, v. 1, pp. 309–311.

29. ADP, NOT, PO1, l. 132, fols. 18v.–20v. (1611-8-2).

30. SAA, 30452: Archief van S. Hart, 478, l. 645, fols. 43v.–44; SR no. 1243; Ebert, "The Trade in Brazilian Sugar," p. 200.

31. Costa, *O transporte no Atlântico*, v. 1, pp. 265–266, 310–312. See also: Moreira, *Os mercadores de Viana*, p. 39, n. 4.

32. ADP, NOT, PO1, l. 138, fols. 74–74v. (1617-2-23).

33. SR no. 952.

34. Moreira, *Os mercadores de Viana*, p. 65.

35. SR no. 3625. According to Costa, the variations in the weight of crates of sugar were not particularly discernible until 1615–1617, each ton being equivalent to four crates. At the time of the WIC's most devastating actions in the Atlantic, from 1623 onwards, the weight of crates of crushed sugar rose to weights higher than 16.6 arrobas, wherein only three crates fitted into a ton (Costa, *O transporte no Atlântico*, v. 1, pp. 265–266, 310–312). However, notary records in Amsterdam reveal that the increase in the weight of crates of sugar was not a linear process. In 1609, a freight contract stipulated that a last would be calculated as ten "normal" crates: SR no. 357. In the following year, 1610, another freight contract stipulated that a last was equivalent to ten large and small crates of common Brazilian sugar, that is, crushed sugar: SR no. 379. A year later, the equivalence was already the familiar figure: eight crates per last: SR no. 475. In 1622, that is, even before the actions of the WIC, two notarized documents mentioned the weight of various crates of sugar: one is referred to as containing 17.5 arrobas, another six crates of white sugar with a total weight of 125 arrobas and 8 pounds, averaging more than 20 arrobas per crate, and a crate of muscovado sugar weighing 20 arrobas: SR nos. 2595, 2675.Nevertheless, the equivalence between a last and eight crates of sugar did not fall into disuse and was used even in 1625 and 1627: SR nos. 3331, 3584.

36. The freight contracts from Viana to Northern Europe analyzed by Moreira also indicate a tendency towards freight arrangements leasing the entire capacity of a vessel: Moreira, *Os mercadores de Viana*, pp. 62–63.

37. For voyages to Porto, see also: SR nos. 39, 50, 284, 354, 426, 641, 1161, 1185.

38. For ships chartered for voyages to Porto, see: SR nos. 25, 40, 41, 47, 48, 49, 76, 89, 291, 362, 379, 1223, 1554. Sometimes with conditions for dead-freight: SR no. 362.

39. SR nos. 2132, 2146.

40. SR nos. 47, 48, 49, 50, 76, 89, 284, 354, 379, 426, 641, 1223.

41. SR no. 284.

42. SR nos. 47, 48, 49, 89, 284.

43. SR nos. 25, 40, 41, 291, 299, 1554.

44. SR no. 39.

45. SR no. 89.

46. SR no. 372.

47. Costa, *O transporte no Atlântico*, v. 1, pp. 377–379.

48. SR nos. 372, 1596; Costa, *O transporte no Atlântico*, v. 1, pp. 377–379, 426; Ebert, "The Trade in Brazilian Sugar," p. 199.

49. Ibid., pp. 129–130, 204. See also: ibid., pp. 201–202. Moreira also highlights how the impact of the political situation was paramount amongst the variables that affected freight rates, linking the changes in rates to diplomatic milestones: Moreira, *Os mercadores de Viana*, p. 64.

50. SR no. 1596.

51. Costa, *O transporte no Atlântico*, v. 1, pp. 271–272. Ebert, however, assumes that the strategy of sailing around the British Isles to avoid Dunkirk privateers made freight charges more expensive: Ebert, "The Trade in Brazilian Sugar," p. 204.

52. Moreira, *Os mercadores de Viana*, pp. 64–65.

53. Costa, *O transporte no Atlântico*, v. 1, pp. 191–192, 379–380.

54. Ebert, "The Trade in Brazilian Sugar," pp. 204–205.

55. Costa, *O transporte no Atlântico*, v. 1, pp. 265–266, 309–312.

56. ADP, NOT, PO2 l. 20, fols. 220v.–223v. (1603-10-15); l. 25, fols. 146v.–150 (1606-5-12); PO1, l. 133, fols. 70–72v. (1612-6-20); l. 133, fols. 77–79v. (1612-6-26); l. 133, fols. 162–163v. (1612-9-22); l. 137, fols. 131–133 (1616-3-11); l. 137, fols. 141–143v. (1616-3-22). Costa mentions a freight contract in which the shipmaster undertook to receive the merchandise in his boat and then load it onto his ship: Costa, *O transporte no Atlântico*, v. 1, p. 331.

57. ADP, PO1, l. 136, fols. 110–112 (1615-8-18).

58. "And should some mishap occur during the stowing or if any wine is lost [neither] he, the shipmaster, nor his men will be obliged to pay anything for the said wine, for which the said trimmer shall be deemed to be liable": ADP, NOT, PO2, l. 20, l. fols. 220v.–223v. (1603-10-15).

59. ADP, NOT, PO1, l. 136, fols. 110–112 (1615-8-18). See also: "...and similarly he will also be paid the customary expenses for ships to enter and exit the harbors [in Bahia]": PO1, l. 138, fols. 133–135 (1617–4–12); "...and the costs of loading and unloading of the said merchandise and said exits and pilots [and] boats and all the other expenses they incur will be paid for by the merchants": PO2, l. 20, fols. 126v.–129v. (1603-8-13); l. 29, fols. 137–138v. (1609-10-13).

60. ADP, NOT, PO2, l. 15, fols. 112v.–116 (1600-12-19); l. 19, fols. 16v.–19 (1602-12-19); l. 20, fols. 126v.–129v .(1603-8-13). In other cases, the onus was on the shipmaster and the crew: PO1, l. 132, fols. 223v.–226 (1612-3-15); l. 135a, fols. 111–113 (1614-7-12); l. 136, fols. 110–112 (1615-8-18).

61. SR no. 7, n. 6.

62. ADP, NOT, PO2, l. 15, fols. 112v.–116 (1600-1-19); l.19, fols. 16v.–19 (1602-12-19); l. 20, fols. 126v.–129v. (1603-8-13).

63. "...with Primage, Petilodeminage, and sometimes Pilotage, according to the accustomed manner in the like Voyages" (Malynes, *Consuetudo: vel, lex mercatoria*, p. 138); "The Merchant likewise doth convenant to pay Pilotage, if a Pilot be used to bring the ship into the harbor; also primage, and petilodmanidge [sic] to the shipmaster for the use of his Cables to the discharge of the goods, and to the mariners to charge and discharge them, which may be sixe pence or twelve pence for the Tunne lading, with some other clauses and agreements made betweene the said Merchants and Master": ibid., p. 141; "Primage and Petilodmanage is likewise due to the shipmaster and Marriners for the use of his Cables and Ropes to discharge the Goods; and to the Marriners for loading and unloading of the Ship or Vessel, it is commonly about twelve pence per Tun": C.

Molloy, *De jure maritimo et navali* II. Ix, 255, in Oxford English Dictionary, entry on: petilodemanage.

64. SR nos. 269, 281, 353, 354.

65. SR nos. 357, 874, 2194.

66. Cape, in SR nos. 281, 3331; flag, in SR no. 3592; hat and flag, in SR no. 357; money for a hat, in SR nos. 2710, 2894; wine, in SR no. 2196; money and a new flag, in SR no. 117 and SR nos. 228, 2894.

67. SR no. 379.

68. SAA, 5075: Archief van de Notarissen ter Standplaats Amsterdam, l. 646A, fols. 178–179. In this Dutch translation of a bill of lading signed in Olinda, the petty averages appear as "ordinarie Lakage," summed up by Hart as "gewone lekkage," that is, "customary leakage": SAA, 30452: Archief van S. Hart, 875; SR no. 2675; ADP, NOT, PO1, l. 133, fols. 162–163v. (1612-9-22). See also: Oxford English Dictionary, entry on: "averages.2." These averages would correspond to the averages for entering and exiting harbors mentioned by Moreira in *Os mercadores de Viana*, p. 66.

69. Costa, *O transporte no Atlântico*, v. 1, pp. 356–358, 429.

70. "...and they, the charterers and shipmaster, are agreeable that all the cargo and wares that are being transported on their account as well as those of the shipmaster and his company, be they sugars or any other wares, which are stowed below decks be transported mixed together so that should there be any damage which is not the fault of the shipmaster, the damage will be shared amongst all parties as general averages": ADP, NOT, PO2 l. 19, fols. 16v.–19 (1602-2-19), fol. 19; l. 25, fols. 146v.–150 (1606-5-12); ADP, NOT, PO2 l. 17, fols. 105v.–108v. (1602-1-9), fol. 108 (1606-5-12). See also: Costa, *O transporte no Atlântico*, v. 1, p. 52.

71. Malynes, *Consuetudo: vel, lex mercatoria*, pp. 157–158; J. Cowell, *The Interpreter: Or Booke Containing the Signification of Words* (Cambridge: John Legate, 1607), entry for "average"; Costa, *O transporte no Atlântico*, v. 1, p. 373. Moreira refers to "general averages," "averages accustomed" and averages that were part of freight together: Moreira, *Os mercadores de Viana*, pp. 66–67.

72. ADP, NOT, PO1, l. 133, fols. 77–79v. (1612-6-26); l. 136, fols. 16v.–18 (1615-7-1); l. 136, fols. 111v; l. 136, fols. 166v.–168v. (1615-9-22); l. 137, fols. 131–133 (1616-3-11).

73. Costa, *O transporte no Atlântico*, v. 1, pp. 266–270.

74. NA, Staten-Generaal, 1.01.02, Loketkas, Admiraliteitsstukken 12561.33.1.

75. Go, "Marine Insurance in the Netherlands," p. 99; Spooner, *Risks at Sea*, p. 18.

76. Costa, *O transporte no Atlântico*, v. 1, p. 266.

77. ADP, NOT, PO1, l. 133, fols. 70–72v. (1612-6-20); l. 135a, fols. 66–68v. (1614-6-23); l. 136, fols. 166v.–168v. (1615-9-22); PO2, l. 7, fols. 131–133 (1616-3-11).

78. SR nos. 657, 663, n. 47.

79. Author's translation into English, with the assistance of Lodewijk Augustinus Henri Christiaan Hulsman.

80. ADP, NOT, PO2, l. 40, fols. 41v.–42v. (1615-1-28). See also: ADP, NOT, PO2, l. 26, fols. 192–194 (1607-4-21); l. 40, fols. 63–64 (1615-2-11).

81. SR no. 1589.

82. Costa, *O transporte no Atlântico*, v. 1, pp. 176, 188, 202, 251–254.

83. Ibid., v. 1, pp. 44–47, 371.

84. ADP, NOT, "Lista dos Antigos Tabeliães da Cidade do Porto [Cópia idêntica do notário Casimiro Curado]." The notary offices which have reasonably complete series are the first office, third series, and the second office, first series. The incomplete series belongs to the fourth office, single series. The offices whose books were mostly lost would have been the eighth and perhaps also the ninth archive.

85. Swetschinski, "The Portuguese Jewish Merchants," pp. 143, 149–151. On these contracts, see: SR no. 1590; Swetschinski, "The Portuguese Jewish Merchants,"

p. 151; idem, "From the Middle Ages to the Golden Age," p. 79; idem, *Reluctant Cosmopolitans*, pp. 109–110; Mauro, *Portugal, o Brasil e o Atlântico*, v. 1, pp. 176, 187; Israel, "Spain and the Dutch Sephardim," p. 359; Israel, "The Economic Contribution of the Dutch Sephardic Jewry," p. 423; Vlessing, "The Portuguese-Jewish Merchant Community in Seventeenth-Century Amsterdam," p. 238.

86. *Ordenações Manuelinas*, book III, title XLV; *Ordenações Filipinas*, book III, title LIX.

87. With regard to the absence of notary registration of simple transactions in Amsterdam, see: Koen, "Duarte Fernandes," pp. 180, 187.

88. Almeida, *Aritmética como descrição do real*, v. 2, pp. 365–366; IANTT, STO, IC 4481, *Documentos apensos*, document no. 5, fol. 1.

89. *Ordenações Filipinas*, book I, title LXXVIII.

90. Freight contracts usually consisted of three or more pages, and in some cases could even reach almost five pages. In one of the latter, a roughly five-page contract referring to a round trip from Porto to Brazil through the Canary Islands, it was stipulated that charterers would pay 11,000 réis per ton, totaling freight charges and averages for both the outward and the homebound journeys, assuming four crates per ton. The length derived from its *sui generis* stipulations; the size of the hired space was flexible and to be decided by the charters or their agents on the spot. On the outward voyage, it could encompass between 50 tons and the entire capacity of the caravel, and on the homeward leg, it would range between any and the total net tonnage. The laytime was also to be agreed upon in Brazil. It could be extended in order to wait for the newly produced sugar after the rainy season was over. The potentially large size of the cargo offset the cost of the notarization, which was an advisable formality under such exceptional conditions of the agreement; see: ADP, NOT, PO1, l. 132, fols. 223v.–226 (1612-3-15).

91. Costa, *O transporte no Atlântico*, v. 1, pp. 53–54, 263–264.

92. SR no. 2560.

93. Costa, *O transporte no Atlântico*, v. 1, pp. 55–75.

94. Idem, "Informação e incerteza: gerindo os riscos do negócio colonial," *Ler História 44* (2003): 55–75, 117–118.

95. Costa, *O transporte no Atlântico*, v. 1, pp. 443–444.

96. Vlessing, "New Light on the Earliest History of Amsterdam Portuguese Jews," p. 63; idem, "The Portuguese-Jewish Merchant Community," p. 233, n. 50; Costa, *O transporte no Atlântico*, v. 1, p. 445.

97. ADP, NOT, PO2, l. 22c, fols. 262v.–264v. (1603-11-5).

98. Costa, *O transporte no Atlântico*, v. 1, pp. 424–425.

99. Ibid., v. 1, pp. 254, 262.

100. SR no. 1456. In regard to this case, see both the previous chapter of this volume and Ebert, "The Trade in Brazilian Sugar," pp. 127–128.

101. Costa, *O transporte no Atlântico*, v. 1, pp. 252–253.

102. Ibid., v. 1, p. 445; K. Morgan, *Bristol and the Atlantic Trade in the Eighteenth Century* (Cambridge: Cambridge University Press, 1993), p. 84; A. Greif, "Contract Enforceability and Economic Institutions in Early Trade," *The American Economic Review 83*:3 (1993): 530; M. Granovetter, "Problems of Explanations in Economic Sociology," in N. Nohria and R. G. Eccles (eds.), *Networks and Organizations* (Boston: Harvard Business School Press, 1992), pp. 36, 42–44; idem, "The Impact of Social Structures on Economic Outcomes," *Journal of Economic Perspectives 19*:1 (2005): 34–35; J. S. Coleman, "Social Capital in the Creation of Human Capital," *The American Journal of Sociology, Supplement 94* (1988): passim; R. S. Burt, *Structural Holes: The Social Structure of Competition* (Cambridge: Harvard University Press, 1992), pp. 14, 18–20, 39; idem, "Structural Holes Versus Network Closure as Social Capital," in N. Lin, K. Cook and R. S. Burt (eds.), *Social Capital: Theory and Research* (New York: Aldine de Gruyter, 2001), pp. 35, 49, 51–52; G. Weimann, "On the Importance of Marginality: One More Step into the Two-Step Flow of Communication," *American Sociological Review 47*:6 (1982): 766.

103. Ebert described the misfortunes of the Dutch shipmaster of the ship *De Hope/A Esperança*, who, in 1617–1618 sailed to Porto and from there to Rio de Janeiro, where he was arrested: Ebert, "The Trade in Brazilian Sugar," pp. 152, 167, 175–176.

104. Greif, "Contract Enforceability," p. 530.

105. Costa, *O transporte no Atlântico*, v. 1, pp. 262, 433–435; Moreira, *Os mercadores de Viana*, p. 89.

106. M. Moschandreas, *Business Economics* (London: Business Press, 1994), pp. 254–284.

107. For further information about this case, see: SR no. 1031.

108. ADP, NOT, PO1, l. 139, fols. 167–169 (1617-9-6).

Chapter Seven

Woman Holding a Balance;
Johannes Vermeer (ca. 1664).

Money Matters

Means and Methods of Payment

How did merchants make payments four centuries ago without having paper money or checks, let alone electronic means of payment? These traders also had to deal with religious, ethical and legal restrictions on charging interest and on payments not made at sight. They traded in commodities at hubs whose derivatives markets, when they existed at all, were still embryonic. They confronted the inherent complexity of the use of coins with an intrinsic metallic value and a poorly mechanized minting process. Likewise, they managed payments or exchanges involving merchandise that were not entirely standardized and whose prices were subject to official regulations.

On Credit

Merchandise, particularly more standardized goods traded in large volumes, was bought and sold with payment being made at sight, in advance, on credit, by means of forward contracts or using mixed methods, with different means of payment, such as currency, products, securities and accounts receivable. Merchants bought directly from producers, distributors and retailers. They also sold to distributors, retailers and, instead of producers, to final users. In the case of sugar, the producers were sugar–mill owners and cane farmers, whereas purchasers included refiners, confectioners, sweet-makers and pharmacists.

Sales and purchases made on credit, as well as payments made in advance, involved interest being paid or charged. When purchasers paid in advance before receiving the goods, they received rebates that compensated for the profits they could have obtained in other investments – the so-called opportunity cost. Advance payment also exposed purchasers to the risk of not receiving the products in accordance with the agreed timeframe, quantity or quality. Even though purchasers could charge the vendor for damages, there was scope for misunderstandings, inconvenience and expenditures in lodging protests and filing lawsuits. Hence, the rebate had to compensate not only for the opportunity cost but also for the risk to the tied up capital. For purchases made on credit, vendors received a premium that functioned in the same way as the rebates in advance payments, but in the opposite direction: the premium compensated for the risk of purchasers defaulting, as well as the fact that the vendor's capital was tied up.

The question of interest was not a trivial matter during that period. Medieval theologians and canonists condemned any sure gain deriving from loans (*lucrum ex mutuo*), which were considered to be usurious, that is, illegitimate and sinful. According to the Scriptures, loans were to be made free of charge, while for medieval theology, money and time were sterile; therefore, they could not be priced; in other words, one could not assign interest to them.

Profits from loans were acceptable when they were the result of random and unpredictable factors, such as an increase or decrease in the value of merchandise with which debts would be paid. Over time, it also became acceptable for creditors to be compensated *a posteriori* for losses and damages incurred for reasons extrinsic to the loan itself. The two acceptable causes were emerging damages (*damnum emergens*) and foregone profit (*lucrum cessans*). The former were damages to creditors caused by defaults, which were only legitimate if it could be proved that they were the direct result of a debtor's fault or fraud.

Foregone profit represented the returns that creditors could have obtained if the sum being lent had been invested in other business activities for the same period. The difference between this latter concept and that of modern-day opportunity costs was the moment used for calculations. Foregone profits were calculated after the term, verifying the opportunities that had effectively been sacrificed by that individual creditor and how much the capital would have actually rendered. In contrast, opportunity cost is estimated beforehand, using the market base interest rate as a benchmark, and setting out from the principle that money yields returns over the course of time, which, as has been seen, was not the prevalent view during that period.[1]

DIVITIÆ FACIVNT FVRES.
Multos perdidit aurem et argentum.
Eccli. 8,
LES RICHESSES FONT DES LARRONS.
L'or et l'argent en a destruit plusieurs.
RYCKDOM MAECKT DIEVEN
Goudt en silver heeft vele bedorve
P. Bruegel Inue
Ioan Galle excudit.
Quid modo diuitię, quid fului vasta metalli
Congeries, nummis arca referta nouis,
Illecebres inter tantas, atq agmina furum,
Inditium cunctis efferus vncus erit,
Pręda facit furem, feruens mala cuncta ministrat
Impetus, et spoliis apta rapina feris.
Men soeckt wel actie om ons te verdoouen,
Maer men souwen niet krygen, waerder niet te roouen.

The Fight of the Money-Bags and the Coffers; *Pieter Breughel, the Elder (1570). The full caption in Latin, French and Dutch, reads: "Riches makes thieves. Gold and silver have destroyed many."*

Over time, however, theologians, jurists and canonists gradually accepted that mercantile activities depended on the flow of capital, and that a merchant who lent to other individuals would undoubtedly forego profits. They realized that by tying up resources, merchants compromised their working capital and exposed themselves to defaults. It was understood that if merchants were not compensated for this, they would not advance credit, which would be very detrimental to the common good. Thus, theologians, jurists and canonists were inclined to extend the concepts of *damnum emergens* and *lucrum cessans*, as long as they were applied exclusively to credit granted by one merchant to another.

Some were of the view that these concepts could be assumed *ex-ante*, equating foregone profit with modern-day opportunity cost.[A/2] This would legitimize charging interest as compensation, as long as this interest was subject to moderate rates and limited to mercantile activities. This was the case of some sixteenth-century Spanish canonists – neo-scholastics from the School of Salamanca.[3] In the seventeenth century, a Dutch jurist and Calvinist, Hugo de Groot (Grotius), went even further and framed these arguments in a more explicit manner.[4] The concepts of Catholics and Protestants were not yet very different, since they mutually influenced each other, primarily those of the former influencing the latter with regard to the way in which theology should relate to the economic and political developments taking place at the time.[5]

The perception that capital needed to be remunerated did not escape the notice of rulers. At the same time, a principle was developed whereby norms, derived from Civil Law, customs or royal orders aimed at preserving and enhancing the prosperity of public matters, could enable subjects to charge a moderate rate of interest.[6] Based on this principle, Charles V promulgated daring and pioneering legislation (ordinance) through which, as the sovereign of the Low Countries, he sought to distinguish usury from interest, banning the former and legitimizing the latter. Only merchants were authorized to charge interest on loans, but at rates limited to 12% per year, and which could not exceed the profits they could have earned by trading with the sum being lent. England followed the same policy; Henry VIII set a limit of 10%, which, after being revoked by his son, was restored by Elizabeth I in 1571 and later reduced to 8% in 1624.

Even after the Dutch Revolt, charging interest continued to be legitimate on both sides of the Low Countries. In practice, in the Republic, the parties agreed upon interest rates among themselves, despite some attempts to impose lower limits, especially when merchants were not involved. Liberality was one of the reasons the United Provinces had one of the lowest interest rates at the time.[7] Those rates fell in direct proportion to the growing security in the market and the supply of capital. The supply of capital increased with the immigration of affluent merchants from the 1590s onwards, and with the profits earned from trade, particularly in the Iberian world, the Mediterranean, Russia, and the Atlantic and Indian oceans. Security improved with a consistent public debt and fiscal policy. With the establishment of the Bank of Amsterdam, as we will see, the city sought to implement a conservative monetary policy and, with the creation of the bourse, the cost of obtaining information was reduced. Municipal authorities and merchants alike strove to ensure that contracts were fulfilled.

Finally, the negotiability of credit instruments and stocks of the India Companies transferred as collateral, provided greater liquidity and coverage for the loans taken out by merchants, expanding the spectrum of investors and contributing towards a reduction in interest rates. Market interest rates for loans to merchants fell from about 8% in 1596 to about 7% in 1610, and below 5.5% at the end of the decade, according to Oscar Gelderblom and Joost Jonker; according to Pit Dehing, from about 10%, between 1600 and 1604, to 6.5%, on average, between 1610 and 1614.[B/8]

In Portugal, as we will see, interest rates of up to 12% per year were allowed on bills of exchange. However, as a rule, it was established that Canon Law would govern these transactions: "Because this is a matter involving sin and the weight of conscience, it is advisable to follow and uphold Canon Law and the decisions of the Holy Mother Church in this regard."[9]

Portuguese Canon Law gradually absorbed the new concepts on interest rates. While the 1639 Synodal Constitutions of the Archbishopric of Braga repeated strict condemnations of usury, particularly those emanating from Rome,[10] they allowed the stipulation of interest rates based on lucrum cessans and damnum emergens.[C] In cases of doubts and gaps, they reiterated that such matters should be referred to learned scholars "who deal with them extensively," and to civil law. In contracts in which money was lent for investment in trade, and the investor-partner and/or insurer shouldered risk in exchange for fixed rates of interest,[11] the Constitutions allowed a maximum interest rate of 5%.[12] However, as we will see in Chapter 9, the interest rates stipulated in these contracts could reach, and even greatly exceed, 30%.[13]

It is important to note that the greatest concern of Portuguese and European jurists and canonists in general pertained to business dealings involving individuals who were not familiar with trade. Those learned individuals were particularly concerned about people who bought, sold or took out loans to cover their needs, such as farmers and artisans. As we will see, in Portuguese mercantile practices, interest rates generally appeared tacitly, and there are no documented cases in which they were contested, although they might have been. However, the custom of built-in interest makes it difficult to assess prevailing market rates.

Returning to the subject at hand, as is the case even today advance purchases could be advantageous to safeguard against price increases in the case of buyers, or a fall in prices in the case of sellers. Purchases were also paid for in advance in order to secure the supply of merchandise of a higher quality than was available for payments at sight. Sellers, in turn, obtained working capital and could reinvest the money received before delivering the merchandise.

Purchases on credit did not strain the liquidity of purchasers, who could avail themselves of the product for immediate consumption or resale. Hence,

A. The concept of *periculum sortis*, which would allow a premium to be charged for taking on another person's risk, was not accepted for loans, since lenders did not incur borrowers' risks but rather their own, considered to be an intrinsic part of the loan.

B. Spufford observes that the VOC used to lend at 8%, prior to 1610, and at 6.25% in 1620, and that a private merchant lent at 5% in 1633: P. Spufford, "Access to Credit and Capital in the Commercial Centers of Europe," in K. Davis and J. Lucassen (eds.), *A Miracle Mirrored: The Dutch Republic in European Perspective* (Cambridge: Cambridge University Press, 1995), pp. 304–305, 310–314, 316–319, 323–329.

C. "...the contract is not usurious: as it likewise is not usurious when the vendor charges a surcharge, which exceeds the just and accurate price, not on account of the wait but instead due to the ensuing losses on account of not having been paid immediately: or foregone profit, which he was likely to have obtained had he sold the merchandise for cash in hand, trading with this ready money, or purchasing other wares" (*Constituiçoens synodaes do Arcebispado de Braga*, title LXVIII).

AVARITIA
· P. brueghel · Inuentor ·
Cock · excud · cum priuileg · 1558
QVIS METVS, AVT PVDOR EST VNQVAM PROPERANTIS AVARI?
Eere / beleeftheÿt / scaemte / noch godlÿck vermaen En siet die scrapende ghierichheÿt niet aen

Avarice, from the Seven Deadly Sins Series; *Pieter Brueghel, the Elder* (1558).

purchases on credit facilitated trade by those who did not have the entire sum available in either cash or merchandise that the vendor would accept as payment. In much the same manner as purchases in advance, the facility served to both ensure the acquisition of a high-quality product and to protect against a surge in price that would exceed the premium paid for the credit.

Another type of transaction involved sales by means of forward contracts, which established that a certain product would be supplied within a given time frame, for a certain sum, to be paid upon delivery of the goods. Apart from guaranteeing the supply and circulation of merchandise, such contracts safeguarded against abrupt price fluctuations.[14]

Purchases using credit were the most common method of payment at the time. An English merchant, Gerard Malynes, who wrote a tradesman's manual during this period, stated that receiving payment within a month was deemed to be excellent terms.[15] In Brazil, as a rule, sugar-mill owners and cane farmers purchased goods on credit from resident merchants or traveling traders who stayed in the colony for some time. As will be seen below, these purchases were usually part of transactions that were not settled in cash but rather in crates of sugar. When the price for sugar was pre-determined, a sale on credit was combined with an advance purchase, wherein the interest paid for credit mingled with that paid on advance payment. When the price was not established beforehand, it was equivalent to a sale on credit using sugar as a means of exchange.[16]

Sugar was sold on credit in Amsterdam too, as done by a Portuguese Jew who sold a Dutchman three crates of white sugar at 18 groten per pound of weight. The gross weight of the crates was measured at 1,604 pounds. However, estimating that the weight of the empty crates (the tare weight) would have been 254 pounds, the parties arrived at a net weight of 1,350 pounds. Hence the total price came to 607 guldens and 10 stuivers.[D] Of this total, the purchaser gave a deposit of 220 guldens and committed to pay the remainder in twelve months. As the sale price included the premium for credit, the purchaser stipulated a rebate at 8% per year in case the payment was settled before the agreed period. Thus, if the debt was paid in six months, for example, the purchaser would receive a rebate of 4%.[E] Portuguese arithmetic manuals taught merchants to calculate such rebates,[17] and Malynes cited a figure of 10% as the average interest rate for sales involving a fixed term.[18]

The risks of creditors – irrespective of whether they were vendors or purchasers – were always assessed in accordance with the reputation, assets and liquidity of the debtor. Thus, it would be reasonable to imagine

D. 607 10 guldens and stuivers = 607.50 guldens = 12,150 stuivers = 24,300 groten = 1,350 pounds x 18 groten.

E. As a guarantee that the vendor would receive the value of the sugar, the purchaser pledged two rental agreements. These agreements referred to a house and a cellar under that house, both near the house with a fleur-de-lis stone tablet on the newly built and prestigious Prinsengracht canal in Amsterdam. The properties had been rented for two years to a surgeon – the house, for 168 guldens a year and the cellar for 100 guldens (SR no. 2084).

that a peasant, artisan or small trader would pay higher interest rates than a well-known and established merchant. In Portugal, the Code *Ordenações Filipinas* tried to prevent individuals with few assets and little experience in financial transactions from venturing into speculative activities such as buying on credit to later also sell on credit. In order to replenish their limited working capital, such neophytes ended up reselling merchandise at prices which were lower than those they had committed to pay. Their purchases on credit probably also entailed interest rates higher than usual to compensate for the risk of default associated with their inexperience and lack of reputation. In order to bridge the gap and pay their expenses, they then resorted to interest-bearing loans, further worsening their situation.[19]

Landowners, particularly sugar-mill owners in Brazil and nobles in Portugal who sometimes lacked liquidity despite their assets, were also charged higher interest rates. Apart from this, their political influence could hinder debt collection.[20] Father Antonil explained that in the context of the late seventeenth century and early eighteenth century, merchants in Brazil demanded high interest rates to buy sugar in advance from planters and farmers since they were exposed to a high risk of default due to droughts, pests, slave revolts, epidemics, and so forth. Apparently, however, the main reason for the high interest rates was the merchants' lack of confidence in the sugar producers.[F] Sugar-mill owners (and cane farmers) contracted debts with many creditors and spent prodigiously. Apart from this, they had become relatively immune to seizures for debts, and even when they could be seized, the cases dragged on for years; during some periods, the Crown granted them a moratorium to pay their debts. From 1612 onwards, sugar mills could no longer be seized and only half of their production could be appropriated to pay debts. In the 1630s, legislation allowed an entire sugar mill to be auctioned, but it could not be partially dismantled. Likewise, its copper tools, oxen and slaves could not be seized on account of a debt that was worth less than the sugar mill's total value, so as not to undermine its ongoing production. Even when all the conditions for a seizure were satisfied, it was not easy to do so in court, and the authorities preferred to seize revenues alone.[21]

If Father Antonil reproached the lack of creditworthiness of many sugar-mill owners, he also disapproved of rebates for purchases of sugar in advance in exchange for cash. According to him, these transactions would not entail "truly foregone profits and emerging damages." This was even worse when "the person providing the advance money would not have employed it elsewhere [in another transaction] before the merchandise was shipped to Portugal," since here too there was no evident lucrum cessans or damnum emergens, that is, the opportunity cost for the money in question.[G]

Future Delivery

Father Antonil frowned upon forward contracts, since he viewed them as a guarantee for purchasers, while vendors submitted to such contracts, "obliged to do so out of need." Without a random element in a purchaser's profits, the contract became usurious. This priest, however, did not consider the hypothesis that the price agreed upon beforehand could be higher than the future price in the market, and that vendors could use this mechanism to safeguard themselves against such a possibility. Such omission suggests that the use of forward contract sales was still incipient in sugar producers' risk management.[H]

However, the lack of credit and liquidity highlighted by Antonil was not applicable to all sugar-mill owners and cane farmers, particularly during the period in question. Then, many straddled both the world of plantations as well as the world of finance, that is, trade, such as well-known figure Ambrósio Fernandes Brandão. Leonor Freire Costa has observed a greater vertical integration between both sectors in the sixteenth century and a greater separation during the first two decades of the seventeenth century, while noting a renewed tendency towards integration at the end of the 1610s and over the course of the 1620s.[22]

In Amsterdam, as the financial market expanded and became increasingly sophisticated, contracts for future delivery proliferated, both with advance payments as well as with forward contracts. Standardized goods that could be substituted by others of a nearly equivalent type, quality and quantity (i.e., fungibility) were better suited to such contracts since purchasers had greater security in terms of the product they would receive. At the same time, the greater volatility of the prices of more popular goods resulted in the use of purchases in advance and forward contracts as instruments offering protection against highs or lows.[23]

In effect, forward contracts were more common in bulk commodities such as grain, salt, wool and dried fish. However, notary records in Amsterdam reveal sales, both advance purchases and forward contracts, of diverse products from the Iberian world, not all of which were bulky and cheap. There are instances of advance purchases of salt from Setúbal[24] and Pero Ximenes wine (from Spain).[25] Deeds also register a forward contract for Andalusian syrup[26] and cinnamon;[27] and sales of sumac[28] and raisins[29] whose records do not allow one to discern whether these were advance purchases or forward contracts.

Even though, as we will see below, the standardization and fungibility of sugar left a lot to be desired, this product also appears to have been sold by means of both forward contracts and advance purchases. Its price fluctuated widely, particularly upon the arrival and departure of ships, or in the absence of traffic.[30]

On December 20, 1600, a merchant from Amsterdam complained, through a notary, about the delivery of fourteen crates of sugar, out of a total of sixty crates, that he had purchased more than three months earlier from a Portuguese who resided in that city. The vendor responded by saying he had already handed over everything that he was supposed to deliver. It is not clear if the deal involved an advance purchase, a forward contract or at sight payment wherein the vendor did not deliver everything he had sold, or

F. "The reputation of a sugar-mill owner is based on his veracity, that is, in his punctuality and dependability in keeping his word.... In other years when revenues are sufficient and there are only moderate losses or no losses at all, there is no reason to let down merchants or the agents who trade on behalf of their principals, to whom they are accountable. Hence it is not surprising if, having for so long experienced hardship while keeping their word with truly foregone profit and extrinsic losses, they raise, with due moderation, the price of the merchandise they sell on credit, God alone knowing when they will actually receive payment for their wares" (Antonil, *Cultura e opulência do Brasil*, pp. 108–109).

G. "To purchase sugar in advance at two cruzados [800 réis], for example, which sugar at the time was commonly worth twelve *tostões* and more [> 1,200 réis], entails difficulties, because the purchaser is sure of making profits and the vendor is morally certain that he will suffer a loss, particularly when the one paying the advance money would not have used it for anything else before the time when the sugar is loaded on board to be shipped to Portugal" (Ibid., p. 109).

H. "Those who buy or sell in advance for the price that the sugar will be worth at the time the fleet departs are entering into a just contract because thus both the purchaser and the vendor are equally at risk. And by this I mean the higher average price that sugar will fetch at that time and not a particular price at which an individual might agree to, compelled by the need to sell their sugar" (Ibid., p. 109). The system of sailing in fleets tended to undermine the producers' position in forward sales agreements entered into between departures and arrivals.

Sale of grain portrayed in the Book of Trades *(1694). Easily standardized products with a lower ratio between value and volume, such as grain, were the most frequently traded items with forward contracts or options.*

if the purchaser suffered damages. The contract had been negotiated by one (or two) broker(s) and had probably been recorded in a private document, depriving us of further details about the transaction. In fact, if a difference had not arisen between the parties leading to notary proceedings, nothing would have been known about this sizable sale of sugar whose full delivery might have taken longer than three months.[31]

Peter Spufford emphasized that Dutch merchants had great advantages over their competitors from other countries because they could use advance purchases extensively due to low interest rates and the easy access to funds in the Republic. Violet Barbour underscored the fact that for the same reasons, merchants from Amsterdam could offer credit to suppliers to ensure their loyalty and could hold larger stocks for a longer period, which enabled them to make purchases during periods when prices were lower and wait to sell when prices peaked.[I]

The truth is that the advantages afforded by low interest rates also had an impact on other centers that traded with the United Provinces, since the volume of business between the various regions involved increased as a whole. Apart from this, foreign merchants could raise money through an agent in the Republic and stock their merchandise there until it was a good time to sell. Likewise, a foreign merchant could have his agent sell the wares in advance purchases or forward contracts. The agent would then remit the proceeds back to the principal, or invest them on the said principal's behalf, while the latter took care of dispatching the merchandise.

Explaining the evolution of contracts for future delivery in Amsterdam, Oscar Gelderblom and Joost Jonker argue that the development of such transactions required that the authorities refrained from imposing many obstacles to setting prices beforehand, aiming at protecting consumers and producers, otherwise the parties could easily repudiate these contracts at the time when they fell due. It is possible to project this situation onto the Brazilian case as well: the growing intervention of local and central authorities in favor of sugar producers was not only detrimental to the merchants but probably also to the producers, who were unable to make use of forward contracts to protect themselves from declines in prices.[32]

Contracts for future delivery resulted in increasingly sophisticated arrangements in Amsterdam, including futures and options. Futures were negotiable forward contracts, that is, the original purchaser could sell his rights to a third party. On the other hand, options guaranteed the right to buy or sell something at a certain time, for a certain sum, in exchange for a

I. Spufford believes that this credit facility was the main reason for the Dutch predominance over English and Hanseatic merchants in the Spanish wool market in the mid-seventeenth century. Similarly, access to cheaper credit enabled Tuscan merchants to surpass Flemish merchants in the wool and textile market in the thirteenth century, and, for the same reason, the Dutch could obtain better prices in Asia than the Portuguese in the seventeenth century (Spufford, "Access to Credit and Capital in the Commercial Centers of Europe," pp. 307, 317–319; Barbour, *Capitalism in Amsterdam in the 17th Century*, pp. 21, 87–93, 95, 100).

Portrait of David Nuyts; *Jonas Suyderhoeff (1631). Sugar refiners and successful merchants, the Nuyts were patrons of the arts and co-founded the West and East India Companies.*

premium paid in the present. When the term was up, the holder of the option could exercise it or relinquish it and lose the premium paid in advance. Options, therefore, functioned as insurance policies against great fluctuations in price, allowing merchants, to safeguard themselves against substantial rises or falls for a small advance amount without committing to purchases or sales. Options became negotiable instruments, as they still are today.

During the sixteenth century, forward contracts and options were widely used in Antwerp and in the trade in grain and herrings in Amsterdam.[J] Gelderblom and Jonker emphasize that such contracts may have been used for other products, but there is no record of them because they were contracted privately on handwritten documents, and the deals were concluded without disputes that would have necessitated registration in official records.[K] The rarity of extant private trading documents in general from merchants of that period suggests that this might well have been the case.[33]

There is no trace of unequivocal options contracts for sugar, however, some notary records show similar arrangements. For the sale of more than thirty crates of muscovado sugar loaded onto the ship of master Theodore Corneille to take effect, it depended on the Portuguese broker who had facilitated the transaction presenting the parties with a document outlining the purchase conditions.[34] Here, it is not clear whether the ship had already arrived in Amsterdam, whether it was on its way or had called in at another port. There is also no trace of the purchase conditions. The apparent future delivery suggests that it was a forward contract or an option.

Four months prior to this, the same Portuguese broker facilitated the sale of fifty crates of panela sugar, which were already in the city, for the same purchaser, Cornelis Nuyts (also written as Nuijts), and his brother David. They were to buy each pound of sugar for 8 groten, with a rebate of 8% per year if they settled the payment before the agreed term. As they were only able to satisfactorily inspect the quality of twenty-eight crates, it was agreed that they would hold the option to purchase the remainder, depending on the quality verified upon delivery.[35] In addition to being sugar refiners, the Nuyts were prominent merchants, founding members of the VOC[L] and patrons of the arts.[36]

The derivatives market developed further with the solution the Dutch municipal authorities introduced for *tulipomania*, the crisis caused by speculation in forward contracts and futures to purchase tulip bulbs in the late 1630s. They transformed forward contracts into options, allowing purchasers to pay a premium to be able to avoid spending the entire amount to which they had committed.[37]

J. Herman van der Wee asserts that even though transactions in futures expanded in Antwerp during the sixteenth century, they still continued to be limited primarily to the trade in grain: H. van der Wee, *The Growth of the Antwerp Market and the European Economy (Fourteenth–Sixteenth Centuries)* (The Hague: Martinus Nijhoff Publishers, 1963), vv. 2, p. 366; O. Gelderblom and J. Jonker, "Amsterdam as the Cradle of Modern Futures and Options Trading, 1550–1650," *Economy and Society in the Low Countries before 1850, Working Paper Series* (2003–2009): 6–7. In the sixteenth century, futures were also common in fairs in Castile: R. Carande, *Carlos V y sus banqueros: la vida económica en Castilla (1516–1556)*, V. 1. (Madrid: Sociedad de Estudios y Publicaciones, 1965), p. 328.

K. A handwritten future contract dating from 1610 has survived along with other papers belonging to a merchant named Hans Thijs. From the 1610s onwards it is possible to find printed forward contracts for shares issued by the Dutch East India Company (VOC). Apparently, options on shares of the India Companies were quite uncommon prior to the 1630s when the VOC began to distribute dividends annually and prices became more volatile. Until the following decade, they would still continue to be a prerogative of wealthier merchants (Ibid., pp. 11–12).

Gelderblom and Jonker linked the emergence of a secondary market, where futures and options were traded, to overcoming the difficulties faced while transmitting maturing credit instruments to third parties, which will be examined in the next chapter. As contracts and procedures became standardized, the market consolidated. A secondary market attracts more participants and speculators when the products are widely accepted, sold in significant quantities and have volatile prices, which guarantees liquidity for derivatives. This was the case with the aforesaid basic food products, but possibly also that of sugar, albeit to a lesser extent. Finally, the existence of markets with continuous and centralized transactions, such as in bourses where price fluctuations were evident, also facilitated the entry of a greater number of investors and speculators without any particular involvement in the trade of the merchandise in question.[38] This resulted in a safer market with fewer price fluctuations and greater liquidity, since futures and options could be transacted at any time.

There are no explicit cases of advance or forward contract sales of sugar in the notary records in the city of Porto. It was, however, possible to identify forward contract sales of wine to be delivered in the Canary Islands[39] and in Madeira,[40] wherein only a deposit was paid in advance and the remainder was to be paid upon delivery. This was also the case with other products, such as sumac from the Douro region.[41] Sales in advance of wine, olive oil and wheat are mentioned in Portuguese canon law: "Do not purchase beforehand for less than what it is worth at the time of delivery, or more than what it can truly be expected from such products to be worth when harvested."[42] It was feared that such contracts would conceal usurious loans made to individuals unfamiliar with the world of commerce.

However, one cannot rule out the possibility that such sales were also prevalent in the sugar trade, assuming that they would have been agreed verbally or by means of private contracts. In fact, notary records in Porto mention situations that bear a great resemblance to sales in advance. One such situation was the sale of sugar that had already been loaded on board but had not yet been delivered because the ship had not arrived at the expected place at the expected time. A resident of a village deep in the countryside of Portugal – Loivos, near Chaves and a short distance away from the Spanish border – sold twenty-four crates and two fechos (small boxes containing the best-quality sugar, as has been mentioned) of white and muscovado sugar to a merchant from Porto and another from Viana, jointly, in exchange for cash. The merchants were appointed as his proxies to charge and collect the sugar from the shipmaster bringing the sugar from Brazil to Portugal, who lived in Viana.[43] In all likelihood the vendor needed to return to the hinterland and preferred to sell the sugar rather than wait for it or collect it elsewhere, even if that entailed a discount on the product's market value.

Another situation, even more akin to sales in advance, was that in which merchants facing cash flow problems sold the sugar they were waiting to receive to soothe the anxiety of their creditors. A merchant in Porto named Paulo Mendes Carvalho transferred to three different merchants, his creditors, a large shipment of merchandise which he had sent to Brazil with a retainer who was to sell the wares and purchase sugar with the proceeds. Each of the creditors was to receive one third of the sugar to be sent by the retainer and would bear the expenses for the homeward voyage. Carvalho, in turn, promised to answer for his retainer's acts. As he owed each of the three merchants a sum smaller than the value of the goods he was transferring to them, they paid him the difference in cash. In truth, the merchandise that had been sent to Brazil had been purchased with money advanced by two of these same merchants.[44] A similar procedure is found in Amsterdam with the transfer of cargoes and all the revenues they rendered in Porto and the Canary Islands and, from there, in Pernambuco.[45]

Use of Cash

Apart from the obvious advantage of not subjecting vendors to possible defaults by buyers, purchases at sight had another fundamental benefit. Itinerant traders did not have the means to purchase in advance, and sales on credit or in forward contracts would require them to extend their stay until the purchase was settled or they would have to rely on credit mechanisms across distances, which generally involved third parties, as shall shortly be seen. It is evident that in Portugal, merchants commonly instructed their agents traveling to Brazil to sell the entrusted cargo in exchange for cash and to avoid selling on credit, hence not leaving any matters pending overseas.[M]

Purchases at sight were paid by handing over cash or products during the act of delivering merchandise. Malynes has emphasized that purchasing with cash was commonly the best and most advantageous method, since buyers paid lower prices for wares than when using credit or bartering goods. However, he also cautioned that a familiarity with the use of coins and their qualities was an indispensable condition for such types of transactions.

Malynes mentions the difficulties involved in ascertaining the quality of coins and knowing how to use them. Nowadays, the value of the coins in our wallets bears no relation to the metal from which they are made, but this was not the case during that period. In theory, the nominal or face value of coins was supposed to reflect the intrinsic value of the metal used in the alloys of gold, silver and copper from which they were made. It was the need to establish this relationship which gave rise to a host of problems and required merchants to be capable of assessing and distinguishing real and counterfeit coins, as well as verifying whether the value of the metal had diminished owing to wear and tear over time or even the deliberate removal of some of the metal.

It was common to extract silver dust by vigorously shaking a sack full of coins. It was even more common to shave (clip) the edge of a coin, its least visible part, a practice facilitated by the minting methods of that period. It was also opportune for merchants to estimate the supply and demand for coins in general, as well as for the precious metals from which they were made, since both influenced the value of money in general and of each coin in particular.[46]

L. The Nuyts brothers also invested in the WIC when it became better established.

M. Francisco Ferreira received the following instructions: "Try and sell diligently for the best circumstances in that land without selling anything on credit either in Brazil [or] in any other land": ADP, NOT, PO2, l. 4, fols. 11–13 (1595-7-5). Merchants from Porto often instructed their agents about to sail to Brazil to sell merchandise at sight, for cash: "You will travel to the town of Olinda, in the captaincy of Pernambuco, where you will unload the said wine and all the other wares you are taking from Portugal and shall then immediately and diligently seek to sell them for ready money according to the circumstances you find in that land, handling the sales and profits as if these were your own property": ADP, NOT, PO2, l. 37, fols. 48–50 (1613-6-10).

Tax Collector and his Wife; *Marinus van Reymerswaele (1538). The disparity between a coin's face value and intrinsic value required considerable expertise to determine the quality and quantity of the metal from which they were made. On the tax collector's desk we see a set of counterweights used to assess several types of coins.*

Sir Thomas Gresham; *Flemish school (1544). An English merchant and financier, Gresham (ca. 1518–1579), who acted as an agent in the Low Countries and was a co-founder of the Company of Merchants Trading to Spain and Portugal.*

'Gresham's Law'

The phenomenon of the disappearance of coins with a greater intrinsic value after depreciation has been known since Antiquity. Yet it became celebrated as Gresham's Law,ℵ for having been mentioned by Sir Thomas Gresham, albeit in a less detailed manner than by other contemporaries, in a letter written on the occasion of Queen Elizabeth I's coronation. In this letter, Gresham recommended that the depreciation of currency be avoided, since it resulted in the migration of good English coins abroad. Having acquired a great deal of experience in Antwerp, a leading commercial hub during the sixteenth century, Gresham advised successive English monarchs on monetary issues. He also oversaw the construction of the first bourse in the English capital, the Royal Exchange, in 1565. In his will, he founded an institution for higher learning bearing his name, and he was also one of the founders of the English Company of Merchants Trading to Spain and Portugal in 1577.[54]

What further complicated the use of coins, however, was depreciation of their official face value vis-à-vis the intrinsic value of the metal from which they were made. The simplest way to do so was for the authorities and mints to reduce the value of the coin's alloy but maintain its face value. Authorities, however, could achieve the same result more effectively, albeit less subtly, without altering the coin's material. As each coin had a fixed rate of exchange with other coins, official rates (tariffs) were often manipulated by raising the exchange rate of a coin with a lower metallic value in relation to other coins in circulation.

These two forms of depreciation, better known as debasement, had a detrimental effect on credit operations and forward contracts. Coins' nominal or intrinsic value might change between the moment the credit was advanced and when it was repaid. Hence, creditors could end up being paid in coins that were worth less than they were when the credit operation had been contracted. In general, payments were made with coins with the lowest metallic value. Nowadays, if we pass on worn notes and keep those in better condition, both with the same face value, we do not become any richer or poorer, since old and new notes have the same market value. During the age in question, however, two coins with the same face value could have different intrinsic values, and anyone who had them would use the coin with a lower intrinsic value to make payments and would keep the other finer coin as a reserve (store of value). This was also the case with coins

ℵ Gresham's Law is also applicable when the intrinsic value of a coin exceeds its nominal value, inducing people to sell such coins as metal and use others as currency.

Capitulo V. 14

Eſtas moedas, alem do valor acima ſempre tem alguma ventagem no troco dellas:por ſem pre ſe pidirem pera muitas partes; a ſaber, para França,ouro,& patacas, pera Cathalunha, toſtoẽs velhos, pera a India patacas, & ſempre ſe ganha nos trocos de dous tè cinco,por cẽto, por maneira que as ditas moedas como ſe foſſẽ mer cadorias, caminhão, & nauegão pera muitas mais partes,& em reſolução a mòr parte, vai ainda que por diuerſas mãos,ter aos theſouros da China,& ſeus Reynos vezinhos.

MOEDAS DO REINO DE Caſtella, que o Anno de 1566. ſua Mageſtade delRey Dom Phelippe noſſo Senhor,que eſtà no Ceo acre centou o ſeptimo.

Hũ ducado, trezẽtos, & ſetenta, & cinco marauedis.
Hum caſtelhano de 22. quilates, 544. marauedis.
Hum eſcudo, quatrocentos marauedis.
Hũ real de prata, trinta, & quatro marauedis.
Hum marauidi, duas bran-

"*Table of coins of the kingdoms of Portugal, Castile, Aragon and Valencia," published in Afonso de Vilafanhe Guiral e Pacheco's Arithmetic manual, printed in Lisbon in 1624.*

At the top of the opposite page, water-powered rollers used to stretch metal into strips and mint coins simultaneously (1620).

Body of a screw press used to mint coins (1678).

On the bottom of the opposite page, a German "Taschenwerk" Press, *probably dating from the seventeenth century. This type of equipment was portable and, therefore, useful in counterfeiting.*

that were over-valued or under-valued in official rates. Holders of such coins would circulate the former and retain the latter, and could have the coins with a higher intrinsic value melted and sell the metal.[51] As private individuals could have their precious metals minted into coins, they gained from depreciation, even after paying the applicable taxes and minting costs.[52]

Apart from this, merchants exchanged better coins for foreign products, since foreigners valued coins according to their intrinsic value as a product and not for their nominal value. Hence, foreigners accepted better coins at a higher rate than the local official rate (agio). During the period in question, a merchant and mathematician named Afonso de Vilafanhe Guiral e Pacheco explained how it was possible to earn between 2% and 5% by exporting various Portuguese and Castilian coins to different Iberian, European and Asian destinations, each of which had their own preferences.[53] The imported products were then resold in the domestic market for baser coins. As a result, depreciation drove coins with a greater intrinsic value out of circulation.

The flight of better coins also occurred within the bi-metallic and tri-metallic systems which prevailed at the time. The sixteenth century saw a great influx of silver from Spanish America. As a result, gold coins gradually ceased to circulate in Europe as a means of exchange. Silver became the European standard, with gold remaining as a store of value. Gold coins began to appreciate in the market, garnering a premium over their nominal value. During the 1620s, the same trend applied to silver coins, which was replaced with copper ones as a means of exchange.[55]

The complications involved in using coins did not stop there. Different monetary systems were legal tender within the same country, and each system was organized with complex fractions and divisions, which required intricate accounting methods. Worse still, foreign coins also circulated, more or less legally. In Portugal, most of the coins in circulation were Castilian, while Flemish coins predominated in the Dutch Republic.

Ideal monetary systems were created to facilitate accounting. Their coins were not minted and hence were not subject to depreciation, merely serving as units of account for conversions among the different coins in circulation. This was the role of the Dutch gulden and this was also how both the Portuguese cruzado and the real gradually began to function. In a certain way, these ideal coins – imaginary or virtual currency, so to speak – functioned like a price index and indexation to the dollar or to the minimum wage, as was common in countries suffering from hyperinflation during the 1980s, with the difference being that the imaginary coins were not a means of exchange, as the dollar is, and hence could not replace actual currency.[56]

Considering all this complexity, it is no surprise that manuals for merchants during this age devoted several pages to long and dreary explanations about how to assess coin alloys and calculate conversions from one coin to another.[57]

Minting methods

The most common minting method used was having two molds, the dies, pressed onto a disc of heated metal. The disc, called a blank, was placed between the two dies, one (the lower one) being stationary and the other (the upper one) being mobile. The mobile die was held with one hand while the other hand was used to hammer the die. The blanks, in turn, were produced by stretching and flattening metal ingots, which were subsequently cut into discs. This method did not produce perfectly smooth and round blanks nor, crucially, blanks with a uniform size and weight. Striking the blanks with a hammer did not improve their morphology: the hammer blows were neither perpendicular to the die nor identical. Thus, the area and thickness of the coins were even more irregular and clipping was less perceptible. In order to avoid this, serrated rims were gradually introduced, engraved onto the coins' sides. However, as long as the area was misshapen, it was not very effective. Producing the blanks by placing molten metal in molds helped, but in addition to being a more complex and costly process, minting coins with hammers ended up making the discs irregular.

From the mid-sixteenth century onwards, more complex and costly processes were invented. The most important of these processes used a machine with two cylinders to flatten the ingots into strips with the desired thickness, which would be cut into discs before or after being minted. If they were cut afterwards, the strips would also be minted by cylinders or half-cylinders. In larger mints, such as the one in the Castilian city of Segovia,[47] cylinders powered by water wheels stretched the metal into strips and minted the coins simultaneously. This mechanism was quite similar – apart from the level of precision, of course – to the hydro-powered rollers used on Brazilian sugar mills.

In some smaller mints, a machine produced the strips while another minted the coins, both operated by hand. Then, the engraved strips were cut in presses, likewise operated by hand. These presses provided a uniform circumference, a technique which gave the coins an undulated surface. Serrated edges, instead of rims, were introduced only at the end of the seventeenth century, and were engraved by another machine. Another later technique molded the sides of coins and serrated their edges in a screw press. This method made the surface flat, but it took some time to be adopted due to the difficulties in forging presses, clamps and screws that could handle pressing bulk quantities of large silver coins.

However, the Portuguese and Dutch coins[48] used during the period in question were all minted with the hammering technique. To be sure, in Portugal, during the reign of King Sebastian, there had been a fleeting attempt to improve the technology used to mint gold coins by smelting and molding a protruding rim, which aimed to prevent coin edges being clipped; this was the "ingenious" idea of a Portuguese inventor, João Gonçalves de Guimarães, and as a result the gold 500 réis coin became known as the "engenhoso" ("ingenious one").[49] In Castile, the most sophisticated method of minting through hydraulic rollers would only be used in Segovia, while the other mints also produced coins with the hammering method.[50]

The Portuguese monetary system

The Portuguese monetary system in effect between 1585 and 1630 was established in 1584 for gold coins and in 1588 for silver coins. Using the real as a standard, coinage was distributed as follows:

Gold

4 cruzados / 1,600 réis
Reign of Phillip II

4 cruzados / 1,600 réis
Reign of Phillip III

2 cruzados / 800 réis
Reign of Phillip II

1 cruzado / 400 réis
Reign of Phillip II

500 réis
Reign of Sebastian

Even though gold cruzados were already rarely being minted and circulated less during the period in question, they continued to be a unit of account, fixed at 400 réis per cruzado. The coin was called a cruzado because it was launched in 1457 when Portugal was mustering forces originally intended for a crusade against the Turks, which were later diverted to the battlefront in Morocco. During the reign of Philip II, golden 500 réis coins were also minted in addition to cruzados. Whether or not they were golden, coins from previous reigns were preserved, mainly as a store of value.[58]

The images of coins in this and the following charts, as throughout the book, do not follow a single scale, and therefore, do not afford a comparison among the actual size of the coins.

Silver

1 *tostão* / 100 réis
Reign of Phillip II and Phillip III

4 *vinténs* or Portuguese *real dobrado* / 80 réis
Reign of Henry and Phillip II

meio tostão / 50 réis
Reign of Phillip II and Phillip III

2 vinténs or Portuguese real / 40 réis
Reign of Phillip II

1 *vintém* / 20 réis
Reign of Phillip II and Phillip III

Copper

10 réis
Reign of Phillip II

5 réis
Reign of Sebastian

3 réis
Reign of Sebastian

1 real*
Reign of Antony

1 *ceitil* / 1/6 to 1/7 réis
Reign of Sebastian

Sources: Almeida, *Aritmética como descrição do real*, v. 1, pp. 175–182; Mauro, *Portugal, o Brasil e o Atlântico*, v. 2, pp. 158–159; C. M. Almeida Amaral, *Catálogo descritivo das moedas portuguesas*, T. 1 (Lisbon: Imprensa Nacional – Casa da Moeda, 1977), pp. 599–642; A. C. Teixeira de Aragão, *Descripção geral e histórica das moedas cunhadas em nome dos reis, regentes e governadores de Portugal*, T. 2 (Lisbon: Imprensa Nacional, 1877), p. 237; J. J. A. Dias, "A moeda," in Serrão and Oliveira Marques, *Nova história de Portugal*, v. 5, pp. 274–275; A. F. Meneses, "A moeda," in ibidem., v. 7, pp.355-363.

**Minted in the Azores when the islands were the Prior of Crato's stronghold, it is an extremely rare coin. Only four or five are believed to remain in existence today.*

The Castilian monetary system

The pairs of coins with the same face value in the double pages show, to the left, blanks minted by hydraulic rollers and, to the right, hammered pieces.

Gold

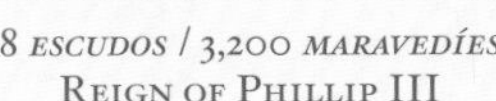

8 *escudos* / 3,200 *maravedíes*
Reign of Phillip III

4 escudos / 1,600 maravedíes
(1,760 after 1609)
Reign of Phillip III

2 escudos / 800 maravedíes
(880 after 1609)
Reign of Phillip III

1 escudo / 400 maravedíes
(440 after 1609)
Reign of Phillip III

Silver

1 *cincuentín*
or 50 reales /
1,700 maravedíes
Reign of Phillip III

1 *real de a ocho*
(8 reales, piece of eight) /
272 maravedíes
Reign of Phillip III

1 real de a cuatro
(4 reales, piece of four) /
136 maravedíes
Reign of Phillip III

1 *real de a dos*
(2 reales, piece of two) /
68 maravedíes
Reign of Phillip III

Silver

1 real /
34 maravedíes
Reign of Phillip III

medio real /
17 maravedíes
Reign of Phillip III

Copper

1 *cuartillo* / 8.5 maravedíes
Reign of Phillip II

8 *maravedíes*
Reign of Phillip III

Cuartos or 4 maravedíes
Reign of Phillip III

Ochavos or 2 maravedíes
Reign of Phillip III

1 maravedí
Reign of Phillip III

Source: Hamilton, *American Treasure and the Price of Revolution in Spain*, pp. 49–52, 59–61, 65, 75.

Portuguese coins did not undergo depreciation during the period. To ensure even greater stability, it was decided in 1612 that any coins that were worn, clipped or whose weight had diminished would be melted and minted anew. Other coins were to receive a stamp authenticating their exact weight. Even more important, orders were issued for Castilian reales to be re-minted as Portuguese coins.[59]

In truth, during the Iberian Union, Castilian coins were legal tender in Portugal, as reflected in the words "I am paying everything in this kingdom's approved and current legal tender, in silver reales" repeatedly recorded by notaries in Porto, where the reales were coins from the neighboring kingdom. The use of Castilian coins, at least those made of gold and silver, continued despite the orders to mint them anew as Portuguese coins, and a Castilian real was rated as being equivalent to 40 Portuguese réis.[60] In Brazil, Friar Vicente do Salvador mentioned a coin of 8 vinténs[61] which did not exist in the Portuguese monetary system but which, very probably, would have been no more than a Castilian *real de a cuatro* coin, which, just like 8 vinténs, would have been worth 160 réis.

One cannot therefore speak of the Portuguese monetary system without also referring to the Spanish system. The latter encompassed gold escudos, silver reales and their multiples. Spanish coins made from precious metals did not suffer depreciation and the 10% increase in the official rate of the gold escudo in 1609 would have served only to update its market value vis-à-vis silver. Only Castilian coins made of copper alloy had a diminished intrinsic value. They were worth less and were generically called *vellón* (*bilhão* or *bolhão* in Portuguese). One of these vellón coins, known as the maravedí, was the Castilian monetary standard; that is, other coins in Castile and its colonies were rated on the basis of the maravedí, despite its low quality and recurrent depreciation.

The vellón underwent sharp and consecutive depreciations in 1597, 1599, 1602, 1603 and 1628, but depreciation only began to have some effect after 1603. From then onwards, however, a surcharge (disagio) over the official rate was demanded in some transactions to receive payments in vellón, requiring more coins to pay the same amount. The great scholar of the Spanish monetary economy during this period, Earl J. Hamilton, affirmed that this surcharge became current from 1619 onwards, with more than an additional 2.5% being charged. In 1624, this surcharge exceeded 10% and in 1627 reached a rate of between 40% and 50%. Consequently, over the decade of the 1620s, copper coins gradually drove silver coins out of circulation and became consolidated as the main means of payment, which was further boosted by a reduction in shipments of silver from America. From 1619 onwards, the mass issuing of low-value coins sparked high inflation.[62]

In Portugal, copper coins were already scarce in the mid-sixteenth century, and the real, minted in copper, its multiples and submultiples were rarely issued during the reigns of the Habsburgs. Consequently, as in the case of the cruzado, the main role of the real was to serve as a unit of account, which, in fact it was until 1911 in Portugal and until 1942 in Brazil. The plural "réis" substituted the word "reais" and became current usage from the mid-sixteenth century onwards, even being spelled so in official documents. Over the course of the following centuries, the depreciation of this coinage meant that accounts were calculated in thousands, *mil-réis*, while millions of réis or thousands of mil-réis were called "*contos*."[63]

"Resello a ocho maravedís": *stamp used to change the face value of a coin from four to eight maravedis (1603).*

Ideal Dutch monetary systems

One of the ideal Dutch systems was based on the *Pond Vlaams* or *Pond groot*, known as pound Flemish, or pound gross, or *Libra de grossos*, as it was called in Portuguese at the time, was worth 20 *schellingen* or *soldos*, in Portuguese. Each schelling, in its turn, was worth 12 groten, known as *dinheiros* or grossos in Portuguese. Hence, each pound Flemish was equivalent to 240 groten. The second system was based on the gulden, or florin, and each florin was worth 20 stuivers (translated into Portuguese as "*placas*"). The exchange between the two systems was fixed: 1 stuiver was worth 2 groten and 1 pound Flemish was equivalent to 6 guldens.[65]

Dutch monetary system
Units of Account

1 *pond Vlaams*, or pound Flemish, or pound gross, pound was equivalent to:	1 gulden or florin was equivalent to:
6 guldens (or florins)	20 stuivers (or placas)
20 schellingen (or soldos)	80 *oortjes*
240 groten (or dinheiros or grossos)	160 *duiten*
	320 penningen

Fractions of the gulden

Although the gulden had virtually gone out of circulation, a fraction of it called the stuiver continued to be minted and was sub–fractioned into 4 oortjes and 8 duiten. All these coins also stayed in circulation, as did the schelling of 6 stuivers and the double stuiver.[66]

Stuiver — Oord — Duit — Schelling of 6 Stuivers (*Roosschelling*) — Double Stuiver

Trade between Brazil and Spanish America

Brazil kept an intense trade with Spanish America, where it resold European and African products and exported Brazilian wares, such as sugar, mainly in exchange for precious metals, whether minted or not. Spanish colonies had a strong demand for European products, because Castile enforced a strictly controlled commercial regime to avoid the flight and smuggling of precious metals, which made the legal supply of these goods insufficient. This was, indeed, an open invitation for smuggling. Yet not all trade with Spanish America was illegal. Part of it took place within the licenses for trafficking in African slaves. Another part was tolerated, such as putting into a harbor by ships that had ostensibly been blown off course and needed supplies or repairs. Castilian authorities were also more accommodating about trade with peripheral regions of its American possessions, which received few outside wares, such as the River Plate during that initial period.[76]

The depreciation of the vellón in Spain aggravated the situation of copper coins in Portugal, since the vast Spanish demand attracted such coins, legitimate and fake alike, over the border. This caused such a shortage of the metal that in 1635 coppersmiths in Lisbon smelted old coins to make their kettles.[64]

From the late sixteenth century onwards, the Republic began to use two parallel monetary systems: the system which the dukes of Burgundy had established for the Low Countries at the end of the Middle Ages and the system instituted by Charles V in the sixteenth century. One of the Dutch systems was based on the pound Flemish, the *Pond Vlaams* or *Pond groot*. The second system was based on the gulden, guilder or florin. During the period in question, these coins were not in circulation but merely served as units of account or "counting coins," as they were known. For example, until 1681, domestic and foreign coins were valued in guldens in the Republic's official rates although the gulden was no longer in circulation by the end of the sixteenth century. It had practically ceased to be minted and was progressively replaced by coins of lesser value.[0]

Half-Rijksdaalder *(1649)*.

Leuwendaalder *(1617), a coin minted according to the standards established by the States-General.*

Grote Gouden Rijder *(1632), standardized by the States-General.*

Patagon *(1631): silver coin from the Southern Low Countries that circulated in the Dutch Republic during the reign of Philip IV (1621–1665).*

Daalder van 30 stuivers *(1602). Coin minted independently in Middleburg by the provincial house of Zeeland, at variance with the Union.*

Counterweight used to assess a specific coin (1623–1644).

After consolidating their independence, the States-General of the United Provinces established the *rijksdaalder* as the nation's standard coin and also issued the *leeuwendaalder*, both minted in silver. However, these coins suffered a rapid process of depreciation. The rijksdaalder began by being rated at 47 stuivers (20 stuivers = 1 gulden) in 1606, but in 1610 underwent a "tolerated" debasement – that is, supposedly provisional – to 48 stuivers and in 1619 was officially fixed at 50 stuivers. The leuwendaalder, in turn, went from 38 stuivers in 1606 to 40 in 1615. Minted in gold, the ducat was issued from 1586 onwards in conformance with the standard produced in Hungary, as was the *gouden rijder* (golden rider) from 1606 onwards, based on an English model, and the double ducat. These gold coins would also be depreciated. The goal of these devaluations was to maintain the coins in circulation and ensure that their official and market rates converged, since base coins, especially from abroad, circulated unofficially in the Republic and tended to drive away from circulation these finer – but underrated – coins.

In effect, many foreign coins circulated in the United Provinces, at first unofficially and later legally. Coins from the Southern Low Countries were prominent. Minted from silver brought from America through Spain, they had a lower metallic value than the coins issued by the Dutch States-General and eventually flooded the Republic, which needed cash for its growing trade and to realize its overseas ven-

tures in the Baltic, the Mediterranean and Asia. After almost a decade trying to fight against them, the Republic's authorities finally assigned them an official rate in 1622. At that time, the Republic also had to deal with the exaggerated debasement of German coins to finance the military expenditure the German states faced on account of the Thirty Years' War (1618–1648).

The debasement of the coins of the newly formed Republic was aggravated by the competition amongst the more than fourteen mints operating in its small territory. The provinces had a great deal of monetary autonomy, as did cities and lords to a certain extent, particularly with regard to small coins used as change. During some periods, they would mint their own types of coins or modeled their coinage on coins from foreign countries. The profit margins of these mints increased the more they issued smaller and baser coins, which, apart from being less controlled, their low value discouraged investing much effort in ascertaining their metallic content. Mints' debasement was often backed by the local governments to which they paid minting fees known as "seigniorage." Debasement was not totally rampant only because a central body oversaw minting and because an overly steep debasement would have ended up discrediting the minter. In any case, a large volume of base, worn, clipped or even counterfeit coins, were in circulation.

As a result – in keeping with Gresham's Law – coins mainly of a dubious quality and purity from various sources continued to circulate within the Republic, and consequently pushed out the good coins minted there from the market. As the official rates lagged behind the real exchange rate, it was common to demand a surcharge to receive debased coins, or for payments to be made in smaller denominations. Hence, whenever it was necessary to pay in minted metal, the question of the real value of the coins was a potential source of discord.

9. Like the gulden, the *penning* had almost gone out of circulation and had become, more than anything else, a reference coin. Sums smaller than one *duit* were probably rounded off in payments. Nevertheless, it is possible that a limited number of penningen (plural of penning) and other coins worth less than one duit were minted in provincial or municipal mints and that such coins were also minted in small numbers and brought illegally from the Southern Low Countries. However, the number of these coins of such low face values in circulation would not have been significant, mainly because the inflationary effects of depreciation would have eliminated the practical use of such small fractions.

Ariſmetica de Affonço de Villaſanhe.

Reynos; poſto que faça menção delles nas contas dos cammus pello meudo.

TABOADA DOS PEZOS, & medidas deſtes Reynos acima declarados.

PORTVGVAL.

Hum quintal, comum, tem quatro arrobas.

Quintal da caſa da India pera eſpecearia. tem 112. arrates.

Cada arratel de pezo grande, 16. onças.

Hũa arroba, trinta, & duas arrates.

Cada arroba deſte quintal piqueno, tem vintoito arrates.

Cada arratel de pezo piqueno, catorze onças.

POr eſte quintal piqueno emtrega ſua Mâgeſtade na caſa da India, a pimenta, gengiure, & outras drogas que vende, & pera a reduzir ao pezo grande: ſe faz, ajuntandolhe a ſeptima parte de ſi meſmo, & pera de grande fazer piqueno; ſe lhe abate a oitaua parte; como a diãte direi, mòrmente que no pezo vzão fazer arrobas de

Suyckeren by ℔.	op tijd.
FYne Rafinad: 2 a 3 po.	30 a 30 ß 2 tyt
dito van 4 pont ——	30 ß ₽
fyne Meliſſen top-ſchoō	29 a 29 ß 2 ₽
dito Lompen top-ſchoō	27 a 27 ß 2 ₽
Breſilſe witte —— cōt	22, 23 a 25 ß
dito Pan-goet ——	22 ß tyt
Maſcobades —— ——	20 ß ₽ tyt
Paneelen —— ——	14 a 14 ß 4 ₽
Sint Thomé ——	12 ß 4 ₽
Wit Candijs ——	42 a 43 ß
Bruyn Candijs ——	29 ß ₽

"Table of weights and measures from the kingdoms of Portugal, Castile, Aragon and Valencia" (1624).

Official prices for Brazilian sugar: ground white, loaf, muscovado and panela, on the Amsterdam Bourse on March 3, 1636.

Bartering and Commodity Money

Alongside coins, payment in goods was also very common. Pure barter, wherein goods were equated directly without resorting to a monetary unit of account, did not take place in the three centers studied, with the exception of exchanges with Amerindians in Brazil. Payments in merchandise were made by commutation, that is, the quantity of goods handed over and received from both sides was determined by the market prices of the respective wares, measured in a monetary unit of account.[67] In other words, in these monetized economies, even though payment was being made in goods, the accounts and prices were set in coins, since these were units applicable to all economic assets.

Even in exchanges with the Amerindians, the Portuguese Crown sought to impose a list of prices on metal tools to safeguard against inflation in the terms of exchange for sourcing brazilwood, contracting labor, obtaining provisions and drugs from the hinterland, and so forth. As far back as the king's regulation (*Regimento*) for the first governor-general of Brazil, dating from 1548, it was decreed that these objects would "circulate as money, as they did until now at the same rates that have been stipulated for them."[68]

Barter had some drawbacks as a means of payment compared to coins. Many goods, such as sugar and wine, were perishable; some were hard to transport, while others could not be divided easily. There were products that evidenced significant differences in quality, involved sharp price fluctuations and, most importantly, could not always be easily sold.

The exchange of wares depended on a coincidence of wants by the exchanging parties. In Amsterdam, which received a greater variety of merchandise, brokers matched demand and supply. Notarized documents in Amsterdam mention an exchange, negotiated by a broker, of 17.5 barrels of Pedro Ximenes wine valued at 30 pounds Flemish per barrel for 96 pieces of cambric valued at 45 guldens apiece, wherein the difference was paid in money. The vendor of the cambric was from northern Europe, while the vendor of the wine and the broker were Portuguese Jews, with all three parties residing in Amsterdam. The exchange resulted in a falling out between the parties and the Portuguese merchant brought three compatriots and fellow Jews before the notary to bear witness on his behalf. The latter unanimously declared that the delivered textiles were not cambric but instead were fabrics from Haarlem – an important textile center in Holland.[P] According to the witnesses, the textiles were not worth the agreed price and would fetch, at most, 25 guldens. Apart from this, the price of the wine in question had soared that year, due to a fall in supply. The broker also lost money on the transaction because he had not checked the goods as he should. Thus, he would only receive commission for the sale of the wine from his Portuguese client and nothing on account of the textiles.[69]

At the time, this exchange of merchandise was called in Portuguese *venda a barato* or, as a verb, *baratar*, which was derived from the same Mediterranean root from which the English language acquired the word "barter." From the same roots developed words denoting fraud such as barratry in English and *baratari*a in Portuguese, perhaps owing to the deception this practice might lead to.[70] It also gave rise to the Portuguese term "*comprar barato*,"[71] i.e., "buying cheap," since payment in goods implied a surcharge; in other words, cash purchases cost less than buying by means of barter. The reason was that the vendor who received goods as payment suffered lower liquidity, since it was possible that the wares received might not be easily resold, a problem that did not exist when payments were made in coins, which circulated without hindrance. This is how a merchant taught his future colleagues to deal with this matter:

> *Two merchants barter, viz. one offering iron and the other offering lead. A quintal of iron is worth 3 cruzados in ready money and while bartering it is assessed at 4 cruzados payable in 3 months. And a quintal of lead is worth 6 cruzados in ready money; and he wants a two-month term. The question is: at what value should the lead be assessed while bartering so that an equal exchange occurs*[72]*?*

Payment in goods was both more relevant and prevalent in Brazil. Many of these exchanges were made in sugar, but this was not due to a shortage of coins in the colony, as Frédéric Mauro observes.[73] In fact, at that time, coins were present in large quantities in Brazil. This is corroborated by the instructions by merchants to their agents traveling to Brazil to sell the merchandise they were taking to the colony for cash, as the one seen above. This is also evident in contracts for maritime transport registered in notary books in Porto, which stipulated that the freight charges for the outward journey were to be paid in Brazil in coins.[74] A significant part of these coins were derived from legal and illegal trade with Spanish America, which at the time was the main source of precious metals also for Europe and beyond.

P. The Dutch settlement that later became the famous New York neighborhood of Harlem was named after this town.

A Frenchman who visited Bahia in 1610 stated, probably with some exaggeration, that: "I have never seen a land where coins are so plentiful, as in this land of Brazil, and they come from the River Plate, which is five hundred leagues away from this bay."[75]

However, sugar functioned well as a means of payment. First, it was easy to price. The product did not suffer from major variations of quality within each of its different types, which could have complicated calculations, and the existing variations were easily ascertainable. Sugar was widely traded and hence its prices in the market were well known. Indeed, the repetitive process of opening and sealing crates, checking goods and weighing the contents was no trivial task,[76] but confidence in the reputation of the parties involved in the chain could dispense with such formalities. Apart from this, assessing sugar did not require the expertise and precision instruments necessary to assess alloys of copper, silver and gold, whether minted into coins or not. Sugar was also easily accepted in payment since it was traded on a relatively large scale. In other words, one could say that it fit the modern concept of a commodity.

As we have seen, there were three main types of Brazilian sugar: white, muscovado and panela. Each of these types was quoted on the Amsterdam Bourse. Each type, however, had its subtypes: the sugar taken from the upper part of the mold tended to be whiter, and became progressively less white and crystallized, and even slightly yellow further down into the mold.[77] Brownish muscovado sugar was extracted from the tip of the mold and was of the worst quality, while panela sugar had varying ratios of crystals and

Detail from Terreiro do Paço in the Seventeenth Century, *by the Dutch painter Dirk Stoop (1662): weighing crates of merchandise, probably sugar, in Lisbon.*

molasses. There were also "beaten" white and muscovado sugars derived from a second processing of the molasses, as well as other inferior types of sugar extracted from byproducts of different phases of the production process. Apart from this, sugar also varied according to its origin and the condition it was in when delivered to the marketplace, as it often arrived damaged by moisture, and even partially washed away. All this influenced the price. Nevertheless, all these variables could be ascertained relatively easily and were mostly visible to the naked eye, as we will see.

According to Ebert, these variations gave rise to the considerable differences in price for the same type of sugar recorded in Lisbon by the Flemish merchant Pedro Clarisse. Ebert highlighted the fact that in Antwerp, during the sixteenth century, the best quality of wares in each product category could be sold at a premium. It is therefore no surprise that merchants insisted that their agents obtain "the best quality goods possible."[78] It is also true that fraud did occur. Opportunities for fraud began from the time the sugar was crated at the sugar mills. Father Antonil warned:

> *And even though the last portion of the sugar, which is called the most expensive sugar in a crate, is rightly the most sought after, it would nonetheless be a great discredit to the sugar mill, a deception and manifest injustice, if a crate was filled with beaten sugar in the middle and covered with a layer of the finest and most expensive sugar on the surface to conceal bad sugar with good, making, therefore, even sugar hypocritical.*[79]

Later on, we will see other cases in which sugar was found to be adulterated at diverse points throughout the supply chain, sometimes openly, and being sold as such, sometimes deceitfully.[80]

There is no doubt that it was easy to ascertain how sugar was crated (in loaves or crushed into lumps), its types, sub-types and origins, as were the prices quoted in trading centers along the route. Two Portuguese men in Amsterdam[R] attested before a notary to the quality of a shipment of fourteen crates of sugar, supposedly consisting of nine crates of white sugar, of which four crates contained good sugar and five contained the worst quality of sugar, while the remaining five crates contained muscovado sugar. Of these last five crates, four did indeed contain muscovado sugar, but the sugar in the fifth crate was of such poor quality that it appeared to be panela sugar. Based on the shape of the crate and the sugar crystals, the merchants were able to affirm that it came from Rio de Janeiro. They also said that

Q. At the end of the seventeenth century, the quality of sugar was also assessed by probes and by sampling the product through holes made in various parts of the crate (A. M. D. Silva, "Introduction and Notes," in Antonil, *Cultura e opulência do Brasil*, p. 168, n. 84).

R. One of these men was James Lopes da Costa, an erstwhile resident of Pernambuco and in whose honor the first synagogue in Amsterdam had supposedly been named as the *House of Jacob* (Costa took up Jacob Tirado as his Hebrew name). The crates had been received by Nicolas du Gardin, a leading merchant whose family came from the southern Low Countries and played a very important role in the Republic's economy, particularly in the sugar trade. For further information about James Lopes Costa (Jacob Tirado) and his family, see: SR no. 22 n. 35; Mello, *Gente da nação*, pp. 9, 12, 19, 51, 97. On Nicolas du Gardin, see: Poelwijk, *In dienste vant suyckebacken*, pp. 267, 272, 283–284; Gelderblom, *Zuid-Nederlandse kooplieden*, p. 86; Lesger, *The Rise of the Amsterdam Market and Information Exchange*, p. 163, n. 83.

they were aware that at the time the two ships which had brought the crates were loaded in Vila Nova de Portimão in the Algarve, the white sugar was selling at 1,850 réis per arroba, muscovado sugar from Bahia at 1,225 réis and sugar from Rio de Janeiro at 1,200 réis.[81]

Apparently, sugar from Bahia was better and more expensive than from any other place along the Brazilian coast. A merchant named Miguel Dias Santiago, whose account book is preserved in an archive in London, recorded lower prices for sugar from the captaincy of Ilhéus, which was loaded in Salvador, compared to the prices of sugar from the captaincy of Bahia.[82] In another documented case, a confectioner complained about a purchase of two crates of sugar loaves from Madeira: ten loaves were broken and mixed with lower-quality sugar.[83]

As for quantities, they were ascertained by means of weight and calculated in arrobas. Crates did not provide a uniform metric, since they came in different dimensions and tended to increase in size, as has been mentioned in Chapter 6, while there were also regional discrepancies. These regional differences, however, were easier to recognize than the weight of its content: a shipmaster taking sugar from Porto and Viana to Livorno and Venice would receive an additional 12 stuivers when the crates transported were from Pernambuco instead of Bahia.[84] As has been seen in the aforesaid case, the shape of the crate indicated that it was from Rio de Janeiro.

In this illustration from the Book of Trades, *the manufacture and sale of weighing scales, key instruments for ensuring fair payment.*

The weight marked on the crates (if it was already marked at that time, as should have been the case at the end of the seventeenth century) and declared to the tax and customs authorities, and perhaps even recorded in bills of lading, did not always correspond to the actual weight of the cargo. This was done to evade paying the full due taxes when these were calculated per weight. In terms of tax planning, it was better to understate the quantity of goods cleared.

Problems arose when a merchant or a consumer received less than expected, which could compromise the reputation of whoever had sent, transported or sold the sugar. However, letters of advice and invoices accompanying the consignments could be used to counter flaws in bills of lading. An agent receiving a consignment with shortfalls would lodge a protest to safeguard himself with regard to his client and, no less important, to avoid paying more duties than were due.[85] In order to ascertain the weight[S] of cargoes, vendors, purchasers and agents used official weighing houses and scales, *haver do peso* in Portuguese[T] and *waag* in Dutch, which were not always placed in the most accessible areas of settlements. Merchants also resorted to other unofficial weighing scales, "outside the 'weighing,'" as Miguel Dias Santiago succinctly affirmed in his account book[86] and as we will see in Chapter 9. It is also possible that they even used the scales of the local customs house.[87]

Calculating the weight of sugar also implied deducting the weight of the crates (tare), which is what Miguel Dias did with five crates of white sugar that he sold to a Frenchman in Lisbon, and which in net terms weighed 63 arrobas and 2 arratéis (32 arratéis = 1 arroba).[88] In Amsterdam, a Portuguese discounted 4½ groten (four and a half groten) from each pound of sugar, originally set at 19 groten, to offset both the moisture and the discrepancy in weight discovered in four crates of white sugar received from Porto when he sold these crates to a Dutchman.[89]

Since sugar was the main merchandise sourced in the colony, it was much in demand. Hence, sugar afforded liquidity and there was generally no shortage of individuals willing to accept it as a means of payment. Even real estate was sold in Brazil in exchange for sugar: three unmarried sisters lost their mother in Porto, while their father was in Paraíba. It appeared that he wished to dispose of a cane field in that captaincy, but the death of his wife made his daughters his partners through their shares either as their inheritance or promised dowries. In order to assuage the fears of possible purchasers that they would contest the sale, the three girls issued a power of attorney authorizing their father to sell cane fields and any other assets in Brazil and to receive the payment in money or in kind, that is, in goods, referring almost certainly to sugar.[U] Miguel Dias Santiago made and received payments in sugar stored in warehouses in the port of Recife ready for shipping.[90]

S. Given the fiscal impact, it was no surprise that merchants resisted the installation of a warehouse with a weighing scale in the lower town in Salvador. The facility was meant to certify sugar crates in exchange for a fee. Still, Salvador also held an official weighing scale in its upper town: AHU_ACL_CU_005-02, Cx. 3, D. 285-291 – [Bahia, prior to November 3, 1623]. At least in Rio de Janeiro, the official weighing of sugar had already been implemented as early as 1617: V. Coaracy, *O Rio de Janeiro no século XVII* (Rio de Janeiro: Livraria José Olympio Editora, 1965), pp. 47–50. See also: Mauro, *Portugal, o Brasil e o Atlântico*, v. 1, pp. 305–307; Costa, *O transporte no Atlântico*, v. 1, pp. 332–333. Even in the late seventeenth and early eighteenth centuries, when the Crown sought to have greater control over the quality and quantity of the sugar being transacted, Antonil stated that: "When a crate of sugar is weighed in order to pay duties, the person doing the weighing weighs the sugar favorably; stating, for example, that a crate actually weighing thirty arrobas weighs twenty-eight. And the king's kindness tolerates and accepts these losses. However, such a crate is not sold for that weight, but rather on the basis of its actual weight, ascertained when it is weighed on the scale placed outside the customs house, which is there to banish all doubt" (Antonil, *Cultura e opulência do Brasil*, p. 110).

T. "Haver-do-Peso" were goods or assets that were sold and taxed by weight, for which official scales were constructed (also known as Aver-do-Peso, Aver-o-Peso or Ver-o-Peso, the name of the famous market in Belém, Pará). The term *avoirdupois* has the same origin, and has given its name to the system of weights based on the 16-ounce pound used in the United States and, to some extent, in the United Kingdom and other former British colonies: OED, *avoirdupois*; A. de Morais Silva, *Diccionario da língua portugueza, aver* (Lisbon: Typographia Lacerdina, 1813).

U. The sisters were Violante Tomas, Maria Tomas and Joana Mendes. They issued a power of attorney in favor of their father, Francisco Tomas, a resident of Paraíba, to "sell, barter, donate, alienate, divide, exchange and in any other way transact any and all goods and real estate he has in the said lands of Brazil... and he can receive the price and money or wares that he is given for the said properties": ADP, NOT, PO2, l. 33, fols. 70–72 (1611-11-5).

Sugar was also the main product exported from Porto – or rather re-exported. Hence, nothing prevented it from being used there too as a means of payment. A merchant from Porto, who also owned a quarter of a caravel, instructed the shipmaster and the pilot of the vessel, which was about to set sail from Lisbon to São Tomé, to bring him his share of the profits of this and all future voyages: "In sugar from São Tomé or muscovado or white sugar from Brazil and if there is no sugar in the lands visited then to bring his share in ready money."[91] In other words, he preferred sugar to cash. Even so, Porto's economy was closely linked to regional and Iberian commerce, where, as has been seen in the "Introduction," the role of sugar was more to attract merchandise from outside the peninsula to be distributed from there and less to be resold locally.

Even though sugar could be subdivided, there were difficulties involved in dividing it for smaller payments. However, it was possible to transmit rights to parts of certain crates through transfers of credits to be liquidated later. The main difficulty in using sugar as a means of payment was not so much its quantification but rather the fluctuations in its price. Used as a form of currency, sugar also tended to be subject to Gresham's Law: whenever possible, it was used as a means of exchange, while coins were hoarded. Advance purchases of sugar from producers in exchange for coins not only involved advancing credit (which, as has been seen, was often problematic for producers) but also attracted a surcharge for accepting sugar instead of coins.[v]

At the time of settling debts, differences regarding the fair value of the merchandise to be handed over as a means of payment often occurred. When the market contracted or transport was scarce traders preferred cash which was prejudicial for debtors who needed to find an outlet for their sugar stocks to avoid storage costs, a loss of liquidity and product spoilage. Antonil warned that sugar could not be stored for very long before being loaded lest it be damaged by humidity: "...sugar that remains [has been allowed to stand] from one year to the next loses its vigor and whiteness, which it never recovers."[92]

In order to resolve the impasse about the product's pricing, in 1614 the government in Rio de Janeiro decreed, that sugar would have to be accepted as a currency and the different qualities of sugar would be priced in accordance with an official rate.[93] However, making it compulsory to accept sugar as money and its official indexation was merely a palliative not a solution since whenever the market price fell significantly a surcharge would be added for payments in sugar in much the same manner as was the case with highly depreciated coins.

Thus, ten years later, it was necessary for the Brazil Court of Appeals (*Relação*), which was located in Bahia, to send a magistrate to Rio to once again decide that all debts except those contracted in currency could be paid in sugar. The local city council was to decide the value of the product annually in the month of June. In Bahia, from at least 1626 onwards, in the aftermath of the losses caused by the invasion and expulsion of the Dutch, the final decision about the price of sugar for paying debts was also entrusted to the city council of Salvador, which was to try to mediate between merchants and sugar-mill owners.[94] This example would be followed by other captaincies from the 1640s onwards.

As has been astutely suggested by the economist Fernando Carlos de Cerqueira Lima, settlers wanted the Crown to increase the supply of money precisely to ensure that the relationship between metallic coins and sugar was reversed, enhancing the value of their terms of exchange.[95] In fact, they even sought to depreciate the currency in circulation in the colony and mint low-value coins. One petition was framed on the grounds of improving public affairs. Dating from 1613, it requested that coins in réis which were already worn out be allowed to circulate freely in Brazil. This was probably a reaction to legislation introduced in 1612 making it compulsory to smelt such coins and mint them anew in Lisbon. In the following year, the high chancellor of Brazil wrote to Philip III asking for permission to mint copper coins in Bahia. He claimed that the increased value of such coins, owing to their being minted anew, had raised prices excessively, affirming "what could earlier be bought for a silver real nowadays costs two." A second petition sent by the Bahia city council in 1626 insisted that the value of Castilian *patacas* should be 40 réis higher, and that minting of low-value copper and silver coins should be allowed in the colony.[96]

In effect, the same French chronicler who had highlighted the abundance of silver coins in Brazil likewise noted that smaller coins were scarce, particularly coins made of copper; that is, precisely those coins that were more susceptible to depreciation. Apart from Portugal not sending them to the colony, the great influx of good silver coins pulled the market up, ensuring that copper coins were rated far below their official value.[W] At the same time, on the other side of the Atlantic, as has been seen, Spain overvalued copper, which thus replaced silver. This resulted in drainage of low value coins to Europe.

However, even silver coins would have flowed offshore. European demand was higher than American demand, while supply witnessed an inverse relationship. Moreover, Portugal and Holland and to a lesser degree Spain, needed silver for their Asian enterprises, since many Asian markets spurned European products and preferred to receive metal in exchange for their wares.[97] Hence, it is not surprising that Portugal devoured the metal and that settlers in the colony preferred to hoard them and use sugar as a means of exchange.[X]

Even within Brazil, the larger centers absorbed coins. Luís Galante noted a document showing how governmental expenditure in the northern captaincies generally tended to be paid more in merchandise and less in coins, the greater the distance from Olinda.[98] Hence, it is not surprising that the most systematic efforts to make sugar more fungible, countable and priceable were spearheaded by the emerging center of Rio de Janeiro.

V. Antonil emphasized that in the late seventeenth century and early eighteenth century, merchants charged high fees to advance credit in cash instead of in wares. To all appearances, they were so high that in 1683 the Crown sought, unsuccessfully, to prohibit receiving money paid in advance for future supplies of sugar (Silva, "Introduction and Notes," in Antonil, *Cultura e opulência do Brasil*, p. 109, n. 106; Schwartz, *Sugar Plantations in the Formation of Brazilian Society*, pp. 204–212).

W. "Small coins are not seen there, but only pieces of eight, four and two reales and their halves, which are worth five soldos; and they seek five soldos and six *branco* coins in Portugal to be sold there [in Brazil] in exchange for small coins and thereby make a profit; because they use very few other coins, apart from those made of silver" (Laval, *Viagem de Francisco Pyrard de Laval*, p. 230).

X. Brandão was probably referring to the shortage of small copper coins or even small silver coins when he complained about the inconveniences of creating the Court of Appeals in Salvador, thus obliging settlers from other captaincies to file judicial appeals in Bahia instead of Lisbon: "Owing to the great expenses they incur on the journey, it being necessary for them to take ready money to this end, which is very difficult to find in Brazil, which is not the case, as I have said, with the papers that are sent to Portugal, because it is enough to ask relatives or friends for help and send a crate of sugar to pay for the expenses." This may be safely inferred, since Brandão repeatedly described how merchants from the River Plate region used to come to Rio de Janeiro, Bahia and Pernambuco, and even settled in Portuguese America, "leaving all the silver and gold they brought in," as well as how Luso-Brazilian merchants sought out the River Plate "with considerable benefit [utility]," i.e., bringing precious metals to Portuguese America (Brandão, *Diálogos das grandezas do Brasil*, pp. 37, 108). About the flight of copper and silver from Portugal, see: M. J. P. F. Tavares, "A moeda de D. João II aos Filipes (1481–1640)," in J. H. Saraiva (ed.), *História de Portugal*, V. 4 (Lisbon: Editorial Verbo, 1983), pp. 277–289.

Money Matters

Chapter Seven

1. R. de Roover, *L'évolution de la lettre de change* (Paris: Librairie Armand Collin, 1953), pp. 55, 72–73, 122–123. This was the opinion of Fernão Rabelo, a Jesuit and professor of theology at the University of Évora: V. Rau, "Aspectos do pensamento económico português durante o século XVI," in idem, *Estudos sobre história económica e social do Antigo Regime* (Lisbon: Editorial Presença, 1984), p. 127.

2. See: ibid, p. 122; R. Muñoz de Juana, "Scholastic Morality and the Birth of Economics: The Thought of Martín de Azpilcueta," *Journal of Markets and Morality* 4:1 (2001): 31–36.

3. Such as the Dominican friar Francisco de Vitoria, the Augustinian monk Martín de Azpilcueta y Jaureguizar (Doctor Navarrus) and the Jesuit father Luis de Molina: Roover, *L'évolution de la lettre de change*, pp. 123–124; D. Melé, "Early Business Ethics in Spain: The Salamanca School (1526–1614)," *Journal of Business Ethics* 22:3 (1999): 181, 183; J. de la Iglesia García, "Martín de Azpilcueta y su 'Comentario resolutorio de cambios,'" *Información comercial española* (2000–2001): 82; Muñoz de Juana, *Scholastic Morality*, pp. 31–36.

4. Roover, *L'évolution de la lettre de change*, pp. 123–124; H. Grotius, *The Rights of War and Peace including the Law of Nature and of Nations (1625)* (New York: M. Walter Dunne, 1901), ch. XII, titles XX–XXI.

5. L. Gómez Rivas, "El pensamiento económico en España y Holanda en el siglo XVII: la Guerra de los Treinta Años y la difusión de ideas: Hugo Grotius," *Cuadernos de Ciencias Económicas y Empresariales* 37 (1999), passim; R. H. Tawney, "Dr. Thomas Wilson," in T. Wilson, *A Discourse upon Usury* (London: G. Bell & Sons, 1925), p. 11; R. de Roover, "Gerard de Malynes as an Economic Writer," in J. Kirshner (ed.), *Business, Banking and Economic Thought in Late Medieval and Early Modern Europe* (Chicago: University of Chicago Press, 1974), passim.

6. Roover, *L'évolution de la lettre de change*, p. 123.

7. Ibid., p. 125; Grotius, *The Rights of War and Peace*, ch. XII, title XXI.

8. O. Gelderblom and J. Jonker, "Completing a Financial Revolution: The Finance of the Dutch East India Trade and the Rise of the Amsterdam Capital Market, 1595–1612," *The Journal of Economic History* 64 (2004), 663, 667–668. Dehing's data was cited by Peter Spufford from an unpublished work: P. Spufford, *Access to Credit and Capital*, pp. 305, 330, n. 6; see also: Barbour, *Capitalism in Amsterdam in the 17th Century*, pp. 23–25, 86–87; P. Dehing and M. 'T Hart, "Linking the Fortunes," in Hart, Jonker and Van Zanden. *A Financial History of the Netherlands*, pp. 52–55.

9. *Ordenações manuelinas*, book 4, title XIV, § 7; *Ordenações filipinas*, book 4, title LXVII, §9.

10. *Constituiçoens synodaes do arcebispado de Braga*, title LXVIII.

11. On *periculum sortis* and *periculi susceptio*, see: Muñoz de Juana, "Scholastic Morality and the Birth of Economics," pp. 31–36; G. Ceccarelli, "Risky Business: Theological and Canonical Thought on Insurance from the Thirteenth to the Seventeenth Century," *Journal of Medieval and Early Modern Studies* 31:3 (2001): passim; D. Melé, "Early Business Ethics in Spain," pp. 182–184; R. de Roover, "The Organization of Trade," in M. M. Postan, E. E. Rich and E. Miller (eds.), *The Cambridge Economic History of Europe*, V. 3 (Cambridge: Cambridge University Press, 1963), pp. 53–57; Roover, *L'évolution de la lettre de change*, pp. 122, 124–125; Wee, *The Growth of the Antwerp Market*, v. 2, p. 358.

12. *Constituiçoens synodaes do arcebispado de Braga*, pp. 692–693.

13. ADP, NOT, PO2, l. 40, fols. 41v.–42v. (1615–1–28).

14. Gelderblom and Jonker, "Amsterdam as the Cradle of Modern Futures," pp. 1, 3.

15. Malynes, *Consuetudo: vel, lex mercatoria*, p. 99.

16. This was valid for Europe, including Portugal and Brasil; ibid., pp. 95–97; IANTT, CC, 1–115–107; ADP, NOT, PO2, l. 37, fols. 48–50 (1613–6–10); Oliveira, *A História do Brazil de Frei Vicente do Salvador*, v. 2, fol. 102. See also: Schwartz, *Sugar Plantations in the Formation of Brazilian Society*, pp. 204–212; Smith, "The Mercantile Class of Portugal and Brazil," p. 370.

17. Almeida, *Aritmética como descrição do real*, v. 2, pp. 174–183.

18. Malynes, *Consuetudo: vel, lex mercatoria*, p. 95.

19. *Ordenações filipinas*, Book 4, Title LXVII, §8.

20. On the growing political power of sugar planters, see: Mello, *Olinda restaurada*, pp. 92–94, 220–221; S. B. Schwartz, *Sovereignty and Society in Colonial Brazil. The High Court of Bahia and its Judges, 1609–1751* (Berkeley: University of California Press, 1973), passim; R. Ricupero, *A formação da elite colonial* (São Paulo: Alameda, 2009), passim.

21. On the exemptions, see: IANTT, CC 1–115–107; Correspondência do governador Dom Diogo de Meneses – 1608–1612, pp. 67–68; AHU_ACL_CU_005–02, Cx. 1, D. 52 – [Lisbon, prior to November 28, 1613]; J. J. de Andrade e Silva (ed.), *Collecção chronologica da legislação portugueza* (Lisbon: Impr. de J. J. A. Silva, 1854–59), v. 2, pp. 130–131; Ferlini, *Terra, trabalho e poder*, pp. 280–281; Mauro, *Portugal, o Brasil e o Atlântico*, v. 1, p. 302; Costa, *O transporte no Atlântico*, v. 1, pp. 59–61, 218–219; Mendes, "A Coroa portuguesa e a colonização do Brasil," passim.

22. Costa, *O transporte no Atlântico*, v. 1, pp. 59–61, 217–220. See also: Mello, "Os livros das saídas das urcas do porto do Recife," pp. 30–35; idem, *Gente da nação*, pp. 5–33; Mello, *Olinda restaurada*, pp. 92–94, 220–221.

23. Gelderblom and Jonker, "Amsterdam as the Cradle of Modern Futures," pp. 3, 6; Barbour, *Capitalism in Amsterdam in the 17th Century*, pp. 74, 90; Dehing, and 'T Hart, "Linking the Fortunes," p. 54.

24. SR no. 913.

25. SR no. 1346.

26. SR no. 2203.

27. SR no. 3035.

28. SR no. 853.

29. SR no. 1397.

30. SR nos. 45, 1600; Ebert, "The Trade in Brazilian Sugar," pp. 142–143, 178–179, 184–185, 189–199; Ferlini, *Terra, trabalho e poder*, pp. 92–94; Schwartz, *Sugar Plantations in the Formation of Brazilian Society*, pp. 173–175; Costa, *O transporte no Atlântico*, v. 1, pp. 61, 89, 218, 220–221, 239–248, 372, 380.

31. SR no. 79.

32. Gelderblom and Jonker, "Amsterdam as the Cradle of Modern Futures," passim.

33. See also: Barbour, *Capitalism in Amsterdam in the 17th Century*, p. 74.

34. SR no. 1344.

35. SR no. 1259.

36. Gelderblom, *Zuid-Nederlandse kooplieden*, p. 219; M. Keblusek, *Boeken in de hofstad: Haagse boekcultuur in de Gouden Eeew* (Hilversum: Verloren, 1997), p. 233; A. J. Lamping, *Johannes Polyander, een dienaar van Kerk en Universiteit* (Leiden: Brill, 1980), pp. 25, 108, 116, 171; Poelwijk, *In dienste vant suyckerbacken*, pp. 88, 167 n. 41, 168, 169 n. 47, 171 n. 51, 203, 264–266;

37. Gelderblom and Jonker, "Amsterdam as the Cradle of Modern Futures," pp. 13–15.

38. Ibid., passim.

39. ADP, NOT, PO2, l. 29, fols. 122v.–125v. (1609–10–3); l. 30, fols. 117–118 (1609-12-24).

40. ADP, NOT, PO2, l. 40, fols. 150v.–151 (1615-6-15).

41. See, for example: ADP, NOT, PO1, l. 148, fols. 148–149 (1624-9-3)

42. D. M. de Lisboa, *Constituições synodaes do bispado do Porto* (Coimbra: 1585), fol. 132v.

43. ADP, NOT, PO2, l. 31, fols. 76–78 (1611-12-1). See also: ADP, NOT, PO2, l. 31, fols. 79–80v. (1611-12-1).

44. ADP, NOT, PO2, l. 39, fols. 157–158v. (1614-11-3); l. 40, fols. 45–46 (1615-1-28).

45. SR no. 1371.

46. Malynes, *Consuetudo: vel, lex mercatoria*, p. 102.

47. G. S. M. Fantom, *El Real Ingenio de la Moneda de Segovia* (Segovia: Cámara de Comercio e Industria de Segovia, 2008), pp. 15–43.

48. H. E. van de Gelder, *De Nederlandse munten: geschiedenis der Nederlandse munten vanaf 500 tot heden* (Utrecht: Het Spectrum, 1972), pp. 135–136.

49. Tavares, "A moeda de D. João II aos Filipes," pp. 277–289; A. H. de Oliveira Marques, "Técnicas artesanais – fabrico de moeda," in Serrão and Oliveira Marques (eds.), *Nova história de Portugal*, v. 5, pp. 63–64; Dias, "A moeda," in Serrão and Oliveira Marques (eds.), *Nova história de Portugal*, v. 5, pp. 256, 273.

50. Fantom, *El Real Ingenio de la Moneda de Segovia*, pp. 15–43.

51. N. Sussman, "Debasements, Royal Revenues, and Inflation in France during the Hundred Years' War, 1415–1422," *The Journal of Economic History 53*:1 (1993): 44–70; idem, "Missing Bullion or Missing Documents: A Revision and Reappraisal of French Minting Statistics: 1385–1415," *The Journal of European Economic History 19*:1 (1990): 147–162.

52. Mauro, *Portugal, o Brasil e o Atlântico*, v. 2, pp. 160–161; Almeida Amaral, *Catálogo descritivo das moedas portuguesas*, t. l. 1, pp. 618, 640; Gelder, *De Nederlandse munten*, pp. 63–129; S. Quinn and W. Roberds, "An Economic Explanation of the Early Bank of Amsterdam, Debasement, Bills of Exchange, and the Emergence of the First Central Bank," *Federal Reserve Bank of Atlanta, Working Paper Series 13* (2006): passim.

53. Almeida, *Aritmética como descrição do real*, v. 1, p. 182; Gelder, *De Nederlandse munten*, pp. 63–129; Quinn and Roberds, "An Economic Explanation of the Early Bank of Amsterdam," passim.

54. About Gresham and the "Law" attributed to him, see: R. A. de Roover, *Gresham on Foreign Exchange* (Cambridge: Harvard University Press, 1949), pp. 18–30, 91–93; V. M. Shillington and A. B. W. Chapman, *The Commercial Relations of England and Portugal* (New York: Burt Franklin, 1970), p. 154; J. W. Burgon, *The Life and Times of Sir Thomas Gresham, Knt., Founder of the Royal Exchange*, V. 2 (London: Royal Exchange, 1839), pp. 500–526.

55. Hamilton, *American Treasure and the Price Revolution in Spain*, pp. 11–103, 211–212.

56. P. E. Guidotti and C. A. Rodriguez, "Dollarization in Latin America – Gresham's Law in Reverse," *International Monetary Fund Staff Papers 39* (1992): 518–544.

57. Almeida, *Aritmética como descrição do real*, v. 2, pp. 212–258; Malynes, *Consuetudo: vel, lex mercatoria*, pp. 284–324.

58. Mauro, *Portugal, o Brasil e o Atlântico*, v. 2, pp. 141–145, 161; Almeida, *Aritmética como descrição do real*, v. 1, pp. 175–176; Almeida Amaral, *Catálogo descritivo das moedas portuguesas*, t. 1, pp. 609–613; Tavares, "A moeda de D. João II aos Filipes," pp. 277–289.

59. Mauro, *Portugal, o Brasil e o Atlântico*, v. 2, p. 162; Maria José Pimenta Ferro Tavares mentions depreciation for silver: Tavares, "A moeda de D. João II aos Filipes," p. 289.

60. Almeida, *Aritmética como descrição do real*, v. 1, pp. 175–182; Tavares, "A moeda de D. João II aos Filipes," pp. 288–289.

61. Oliveira, *A História do Brazil de Frei Vicente do Salvador*, v. 2, fol. 174.

62. Hamilton, *American Treasure and the Price of Revolution in Spain*, pp. 20 n. 3, 24, 26 n. 5, 29 n. 7, 31, 32 n. 2, 34–35, 62–81, 93–103, 211–212, 318; J. de Santiago Fernández, "El documento monetal del vellón en el reinado de Felipe II: su ordenación y trascendencia," *Revista General de Información y Documentación 11*:2 (2001): 134–138; J. I. García de Paso, "The 1628 Castilian Crydown," *Hacienda pública española/Revista de economía pública 163*:4 (2002): 74.

63. Almeida, *Aritmética como descrição do real*, v. 1, pp. 177–178; Tavares, "A moeda de D. João II aos Filipes," pp. 277–289.

64. Hamilton, *American Treasure and the Price of Revolution in Spain*, p. 97; Mauro, *Portugal, o Brasil e o Atlântico*, v. 2, p. 163; Almeida, *Aritmética como descrição do real*, v. 1, p. 179; Almeida Amaral, *Catálogo descritivo das moedas portuguesas*, t.1, p. 640.

65. On the Dutch monetary system, see: Gelder, *De Nederlandse munten*, pp. 63–129; J. G. van Dillen, "The Bank of Amsterdam," in idem (ed.), *History of the Principal Public Banks* (London: Routledge, 1964), pp. 81–83, 87–88; Dehing and 'T Hart, "Linking the Fortunes," pp. 38–40; W. G. Wolters, "Managing Multiple Currencies with Units of Account: Netherlands India 1600–1800"; paper contributed to the XVI International Economic History Congress of the International Economic History Association, Helsinki, 2006, pp. 1–10; Quinn and Roberds, "An Economic Explanation of the Early Bank of Amsterdam," passim. I am grateful for the information provided by Arent Pol, curator for medieval and modern coins at the Geldmuseum, Utrecht.

66. See the equivalence between imaginary guldens and actual groten; one to 40, in a shipping contract for a journey between Amsterdam and Faro in 1625: SR no. 3330.

67. Malynes, *Consuetudo: vel, lex mercatoria*, pp. 83–84.

68. "Regimento de 17 de dezembro de 1548 do governador geral do Brasil," in *Documentos para a história do açúcar*, V. 1. (Rio de Janeiro: Instituto do Açúcar e do Álcool, 1954), pp. 45–62; A. Marchant, *Do escambo à escravidão: as relações econômicas entre portugueses e índios na colonização do Brasil (1500–1580)* (São Paulo: Companhia Editora Nacional, 1980), passim.

69. SR nos. 1116, 1117, 1318.

70. Almeida, *Aritmética como descrição do real*, v. 1, pp. 264–269; OED, entry *barrat*.

71. A. de Morais Silva, *Novo dicionário compacto da língua portuguesa* (Lisbon: Editorial Confluência, 1961), entries on "Baratar" and "Barato"; J. S. R. de Viterbo, *Elucidario das palavras, termos e frases que em Portugal antigamente se usaram e que hoje regularmente se ignoram*, T. 1 (Lisbon: A. J. Fernandes Lopes, 1865), entries on "Baratar" and "Barato"; R. Bluteau, *Vocabulario portuguez & latino* (Coimbra: Collegio das Artes da Companhia de Jesus, 1712–1728), entries on "Baratar" and "Barato"; A. Houaiss and M. S. Villar, *Dicionário Houaiss da língua portuguesa* (Rio de Janeiro: Objetiva, 2001), entries on "Barata," "Baratar," "Barataria" and "Barato."

72. Almeida, *Aritmética como descrição do real*, v. 2, p. 138.

73. Mauro, *Portugal, o Brasil e o Atlântico*, v. 2, p. 136. Schwartz's analysis of coins and credit refers to the period after the Portuguese Restoration, when both the extraction of metals in Spanish America and the access by Luso-Brazilians to the region had diminished: Schwartz, *Sugar Plantations in the Formation of Brazilian Society*, pp. 202–212.

74. The following records can be mentioned as an example: ADP, NOT, PO2, l. 20, fols. 126v.–129v. (1603-8-13); l. 24, fols. 71–74 (1605-9-14); l. 26, fols. 163–166 (1607-3-16); l. 43, fols. 113–114v. (1616-9-4). Ebert follows Schwartz, projecting the latter's analysis of a later period on the early seventeenth century, and emphasizing the shortage of currency in the colony. Such a shortage would have meant that residents preferred to make payments in cash and credit transfers in European centers, while in the colony they essentially used sugar and credit instruments. However, Ebert did confuse some elements while interpreting the sources. One of these sources pertained to a transfer of a credit between two merchants living in Amsterdam and not in Brazil. The credit was the result of the sale of nineteen pieces of linen textiles from Rouen in Bahia by the local agent of the individual transferring the credit in Amsterdam and could have included some types of sugar purchased with proceeds of the sale and then sent to Lisbon or elsewhere. Ebert believed that the transfer was made on behalf of the merchant in Bahia, who Ebert considered a partner and not a debtor of the person transferring the credit in Amsterdam: Ebert, "The Trade in Brazilian Sugar," pp. 140–141; SR no. 2010, n. 10; Archief van de Notarissen ter Standplaats Amsterdam, l. 625, fols. 430–432; l. 645a, fols. 909–910.

75. Laval, *Viagem de Francisco Pyrard de Laval*, p. 230. Later, Laval reiterated: "Thus, this is the land in which one sees more money than in any other place which I have visited and it all comes from the River Plate": ibid., p. 231.

76. Canabrava, *O comércio português no Rio da Prata*, passim; D. M. Swetschinski, "Conflict and Opportunity in 'Europe's Other Sea: The Adventure of Caribbean Jewish Settlement," *American Jewish History* 72:2 (1982): passim; Barros, *Porto: a construção de um espaço marítimo*, v. 1, p. 816, n. 2012; L. A. V. Galante, "Uma história da circulação monetária no Brasil no século XVII," PhD dissertation, University of Brasília, 2009, pp. 9–38.

77. Antonil, *Cultura e opulência do Brasil*, p. 167; Schwartz, *Sugar Plantations in the Formation of Brazilian Society*, pp. 119–125.

78. ADP, NOT, PO2, l. 37, fols. 48–50 (1613-6-10); Ebert, "The Trade in Brazilian Sugar," pp. 187–188.

79. Antonil, *Cultura e opulência do Brasil*, p. 166.

80. PRO, SP, 9/104, fol. 126.

81. SR no. 396; for further information about this case, see also: Ebert, "The Trade in Brazilian Sugar," pp. 187–188. Ebert presumes that the sugar from Pernambuco had a higher quality and price than that of Bahia, without presenting any source thereof. The chronicle of the Jesuit Fernão Cardim contradicts it, stating that at the end of the sixteenth century the sugar mills of Bahia produced the best sugar of the entire Brazilian coast: Cardim, *Tratados da terra e gente do Brasil*, p. 217.

82. PRO, SP, 9/104, fol. 3v.

83. SR no. 282.

84. SR no. 952.

85. PRO, SP, 9/104, fol. 127v.

86. PRO, SP, 9/104, fols. 88v., 98v., 121v., 132v.

87. With regard to the weighing regulation, from the second half of the seventeenth century onwards, see: Schwartz, *Sugar Plantations in the Formation of Brazilian Society*, pp. 121–125.

88. PRO, SP, 9/104, fol. 115.

89. SR no. 906.

90. PRO, SP, 9/104, fols. 78–83v.

91. ADP, NOT, PO2, l. 27, fols. 188–189 (1609-5-27).

92. Antonil, *Cultura e opulência do Brasil*, pp. 163–165.

93. Coaracy, *O Rio de Janeiro no século XVII*, pp. 47–48, 63; Mauro, *Portugal, o Brasil e o Atlântico*, v. 2, p. 136; F. C. G. C. Lima, "Sugar and Metals as Commodity Money in Colonial Brazil," Economic History Society Annual Conference, University of Durham, 2010.

94. AHU_ACL_CU_005-02, Cx. 3, D. 423 – 424 – [Bahia, May 16, 1626]; Schwartz, *Sugar Plantations in the Formation of Brazilian Society*, pp. 197–198.

95. Lima, "Sugar and Metals as Commodity Money"; idem, "Uma análise crítica da literatura sobre a oferta e circulação de moeda metálica no Brasil nos séculos XVI e XVII," *Estudos Econômicos* 35:1 (2005): 169–201.

96. AHU_ACL_CU_005-02, Cx. 1, D. 67 – [Bahia, May, 26, 1614]; Mauro, *Portugal, o Brasil e o Atlântico*, v. 2, p. 174. The mechanism of devaluing currency to compensate for a drop in prices would be used in the late nineteenth-century Brazil with coffee: C. Prado Jr., *História econômica do Brasil* (São Paulo: Editora Brasiliense, 1978), p. 228.

97. On the flight of copper and silver from Portugal and Brazil, see: Tavares, "A moeda de D. João II aos Filipes," pp. 277–289

98. Galante, *Uma história da circulação monetária no Brasil*, pp. 24, 63–66.

Chapter Eight

The Tax Collector *or* Village Lawyer (detail), *Pieter Brueghel, the Younger (1621).*

Cash Flow

Credit and Liquidity

The medium of exchange used in commerce extended far beyond hard cash and commodities used as currency. Merchants themselves created their own form of currency in their financial activities, private fiduciary money which was not physically minted in metal, but was only recorded in securities and credit transfers, in investments and loans with third parties' deposits.

Trade likewise established an infrastructure for a range of financial operations. In practice, merchants acted as banks, they maintained current accounts for third parties and with third parties, transferred funds from one account to the other, made and received payments on behalf of others, and, through their correspondents, sent funds to some parties on behalf of others.

These banking activities were supported by commerce, which provided real coverage in terms of merchandise and money, established a network of counterparts, and provided experience and expertise in transactions and calculations. However, the most important aspect is that financial activities injected capital into the accounts of these merchants and expanded the capacity of their mercantile operations. Hence, understanding these transactions is not secondary but is rather a key part of any study of trade.

Cashless Transactions

Sales on credit commonly took place using a tab. Buyers had a credit account with the vendor, who recorded the debit in his account books or papers, in which the purchaser generally acknowledged the debt by appending his signature. When the debt was paid, it was the turn of the vendor to attest to this fact, signing the release in the purchaser's account books or on individual slips of paper.[A]

In the engraving, The Merchant, *from the* Book of Trades *(1694), the signs in the background – England, France, Spain, Italy and Smyrna (now Izmir) – suggest that the merchant traded in all those marketplaces and engaged in financial transactions with them as well. This would be the type of setting in which an important businessman would work, along with his clerks and retainers.*

Another means of purchasing on credit was by issuing credit securities. These were pieces of paper which constituted private credit instruments and contained the acknowledgement of the debt and a promise that the person or persons named therein would pay a certain sum, in a certain currency, to a certain person or persons, at a stipulated time and place. The two most common credit securities were IOUs, or "bills-obligatory" or "bills of debt," and bills of exchange.

In bills-obligatory, known in Portuguese as *assinados*, or as *conhecimentos*,[1] *escritos*[2] or *livranças*,[3] the purchaser acknowledged owing a given value for merchandise, money or services received from a certain person, and promised to pay this sum to the creditor on the date established therein.[B] Thus, a Portuguese Jewish merchant signed one of these documents in Amsterdam, acknowledging that he owed a Dutch merchant the sum of 875 guldens and 12 and a half stuivers for goods he had received.[4] The only difference between bills-obligatory and modern promissory notes (or *livranças*, as they are known in Portugal) is that a promissory note is an instrument that is fully transferrable to third parties, which was not exactly the case with bills-obligatory, as we will see. With some variations, assinados were the Portuguese equivalent of English bills of debts, acknowledgements of debt and IOUs; Italian *pollizze*; Spanish *libranzas* and *cédulas*; French *cédules obligatoires,* and Dutch *obligaties* and *bekentenissen*. The multiple and imprecise nomenclature in many regions indicates that the instrument's characteristics and properties were still developing.[5]

The interest rate was generally incorporated in the instrument's face value,[6] which avoided judicial disputes about its legitimacy.[C] The fact that interest was not specified in the documents may raise doubts as to whether it was indeed charged. However, it appears to be highly unlikely that sales on credit would forego interest, when merchants were so keenly aware of their opportunity cost. The arithmetic manuals of the age were clear in this regard, and one of them posed the following question:

> *A merchant sold a length of fabric for 20 cruzados on four months' credit and thereby earned 8 cruzados and sold another for 25 cruzados, also on credit, though the period is not known, thereby earning 18 cruzados. Question: when this merchant sold the second piece of cloth how long was the period of credit as compared to the first piece?*[7]

A. Thus, a merchant in Porto authorized his counterpart in Pernambuco to "give releases for what you receive and sign on any account books, sheets, tabs [and] rolls of records"; see: ADP, NOT, PO2, l. 29, fols. 94v.–96v. (1609-9-1).

B. "Assinados" and "escritos" were generic Portuguese terms for private legal instruments written in one's own handwriting, for various purposes, including acknowledgement of debts and promises of payment. The term "*conhecimentos*" referred to acknowledgments and confessions of assumed obligations, such as debts to be paid or cargos to be delivered, as in the case of bills of lading (*conhecimentos de carga*), mentioned earlier (Roover, *L'évolution de la lettre de change*, pp. 110, n. 111, 87–88). The term "*livrança*" possibly derives from the Castilian *libranza*, designating payment orders issued by treasury authorities to leaseholders of the Crown's revenues, to release payment to a beneficiary, and also began to be used to refer to notes containing acknowledgment of debts and promises to pay used in large Castilian fairs, which were important for the entire Peninsula. This was perhaps how the term began to be used in Portugal, where, to date, promissory notes are still called "livranças." This study has chosen to use the term "assinado" to refer to bill-obligatory in Portuguese because this is the term that appears most frequently in the sources (Bluteau, *Vocabulario portuguez & latino*, entry "Assinado"; Carande, *Carlos V y sus banqueros*, pp. 224, 229).

C. Manuel António Fernandes Moreira transcribed a bill of exchange dating from 1664, issued in Goa to be paid in Lisbon to a trader from Viana. The bill mentions an interest rate of 16 and 2/3 % (16.66%), which is justified (in the text of the bill itself) on the basis of the risk of the voyage (Moreira, *Os mercadores de Viana*, pp. 128–129). As we have seen in the previous chapter, the risks of a voyage could be viewed as legitimate, since they were random and extrinsic to the loan, unlike opportunity cost and default.

The same manuals taught prospective merchants how to calculate interest due on the basis of years, months, days and hours. While these were merely exercises to hone arithmetic and accounting skills, and were not necessarily applied to actual situations with the same precision and rigor, the underlying idea, that is, the remuneration of capital over the course of time, would undoubtedly not have gone unheeded. In fact, as we will see in the next chapter, Miguel Dias Santiago charged different prices in Brazil and Portugal depending on the timeframe, method and means of payment, and the reputation of the payer.[8]

Bills-obligatory worked well in transactions that began and ended in the same marketplace. So, how could a traveler who neither had nor could have access to sufficient funds at that moment trade in a foreign location? He could obtain credit if he had access to such funds back home via third parties. A merchant, probably called Jan van Lancker, said to be Flemish and possibly a Dutchman, was passing through Porto when he issued three bills of exchange to pay for merchandise he had received from a local merchant. At least one of the three bills was issued in payment for purchases of sugar. In one of them, issued on December 4, 1614, Van Lancker instructed a merchant in Hamburg and another one in Amsterdam to pay a Portuguese Jew 400 cruzados, at a rate of 114 groten per cruzado.[9]

As has been seen, the operations of bills of exchange were slightly more complex than those of bills-obligatory. While the latter involved only the debtor and the creditor, bills of exchange, in principle, involved four people, two locations and two currencies. The first was the deliverer, who delivered the funds by selling wares, transferring assets or providing services to the drawer (or taker), who issued the bill. Both deliverer and drawer were at the same location, while the bill was to be paid elsewhere by the party on whom it was issued, that is, a drawee (or payer), normally a counterpart of the drawer, to the payee, a counterpart or debtor of the deliverer in the other mercantile center. Once the bill of exchange had been issued, the deliverer sent it to the payee. The payee then presented the bill to the drawee, who was to sign and date it as a signal of acceptance. The moment the bill was presented for acceptance was called "sight," and the period in which the payee was to be paid started from this date onwards, generally stipulated in the document, along with the rate of exchange. The bill might specify the maturity period or leave it "at usance," that is, in accordance with the customary periods for bills issued in the first marketplace and paid in the second.[10]

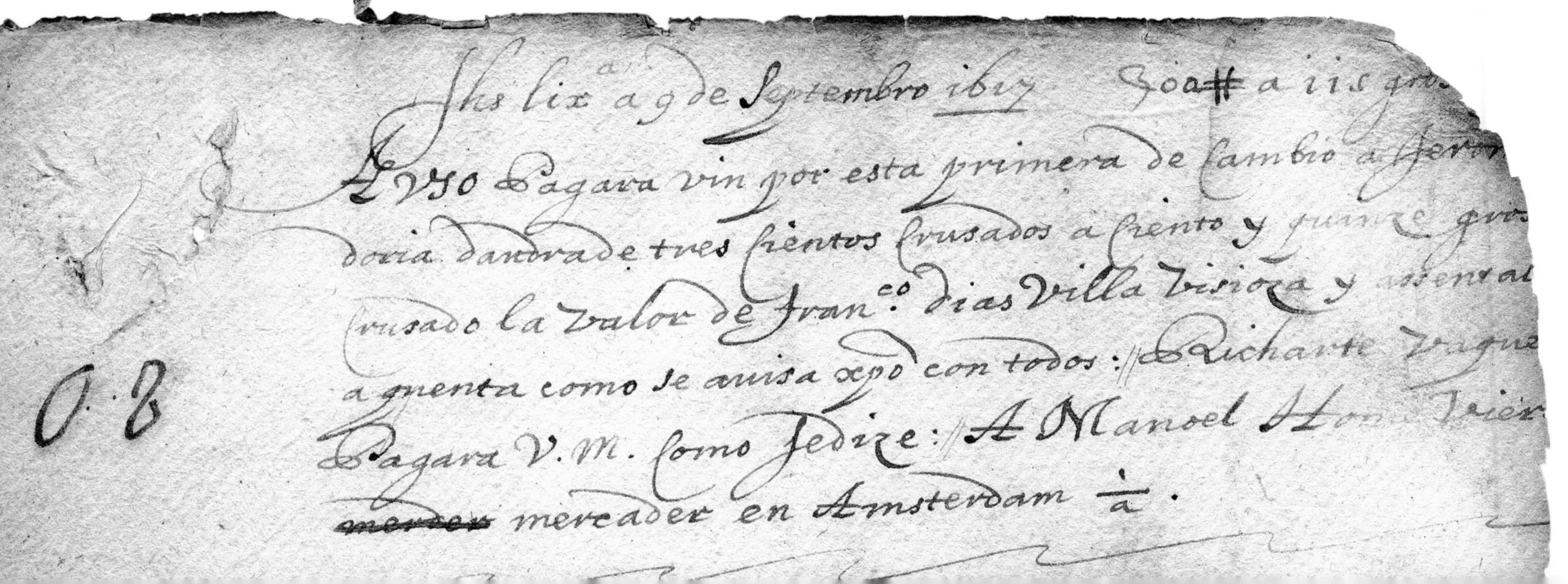

Jhs lix.a a 9 de Septembro 1617 — 300# a 115 gro[illegible]
A vso pagara vm por esta primera de cambio a Jero[illegible]
doria dandrade tres cientos crusados a ciento y quinze gro[illegible]
crusado la valor de fran.co dias villa visioza y asentai[illegible]
a quenta como se auisa xpo con todos:// Richarte Vaque
Pagara V.M. como se dize:// A Manoel Hom[illegible] Vieir[illegible]
~~mercader~~ mercader en Amsterdam

O. B

Copy of a bill of exchange payable "at usance" prepared by a notary in Amsterdam in November 1617. Richarte Vaque (drawer) had issued the bill in Lisbon in September of that year, instructing Manuel Homem Vieira (drawee) to pay to Jerónimo Dória de Andrade (payee) in Amsterdam 300 cruzados (at 115 groten to the cruzado), the same amount that Francisco Dias Vila Viçosa (deliverer) had handed over to the drawer.

"Rule for multiplication," from the Arithmetic manual by Afonso Vilhafane Guiral e Pacheco (1624).

Capitulo VII. 28

1 vez 2 são 2
2 vezes 2 são 4
2 vezes 3 são 6
2 vezes 4 são 8
2 vezes 5 são 10
2 vezes 6 são 12
2 vezes 7 são 14
2 vezes 8 são 16
2 vezes 9 são 18
2 vezes 10 são 20

---

3 vezes 3 são 9
3 vezes 4 são 12
3 vezes 5 são 15
3 vezes 6 são 18
3 vezes 7 são 21
3 vezes 8 são 24
3 vezes 9 são 27
3 vezes 10 são 30

---

4 vezes 4 são 16
4 vezes 5 são 20
4 vezes 6 são 24
4 vezes 7 são 28
4 vezes 8 são 32
4 vezes 9 são 36
4 vezes 10 são 40

---

5 vezes 5 são 25
5 vezes 6 são 30
5 vezes 7 são 35
5 vezes 8 são 40
5 vezes 9 são 45
5 vezes 10 são 50

---

6 vezes 6 são 36
6 vezes 7 são 42
6 vezes 8 são 48
6 vezes 9 são 54
6 vezes 10 são 60

---

7 vezes 7 são 49
7 vezes 8 são 56
7 vezes 9 são 63
7 vezes 10 são 70

---

8 vezes 8 são 64
8 vezes 9 são 72
8 vezes 10 são 80

---

9 vezes 9 são 81
9 vezes 10 são 90

---

10 vezes 10 são 100
10 vezes 100 são 1000
1 vezes 100000 1 conto.

Rekenpenning: *a "jeton," copper counting token used on lined surfaces similar to an abacus. These lines were often scratched, painted, engraved or encrusted on boards, tables or counters. Tokens such as these were also called "contos para contar" and "tentos de contar" in Portuguese. The coin shown here was minted in Dordrecht in the Dutch Rebel Provinces in 1587 to commemorate the famine that was scourging the county of Artois, then controlled by Hispanic forces. On one side, we see a Spaniard flanked by starvation and death, associating the region's sufferings with Catholic impiety. On the reverse, bounty is connected with the true faith.*

So how could a vendor be sure that a bill of exchange issued by a buyer would be honored by someone else, at a certain time in a foreign land? Generally the drawer was either a counterpart of the drawee, and had access to the latter's assets, or was the drawer's employee – factor, retainer, for example – being publicly known as such. However, when the drawee was not a habitual counterpart of the drawer, bills of exchange were preceded by letters of credit, in which the prospective drawee pledged to honor the bills of exchange drawn on him by the drawer for given purposes and up to a specified amount.[11] On the other hand, bills of exchange were generally accompanied by letters of advice, whereby the drawer informed the drawee of the reasons and purposes why the bill of exchange was issued, and which of the credits kept with the drawee was to be deducted to settle the said debt. In reality, these notices essentially authorized both the payment to the payee and the debit of that amount from the drawer's current account.[12] At the same time, the drawer inserted the expression "as per advice" on the bill of exchange to notify the drawee that he was to receive a letter of advice from him. If the letter and the bill revealed a discrepancy as to which of drawer's credits the value should be debited, the drawee was to lodge a protest about such an inconsistency to avoid the drawer subsequently claiming damages.[13]

The exchange rates cited in the bills included incorporated interest. However, exchange rates, unlike interest, were considered to be legitimate by medieval jurists, theologians and canonists. The proceeds of exchange operations depended on a random difference between the exchange rate stipulated in the bill of exchange and the actual exchange rate current at the place and time of payment. If anyone profited in this process, it was considered legitimate because they could similarly incur losses. Hence, in principle, bills of exchange were to be used only in transactions involving disparate currencies or, at least, different places.[14]

With time, theoreticians progressively allowed bills of exchange to be used in the same territories where there was no disparity in the exchange rate but merely a physical distance. A consensus emerged that a spatial hiatus could give rise to an "exchange rate," even if both locations used the same currency, since, if many individuals sought out businessmen in one location asking bills to be issued in other locations in exchange for money or goods, then the said businessmen would charge a premium for providing the limited assets they had in the remote location. Hence, the balance of payments between the two locations in the same realm created an "exchange rate."[15] The difference between supply and demand for coins in two locations also gave rise to an "exchange." Apart from this, by safely transferring resources, these businessmen acted as transporters and insurers, activities which, according to theologians and canonists, warranted legitimate remuneration.[16]

In effect, in sixteenth-century Spain, there was an intense flow of remittances through bills of exchange within the dominions of the same Crown, especially between the different fairs that were held over the course of the year in the cities of Castile, and between these fairs and Spain's main Atlantic port, Seville. Nevertheless, in 1552, owing to the influence of rigid theologians, an edict was issued banning bills between regions where the same currency circulated in which exchange rates differed from the par value. It was a significant setback for the nascent doctrine, but ended up by further stirring the debate on this matter in vibrant Iberian neo-scholastic schools.[17]

Portuguese legislation differed from Spanish law, and continued allowing the use of bills of exchange within the realm and its overseas territories. Going even further, King John III complained to Prince

Philip of Spain, the future Philip II, that this edict was extremely inconvenient for Portuguese merchants in Castile, who could not resort to this financial mechanism, and that since Portugal permitted such practices in its domains, the edict stained the image of Catholic orthodoxy that the Portuguese Crown took pride in.[18]

However, John III's successor, King Sebastian, tried to follow the Spanish lead. For seven years, he forbade bills of exchange from being drawn for the payment of a value different from the one received in transfers within Portuguese dominions, either in Europe or overseas. He was obliged to reverse this decision in 1577, authorizing such bills to be issued with a premium of up to 12% per year at fairs held in Lisbon in June and December until the next fairs held in the Algarve in April or October, and vice versa. The same rate was applied to bills from and to Seville. Higher rates could only be agreed with other foreign marketplaces.[19] Once again, the legislation had to adjust and the code *Ordenações Filipinas*, published in 1603, authorized profits for exchanges between different places, even without fairs being held there, legitimizing this on the basis of the expenditure merchants incurred to keep funds in other locations.[20]

In practice, such bills were freely and widely issued from Brazil to Portugal, and vice versa, as well as between Portugal and its African and Asian colonies, between different colonies and within Portugal itself.[D] Miguel Dias Santiago, a merchant whose operations are examined in greater detail in Chapter 9, issued bills of exchange on Pernambuco from Bahia and, subsequently, on Salvador from Olinda, from Brazil on Portugal and vice versa.[21]

Contravening the law, bills of exchange were even issued for operations limited to a single location. If it were not for the difference in the places and the currency, a bill of exchange involving just two individuals was equivalent to a bill-obligatory.[E] In fact, in Portugal, the term "bill of exchange" often designated instruments used in operations between two people in a single trade center. Thus, an instrument issued by the above-mentioned Jan van Lancker to pay for a certain quantity of sugar, which the notary called a bill, was in truth a bill-obligatory, by which Van Lancker committed to pay the seller 225,500 réis within eight days of signing the instrument.[22] There is an example of another bill of exchange/bill-obligatory issued by a merchant in Porto in his own favor, to purchase textiles. The subscriber, who was simultaneously both the drawer and the drawee, accepted paying his own bill of exchange and paid for his part of the textiles purchased.[23]

D. Manuel António Fernandes Moreira called "credit missive bills" (*carta missiva de crédito*), bills of exchange in which there was no exchange of currency but just a transfer to another location, although he does cite a document in whose text the word "*cambeo*" ["exchange"] is expressly mentioned (Ibid., pp. 124–125).

E. Moreira called bills-obligatory "simple bills," noting that the sole difference between these and the "credit missive bills" was that "simple bills" were issued and paid in the same location, ignoring the fact that the drawer was also the drawee. In the example cited by Moreira too, the subscriber accepted his own bill (Ibid., pp. 127–129).

Recovering Payments

The main difficulty with sales on credit was safeguarding the creditor's rights. Innumerable powers of attorney were issued by merchants to recover unpaid debts.[24] Records of debts in public and private contracts, account books, rolls, tabs, and so forth, served as admissible evidence in the judicial system, even more so if these were acknowledged and signed by the debtor. However, judicial enforcement entailed a prior judgment of the creditor's claims, which implied slow and expensive proceedings, often with an uncertain outcome. Hence, in most contracts registered at the notary offices in Porto, there was a clause in which the parties stipulated that the contract:

> *is to be valid in and out of court as though* res judicata*, which was adjudicated by a competent judge, requested, consented to and accepted by the parties and thus they request any of His Majesty's courts where this document is presented to judge and decide upon it as a final judgment which cannot be appealed.*[25]

Purchases on credit using bills of exchange skirted the inconveniences of legal proceedings resulting from the judgment of disputes over debts. Bills of exchange conferred the same right to proceed to enforcement as a judgment did.[F] In case of default, the creditor of the instrument demanded seizure of the debtor's assets immediately, without the debt needing to be validated by the judicial system. Just like checks nowadays, the right to the value of the bill was unconditional and autonomous with regard to the transactions from which it stemmed.

The same decree that had again allowed bills of exchange to be issued within Portugal, with incorporated interest, for transfers from one fair to another, established that drawees who had already accepted the bill for payment, and their drawers, would only be heard by magistrates after they had paid the sums in question. If, by the end of the fairs, which lasted a month, neither the drawees[G] nor the drawers had paid the amount due, both would be immediately subject to enforcement. No merchant who had issued or accepted a bill at a fair could claim being under a privileged jurisdiction or delay enforcing the bill under any pretext.[26] Given that bills were allowed to be drawn from one location on another, without fairs taking place at the site, it seems that these provisions on enforcement were extended to any time period stipulated in them. The automatic right to proceed to enforcement conferred by bills of exchange is evident in some of the contracts recorded in the notary books in Porto which, instead of equating the document to a final and unappealable judgment as above, while seeking to avoid lawsuits in cases of default, simply stipulated: "this document shall be valid as a bill of exchange."

Despite the summary procedure used to enforce debts incurred by means of bills, enforcing a bill was still a laborious process. The drawee could refuse to accept the bill if the drawer's credit with him was not sufficient, or if he had not been instructed by the drawer to pay it. In such cases, as soon as the payee received a refusal from the drawee, he would lodge a protest for non-acceptance. The protest served to demonstrate to the drawer that the drawee had refused to satisfy the drawer's order. In the Low Countries, protests were lodged with notaries, while in Portugal and in Brazil they were lodged with a court.[H/27]

Re-exchanging bills

The value of a new bill, once reissued, would be equal to that of the previous bill, already exchanged, that is, already incorporating the interest (justified on account of the distance) and converted, as the case might be, into the currency of the location on which it had been drawn. The re-exchanged bill would add a new exchange rate to this value for the return to the original location. Furthermore, it would include damages for losses incurred due to the two currency conversions, if any, forgone profit, and all the other costs on account of protests, postage, brokerage and commissions. Looking for another way of obtaining the funds that had not been paid, the original payee, and drawer of the second bill, might have to resort to the assistance of a creditor inclined to exchange current funds for credit to be received elsewhere. The ex-payee might also need the services of a broker to find such a deliverer and to verify the creditworthiness of all the parties involved in the transaction.[28] The fee paid to brokers for these services was also added to the value of the new bill, even if their services were not used, along with the commission likewise charged by deliverers from payees for taking care of their remittances by means of bills. The commission was charged even if no third party was a deliverer for a re-exchanged bill, but rather the deliverer was the new drawer (and ex-payee) himself, damaged by the lack of payment. Between Brazil and Portugal, this commission was usually 5%.[29] All these items would be included in the protest for non-payment. A rate of 25% was charged for the re-exchange of a bill from Porto back to Paraíba.[30]

Such protests generated a certificate recording that the drawee had been notified to pay, along with any response or absence of a response. Sometimes, after a protest for non-acceptance had been lodged, someone offered to pay the bill on behalf of and for the honor of the drawer. In such cases, the protest served to safeguard the rights of the person making such a payment against both the deliverer and the drawer abroad.

Once a protest for non-acceptance had been lodged and the period stipulated in the bill for payment had elapsed, if nobody came forward to pay it or, if, even after accepting the bill, the drawee refused to make payment, the payee (the local correspondent of the deliverer who had originally received it as payment) would lodge a second protest for non-payment and re-exchanged the instrument; that is, he would draw a second bill on the drawer of the first bill on behalf of either the original deliverer or someone else.

Thus, a merchant from Porto granted a power of attorney to a resident of Aveiro who was going to Pernambuco, or was already there, to charge and recover 70,000 réis from a merchant living in that captaincy. The amount pertained to a bill of exchange that the latter had issued on his own brother, who lived in Porto. Yet, since the said brother "neither paid the sum, nor did he wish to pay it and he, the grantor, re-exchanged it and it is being re-exchanged and you shall appear in legal proceedings against him and all the other debtors."[31] The brother living in Pernambuco had probably gone bankrupt, and lacked sufficient funds to back the bill. This is what can be deduced from another power of attorney granted five days prior to this by another merchant from Porto on behalf of the same individual to recover

F. See: ADP, NOT, PO2, l. 36, fol. 294 (1613-4-12).

G. Only drawees who had accepted bills for payment were covered by this decree.

H. In Portugal, protests were lodged in courts associated with trade, such as the Customs House magistrates, the Magistrate for India, Mina and Brazil and the [Mercantile] Consulate, when the latter existed.

everything that the said merchant in Pernambuco owed him.[32] Apart from having to face the legal consequences, the drawer of a re-exchanged bill who tried to avoid paying a bill he had originally issued would become discredited in commercial circles, unless it was publicly known that the deliverer, his immediate creditor, had also not fulfilled his obligations towards him.[33]

In Portugal, the decree determining the prompt enforcement of due and unpaid bills of exchange in fairs extended the same procedure to bills-obligatory issued for the purchase of merchandise whose signatures were acknowledged by the respective subscribers: "And the same enforcement procedure will be applicable for bills-obligatory that some individuals issue to pay the sums declared therein in the said fairs, being acknowledged by the parties and proceeding from merchandise that has been bought."[34]

The proceedings for enforcing bills-obligatory in mercantile hubs of the Low Countries and along the German and Baltic coasts were even more summary. Here, bills-obligatory with the clause "payable to the bearer" were commonplace, and, according to Malynes, magistrates would summon defaulters and immediately ask them: "My friend, what is the reason that you have not payed this your Bill to C. D. [the payee]'?"[35] Malynes affirmed that the main reason for honoring a bill-obligatory was not the fact that it could be enforced promptly, but was rather the drawer's reputation. By refusing to pay a debt, the debtor reneged upon his own signature and, thus, "he is not only utterly discredited, but also detested of all Merchants." Hence, merchants, both local and foreigners from all nations, sought to interact sincerely and honestly.[36] In effect, sources reveal several powers of attorney in which subscribers of bills-obligatory issued in Amsterdam empowered and instructed their representatives to acknowledge and confirm both the validity of the instruments being transacted and their signatures.[37]

If receiving credit instruments as payment implied the risk of default, which was not a factor when payments were made in cash, the loss of these documents was not irreversible, as was the case with coins. To guard against loss, bills of exchange were generally issued in triplicate. Moreover, it was possible to make authenticated copies of the instruments and even to reissue them when good faith and understanding prevailed among the parties. Thus, a mariner brought two copies of a bill of exchange for 20,000 réis from Olinda and lost one of them after the payee had appended his acceptance on the document. He presented the second copy in Porto for payment and, to prevent any future doubts, released the payee, revoking the validity of the first copy.[38] Of the bills issued by Van Lancker, mentioned above, the seller had already sent the first two copies abroad, without receiving payment. He made a notarized transcript of his third copy, keeping the originals in case the authenticated copy was destroyed or mislaid.[39]

One could say that the preferences of merchants with regard to means of payment to be used in transfers overseas observed the following hierarchy: first, bills of exchange, followed by merchandise and, finally, coins. This is clearly evident in the instructions given by a merchant from Porto to his agent on how to use any remaining proceeds from the sale of merchandise he was taking to Pernambuco after buying enough sugar to fill the space that had been leased beforehand for the homebound voyage. First of all, the agent was to look for "a good bill of exchange" and, through it, was to remit the surplus funds back. If he was unable to find a creditworthy individual who had funds in Portugal and was inclined to issue him a bill of exchange for that amount, then the agent was to buy white sugar and load it onto another carrack or ship about to set sail to Portugal. He was to send the funds back in cash only as a last resort. If this was the case, then the coins were to be loaded onto hulks sailing for Lisbon or Viana. The merchant probably specified the type of vessel as a security measure. Often requisitioned to transport governors-general and other authorities traveling to Brazil, hulks were larger and, when well-armed, had a better capacity to ward off pirate attacks.[40] The instruction to use a vessel bound for Lisbon or Viana could indicate that no hulks were expected to be sailing to Porto at the time when the coins would be sent.[41] Obviously, this preference for sugar over coins could change according to variations in the terms of trade for sugar and silver.

The same order of priorities had already been indicated in a charter dating from 1515 in which the monarch established a mechanism for remitting the proceeds derived from the sale of merchandise sent on his behalf to Asia, where silver undoubtedly had far more advantageous terms of trade.[42] It also seems symptomatic that Ambrósio Fernandes Brandão, a merchant and sugar planter, when describing the activities of silver merchants – known as *peruleiros* – who established themselves in the River Plate region and later settled in Brazil, cited the same order for methods of transferring funds from Brazil to Portugal:[I] "deliver their money against bills of exchange, or they buy sugar, or take [the funds] with them to Portugal."[43]

The fact that goods were preferred over coins is also no surprise. Coins were far more coveted and more easily stolen, kept hidden and circulated than bulkier sugar. To a lesser degree, the same held true even for spices. Moreover, ascertaining discrepancies between qualities and quantities of sugar was easier than distinguishing between metal alloys or coinage. When coins were transported, a lot depended on the good faith of the people sending or transporting them. Hence, the fact that merchants preferred sugar, or rather shunned coins, in international transfers in favor of bills of exchange and goods was evidently due, above all, to a question of security and trust.[J]

Transferring Credit Instruments

As has been seen, sales on credit were the general rule. The disadvantages of sales on credit were the risk of default and a loss of liquidity. The use of credit instruments lessened the risk of default, given that these instruments allowed for automatic enforcement. There were also solutions to mitigate the loss of liquidity. Bills-obligatory could be transferred to third parties before maturity, a practice vividly described by Malynes:

I. Fernando Carlos de Cerqueira Lima states that different documents mention instances of colonial authorities ordering the taxes collected in Brazil to be remitted to Portugal by means of bills of exchange, stipulating that metals should only be sent as a last resort. Unfortunately, he did not indicate the sources (Lima, "Sugar and Metals as Commodity Money," pp. 6–7).

J. Studying the sugar trade in Viana (do Castelo), Manuel António Fernandes Moreira had a different perspective. He noted the infrequent appearance of transcriptions of bills of exchange referring to dealings with the rest of Europe in the notary books in Viana. Moreira interprets this scarcity of transcripts as a fear that bills of exchange would not be settled abroad, particularly during periods of hostility between the country where they had been issued and the country in which they would be paid. Being wary, merchants preferred to receive payments at sight and in their town. Moreira observes: "Bills of exchange are rarely transcribed in notary books in Viana. I think that merchants sought to avoid them. They entailed a slow and dangerous process, at a time when services [of funds transfer] were almost exclusively carried out by private individuals. They preferred prompt payment, in dealings with [the rest of] Europe. It would undoubtedly not be far from the truth to say that hostility between states caused merchants to be wary" (Moreira, *Os mercadores de Viana*, p. 128). This hypothesis makes sense within the scenario that Moreira suggests for Viana: local merchants exported little to northern Europe on their own account, and hence did not have credits to receive abroad. It was thus natural that they preferred to receive payment at sight: ibid., pp. 35–36, 181–182. However, had there been monies to receive or pay abroad, the advantages of transferability and the reissuing of bills were clear, especially in situations of war. The risks of default could be avoided, as can be seen in ch. 10.

> *Suppose A. B. the Clothier selleth to C. D. the Merchant one pack of Clothes, for the summe of one hundreth pounds paiable at six moneths, and doth condition with him to make him a Bill in the name of such a man as hee shall nominate unto him: A. B. the Clothier buyeth of D. E. the Gentleman, so much Wooll as amounted to one hundreth pounds, and doth intend to deliver him the bill of C. D. the Merchant, in full payment of his Woolls, and to cause the same to be made in his (this Gentlemans) name: But D. E. the said Gentleman, caused him to make the Bill payable to E. G. the Mercer, and the Mercer is contended with the like condition to accept thereof; but he caused the same to be made payable to C. D. the Merchant, of whom hee buyeth his Velvets and Silkes; and so in payment of them, hee delivered him (by Intermissive time) his owne Bill, which he first should have made to the Clothier's*[44]

By transferring credit, merchants could reinvest the sums in new operations and ensure a greater circulation of assets. Malynes provided a description of how English merchants transferred bills-obligatory they received in payment during business trips to the Low Countries and Hamburg:

> *For when they have sold their Clothes unto other Merchants, or others, payable at 4, 6, 8, or more months; they presently transferre and set over these Billes (so received for the payment of their Clothes) unto other Merchants, and take for them other commodities at such prices as they can agree with the Seller of them, be it Velvets, Silkes, Satains, Fustians, or any other wares or commodities, to make returne of the provenue [proceeds] of theirs; and so selling those forraine commodities here in England, they presently buy more Clothes, and continue a Revolution of buying and selling in the course of Trafficke and Commerce....*[45]

Hence, when a merchant sold on credit and then transferred this credit to someone else, he increased his working capital. This is why Malynes emphasizes the benefits of this expedient for young merchants who still had very little capital of their own, thereby lowering the barriers to their entry into the market.[46] The transferability of instruments also increased both the liquidity and the velocity of circulation in the market. Furthermore, it improved cash flow management, thereby decreasing the costs and risks of keeping large amounts of cash or merchandise on hand for use as means of payment. Thus, the increasing transferability and greater enforceability of the instruments reduced their shortcomings as a means of payment as compared to coins. These instruments ended up serving as fiduciary money – paper money issued by the subscriber.

However, instruments were not always transferrable. Such transfers varied according to the type of instrument, local laws and customs, and the level of trust among the parties. The juridical doctrine of the age hindered transferability. Roman and Germanic law – the sources of medieval and early modern European law – prohibited transferring an instrument before maturity. Only instruments which had fallen due could be recovered and received by third parties who were deemed to be representatives in good faith of the payee cited in the instrument: relatives, factors, retainers, agents, proxies, and so on. If the due instrument had to be enforced judicially, such bearers-representatives would not be heard without producing a power of attorney issued by the original payee.[47] The transferability of bills of exchange was

"Vanitas": Still Life with the "Spinario"; *Pieter Claesz* (1628). *The artistic genre of* vanitas *alludes to the fleeting nature of glory and earthly pleasures.*

even more complex, as shall shortly be seen. Nonetheless, the expansion of commercial activities required mercantile practices to facilitate the transferability of credit instruments. As in the example cited by Malynes, traveling merchants often could not remain at a trade center abroad until the maturity of the bills-obligatory received for the sale of their wares. Transferring them to individuals who stayed longer or lived there solved the problem, at least for those individuals who were about to leave.

Legal doctrine evolved in the wake of mercantile practices. Even though the former often hindered the latter, at the end of the day theory was forced to legitimize practice. One of the ways found to ensure transferability was to formally cede, before a notary, the rights to an instrument that had yet to become due, accompanied by a power of attorney on the attorney's own behalf as if the credit was his (*in rem suam*). Another method was a novation (substitution of a new contract for an old one): recording the debtor's consent to make the payment cited in the instrument to a third party named by the creditor. At the same time, bills-obligatory payable to the bearer, irrespective of whether the bearer's name figured on the document or not, circulated in fairs in the Low Countries during the early sixteenth century. They were transferred by means of tradition, simply changing hands, a practice that ended up being regulated by the authorities. The circulation of bills-obligatory also became established at the fairs in Castile and, in all likelihood, also at the Genoese fairs held in Lyon, Besançon and Piacenza. This would have been necessary due to the constraints of itinerant commerce and the fact that merchants traveling to foreign marketplaces generally only stayed for a short while.[48]

Although instruments payable to the bearer spared lengthier and more costly transference procedures, they also presented a serious drawback to the last bearer by precluding action against the previous bearers in case the (original) subscriber defaulted. On the other hand, this lack of joint liability among the successive transferors offered an interesting advantage for the market in general. Since intermediary bearers could not be sued if the subscriber did not honor the debt, they did not hesitate to receive such bills-obligatory and hand them on, which increased the instrument's liquidity and made it more akin to paper money.[49]

This was how bills-obligatory functioned. Bills of exchange faced greater doctrinal obstacles to their transferability. According to one of the leading experts on their development, Raymond de Roover, medieval traditions affirmed the drawer (issuer) was a debtor only with regard to the deliverer who had supplied him assets (a seller for example), while the drawee (payer) and the payee were their respective agents abroad. Hence, if the amount due was not paid, the payee could only sue the drawee, never the drawer. That was the prerogative of the deliverer, who, in certain circumstances, could revoke the payee's rights to charge and collect the payment. Hence, in order to be enforceable in court, the rights of anyone to whom the bill had been transferred by the payee (transferor) were contingent on the deliverer's good will and good faith.[K]

Let us return to the two bills of exchange and the bill-obligatory Jan van Lancker issued while passing through Porto to pay a local supplier. The vendor decided that the original payees named in the instruments would not receive the respective sums, but the monies would instead be paid to a "Flemish youth" returning from Porto to the Low Countries. It appears that Van Lancker had left the city without paying the bill-obligatory, nor had he ensured that the bills of exchange were paid in northern Europe. As has been seen, the first and second copies of both these bills of exchange had been sent back a long time ago. Thus the supplier had changed his mind about the best way to use those instruments.[50]

The attempts made in the Low Countries during the sixteenth century to extend to bills of exchange the transferability already allowed for bills-obligatory met with fierce resistance.[L] However, the authorities ended up allowing the credit contained in such bills of exchange to be transmitted by an assignment to be recorded in the account books of the transferor, the recipient and the drawee, whereby the transferor was also jointly liable for the payment of the bill of exchange. Thus, credit could circulate by means of successive assignments. However, this was a rather complicated mechanism, since the final recipient had to verify if the sum transmitted had been correctly recorded in the account books of those who became his debtors.[51]

Finally, the assignment of bills of exchange paved the way for endorsement, a mechanism which began to appear in the main European marketplaces at the turn of the seventeenth century and became consolidated during the early decades of this century, although its full legitimization would have to wait until much later. In the period in question, endorsement, when accepted, did not mean the full transmission of the rights enshrined in a bill of exchange to the endorsee (in whose favor the instrument was endorsed), but was rather an instruction by the payee to the drawee to pay the endorsee. This was sufficient when there was good faith, trust and funds. The sequence of endorsers was recorded on the bill of exchange itself, generally on the back of the document. Just as with assignments, the most recent payee reserved the right to sue all the endorsers listed on the bill of exchange.[52]

In Porto, transmissions of instruments registered in any manner whatsoever in notary documents generally referred to powers of attorney for a proxy to recover and receive the value of the instrument, on their own account (in rem suam), as well as in the name of and on behalf of the grantor. This would have been the case with an instrument payable to Pedro Rodrigues da Veiga, who lived an itinerant life between Antwerp, his birthplace, Amsterdam, Rotterdam, Hamburg, Brazil, West Africa, Porto and other parts of the world. Coming from the Low Countries, on March 20, 1603, he passed through Porto, where he bought sugar worth 104,780 réis and, as payment, wished to transfer a bill-obligatory[53] for the same amount,

K, Regarding the Low Countries, Roover stated that at the end of the sixteenth century, Antwerp's customs – codified and made binding by Charles V and the foundation for all mercantile law in the region – allowed deliverers the right to appeal against the drawer of a bill that had not been honored by the drawee. The payee could only avail himself of this right if he could prove that he had delivered the sum cited in the bill and that he was not a mere representative of the deliverer. Moreover, the deliverer had the right to oppose the payment of a bill, even after it had been accepted by the drawee. Finally, if the payee went bankrupt before a payment fell due, the payment order was deemed to have been revoked. Consequently, drawees who made payment for bills which had not yet fallen due did so at their own risk (Roover, *L'évolution de la lettre de change*, pp. 92–94).

L, According to Roover, Hanseatic cities allowed greater flexibility in the transfer of bills of exchange, allowing bills to be issued with a clause "payable to so-and-so or to the bearer." Roover attributed this to the fact that Germanic merchants made little distinction between bills-obligatory and bills of exchange. Germanic merchants regarded the latter more as payment orders rather than currency exchange contracts. Moreover, Hanseatic trade was based on periodical journeys by merchants to other locations. Before setting out, merchants transferred instruments about to fall due to compatriot innkeepers who lived there and hosted seasonal visitors. Even if this Hanseatic tradition had influenced informal practices in the Low Countries, it would take time to be approved and become common practice there and in the rest of Europe (Ibid., pp. 97–98, 114). Hanseatic cities were Germanic mercantile cities, mainly on the Atlantic and Baltic coasts, which formed a league known as the *Hansa*, meant to protect the interests and rights of merchants from allied cities from the authorities in the locations where they traded. Despite vicissitudes, the league endured from the early Middle Ages to the beginning of early modern times: P. Dollinger, *The German Hansa* (London: Macmillan, 1970), passim.

Portrait of Maria Trip (1619–1683); *Rembrandt van Rijn (1639). Note the abundance of passementerie (fabric adornments), an important item of international trade, trimming the sitter's clothing.*

payable the following June. Veiga had received the instrument from another merchant from Porto as payment for some passementerie (fabric adornments) that a third Porto merchant had sold on Veiga's behalf.[54] To ensure the transfer, he issued a power of attorney in rem suam to the sugar vendor, so that the latter could charge and collect the sum specified in the instrument at the time the payment fell due.[55]

While, on the one hand, the need for such powers of attorney hindered the transferability of instruments, on the other hand it enhanced stability in the market. The payer was not pressed by the legitimate payee after having already paid a putative payee (not legitimate, but who could be considered to be legitimate in good faith). Similarly, armed with a power of attorney, the new payee could take all steps against a recalcitrant, defaulting or bankrupt debtor. Such powers of attorney frequently included a formal ceding of the instrument and all rights deriving from it, which further increased the security of the instrument for the person to whom it was being transferred. In some instruments, the new payee also provided an acquittance to the previous payee, releasing him from any obligations, in case the signatory or the drawee did not pay the debt and undertaking the risks and costs, losses and damages, if any.[56]

One of these cases refers to a bill of exchange drawn by the same merchant from Porto who had refused to pay the bill of exchange that his brother, who lived in Pernambuco, had drawn on him. He subsequently also moved to Pernambuco and from there drew another bill of exchange on another brother in Lisbon. The payee of this bill of exchange brought it with him from Pernambuco to Porto. On the banks of the Douro, he supposedly received the same sum specified in the bill of exchange, 82,000 réis, in cash and goods, from a merchant in Porto and, in exchange, ceded the bill of exchange to the seller before a notary and granted a power of attorney to the seller to collect the respective payment from the drawee in Lisbon, declaring himself to have been paid and satisfied with regard to the said bill of exchange and that he was withdrawing from the instrument. The transferor was apparently on the verge of going back to Brazil. Having transferred the receivable to another party he could go happily on his way.[57]

It would not be wrong to say that it was advisable for transfers to be accompanied by such formalities whenever there was a lack of trust among all the parties involved. These were prudent precautions when difficulties were anticipated – for example if the transferor was to leave the city[58] or the drawee or drawer lived elsewhere.[59] Formalities were also recommended, if not legally required, when the transfer was part of a large, complex, or formal transaction – such as transferring an inheritance.[60] Hence, a lack of familiarity among the individuals who were to pay and receive the amounts stipulated in the instrument could explain such formalities.

Endorsements were practiced in Porto.[M] However, records of protests for non- acceptance or payment in the city, which could have been an important source of information regarding transfers of bills of exchange, have not survived for posterity. In Portugal, they were registered in court and not a notary public office, and the documentation pertaining to courts in Porto for this period has been lost.[61] Thus, the sole case of endorsement found amongst documents examined is a bill-obligatory, and not a bill of exchange, and the endorsement was followed by a novation, an act in which, as has been seen, the debtor had to consent to pay a new beneficiary.[N] The endorsement and novation, both informal, were followed by a power of attorney in rem suam.[62] It is possible that all these formalities were conducted due to the fact that the transaction involved a large inheritance. Inheritance laws required more formal acts to avoid future disputes among heirs, or among heirs and their debtors or creditors, all the more so if an heir was a minor or was absent.

In fact, nothing prevented less formal methods of transfer, such as endorsement and tradition, from being more widely used – on the contrary. It is possible that transactions that did not require formal actions and whose parties trusted each other were never registered in public records.[O] As will be seen in the next chapter, Miguel Dias Santiago received "warehouse scripts," that is, bills-obligatory from wholesale merchants in payment for the sale of sugar. Even though he was not expected to refer to powers of attorney or ceding of rights in his account books, the absence of further details about the way in which the right to the credits mentioned in such instruments was transferred suggests that these were informal transfers.[63]

Informal transfers were probably more common when the debtor (subscriber or drawee), the transferor and the recipient all lived in the same location, as in the scenario imagined by Malynes, in which a bill-obligatory was returned to the merchant who had issued it after having changed hands three times. Since the same location was the setting for all the exchanges, concerns could easily be assuaged and the rights of all three – transferor, transferee and payer – acknowledged by all parties involved. Malynes affirmed that in Amsterdam, vendors promptly accepted payments made by means of bills-obligatory issued by third parties whom they knew. However,

M. Moreira states that in this period, the endorsement of "credit missive bills, as well as simple bills" was practiced in Viana, without however referring to sources in which this was explicitly mentioned (Moreira, *Os mercadores de Viana*, p. 125).

N. This was a method commonly used in England to skirt the obstacles imposed by Common Law on transfers of instruments before maturity (Roover, *L'évolution de la lettre de change*, pp. 88–89; Malynes, *Consuetudo: vel, lex mercatoria*, p. 99).

O. It is possible that the transfer of the bill-obligatory of Pedro Rodrigues da Veiga, that merchant from Antwerp who wanted to transfer the credits he had received from a merchant in Porto to another Porto merchant, was effected unofficially and that is why the drafted contract was never signed in a notary's office.

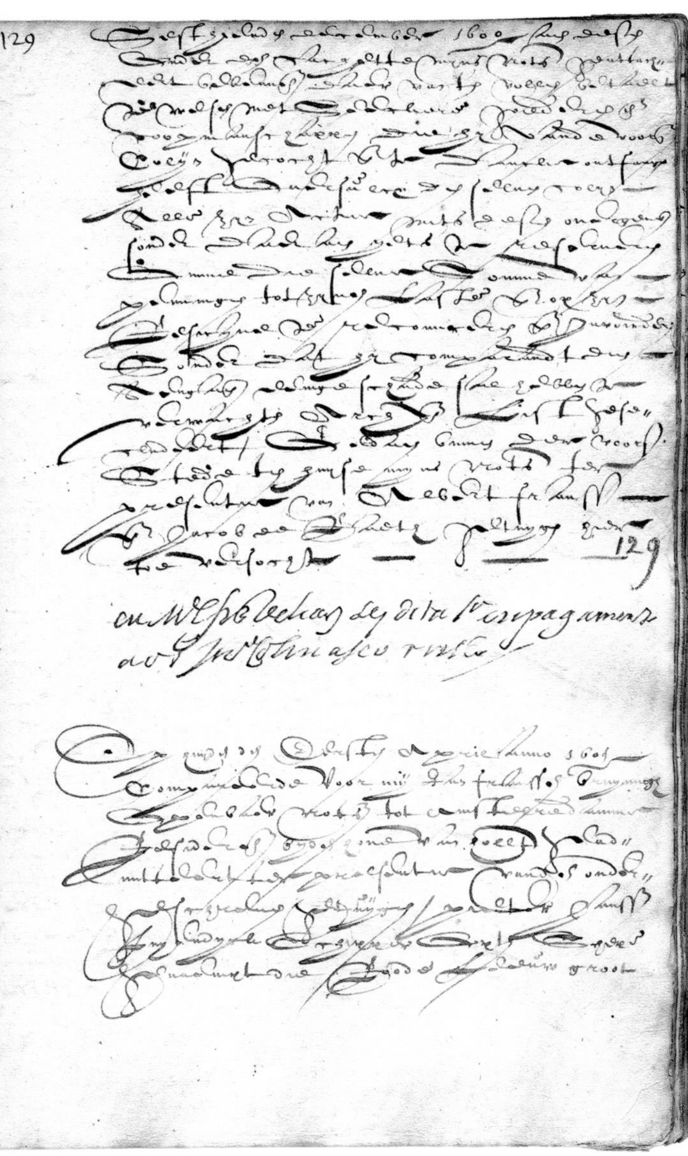

On March 31, 1601, the notary Jan Fransz. Bruyningh of Amsterdam authenticated the seal of the notary Nicolaas de Witte of Leiden in a document produced three and a half months earlier, in which the merchant Jan Colijn had undertaken all the risks of the bill-obligatory that Manuel Fernandes de Leão had transferred to him in payment for merchandise supplied by Colijn. In his own hand, Fernandes de Leão confirmed the transfer of the instrument in the Amsterdam notary's book.

Printed standardized contract for the purchase and sale of shares of the Dutch West India Company (WIC). The details of the shares transacted, of the parties and of the transaction itself were filled in by hand (1629–1630).

if they were unknown, the future recipient or a broker would make inquiries about the solvency of the subscribers. To further guarantee the creditworthiness of the document, they would ask the subscribers to confirm their willingness to pay the sum stipulated therein. Even if they did not take care to meet the subscriber, a climate of security prevailed, since both the legal system and the mercantile circles had an extremely low tolerance for recalcitrant debtors and those who reneged on their own signatures.

In fact, Malynes examined the enforcement of bills-obligatory in the northwest region of mainland Europe within a regional context of safe transferability. He stated that bills-obligatory functioned like cash and were the most common means of payment in Amsterdam, while coins served to make up the difference between the value of the merchandise and that of instruments being transferred or issued. Malynes could have exaggerated in his description of the transferability of bills-obligatory in Amsterdam, since his entire discourse in this regard had a single agenda: he sought to convince the English government to follow continental Europe's example and hence he highlighted the advantages of the procedure.[64]

Few cases of endorsements are mentioned in Amsterdam notary records, and many of them refer to endorsements carried out in other locations. This scarcity of examples perhaps reflects the informal nature of both the practice as well as the means adopted to solve the related disputes, when limited to the same location.[65] In effect, the following case suggests that, for transfers within the same city, the more formal procedures, such as written acceptance by the drawee, were used when the transferee had good reason to be apprehensive.

A Portuguese broker in Amsterdam stated that a Portuguese merchant had issued a bill of exchange for 300 guldens on another Portuguese in the city, in favor of his own son-in-law. After deducting the sum of 93 guldens, which his father-in-law owed him, from the bill of exchange, the son-in-law handed it over to a silk supplier who was not Portuguese, to repay an existing debt and to purchase more silks for his father-in-law. However, the supplier was reluctant to accept such a transaction and only agreed after the drawee (a third Portuguese party) wrote on the bill of exchange that he would pay him in seven months. Even so, the supplier eventually felt that he had risked too much and, in the absence of the son-in-law, took back all the silk he had delivered to him, and said he would only return the bill of exchange after he was paid what he was owed.[66]

Bills of exchange and bills-obligatory which had already fallen due were also transferred.[67] Obviously, the transfer of matured (and hence more liquid) credit did not offer the same advantages as the transfer of credit that had yet to fall due. Nevertheless, it could prove to be a good business decision to transfer an instrument to someone who could recover the debt more easily, such as a compatriot of the debtor or someone traveling to their place of residence. This saved time and expenditure on travel, which also represented liquidity and opportunity costs.

Moreover, other instruments that also conferred the right to automatically proceed to enforcement (enforceable instruments) were also transmitted, such as assets due as a result of judicial sentences,[68] orders of payment against royal treasury bonds and insurance policies[P] whose indemnities had already been adjudicated by the Amsterdam Insurance Board. There are cases where saffron was bought in Porto by means of transferring rights over an order of payment against the treasury,[69] and baize textiles were purchased in Amsterdam by transferring an insurance policy.[70] In fact, there was a veritable secondary market in insurance policies. Following the course of one such policy reveals that after having been adjudicated it changed hands twice, having been transferred the first time to pay out a bill-obligatory.[71] In addition, shares in the East India Company (VOC) and later the West India Company (WIC) were also transferred.[72]

P. The use of insurance policies as a means of payment in Venice was emphasized by A. Tenenti: "The *polizza* is a negotiable and negotiated instrument; there is almost absolute confidence in its validity. There is no shortage of examples. On April 29, 1594, the clerk of the ship *Stella et Marchina*, Simon Sassonello, borrowed 100 ducats from a Portuguese named Nuno Bernardes and gave him a polizza for 10 pounds of gross weight as collateral. Generally, the credit represented by the polizza is transferred by holders who cannot obtain it in payment" (Tenenti, *Naufrages, corsaires et assurances maritimes à Venise*, p. 63).

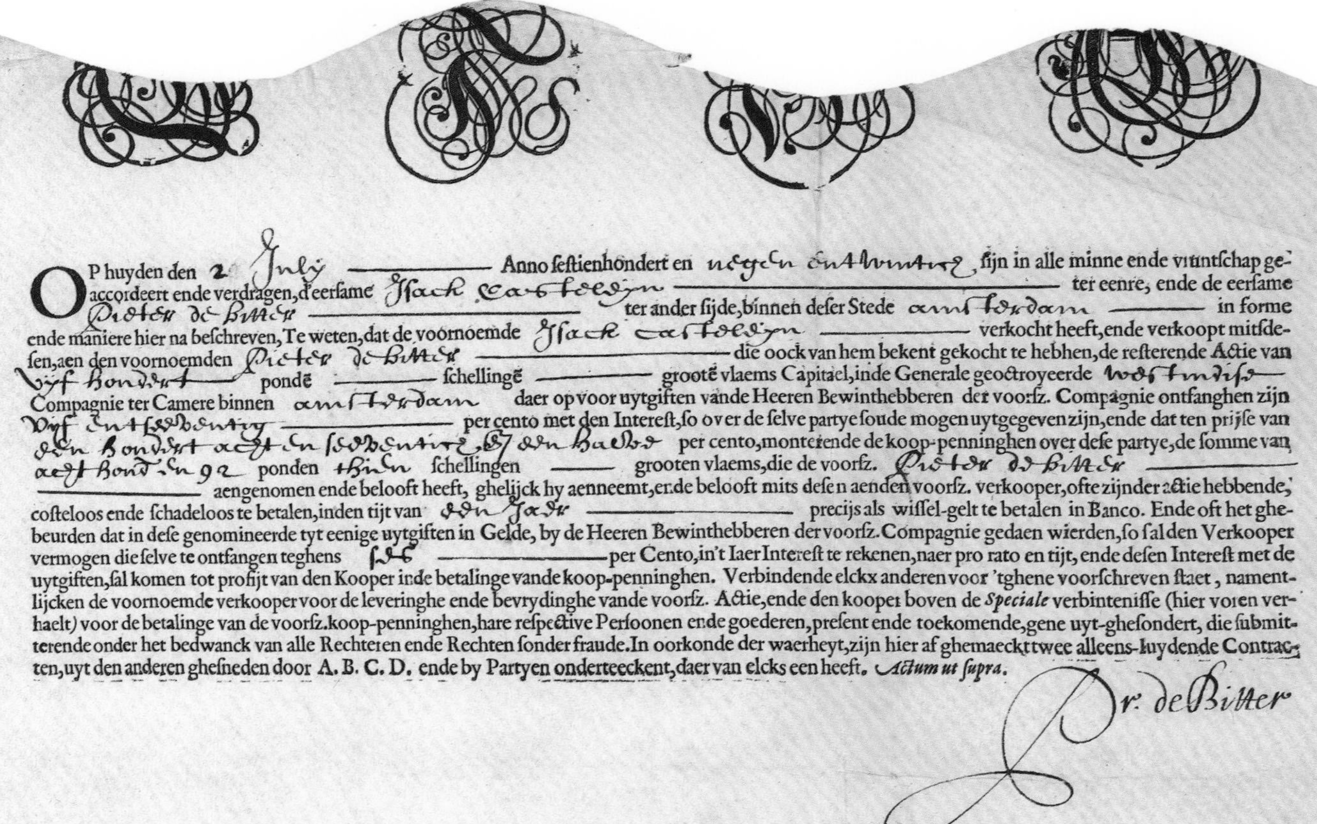
OP huyden den 2 July Anno sestienhondert en negen entwintich, sijn in alle minne ende vriintschap geaccordeert ende verdragen, d'eersame Isack Castoleyn ter eenre, ende de eersame Pieter de Bitter ter ander sijde, binnen deser Stede amsterdam in forme ende maniere hier na beschreven, Te weten, dat de voornoemde Isack Castoleyn verkocht heeft, ende verkoopt mitsdesen, aen den voornoemden Pieter de Bitter die oock van hem bekent gekocht te hebben, de resterende Actie van vijf hondert pondẽ schellingẽ grootẽ vlaems Capitael, inde Generale geoctroyeerde west indise Compagnie ter Camere binnen amsterdam daer op voor uytgiften vande Heeren Bewinthebberen der voorsz. Compagnie ontfanghen zijn vijf entseventich per cento met den Interest, so over de selve partye soude mogen uytgegeven zijn, ende dat ten prijse van een hondert acht en seventich en een halve per cento, monterende de koop-penninghen over dese partye, de somme van acht hondert en 92 ponden thien schellingen grooten vlaems, die de voorsz. Pieter de Bitter aengenomen ende belooft heeft, ghelijck hy aenneemt, ende belooft mits desen aenden voorsz. verkooper, ofte zijnder actie hebbende, costeloos ende schadeloos te betalen, inden tijt van een jaer precijs als wissel-gelt te betalen in Banco. Ende oft het gheburden dat in dese genomineerde tyt eenige uytgiften in Gelde, by de Heeren Bewinthebberen der voorsz. Compagnie gedaen wierden, so sal den Verkooper vermogen die selve te ontfangen teghens ses per Cento, in't Iaer Interest te rekenen, naer pro rato en tijt, ende desen Interest met de uytgiften, sal komen tot profijt van den Kooper inde betalinge vande koop-penninghen. Verbindende elckx anderen voor 'tghene voorschreven staet, namentlijcken de voornoemde verkooper voor de leveringhe ende bevrydinghe vande voorsz. Actie, ende den kooper boven de *Speciale* verbintenisse (hier voren verhaelt) voor de betalinge van de voorsz. koop-penninghen, hare respective Persoonen ende goederen, present ende toekomende, gene uyt-ghesondert, die submitterende onder het bedwanck van alle Rechteren ende Rechten sonder fraude. In oorkonde der waerheyt, zijn hier af ghemaeckt twee alleens-luydende Contracten, uyt den anderen ghesneden door A. B. C. D. ende by Partyen onderteeckent, daer van elcks een heeft. *Actum ut supra*.

Pr. de Bitter

Legal theory gradually followed mercantile practice and legislation eventually regulated established usage.

Godinnen ſlibberglad des Aemstels, die de voet
Van dit ſwaerlyvich werck belickt, wilt u niet belgen
Dat ghy benauwder ſpeelt met uw ſwierende vloedt,
Hier, daerſe keelen vyf met cunst gemetst verſwelgen.
De Burse ryster. tot ontfang der volcken vremdt
Vande langarmde Zee den vader aller meeren.
En van uw maechſchap, dat aen 'sWerelds bodem swemt,
Geſonden om uytheemſch uw ſchulpen te stofferen.
P. C. Hooft Amsterdammer

The Amsterdam Bourse in an engraving by Claes Jansz. Visscher (1612).

SA AMSTERO DAMENSIS

Even though juridical doctrine did not prevent the transmission of debts that had fallen due,[73] these enforceable instruments were often transferred by means of a formal ceding of rights and powers of attorney – clearly a precaution in case it became necessary to demand payment from the debtor in court. In effect, transfers of such debts without formally ceding rights or obtaining the consent of the debtor could result in bad faith. This is suggested by an episode involving a merchant from Porto arrested by the Holy Office. He alleged before his inquisitors that one of his debts pertaining to customs duties had been given in payment for a bill issued on the customs house treasurer in favor of one of his rivals. Instead of requesting payment from him, the rival had proceeded directly to enforce the recovery of the debt. Affronted, the merchant had taken the money to the customs house and said that he did not owe anything to that rival but instead to the customs house and that he had brought cash with him to pay for it.[74]

Along with interest, the practice of discounting began to be justified as early as the fourteenth century, in Italy, being better accepted by some Iberian canonists in the sixteenth century. Rather than a profit on a loan, i.e., usury, these scholars tended to view discounting as purchasing the utility of using money in the present, that is, liquidity.[75] Discounting a bill of exchange was more complicated, since it implied reducing the rate of exchange, which risked leading to interpretations that the exchange, until then consecrated as being legitimate, was in fact usury.[76] The process of understanding these operations was still underway.

In practice, however, signed bills issued in the same location (payment orders) were already discounted in Amsterdam at 8% a year. In some cases, the recipient took on the risk of default and forewent judicial proceedings against the transferor.[77] With regard to bills-obligatory, Malynes related that in northwestern mainland Europe it was possible to "sell them to other merchants that are moneyed men, and abating for [discounting] the interest for the time." In Portugal, sources do not habitually mention the rates of discount while transferring credits[78] and likewise do not mention interest rates. However, it does not seem reasonable that neither interest nor discount rates in transfers of credit was charged, since, as is evident, merchants clearly understood the concepts of opportunity cost, liquidity and the risk of default.[79]

Moreover, matured instruments paid in cash instead of transfers of credit resulted in a reduction. In sixteenth-century Amsterdam, when a credit instrument – bill of exchange or bill-obligatory – was paid in cash to third parties and not by means of assignment, the payee was subject to a deduction in conformance with the rate at the Bourse. According to Herman van der Wee, this deduction (agio) could be as high as 2.5%.[80] In Portugal, even though the Crown tried to check this practice, it tacitly acknowledged it as a convention. In a charter dated August 12, 1553, King John III forbade deductions being charged for paying instruments in cash and mentioned the existence of a current market rate for payments in instruments, i.e., transfer of credits. As the charter was incorporated into the code *Ordenações Filipinas* along with the laws pertaining to "usury contracts," it probably had a similar purpose: to protect ordinary people unfamiliar with commerce – farmers, artisans, and so forth – from the complexities of dealings in transfers of credit, exchanges and financial speculation.

Payments by means of other credits receivable, such as insurance policies, judicial sentences and various kinds of debts, could also involve reductions, even in the case of credits which had fallen due, since the time, effort, and expenditure involved needed to be remunerated.

Current Accounts

Perhaps the most common way of transferring credits as a means of payment was to offset debts, possibly even in preference to credit instruments. Every merchant had current accounts with various other merchants, which were recorded in ledgers. Thus, a merchant would buy goods on the account of a colleague and would debit the value from either the merchandise or the credits he held with him. If he sold products on behalf of the colleague, he would likewise credit his account with the proceeds. The colleague, in turn, would also adjust the assets and liabilities with the merchant in his own ledgers. As has been seen, such accounting transactions were also done by means of bills of exchange issued against each other. From time to time, both parties settled their accounts and pending balances. This was a simple method, which avoided having to deal with coins or credit instruments. On the other hand, it involved the costs and risks inherent in agency relations (principal-agent problem), as we will see in Chapter 9.

The following case is an excellent example of how this system of credit transfers functioned: a master who manufactured cauldrons and kettles, which were essential equipment for sugar mills in Brazilian and confectioners everywhere, had bought some of these utensils, perhaps for resale, from a merchant in Porto for the substantial sum of 1,268,466 réis. This sale, on credit, was registered in a public record. Eighteen months later, the vendor had already received 672,000 réis from the cauldron-maker, for which he issued a release at the same time as he transferred the outstanding credit of 596,466 réis to another merchant in Porto. The transferee had a power of attorney from a third Portuguese merchant, living in Antwerp, which authorized him to receive everything that the cauldron vendor owed him, including the said sum. As a result, the cauldron-maker would be paying indirectly to the merchant in Antwerp. To formalize this transfer, the cauldron-maker agreed to pay the remaining debt to the proxy, who, in turn, was to record these payments in his account books as they were received: "He shall enter these payments in his account books, which entries will be valid as though made in public records." The vendor, in turn, issued a release to the cauldron maker for all accounts between them, striking them all out in his account books.[81]

The following case was even more curious. A petty trader or perhaps a seafarer, possibly even being both simultaneously, received a bill of exchange for a sum of 322,000 réis from a sugar-mill owner in Paraíba – Afonso Neto, one of the conquerors of the captaincy (to the Amerindians)[82] – to

Q. Malynes, *Consuetudo: lex mercatoria*, p. 99. In a case found in the archives in Amsterdam, the haste of the drawer and the drawees to ensure that the payee received the payment before maturity shows that they did not deem the value of time to be negligible. On July 20, 1622, a notary served a notice on a Portuguese Jew at the request of a Dutch merchant who had bought sugar from him. The sugar was sold on the third of the same month for about 2,000 gulden, but with a rebate in case of prepayment. Four days later, the buyer paid most of the value of the goods with two orders of payment on other Dutchmen and, on the 14th of the month, he paid the remainder in cash. Now, six days later, he was asking the seller to collect payment of the orders of payment, as the drawees were willing to pay promptly. The seller replied that he had transferred the orders of payments to third parties and, if they were not collected soon, he would be willing to collect them himself directly from the drawees, take them back from the transferees, and return them to the buyer. It seems that there was good faith and trust among the parties, who collaborated to save on the opportunity cost for all concerned (SR no. 2671).

R. When sums were given or received by means of a currency exchange – i.e., by transfers from one location to another involving a conversion or exchange of currency – the amounts could not be changed when they were paid out by means of transfer of bills of exchange or livranças, i.e., bills-obligatory instead of cash: "while giving and paying by means of bills or bills-obligatory, charging a greater interest [agio] for paying in cash as to the rate at which livranças were exchanged and circulated in the marketplace at the time" (Rau, "Aspectos do pensamento económico português," p. 97). The charter was later incorporated into the *Ordenações Filipinas: Ordenações Filipinas*, book 4, title LXVII, §7.

be paid by a merchant in Porto or another merchant in Lisbon. The bill of exchange still had more than six months to go before becoming due, when the individual stipulated as being responsible for payment (drawee) in Porto sold the payee various lengths of fabric: serge, iridescent (*cangiante*) textiles, fustian, and so forth. According to the parties, the value of the fabrics was equivalent to the sum specified in the bill of exchange at the current market value of the textiles. Then, before a notary in Porto, the payee transferred his rights contained in the bill of exchange to the drawee and vendor in Porto, granting him a power of attorney to receive the sum specified therein from the merchant in Lisbon "or from himself"[83] [sic]. It was understood that, in the latter case, the merchant in Porto would only offset the value of the bill of exchange with the sold merchandise in the accounts that he held with the sugar-mill owner. These current accounts between them did not last long, since two years later the merchant in Porto granted a power of attorney to three merchants in Pernambuco to recover from the sugar-mill owner in Paraíba everything that he still owed him.[84]

Bills of exchange were not necessary to issue payment orders. Counterparts sent them to each other through letters of advice. This was how a prominent sugar-mill owner in Pernambuco, João Pais Barreto, whose family saga has been recounted by Evaldo Cabral de Mello in *O nome e o sangue*,[85] paid the widow of his late boatman, who was owed money:

> *[Letterhead:] Antonio Pereira[,] may God keep him [,] Porto[,] first copy*
>
> *[Text:] Please order that Maria Fernandes, the wife of the late Sebastião Dias, who used to be my boatman and who is with God, be given thirty one thousand three hundred and forty réis, which is what I owe him for the remainder of all the accounts I had with him and demand a public release [from her] certifying how she has received this sum from me on behalf of her husband and I declare that I have issued two copies [of this document] with identical contents, of which only one will be valid; Olinda, April 27, 1615 João Pais Barreto.*[86]

The addressee of this letter of advice gave the widow the said sum in Castilian double reales, that is, *piezas de a dos*, and Portuguese tostões, all in silver, and obtained a release from her.

Certified manuscript copy dated 1597 of an excerpt from the account book of the merchant Manuel Rodrigues Vega, recording the sale of a load of woad to Hans Staes and Hans de Verne, and corroborated by the sworn testimony of Balthasar van Nispen and Joost Brest on behalf of the seller.

Payment order issued by Gaspar Dias in Lisbon to Afonso Rodrigues Cardoso in Amsterdam instructing him to pay 166 pounds Flemish after deducting the amount paid for insurance to Alberto Velecker in Amsterdam, due to a settlement of accounts between Dias and a certain Harman Geraldez (Herman Gerritsz.).

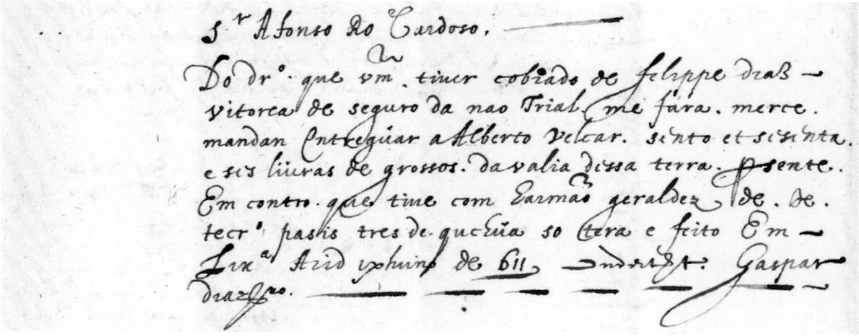
Sr Afonso do Cardoso.
Do dro. que vm. tiver cobrado de felippe dias vitorca de seguro da nao Trial me fara merce mandar entreguar a Alberto Velcar. sento et sesenta e seis liuras de grossos. da valia dessa terra. presente. Em contro. que tive com Darmas geraldez de. de. tecr. pashs tres de quereña so tera e feito Em Lixa. A 20 yohuno de 611 ... Gaspar diaz ...

Merchants maintaining current accounts with each other were sought after for transferring funds by individuals outside the mercantile universe, and even from humble sections of society.[S] Returning to the case described above, in which the first copy of a bill of exchange was lost and the payee presented the second copy thus annulling the first copy, this bill of exchange had been issued against a sum handed over by an abbot of the São Bento monastery in Olinda (deliverer) to be paid to sailors living in the outskirts of Porto (payees).[87] The drawer and the drawee, on the other hand, were well-established merchants in Olinda and Porto. The drawer instructed the drawee to debit the value of the bill of exchange from his account: "and please enter it into my account."[88]

These two incidents show how merchants offered services which resembled banking services, as mentioned at the beginning of this chapter. They maintained current accounts for and with third parties; they transferred money from one account to another; made and received payments on behalf of others; received funds from parties to issue bills to be paid to other parties indicated by the deliverer and settled instruments issued by individuals who maintained current accounts with them.[T]

These assets belonging to third parties entrusted to merchants increased their working capital and expanded their operating capacity. More importantly, in all these financial activities, they themselves created fiduciary money, just like banks lending the deposits received from account holders. By issuing credit on their own assets and on the assets of third parties in their possession, they could engage in a far larger number of transactions[U] than would have been possible if they only used coins and merchandise.[89] However, they risked bankruptcy if they were unable to pay their debts when demanded by creditors. If all creditors demanded payment simultaneously, due to, for example, rumors of insolvency, it could result in financial ruin, which, in its turn, could generate a domino effect in the market.[90]

S. Moreira highlighted the role played by merchants and their credit instruments in repatriating funds earned by emigrants from Viana in Brazil (Moreira, *Os mercadores de Viana*, p. 126).

T. A shipmaster from Biscay allowed his debtor, a merchant from Porto, to draw a bill of exchange in favor of another merchant in Porto with whom the shipmaster had a current account: ADP, NOT, PO2, l. 39, fols. 96v.–98v. (1614-9-20).

U. Roover, a seminal scholar of the development of bills of exchange, overlooked the key role played by these instruments in the growing trade in merchandise during the sixteenth century. He emphasized that the expansion of the international banking system in the sixteenth century was not rooted in the trade in goods, even though it had a significant impact on this trade, but rather was due to the influx of precious metals from the Americas, loans to European treasuries and transfers of money in favor of the Habsburgs and their ventures in the Old World. All these were large-scale transactions, the prerogative of leading banking-merchant houses (Roover, *L'évolution de la lettre de change*, p. 67). However, the trade in merchandise, carried out in large measure by medium-scale merchants, laid down the foundations (and provided the coverage) for financial transactions, which, on the other hand, not just facilitated their activities but even fueled them.

Banker, *attributed to J. Wildens (seventeenth century).*

Banking Activities

From the late Middle Ages, European rulers had sought to prevent crises caused by private currency supply. To this end they restricted or banned the activities of money-changers and private bankers (money-dealers) – who received deposits, often paying interest, and made transfers at the same fair or location, and from one location to another – the most clearly identifiable creators of fiduciary money. Being banned, bankers and money-changers were replaced by merchants and more subtle financial operations.[91]

At the same time, attempts were made to regulate the operations of private banks which were monopolies or virtually monopolies. Such banks were to maintain most of their deposits in coins in their coffers (high cash reserve ratios), stay away from risky investments and deny overdrafts to their account holders. All this was in vain. Even authorized banks repeatedly broke the rules and ended up going bankrupt.[92]

More systematic efforts were gradually introduced, organizing public banks operating on an exclusive or semi-exclusive basis. These banks were to follow conservative banking practices and thus ensure a stable and organized monetary system, maintaining high reserves of precious metals. The process began within the Crown of Aragon and in its sphere of influence; first, in Barcelona (1401), and then in Palermo (1552) and Naples (1584). The movement continued northwards: Genoa (1586), Venice (1587 and 1619), Milan (1597), Rome (1605) and Sienna (1624). It reached its zenith in northwest Europe; in Amsterdam (1609), Middelburg (1616), Delft (1621), Hamburg (1619) and Rotterdam (1635).[93]

The main objective behind the creation of the Amsterdam Exchange Bank, the Wisselbank, in 1609, was not to contain collapse of private banks but rather to prevent the flight of precious metals and the growing use of debased coins in the chaotic monetary system that prevailed in the young Republic. To this end, efforts were made to keep the bulk of the financial flow and good quality coins within the walls, ledgers and coffers of the bank itself. Only the bank was allowed to exchange coins, maintain deposits in current accounts and pay out bills of exchange worth more than 100 pounds Flemish (equivalent to 600 guldens). All calculations were based on guldens, which, as we have seen, were not in circulation but merely served as fixed units of account. The activities of money-changers and private banks were banned, as was assignment of bills of exchange in merchants' account books. Anybody could open an account, as long as they deposited a sum of more than 300 guldens, of which only 3% could be in small or debased coins.[94]

The public placed great trust in the bank. It had, after all, been established in the image of a successful institution, the Banco della Piazza di Rialto, in Venice. Apart from this, it was a municipal body in a city governed by an urban section of society that favored trade and mercantile institutions which supported its expansion. People believed that the municipal authorities would supervise the bank's management and, in case of a crisis, would intervene to ensure solvency. As a public institution, it was expected that the bank would not venture into risky investments as private enterprises tended to do.

The solvency and liquidity of the institution in general, and of the account holders in particular, were guaranteed by the extremely conservative credit policy followed by the bank. In principle, the bank did not lend its deposits and, if it did so, it was generally only to another public or semi-public institution. The bank prohibited its account holders from taking on liabilities without sufficient funds and levied a

3% fine on negative balances. These guarantees were reinforced by the privilege that sums deposited in the bank were exempt from judicial seizure. Moreover, the bank's coffers were also safer than those in any house, office or store.

For merchants, financial operations conducted through the bank offered great advantages. Apart from the aforesaid guarantee of solvency and liquidity, the institution offered reasonable protection against the constant debasement of coins in circulation in the Republic. In addition to the fact that all the accounts were indexed to imaginary guldens, as was common for all types of accounts in the Republic, payments and bills issued were only made in good silver coins. Hence, when receiving payment of a credit at the bank, the creditor ensured its value at official rates, far better than those prevalent in the market; in other words, they were always paid, and they received more silver for their guldens.[95] Hence, it is not surprising that drawees of bills of exchange did their best to pay in cash outside the bank, that is, in coins with a lower metallic value. In notary records in Amsterdam, there is a case of the widow of a Dutch merchant who took advantage of the fact that the value of a bill was less than 600 pounds Flemish to refuse to pay the Portuguese payee through the bank.[96]

On the other hand, bank transactions entailed a series of vexations. Whether it was to draw upon an available balance, transfer money to another person's account, issue a payment order to someone who did not have an account or pay and receive payment for bills of exchange, the account holder had to fill out an application at the bank's premises personally or through a proxy. Furthermore, to receive payment for a bill worth 600 guldens, both the drawee and the payee had to have at least half that sum already deposited in the bank. Often, the promptness and flexibility of being able to issue, settle and transfer instruments and funds privately seemed to be more important than the trust and stability associated with the bank. It was enough for debtors to simply be reliable and solvent and credits not to be converted into baser coins. As a result, bills continued to be paid outside the bank and private banks never ceased operation.

Another no less important matter was the fact that money deposited in the bank did not provide revenue, while, if deposited with other merchants it could be remunerated with interest or profit sharing. Thus, it is reasonable to suppose that an account holder would only keep the money necessary for payments and a reserve for contingencies in the bank in Amsterdam, while investing surplus funds in ventures that could generate greater profits. This was another reason for the resilience of private banks, the so-called *kassiers*, which even used their accounts in the official bank to carry out their private operations such as receiving and making payments from or to individuals having an account at the official bank and wishing to operate in this way, thus keeping their funds safe. After persisting clandestinely for twelve years, the kassiers were readmitted in 1621, subject to the condition that they maintained an account at the public bank, which ensured some cash reserve ratio for their operations.[97]

Ground floor plan of the former City Hall of Amsterdam (1639), showing the area occupied by the Wisselbank on the bottom left.

In Portugal, it was common for wealthy individuals to entrust part of their capital to merchants who invested these funds in their business ventures, by means of silent partnership contracts, or "profit and loss contracts" as they were known. Investors received half the profits the merchant obtained from the capital, but were liable for losses according to the damage. The half of the profits paid to investors compensated them for tying up their capital and the risk, while the merchant's half compensated his industry and the efforts of his agents.[98] If there were no profits, the merchant only returned the principal, without receiving any compensation for his work.

When losses were incurred, merchants could not charge investors more than the capital invested, no matter how much had been lost in the transaction, and would have to repay the loss in full if they or their agents were liable. To avoid any doubt, losses to be incurred by investors had to be justified by two individuals of good standing within a few days. In some cases, merchants were obliged to underwrite capital equal to that of investors and were responsible for half the losses caused by force majeure.[99] In such cases, however, investors would not receive any part of the profits on the capital underwritten by the merchant but only half the profits on the capital that the investors themselves had underwritten. The contracts established that the merchant was responsible for paying all taxes and duties due. They also forbade transactions in prohibited goods and banned investing the loans in maritime, river, or border trade.

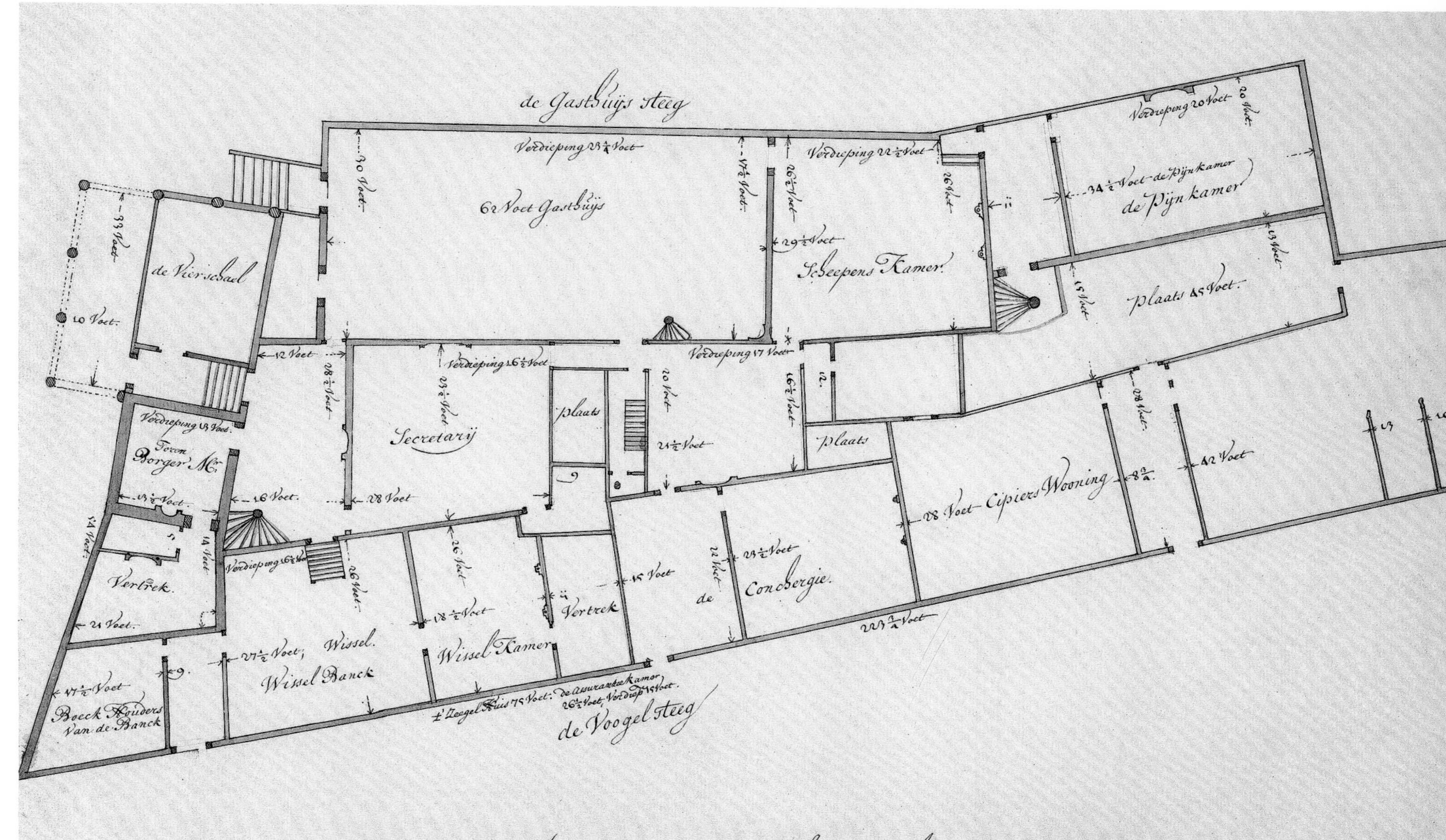

Chest and cart belonging to the Wisselbank in Amsterdam (seventeenth century), used to transport money.

Unlike loans with predefined interest rates, these arrangements were deemed to be legitimate by canonists, who did not view them as loans but rather as partnerships in which both parties were subject to risk. Investors assumed the majority of the risk in the venture (*periculi susceptio*) and hence deserved to be compensated even without working. This type of contract also contributed towards the common good and enabled far more individuals, particularly from the less wealthy sections of society, to participate in trade[v] without having all the capital or shouldering all the risk.[100] These canonical and juridical doctrines explain the designation "profit and loss contracts," which emphasized the random nature of the remuneration for the loan, which could result in profits as well as losses, even though the contracts served to protect the capital and they could conceal interest. This was also true in the case of "partnership contracts"[101] or "companies,"[102] which underscored the fact that these were not loans. Finally, the contracts' format explicitly stated that the profits earned by the investor were legitimate as they were derived from bearing risk in the venture.

These contracts usually had a relatively short duration, generally established on an annual basis, and could be renewed for similar periods.[103] It was common for such contracts to be renewed several times.[104] Some contracts stipulated automatic renewals at the outset in case investors did not provide a notice of non-renewal shortly before the contract elapsed,[105] or enabled the merchant to use the capital continuously until the investor asked for accounts to be settled.[106]

It is almost certain that these operations were far more profitable than other investments available to the urban patriciate and aristocracy at the time, which generally consisted of different types of leased properties and rights.[107] It is therefore reasonable to suppose that investors wished to increase the performance of their portfolios by including a riskier component, which had the potential to generate higher profits. Moreover, the short duration of such contracts meant the investments had greater liquidity and could be better adjusted to the debasement of currency and inflation than rentals or leases generally spanning several years, and even to lifelong or perpetual arrangements. However, it was essential for investors to trust in the integrity and commercial skills of the merchants to whom they entrusted their capital.

Thus, a widow in Porto invested 100,000 réis in cash in the activities of a merchant in her city for a one-year period.[108] The contract was renewed and the widow asked the merchant to settle her accounts and pay her what was due only a year and a half after loaning the sum,[109] when she needed the money.[110] Another widow, this time an aristocrat, invested a sum that was more than five times greater than that of the first widow, for a period of almost five years, until she asked for her accounts to be settled.[111] Not all investors, however, belonged to the upper echelons of society. There were also professionals, such as basket weavers,[112] phlebotomists[113] (specialists in drawing blood from patients for therapeutic purposes), and silk weavers,[114] who probably sought to extract greater profits from their savings by means of mercantile transactions and were willing to take the inherent risks.

v. In the same ordinance, dated October 4, 1540, that authorized moderate interest rates in transactions between traders up to a limit of 12% in the Low Countries, Charles V forbade individuals who were not traders to deposit funds with merchants and enter fixed-profit silent partnership contracts. However, deposits were allowed in companies in which individuals who were not traders associated with a merchant on a "profit and loss" basis. Anyone infringing these rules was subject to having their money confiscated and being declared public usurers (Roover, *L'évolution de la lettre de change*, pp. 124–125; Van der Wee, *The Growth of the Antwerp Market*, v. 2, p. 358).

Portrait of a Merchant, *supposedly Egbert Gerbrantsz., and his wife, attributed to Dirck Jacobsz. (1541).*

It is not known if the ban on investing in foreign, maritime or river commerce, which was standard practice in these contracts, was followed diligently. The fact is that even if merchants used the loaned money in domestic operations, this released a corresponding part of their own capital to invest wherever they wished. In some cases, it even seemed contradictory: a contract stipulated that the merchant was to invest the money in sugar and other wares, legitimate and current in Portugal, but could not use it or risk it in maritime trade or banned goods. Perhaps the loan was meant to be invested in the resale of sugar and wares within Portugal or perhaps the Iberian Peninsula. However, it was more likely to be a monotonous repetition of a conventional formula, as notary formulas often tend to be.[115]

There were also individuals who deposited sums with merchants at fixed interest rates. Notwithstanding civil and canonical prohibitions, these transactions were justified as being investments in trade and hence, in principle, involved risk, at least that of the merchant going bankrupt. The assets left by Diogo Dias Querido,[w] who had been an important merchant in Bahia and died in Amsterdam, included the considerable sum of 3,000 cruzados that had been entrusted to his brother-in-law, yielding 6.25% per year. As the sum was indicated in a Portuguese monetary unit, viz. the cruzado, accompanied by a conversion into pounds Flemish, it is highly likely that the investment would have been made still in Portugal or in Brazil.[116] In fact, various sources suggest that money was deposited at that interest rate[x] with merchants, who then used them in their mercantile activities or even lent them to third parties at higher rates of interest. An intermediate formula was to invest at fixed interest rates in a company.[117]

Merchants everywhere lent each other money by other means, using the exchange rates between different locations and the incorporated interest, exporting and repatriating sums through bills of exchange,[118] or simply against bills-obligatory. In Amsterdam, loans against bills-obligatory paid 5% to 8% interest. From 1602 onwards, shares in the East India Company (VOC) could accompany such loans as collateral. Oscar Gelderblom and Joost Jonker have affirmed that the growing solidity of the VOC, supported by the States-General, and whose shares could easily be transferred or judicially seized to pay debts, facilitated the use of its shares as collateral for loans through bills-obligatory. This mechanism would have encouraged an increasingly wider circle to invest in trade, since it not only offered coverage for the loans but also liquidity since creditors had the option of transferring the credit instrument to third parties along with the collateral.[119]

W. As will be seen, Diogo Dias Querido was a partner of Miguel Dias Santiago when the former was in Bahia and the latter in Pernambuco.

X. According to Eddy Stols, in Antwerp in the first half of the seventeenth century, short-term interest rates among merchants ranged from 5% to 6.25%, while deposits earned 5.5 to 6% (Stols, *De Spaanse Brabanders*, v. 1, pp. 320–321).

Cash Flow

Chapter Eight

1. ADP, NOT, PO1, l. 131, fols. 250–251 (1611-6-17); PO2, l. 25, fols. 19–20v. (1606-3-3).

2. PRO, SP, 9/104, fols. 110, 111, 128v.–129v.

3. *Ordenações Manuelinas*, book IV, title XIX, §§1, 6 and 7; Rau, "Aspectos do pensamento económico português," p. 97; *Ordenações Filipinas*, book IV, title LXVII, §7.

4. SR No. 1977.

5. Gelderblom and Jonker, "Completing a Financial Revolution," pp. 646, n. 26, 647 n. 33.

6. Malynes, *Consuetudo: vel, lex mercatoria*, p. 102.

7. Almeida, *Aritmética como descrição do real*, v. 2, pp. 165–166.

8. Ibid., pp. 174–183.

9. "Jesus, in Porto, on December 4, 1614, you shall pay 400 cruzados at sight for this third [copy] of this [bill of] exchange, if you have not paid either the first or the second copy, to Mister Manuel Lopes Nunes, 400 cruzados at 114 groten per cruzado, the sum received here from Mister Luís Mendes, and enter it into the account as per advice. [May] Christ [be] with all, Jan van Lancker to Melchior Werner, may God keep him, [in] Hamburg, [or] to Volbert Vaninge, Flemish merchant, may God keep him, [in] Amsterdam": ADP, NOT, PO2, l. 41, fols. 36v.–38 (1615-6-18).

10. Roover, *L'évolution de la lettre de change*, pp. 43–45; J. F. Marnoco e Souza, *Das letras, livranças e cheques* (Coimbra: França Amado, 1905–1906), v. 1, pp. 2–190.

11. ADP, NOT, PO2, l. 40, fols. 150v.–151 (1615-6-15); Malynes, *Consuetudo: vel, lex mercatoria*, p. 104.

12. ADP, NOT, PO2, l. 19, fols. 51v.–53v. (1603-1-8).

13. Malynes, *Consuetudo: vel, lex mercatoria*, pp. 394–400.

14. Roover, *L'évolution de la lettre de change*, pp. 44–45, 55, 72–73.

15. Ibid., pp. 50–52.

16. Rau, "Aspectos do pensamento económico português," p. 92.

17. Carande, *Carlos V y sus banqueros*, pp. 345–348; F. Rico, "Resolutorio de cambios de Lázaro de Tormes (hacia 1552)," *Dicenda: Cuadernos de Filología Hispánica* 7 (1987): 117–131, passim; Roover, *L'évolution de la lettre de change*, pp. 108–109.

18. Almeida, *Aritmética como descrição do real*, v. 2, p. 368.

19. Rau, "Aspectos do pensamento económico português," pp. 99, 115.

20. *Ordenações Filipinas*, book IV, title LXVII, §5.

21. See, for example: PRO, SP, 9/104, fols. 35v., 43–54, 85. See also: Mello, *Gente da nação*, pp. 46–48.

22. "Jesus, in Porto, on September 12, 1614, I, Jan van Lancker, Flemish merchant shall pay 225,500 réis for this first copy of this [bill of] exchange to Mister Luís Mendes [viz.] 225,500, the sum received from him in sugars to my satisfaction, which I shall pay to him within eight days after this document is prepared and I will ensure good payment to him in that period. [May] Christ [be] with all, Jan van Lancker...": ADP, NOT, PO2, l. 41, fols. 36v.–38 (1615-6-18).

23. ADP, NOT, PO2, l. 10, fols. 105–107 (1598-3-10).

24. See ch. 10.

25. ADP, PO2, l. 29, fol. 47 (1609-8-6).

26. Rau, "Aspectos do pensamento económico português," p. 116.

27. Moreira, *Os mercadores de Viana*, p. 126; Almeida, *Aritmética como descrição do real*, v. 2, pp. 366–367; ADP, NOT, PO2, l. 16, fols. 49–51v. (1601-4-14); charter dated July 30, 1592, in *Documentos para a história do açúcar*, v. 1, p. 397; "Provizão e Regimento do Consulado Portuguez," in J. F. Borges, *Fontes, especialidade, e*

excellencia da administração commercial. Segundo o Código Commercial Portuguez (Porto: Typ. Commercial Portuense, 1835), pp. 35, 43, 59; D. N. Leão, *Leis extravagantes collegidas e relatadas pelo licenciado Dvarte Nunes do Liam per mandado do muito alto & muito poderoso rei Dom Sebastiam Nosso Senhor* (Lisbon: Antonio Gonçalvez, 1569), fol. 33v. ff; *Ordenações filipinas*, book I, title LI.

28. Go, "Marine Insurance in the Netherlands," pp. 76–77.

29. PRO, SP, 9/104, fol. 85v.; Malynes, *Consuetudo: vel, lex mercatoria*, p. 116.

30. ADP, NOT, PO2, l. 47, fols. 97v.–98v. (1617-12-9).

31. ADP, NOT, PO2, l. 29, fols. 181v.–183 (1609-10-29).

32. ADP, NOT, PO2, l. 29, fols. 166–67v. (1609-10-24).

33. Malynes, *Consuetudo: vel, lex mercatoria*, pp. 398–406; Almeida, *Aritmética como descrição do real*, v. 2, pp. 340–341.

34. Rau, "Aspectos do pensamento económico português," p. 116.

35. Malynes, *Consuetudo: vel, lex mercatoria*, pp. 101–102.

36. Ibid.; Roover, *L'évolution de la lettre de change*, pp. 94–96.

37. SR nos. 3210, 3620.

38. The text of the bill of exchange reads as follows: "To António Fernandes Esteves in the Porto. Olinda, February 28, 20,000 réis two months after sight. If the first [copy] has not been paid, you will pay against this second copy of [bill of] exchange to Pedro Duarte or Marcos Dias 20,000 réis, the sum received from the Reverend Father Friar [sic.] Paulo Peixoto, abbot of São Bento, and enter it into my accounts. Christ [be] with all, Francisco Gomes Pina": ADP, NOT, PO2, l. 39, fols. 6–6v (1614-7-8 [sic])

39. ADP, NOT, PO2, l. 41, fols. 36v.–38 (1615-6-18).

40. Sluiter, *Os holandeses no Brasil antes de 1621*, p. 201.

41. "...And whatever remains you will load or send in any other carrack or ship sailing to this kingdom [Portugal] if you do not find any safe bill of exchange by which to send them [proceeds] and if you are unable to find neither a bill of exchange nor space aboard a ship you will send them in cash aboard the hulk that you deem fit bound for Lisbon or Viana": ADP, NOT, PO2, l. 4, fols. 11–13 (1595-7-5). See also: Costa, *O transporte no Atlântico*, v. 1, p. 189

42. "...And send us everything that you can send to us through bills of exchange, as long as they are drawn by safe and reliable individuals; and ensure that they will be payable at two months after sight or at most three months and if possible in less time [...] And when you cannot send them [the proceeds] via bills of exchange, then send them in pepper in the first good passages [i.e., homebound ships]": Almeida, *Aritmética como descrição do real*, v. 2, p. 357.

43. Brandão, *Diálogos das grandezas do Brasil*, p. 108; Lima, "Sugar and Metals as Commodity Money," pp. 6–7.

44. Malynes, *Consuetudo: vel, lex mercatoria*, p. 97.

45. Ibid., pp. 96–97.

46. Ibid., p. 99.

47. Roover, *L'évolution de la lettre de change*, pp. 87–88, 90.

48. Ibid., pp. 94–100, 114; Van der Wee, "The Influence of Banking and the Rise of Capitalism in North-West Europe," in A. Theichova, G. K. Hentenryk and D. Ziegler (eds.), *Banking, Trade and Industry: Europe, America and Asia from the Thirteenth to the Twentieth Century* (Cambridge: Cambridge University Press, 1997), pp. 181–184, 188, n. 9; Van der Wee, *The Growth of the Antwerp Market*, v. 2, pp. 340–349, 343; Malynes, *Consuetudo: vel, lex mercatoria*, pp. 98–99; Carande, *Carlos V y sus banqueros*, v. 1, pp. 323–324.

49. Malynes, *Consuetudo: vel, lex mercatoria*, pp. 99–100; Roover, *L'évolution de la lettre de change*, pp. 84, 92, 98.

50. ADP, NOT, PO2, l. 41, fols. 36v.–38 (1615-6-18).

51. Roover, *L'évolution de la lettre de change*, pp. 86–87, 94, 96–99; Malynes, *Consuetudo: vel, lex mercatoria*, p. 394; Van der Wee, *The Growth of the Antwerp Market*, v. 2, pp. 334–339; Van der Wee, "The Influence of Banking," pp. 182–183; Roover, *L'évolution de la lettre de change*, pp. 97–98, 114.

52. Roover, *L'évolution de la lettre de change*, pp. 99–118.

53. The document called it a bill of exchange, but in truth it was a bill-obligatory.

54. For some reason the contract stipulating the transaction was not signed, at least not before the notary: ADP, NOT, PO2, l. 19, fols. 173–174v. (1603-3-20).

55. On Pedro Rodrigues da Veiga, see: SR nos. 31, 68, 98, 214, 237, 431, 448, 449, 450, 471; Swetschinski, "Kinship and Commerce – The Foundations of Portuguese Jewish Life in 17th-Century Holland." *Studia Rosenthaliana 13*:2 (1979): 66.

56. Such as, for example, in ADP, NOT, PO1, l. 146, fols. 209–210v. (1623-6-10); fols. 218v.–219v. (1623-06-13); PO2, l. 23, fols. 82v.–85v. (1605-4-2).

57. ADP, NOT, PO2, l. 42, fols. 81v.–82v. (1616-2-29).

58. ADP, NOT, PO1, l. 146, fols. 209–210v. (1623-6-10); fols. 218v.–219v. (1623-06-13); PO2, l. 19, fols. 173–174v. (1603-3-20); l. 23, fols. 82v.–85v. (1605-4-2); l. 25, fols. 19–20v. (1606-3-3); l. 37, fols. 154v.–155 (1613-8-17); l. 42, fols. 81v.–82v. (1616-2-29).

59. ADP, NOT, PO2, l. 28, fols. 125v.–127 (1609-7-13).

60. ADP, NOT, PO2, l. 29, fols. 44v.–47v. (1609-8-6).

61. The sources for the district of Porto are available only from 1818 onwards, and the sources for the Court of Appeal of Porto from 1755 onwards: ADP/JUD/TCPRT; ADP/JUD/TRPRT.

62. ADP, NOT, PO2, l. 29, fol. 45.

63. PRO, SP, 9/104, fols. 110, 111, 128v–129v.

64. Malynes, *Consuetudo: vel, lex mercatoria*, pp. 96, 98–102.

65. In Antwerp: SR nos. 293, 756, 2389, 2407 and 2424, 2781, 2893 and 2914, 3202 and 3261. In France: SR nos. 2188 and 2532; first in Middelburg and later in Antwerp: 1329, n. 109. Apparently in Amsterdam: SR nos. 2753, 3156. For instances of bills-obligatory being formally ceded in notary records in Amsterdam, see: SR nos. 799, 1459, 1985, 2377, 2796, 3210, 3323, 3449 – they refer to instruments which had not been paid yet and the deeds probably sought to formalize the right of the transferees to recover the monies from the respective drawees or drawers abroad, or which were part of larger and more complex agreements.

66. SR no. 778.

67. ADP, NOT, PO2, l. 6, fols. 29v.–31 (1596-8-23); SR nos. 2033, 2044.

68. ADP, NOT, PO2, l. 31, fols. 20–21v. (1610-1-13); l. 43, fols. 62v.–63v. (1616-7-10).

69. ADP, NOT, PO2, l. 15, fols. 23v.–25 (1600-10-19).

70. SR no. 1703. See other cases in SR nos. 1413, 1656, 1685, 1699, 1710, 1703, 2002, 2157, 3027, 3110, 3268. Although some notary records do not explicitly cite a decision by the Amsterdam Insurance Chamber, the context suggests that the policies had been adjudicated: SR nos. 1838, 2012, 2075, 2201, 2270, 2976. With regard to the use of insurance policies as a means of payment in Venice, see: Tenenti, *Naufrages, corsaires et assurances maritimes à Venise*, p. 63. For payments with transfers of cargoes, insurance policies and debts fallen due overseas, see also: Ebert, "The Trade in Brazilian Sugar," pp. 140–141.

71. SR nos. 1699, 1710.

72. SR no. 3111. Violet Barbour describes (probably with regard to the second half of the seventeenth century) a range of business dealings with numerous credit instruments: Barbour, *Capitalism in Amsterdam in the Seventeenth Century*, p. 55. See also: Dehing and 'T Hart, "Linking the Fortunes," pp. 54–55; Gelderblom and Jonker, "Completing a Financial Revolution," passim.

73. Roover, *L'évolution de la lettre de change*, pp. 90–94, 105–106, 109–110; Malynes, *Consuetudo: vel, lex mercatoria*, pp. 97, 99.

74. IANTT, STO, IC 11260, fols. 158v.–159.

75. J. Huerta de Soto, "La teoría bancaria en la Escuela de Salamanca," in *Nuevos estudios de economía política.* (Madrid: Unión Editorial, 2002), pp. 73–99; M. de Azpilcueta, L. Ortiz, M. Grice-Hutchinson, E. Lluch and B. Schefold, *Comentario resulutorio de cambios* (Dusseldorf: Wirtschaft und Finanzen, 1998), p. 281, n. 231, through the writings of Muñoz de Juana, "Scholastic Morality and the Birth of Economics," p. 32; Roover, *L'évolution de la lettre de change*, p. 129; Grotius, *The Rights of War and Peace*, XII: XX–XXI.

76. Roover, *L'évolution de la lettre de change*, pp. 55, 72–73, 129–130, 144.

77. SR nos. 2559, 2394. For the risk shouldered by the transferee, see: SR no. 2559. It is evident that discounts were practiced before the period mentioned by Raymond de Roover: "In truth, the practice of discounting was relatively recent: no trace of it can be found before the seventeenth century in England and before the eighteenth century in continental Europe": Roover, *L'évolution de la lettre de change*, p. 119. In effect, Van der Wee stated that discounts were already an established practice in Antwerp during the early seventeenth century: Van der Wee, "The Influence of Banking," pp. 183–184.

78. Moreira affirms that endorsements was practiced in Viana in the transfer of bills-obligatory, which he called "credit missive bills," as well as of bills of exchange that did not involve a currency exchange, which he called "simple bills." Moreira further states that such endorsements were done "by means of certain discounts." He referred to a transfer, without expressly mentioning endorsement, in which the bill was worth 17,000 réis and was transferred for 65,000! Could this bill have been only one of the means of payment for the higher sum?: Moreira, *Os mercadores de Viana*, p. 125.

79. Stols states that the sale of merchandise at a "rebate" was a common practice in Antwerp during the first half of the seventeenth century, interest of 7% to 8% being deducted per year. However, according to a coeval Flemish report, this practice was not in vogue in Portugal. The author also emphasized that mercantile rebates (on the sale of goods) should not be confused with financial discounts, evidence of which he found in only a single case. On the other hand, Stols avers that endorsements were not rare and that a vendor who had received a bill of exchange in payment drawn on a location with which the vendor had little or no dealings could transfer it to another merchant who had greater contacts in a larger number of locations, and could hence recover the funds more easily. Wouldn't this amount to a discount of the instrument without deducting interest? It is possible that the absence of signs of discounts, *strictu senso*, i.e., the rebate of interest, was due to the informal nature of such operations, and the custom of concealing the interest: Stols, *De Spaanse Brabanders*, v. 1, pp. 322–324 and nn. 250, 258, 261.

80. Van der Wee, *The Growth of the Antwerp Market*, v. 2, pp. 345–346, 358–360.

81. ADP, NOT, PO2, l. 6, fols. 160v.–162v. (1596-11-13). See another case in: ADP, PO2, l. 26, fols. 180v.–183v. (1607-4-6).

82. Gonçalves, *Guerras e açúcares*, p. 240; Ricupero, *A formação da elite colonial*, pp. 309–310.

83. ADP, NOT, PO2, l. 37, fols. 154v.–155 (1613-8-17).

84. ADP, NOT, PO2, l. 41, fols. 57v.–58v. (1615-7-26).

85. It is not clear if this referred to the father or, more probably, to his son of the same name: E. C. de Mello, *O nome e o sangue: uma parábola familiar no Pernambuco colonial* (Rio de Janeiro: Topbooks, 2000), pp. 23–24, 49, 56, 64, 71, 101, 163, 198, 294–296.

86. ADP, NOT, PO2, l. 41, fols. 53–54 (1615-7-17).

87. The information that the beneficiaries of the bill – Pedro Duarte, living in Massarelos, and Marcos Dias – were sailors is derived from other documents, but it is possible that these other documents refer to individuals with identical names living in the same suburbs of Porto: ADP, NOT, PO2, l. 15, fols. 62–63v. (1600-11-8); fols. 112v.–116 (1600-12-19); l. 35, fols. 138v.–142 (1612-7-16).

88. ADP, NOT, PO2, l. 39, fols. 6–6v. (1614-7-8 [sic]).

89. Van der Wee described the importance of fiduciary money for the development of Europe in the sixteenth century: Van der Wee, *The Growth of the Antwerp Market*, v. 2, p. 366. See also: Roover, *L'évolution de la lettre de change*, pp. 117–118.

90. Huerta deSoto, "La teoría bancaria en la Escuela de Salamanca," pp. 88–94; Carande, *Carlos V y sus banqueros*, v. 1, pp. 319–323, 338–339; Van der Wee, *The Growth of the Antwerp Market*, v. 2, p. 333.

91. R. de Roover, "New Interpretations of the History of Banking," in J. Kirshner (ed.), *Business, Banking and Economic Thought in Late Medieval and Early Modern Europe. Selected Studies of Raymond de Roover* (Chicago: University of Chicago Press, 1974), pp. 219–223; Spufford, "Access to Credit and Capital," pp. 320–321. Malynes described the process thus: "Many Merchants trafficking only in Exchanges become good observers, and as ingenious as the Bankers themselves, according to the Adage *Fabricando fabric simus*": Malynes, *Consuetudo: vel, lex mercatoria*, p. 406.

92. Roover, "New Interpretations of the History of Banking," pp. 217–219; Van Dillen, "The Bank of Amsterdam," pp. 83–86; Spufford, "Access to Credit and Capital," p. 322.

93. Roover, "New Interpretations of the History of Banking," pp. 223–229; G. Luzzato, "Les banques publiques de Venise (siècles XVI–XVIII)," in J. G. van Dillen (ed.), *History of the Principal Public Banks* (London: Routledge, 1964), pp. 39–64; Spufford, "Access to Credit and Capital," pp. 322–323.

94. Van Dillen, "The Bank of Amsterdam," pp. 84–92.

95. Quinn and Roberds, "An Economic Explanation of the Early Bank of Amsterdam," pp. 2–8; Barbour, *Capitalism in Amsterdam in the Seventeenth Century*, pp. 44–46; Dehing and 'T Hart, "Linking the Fortunes," pp. 45–46.

96. SR nos. 1684; 2654.

97. Van Dillen, "The Bank of Amsterdam," pp. 84–86, 92; Spufford, "Access to Credit and Capital," pp. 305–307; Dehing and 'T Hart, "Linking the Fortunes," pp. 43–44.

98. "...and the profits that Our Lord may provide by means of trade and the use of the said 200,000 réis will be divided, half going to him, Simão Vaz da Costa, in return for the efforts and industry of his person to keep for himself and his factors and agents, and the other half of the said profits will be handed over to Manuel Francisco as his profit for investing his money, and risking and venturing it...." ADP, NOT, PO2, l. 134, fol.103. This was a vestige of the medieval *commenda* and *societas maris* contracts, see R. S. Lopez and I. W. Raymond (eds.), *Medieval Trade in the Mediterranean World* (New York: Columbia University Press, 2001), pp. 174–175; J. H. Pryor, "Commenda: The Operation of the Contract in Long-Distance Commerce at Marseilles during the Thirteenth Century," *Journal of European Economic History* 13:2 (1984): passim.

99. ADP, NOT, PO2, l. 134, fols. 102–105 (1613-2-26).

100. Ceccarelli, "Risky Business," passim; Roover, "The Organization of Trade," pp. 53–57; Melé, "Early Business Ethics in Spain," pp. 182–184; Roover, *L'évolution de la lettre de change*, pp. 124–125; Van der Wee, *The Growth of the Antwerp Market*, v. 2, p. 358.

101. ADP, NOT, PO1, l. 131, fols. 184v.–185v. (1611-3-29).

102. ADP, NOT, PO1, l. 139, fols. 138–139v. (1617-8-18).

103. ADP, NOT, PO2, l. 8, fols. 105–107 (1597-6-18); l. 35, fols. 178–180 (1612-8-14).

104. "...and because they were bound by contract for forming the said company between them [...]in the manner in which it has been operating until now, each of them was paid their due share of the profits remaining after accounts were settled": ADP, NOT, PO2, l. 23, fols. 101–104v. (1605-4-19); l. 22a, fols. 29–30v. (1606-12-11). ADP, PO1, l. 139, fols. 138–139v. (1617-8-18).

105. ADP, NOT, PO2, l. 134, fols. 102–105 (1613-2-26).

106. ADP, NOT, PO2, l. 14, fols. 242v.–244v. (1600-9-7).

107. Moreira, *Os mercadores de Viana*, pp. 104–124

108. ADP, NOT, PO2, l. 23, fols. 101–104v. (1605-4-19).

109. ADP, NOT, PO2, l. 22a, fols. 29–29v.

110. ADP, NOT, PO2, l. 22a, fols. 29–30v. (1606-12-11).

111. ADP, NOT, PO2, l. 14, fols. 242v.–244v. (1600-9-7).

112. ADP, NOT, PO1, l. 131, fols. 89v.–91v. (1610-12-30); ibid., fols. 184v.–185v. (1611-3-29).

113. ADP, NOT, PO2, l. 41, fols. 70–71v. (1615-9-9).

114. ADP, NOT, PO1, l. 134, fols. 102–105 (1613-2-26).

115. ADP, NOT, PO1, l. 136, fols. 66–67v. (1615-7-29).

116. SR no. 3039. On Diogo Dias Querido, see: SR no. 574 n. 51; Mello, *O nome e o sangue*, pp. 37, 47; *Primeira visitação do Santo Officio às partes do Brasil: denunciações da Bahia*, pp. 86, 122–124; *Segunda visitação do Santo Ofício às partes do Brasil, confissões da Bahia*, pp. 150, 509; Oliveira, *A História do Brazil de Frei Vicente do Salvador*, v. 2, fols. 128v.–129.

117. With regard to these practices, see: Almeida, *Aritmética como descrição do real*, v. 1, pp. 197, 251–252; v. 2, pp. 100–106; Moreira, *Os mercadores de Viana*, pp. 121, 123, 127; Gelderblom and Jonker, "Completing a Financial Revolution," p. 646. See also: Costa, *O transporte no Atlântico*, v. 1, pp. 232–233; Stols, *De Spaanse Brabanders*, v. 1, pp. 320–321.

118. Roover, *L'évolution de la lettre de change*, pp. 74–82; idem, "What is Dry Exchange? A Contribution to the Study of English Mercantilism," *Journal of Political Economy* 52:2 (1944): passim; Rau, "Aspectos do pensamento económico português," passim; Almeida, *Aritmética como descrição do real*, v. 1, p. 253, v. 2, pp. 340–341; Gelderblom and Jonker, "Completing a Financial Revolution," pp. 645–646; Stols, *De Spaanse Brabanders*, v. 1, pp. 324–325.

119. Gelderblom and Jonker, "Completing a Financial Revolution," pp. 646–648, 651, 660.

Chapter Nine

The Merchant Georg Gisze; *Hans Holbein, the Younger (1532). A member of the urban patriciate of the Hanseatic city of Danzig (Gdansk), this merchant's portrait is set in his office in London, to where he emigrated. He is holding a letter from his brother, and in the Baroque spirit, the Latin motto on the wall reminds us: "No pleasure without regret."*

Overseas

Agents and Agency Relations

By definition, overseas trade required that goods, cash or credit be transferred abroad, to be exchanged for other products, currency or funds, which, in their turn, would be sent back or remain abroad at the merchant's disposal. Merchants could handle these operations themselves, traveling along with their wares, but were then exposed to risks along the way and wasted a lot of time in transit. Moreover, their capital would be tied up a single voyage at a time, the risk was concentrated and business opportunities were limited. The use of agents made trade more efficient and flexible, and possibly less risky. From their offices, merchants could oversee a range of simultaneous operations and adjust them as circumstances changed.

Illustration from The Costume Book *(1520–1560), by Matthäus Schwarz, showing him in his office with Jacob Fugger (right). Schwarz was Fugger's accountant. One of the wealthiest men of his time, a member of a German banking family, Fugger loaned money to governments, financed armies and leased mining rights. The signs in the background show some of the cities where the Fuggers had agents, including Lisbon (below, right).*

However, merchants' relations with their agents were not all rosy. Agents posed a series of challenges and risks for merchants. Ineptitude, neglect, delay, indecision or undue haste could be just as detrimental to invested capital as malicious fraud. Merchants were vulnerable to an agent's personal travails, such as bankruptcy, illness or death, even if these misfortunes had nothing to do with the service being provided.

At this time, the sugar trade was not based on hierarchically organized firms with head offices in one market and branches in others. In general, merchants traded individually. Even though the term appears often in the sources[1] and the literature, during this period there were no proper factors[A/2] – i.e., salaried representatives who generally worked exclusively for a merchant in a foreign marketplace, lending greater rigidity to the organization of trade.[3] In practice, the individuals who were generally designated "factors"[B] were counterparts whose role is analyzed in the following pages.[4] At the time, merchants favored a more flexible and adaptable model than the companies and factors that characterized the period between the fourteenth and sixteenth centuries, and were frequently adopted by large merchant-banker families such as the Medicis, Affaidatis, Schetzes and Fuggers, and, subsequently, the India companies, albeit with considerable differences.[5]

In this context, as we will see at the end of this chapter, merchants generally traded with different marketplaces through a portfolio of agents, each with different characteristics, who were linked to the merchants through various types of agency arrangements. The composition of this portfolio changed constantly, so as to better correspond to a merchant's interests. Those interests were often contradictory

– dilemmas that were resolved within the prevailing legal, political, social and religious constraints.

The different types of arrangements can be divided into two main groups: those in which the hired agent lived in the foreign marketplace and those in which he managed the capital entrusted to him during a voyage. The first group was made up of merchants who lived continuously in a trading hub, where they carried out a wide range of mercantile, financial and bureaucratic operations on behalf of their overseas principal. Of course, established residency in a trading center did not mean staying there continuously and forever, and it was common for merchants to relocate from one trading center to another, and to travel on business.[6] However, this did not imply that they were traveling agents, whose function as intermediaries was inextricably linked to their travels and short sojourns in overseas marketplaces. Fixed agents were often well-established merchants, while traveling agents were typically modest traders. Here, the term trader is used arbitrarily to designate individuals who engaged in mercantile activities at some point, but were not wholesale merchants rooted in a trading center.[7]

The most common agency arrangement between two well-established merchants was that of counterparts – one carrying out transactions on behalf of the other on a reciprocal basis, and being remunerated by means of commissions on the commercial and financial transactions entrusted to them.[8] Counterparts often engaged in joint commercial ventures from time to time, and it was not uncommon for them to form long-term partnerships lasting several years. The fact of being partners in certain ventures did not preclude individual business operations, which were kept separate; nor did it affect their relationship as counterparts.

In partnerships, they divided the capital, the risk, the profits and the losses, generally on an equal basis, although sometimes the remuneration of the capital and the labor invested by the partners were in different proportions. It was also common for the diverse expenditure and revenues to be distributed between them according to the comparative advantages of each merchant or their respective trading centers, and the purpose of the partnership.[9]

Among traveling agents, "supercargoes" were somewhat similar to partners: they were entrusted with large sums, and all indications are that they were entitled to a share in the profits. They were employed when one or more merchants chartered space for a large cargo or even chartered the entire capacity of a ship ("voyage charter"). They were meant to oversee all as-

A. Malynes described factors thus: "a Factor is created by Merchants Letters, and taketh Salarie or provision of Factoridge: [...] a Factor is bound to answere the losse which happeneth by overpassing or exceeding his Commission [...] Factors therefore must bee very carefull, to follow the Commissions given to them, very orderly and punctually [...] Factors doe deale most commonly for divers men, and every man beareth the hazard of their actions [...] which is the cause that Intimations, Citations, Attachments, and other lawfull courses [...] take no place against Factors unlesse they have Procurations" (Malynes, *Consuetudo: vel, lex mercatoria*, p. 111).

B. In truth, sources mention the term far more with reference to the representatives of consortiums which leased rights, taxes and monopolies from the Crown, such as those for salt and brazilwood. They were the sole representatives for given regions and acted on behalf of the entire consortium or one of its members; Cornelis Snellinck, for example, originally from Antwerp, was the factor in Amsterdam for the consortium which leased brazilwood exports (SR no. 138). Francisco Rodrigues Ribeiro and António Dias Ribeiro were both factors of André Lopes Pinto, who leased a salt contract (SR no. 987).

pects of the voyage except for the technical aspects of navigation; they established which ports the vessel would visit, the itineraries to be followed, the time spent waiting at ports, and departures. They decided which part of the merchandise would be loaded and unloaded at each port, often in conjunction with their principal's counterparts or partners living in the respective center, from whom they received, or to whom they transmitted instructions. Furthermore, if the principal also owned the vessel, the supercargo could be entrusted with the task of supervising the vessel's administration.

Most traveling agents – i.e., traveling commissioners – however, took small consignments and/or letters of credit with strict limits, and brought the proceeds of the transactions back to their principal after deducting sale and purchase commissions, in the same manner as counterparts. There were also arrangements that combined both transport and agency services, wherein the shipmaster and/or the pilot were entrusted with the tasks of an agent, and were remunerated for both services. There were also relationships combining agency services and mercantile credit into a single venture. These were the so-called sea loans (or more specifically "bottomry" contracts), in which the merchant lent a certain sum – in goods, cash and/or credit – for an agent to invest during a voyage. In exchange, if the agent returned safe and sound with the proceeds from the venture, he would return the sum along with a fixed rate of interest, irrespective of the profits or losses of the enterprise. The merchant bore the risks of force majeure – fire, water and predators – while the agent, often the shipmaster, pilot, and other owners, typically pledged their share in the vessel as a guarantee for the payment.

It is important to emphasize that these roles were not professions but rather forms of agency relations which co-existed with the agent's other activities – such as trading, shipping, minor itinerant commerce, practice and artisanship – and they often occurred alongside other commercial relations with different merchants, employing either the same or other modalities.

Resident Agents

Previous chapters have mentioned some activities linked to transport and the methods and means of payment provided by, or relying on, counterparts and partners. It would now be opportune to examine these and other functions at greater length. An account book belonging to a merchant named Miguel Dias Santiago (or "de Santiago") recorded his transactions, such as debts, credits, payments, receipts, the dispatch and arrival of shipments, revenues and expenditure associated with these operations, and so forth. These records span the period between 1596 and 1617, during his sojourn in Salvador, Olinda and Lisbon. This is not the only record of the merchant's accounts and therefore does not cover all his transactions or the entire period. Furthermore, the series are not continuous, and some deal more with certain types of transactions and specific kinds of trade relations. Still it clearly illustrates the activities of a fixed agent living overseas. Santiago's account book has already been the subject of a preliminary study by the historian of Pernambuco José Antônio Gonsalves de Mello,[10] and some of its data has been examined by other authors – Harold Livermore, Engel Sluiter, Frédéric Mauro, Stuart B. Schwartz and James C. Boyajian.[11] Yet it still merits more in-depth research.

Indian chest made in Cochin in the first half of the seventeenth century. Items like this, taken from Portuguese India to Europe, were both goods in themselves and containers for other wares, such as textiles.

Santiago was probably born in northern Portugal, his family's homeland. In 1596, he was living in Salvador (Bahia) and he remained there until the first half of 1599, when he moved to Olinda (Pernambuco). In mid-1601, on his return to Portugal, he settled in Lisbon. It is not clear whether he relocated to Antwerp between the second decade of the seventeenth century, when the entries in his account book become scarcer, and 1627, when he or a namesake held the office of consul of the Portuguese nation there, the equivalent of the head of the body representing Portuguese merchants in Flanders.[C] In 1628, he or a similarly named individual also appeared to be living in Porto, with ties to Old Christian families.[12]

One of the consignments that Santiago received in Pernambuco in 1600 arrived aboard the Norwegian hulk *Adam and Eve,* and had been shipped from Lisbon by Paulo de Pina.[13] The products were accompanied by their respective bill of lading and an invoice recording their prices and diverse costs incurred in Portugal while loading them "under decks," based on which the "profits" were calculated. In this case, these costs included various charges associated with clearing the goods through customs and the averages paid to the shipmaster before setting sail from Lisbon. Insurance contracts were also mentioned within the costs of other consignments Santiago received in Brazil.[14]

C. Hans Pohl indicates that Miguel Dias Santiago, the same merchant mentioned in the records analyzed here or a namesake, was one of the "consuls of the Portuguese nation" in Antwerp in 1627; see: H. Pohl, *Die Portugiesen in Antwerpen (1567–1648)* (Wiesbaden: Steiner, 1977), p. 354.

The cargo was shipped in diverse numbered containers, some in chests from India used as furniture to store domestic items, occasionally carved, painted and inlaid with mother-of-pearl or lacquered, which were also merchandise. One of the chests from India received in this consignment contained basic cotton and woolen textiles; tammy, baize and serge. The following table provides a more precise idea of the composition of a consignment shipped to Brazil to be sold in order to generate funds to purchase sugar.

Number of pieces	Product	Quality	Length	Value per unit of length (réis)	Total value (réis)
5	tammy	dyed	286 ells	255	72,930
2	baize	with a thread count of 80	107 cubits	390	41,730
1	baize	with a thread count of 100	44 cubits	490	21,560
3	serge	–	–	–	6,000
1	chest	From India with a key	–	–	3,000
Total	–	–	–	–	**145,220**

This hulk's consignment also included another chest from India, which was simpler and held together with nails, which reinforced the structure and also served as decoration. Likewise, this second chest contained simple fabrics, primarily baize, and 80-quintal containers (320 arrobas each) of salted codfish.

All told, the consignment sent aboard the *Adam and Eve*, and another consignment, also received by Santiago, shipped aboard a German hulk, the *Wild*, from Lübeck, were worth a total of 1,870,700 réis. At least five individuals invested different sums in both consignments, including Santiago himself. In all likelihood, these hulks also transported consignments for other people – and, here, it is possible to clearly discern the strategy of spreading cargoes over different vessels to mitigate risks.

Acting as a counterpart for this five-man consortium headed by Paulo de Pina, the merchant who shipped the goods in Lisbon, Santiago sold both cargoes, except for the portions earmarked for two other investors who lived in Brazil, and other shares which he handed over to agents of Portuguese investors – not including almost one-third of the codfish, which was spoiled.[D] The goods were sold to various individuals on different terms and with varying profit margins. The 107 cubits of 80-count baize mentioned above, for example, were sold to four individuals for different prices: 650, 700, 730, and 800 réis, per cubit. Prices were probably set in accordance with the variables associated with selling on credit: the period, means of payment (coins, sugar, etc.) and the buyer's reputation.[15]

Made of angelim *wood and tinplate, this is the same chest shown open on the previous page, now shown closed.*

From the proceeds he obtained by selling the consignments shipped on these two hulks, Santiago deducted the freight charges for the incoming journey, various customs charges, payments for the trans-

port from the port located in Póvoa do Recife to the dock in Olinda, and cartage charges for carting the goods from the dock up a steep hill to his home. Known as the Varadouro to this day, the dock was the site where the boats, caravels and galliots arriving at Olinda on the Beberibe River (generally from the port of Recife) unloaded their cargo. Even though Santiago said the goods had been transported from Recife to the dock by "cart," they would almost certainly have been transported by river, or else would have traveled overland through the isthmus that linked Recife to Olinda.[16] Finally, he deducted from the revenue his commission for the sale as a counterpart, at the rate of 8%. These costs amounted to 190,700 réis, and both shipments together rendered a profit of 1,109,498 réis in Brazil, almost 60%.

D. For example, the Brazilian stakeholder, António Ribeiro, who owned a smaller share, would receive 30,000 réis divided in the following manner: 10,000 in codfish, another 10,000 in passementerie (fabric adornments) of his choice, 4,000 in Segovia hats and 6,000 in a length of raxa (coarse woolen fabric), silk skeins or ribbons, as he wished; products which arrived aboard the *Wild*, a German hulk (PRO, SP, 9/104, fol. 58v.).

Allegory of Autumn: Saleswoman Serving Distinguished Clients in the Frankfurt Weinmarkt; *attributed to Lucas van Valckenborch and Georg Flegel (1594).*

Gonçalo Gonçalves, the Younger, and his wife, Maria Gonçalves, *in seventeenth-century dress (1620). This work is one of the rare portraits of members of the colonial elite.*

The merchandise received was not always sold to end users. Many buyers were also merchants, possibly interested in stocking up on the goods or satisfying orders from their customers. Even so, merchandise was also sold directly to sugar-mill owners, and even to the governor of the captaincy at the time.[17]

Santiago also consigned merchandise to retailers. Basic foodstuffs, which were controlled by the authorities, tended to entail complications. He therefore had to go to court to secure the release of barrels of wine – whose volume was less than they were meant to contain – which had been sent on behalf of his principals.[18] Storing wine, as well as other bulky products, often required renting space in a "lodge" (*logea*), or warehouse, as Santiago did to store the forty-four casks of wine that arrived aboard the same caravel that had brought a consignment of twenty-four barrels of tuna.[19]

Perishable products were also problematic. Of those barrels of tuna Santiago received in Olinda on behalf of the same Paulo de Pina, only one could be sold at a good price. Four barrels were never even put up for sale. Five were handed over on consignment to four retailers – one male and three female. Two of them never paid, since the tuna had spoiled, and one retailer even had the fish thrown into the sea. Finally, Santiago handed over eight barrels to another of Pina's agents, who sold them on credit for a third of the price, "so that they would not be written off entirely." The best price obtained for one of those barrels, which, at the port of departure, before being loaded, had cost 1,240 réis each, after deducting all the other expenses, was 3,000 réis. The others were sold at 1,800, 1,600, and even at 1,000 réis on credit![20]

Santiago bought sugar with the proceeds of these sales, received sugar as payment, and even purchased sugar at his principals' request with funds from their current accounts. From the sugar he purchased on their behalf, Santiago deducted a commission of 5%.[21] In Brazil, the counterparts' commission for purchases was 5%, and was generally 8% for sales,[22] even though there were cases[23] in which these commissions did not exceed 4%, perhaps because the goods were wine and tuna, marketable products with low value per unit and, which afforded narrow profit margins.[E] The fact that the commissions for sales were higher than those for purchases was probably justified because it was relatively harder to sell the various products sent to the colony than to buy the goods requested, usually sugar.[24]

Apart from his purchasing commission, Santiago also deducted other costs incurred on account of the goods being exported: leasing warehouses where the sugar was stored before being loaded, customs duties and expenses for transferring the goods from the warehouse to the "well" – the deepest area between Recife and the reefs beyond which ships anchored.[25] In addition, he paid the shipmasters averages before departures and demurrage[26] – and, in order to ensure that there were no delays, he had to make arrangements to load the return cargo within the laytime his principals had agreed with the shipmaster.[27]

While he was carrying out all these operations on behalf of his principals[F] – counterparts and partners – in Portugal, the latter also served as his agents in Portugal. He shipped them sugar and merchandise for them to sell there or re-export to other marketplaces,[28] and they also received sugar he sent on behalf of his principals in other trading centers. Aboard one ship that set sail from Pernambuco for Viana, for example, he loaded four crates in partnership with a cousin and two sacks of cotton in partnership with a merchant in Salvador,[29] Diogo Dias Querido. With Querido, he also traded in a partnership within the colony, sending goods to Espírito Santo and Rio de Janeiro.[30] Prior to this, when he lived in Salvador, Santiago re-exported sugar from Ilhéus.[31]

Financial transactions played quite an important role within the activities of fixed agents. Santiago accepted and paid bills of exchange drawn by his principals on him; in the other direction, he also received sums from third parties (deliverers) and issued bills of exchange requesting his counterparts and partners – his agents – to pay others. Similarly, he and his partners and counterparts remitted sums to each other through bills issued by third parties on their respective counterparts.[32] For collecting debts and taking care of transferring funds through bills of exchange drawn by third parties, Santiago received a commission equivalent to that which he received for purchases, that is, 5%.[33]

Santiago acted in different ways at the request of his principals. He often facilitated operations in which he only had a small stake, in some cases the activities of other agents, some of them traveling ones, and even concluded operations which had been begun by principals before leaving Pernambuco, to which Santiago had moved from Bahia. Such operations included payments, customs clearance, freights, renting warehouse space, hiring guards for wares, donations to religious brotherhoods, judicial proceedings, and so forth. As for revenues, he charged and collected payments on account of loans, sales made on credit, rentals, revenues from plantations and leased rights.

He received some of these revenues in the form of sugar, some in cash and some in credit instruments; bills of exchange, offsetting entries in current accounts and diverse types of credit transfers from third parties. Sometimes parties transferred to him securities whose value was more than or less than the debt, which meant that he had to adjust for the remainder. While matching accounts, outstanding debts could be paid off through accounting entries, offsets and assignment of credits which the debtor was due from third parties.[34]

Sugar in warehouses ready to be loaded was used as a means of compensation. Santiago received slaves and merchandise as payment, which he later resold. All these payments involved time and risk, and required considerable mathematical skills. In the case of payment in sugar, he sometimes received from the same debtor "sugar at different prices," which had to be duly calculated. He also sued recalcitrant debtors.[35]

E. Sometimes, the commissions on sales and purchases could add up to 15% altogether. On the other hand, Manuel António Fernandes Moreira, writing with regard to the sugar trade in Viana (do Castelo), stated that counterparts deducted a commission of up to 10%, not on sales and purchases but on the profits of the entire operation (Moreira, *Os mercadores de Viana*, p. 206).

F. The term "principal" here is used generically to indicate any merchant who entrusted another party with managing his capital, even if in a joint partnership and irrespective of the structure (horizontality) of the relationship between the parties.

Back in Portugal

In Lisbon, Santiago carried out similar activities as in Brazil, the difference being that he now did so on behalf of his principals in the American colony and other trading centers. First, he negotiated payments for transport costs with shipmasters bringing sugar and other goods from Brazil.[36] The solubility of sugar meant that it was highly susceptible to mishaps during the journey – often part or even all of the contents of crates were destroyed by water. In such cases, Santiago ensured that the shipmaster discounted the freight charges for the respective goods, and included the value of the lost arrobas in the general averages, which, as we have seen, served to distribute damages among all consignors as well as the shipmaster.[37] In one such case, of the forty-five crates that Santiago received from a shipmaster named Francisco Tomé, one crate arrived empty while eight crates were damp.[38]

The merchant also had to verify whether the goods that the shipmaster delivered to him matched what the senders had shipped. On one occasion, it was found that he had received a crate of panela sugar instead of the muscovado sugar which had been sent. The crate in question had been switched and, even worse, another five crates were found to be missing. Santiago noticed the discrepancy in time, and the shipmaster promised to pay the difference, pledging his "keep" (*refeição*) as a guarantee – which probably corresponded to revenues he was entitled to receive for the voyage: his "advantages," salary to top crewmembers; his share in the profits of the voyage; and/or his "plate" (*prato*), the food allowance which crew members were entitled to receive while sailing or while waiting in ports, in the latter case commonly paid in cash.[39]

The solubility and relatively high value of sugar necessitated prompt action even when the product was on land. Santiago had to pay to remove twenty-two crates in the customs complex from the rain.[40] On another occasion, he paid customs officials to remove the crates from the yard and "sleep with them"[41] – here it is not quite clear whether the danger was expected from the weather or from thieves.[G]

Santiago strove to minimize damage to his principals' sugar as well as his own. Of the consignment of forty-five crates received from Francisco Tomé, he sold the dry crates and removed the contents of the damp crates, repackaged what he could salvage, and shipped it on to Hamburg and Holland. The fact that he sent damp sugar to northern Europe is not surprising. Once there, it would probably have been refined, and the damage caused by salt water would have been mitigated.[42] Similarly, a damp crate that had arrived in a consignment of four containers was sold to a confectioner, where it would be cooked and mixed with other ingredients.[43] On another occasion, Santiago found a more unusual solution: a crate of muscovado sugar made from "dregs" (*somenos*), that is, from the scum or from molasses left over from the purging process (normally sold at a much lower price),[44] "was refilled and mixed with the damp white [more valuable] sugar that remained in the crates classified as general averages [being damaged]."[45]

Clearing goods through customs involved further expenditure and care. A large number of customs duties were payable in Portugal, which, as with other costs, the agent later deducted from the principal's proceeds. Santiago's records suggest that payments made in Portugal were often based on weights recorded in the colony. However, when a crate arrived without a weight certificate or the certificate diverged greatly from the physical consignment, goods were weighed at the customs house in Portugal and

In this scene of the famous display of saffron and spices in Nuremberg, we see activities characteristic of both customs and weighing houses: declaration, examination and, when necessary, certification of goods.

the merchant recorded the results to show his principal any discrepancies that might be found.[46]

Santiago also hired workers to unload cargoes, paid cartage up to the "lodge," and rented space when necessary. For goods being sold, he paid cartage for taking goods to the official weighing scale and paid workers for weighing the goods. He sometimes also had the buyer's mark[47] stamped on the crates.[H] On occasion, he paid for the goods to be delivered to the purchaser.[48] Finally, he deducted the "brokerage" fee for the sale, which, more than being a fee for broking deals properly speaking, was an emolument paid to a city official who certified the sale and served as a witness in cases of disputes.[49]

As in Brazil, Santiago received cash, goods and credits as payment in Portugal as well. In Lisbon, he sold sugar on credit to foreigners in exchange for "scripts," i.e., bills-obligatory, and he received scripts from third parties as collateral for the payment for twenty-five crates of sugar sent to him by

G. This was also the case with expenditure incurred to "take crates in the customs complex indoors at night" (PRO, SP, 9/104, fol. 39v.).

H. With regard to the late seventeenth century and the early eighteenth century, Antonil states: "The mill's mark, even using a heated brand, is stamped on the crate's front panel, near the bottom, in the right corner, so as to ascertain any shortcomings that might have occurred while packing the sugar.… If the mark of the sugar-mill owner or merchant on whose behalf it is being shipped is stamped with a heated brand, it is stamped in the middle of the said crate's front panel. If it is not stamped with a heated brand, the person's name is put in the same spot with ink, which can be removed with an adz when the crate is sold to another merchant, replacing it with the name of the person buying the crate" (Antonil, *Cultura e opulência do Brasil*, p. 168).

The Calling of Matthew; *Jan van Hemessen (1536). The theme of Jesus summoning Matthew (a tax collector and future apostle and evangelist), gave early modern artists an opportunity to portray the activities of the businessmen of their time. In this scene, we see merchants, leaseholders, and bankers or moneylenders receiving payments in cash and credit, checking and entering accounts and putting away ledgers.*

a cousin living in Pernambuco.[50] In the context of his partnership with this cousin, he sold four crates of white sugar to a foreigner, "in exchange for warehouse scripts" that the foreigner had received for selling his own goods to third parties, that is, wholesale merchants.[51] He also sold goods in Lisbon on credit.[52]

As a counterpart, he received commissions on sales, which, in Lisbon, were much lower than in Brazil, generally being 3%,[53] and sometimes 4%.[54] One can only speculate whether this lower percentage could be explained by the higher absolute prices of sugar in Portugal. Furthermore, the higher commissions paid in Brazil were probably meant to cover opportunity costs and compensate for the inconvenience of traveling to and even residing in the colony. In some cases, without explaining why, Santiago decided to forego his sales commission and the rental charges for leasing space in his store, where the sugar was kept: "And there is no extra charge for commission and storage."[55] He did not enter any sugar that he was unable to sell immediately – owing to its poor condition – in the accounts of his principals or partners, but instead waited to see what price they could fetch.[56]

In Lisbon, Santiago also re-exported sugar that had been sent to him from Brazil. Of a shipment of nine crates sent from Paraíba on behalf of a merchant living in the colony, he sold five crates of white sugar to a Frenchman and one crate of muscovado sugar to another foreigner. He sent the three remaining crates to a New Christian merchant in Antwerp, to whom he also transferred the proceeds from the sale of the other (aforementioned) six crates from this consignment, after deducting costs.[57] The transfer was made through a bill of exchange drawn by a third party, whose value, recorded in cruzados, would be paid in Antwerp by the brother-in-law of the drawer in pounds Flemish in accordance with the exchange rate stipulated in the credit instrument.[I]

Santiago also re-exported goods to the Mediterranean. He shipped a valuable cargo – worth 512,335 réis – to Venice, on a carrack that was apparently Dutch, on behalf of one of his nephews in Brazil, João de Paz.[58] In the opposite direction, he sent products to Brazil, some on behalf of merchants in the colony, others on behalf of their partnerships with third parties, and yet others for himself. Half of the forty quintals of codfish he sent to João de Paz were sent on De Paz's behalf, while the other half was sent on his own account.[59] Santiago also sold products from northern Europe in Lisbon on behalf of his principals in Brazil. He sold sixty pieces of serge from Dunkirk, in a 50-50 partnership with his cousin in Pernambuco.[60] He shipped peaches and pears, European products, to the Low Countries[J] on behalf of João de Paz.[61]

He carried out some transactions – buying, selling and re-exporting – on the instructions of his counterparts and other parties, which he called "commissions." He conducted other transactions at his own initiative, probably because he thought these deals would be profitable for his principals. In addition, he took care of transactions – planned and unplanned alike – for his principals in other trading centers. Sugar shipped on behalf of Diogo de Paiva, who, to all appearances, lived in Pernambuco, ended up in Porto. Santiago made sure that one of his nephews who lived in that city unloaded, cleared, stored and sold the merchandise, for which he paid him a commission of 2% after deducting his own commission.[62]

The interdependence of Portuguese trading centers meant that Santiago maintained counterparts in other ports around Portugal. Thus, on another occasion, he charged a commission of 2% from that same nephew in Porto. This commission was on account of the sale of another shipment of sugar, from Paraíba, to a foreigner, who paid for the goods by transferring some "warehouse scripts." Santiago entered the value of the credit instruments to

I. The costs deducted from the sale price consisted of similar expenses as those mentioned in the context of imports into Portugal along with other costs associated with exports and sales, such as brokerage fees for the six crates, customs duties and expenses incurred while loading the crates being re-exported – bands and nails to secure the containers, a boat to take the crates to the ship, cartage up to the boat and a clerk. Finally, Santiago also charged 3% commission for selling the goods in Portugal and re-exporting them (PRO, SP, 9/104, fols. 114v.–115).

J. He generally called the region Flanders, which could designate the southern Low Countries, the Dutch Republic or the entire northwest area of continental Europe.

the account of his aforesaid nephew's brother-in-law.[63] Another merchant, this time from Viana, sent merchandise to Bahia and Pernambuco on Santiago's behalf, being paid a commission of 2% for his services, apart from costs, which, in this case, included expenditure on account of pitch, nails and caulking.[64]

He also took out insurance or ordered it be purchased in the Low Countries for his partners and counterparts,[65] and carried out financial transactions on behalf of principals in Brazil. On a single day, he made two payments in Lisbon on behalf of his nephew in Pernambuco. The first was for a payment order that his nephew had sent him in favor of a merchant who was related to both of them. The second payment comprised the settlement of a bill of exchange drawn by the nephew on Santiago, which was presented to him by the payee.[66] Santiago sometimes credited the profits from a mercantile transaction carried out on behalf of a principal in Brazil to the account of another merchant, a counterpart of the former and his own counterpart as well, who lived in another trading center in Portugal, probably following instructions.[67]

As his own account book entries indicate, Santiago recorded transactions realized on behalf of his principals. He must also have kept other papers documenting these transactions, such as bills of lading, letters of credit, insurance policies, receipts and releases, and even other journals and ledgers. He kept in touch with his partners and counterparts,[68] rendered accounts to them and received accounts from them. From time to time they settled the relevant account on request, or if any of them died.[69]

All these activities were tiring and time consuming. To assist him, Santiago had at least one Flemish retainer, that is, a Dutch-speaking assistant.[70] It was common for merchants to employ cashiers to take care of their ledgers and accounts, perhaps the most tiresome and tedious part of their activities. The different handwritings and styles in Santiago's account book suggest that he, too, used the services of such assistants.[71]

Assigning Supercargoes

Let us examine the case of the supercargo. On behalf of ten investors, Álvaro de Azevedo, a prominent merchant in Porto, entrusted an enormous sum in credit and merchandise to Paulo Rodrigues de Aguiar, a young trader living in Aveiro, who was to act as their agent on a voyage to Pernambuco with a stopover in the Canary Islands.[72]

As Aguiar (the supercargo) himself invested resources in the venture, there were thus a total of eleven investors. Eight participated with goods alone, from which Aguiar was to trade for profit; two only invested by means of letters of credit entitling the agent to draw bills of exchange on them or receive funds from their other agents in the Canary Islands. The agent was to use the assets to buy twenty-three casks of wine. Azevedo, who was the head of the consortium and served as the interface with the other investors, was also the largest investor in the venture. Apart from merchandise, he gave the agent a letter of credit with a limit of up to 500,000 réis, allowing him to draw bills and have funds available should money fall short to purchase the eighty casks of wine the agent was to purchase in the Canary Islands, which were later to be sold in Brazil. The agent pledged to comply scrupulously with the agreement – written down in an "instruction signed by both parties."

Investors with merchandise	***Residence***	***Value (réis)***
Álvaro de Azevedo	*Porto*	617,100
Paulo Rodrigues de Aguiar	*Aveiro*	150,000
Paio Rodrigues de Paz	*Viana*	
Marçal Saraiva	*[Pontevedra]*	360,000
Domingos Pereira	*[Madrid]*	
Domingos Lopes Vitória	*Porto*	160,000
Paulo Nunes Vitória	*Vila do Conde*	100,000
Francisco de Lima	*Figueira da Foz*	100,000
Antonio Mendes Ribeiro	*Porto*	50,000

Investors with letters of credit	***Residence***	***Value (réis)***
Gonçalo Cardoso da Fonseca	*Porto*	*Credit equivalent to 23 casks of wine in the Canary Islands*
Antonio Fernandes Esteves	*Porto*	
Álvaro de Azevedo	*Porto*	< 500,000 *To supplement shortages in the other shares*

Let us see what was stipulated in the instructions. The agent was to travel aboard the ship on which the goods had been loaded, as stated in the shipmaster's bill of lading. The vessel would first go to Santa Cruz or Garachico, on the island of Tenerife, where he was to try to sell whatever he could for the highest possible price. At any rate, he was to fill the eighty empty casks he was taking with him. Fifty-seven casks were to be filled with wine purchased with the proceeds from the merchandise he sold, and twenty-three from funds obtained by means of the two letters of credit. The wines to be purchased were to be "of the best possible quality."

If the agent managed to obtain more money from the sales than was necessary to fill the fifty-seven casks, he was then to buy as much wine as possible. If the opposite scenario happened, and the proceeds from the sale were not enough to fill the fifty-seven casks, then he was to use Azevedo's letter of credit. This letter authorized him to draw bills of exchange until he managed to purchase the fifty-seven casks for up to 500,000 réis and was able to set sail as soon as possible – "not exceeding this order in any manner whatsoever, with neither a greater nor lesser quantity, always seeking to be on your way as soon as possible." If the two letters of credit issued for the purchase of the other twenty-three casks were not honored, the shortfall could be bridged both by the letter of credit issued by Azevedo and the proceeds of the merchandise being sold there. However, everything to be purchased with supplementary credit from Azevedo would be sent exclusively on his account and not on behalf of the "company," that is, with the other merchants.

The agent was to continue from the Canary Islands on to Pernambuco as soon as the wine casks had been filled. He was to unload them at the destination along with the rest of the goods taken from Portugal, "seeking to sell them immediately and diligently" for cash at current prices: "according to circumstances in that land." Furthermore, he was instructed to sell as little as possible on credit and to extend credit only to merchants "with lodges," that is, well established wholesalers, whose securities would be more easily negotiable and recoverable. Such credit was only to be extended for a short period, which would not oblige him to tarry in Brazil. In other words, the investors felt that it was best to realize their earnings as fast as possible rather than to charge interest for selling goods on credit. Any debts that could not be recovered in time would be entrusted to two resident merchants who were Azevedo's agents. Any poor-quality goods that were not sold in time would likewise be handed over to them instead of selling them at a loss. Finally, as per the same instructions, these merchants would take the agent's place in case of his absence, illness or death.

With the proceeds of these sales he was to buy the best sugar available, be it white, muscovado or panela, as long as it was of the best quality he could find. He was specifically instructed that under no circumstances was the white sugar to be "round," that is, from the middle of a sugar loaf, which was of inferior quality compared to the upper part of the loaf,[72] "but only from the whitest and driest, the good ones, or the more or less all right." In the case of panela sugar, the concern was that "it should not be sticky," which probably meant that such sugar should contain a higher ratio of sugar crystals to molasses.[73]

In order to spread the risk, Azevedo instructed his agent to ship the merchandise back to Portugal in batches of up to twenty assorted crates, wherein such lots combined different types of sugar: white, muscovado and panela. Each lot was to be loaded onto a different ship. Azevedo hoped that his agent would do his best "to load on the best ships," aboard which space would be leased with freight charges and averages "as is customary." The agent was to take steps to advise him beforehand which cargoes had been loaded on which ship, and who the respective shipmasters were, so that he or another of the investors would have enough time to insure the goods.

On the homebound journey, the vessels were to sail to either Porto or Viana. If they went to Porto, the crates were to be consigned to Azevedo, and if they went to Viana, then they were to be sent to an investor who lived there. In case the goods had to be shipped to Lisbon, owing to a lack of options or circumstances, they were to be consigned to a merchant who was a cousin and brother-in-law of two other investors, and the nephew of a third investor. The bills of lading were to specify whether the goods were being shipped on behalf of the "company" or just in Azevedo's name, having been purchased with the proceeds of the wine bought in the Canary Islands with his supplementary credit. To avoid confusion, the agent was to do his best to separate crates purchased from the sale proceeds from those purchased with the letters of credit issued by the two merchants and goods bought with Azevedo's credit.

Between twenty and thirty assorted crates purchased with the proceeds from the sale of merchandise were to be loaded onto the ship on which the agent would return to Portugal. Furthermore, as it had been agreed with the shipmaster of the vessel that had taken the cargo on the outward journey that it would bring back sixty crates on the homebound voyage, the agent was instructed to fill the remaining space with cargo belonging to third parties, possibly Alvaro's fixed agents there – "You shall try and fill the remaining space [with goods shipped] by friends."

Aguiar promised to comply with all the clauses of his instructions and pledged all his assets, particularly the goods he was taking with him, which could be seized, wherever they were, until the investors had received their due. He also undertook to render accounts for the entire venture to Azevedo, or anybody else he appointed. However, he would not have to report to the other investors, "companions and associates," which would be Azevedo's responsibility. The merchant and the agent presented these "instructions" to the notary, who copied them in a public deed which both parties signed. The text emphasized that each party kept an identical transcribed copy of the document. It is curious to note that the deed was witnessed by a priest and a "Flemish" retainer in the merchant's employ.

Here, unlike Santiago's account book, the source only describes what the agent should do, and not what he purportedly did. There are no clues as to the actual outcome of the voyage.[L] In most cases, the arrangements with and instructions to agents were not issued as public deeds, and possibly not even written down as private documents. The fact that this specific case was formally documented probably had to do with the large sums being invested and the extensive network of geographically scattered investors.[M]

Aguiar was entrusted with a substantial cargo and credit. Other agents taking such valuable assets often operated as "supercargoes." Supercargoes[N] were more commonly employed on longer voyages, with lengthier stopovers and/or on routes that entailed many ports of call – particularly routes infested with pirates – and voyages whose itineraries were subject to changes along the way, according to the anticipated conditions. The presence of supercargoes on the route between Brazil, Portugal and the Low Countries was more common when various stops were made in Portuguese and Galician ports (in northwest of the Iberian Peninsula), first heading for a port further north or to the largest port. Once there, they would decide whether to continue on to the next harbor, and which port that would be. This was also the case with voyages to the Algarve and with the triangular trade with Brazil, via Africa,[O] during which long sojourns were common, and various ports could be either included or excluded.[74]

Unfortunately Azevedo's instructions shed no light on how Aguiar would be paid for his services. This is also the case with most sources mentioning supercargoes and agents accompanying large consignments, who could also have served as supercargoes.[75] However, some agreements for journeys from

K. "There are different qualities of white sugar, namely, fine sugar, round sugar and low sugar. All these are 'male' sugars, i.e., purged in a mold. Fine sugar is whiter, more crystallized and heavier, and hence it is normally the first part of the loaf, which is called the 'face' of the loaf. Round sugar is slightly less white and is less crystallized, and is commonly found in the second part of the mold, and I say commonly because this is not an infallible rule; it can happen that the face of some loaves are less white and less crystallized than the second part of another loaf" (Antonil, *Cultura e opulência do Brasil*, p. 167).

L. This agreement was signed in June 1613, when Paulo Rodrigues de Aguiar was possibly less than twenty years of age. The only other information available about Aguiar is that he had passed through Cartagena de las Índias (now in Colombia) prior to October 1615; in November 1616, he was back in Porto, where he was a witness to a marriage dowry; he had already returned to Pernambuco in November 1617 and April 1618, where he received powers of attorney from individuals in Porto; and, in September 1618, he was supposed to send sugar from Pernambuco to Álvaro de Azevedo (ADP, NOT, PO2, l. 42, fols. 24–24v. (1615-10-31); l. 44, fols. 50v.–52 (1616-11-24); l. 47, fols. 54v.–56 (1617-11-18); l. 48, fols. 151v.–153 (1618-4-20); IANTT, STO, IL 728, fols. 5v.–6; IL 11867 (session dated 22.7.1620); IL 1159, fol. 12v.).

M. As mentioned, few contracts for freight and for transmitting credit instruments were registered with notaries when transactions were conducted between parties who trusted each other. This will be examined in further detail in the next chapter.

N. Beyond the geographical scope of this study, the use of supercargoes was even more frequent on voyages from Amsterdam to the Algarve and to the Mediterranean basin, as well as on voyages departing from Portugal and the Low Countries which included ports in West Africa. It was common for various ports to be visited during voyages from the Republic to the Algarve, and ships often stopped first in Lisbon or in a port in the Algarve before deciding whether or not to continue the journey and if so to which ports (SR nos. 190, 281). Voyages to the Mediterranean could last more than a year when ships called in at numerous ports, north and south, in a sequence defined during the course of the voyage (SR no. 880). The slave trade both to Brazil and to Spanish America entailed long laytimes in African ports, where decisions were made and instructions were often received regarding the port that would serve as the destination in the Americas.

O. Voyages from the United Provinces to West Africa, with or without a stopover in Portugal, whether returning to the Republic or continuing on to Italy, could include more than one African port, with laytimes of more than six months and the presence of several supercargoes (SR nos. 363, 448, 445, 525, 574).

Wolgemeinte Erinnerungs Regeln
Für einen Jungen Kauff-und Handelsmann / darnach er sich zu richten/
wann er nicht verderben will.

Medieval arrangements similar to supercargoes

Profit-sharing meant that arrangements involving supercargoes were somewhat similar to a form of mercantile association common in the Middle Ages, known as a *commenda*, and its equivalents and variants, *collegantia* and *societas maris*. These arrangements typically comprised two partners – a "passive" (or "sedentary") investor and an "active" and traveling partner, who could also be an investor. If the traveler did not invest any capital in the venture, he would receive a quarter of the profits; if he invested up to one-third of the costs, he would receive half the profits. In case of losses, the traveler would bear losses proportional to the capital he invested, if any, and would not be remunerated for his efforts.[79]

Amsterdam to West Africa and to the Canary Islands, possibly extending up to Brazil, stipulated that at the end of the venture, the supercargoes would receive a share in the profits at the principal's discretion.[76]

Research found only one case of a voyage undoubtedly bound for Brazil that clearly mentions this sharing arrangement. If the venture was profitable, after the sugar was sold in Porto, the profits would be divided between the merchant, on the one hand, and the carrack's shipmaster and pilot, on the other. The two last-mentioned would accompany and bring back the goods, as well as serve as supercargoes.[77] However, nothing precluded supercargoes from also receiving commissions in other ventures, and it is not unlikely that some cashiers and retainers who served their employers also as supercargoes would have received commissions or a share in profits, in addition to their salaries.[78]

Commissioning Consignments

Most traveling agents, however, were entrusted with far smaller cargoes than the consignment to assigned to Aguiar, and had even less discretionary authority over the principal's capital than that delegated to Aguiar. This was generally the rule among the aforesaid traveling commissioners, who traded small consignments on behalf of their principals and, just like counterparts, deducted commissions for sales and purchases.[80]

Santiago employed two of his traveling agents probably as commissioners. In 1597, in Salvador, he entrusted one with a consignment comprising various imported products, which the agent was to take to Espírito Santo. The cargo, estimated to be worth 112,000 réis, was shipped on behalf of Santiago himself, and of Diogo Dias Querido, who also lived in Bahia.[81] Two years later, in Olinda, Santiago entrusted four crates of sugar to a shipmaster from Viana. Including other costs, the consignment was worth 55,700 réis – in sharp contrast to the more than 1,537,100 réis managed by Aguiar just in merchandise, apart from

The Education of a Young Merchant; *Mathias Van Somer (ca. 1650). Good faith, diligence and discernment were key virtues required of any agent. Employment as supercargoes often served as training for young members of merchant families.*

the funds contained in the letters of credit. Of the four crates taken by this shipmaster, two were sent on Santiago's behalf while the other two were shipped on behalf of his cousin, who apparently also lived in Pernambuco. The same shipmaster was further entrusted with two sacks of cotton, together worth 22,215 réis, again on behalf of Santiago and the aforesaid Diogo Dias Querido, the latter in Bahia.[82]

Whether it was on their own account or as agents, travelers were a crucial part of overseas commerce, since merchants in Brazil preferred to buy goods after inspecting the quality and quantity of the items, instead of risking ordering them sight unseen from Portugal or other parts. This ensured more tangible and safer profits. Ambrósio Fernandes Brandão, himself a merchant and sugar-mill owner, who would also be one of Santiago's counterparts when the latter moved to Lisbon,[83] stated:

> *Many order [goods] from Portugal, but most of them buy them from other traders who bring them from there, allowing the latter to mark up forty to fifty percent over the purchase price, depending on the type and quality of the merchandise, or the scarcity or abundance of those products in the marketplace.*[84]

In effect, this penchant for buying goods in the colony was also evident in Santiago's business dealings when he was a fixed agent in Brazil, selling most of his merchandise to fellow merchants instead of end users.

As has been shown, it was common for seafarers to serve as mercantile agents. On occasion, they negotiated arrangements combining both transport and mercantile agency services.[P/85] In one such agree-

The Damrak in Amsterdam; *Jacob van Ruisdael (ca. 1670).*

ment, the sailors promised to buy a certain quantity of sugar whose value would be covered (along with all related costs in Brazil) by a bill of exchange to be drawn on the principal. They would not receive any commission, and apparently would not have a share in the profits either. Nevertheless, they made sure that the bulk of the freight space available on their caravel would be booked for the homeward voyage, even if at a price equal to the lowest rate paid by other consignors they could find. They would thus earn more if they managed to attract other consignors at higher rates.[86]

Sea Loans

The so-called sea loans (bottomry contracts) mentioned at the beginning of this chapter were a common form of mercantile agency arrangement, generally involving seafarers. Even if they were often contested, their fixed interest rates were justified canonically and legally because the merchant bore the risk of losses resulting from force majeure, viz., shipwrecks, fires or seizure.[87] Consequently, these contracts were compared to insurance. Such arrangements also involved a credit operation, since, except in cases of force majeure, the merchant (or investor) would either receive the initial capital along with the interest, or would enforce the guarantees. In practice, such agreements entailed a mercantile agency relationship, as the merchant's profitability was subject to the traveling agent's commercial conduct and performance. Payment was made upon returning, on an unspecified date, and in goods acquired overseas, at variable prices, often with the proceeds from the sale of other products being acquired in the same way, and whose shipment was arranged by the traveling agent.

One such contract was signed by a merchant in Porto, on the one hand, and the shipmaster of a carrack and a small trader who would travel aboard the carrack, on the other.[88] The latter received a number of textiles from the merchant – a piece of velvet, three of taffeta and two of grosgrain – which were together worth 120,600 réis. Not only were these goods in their possession, but they had already been loaded aboard the carrack. The parties declared before the notary that they were satisfied with the quality, quantity and prices of the wares. The travelers promised that they would set sail with the first favorable winds for Pernambuco or "wherever the said vessel will unload" in Brazil, with a stopover in Santa Cruz in the Canary Islands. Apart from the merchandise, they also received a bill of exchange from the merchant. The bill was worth 100,000 réis, payable eight days after sight by another trader from Porto who had already left for Santa Cruz. In case they did not receive the payment from this party, or another party for the honor of the drawer, within the stipulated eight days, they could raise that sum in the said town by drawing a bill of exchange on the merchant in Porto. They thus received 220,600 réis in all, which they would pay back in Porto, along with 30% interest.

Everything was to be paid in white sugar to be acquired in Brazil with the proceeds from selling the merchandise and the wine, which they were almost certainly meant to buy en route using the credit in the Canary Islands. On top of the 30% interest, the travelers were also to give the merchant half an arroba of additional sugar per crate after the crates were weighed if the crates were sourced from Pernambuco, or a quarter of arroba if the crates had come from Bahia. The contract specified the type of sugar to be bought: "The best available in the land as if bought with cash." The document suggests that vendors preferred to exchange their best sugar (premium) for currency, and that was the quality of sugar that the merchant in Porto expected to receive. Therefore, even if the travelers bartered the goods they were taking for sugar, they were to ensure that they acquired sufficient sugar of that fine quality.

The sugar was to be shipped on the same carrack that made the outward journey. However, if the vessel was chartered to return to a port other than Porto, or if it did not return in that same year, the travelers were to ship the sugar within a span of four months from their arrival in Brazil on another vessel. This other vessel should be a "very good ship coming to this city," and the travelers were to advise the merchant on which vessels the goods had been loaded so that he could make sure that the necessary insurance would be purchased. The crates were to be stamped with his mark, and the travelers were to ask for four copies of the bill of lading for each consignment. They were to send the merchant two copies, and would keep the third with them, while the fourth would remain in Brazil. Both the external marks and bills of lading would enable the merchant to have the shipments insured.

The travelers would have to repay the principal and the interest irrespective of their commercial success in the Canary Islands and Brazil: "whether more or less profits are made." In case the sugar was found to be wanting in terms of quality, within the time frame and manner that had been agreed upon, they would compensate the merchant for his losses and damages. Apart from this, the risks borne by the merchant, both for the outward as well as the homebound journey, only comprised the following events of force majeure: fires, shipwrecks, taking water on board and seizure ("fire, sea and thieves"); all other risks were the travelers' responsibility. Finally, the travelers would not receive any commission for selling or buying goods, and were also liable for customs duties and "all other expenditure."

As a guarantee, the travelers pledged all their assets, and the merchant could recover the principal and interest from the "most suitable" assets, that is, those that could most easily be seized. To this end, the notary deed would be valid as a final and unappealable judgment, conferring the right to automatically proceed to enforcement. In this latter clause, the contract differs somewhat from customary agreements in which a share of the vessel was generally pledged – in this case, probably because one of the travelers, the trader, might not have been a co-owner of the carrack.[R/89]

P. David G. Smith also described some cases of individuals who combined the services of both shipping and mercantile agency. However, he emphasized that "Merchants usually resorted to this type of arrangement when they were trading to ports in which they had no permanent correspondent or procurator" (Smith, "The Mercantile Class of Portugal and Brazil," p. 360). As shall be seen shortly, this was not the rule – far from it. Merchants used to trade with other mercantile centers through various agents employed by means of different types of arrangements, and could simultaneously have more than one fixed counterpart and other traveling agents, including seafarers, to the same marketplace.

Q. The interest charged in sea loans (termed "contratos de dinheiro a ganho e risco," i.e., "money at profit and risk contracts" in Portuguese) was justified by canonists and jurists precisely because of the assumed risks, which were understood to be extrinsic to the loan per se. The interests charged were not deemed to be usurious, but rather recompense for the ***periculum sortis*** (danger to capital), a category (title) which allowed charging a premium for assuming other people's risk, such as in the case of insurance. This would not be the case of contracts in which there was a fixed return and in which the person extending the credit took on only the risk of default by the debtor, because scholars considered risk to be an intrinsic part of such a loan. In such cases, it was only possible to use the concepts of lucrum cessans and ***damnum emergens*** ex-post. As has been seen, these two exceptions were then increasingly deemed to be acceptable ex-ante too. In his ordinance issued on October 4, 1540, Charles V regulated interest being charged in the Low Countries, forbidding deposits by non-merchants with merchants and companies and authorizing moderate interest rates being charged in transactions between merchants up to a limit of 12%, as well as sea loans in which the investors were not merchants.

R. Leonor Freire Costa has pointed out the futile attempts by the Portuguese authorities, in the 1620s, to try to put an end to this practice, affirming that such contracts, when accompanied by insurance, meant that all stakeholders put up little resistance to attacks by pirates and corsairs, which abounded at the time. She emphasized that, during this period, shipowners used this mechanism even more frequently to protect their investments, even at higher rates of interest (Costa, ***O transporte no Atlântico***, v. 1, pp. 227–235, 387–388). Christopher Ebert interpreted these arrangements merely as a mechanism to mitigate risk and not to finance trade or to govern mercantile agency overseas (Ebert, "The Trade in Brazilian Sugar," pp. 153–155).

This illustration from the Book of Trades *(1694) shows a ship being loaded under the supervision of a merchant or shipmaster.*

As previously shown, the merchant's profits or losses depended on the quality and the prices at which the wine would be bought and the sugar sold, as well as the cost at which the bill of exchange was drawn, if a bill was to be drawn at all. Apart from this, hiring vessels in poor condition or neglecting to inform the merchant about the shipments could result in the total loss of the capital invested. Delays increased opportunity costs – so much so that the merchant made a point of noting all these issues in the clauses of this contract. The fact that the merchant's profits were subject to the travelers' good faith, diligence and discernment meant that they were mercantile agents no less than borrowers.

Entrusting One's Capital

As we can see from the aforesaid examples, fixed agents did or could carry out a much broader range of transactions on behalf of their principals than traveling agents.[90] The fixed agents' continuous presence in a trading center made it possible to engage in lengthier transactions, to offer longer periods of credit for sales, to stock up on goods in order to sell them at the best terms, to use the proceeds of sales for future purchases or financial transactions, to sue, to both sell and receive purchase orders in advance, and so forth.

It is true that some traveling agents spent longer periods overseas[91] and could therefore offer purchasers a few months of credit.[92] However, even Aguiar, in whose case the principals had not specified a time frame for remaining in Brazil or for shipping them the sugar, had clear instructions to sell as little as possible on credit, for the shortest possible time, and only to the merchants of highest standing. If necessary, he was to entrust the task of collecting debts to fixed agents and wholesalers so that his return was not delayed.[S/93] Other traveling agents may have paid third parties with bills-obligatory or other credits received from wholesalers in payment for their merchandise, which could, however, entail a discount. Such agents would have had to decide whether the discount and the liquidity risk compensated for losses due to unsold goods.

Short sojourns of travelers abroad were often also advantageous for the principal. As David G. Smith aptly suggests,[94] this ensured quicker returns on the capital, instead of leaving the outstanding credit in the agent's custody. It was consequently harder for agents to improve their cash flow or make their own investments with the capital held from their principals, who thus did not have to continuously oversee how this capital was used.[T]

S. Ambrósio Fernandes Brandão, writer, merchant, tax collector and sugar-mill owner in the captaincies of Pernambuco and Paraíba, emphasized the importance of time. He alleged that wholesalers in Pernambuco stored the sugar they commonly received from the inhabitants of Paraíba as payment for the merchants' sales in their warehouses ready to be shipped and, as a consequence, the ships which called in at Paraíba ports did not find much sugar there, nor could they obtain it during reasonably short sojourns in exchange for the goods they had brought. In this manner, ships arriving from Portugal went directly to Pernambuco, instead of stopping over at Paraíba (Brandão, *Diálogos das grandezas do Brasil*, p. 25).

T. Beyond the route examined here, supercargoes who wished to remain more than six months in the ports of West Africa had to obtain the approval of their principals beforehand, while in the Mediterranean they could sail from port to port for more than sixteen months (SR nos. 455, 880).

N.
MAES

The time available in a marketplace was one of the factors to be considered when hiring an agent, but it was not the only important aspect. In fact, merchants sought to hire agents with a number of qualities which were not always compatible. They wanted their agents to be as talented, knowledgeable, well- funded and equipped as possible, endowed with expertise and highly motivated to generate profits, averse to taking unnecessary risks, trustworthy and cheap. Some of these characteristics depended on personal qualities, while others were the result of the combination of these characteristics and the types of arrangements through which they were employed.

Resident merchants had the opportunity to accumulate broader and more diversified experience in the various activities associated with commerce, given the wide range of transactions they conducted.[95] It took practice to master complex exchanges, measurements, sorting, coins, interest rates, foreign exchange, transport costs and means, insurance, accounting, and so forth. Moreover, well-established merchants could rely on a network of clients and suppliers of goods and services, who kept the merchants up to date and gave them a more comprehensive outlook on market trends. This enabled the merchants to keep their overseas principals abreast of what was going on in their trading centers and better coordinate chains of supply and demand.

Well-established merchants were able to mobilize an infrastructure of warehouses, boats, ships, retainers, cashiers and slaves which they could include in their services, streamlining their principals' commercial operations. They might possibly offer such services at a lower cost than the principals would have had to incur if they had hired them from third parties. Indeed, Santiago provided these services at no extra cost on at least one occasion. The capital of affluent merchants employed as agents was a major asset for their principals, since the agents could extend credit to the latter and cover imbalances in current accounts between the two parties. Thus, such agents could settle payments and make purchases in advance on behalf of their principals.

The most important factor was the credit and reputation of those employed as agents, as well as of all those who were involved in trade in some way. Creditworthiness depended on one's capital and liquidity, which enabled the individual to fulfill his obligations punctually, overcome shortages in his own cash flow, raise funds on the market, offer guarantees, and have enough assets to be seized, if necessary. One's reputation as a skillful and honest businessman could extend well beyond one's place of residence and the centers with which one traded.

Above all, an agent's capital and reputation influenced his relationship with his principals. When the agent was an affluent, well-established and respected merchant, relations generally tended to be more horizontal. He was entrusted with larger transactions or various small sums simultaneously, and was subject to fewer restrictions with regard to how to manage business deals. Such agents also served their principals for periods encompassing successive ventures.

On the negative side, there is no doubt that the volume of capital and the latitude allowed in terms of discretionary power entrusted to counterparts and partners meant that these agents could cause greater losses for their principals. The longer and more complex transactions they were allowed to perform, often on their own initiative, were more difficult to be verified. However, losses caused to the principal would

The Account Keeper; *Nicolas Maes (1656).*

DOVE L' ORO PARLA, OGNI LINGVA TACE.
13
M. Mitelli. I. e. F.
Conuinta ogni ragion, muto ogni foro
Resta, doue la Borsa apre la bocca,
Ch'Orator non si troua eguale à l'Oro.

Where Gold Speaks, Every Tongue Is Silent; *Giuseppe Maria Mitelli (1678). By employing an agent, a merchant exposed himself to the risk of opportunism.*

jeopardize agents' reputation, which was their chief asset as merchants themselves. Relationships with counterparts and partners usually either had a predetermined duration or were subject to termination at the request of one of the counterparts or partners. Principals could entrust further and larger assets or fewer and smaller, as well as demand repatriation of capital and proceeds. Furthermore, as we will see, merchants were usually counterparts and partners of more than one principal. Thus, both the revenues generated by one's activities as an agent and those resulting from the reciprocity of one's counterparts and partners could either shrink or expand, depending on how the agent's current and prospective principals, individually and collectively, perceived the agent's actions and conduct. Finally, the horizontal and reciprocal structure of these arrangements meant that the agent had assets entrusted to his principals which could be withheld or seized in case of the agent's misconduct.

On the other hand, the great mobility of seafarers and small traders generally employed as traveling agents, coupled with a lack of commitment by the merchant in rehiring them for new ventures, could tempt them to act opportunistically. Furthermore, their modest capital and relative anonymity minimized the damages that informal and legal mechanisms could inflict on their reputations and assets. It was precisely to reduce this moral hazard that merchants employed these modest and itinerant individuals on particular ventures involving small sums, allowing them little autonomy within a limited timespan. Even though they could be repeatedly hired by the same merchant, this did not alter the fleeting nature of these arrangements, whose transience and narrower autonomy entailed a greater verifiability of agents' actions, and whose volume of entrusted assets, if embezzled, did not suffice to live on them for long.

These attributes and the frequent requirements for guarantees, sureties and pledges in the arrangements through which they were employed served to inhibit and prevent possible frauds, but were unable to eliminate them entirely. Nevertheless, these individuals were expected to be highly motivated not just to act properly but also to ensure profits for their principals. The remuneration obtained from each venture had a far greater impact on their modest earnings than on the revenues of agents who were well-established merchants. Ensuring profits for their principals was the former's greatest guarantee that they would be entrusted with new ventures from the same and other merchants. As they built their reputations in mercantile circles, they themselves could become merchants and thrive, both financially and socially.

Employing supercargoes entailed risks more similar to those in relationships with counterparts and partners than other kinds of arrangements with traveling agents. This was because, although the sporadic and itinerant nature of their jobs limited their autonomy and the volume of capital entrusted to them, they had slightly more discretionary power and could carry out a greater number of transactions on behalf of their principals. The latter, in turn, entrusted them with more assets than those given to other traveling agents.

It is also important to note that not all fixed agents were affluent. There was a continuum between more moneyed agents and humbler ones. Arrangements with agents, both resident and traveling, whose capital and reputation were more modest limited their autonomy in various aspects: the sums entrusted to them, the freedom to draw bills of exchange on the principal or keep the proceeds in their current accounts without remitting them to the principal, and the initiative and discretionary power on how to use the principal's capital.[U] It was also common for merchants to oblige lowlier agents to hand over the capital to other agents in the same center if they were unable to fulfill the stipulated conditions. Furthermore, it was customary to require them to provide real and fiduciary guarantees to ensure strict compliance with the principals' instructions.[96]

This confirms that capital and reputation were decisive qualities in relations between agents and principals. Indeed, arrangements involving humbler counterparts were more like those of commissioners than counterparts who were affluent merchants living in the same trading center. The differences between these minor counterparts and commissioners were limited to the fact that the former did not travel with consignments, and they were promised new assignments as long as they complied with their instructions.[97]

The ways in which agents were remunerated also depended on variables that needed to be taken into account. In sea loans, merchants preferred the predictable profits from fixed rates of interest over the possibility of greater profits in other types of overseas agency arrangements. With profit sharing, the division of risks offset a possible loss of profitability, while commissions entailed foregoing the predictability of profits, as well as the sharing of risks, with a view to greater returns. In the case of agents who did not receive remuneration, as was the case of some arrangements involving shipmasters and travelers, merchants risked agents lacking motivation.

In order to balance all these pros and cons, merchants used to entrust their business with the same trading center to more than one agent and employed agents with diverse qualities through different types of arrangements according to the characteristics of each transaction or series of transactions.[98]

Trading 'Nations'

Prospects of prosperity or decline as a result of a better or worse professional reputation, on the one hand, and limiting conditions, whether real or contractual, on the other, reduced the possibility of negligence and fraud, but did not eliminate them. As already noted, counterparts, partners and supercargoes were the individuals who could cause the greatest damage to merchants, considering the volume of capital and the latitude of autonomy they were entrusted with. Likewise, these arrangements entailed a lower verifiability of agents' actions. This was precisely why many of these agents were related to the merchants.[99] Some of Santiago's main partners and counterparts included his nephews, cousins and sister.[100]

It was also quite common to find more horizontal arrangements with agents who, even if they were not relatives, came from the same locality, region or country, or shared the same ethnicity or religion. Among these affinity groups that played an active role in the sugar trade, the merchants from the town of Viana (now Viana do Castelo), in northern Portugal, stood out. Entrepreneurs from this vibrant port town played a leading role in the early stages of the colonization of Brazil. Such a role was even more significant considering the population of the town, which, in around 1530, had fewer than 1,000 households, while Porto already had about 3,000 and Lisbon more than 13,000.[101] It is, however, true that merchants from Viana availed themselves of the services of their peers from other groups to trade with northern Europe.[V] Various groups of non-Portuguese were also important, especially the "Flemish" (a term that applied to people from

Passover Seder of the Portuguese Jews; *Bernard Picart (1725). Portugal was the destination of a large number of Jews fleeing persecution on the Iberian Peninsula and even France during the Middle Ages. Later on, Jews were forced to convert to Catholicism in Portugal and their descendants who settled abroad were identified in many countries as being from the "Portuguese Nation."*

the Low Countries in general, and even to German speakers from northwestern continental Europe). "Flemings" were present in Portugal, the Atlantic islands and Brazil, to a greater or lesser extent, until foreigners were banned from that colony in 1605, and even after the ban. "Flemings" and other foreigners continued to stay on in Brazil as late as 1618, and the highest colonial authorities were aware of their presence.[102]

However, the most prominent group plying the sugar trade during this period was comprised of, to all appearances, merchants of Jewish descent. The Jewish-New Christian diaspora in Brazil, Portugal and the Netherlands had a strong group identity. Such identity derived from their common history, the external constraints to which they were subjected, and extensive endogamy. These factors were sometimes combined with a desire to maintain their Jewish practices and beliefs, and their sense of distinctiveness. Some of them viewed this distinctiveness as superiority.[105] They were also identified as a specific group by the Old Christian majority in both the Iberian Peninsula and the Low Countries. In the Portuguese world, they were

U. This category could also include merchants' retainers who looked after their business dealings overseas (ADP, NOT, PO2, l. 29, fols. 47v.–49 [1609-8-7]). An example is the case of a partner with these limitations in a company formed by merchants from the Low Countries to trade between Bahia, Lisbon and Amsterdam: the partner who went to Bahia was subject to quite restrictive conditions, probably due to his lower capital and reputation, as well as the greater distance from the other centers (SAA, 5075: Archief van de Notarissen ter Standplaats Amsterdam, l. 33, fols. 390v.–392). On this case, see also: Stols, "Os mercadores flamengos," p. 37; Ebert, "The Trade in Brazilian Sugar," p. 99. Ebert, however, mentions that the trader in Bahia would be paid commissions without specifying that he would receive them only after the company was liquidated.

V. There were New Christians in Viana, but, according to Moreira, they would have been a minority among the town's businessmen (Moreira, *Os mercadores de Viana*, pp. 35, 144–145).

Military Orders and Portuguese social status

Titles and rewards (*mercês*) bestowed by the military orders were a central mechanism of the early modern Portuguese state to reward services rendered, especially entailing the use of arms. The bestowal of such honors implied important social and economic advantages; recipients were exempted from taxes and enjoyed other privileges including the right to demonstrate signs of nobility, such as riding horses, bearing arms, wearing silk garments, and so forth. Moreover, such titles attested to the purity of their blood. At the beginning, they were also granted pensions or revenues from specific properties owned by the order, and privileged jurisdiction. The rules trying to limit the Crown's power to bestow these honors were repeatedly disregarded, since these grants served to reinforce the Crown's ties with the elite, particularly with marginal and emerging elite segments, thus inducing individuals to render services on the basis of expectations. Apart from seeking to rise to the expectations of merited subjects, the Crown strove to ensure that both the distribution of rewards was equitable and the symbolic value of the honors was upheld. Nevertheless, as these honors were often exchanged (whether overtly or covertly) for donations, loans or other financial services, they were an important source of revenue in times of crisis – a venality that clashed with the chivalrous image these honors sought to promote.[114]

collectively known as "people of the Hebrew nation," or other versions of this expression. Outside Portuguese territories, they were deemed to be from the "Portuguese nation" – an interesting coincidence, whereby being Portuguese abroad was confused with having Jewish origins.[106] The importance of New Christians and Jews in the sugar trade and the importance of this trade in the economic activities of the group are clearly evident both in the literature – in almost all the studies on this subject – as well as in primary sources,[107] albeit, perhaps, in a slightly exaggerated manner.

During the Middle Ages, Portugal hosted a growing community of Jews. Portugal absorbed immigrants from other Iberian kingdoms attracted by the development of the western region of the peninsula, and fleeing from persecution in the east. Jews settled primarily in towns, and engaged in urban professions: artisanship, medicine, trade and finance. In 1492, Portugal was the destination for a significant number of Jews who had been expelled from Spain. However, in December 1496, Portugal also decreed the expulsion of its community.

Nevertheless, few Jews were actually able to leave Portugal, since the monarch wished to be rid of Judaism but wanted to retain the Jews. He tried to induce them to convert. He forced all those who refused to be baptized to hand over their children to be raised by Christian parents, chosen by their biological families, to whom they were to also hand over two-thirds of their assets during their lifetime. The king prevented Jews from leaving Portugal but guaranteed that they would be protected against inquisitional enquiries about their beliefs for the next twenty years if they converted. Finally, the monarch ended up forcing baptism (although details about this measure are sketchy), in a phenomenon that became known as the "General Conversion" or "Standing Baptism."[108]

Over the course of subsequent centuries, these converts and their descendants continued to be known as New Christians in Portugal and its dominions. In principle, the term was also used for Muslims and heathens who converted and their descendants. However, it was used far more frequently to designate individuals of Jewish ancestry, and ended up being associated primarily with this group because they were more numerous, and were deemed to pose a more serious threat to the Church, the State and society, at least in Portugal and in the more Europeanized areas of its colonies.[w]

Protection against inquiries into converts' conscience initially granted by King Emmanuel in 1497 was extended for another twenty years, resulting in forty years with little interference in the private religious beliefs and practices of converts and their progeny. This calm came to an end after a lengthy dispute between the Crown, on one side, and the Holy See, representatives of New Christians in Rome and sectors of the Portuguese clergy, on the other. In 1536, the pope sanctioned, somewhat reluctantly, the establishment of a Portuguese national Inquisition.

'Flanders' and the 'Flemish'

The term "Flanders" was used generically to refer to the entire coast of northern Europe, from Dunkirk to Danzig/Gdansk, and more specifically to the Low Countries, both the southern Low Countries, ruled by the Habsburgs, as well as the northern Low Countries, which formed the Dutch Republic.[103] This confusion was rooted in history: the primacy of Flanders and Brabant in European and Portuguese trade in the previous four centuries, and the similarity between Dutch and German, which also enabled them to have joint representatives and enjoy the same privileges in Portugal.[104] This ambiguity came in handy when Portugal and the Dutch Republic found themselves in opposite camps. As a result, citizens of the "Rebel Provinces" were able to move more freely in Portuguese territory under the guise of being from Flanders, a province loyal to the Habsburgs.

Commissioners and familiars of the Holy Office

Once the stage of organizing the Tribunal of the Holy Office of the Inquisition was concluded, a period characterized by the expansion of its activities began (1573–1615). The Tribunal's consolidation within Portuguese society was accompanied by an increase in the inquisitors' workload and the reorganization of its bureaucratic structure. New posts were created, and the number of officials increased. Permanent representatives were appointed to serve at different locations in Portugal and its overseas dominions. The latter formed a complex network of agents that sought to bring the entire Portuguese Empire within the purview of the inquisitors.

The offices of "commissioners" and "familiars" were a prominent feature of this new organization structure. Commissioners were clergymen who were to represent the Holy Office, and serve it in the more important locations of each of the Inquisition's districts, particularly in seaports, the Atlantic Islands and the captaincies of Brazil. Their functions included keeping the inquisitors informed of all matters within the Tribunal's jurisdiction, especially regarding offenses related to the purity of the faith, interrogating witnesses according to prior instructions, ensuring compliance with arrest warrants, sending detainees to the Tribunal, monitoring convicts serving their sentences in their area of residence, and so forth.

In turn, familiars were lay aides of the Tribunal and were to be appointed in all cities and towns, especially port towns, in numbers that the inquisitor-general deemed to be sufficient. They were the secular and local arm supporting the Tribunal's activities and ensuring the vigilance that it sought to impose on society. Like the members of the military orders, the Inquisition's familiars enjoyed various social, economic and legal privileges.[115]

The objective of this Inquisition was primarily to curb the Jewish practices that New Christians supposedly maintained, with a greater or lesser degree of secrecy, and to forcibly integrate them into the Catholic majority. The tribunal only began to persecute the subjects of their inquiries in the 1540s and, from then on, any New Christian, whether "entire," "half, "a quarter," and so on, was deemed to be a potential heretic, liable to be imprisoned, judged and convicted by the tribunal. Their assets were seized when they were arrested, and if they were convicted, as was usually the case, those assets were confiscated.[109]

w. Hinduism and Amerindian religions ended up overshadowing Judaism as the focus of inquisitorial activities in Asia and the Amazon Basin in the eighteenth century; see: *Livro da visitação do Santo Ofício da Inquisição ao Estado do Grão-Pará (1763–1769)* (Petrópolis: Vozes, 1978), passim; F. Bethencourt, "A Inquisição," in C. A. Moreira de Azevedo (ed.), *História religiosa de Portugal*, V. 2 (Lisbon: Círculo de Leitores, 2000), pp. 128–130. Until then, Judaizers comprised the vast majority of defendants and those convicted by the Portuguese Inquisition; see: A. B. Coelho, *Inquisição de Évora* (Lisbon: Editorial Caminho, 2002), pp. 215, 221, 230–231, 585–626; F. Bethencourt, "Rejeições e polémicas," in Azevedo, *História religiosa de Portugal*, pp. 49–62.

Auto-da-Fé held in Plaza Mayor, Madrid; *Francisco Rizi (1683).*

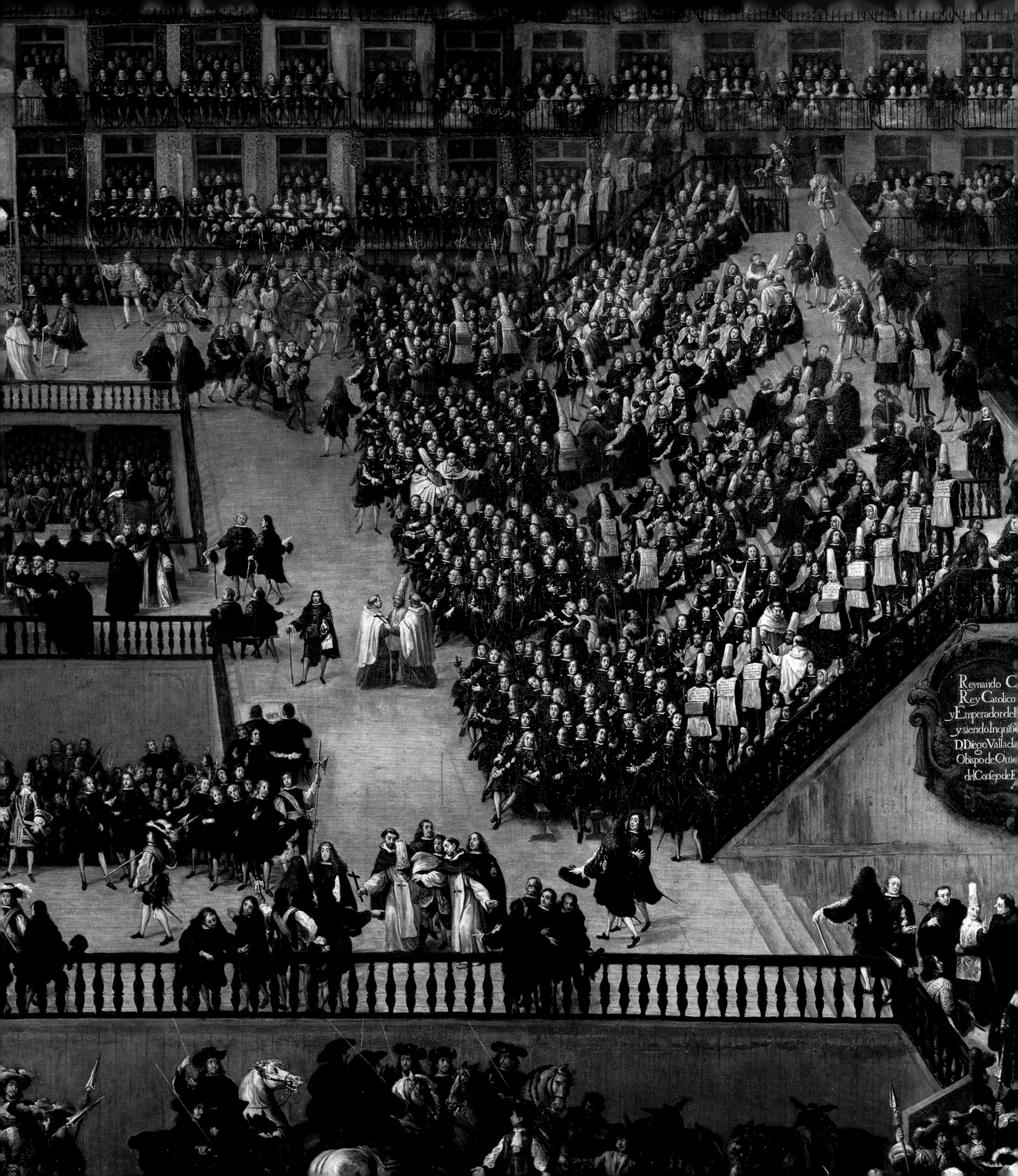
Reynando
Rey Catolico
y Emperador del
y siendo
D. Diego
Obispo de
del Consejo de

Apart from inquisitorial persecution, New Christians were subject to a growing number of discriminatory restrictions barring their entry, at least in a pro-forma manner, into religious and secular institutions, such as regular orders, secular clergy, the Inquisition itself, the prestigious military orders, charitable institutions known as *misericórdias*, universities, brotherhoods, royal and municipal service, the courts, being granted nobility and honorific titles; and that was just the beginning of a longer list.[110] These bans fell under the category statutes of "purity of blood."[111] The origins of candidates wishing to enter these institutions were subject to varying degrees scrutiny. Military orders enjoyed great prestige in Portuguese society, largely due to a guarantee of the purity of the blood of their members thanks to the rigor of their investigations. This was even truer for auxiliary offices in the Inquisition, such as the lay aides known as "familiars," and clerical "commissioners," viewed as being the first step toward becoming part of a military order, and perhaps even joining the ranks of the nobility, for such individuals or their relatives. Ethnic origin thus came to be one of the main criteria for social status.[112] In most cases, discriminating restrictions were only imposed from the 1570s onwards. At that time, many of the children and grandchildren of converts had already attained important positions after having their rights deemed equal to Christians' upon baptism. Such restrictions were similar to the bans on Jews joining lay corporations during the Middle Ages, and hence were of a clearly reactionary nature.[113]

A secondary effect of the statutes of purity of blood was that more aristocratic families, nobles, gentlemen, members of urban patriciate, Brazil's governing stratum and wealthy families consulted genealogists before accepting marriage proposals, so that no stigma affected their offspring, even through collateral kinship.[116] This discrimination and persecution resulted in a considerable sense of "otherness" among New Christians, which, along with the desire of some of them to maintain their ancestral beliefs and observances, led to the practice of endogamous marriages.[117] There is certainly no doubt that marrying within one's own distinct social group was a common practice in the early modern times. That included marriages among families with the same occupations, immigrants from the same localities, and so forth.[118]

Persecution, "otherness," and endogamy did not mean segregation. New Christians socialized with Old Christians, and intermarriages were not uncommon. Over the course of a few generations, some New Christians even managed to shed their New Christian identity and climb the social ladder, marrying into illustrious families, and subsequently reinventing their origins and obliterating "blood defects." Success in this endeavor was acknowledged when an individual was awarded a membership into a military order or was made a lay aide (familiar) of the Holy Inquisition.[119] It is also not possible to generalize and say that all New Christians secretly maintained Jewish practices and beliefs, although many did so. Practices, beliefs, and identity varied greatly, even within the same family. There were sincere Catholics, crypto-Jews, skeptics to a greater or lesser degree, and a variety of different belief combinations and other idiosyncrasies.[120] In Brazil, integration and mixed marriages would almost certainly have been far more frequent than in Portugal, since the greater porosity and openness of the social fabric, which was still being formed in the colony, enabled these discriminated against individuals to attain important offices during the period under review.[121]

This eighteenth-century engraving shows the end of the procession that followed the reading out of sentences at an auto-da-fé and the punishment of the condemned in Terreiro do Paço, Lisbon. The Italian legend reads: "Method of burning those condemned by the Inquisition."

Apart from the aforementioned restrictions, the freedom of movement of New Christians was also curtailed. Concerned about an exodus to lands where they could freely embrace Judaism, taking their

Maniera di bruciare quelli che furono condannati dalla Inquisizione.

capital, manpower and potential skills with them, the Crown and the Church repeatedly forbade them to leave Portugal, even to go to the colonies.[122] The last ban, dating from 1580, hence prior to the period in question here, was revoked in 1601 and reinstated in 1610.[123] In theory, mercantile journeys were only authorized by means of licenses, for which guarantees for their return had to be provided. At least within the boundaries of the Iberian world, these restrictions were widely disregarded. In all likelihood, this could have been the case with Miguel Dias Santiago. Nevertheless, being apprehended fleeing from Hispanic domains, particularly someone wanted by the Inquisition, had serious consequences, being tantamount to a confession of guilt.[124]

The Low Countries was one of the regions to which New Christians emigrated. From the first half of the sixteenth century onwards, they lived as Catholics in Flanders and in Brabant, where, from time to time, the Habsburg authorities persecuted them for Jewish practices. In the 1579 treaty of the Union of Utrecht (the constitutive act of the Dutch Republic) allowed its inhabitants freedom of conscience, which should not, however, be confused with religious freedom. In private, every individual could believe what he or she wished, without being investigated, persecuted or coerced. Collectively, and especially in public, only the Dutch Reformed Church was allowed.[Y] It was in this context that New Christians began to

X. Evaldo Cabral de Mello argues that it was only after the Dutch were expelled from Brazil (1645) that the rural aristocracy in Pernambuco became a restrictive and entrenched group, but that until then mixed marriages were common (Mello, *O nome e o sangue*, pp. 174–181, 220–230). Similarly, Russell-Wood states that discrimination in Bahia brotherhoods only began to be a real issue from 1618 onwards; see: A. J. R., Russell-Wood, *Fidalgos and Philanthropists: The Santa Casa da Misericórdia of Bahia, 1550–1755* (Berkeley: University of California Press, 1968), pp. 136–137.

Y. The Religious Peace proposed by William of Orange, the leader of the insurgents, to the States-General in 1578 established a precedent of toleration but which only encompassed Catholics and Protestants (Swetschinski, "From the Middle Ages to the Golden Age," pp. 62–63; Israel, *The Dutch Republic*, pp. 184–196).

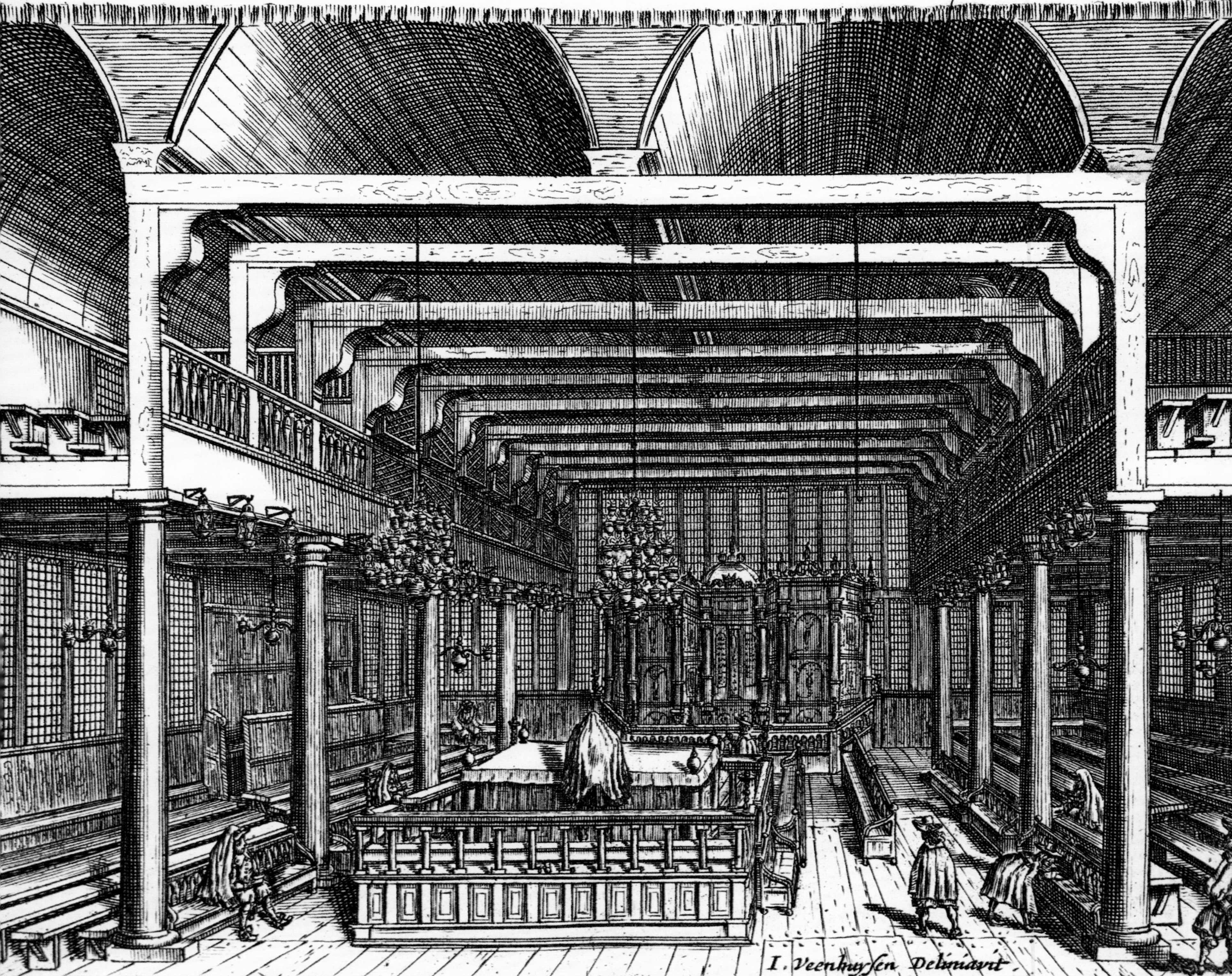

Interior of the Portuguese Synagogue in Amsterdam; *Jan Veenhuysen (ca. 1660). The Talmud Torah congregation was formed in 1639 with the unification of the three Portuguese congregations established in the city between 1595 and 1630. The famous building where it is housed today was inaugurated in 1675; then the synagogue shown here was deactivated as such.*

The status of Jews in Amsterdam

Everything indicates that there was a certain understanding between the municipal authorities and New Christians/Jews to allow the practice of Judaism, as long as it wasn't publicly visible.[127] Jews' status continued to be vague for quite some time, long enough to establish synagogues, purchase land for cemetery outside the city, set up a service to supply kosher meat (slaughtered according to Jewish rites), and organize learning of Judaism for newcomers from the Iberian world and their children, in additional to several confraternities with various specific purposes.

As could be expected, their presence did not go unnoticed. More fiery Calvinists resented these discreet congregations, and non-Calvinist Christians complained that Jews were allowed to do what they, despite being Christians, could not. The tone of these protests became even more heated when a few Dutch Christians converted to Judaism, and cases of sexual relations between Jewish men and Christian women came to light.[128]

These protests obliged the authorities to take a stand. In 1616, in the aftermath of one such scandal, the burgomasters of Amsterdam issued a bylaw which set out a number of behaviors deemed to be unacceptable: blasphemy against Christianity, proselytizing among Christians and their circumcision (implicitly excluding New Christians from the ban on circumcision) and sex with Christian women (even prostitutes). Jews were to obey all relevant municipal and provincial legislation, including a ban on building public synagogues, which had been decreed earlier, and a specific formula was prepared for Jewish oaths. In 1619, the States of Holland finally decided upon the matter, which had already been analyzed for about five years, and in which regard Amsterdam's bylaws were to temporarily remain in effect until a provincial resolution. The States of Holland's decision ended up transferring the issue back to the municipal level, stipulating only that cities might earmark an area to settle Jews, if they wished, but could not force them to use outward distinguishing marks. This measure sanctioned the precedents and reinforced tolerance, leaving scope for future negotiations at a local level.ζ

Such compromise was possible because Portuguese Jews were perceived as potentially bringing considerable profits to these cities, while less likely to provoke antagonism with the Reformed Church. The greatest challenge to this new Church in the early seventeenth century proved to come from Catholics, non-Calvinist Protestant denominations and, primarily, the heterodox and non-conformist currents within the Reformed Church itself. The latter were banned at the time the Dutch province pronounced its decision. Jews were far from center-stage, and could continue to maintain their discreet presence as long as they did not injure Christian or civic sensibilities, attract attention or make trouble. Some idiosyncrasies would also have contributed towards this tolerance. Humanism, the Reformation and Christian Hebraism sometimes resulted in a positive image of Jews and Judaism, while the discord with Catholicism, the Hispanic Monarchy and religious repression generated a certain amount of empathy between some Dutchmen and the Jews.

arrive in the Republic's cities, particularly Amsterdam, during the last two decades of the sixteenth century. By the end of the second decade of the seventeenth century, between 500 and 1,000 New Christians were already living in Amsterdam.[125] Most of them embraced Judaism in an increasingly open manner, and gradually formed community institutions.[126]

However, not all New Christians joined the community in Amsterdam, and not all of those who did became devout Jews and conformed to rabbinical norms. Be that as it may, the group of Portuguese immigrants of Jewish extraction had a strong feeling of belonging to the group, and the creation of the community was, to a large extent, a response to the discrimination and persecution they suffered in the Iberian world. With the gradual con-

ζ It is worth noting that, in 1581, the States-General of the insurgent provinces agreed to issue Portuguese merchants and their goods the same safeguards granted to other merchants. In 1598, the burgomasters of Amsterdam allowed the status of burghers to be granted to Portuguese immigrants. Magistrates affirmed their confidence that they were Christian merchants, whom they forbade to pray publicly outside authorized places of worship. It is unclear whether the burgomasters feared Catholic masses or Jewish prayers. Other cities promised religious freedom to Jews if a specific number of well-to-do families established residence there: Alkmaar (1604), Harlem (1605) and Rotterdam (1610). Because that number of families was never reached in those cities, the main result of the privileges granted was the creation of a precedent for Amsterdam.

Juramento dos Burgezes.

YSto jurais, que vos ſereis hu bom e fiel Poorter, Burgez deſta Cidade, e em todo tempo obidiente à os Señores ſeus Burgameſtres e Regidores, em guardas, picar gellos, e outras deffenſas esbriguacois deſta Cidade, com expontania vontade, advertindo eſta boa Cidade do mal que entenderdes; que atende reis e ajudareis com todo voſſe poſſivel à ſua proſperidade, com conſelho e obra, e aſſi mais fazendo, ou deixando tudo acquillo que hu bom Burgez deve fazer ou deixar.

Tuo verdadeiramente: os ajudo Deos todo poderoſo.

BUrgermeeſteren en Regeerders der Stad Amſterdam, hebben tot Poorter deſer Stede aangenomen

ſijnde van de Joodſche Natie, met dien verſtande, dat hy volgens de Keure deſer Stede, ten opſicht van de Jootſche Natie genomen, geen Winkel-neeringe hier ter Stede ſal vermogen te doen; mitsgaders dat het ſelve Borger-regt alleen gegeven word voor ſijn perſoon, ſonder dat het over ſal gaan aan ſijne kinderen, ende heeft daar op gemelte

ſijn Eed gedaan, en aan de Heeren Threſorieren het Poorter-regt betaalt. Actum

Oath taken by those who attained the rank of burghers in the city of Amsterdam [ca. 1690]. At the top of the page, in smaller type, the Jewish version, in Portuguese.

Marriage Contract [ketubbah] *signed in 1617. The couple David Curiel and Rachel Curiel, residents of Amsterdam, one of the main destinations for the Jews who left the Iberian Peninsula.*

solidation of community institutions, most immigrants joined them, even though some evidenced dissident behavior and attitudes, and even lived apart from the community for a while.[129] Others returned to the Iberian world with a view to remaining there.[130]

The vast majority of Miguel Dias Santiago's partners and counterparts who were not his relatives were New Christians, a group to which he himself belonged. As Gonsalves de Mello notes, Santiago's relocation from Salvador to Olinda appears to have occurred after his counterpart, Paulo de Pina, moved from Olinda to Lisbon in 1599. Santiago similarly moved from Olinda to Lisbon in 1601 after Pina's death. These relocations, the care Santiago took with the transactions his counterpart left behind in Olinda, and later in Lisbon, as well as his attention to a series of business deals in favor of Pina's wife and subsequently his widow, reveal a very close relationship. Pina may have been related to Santiago, but would not have been close kin. Had he been, Santiago would undoubtedly have mentioned their degree of kinship on one of the many occasions when he referred to Pina, as he often did in the case of his nephews, cousins and sister.[131]

This does not mean, however, that all Santiago's agents were either relatives or New Christians. His counterparts even included foreigners. From Salvador and Olinda, Santiago sent some consignments of sugar to a "Fleming" in Lisbon, whom he called Diogo Nidrofe.[132] Hence, these numerous and varied agents included people of diverse ethnic, religious and geographic origins.

This diversity is even more evident in another example: Santiago employed António Maciel,[133] probably an Old Christian,[134] from Olinda to Viana in 1599 as a traveling agent, presumably a commissioner. The following year, he sent more sugar to the same port of destination, this time consigned to Jorge Esteves, a well-established New Christian merchant in Porto, who would presumably have gone to Viana to receive the cargo or directed someone there to do so in his stead.[135] Again in 1600, Santiago shipped another consignment to the same António Maciel who had been his traveling agent the previous year. It is not clear whether Maciel had set up residence in Viana, or travelled back to the colony to be once again employed as a traveling agent. In either case, in Maciel's absence, the consignments were to be handed over to two resident merchants. The first was António Sanches, a wealthy Old Christian merchant and a member of the town patriciate, according to Manuel António Fernandes Moreira,[136] while the second was Miguel Rodrigues de Azevedo, a New Christian, and possibly a relative of Santiago and a resident of Porto.[137]

ושמח מאשת נעוריך
יהי מקורך ברוך
יתן ה' את האשה הזאת הבאה אל ביתך כרחל
וכלאה אשר בנו שתיהם את בית ישראל
תנו לה מפרי ידיה ויהללוה בשערים מעשיה

Portrait of Cornelis Pietersz Hooft (1547–1626); *Cornelis van der Voort (1622). Merchant and politician, moderate and tolerant in religious matters, Hooft had relatives who were also merchants in Danzig (Gdansk), La Rochelle, Aveiro (Portugal) and in Norway.*

Portrait of a Man Believed to Be Dr. Ephraim Bueno (1599–1665), *Rembrandt van Rijn (ca. 1644). A famous physician and author, Bueno was born a New Christian in Portugal, studied Medicine in Bordeaux, France, and openly embraced Judaism in Amsterdam.*

Overseas

Chapter Nine

1. IANTT, STO, IL 3068, fol. 37v.; IL 12999, fol. 223; SR nos. 29 n. 37, 45 n. 48, 138, 1437, 1442, 1767, 1905.

2. Costa and Moreira strongly emphasize the absence of a hierarchy both among mercantile centers as well as among counterparts, underscoring that these were counterparts and not factors. Eddy Stols describes the new organization of the trade that emerged around the mid-sixteenth century in the following manner: "This was no longer based on monopolies (for example the Venetian or subsequently the Portuguese monopoly of the spice trade) nor on fixed axes and two poles (such as, for example, Lisbon-Antwerp), but on multiple and continuous alternatives, in a true competition [...] Italian or German style firms such as the Affaitadis or Fuggers, with their company contracts and salaried factors, were not sufficiently mobile to continually adapt to the arrival of colonial goods to different markets and to price fluctuations. The system of counterparts scattered over all the important trading centers, linked to each other not by strict contractual obligations or salaries but rather through reciprocal services and commissions, a mutual participation in limited and temporary business dealings and almost feudal ties of kinship and friendship, proved to be far more suitable": Stols, "Os mercadores flamengos," pp. 29–30. As for retainers, Stols notes the difficulties faced by the Schetzses, a great Flemish family of businessmen, in ensuring that the factors looking after their sugar mill in São Vicente complied with their orders and behaved in an acceptable manner: "If with regard to the latter problem the Schetzses appealed to the Jesuits for assistance, in the case of the former they made the mistake of not supplementing the factor's salary with a stake in the sugar mill. An even greater mistake considering that, during that age, international trading relations were increasingly being conducted on the basis of counterparts and joint ventures and less on the basis of factors and salaried service": ibid., pp. 20–27 and 42. The hierarchy among trading centers and their merchants, even with a flexible structure based on kinship ties and centered in the Iberian Peninsula, has been defended by some authors. To become better acquainted with the opinions of these authors who defended the hierarchy between the trading centers and their traders, see: Swetschinski, "The Portuguese Jewish Merchants of Seventeenth-Century Amsterdam," pp. 65, 67, 140–141, 149–151, 164–165; Mello, *Gente da nação*, pp. 15–17; idem, "Introduction and Notes," in "Os livros das saídas das urcas do porto do Recife," pp. 33–34; Israel, "The Economic Contribution of the Dutch Sephardic Jewry to Holland's Golden Age," pp. 418, 420, 429; J. I. Israel, "Manuel Lopez Pereira of Amsterdam, Antwerp and Madrid: Jew, New Christian, and Adviser of the Conde-Duque de Olivares," in idem, *Empires and Entrepots*, pp. 251–253; J. C. Boyajian, "New Christians and Jews in the Sugar Trade, 1550–1750: Two Centuries of Development of the Atlantic Economy," in P. Bernardini and N. Fiering (eds.), *The Jews and the Expansion of Europe to the West, 1450–1800* (New York: Berghahn Books, 2001), p. 473. Some historians also identified the headquarters in the Low Countries: França and Siqueira, "Introduction and Notes," pp. 134–136, 153–158. For a review of the literature on the subject, see: Strum, "The Portuguese Jews and New Christians in the Sugar Trade," pp. 140–142.

3. Costa, *O transporte no Atlântico*, v. 1, pp. 91–100, 123, 129–130, 156–158; Moreira, *Os mercadores de Viana*, p. 206. In this regard, see also: Smith, "The Mercantile Class of Portugal and Brazil," pp. 345–346; Ebert, "The Trade in Brazilian Sugar," p. 77.

4. Rau, *Estudos sobre a história do sal português*, p. 178; Swetschinski, "The Portuguese Jewish Merchants of Seventeenth-Century Amsterdam," p. 151; idem, "From the Middle Ages to the Golden Age," p. 79; idem, *Reluctant Cosmopolitans*, pp. 10–110; Mauro, *Portugal, o Brasil e o Atlântico*, v. 1, pp. 176, 187; Israel, "Spain and the Dutch Sephardim," p. 359; idem, "The Economic Contribution of the Dutch Sephardic Jewry," p. 423.

5. Lopez and Raymond, "Introduction and Notes," in idem, *Medieval Trade in the Mediterranean World*, pp. 185–211, 213, 215–217; Roover, "The Organization of Trade," pp. 70–105, 109, 115–116; E. S. Hunt and J. M. Murray, *A History of Business in Medieval Europe, 1200–1550* (Cambridge: Cambridge University Press, 1999), pp. 55–57, 62, 99–122, 155–156.

6. Costa, *O transporte no Atlântico*, v. 1, pp. 129–130; Stols, "Convivências e conivências," p. 122.

7. Moreira, *Os mercadores de Viana*, p. 17; Smith, "The Mercantile Class of Portugal and Brazil," pp. 350–351, 376, n. 1; Strum, "The Portuguese Jews and New Christians in the Sugar Trade," pp. 82–84.

8. "...and for other expenditure and costs incurred on account of his goods and my commissions": ADP, NOT, PO2, l. 29, fols. 3v.–7 (1609.7.19); SR no. 1905; Malynes, *Consuetudo: vel, lex mercatoria*, pp. 111, 113, 116, 368.

9. SR no. 644; ADP, PO2, l. 36, fols. 115v.–117 (1612-11-20); SAA, 5075: Archief van de Notarissen ter Standplaats Amsterdam, l. 33, fols. 390v.–392. For further information about partnerships, see: Smith, "The Mercantile Class of Portugal and Brazil," pp. 135, 347–350; Strum, "The Portuguese Jews and New Christians in the Sugar Trade," p. 84; Ebert, "The Trade in Brazilian Sugar," p. 99.

10. Mello, *Gente da nação*, pp. 35–50.

11. Livermore, "A marinha mercante holandesa no comércio do Brasil," p. 496, n. 3; Mauro, *Portugal o Brasil e o Atlântico*, v. 1, p. 316; Schwartz, *Sugar Plantations in the Formation of Brazilian Society*, pp. 121, 171; Boyajian, "New Christians and Jews in the Sugar Trade," passim.

12. Costa, *O transporte no Atlântico*, v. 1, p. 415; idem, "Redes interportuárias nos circuitos do açúcar brasileiro. O trajecto de Gaspar Pacheco, um banqueiro de D. João IV," in M. S. da Cunha (ed.). *Do Brasil à metrópole: efeitos sociais* (Évora: Universidade de Évora, 2001), p. 20.

13. PRO, SP, 9/104, fols. 58 ff.

14. Ibid., fol. 76. For further information about this and other consignments received and handled by this merchant, see also: Mello, *Gente da nação*, pp. 45–46.

15. PRO, SP, 9/104, fol. 62v.

16. On Olinda and Recife, see the next chapter.

17. Mello, *Gente da nação*, pp. 45–46.

18. PRO, SP, 9/104, fol. 74v.

19. Ibid., fol. 75v.

20. Ibid., fol. 75v.

21. Ibid., fols. 3, 13v., 19v.

22. SR no. 314; SAA, 5075: Archief van de Notarissen ter Standplaats Amsterdam, l. 33, fols. 390v.–392; Mello, *Gente da nação*, p. 41.

23. PRO, SP, 9/104, fol. 75.

24. It should be recalled that Stols criticizes the use of factors and retainers, who had little incentive to seek profits for their principals: Stols, "Os mercadores flamengos," pp. 20–27.

25. PRO, SP, 9/104, fols. 11, 11v, 14, 20. See also: AHU_ACL_CU_005-02, Cx.3, D.285–291 – [Bahia, before November 3, 1623]; Costa, *O transporte no Atlântico*, v. 1, pp. 332–333; Mauro, *Portugal o Brasil e o Atlântico*, v. 1, pp. 305–307.

26. Ibid., fol. 13v.

27. On these activities, see also: Mello, *Gente da nação*, p. 41.

28. PRO, SP, 9/104, fols. 25, 28.

29. Ibid., fols. 12, 50, 59; Mello, *Gente da nação*, p. 37.

30. PRO, SP, 9/104, fols. 6–6v.

31. Ibid., fol. 1.

32. Ibid., fols. 43–54, 84–85v.

33. Ibid., fol. 85v.

34. See also: Mello, *Gente da nação*, pp. 46–48.

35. PRO, SP, 9/104, fols. 78–83v.

36. Ibid., fols. 87v., 94v., 98v.

37. Ibid., fols. 95, 104, 108, 129v.

38. Ibid., fols. 128v.–129.

39. Costa, *O transporte no Atlântico*, v. 1, pp. 356–359, 429–430, 441; Moreira, *Os mercadores de Viana*, pp. 50–55, 91–92.

40. PRO, SP, 9/104, fol. 123.

41. Ibid., fol. 88v.

42. Ibid., fols. 128v–129.

43. Ibid., fol. 180.

44. Antonil, *Cultura e opulência do Brasil*, pp. 147–148.

45. PRO, SP, 9/104, fol. 111.

46. "As on 14 November they owe 12,861 for the duties of 86@ [arrobas] with the Consulate charges, since that was the weight ascertained when they were weighed in the customs house as they were not accompanied by a certificate": ibid., fol. 131v. See also: ibid., fol. 108v.

47. Ibid., fols. 98v, 121v.

48. PRO, SP, 9/104, fol. 39v.

49. Ibid., fols. 114v., 116v.; *Ordenações manuelinas*, book 3, Title XLV, Art. 17; *Ordenações filipinas*, book 3, Title LIX, Art. 19; Costa, "Informação e incerteza," pp. 112–114; Silva, *O Porto e o seu termo*, v. 2, pp. 661–666; Barros, "Porto: a construção de um espaço marítimo," v. 1, pp. 102–105;

50. PRO, SP, 9/104, fols. 101, 107, 108.

51. Ibid., fol. 110. See also: ibid., fol. 111.

52. Ibid., fol. 123.

53. Ibid., fols. 87v., 96v.

54. Ibid., fol. 96v.

55. Ibid., fol. 125v.

56. Ibid., fol. 123.

57. SR no. 206 n. 59.

58. PRO, SP, 9/104, fol. 38v. João de Paz lived in Olinda: Mello, *Gente da nação*, pp. 37, 49.

59. Ibid., fol. 36v.

60. Ibid., fol. 132v.

61. PRO, SP, 9/104, fol. 39v.

62. Ibid., fol. 95v. On behalf of this nephew in Olinda, he paid the expenditure incurred in Porto for the entry and exit of eleven crates that the nephew had sent there in a caravel and which were reloaded onto a hulk bound for the Low Countries ("Flanders"): ibid., fol. 37v.

63. Ibid., fols. 128v.–129. On the interdependence of Portuguese ports, see: Costa, *O transporte no Atlântico*, v. 1, pp. 81–100.

64. Ibid., fols. 143–143v.

65. Ibid., fols. 35v., 39v., 133v.

66. Ibid., fol. 35v.

67. Ibid., fol. 128v.

68. Ibid., fols. 136, 140, 144v.

69. Ibid., fols. 33v.–42; 78 ff.

70. Ibid., fols. 86v., 91v., 97v.

71. For further information about the activities of retainers and cashiers of merchants in Bahia, see: Smith, "The Mercantile Class of Portugal and Brazil," pp. 373–374.

72. ADP, NOT, PO2, l. 37, fols. 48–50 (1613-6-10). On this case see also: Costa, *O transporte no Atlântico*, v. 1, p. 96.

73. Schwartz, *Sugar Plantations in the Formation of Brazilian Society*, pp. 120–121, 162.

74. SR nos. 157, 284, 299, 412; IANTT, STO, IL 728, p. 168v. Among many other cases, see: ADP, NOT, PO2, l. 40, fols. 63–64 (1615-2-11).

75. Some documents mentioning traveling agents entrusted with large consignments or traders traveling with many wares give the impression that these agents were supercargoes: ADP, PO2, l. 40, pp. 150v.–151 (1615-6-15). However, in other instances it is hard to tell whether the traveler traded the cargo or merely accompanied it, leaving the remaining transactions in the hands of a fixed agent at the destination port: ADP, NOT, PO1, l. 136, fols. 16v.–18 (1615-7-1).

76. SR nos. 387, 447, 448, 455.

77. ADP, PO1, l. 149, fols. 12v.–13v. (1625-10-21).

78. ADP, NOT, PO2, l. 38, fols. 68v.–70 (1614-5-17); l. 39, fols. 157–158v. (1614-11-3); l. 40, fols. 45–46 (1615-1-28); IANTT, STO, IL 728, fols. 5v., 58v., 230.

79. Lopez and Raymond, "Introduction and Notes," pp. 174–176; Roover, "The Organization of Trade," pp. 49–54; Pryor, "Commenda," passim; B. Z. Kedar, *Merchants in Crisis: Genoese and Venetian Men of Affairs and the Fourteenth Century Depression* (New Haven: Yale University Press, 1976), pp. 21–42; Hunt and Murray, *A History of Business in Medieval Europe*, pp. 60–61. For a clearer parallel between medieval commenda and early modern supercargoes, see: Moreira, *Os mercadores de Viana*, pp. 207–209.

80. SR no. 314; SAA, 30452: Archief van S. Hart, l. 253, fol. 151v.; ADP, NOT, PO2, l. 4, fols. 11–13 (1595-7-5); Costa, *O transporte no Atlântico*, v. 1, p. 189; Strum, "The Portuguese Jews and New Christians in the Sugar Trade," pp. 86–88; ADP, NOT, PO1, l. 148, fols. 62–63 (1624-6-12).

81. PRO, SP, 9/104, fol. 6.

82. PRO, SP, 9/104, fol. 12.

83. On Brandão, see: Mello, *Gente da nação*, pp. 26–27; Gonçalves, *Guerras e açúcares*, pp. 219–223.

84. Brandão, *Diálogos das grandezas do Brasil*, p. 105.

85. Costa, *O transporte no Atlântico*, v. 1, pp. 442–448; Polónia, "Os náuticos das carreiras ultramarinas," pp. 125–126; Strum, "The Portuguese Jews and New Christians in the Sugar Trade," pp. 88–89. On the mercantile activities of seafarers, who also operated on their own account, see: Costa, *O transporte no Atlântico*, v. 1, pp. 445–448.

86. ADP, NOT, PO2, l. 26, fols. 192–194 (1607-4-21).

87. Roover, *L'évolution de la lettre de change*, pp. 122, 124–125; idem, "The Organization of Trade," pp. 53–57; Muñoz de Juana, "Scholastic Morality and the Birth of Economics," pp. 31–36; Melé, "Early Business Ethics in Spain," pp. 181–183; Ceccarelli, "Risky Business," passim; Grotius, *The Rights of War and Peace*, XII–XXIII; Van der Wee, *The Growth of the Antwerp Market and the European Economy*, v. 2, p. 358.

88. ADP, NOT, PO2, l. 40, fols. 41v.–42v. (1615-1-28).

89. For further information about sea loans, see: Moreira, *Os mercadores de Viana*, pp. 121–122; Israel, *Dutch Primacy in World Trade*, pp. 76–77; Strum, "The Portuguese Jews and New Christians in the Sugar Trade," pp. 89–91.

90. For a more detailed analysis of the advantages of the different types of agency arrangements, see: ibid., pp. 70–111; Costa, *O transporte no Atlântico*, v. 1, pp. 91–100, 123, 129–130, 156–158, 184, 189, 203, 232–235; 338–339, 442–448; Ebert, "The Trade in Brazilian Sugar," pp. 153–155; Israel, *Dutch Primacy in World Trade*, pp. 76–77; Moreira, *Os mercadores de Viana*, pp. 17, 121–122, 132–133, 143, n. 6, 206; Polónia, "Os náuticos das carreiras ultramarinas," pp. 125–126; Smith, "The Mercantile Class of Portugal and Brazil," pp. 135, 347–351, 360, 373–374, 376, n. 1; Stols, "Os mercadores flamengos," pp. 29–30.

91. ADP, NOT, PO2, l. 37, fols. 125v.–126v. (1613-7-31); ibid., fols. 126v–127v. (1613-7-31).

92. Brandão, *Diálogos das grandezas do Brasil*, p. 25. Friar Vicente do Salvador made a similar observation: Oliveira, *A História do Brazil de Frei Vicente do Salvador*, v. 2, fol. 136v.

93. ADP, NOT, PO2, l. 37, fols. 48–50 (1613-6-10).

94. Smith, "The Mercantile Class of Portugal and Brazil," p. 361.

95. Malynes, *Consuetudo: vel, lex mercatoria*, p. 111.

96. ADP, NOT, PO2, l. 20, fols. 90–91v. (1603-7-7); l. 29, fols. 76–77v. (1609-8-26).

97. Moreira attributes great importance to powers of attorney in agency relationships, which was not evident in the documents examined; Moreira, *Os mercadores de Viana*, pp. 17, 132–133, 143, n. 6.

98. Ibid., p. 54, n. 66.

99. For a systematic discussion on the question of kinship and affinity in agency relationships in the sugar trade, see: Strum, "The Portuguese Jews and New Christians in the Sugar Trade," pp. 112–186; França and Siqueira, "Introduction and Notes," pp. 151, 153–158, 160, 169–173; Swetschinski, "The Portuguese Jewish Merchants of Seventeenth-Century Amsterdam," pp. 134–291, 215–221, 273–274; idem, "Kinship and Commerce," pp 52–74; idem, "From the Middle Ages to the Golden Age," p. 81; Mello, "Os livros das saídas das urcas do porto do Recife," pp. 33–34; idem, *Gente da nação*, pp. 5–79; Costa, *O transporte no Atlântico*, v. 1, pp. 130–140, 160–161, 291–293, 413–437, 515–587; idem, "Merchant Groups in the Seventeenth-Century Brazilian Sugar Trade, Reappraising Old Topics with New Research Insights," *E-Journal of Portuguese History 2*:1 (2004), passim; Israel, "The Economic Contribution of the Dutch Sephardic Jewry," pp. 418, 420, 429; idem, "Manuel Lopez Pereira of Amsterdam, Antwerp and Madrid," pp. 251–253; idem, "Diasporas Jewish and Non-Jewish and World Maritime Empires," in I. B. Mccabe, G. Harlaftis, and I. P. Minoglou (eds.), *Diaspora Entrepreneurial Networks: Four Centuries of History* (Oxford: Berg, 2005), pp. 3–26; Smith, "The Mercantile Class of Portugal and Brazil," pp. 103–104, 119, 125–127, 137–138, 145, 153–155, 168–169; idem, "Old Christian Merchants and the Foundation of the Brazil Company," passim; Mauro, *Portugal o Brasil e o Atlântico*, v. 1, pp. 279–298; Ebert, "The Trade in Brazilian Sugar," pp. 14, 80, 82–83, 88, 90, 97–98, 217; Stols, "Os mercadores flamengos," pp. 30, 42; idem, "Convivências e conivências," pp. 134–141; Moreira, *Os mercadores de Viana*, pp. 35, 144–145, 206–207; C. Antunes, *Globalisation in the Early Modern Period* (Amsterdam: Aksant, 2004), p. 137; Boyajian, "New Christians and Jews in the Sugar Trade," passim.

100. Mello, *Gente da nação*, pp. 36–41. However, it is not clear why Gonsalves de Mello did not point out that Santiago's cousin, called Duarte Fernandes, might not have been the brother of Diogo Fernandes Camarajibe but just a namesake, since there is no other reliable genealogical reference to the kinship ties between them, apart from Duarte Fernandes being mentioned as a cousin in Miguel Dias Santiago's account book: PRO, SP, 9/104, fol. 36.

101. T. F. Rodrigues, "As estruturas populacionais," in Mattoso, *História de Portugal*, v. 3, pp. 206–210. On Viana's role in the context of colonization, see: Moreira, *Os mercadores de Viana*, pp. 7–23. See also the bibliography in: M. A. F. Moreira, "O porto de Viana do Castelo na época dos Descobrimentos, abordagem das fontes," *O Litoral em perspectiva histórica (sécs. XVI–XVIII): actas* (2002): 41–46.

102. BA, 51-VIII-5, fol. 123; 51-VIII-9, fol. 97, 51-V-71, fol. 84; *Livro primeiro do governo do Brasil*, doc. 46, pp. 221–223, doc. 65, pp. 241–242, doc. 68, pp. 246–247, doc. 69, pp. 247–248, doc. 75, pp. 259–260; Silva, *O Porto e o seu termo*, v. 1, pp. 330, 338–339; Stols, "Os mercadores flamengos," pp. 36–37; idem, "Convivências e conivências," passim.

103. Silva, *O Porto e o seu termo*, v. 1, pp. 338–339.

104. BA, 51-VIII-9, fol. 103; 51-VIII-19 n. 284, fols 176–176v.; 51-VIII-21, fols. 110, 150v.–152v.; Silva, *O Porto e o seu termo*, v. 1, pp. 343–345.

105. M. Bodian, *Hebrews of the Portuguese Nation: Conversos and Community in Early Modern Amsterdam* (Bloomington: Indiana University Press, 1999), pp. 14–15, 29; Y. Kaplan, "Deviance and Excommunication in the Eighteenth Century:

A Chapter in the Social History of the Sephardi Community of Amsterdam," in Michman, *Dutch Jewish History*, v. 3, p. 104; Y. Kaplan, "The Portuguese Community in Seventeenth-Century Amsterdam and the Ashkenazi World," in Michman, *Dutch Jewish History*, v. 2, passim; Y. Kaplan, "The Self-Definition of the Sephardic Jews of Western Europe and their Relation to the Alien and Stranger," in B. R. Gampel (ed.), *Crisis and Creativity in the Sephardic World – 1391–1648* (New York: Columbia University Press, 1997), passim; Y. Kaplan, "Jewish Amsterdam's Impact on Modern Jewish History," in M. Graetz (ed.), *Shöpferische Momente des europäischen Judentums in der frühen Neuzeit* (Heidelberg: Universitätsverlag C. Winter, 2000), pp. 38–44.

106. See, among others: J. L. Azevedo, *História dos cristãos-novos portugueses* (Lisbon: Clássica Editora Distribuição, 1989), passim; Bodian, *Hebrews of the Portuguese Nation*, passim.

107. See, among innumerable others: AHMP, A-PUB-45, fols. 323v.–324v.; Smith, "The Mercantile Class of Portugal and Brazil," pp. 15–19; Mello, *Gente da nação*, p. 26; A. Novinsky, *Cristãos novos na Bahia* (São Paulo: Perspectiva, 1972), pp. 67–69; Israel, "Spain and the Dutch Sephardim," pp. 355–383; Vlessing, "New Light on the Earliest History of Amsterdam Portuguese Jews," pp. 53–60; idem, "The Portuguese-Jewish Merchant Community in Seventeenth-Century Amsterdam," pp. 223–225, 231–232.

108. Lipiner, *Os baptizados em pé. Estudos acerca da origem e da luta dos cristãos-novos em Portugal* (Lisbon: Vega, 1998), passim; Tavares, *Os judeus em Portugal no século XV*, passim; F. Soyer, *The Persecution of the Jews and Muslims of Portugal: King Manuel I and the End of Religious Tolerance (1496–7)* (Leiden: Brill, 2007), pp. 182–240.

109. A. Herculano, *História da origem e estabelecimento da Inquisição em Portugal* (Lisbon: Imprensa Nacional, 1864–1872), passim; Azevedo, *História dos cristãos-novos portugueses*, pp. 17–235; F. Bethencourt, *História das Inquisições: Portugal, Espanha e Itália, séculos XV–XIX* (São Paulo: Companhia das Letras, 2000), pp. 17–33.

110. Andrade e Silva, *Collecção chronologica da legislação portugueza*, v. 1, pp. 42, 128, 271–273, 314–315; v. 2, pp. 278–279; Mea, "A Igreja em reforma," pp. 441–444; Almeida, "As misericórdias," pp. 169–176; F. Olival, "Rigor e interesses: os estatutos de limpeza de sangue em Portugal," *Cadernos de Estudos Sefarditas 4* (2004): 153–155, 156–160, 163; idem, "Juristas e mercadores à conquista das honras: quatro processos de nobilitação quinhentistas," *Revista de História Económica e Social, 2nd series, 4*:2 (2002): passim; idem, "Structural Changes within the 16th-Century Portuguese Military Orders," *E-Journal of Portuguese History 2*:2 (2004): 15; M. L. Tucci Carneiro, *Preconceito racial: Portugal e Brasil-Colônia* (São Paulo: Editora Brasiliense, 1983), pp. 108–109, 121–123.

111. Y. Baer, *A History of the Jews in Christian Spain* (Philadelphia: Jewish Publication Society, 1992), v. 2, pp. 277–283, 325; Tucci Carneiro, *Preconceito racial: Portugal e Brasil-Colônia*, pp. 43–48; Olival, "Rigor e interesses," pp. 151–155.

112. Ibid., pp. 161–164, 166–179, 182.

113. Olival, "Juristas e mercadores à conquista das honras," pp. 8–23, 43–53.

114. Idem, *As ordens militares e o estado moderno. Honra, mercê e venalidade em Portugal (1641–1789)* (Lisbon: Estar Editora, 2001), passim; idem, "Mercado de hábitos e serviços em Portugal (séculos XVII–XVIII)," *Análise Social: Revista do Instituto de Ciências Sociais da Universidade de Lisboa 38*:168 (2003): passim; idem, "Rigor e interesses," passim; N. G., Monteiro, "Elites locais e mobilidade social em Portugal nos finais do Antigo Regime," *Análise Social: Revista do Instituto de Ciências Sociais da Universidade de Lisboa 32*:141 (1997): 344; I. M. de Sousa e Silva, "A Igreja e a Ordem de Cristo no primeiro quartel do séc. XVI: a criação das comendas novas," in *Estudos em homenagem ao professor doutor José Marques*, V. 2 (Porto: Flup, 2006), p. 255, n. 21.

115. A. M. Pereira, A Inquisição no Brasil.Aspectos da sua actuação nas capitanias do Sul (de meados do séc. XVI ao início do séc. XVIII) (Coimbra: Fluc, 2006), pp. 93–94, 101, 115–117; *Traslado autentico de todos os privilégios concedidos pelos Reys destes Reynos, and Senhorios de Portugal aos Officiaes, & Familiares do Santo Officio da Inquisição* (Lisbon: Miguel Manescal, 1691), passim; J. E. Franco and P. de Assunção, *As metamorfoses de um polvo: religião e política nos regimentos da Inquisição portuguesa (séculos XVI–XIX)* (Lisbon: Prefácio Editora, 2004), passim; I. R. Pereira, *Documentos para a história da Inquisição em Portugal* (Porto: Arquivo Histórico Dominicano Português, 1984), pp. 95–98.

116. Olival, "Rigor e interesses," pp. 152–153, 158; Mea, "A rotura das comunidades cristãs novas do litoral – século XVII," p. 268.

117. Smith, "The Mercantile Class of Portugal and Brazil," pp. 31, 101–104, 138, 179–184, 210–214; H. Salomon (ed.), "The 'De Pinto' manuscript. A 17th-Century Marrano Family History," *Studia Rosenthaliana* 9:1 (1975): 20–27; Révah, *Uriel da Costa et les marranes de Porto*, passim; Silva, *O Porto e o seu termo*, v. 1, pp. 281–309.

118. Lesger, *The Rise of the Amsterdam Market and Information Exchange*, pp. 159–160; Poelwijk, *In dienste vant suyckerbacken*, pp. 200–209; J. F. Afonso, *A Rua das Flores no século XV: elementos para a história urbana do Porto quinhentista I* (Porto: FAUP, 2000), pp. 119–120, 135; Silva, *O Porto e o seu termo*, v. 1, pp. 432–433; P. de Brito, *Patriciado urbano quinhentista: as famílias dominantes do Porto (1500–1580)* (Porto: Arquivo Histórico, Câmara Municipal do Porto, 1997), passim; Smith, "The Mercantile Class of Portugal and Brazil," p. 88; Stols, "Os mercadores flamengos," p. 31.

119. Mello, *O nome e o sangue*, passim; Olival, "Juristas e mercadores," passim; Smith, "The Mercantile Class of Portugal and Brazil," pp. 204–205.

120. Much has been written, and continues to be written, about the identity, faith and practices of New Christians, often following the polemics between António José Saraiva and Salvador Israël Révah. Both this polemic itself and a fairly extensive bibliography on the subject can be found in H. P. Salomon and I. S. D. Sassoon, "Introduction," in A. J. Saraiva, *The Marrano Factory: The Portuguese Inquisition and Its New Christians* (Leiden: Brill, 2001), pp. IX–XIV, 231–341.

121. Mello, *Gente da nação*, p. 6; Schwartz, *Sovereignty and Society in Colonial Brazil*, pp. 108–110; Schwartz, *Sugar Plantations in the Formation of Brazilian Society*, pp. 265–275; Smith, "The Mercantile Class of Portugal and Brazil," pp. 334–356, 400–402, 416; Siqueira, "A Inquisição portuguesa e a sociedade colonial," pp. 149–151; Novinsky, *Cristãos novos na Bahia*, pp. 57–102; Mello, *O nome e o sangue*, pp. 174–181, 220–230; Russell-Wood, *Fidalgos and Philanthropists*, pp. 136–137.

122. Israel, "Spain and the Dutch Sephardim," pp. 355–383.

123. BA, 44-XIII-50, fols. 9–10. Some changes were made in 1583 to the conditions of the 1580 law: Azevedo, *História dos cristãos-novos portugueses*, pp. 120–121; Tucci Carneiro, *Preconceito racial: Portugal e Brasil-Colônia*, pp. 74–79.

124. H. P. Salomon, *Portrait of a New Christian. Fernão Álvares Melo 1569–1632* (Paris: Fundação Calouste Gulbenkian, 1982), pp. 41–117; idem, *Os primeiros portugueses de Amesterdão: documentos do Arquivo Nacional da Torre do Tombo, 1595–1606* (Braga: [n. n.], 1983), pp. 21–22; Révah, *Uriel da Costa*, pp. 420–442.

125. H. P. H. Nusteling, "The Jews in the Republic of the United Provinces: Origin, Numbers and Dispersion," in J. Israel and R. Salverda, *Dutch Jewry: Its History and Secular Culture (1500–2000)* (Leiden: Brill, 2002), p. 48; Y. Kaplan, "The Portuguese Community of Amsterdam in the 17th Century: Between Tradition and Change," in A. Haim (ed.), *Society and Community* (Jerusalem: Misgav Yerushalayim, 1991), p. 26; idem, "Jewish Amsterdam's Impact on Modern Jewish History," pp. 31, nn. 37, 38; Israel, "Spain and the Dutch Sephardim," p. 359, n. 16.

126. Kaplan, "Jewish Amsterdam's Impact on Modern Jewish History," passim; Swetschinski, "From the Middle Ages to the Golden Age," passim.

127. A. H. Huussen Jr., "The Legal Position of the Sephardi Jews in Holland, Circa 1600," in Michman, *Dutch Jewish History*, v.3, pp. 19–41; Vlessing, "New Light on the Earliest History of Amsterdam Portuguese Jews," pp. 44–46.

128. For further information about the status of Jews in Amsterdam during this period, see: A. H. Huussen, "The Legal Position of the Jews in the Dutch Republic c. 1590–1796," in Israel and Salverda, *Dutch Jewry: Its History and Secular Culture*, pp. 25–41; Huussen, "The Legal Position of the Sephardi Jews in Holland circa 1600"; Kaplan, "Jewish Amsterdam's Impact on Modern Jewish History"; Swetschinski, "From the Middle Ages to the Golden Age."

129. Y. Kaplan, "The Social Functions of the Herem in the Portuguese Jewish Community of Amsterdam in the Seventeenth Century," in Michman, *Dutch Jewish History*, v. 1, pp. 111–155; Kaplan, "The Intellectual Ferment in the Spanish-Portuguese Community of Seventeenth-Century Amsterdam," pp. 288–314; idem, "Wayward New Christians and Stubborn New Jews: The Shaping of a Jewish Identity," in L. Gartner and K. Stow (eds.), *Jewish History – The Robert Cohen Memorial Volume* (Haifa: Haifa University Press, 1994), v. 8, nn. 1–2, pp. 27–41; Y. Kaplan, "An Alternative Path to Modernity," in idem, *An Alternative Path to Modernity: The Sephardi Diaspora in Western Europe* (Leiden: Brill, 2000), pp. 16–22; idem, "Jewish Amsterdam's Impact on Modern Jewish History," pp. 61–62; Bodian, *Hebrews of the Portuguese Nation*, pp. 32–33. See also the bibliography in: Costa, *Exame das tradições farisaicas*; Révah, *Uriel da Costa et les marranes de Porto*.

130. Y. Kaplan, "The Travels of Portuguese Jews from Amsterdam to the 'Lands of Idolatry,'" in idem (ed.), *Jews and Conversos* (Jerusalem: Magnes, 1985), passim; D. L. Graizbord, *Souls in Dispute: Converso Identities in Iberia and the Jewish Diaspora, 1580–1700* (Philadelphia: University of Pennsylvania Press, 2004), passim; Salomon, *Os primeiros portugueses de Amesterdão*, p. 21 ff.; Israel, "Manuel Lopez Pereira of Amsterdam, Antwerp and Madrid," passim.

131. While still in Salvador, Santiago dealt with Francisco de Ataíde, resident in Portugal, who Gonsalves de Mello identified as a brother of Paulo de Pina: Mello, *Gente da nação*, pp. 36, 40, 43–44, 47–48. For Santiago's genealogy, see also: IANTT, STO, IL 9892; I. S. Révah, "Pour l'histoire des nouveaux-chrétiens portugais: la rélation généalogique d'I. de M. Aboab," *Boletim Internacional de Bibliografia Luso-Brasileira* 2:1 (1961):passim.

132. PRO, SP, 9/104, fols. 19v., 23v., 28v. Stols believes that he could have been called Nieuwhof: Stols, *De Spaanse Brabanders*, v. 2, p. 50, n. 394; Mello, "Os livros das saídas das urcas do porto do Recife," p. 45.

133. PRO, SP, 9/104, fol. 12.

134. PRO, SP, 9/104, fol. 29. It would seem more plausible that he returned to Brazil to be employed once again as a traveling agent, since on the first voyage António Maciel sailed aboard a vessel commanded by a shipmaster named Gaspar Maciel, while on this trip he sailed on Francisco Maciel's vessel, which would suggest that this was a family of seafarers and traders, mostly Old Christians, according to Moreira's notes about other individuals bearing the surname Maciel from Viana at that time and the records of the Inquisition's visit to the town in 1618, studied by Susana M. V. Carvalho. Of course, this is clearly conjecture: Moreira, *Os mercadores de Viana*, pp. 147, 153, 159, 165, 171–172; S. M. V. Carvalho, "Viana seiscentista, a visita inquisitorial de 1618," Master's thesis, Universidade do Porto, 2000, Appendix IV.

135. PRO, SP, 9/104, fol. 17v.

136. Moreira, *Os mercadores de Viana*, p. 147.

137. IANTT, STO, IL 728.

Chapter Ten

A Lawyer in His Study;
Adriaen van Ostade (168?).

The Word

Communications and Norms

The hiring of agents, contracting shipping and insurance, selling on credit and using credit instruments, among other transactions, depended on everyone involved upholding agreements, promises, terms and clauses. Counterparties were also to comply with a series of norms, which were posited, enacted, consuetudinary, agreed and implicit. In other words, the stability, expansion and efficiency of trade depended on the players' compliance with established rules. In effect, different mechanisms sought to ensure this compliance and guarantee that transgressors did not get away scot free.

In the Solicitor's Office; *Marinus van Reymerswaele (1542). Businessmen and seafarers turned to the courts and granted powers of attorney to lawyers, pleaders and solicitors to defend their rights.*

Courts and Contracts

Merchants, seafarers and trade-related professionals often went to court to solve disputes. This is evident from the numerous powers of attorney registered at notary offices in Porto and Amsterdam that were granted to enforce judgments that had already been decided. The resort to the legal system can also be inferred from the powers of attorney granted to lawyers, pleaders or solicitors to defend the rights of the grantor in court. Perhaps some of these powers of attorney were just preventive measures, without any lawsuits actually being filed. However, they suggest that parties seriously considered the possibility of resorting to judicial proceedings.[A] In Brazil, the previously mentioned Ambrósio Fernandes Brandão, merchant, sugar-mill owner and tax farmer, stated that he had appealed to the Court of Appeal in Salvador against various sentences issued by the magistrate in Pernambuco.[1]

Various other types of procedures were carried out with possible lawsuits in mind. This was the case with the certificates and protests issued for merchandise that arrived with a shortfall, or whose quality was different from what was expected. Miguel Dias Santiago had such certificates produced for consignments of wine and sugar. Such testimonies *in perpetuam rei memoriam*, prepared by notaries or customs and official scales officials, served as proof in case of disputes between the merchant receiving the goods and other parties, such as the consignor, the shipmaster or any overseas agent.[2] These testimonies were often accompanied by affidavits from shipmasters, loaders and depot staff, among others. Protests for non-acceptance or non-payment of bills of exchange, or for not having the chartered cargo loaded during the laytime, were also drawn up with lawsuits in mind. In case of lack of acceptance or payment, these protests served to charge the sum mentioned in the bill, plus re-exchange and other costs and damages. When shipments were not loaded, even if such protests were not necessary, they helped the shipmaster charge the charterer for shipping. The charterer, in turn, would resolve the matter with the individual responsible for loading the merchandise.

Trade and shipping involved tremendous mobility, which facilitated absconding and concealment, or diversion of debtors' assets. In one case, two Portuguese youths appeared as translators on behalf of a Portuguese merchant in Amsterdam. A year and a half earlier, the merchant had sold a shipment of Brazilian tobacco to a Dutchman who still owed him part of the agreed sum which the latter had promised to pay by transferring a bill

A. Other powers of attorney were granted to non-pratictioners to recover outstanding credits, authorizing them to use legal means, if necessary. As already seen, there is no doubt that many of these powers of attorney only sought to transfer the credits to the proxy and were not related to existing disputes, and even less to ongoing lawsuits. Be that as it may, going to court was a real possibility. In Portugal, powers of attorney tended not to describe the matter in dispute explicitly. However, the abundance of powers of attorney issued by merchants suggests that many were related to mercantile or financial issues (Strum, "The Portuguese Jews and New Christians in the Sugar Trade," pp. 294–307).

obligatory. However, the purchaser, who lived in an attic with his family, fled the city, leaving numerous debts behind. A month later, he was located in Zeeland, so the creditor granted a power of attorney to an individual living in that province to recover the debt.[3]

In order to avoid defaults and fraud, it was a common practice to seize assets and even imprison fraudsters and defaulting debtors. Contracts signed in Porto habitually contained a clause issuing a power of attorney to the warden of the city jail[B] (a kind of police officer), authorizing him to seize assets or arrest the defaulting debtor.

Lawsuits, protests, arrests and seizures were lodged, filed and enforced overseas, in foreign lands and even in enemy territories. Many powers of attorney were granted in Porto for the purpose of suing or seizing the assets of residents and visitors in Brazil.[4] A resident of the village of Linhares, in the Portuguese hinterland (probably from Beira province), enforced his rights against a defaulting debtor living in Pernambuco. The creditor ensured that the customs house magistrate in Porto seized some sugar and had it trusteed in the hands of two merchants in Porto. The creditor in Linhares instructed his proxies in Porto – a lawyer, two merchants and one of his retainers – to seize any and all of the debtor's assets that should arrive in that city or the surrounding region. This debtor was none other than Ambrósio Fernandes Brandão.[5/C]

The Southern Low Countries – both Catholic and loyal to the Habsburgs – and the neutral nations served as a judicial bridge between the Dutch Republic and the Iberian world. In 1625, at the height of the war, a merchant based in Amsterdam granted power of attorney to a counterpart in neutral Hamburg. The former authorized the latter to seize all the goods belonging to a Lisbon businessman to be found in Hamburg (he also knew or suspected that some items were in the hands of a certain trader). The grantor expressly stated that he hoped to obtain the payment due to him by proceeding in this manner.[6]

The Southern Low Countries were very close to the Dutch Republic, both geographically and economically. Many businessmen divided their time between both territories, which further complicated the definition of the boundaries of "Flanders" from the Iberian point of view. This blurring was more intense in the period preceding the Twelve Years' Truce, when the reunification of the rebel provinces with the Southern Low Countries was still a possibility. Hence, in their disputes with Porto and Lisbon, plaintiffs and defendants based in the northern provinces took action and responded through the judiciary in Antwerp and Brussels. The judgments of these courts were deemed to be valid on both sides, both Iberian and Dutch, due to political-religious legitimacy on one side, and to national legal traditions on the other.[7]

Thus, if a defaulting or dishonest businessman or seafarer wished to continue to trade in the port where his principals or creditors lived, or in a neutral port, he was exposed to having his goods seized there and or to being arrested.[8] If war broke out, a party could be harassed while finding himself in an enemy nation, and forced to acquiesce to an unfavorable and perhaps unjust solution. Nevertheless, after returning home or reaching a neutral port, he could appeal, claiming that he had acted under duress, and win.[9]

While imprisonment and the seizure of goods were powerful means of dealing with absconders and defaulters, they hindered exchange when used excessively, precipitately or frivolously.[10] In order to avoid excesses the plaintiff would be liable for reparations for losses, damages and foregone profits if the defendant was found to have been arrested unjustly.[11] Whenever necessary, the intervention of guarantors and trustees enabled individuals, vessels, goods and currency to continue to circulate until the matter was settled.

If the debtor had neither domicile nor credit in the town, and filed an appeal (which could potentially be a maneuver to gain time and abscond), the Dutch courts allowed such individuals to remain free as long as they reported to the authorities periodically until the appeal was heard and judged. This reflects how capital and the capacity to obtain credit were critical, even to an individual's physical liberty.[12]

With the economy becoming more market-oriented, the authorities became increasingly concerned about bankruptcy frauds, which precipitated extensive domino effects. As far back as the early sixteenth century, Portuguese law stipulated that anyone who maliciously failed to pay their debts or became insolvent would be imprisoned until they had paid everything they owed.[D] A law enacted 1597 specifically dealt with fraudulent default and bankruptcy.[13] Philip II justified it as follows:

> *...because I have been informed that... some merchants collapsed, maliciously going bankrupt, with merchandise bought on credit and having taken a lot of money on loan through exchange operations. In addition to absconding, they conceal their assets to such an extent that they will never be found and have their credits under the name of third parties. In order to claim losses, they pretend to have made shipments to India and other places, which they do not declare until after news arrives of some cargo being lost. When individuals from outside the realm go bankrupt, they pretend to be major stakeholders as though they were creditors. With these subterfuges and collusion they attempt to cover up their bankruptcy frauds, believing that by these methods they will not be punished; and that thereby they could more easily reach a settlement with their creditors, asking them instead to acquiesce to a voluntary agreement for most of their debts.*[E]/[14]

The Hispanic monarch equated such acts with theft and subjected them to the same penalties. These were also applicable to any accomplices, including the merchant's agents (factors) and all those who helped him conceal or divert the goods, or hid people who had fraudulently gone

B. The "minor warden" was responsible for making arrests – when equipped with a judicial warrant, when the perpetrator was caught red-handed, during serious disturbances to public order, or if a suspect was found on the streets after a curfew – serving as a jailor to prisoners and bringing them to hearings, enforcing debts and watching over the city day and night, patrolling it with the assistance of his men. The royal judge's bailiff also had very similar functions such as making arrests, collecting fines and auditing regulated activities and prices (Silva, *O Porto e o seu termo*, v. 2, pp. 667–677).

C. The trustees were two brothers who became the brothers-in-law of a nephew of Miguel Dias Santiago, and later embraced Judaism in Amsterdam and Hamburg: ADP, NOT, PO2, l. 27, fols. 142–143v. [1609-5-6].

D. When an item is transferred or sold by the debtor to a third party, one-third would remain with the new owner, another third would go to the damaged party and the last third to the Crown (*Ordenações Manuelinas*, Book 5, Title LXV). This procedure was also maintained in 1603 in the *Ordenações Filipinas* (*Ordenações Filipinas*, Book 5, Title LXV).

E. This excerpt has been provided in modern English to facilitate understanding.

bankrupt. Individuals who had failed after gambling with or frittering away other people's money were also classified in the same category. They would only be exempted from more severe penalties if they had been lead to ruin as a result of force majeure.[F] In such cases, they were entitled to reach voluntary agreements arbitrated under the auspices of tribunals with exclusive jurisdiction over mercantile and shipping matters, as we will see shortly.[G]

In effect, when a bankruptcy was not a fraud, it was in everyone's interests, especially the creditors', for the debtors to recover. Hence, it did no one any good to keep them in jail.[15] In the Low Countries, a bankrupt party who had hopes of a quick recovery could ask the legal authorities for a few months' grace before being subject to imprisonment and seizures. This process was called *sûretés de corps* and was frequently used by the merchants in Amsterdam examined in this volume. If such an individual wanted more time, he would have to file for a moratorium (respite), applying to the Court of Holland for a letter of attermination allowing him a few years to repay the debts, at the judge's discretion. He had to provide guarantees and obtain the consent of his major creditors. Another way of avoiding arrest was to hand over all assets to creditors in a process akin to modern-day bankruptcies. This depended on obtaining the approval of the competent magistrate, notifying all creditors and bringing in an assignee. This was not applicable to bankruptcy frauds however, and, until creditors were fully repaid, the debtor could only keep enough earnings to provide for his subsistence.[16]

Despite all this, resorting to the legal system consumed time and money as it does today. Moreover, magistrates often did not understand the matters that they were to adjudicate.[17] Notwithstanding these limitations, merchants must have believed that the system was somewhat effective, otherwise they would not have repeatedly resorted to such an onerous mechanism. The legal system also had a discouraging effect, since awareness of the possibility of judicial punishment, at home or abroad, in times of peace or war, would have somehow served as a deterrent to fraud. Going to court was more relevant in disputes involving larger amounts.

It is also important to note that merchants anticipated relying on the courts when they entered into contracts. As we have seen, Portuguese legislation required that contracts involving sums of more than 60,000 réis be registered with notaries to be considered admissible evidence in court.[18] Nevertheless, Portuguese jurisprudence and doctrine held that "the promptness [haste] in contracts between merchants exempts registering them before a notary."[19] Instead, admissible evidence could be provided in the form of private documents and witnesses.[20] This was also the case in Holland.[21] While examining freight contracts, we have seen that merchants and shipmasters often used private contracts and even relied on oral agreements. Merchants appeared before notaries, mainly in matters that required greater formality such as those involving individuals who were absent, orphans, widows, minors, and so forth. Notaries were also resorted to in transactions that were not habitual between the parties, in situations of greater risk or when familiarity or trust did not prevail among the interested parties. This was true for mercantile agreements in general, and not just freight contracts. There is no doubt that the decision to spend time and money having documents recorded before notaries derived from the anticipated usefulness of the deed in court, even though it was not compulsory as admissible evidence.

Mercantile Usage

Just as it is today, contracts were not a panacea, and could not anticipate all the exigencies that might arise. At the very least, however, the parties covered what they believed to be the most pertinent concerns, as well as the variables inherent to the agreement itself, such as the size of the cargo and the port of destination in the case of freight contracts. However, the drawbacks of and gaps in contracts and legislation were supplemented by fairly well-established mercantile custom that was relatively uniform and universal throughout Western Europe and its overseas possessions, with few regional differences. The latter was the result of centuries of experience, and the interests of both businessmen and authorities in the ensuing scalability and stability of trade. Examples of such uniformity and universalization have been seen in the case of both bills of lading and bills of exchange.[22]

Individuals dealing in such matters and in foreign marketplaces were familiar with regional differences in mercantile and shipping usage and custom. Such differences were described at length in merchants' manuals and attested to by experts on request.[23] Such disparities were also mentioned in contracts, such as in the case of freight contracts, which typically stipulated that goods would be loaded and unloaded in accordance with the "land's custom."[24]

Attitudes that went against or questioned established custom were repudiated.[25] Hence, clauses of agreements and contracts, whether registered at notary offices, prepared privately or agreed upon orally, were implicitly supplemented by a comprehensive, well-known and binding system of norms.[26]

Usage and custom influenced the decisions of magistrates, arbiters and mercantile tribunals. In the 1530s, Emperor Charles V had the customs of Antwerp codified and made them binding, seeking to resolve issues where they clashed with Roman and Germanic law.[27] In 1592, his son Philip II created the Consulate in Portugal, which was a kind of professional corporation for merchants, and was hence also known as the Merchants' University or Mercantile Business House. The Consulate maintained a tribunal[H] with exclusive jurisdiction over mercantile matters. Its magistrates of first instance (primary or original jurisdiction) were not jurists but rather merchants elected by their peers, with the assistance of a legal advisor. This institution was created after merchants' corporations with the same name that had been established centuries before in the Crown of Aragon and elsewhere, and its statutes were regulated two years later.[I]

F. "...if they suffer heavy losses at sea, or on land, in the course of their lawful trade & business, without there being any malice or willfulness in this regard, they will not be subject to any criminal penalty...." (BNP, RES. 84//16 A: *Ley sobre os mercadores que quebram* [1597-03-08], p. 41).

G. "... the matter shall be referred to the prior and consuls of the Consulate, who will seek to settle and reconcile the debtor with his creditors, according to the regulations" (Ibid.).

H. With regard to the functions of this tribunal, the charter that created the Consulate also states: "...they will adjudicate all business matters, which henceforth arise between merchants and their factors [agents], and any and all matters regarding, concerning and subordinated to mercantile matters, trade and commerce between merchants, including purchases and sales between them, as well as debts derived from exchanges, and the way these should be processed, as well as insurance taken out in this city, accounts with companies, both existing and to be established, and mariners' remuneration for which money is paid to the owners and shipmasters of the carracks and ships...." (Charter dated July 30, 1592 in *Documentos para a história do açúcar*, p. 397). Another law referred to its functions as being: "The way in which foreigners and locals who have companies in this city should trade, & what should be settled in terms of insurance, & exchanges, & accounts, what factors should render to their principals, & how the carracks & ships should depart from the port in this city, & from other ports in the realm" (BNP, RES. 84//16 A: *Ley sobre os mercadores que quebram* [1597-03-08]).

I. These magistrates were chosen indirectly by a college of thirty members, elected by registered merchants, and, in turn, appointed the officials: J. F. Borges, *Fontes, especialidade, e excellencia da administração commercial*, p. 48 ff.

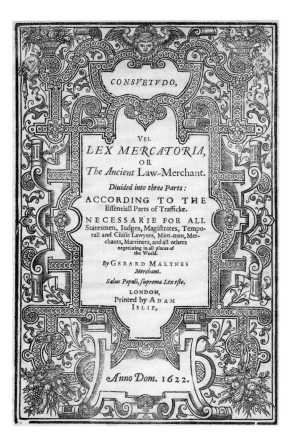

Title page of Consuetudo: vel, lex mercatoria, *by the merchant Gerard Malynes (ca.1586–1641); printed in London in 1622, it proclaims its indispensability for authorities, judges, magistrates and lawyers, among other professionals.*

Principals and major partners[28] could also sue their agents (factors) and associates (partners) through the Consulate, even if they lived in the overseas colonies or were only there temporarily. In such cases, account books, letters and witnesses were to be considered admissible as evidence. If the agent failed to attend, he would be judged and sentenced by default, as long as the principal left a guarantee in case the accused arrived with new evidence. Once again, the primary objective was to achieve a speedy outcome, leaving scope for an equitable solution in case the accused had been unjustly convicted without having been able to duly present his case or defend himself. Defendants could default owing to either personal difficulties or transport and communications shortcomings, which were more acute in some parts of the Portuguese world than in others.[29]

The Consulate's functions also included deciding cases of bankruptcy; regulating the insurance and exchange markets, as long as this was in conformance with the laws on usury of both the realm and the church; monitoring the work of the brokers who certified sales and purchases, particularly by foreigners; supervising the distribution of cargo salvaged from shipwrecks amongst involved parties; and registering all sea loans (described in the previous chapter), so as to ensure greater control over credit transactions.[30]

Since this tribunal primarily aimed to adjudicate disputes speedily based on practical expertise, its magistrates were to produce "a succinct and well-founded report [judgment] by individuals well versed in this profession."[31] Suits were brought orally, as were the replies by the opposing party, and attempts would be made to reconcile the litigants. If these attempts failed, the parties would present their case in writing. In order to avoid time being wasted with intricate juridical digressions, such presentations were not to be prepared by qualified lawyers even though they could be consulted.[J] Magistrates, in turn, would follow the mercantile custom, and not Civil Law: "They will proceed and decide everything succinctly and summarily, in the manner of merchants, as they deem to be fair, with the truth coming to light and good faith being safeguarded."[32]

Appeals were allowed only in disputes involving larger sums and were first heard within the Consulate, which had a magistrate to hear appeals appointed by the monarch. This magistrate should be an individual with both mercantile experience and some legal training, who was to summon two experienced merchants to adjudicate each appeal along with him. Their decisions could only be appealed in higher courts outside the Consulate only if the dispute involved amounts of more than 1,600,000 réis.[33]

As we saw in Chapter 1, the establishment of the Consulate also entailed the creation of a new 3% tax on imports and exports in order to finance both the operations of the tribunal and a fleet to defend the coast. While the tribunal was abolished in 1602 for various reasons, the 3% tax was maintained, and allegedly continued to be used to safeguard the coast and combat piracy.[K]

After the Consulate's abolition, trading and shipping disputes fell within the purview of the customs house magistrate, as long as the cases in question involved small amounts. This magistrate's profile, however, was closer to other royal officials, being a bureaucrat, than to merchants. Nevertheless, neither the Consulate nor the customs house magistrate excluded civil magistrates, who continued to decide mercantile disputes by themselves and with the assistance of merchants and trade-related professionals. Despite the Consulate's brief existence, Portuguese jurisprudence would continue to regard trade usage and custom as legally binding.[34]

Had it not been for the premature abolition of the Consulate as a merchants' corporation, Portugal would have preceded the United Provinces in the field of specialized mercantile jurisdiction. In Amsterdam, tribunals of peers (colleges), subordinate to the municipal administration and appointed by the latter, gradually began to regulate and resolve commercial and financial disputes. A tribunal of reconciliation handling minor disputes was created in 1598 and professionalized in 1611. As has been seen, the Insurance Chamber was also founded in 1598, and was to decide upon cases pertaining to policies signed within the city's jurisdiction. The Chamber's decisions were appealable to the city's magistrates, and cases suspected of fraud were referred to the regular court. The Chamber of Maritime Affairs was only created in 1641 and the Chamber of Bankruptcy was instituted three years later.[35] In Amsterdam, it was common for magistrates to appoint merchants to arbitrate mercantile disputes, thus sanctioning usage and custom.[36]

Arbitrating Disputes

Using arbiters was a common practice. Their advantages were similar to those of modern day arbitration: saving time and money and being able to rely on experts in the matter at hand. These advantages were openly expressed in documents registered with notaries: "in order to avoid chagrin, expenses, differences and claims and other consequences that might result from litigations, and because their outcome is uncertain."[37] Generally, each party appointed an arbiter with the consent of the other party.[38] If the two arbiters were unable to arrive at a decision by consensus, a third arbiter could be chosen by the two arbiters or appointed by the parties. There were cases in which this third arbiter was appointed by the parties together with the first two arbiters, although he would only be summoned to provide a

J. "...because it would not be opportune in such matters for opinions to be issued by them [lawyers] based on Law, since it is aimed to ensure that there are no delays in resolving ordinary cases in this Tribunal, especially in routine matters which are better understood by those in the profession than by lawyers"; "Provizão e regimento do consulado portuguez," p. 44.

K. A plan for a Consulate had been already considered during the reign of King Henry (Henrique).

deciding vote if the first two were unable to make a decision. On other occasions, the parties nominated the third arbiter only after the proceedings had reached an impasse.[39]

Cases could involve an even larger number of arbiters, including up to three per side, for a total of seven.[40] Arbiters were generally chosen amongst more prominent merchants in the city, or from larger mercantile centers. The selection sometimes extended to lawyers, professionals whose activities made them experts and other figures with moral authority. Businessmen and seafarers resorted to arbitration abroad through proxies.[41]

Arbitration was formal when the parties expressly committed to abide by the arbiters' decision, which was binding and could be enforced by public officials, while appealing these decisions necessitated the prior payment of heavy fines to the opposing party. If, in formal arbitrations, arbiters had to comply with certain procedures these were still far quicker than those involved in legal proceedings.[42] They were often remunerated, but undoubtedly received smaller sums than the costs involved in lawsuits.

Celebration of the Peace of Münster, 1648, at the Headquarters of the Crossbowmen's Civic Guard, Amsterdam; *Bartholomeus van der Helst (1648). The civic militia of Amsterdam celebrates the Peace of Münster, as the treaties that brought the Eighty Years' War between the Dutch and Spaniards to a close became known, and the Dutch Republic was recognized de jure as a sovereign state. The accords signed in Münster were also a stage of the so-called Peace of Westphalia, the series of treaties that ended the Thirty Years' War in Europe.*

An excellent example is the dispute between Francisco de Cáceres, a leading merchant in Porto, and Diogo de São Pedro and Amador Álvares, traveling agents and co-owners of a carrack. They had taken Francisco de Cáceres's merchandise on their carrack from Porto to Angola, where they apparently had bought slaves, later selling them in Bahia, and bringing back the proceeds of these transactions in sugar. The dispute over the value of the proceeds had been decided by the royal civil magistrate (*corregedor do cível*) of Porto, but doubts arose between the parties when the verdict was to be enforced. To avoid further delays with judicial proceedings, Francisco de Cáceres appointed another merchant living in the city, Diogo Henriques Cardoso, as his arbiter and the other two similarly appointed someone they trusted. In case the arbiters felt it necessary to appoint third parties, they could do so without needing the consent of the litigants. The litigants pledged their assets to comply with the decision and appointed the warden of the prison in Porto as their proxy to enforce the decision and arrest them, if necessary. A penalty of 300 cruzados (1,200 réis) was stipulated for any party appealing the arbiters' decision and the two former agents withdrew the appeal they had filed with the royal civil magistrate against the sentence.

The arbiters went through the accounts of the venture, deducting the ordinary expenditures, the costs incurred while purchasing twelve crates of panela sugar and the freight charges for transporting these crates from Bahia to Porto. The crates had already been received and cleared through customs by Francisco de Cáceres, who had paid the respective duties and taxes in Porto.[43] The most interesting element of this document is what followed. The net value to be decided as due to the merchant would be reinvested in another consignment to be entrusted to the same agents. With the proceeds from the sale of these wares, the agents were to buy slaves in Angola and sell them in Brazil, likewise deducting the expenditure and costs incurred in this operation. The net proceeds of this new transaction were to be paid in cash, in Porto, on the date to be stipulated by the arbiters. Hence, the parties were not just interested in continuing the circulation of money, vessels and people but also in maintaining their own commercial relationship. The result represented a second chance, which would hopefully be profitable for both sides or, at the very least, less onerous than litigation.

In Amsterdam, brokers served as arbiters in transactions that they had facilitated, since they were responsible for assessing the creditworthiness of the counterparties and should not allow contracts to be signed by those unable to fulfill their side of the deal.[44] A notary in Amsterdam served a notice to a Portuguese merchant at the request of a confectioner to whom the merchant had sold white sugar loaves from Madeira – that is, the white bases of loaves – in two crates. The confectioner complained that ten loaves were broken, and had mostly been mixed with lower-quality types of sugar. He refused to take delivery at the agreed price and demanded they be replaced with good-quality product. The merchant responded that he would abide by the decision of the broker who had served as the intermediary in the sale.[45]

The use of informal arbitration was suggested in the clauses pertaining to the distribution of the general averages in some shipping contracts in Porto, which stipulated that this would be done "amicably by two men well versed in these matters without disputes or magistrates."[46]

Through informal arbitration, the parties probably dispensed with formalities and gave up binding decisions that conferred the right to proceed to enforcement in favor of simplicity, swiftness and lower costs. Informal arbitration was more common in simpler cases involving smaller sums. Formal arbitration, on the other hand, was more often used as a substitute for legal proceedings that had already begun or were to be enforced, as in the aforesaid example. It was also used during disputes requiring a greater degree of formality such as those involving real estate, inheritances or third parties, especially minors, widows and absent heirs.[47]

Both civil and mercantile courts and, primarily, arbiters tried to reconcile the parties, which would save the time, effort and circumspection required to decide the matter. In effect, the simplest way of solving conflicts was an "amicable agreement," when the parties settled and reached an accommodation, ending the dispute. These agreements were often formalized by a notary in which the parties agreed would be binding and in effect as though they were a final and unappealable judgment. Apart from magistrates and arbiters, families and the social milieu played a role, exerting pressure for parties to reach an agreement. In his campaign against the court of appeal being established in Bahia in 1609, Ambrósio Fernandes Brandão alleged:

> *...all the residents of this State [i.e. Brazil], in the captaincies where they live, are linked to each other by kinship or friendship, and they never take their pleas so far that it is necessary for them to file an appeal at the Court of Appeal in Bahia, because before it can get to that stage friends and relatives get involved, reconciling them and forging an agreement, so that their disputes come to an end and as a result few appeals [from other places in Brazil] are filed in Bahia; and with regard to those that are filed there, it would be better if all the residents of Brazil sent their appeals to Portugal.*[48]

In any case, a settlement was preferable, above all, for the parties themselves. They saved time, animosity and incalculable risks in getting involved in interminable proceedings or intricate arbitration. This is what they voiced repeatedly in documents formalizing amicable settlements:

> *"Since they [parties] were related and in order to avoid qualms, animosity, hatred, costs and expenditures, which usually are entailed by such lawsuits, whose outcome is doubtful and uncertain... they have arrived at a settlement through a transaction and an amicable composition."*[49]

Often, the parties realized that no magistrate or arbiters would find a precise solution for their dispute or that such a solution "would not be reached without much dispute and cost."[50] Hence, it was better to be content with a partial, but at least speedy, solution. Sometimes, however, this realization dawned quite late in the process, when the parties were already tired of their disputes and decided to concede some of their uncompromising demands.[51]

Building a Reputation

Prominent merchants, small traders, shipmasters, insurers, brokers, boatmen, stowers, and so forth, generally acted correctly. They did so not just to avoid lawsuits and quarrels but above all to preserve and expand their commercial relationships with old and new counterparties, in the same city as well as in other trade centers. An individual's reputation was one of the most important assets for men involved with trade, if not *the* most important.

The following example is a case in point: on October 2, 1626, a notary registered a statement in Amsterdam at the request of the Portuguese Jewish merchant Jerônimo Rodrigues Mendes. Mendes claimed that, a little over a week earlier, a Dutch insurer had come up to him at the Bourse and handed him a letter from the English shipmaster John Stevens. In it, Stevens complained that certain London merchants had stated that Mendes had told the insurers of the vessel *London* – including the Dutchman who handed him the letter – that Stevens had allegedly fled with the vessel. The insurers and the notary himself affirmed that they had never had this impression of the shipmaster. Mendes further declared that he had always

Title page of The Perfect Merchant, *a trade manual by the French merchant Jacques Savary, printed in Paris in 1675.*

had a good impression of Stevens, whom he believed to be an honest and reliable man, and that he would be inclined to give him a recommendation if he returned to Amsterdam.[52]

The rumors about the shipmaster's flight raised suspicions as to the good faith of the parties: whether it was true that Mendes had really harbored suspicions about him or whether he had actually made up the story to defraud insurers. The underwriters might have been wary of collusion between the policyholder with the shipmaster to benefit from both the insured goods and the indemnity. On the other hand, it may have been the insurers who had spread the rumor to avoid paying indemnity. The shipmaster, in turn, had good reason to be upset, since he had a respectable record of services provided to this merchant, other Portuguese Jews in Amsterdam and businessmen in the Dutch, English and Iberian trading centers he plied.

In March 1623, that is, three and a half years before this statement in which everyone affirmed their confidence in the English shipmaster, a certain John Stevens, who can be assumed to be the same man, set sail from Amsterdam for Malaga, in Spain, with a ship called the *Hope*, owned by the same Jerônimo Rodrigues Mendes. However, in May, seven pirate ships approached his vessel off Cape Roca, along the Portuguese coast, and seized all the cargo. According to the shipmaster, the pirates also took his sails, rigging and anchors, abandoning the ship's hull and setting it adrift. The entire crew was taken to Algiers and sold as slaves. Only Stevens managed to escape and reached Amsterdam before the end of June 1624, while the other men remained captive.[53]

Almost a year later, in April 1625, another Portuguese Jewish merchant, Jerônimo Rodrigues de Souza – *Souza*, not Mendes – asked two English sailors to make a statement before a notary with the help of a translator. Both of them affirmed that a month earlier they were in the port of Plymouth, when John Stevens arrived from London, and stayed for two or three days. During this laytime, he loaded some fardels (bundles) of goods for two non-Portuguese merchants to be delivered in Viana, and took on a pilot to guide the ship to Aveiro.

In July the same year, Stevens was already back in the Low Countries. He called in at Veere, in the province of Zeeland, with his ship *London*. He brought salt, olive oil and other wares from Aveiro. Jerônimo Rodrigues de Souza gave his son power of attorney to fetch these goods. At least four other Portuguese merchants did the same.[54] For another three Portuguese,

Stevens transported from Plymouth textiles salvaged from a different vessel that had been shipwrecked off the English coast en route to the Algarve. A notary witnessed the arrival of these textiles from Zeeland to Amsterdam, aboard a *smak* – a Nordic ship akin to a small caravel[55] – from where they were loaded on a boat that delivered the wares to the houses of the respective merchants.[56]

All this monitoring of Stevens' movements by consignors, shipowners and insurers could have been rooted in misgivings. The prevailing scenario favored caution: a war at sea and on land between the Dutch Republic and the Hispanic Monarchy alongside an infestation of Muslim pirates. In this environment, a shipmaster who was neither Portuguese nor Dutch, but English, could travel more easily between the two political spheres. Yet he could also flee or sell goods to pirates and corsairs. In fact, he had already lost an entire ship and its cargo under his responsibility, claiming they were seized by force. Anchoring as he did at the small port of Veere at the height of summer, when there was no ice in Amsterdam's harbor, could also have raised suspicions. Clearly, a shipmaster could be closely monitored, and fear that rumors about him could damage his reputation would have driven him to act with alacrity.

Both in this instance as well as in the arbitration case between Francisco de Cáceres and his former agents, we can see that merchants repeatedly contracted the services of agents and other trade-related professionals. It is reasonable to suppose that personal relations often developed which forestalled bad faith. Moreover, as has been seen in the case of Stevens, and will be clear in even further detail shortly, marketplaces were closely connected, and within each of them information about the conduct of its actors flowed at relatively great speed, volume and accuracy. Professionals involved with trade and shipping tended to shun those whom they knew to have openly flouted the standards of conduct shaped by mercantile usage and custom, especially if they had done so opportunistically. As previously noted, merchants kept multiple relationships with professionals who performed similar tasks – overseas agents, shipmasters, insurers, brokers, suppliers and consumers, creditors and debtors, and so forth. Such relations were either short-term and renewable or long-term, but could be terminated at the request of one of the parties. Thus, the past conduct of these professionals in trade and shipping was key to ensuring future revenue, which could either expand or shrink according to the reputation of those involved. Furthermore, tradesmen and seafarers were concerned about their reputation among people with whom they had established significant, long-lasting relationships. Hence, a confirmation that Stevens intended to flee would have had disastrous consequences for his career.

Compliance with norms was secured mostly by these informal mechanisms based on reputation and economic and social incentives and pressures. In all likelihood, the legal system – and other mechanisms contingent on it – mostly supplemented the former when they had failed or were feared to be insufficient. This can be inferred from the informality that was often characteristic of maritime transport contracts, credit transfers and relationships with overseas agents. These mercantile arrangements frequently dispensed with notarized documents and favored private instruments and even verbal agreements, as we discovered in previous chapters.

It is difficult to ascertain whether and to what extent mercantile custom became entrenched to the point of becoming a generalized morality in such circles, capable of inhibiting opportunism a priori, and dispensing, at least in part, with other incentives or penalties, whether economic, social or legal.[57] It is easier to identify improper rather than moral conduct in the sources. Nevertheless, it is possible to discern signs of this internalization in dying declarations. Declarants' remaining time on earth no longer allowed them to enjoy advantages or suffer penalties, although they could always worry about their offspring or the afterlife.[58]

Walls Have Ears

Except in the case of generalized morality, the effectiveness of all other mechanisms for compliance with norms – dishonor, courts, mercantile tribunals and arbitration – depended on information to punish transgressors or, at least, to stop cooperating with them, or never establish a relationship with them in the first place. Information was crucial for hiring and monitoring agents and contracting parties, adjudicating disputes, proving fault and punishing transgressors. No less so, information was critical to making business decisions: which goods to ship and which goods to order, what price to pay and what price to accept, when to insure or arm a vessel, and so forth. Merchants also needed to keep abreast of the progress of their overseas ventures, the results of transactions, the costs involved, the terms of exchange, payment terms, mishaps and incidents, and so on.

Notwithstanding the distances and transport technology of the age, one could say that merchants and people associated with trade and shipping generally had access to a large amount of detailed and updated information about the state of affairs in foreign trading hubs and the outcome of their business ventures. The flow of this information was supported by frequent sailings, intense correspondence, a large number of travelers and the close-knit urban and mercantile fabric of cities during that period. Such relative intimacy was coupled with mechanisms that reinforced these ties at a personal, social and mercantile level. Furthermore, organizations compensated, often intentionally, for the loss of cohesion engendered by growth, as was the case in Amsterdam, by far the largest of the four trading centers this study has analyzed in detail (Amsterdam, Porto, Salvador and Olinda-Recife).

Between 1578 and 1622, Amsterdam's population more than tripled, increasing from about 30,000 to 100,000 inhabitants. As was noted in Chapter 1, the turmoil that wracked the southern provinces in the Low Countries during the last quarter of the sixteenth century, especially Flanders and Brabant, brought qualified refugees and immigrants to the city. These newcomers contributed even further to the growth in commercial, manufacturing and shipping activities in Amsterdam in particular, and in the Republic in general. This progress attracted even more new arrivals, resulting in a shortage of space.

When, in 1578, Amsterdam sided with the Revolt and the Reformation, in the so-called "Alteration," areas of the city previously occupied by churches and monasteries were freed up for civil, manufacturing and residential use.[59] It was still not enough, and by 1615 the city had undergone three expansion plans. The third resulted in the first section (West) of the city's famous canals semicircle. Nevertheless, this territorial expansion never kept pace with the city's demographic growth, and Amsterdam continued to suffer from a shortage of space. In fact, some of the new areas incorporated into the city were not residential, but rather reserved for the shipyards, port facilities, warehouses and manufacturing.[60]

Porto was and continued to be much smaller than Amsterdam. It had between 14,000 and 20,000 inhabitants, including some small parishes outside the city walls.[L] The walls surrounded its scant 44,500 m^2, which encompassed two hills overlooking the Douro River, with a small stream called the Rio da Vila (literally "town stream") running between the two hills. The eastern hill housed the older district, the seat of the main municipal and episcopal institutions. The other hill was settled more recently and, along with the Lower Town and riverside areas, housed royal institutions. To a certain extent, they reflected the political forces jockeying for supremacy and power in the city over the centuries: the bishopric, the city council and the monarchy.[61]

Not all of the intramural areas were inhabited. A significant swathe of land was located within the monastery walls, where the monks had their kitchen gardens, orchards and areas for contemplation. Many open areas could be found in the backyards of private homes, and there were empty lots in the center of city blocks. Food crops and ornamental plants were also grown in these areas, which were known as "*enxidos*."[62]

Salvador and Olinda[M] were the main urban centers in Brazil, later joined by Rio de Janeiro. Both had small populations and areas. Until 1618, there were no more than 3,000 men of European descent fit for combat in either Olinda or Salvador. This figure possibly included men who came from various backgrounds, but were free and Europeanized. Even if we included other individuals of the same origins living in the outskirts of these urban centers, on the sugar mills and in neighboring settlements, it is unlikely that this population would have reached 9,000.[N/63] During this period, there was no clear distinction between the urban and rural population, especially in the upper social echelons, since sugar-mill owners and cane farmers lived in urban centers for varying periods of time, and free men often visited these centers to do business.

Apart from this, most of the settlements, sugar mills and cane farms were located near the coast. In Pernambuco and Bahia, they were a short distance from Olinda and Salvador. They were linked to these urban centers by waterways running into the Capibaribe, the Beberibe and other basins north and south of these rivers in Olinda, and, in the case of Salvador, into Todos os Santos Bay.

Along with the sea, rivers large and small provided economical and easy means of transport to these export hubs, as well as powering water mills

L. The parishes of Miragaia and Santo Idelfonso. Apart from these two parishes, Porto had other suburbs along the Douro and the Atlantic coast, such as Vila Nova da Gaia, Massarelos, São João da Foz, Matosinhos and Leça, all of which were less than 13 km from the city. Their close ties with urban life made them part of the city's space, and many of the trade-related professionals who worked in or served Porto lived in these suburbs (Silva, *O Porto e o seu termo*, v. 1, pp. 86–107).

M. Even the inhabitants of the captaincies of Itamaracá, Paraíba and Rio Grande resorted to Olinda's marketplace for supplies, mainly because their own marketplaces were still too small to justify varied inventories. However, there may have been other reasons for that, such as the fact that many early settlers came from Pernambuco.

N. The data is derived from chroniclers whose accuracy is doubtful. Some referred to all inhabitants, and others only to the population which could be mustered for combat. They did not always distinguish between individuals of European descent and the free population of Amerindian and African descent. Moreover, some included the entire city limits and the areas they believed such limits encompassed, incorporating the rural and semi-urban communities that surrounded the urban centers, even including distant settlements such as Igarassu among the inhabitants of Olinda!

The city of Amsterdam is portrayed during the last of three expansion plans it underwent between the mid-sixteenth century and 1615. This third expansion resulted in the Western section of the semicircles formed by its famous canals.

Illustration by Pier Maria Baldi for the Voyage of Cosimo de' Medici in Portugal and Spain, *written by Lorenzo Magalotti (1668–1669). This engraving shows a view of the city of Porto, taken from the village of Gaia.*

used to produce sugar. Much of the colony's mercantile and manufacturing life relied on these waterways, which is clearly evident in the maps shown in this book.[Ο] Boats, skiffs, canoes, rafts, small caravels and galliots quickly and regularly transported sugarcane, sugar crates, merchandise, people, messages, notes and letters.[64]

Based on urban models of defense, health and symbolism imported from the Mediterranean, both Salvador and Olinda had an Upper and Lower Town. The Upper Town was the noble and sacred district containing administrative and ecclesiastical institutions; the Lower Town was linked to transport and trade. Salvador was the capital of the colony, where the governor-general and his entourage, the central bureaucracy, the bishop, chapter of canons, several convents and monasteries, and the only court of appeal were located. The few streets in the Upper Town housed all these institutions and authorities, apart from a large number of common folk. The upper and lower parts of town were separated by a cliff, and were initially linked by two steep paths used by animals, carts and pedestrians. Later, two elevators with large gears and counterweights hoisted cargo up ramps built with planks.[65]

Ο. It is worth noting that the use of river and maritime transport would not have been as easy in Bahia and Pernambuco, where not all the sugar mills were located in the basin of the Capibaribe and Beberibe rivers, which ran into the sea at Recife (AHU_ACL_CU_005-02, Cx. 3, D. 285–291 – [Bahia, before 1623, November 3]; Costa, *O transporte no Atlântico*, v. 1, pp. 332–333).

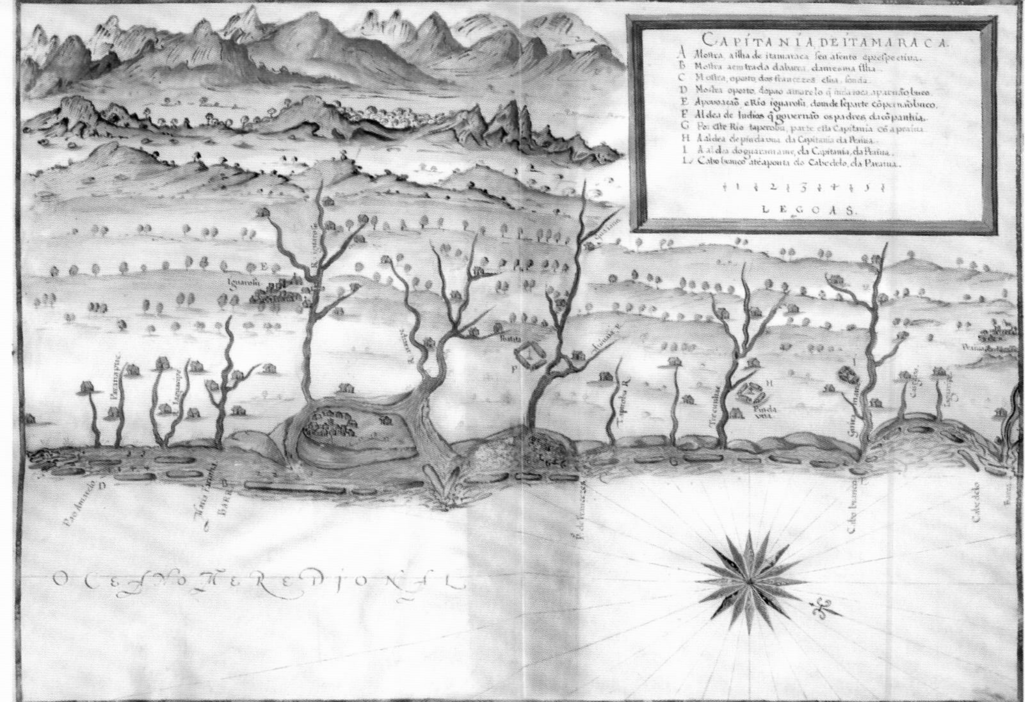

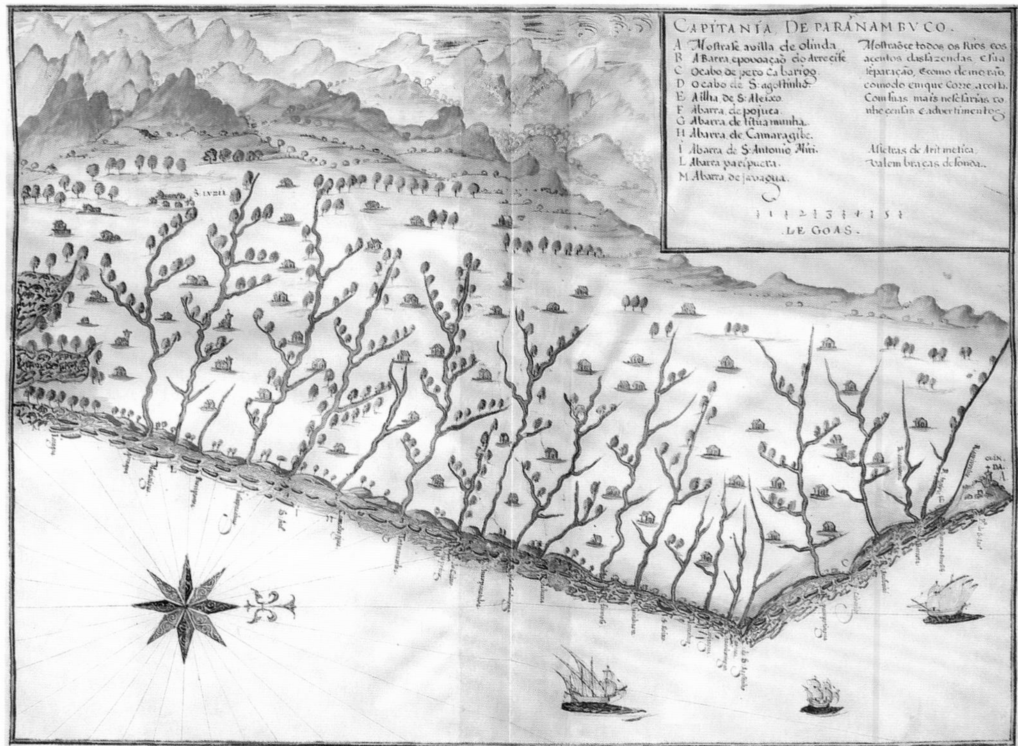

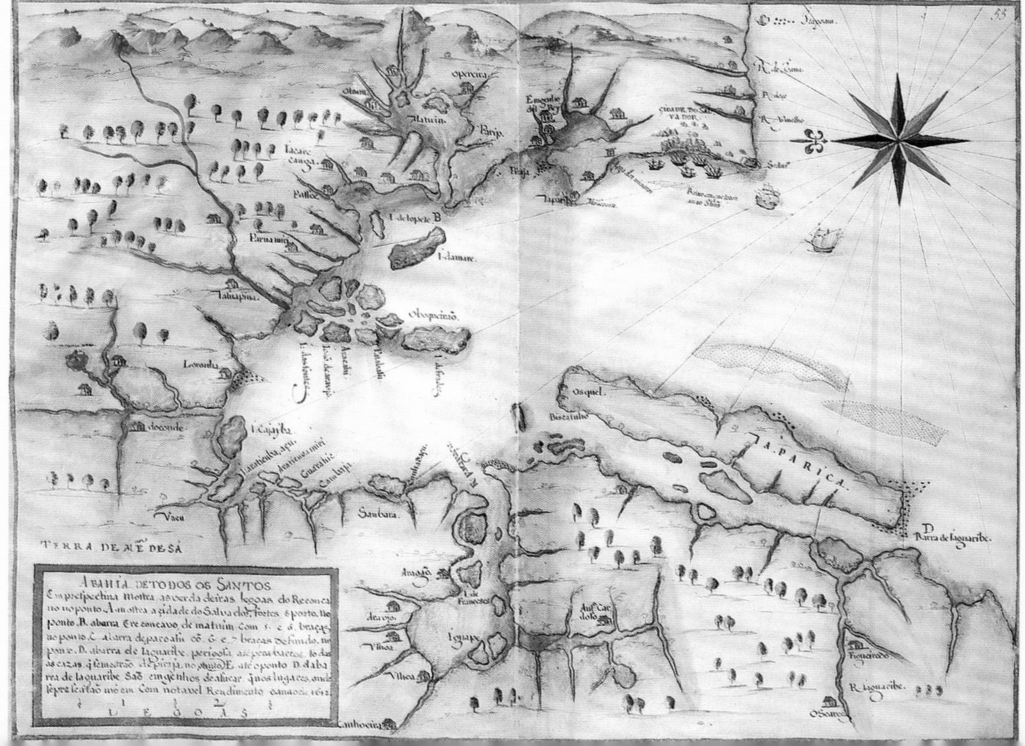

On this page, three sea charts drawn by João Teixeira Albernaz, the Elder, around 1616, highlighting the sugar mills located along waterways. The first two show the northeastern coast to the north and south of Olinda. In the first, we see the coast of the captaincies of Itamaracá and Paraíba as far as the town of the same name (now the city of João Pessoa). At least commercially, both captaincies were extensions of Pernambuco. In the second chart, we see Olinda and the southern coast of Pernambuco. The third portrays the city of Salvador, the Recôncavo and Todos-os-Santos Bay.

Depiction of the coast of Pernambuco, with plans of Olinda, the City of Maurícia (Mauritsstad) and Recife, and views of the Palace of Vrijburg (Fribourg), built by Johan Maurits of Nassau-Siegen, drawn by Cornelis Golijath (1648). Although the period portrayed here – the Dutch – came after the one described in this book and the urban layout was different, we can see that villages, sugar mills and cane farms were connected by waterways and sea routes.

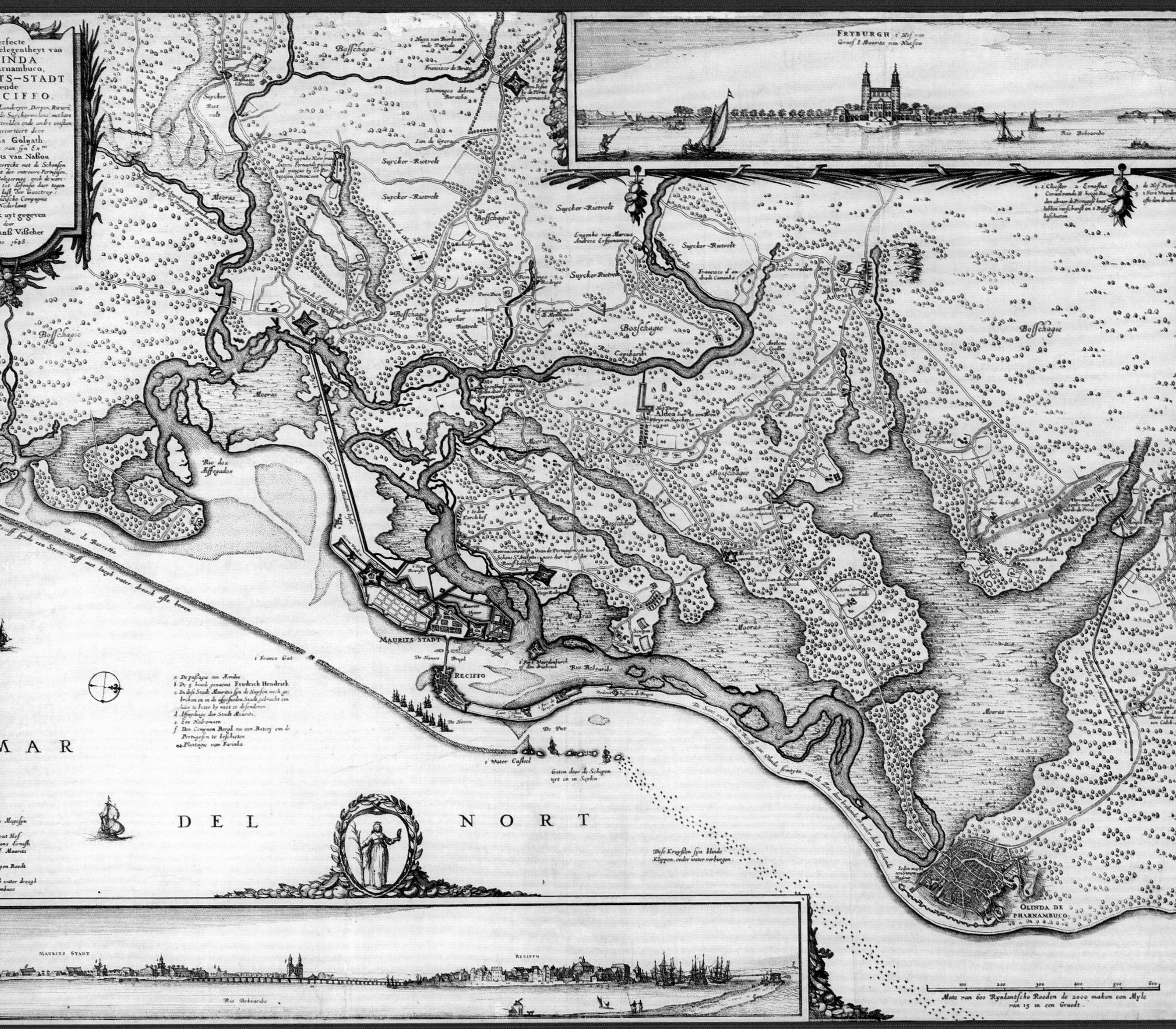
FRYBURGH
MAURITS STADT
RECIFFO
OLINDA DE PHARNAMBUCO
MAR
DEL
NORT
Bosschagie
Moeras
Rio Beberibe
Mate van 600 Rynlantsche Roeden de 2000 maken een Myle van 15 in een Graedt.

Plan of the Recovery of Bahia; *João Teixeira Albernaz, the Elder (1631). Here we can clearly see the vacant areas of the city of Salvador, the "enxidos" or backyards, and the buildings with shared walls, after Bahia was regained from the Dutch.*

Plan of Olinda; *Johannes Vingboons (1665). According to the scholar José Luiz Mota Menezes, this plan is probably a proposal to rebuild the town during Dutch rule and after the great fire of 1631, and not a map of the lots that existed prior to the blaze, when the actual built-up areas would have been much smaller. The envisaged layout, however, maintained the same standard of urban development, with shared walls in the occupied areas.*

Olinda was built on five small hills – not rivaling the seven hills of Rome. It started on the hill where, supposedly, a retainer employed by the city's founder, Duarte Coelho Pereira, coined the town's name: "walking through the jungle with some other people, looking for a suitable building site and finding this place, which is set on a high hill, he exclaimed with joy: *O'linda* ['How beautiful!']."[66] One of its neighborhoods descended the slope down to the Beberibe River. Both the river and a sandy isthmus linked the town to the settlement of Recife, then a small townlet that served as a harbor for ocean-going vessels.[67]

Even though not all the intramural areas in Porto, Salvador, Olinda and Amsterdam were inhabited, the built-up areas were densely constructed, and the streets were quite narrow. Houses were built with shared walls, and it was common for a single edifice to

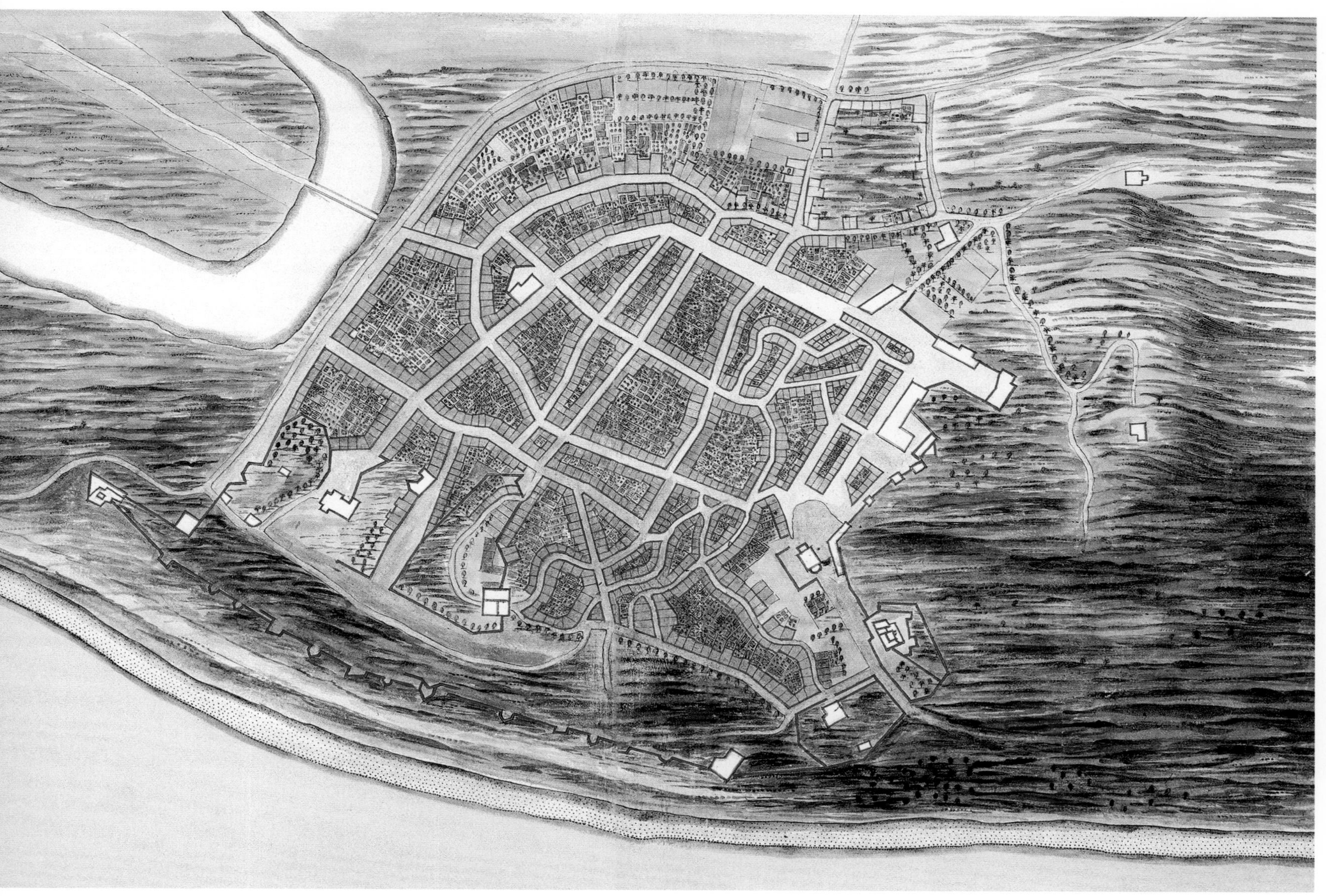

contain several residences, commercial establishments and workshops. Such urban settings were hotbeds for gossip and rumors in settlements where many of the inhabitants knew each other, and often knew far too much about other people's lives.[68]

In Amsterdam and Porto, each building contained several homes. As Porto's population grew, the vacant lots and backyards began to be occupied, and more floors were added.[69] In Amsterdam, backyards were more common in the residential areas created under the third expansion plan, since the oldest quarters, which were so densely populated – often utilizing basements and attics [70] – did not allow that luxury.[71] In Olinda and Salvador, the urban layout followed the same model of row houses, albeit with fewer floors, even though both had more empty intramural spaces than Porto, including vacant lots, uninhabited steep slopes, public squares, vast convent grounds and extensive backyards.[72]

Not only the urban model of these cities but also their recreational and socialization practices facilitated the flow of information within urban centers. Leisure generally consisted of collective activities shared with family, friends and acquaintances in the form of spontaneous visits, reciprocal invitations[P] and scheduled gatherings,[73] in which sweets played an important role.

In the Low Countries, as well as in Portugal and in Brazil, men usually got together in the evenings to play[Q] cards, dice, backgammon and other games.[74] Going shopping, taking a stroll through commercial areas,[75] and seeing the sights around town[76] were common pursuits. The same was true of walks and picnics, boat rides, fishing and hunting in forested areas and along waterways in or around the cities.[77] People met up in houses of worship, before and after prayers,[78] and fraternized in religious and lay brotherhoods formed for pious, charitable, social, educational and cultural purposes.[79] They also flocked to processions, bazaars, bull runs, cavalcades, festivals and celebrations.[80] In the Dutch Republic, participation in professional guilds, which organized meetings, events, celebrations, rituals and processions, played an important role in civic life, while rhetoric chambers, very popular in the Low Countries, held declamation, reading and theater sessions.[81]

A great deal of information about other people's lives also came from social control and vigilance mechanisms that were introduced over time. In Amsterdam, "neighborhood watches" formed by residents patrolled the streets, especially at night, and held suspects until the city's sheriff (*schout*) arrived, or took them to magistrates and even to the consistories of the Reformed Church. Policing depended heavily on these paid patrols, since both the sheriff and his men, and the civic militia (*schutterij*, a very prestigious and important association in the Republic's cities, formed by members of the urban middle class), which were responsible for maintaining public safety and law and order, had few active members, and were only summoned in cases of serious disturbances. Apart from crime, the neighborhood watches kept an eye on all types of behavior considered improper by an increasingly regulated and moralistic society. This strict social control was further reinforced by neighborhood visits by the Reformed Church to check on its communicants.[82]

A Portuguese institution akin to the Dutch neighborhood watches known as *quadrilheiros* was not as prestigious or effective in identifying individuals and behavior that deviated from the law, order or morality, at least in Porto. In this city there were years when the twenty-two men set for the job were not elected and when they were, sought to avoid these duties on the pretext of various privileges and other subterfuges. On pain of imprisonment, some of them, generally professionals of a lower social standing, such as shoemakers and tailors, were obliged to accept and carry out these duties for three long years. They received no pay, therefore had little incentive to carry out actual social control.

Two Women in Conversation at a Doorway; *Jacobus Vrel (1650–1662). Socialization – including visits and meetings, both scheduled and casual – the pattern of urban planning and social control mechanisms enhanced the informal flow of information.*

The Listening Housewife (The Eavesdropper); *Nicolaes Maes (1656). This painting is part of a series that warns of the difficulty of keeping sins secret and stresses the tenuous line between the public and private spheres, even at home.*

The Company of Captain Roelof Bicker and Lieutenant Jan Michielsz Blaeuw, Amsterdam, 1639; *Bartholomeus van der Helst, 1639.*

The surviving documents, especially inquisitorial records, repeatedly emphasize the lack of privacy in Brazil and in Portugal, not to mention that it was impossible to remain anonymous. It was hard to keep secrets for long regarding people's business, love and sex lives. Even one's activities in the privy could become public knowledge. However, there was still scope for some secrecy, and the growing social vigilance engendered by the development of the Inquisition's activities tended to instill reserved and wary behavior.[83]

Clearly, the relative intimacy of urban centers emphasized above was lessened by the fact that these port cities received many outsiders who were just passing through. Moreover, Brazilian towns hosted individuals who only stayed there long enough to get on their feet before returning to Portugal or settling in the countryside,[84] whereas Amsterdam continually attracted immigrants.[85] Nevertheless, this newly arrived or floating population usually knew people who had already settled there, and soon established relations with the local population, even if just in the port, and with their new neighbors. In the case of Amsterdam, the largest of these centers, immigrants and visitors were soon identified by their neighborhood watches.

As the case of the fugitive tobacco buyer mentioned at the beginning of this chapter makes clear, it was hard to abscond for long periods, and doing so entailed a high personal, social and mercantile cost.[86]

P. Except when another context has been expressly indicated, the references to leisure and socialization habits mentioned here pertain to Porto. Most of them come from statements in which the defendants accused of Jewish practices in inquisitorial cases described occasions when they had confessed to their "accomplices" or fallen out with enemies who could have denounced them. However, there is no reason to believe that such customs differed between Old and New Christians (IANTT, STO, IC 8658, fol. 69v.; IL 11260, fol. 145). With regard to this subject in Brazil, see: IANTT, STO, IL 3080, n/n (session dated 1621.11.17).

Q. Enmities arising from gambling disputes were a common theme in inquisitorial defenses, and there are too many to list here. With regard to this subject in Brazil, see: IANTT, STO, IL 5395, fol. 57v.; Stols, *Dutch and Flemish Victims of the Inquisition in Brazil*, p. 52. Despite official opposition, games of chance persisted as a popular pastime in the Dutch Republic; see: Israel, *The Dutch Republic*, p. 952; B. Roberts, *Sex and Drugs before the Rock'n' Roll. Youth Culture and Masculinity in Holland's Golden Age* (Amsterdam: Amsterdam University Press, in print), passim.

AMSTELODAMI EMPORII TOTIUS ORBIS CELEBERRIMI, HO
AMSTERDAM
De Zuyder Kerck
De Oude Kerck
Monkelbaens Toorn
Schreyerhoeks Toorn
TYA FLUVIU

The Bourse's Patio

If cities were or sought to be close-knit places, the same could be said about their marketplaces. As seen earlier, during the period examined herein, Amsterdam traded a far vaster range of products and services with many more markets than any other center on the sugar route. Gradually, Amsterdam became the main commercial hub in the West. According to Clé Lesger, between the penultimate decade of the sixteenth century and the second decade of the seventeenth century, the city's mercantile circle lost its erstwhile cohesion. It was no longer possible to identify people by their given names and father's name alone, without the need for surnames.[87] Towards the end of this period, there were already hundreds of traders in Amsterdam, and if one included petty traders, that figure would have surpassed a thousand.[88] Nevertheless, most mercantile activities took place within a fairly limited space, roughly corresponding to the city's medieval perimeter.[89]

The main axis of Amsterdam's commercial center was the Damrak canal, which links the dam on the Amstel River (the Dam) to the Ij River, of which the former is a tributary. Dam Square was located to the south, while to the north the Nieuwe Brug (New Bridge) crossed the canal. The *paalhuis,* or post office, was located on the western side of the bridge, in front of the Ij anchorage. As soon as shipmasters disembarked, they were supposed to hand over all the letters they were bringing to a post office official.

One of the scales on which wares brought to the city were weighed for taxation and certification purposes was located at the heart of Dam Square. This weighing scale was called the Waag, and was equivalent to the Haver do Peso or Ver o Peso in the Portuguese world. Behind it was the modest municipal building, the Stadhuis, which at the time encompassed the Exchange Bank or Wisselbank,[90] and the Insurance Chamber, that is, the Assurantiekamer, apart from other bureaucratic services which merchants occasionally had to use.[91] The Wisselbank disseminated news about defaults and insolvency pertaining to account holders. The bank also monitored accounts and disclosed any shortfalls.[92] Information about damage to ships and cargo converged at the Assurantiekamer.

Even before the Bourse was founded with its own buildings and norms, meeting spaces for people who had goods or services to either offer or acquire had already emerged in the city. When the weather

The Paalhuis and the Nieuwe Brug in Amsterdam in Winter; *Jan Abrahamsz. Beerstraaten (1640–1666). The New Bridge across the Damrak canal and the post office.*

Amsterdam, Seen from the IJ River; *Pieter van der Keere (1618).*

Dam Square in 1604, during the Procession of Lepers in Koppertjesmaandag; *Adriaen van Nieulandt (1633). Left, the city hall (*Stadhuis*), with its tower; center, the Waag, the official weighing house, and right, the* Damrak *canal, with boats heading to the port and the warehouses.*

PERTIES MAANDAG OPGEHOUDE IN't JAARI604

Cours van Negotie t'Amsterdam den 3 Maert.

ANNO 1636.

Waren by ℔.	
Primaes peper grof c.	
Dito gemeyn — cōt	23 ß 4 a 6 p
Portugaels grof, cont.	
Bresily Peper	
Geneets Greyn het ℔	6,4 p a 7 ß cōt
Nagelen in soorten – cōt	8 ß 9 a 10 ß
Engelse Naghelen	
Cappeletten	ß cōt
Macis schoon	cont
Dito tweede soorte	20 ß con
Dito derde soorte	16 ß 6 a 8 ß cō
Noten in Soorten	50 stuy tijt
Rompen	34 a 35 st cont
Caneel in soorten	39 a 40 st cont
Engels Saffraen N. con	37, 10 a 38 gl
Gember van Porto Rico	25,10 a 26 ß cō
dito Doming.	ß cōt
Dito de Brasil geconfijt	17,4 a 18 ß cōt
Madery Sucaten	23 a 24 ß cont
Chinese Gember	9 a 10 ß cont
Olyphants Tanden	cont

Suyckeren by ℔.	op tijd.
Fyne Rafinad: 2 a 3 po.	30 a 30 ß 2 tyt
dito van 4 pont	30 ß p
fyne Melissen top-schoō	29 a 29 ß 2 p
dito Lompen top-schoō	27 a 27 ß 2 p
Bresilse witte — cōt	22, 23 a 25 ß
dito Pan-goet	22 ß tyt
Mascobades	20 ß p tyt
Paneelen	14 a 14 ß 4 p
Sint Thomé	12 ß 4 p
Wit Candijs	42 a 43 ß
Bruyn Candijs	29 ß p

Verwen by ℔.	en 100 ℔.
Coucenilje Mestique	70 a 72 ß
dito commune	55 a 56 ß
Indigo Guatimalo	12 a 13 ß tyt
dito Laure	61 a 62 stu tyt
dito Karkees en Tripoli	67 st cont
Spaens Groen	17 a 18 st tyt
Ferneboucq	34 a 35 gl cont
Sint Martens Hout	12 gl cont
Ficet hout	7 gl tyt
West-Indisch Hout	
Campets hout	24 gl cont
Geel-hout	2, 15 a 23 gl cōt
Crappen — nieuw	34 gl cont
Ghemeyne	24 gl tyt
Breslause — nieuw	23 gl
Wijnsteē van Duytsland	32 gl cont
Italiaensen Wijnsteen	14 gul tyt
Groote Gal-noten	32 a 33 gl cont
Grove Gomme	21 gl cont
Pastel vā S.Michiel, bael	16 gl
dito Thoulouse, de bael	gl tyt
Smack de Port a Port	28 ß tyt
dito de Mallega	tyt
Engels Coper-root	gl con
dito Luyckx	4,10 a 5 gl con
Roomsen Aluyn	39 a 40 ß cont
dito Luycksen Aluyn	28 ß cont
dito Engelschen Aluyn.	ß cont

Drooghen	op tijd.
Quickfilver 't pōt.	22 stuy tyt
Seduwaer fijn 't pōt	gl cōt
Benjuin 't pont fijn	3 gul
Robarber het pont fijn	10 a 12 gl tyt
Radice China	63 st ℔ tyt
Seversaet het pont	32 a 38 stuy tyt
Galanga 't pont	12 a 13 stuy tyt
Lange Peper	10 stuy cont
Senebladeren	35 a 36 st tyt
Salse Parille	36 a 38 stuy
dito Salvatico	20,26 a 28 st
Opoponar	16 a 17 gl cont
Cardemom	36 st tyt
Coloquint.	20 stuy tyt
Bitter Amandelen	22, 23 gl 'thōd.
Witte Wieroock	16 a 18 st tyt
Euforbium — 100 ℔	
Mechoacan	tyt
Besar Steē Oriental. cōt	20 a 22 gl d'ōz
Dito Occidentalis	5 gl 2 a 8 st cōt
Ambre Grisa — cōt	38 a 40 gl d'ōz
Coculus — oude	18 a 19 st cōt
Corcuma	16,17 a 18 st
Gom Tragant	9 a 10 stuy tijt

Huyden by de ℔.	
Ivchten	15 a 16 st tyt
Schevincken	5 st 4 p tyt
Dansicker Banck-huydē	6 st p cōt
Inlandse gesoutē huydē	3 st 2 p cōt
West-Indische Huyden	7 st cōt
Yrlantsche Huyden – cōt	2 st 10 p cōt
Vriesse Koe-huyden, cōt	2 st 6 a 8 p cōt
Vriesse Bul-huyden	3 st p cont
Spaens Leer — cōt	34 a 35 stu con

Waren by 100. ℔.	
Melaensen Rijs	52,10 a 53 ß cō
Levantsen Rijs	42,10 a 43 ß cō
Corinten in booten ni.	15 a 16 gl tyt
Dito Oude	
Lange Amandelen	gul cōt
Valence Amandelē nieu	29 a 30 gl tyt
Ambrozijnse	gl tyt
Dito Provence	21 a 22 gl tyt
dito de Barbaria	
Alecantse Zeep,	gl cont
dito geconterfeyte	gl tyt
Veneetse Annys	36 a 37 gl cont
Dito Alecantse	40 gl tyt
Maltes Annys	gl tyt
Poulsen Commijn	gl tyt
dito Cecilse	cōt
Cappers de Majorque	24 a 25 gl
Dito de Tolon	24,10 a 25 gl ty
N. Lang Rozijn, — tyt	gl st
N. Corf-rozijn	12 gl 5 st tyt
Tonnekens Vygen	19 a 20 gl cont
Vygen de Coppel	37 a 38 ß tyt
Lange Pruymen	ß tyt
dito ronde	ß tyt

Syroop/ Honigh en	Was.
Madrilse Syroop, 't vat	55 a 56 L cōt
Suyck. Syroop 100.	59 a 60 ß cōt
Bord. Honig, 't vat Nieu	45 a 46 L tyt
Honig van S. Malo, 100.	10,10 a 11 gl
Bajoensen Honig, 100	gl ty
Honig vā Bretaēs 100, cō	gl
Inlandsen, de ton	gl cōt
Inlands Was, cōt. b.	72 gl cont
Droog Oosters Was,	70 a 71 gl cōt
Ghemeen Oosters	68 gl cont
Oosters Vet-Was	64 gl cont

Talck en Traen.	
Osters Talck — cōt	18 a 19 gl
Soeten Talck — cōt	22 a 23 gl
Moscovise Talck	17 a 18 gl tyt
Lever Traen	40 a 41 gl
Groenlandse Traen,	42 a 43 gl tyt
Robbe Traen	39 a 40 gl st
Inlandse Traen cōt	22 a 23 gl st

Olyen by 't vat / en	by d'Aem.
Malegomse Oly, 't vat	L tyt
Poulse Oly, 't vat	73 a 74 L tyt
Majorxe Oly, 't vat — tyt	69,10 a 70 L
Groote Olyvē 't quarteel	36 a 37 gl cōt
dito Kleyne, 't quarteel	24 a 25 gl cōt
Lemoenen de Pijp	gl cont
Rijgs Lijnzaet — cōt	16, 10 a 17 gl
Oly van Lijnzaet	39 gl st
Oly van Raepzaet	48 gl st
Oly van Hennipzaet	41 gl

Spaense Wynen.	Op Tijdt.
Serese Secken 't vat	46 a 50 L
Condaetse Secken	L
Piere Semenes Nieuw	50 a 53 L
Canary-Wijn	
Condaetse Bastert	38 a 40 L
Sipioense Bastert	56 a 60 L
Wijn Tinte	68 a 70 L
Malveseyen	
Alecantse	L
Spaēs Brādew: 30 virtel	10 a 11 L ß

Franse Wynen 't Vat/	op tyt.
Petouwen — N.	10 a 11 L
Conjacken	13 a 14 L
Bordeeuse — Nieu	20 a 22 L
Libornse	18 a 19 L
Hooghlandse	L
Tosanen	L
Anjouwen — schoon	14 a 15 L
Vin Courte	14 a 16 L
Nantese — Nieu	13 L 10 ß
Nantse Brandw: 30 vier	12 L 5 ß
Bord: Brand: 30 virtel	11 L 10 ß

Oosters Vlas en	Hennip.
Heylig Vlas schip – ℔	32,36,48,80 gl
Pruys nieu	42 a 44 gl
Hekelt Lettouws Nieu	48, 50 gl
Boutsnicker Vlas – N 44,	45 gl O
Paternosters — N 45,46	Oud gl
Ezens — Nieu 52,54	Oud gul
Tils Vlas nieu	Oud gul
Memels Oud	gul
Memels Nieu	40,42 a 46 gl
Drie band out 44 a 45.	N. 45 a 46 gl
Reyn Hennip, Ryg.	34 a 35 gl cont
Pas Hennip nieu	26 gul cont
Hollands gewas schip ℔	29 a 30 gl cont
Koningsberger Rijs,	34 gl tyt
Kleyn Band, — cōt	24 gul cōt
Rus band	gul cōt
Torsen	

Official price list for several products on the Amsterdam Bourse on March 3, 1636. Several types of sugar appear in the second block in the left column.

Courtyard of the Amsterdam Bourse Building; *Job Adriaensz. Berckheyde (1670–1690). Note the announcements posted on the pillars and the groups gathered to negotiate for different types of merchandise and services in several spots of the courtyard and arcade.*

was good, they met outdoors, on the eastern side of the Nieuwe Brug. On rainy days, they sought shelter nearby, under the eaves of houses on northern end of the Warmoesstraat thoroughfare or in Sint Olofskapel (St. Olaf's Chapel), also in that part of town; in the Nieuwe Kerk (New Church) near Dam square or in the Oude Kerk (Old Church).[93]

In 1611, the building housing the Amsterdam Bourse was finally inaugurated on Dam Square.[94] Following the model used in Antwerp and London, it had an internal courtyard flanked by an arcade. Here, traders and brokers bought and sold, extended and took loans, chartered ships, hired services, insured merchandise, traded securities issued by private individuals, dealt in government and India companies' bonds and in shares of these companies, and so on. Gradually, different parts of the courtyard and colonnade began to specialize in transacting specific goods and services.ᴿ Letters were also delivered at the Bourse. Post office officials brought the correspondence they had received from shipmasters, numbered them, listed them, and then announced the list at the Bourse. Any mail that was not collected before the next close of business was delivered to the merchants' residences. This convergence of information through all these functions was reinforced by the brief working hours of the Bourse. It was open for just one hour, and the city authorities, sought to prevent meetings near the Bourse after closing time to prevent speculation.[95]

Hence, the Bourse was the city's commercial nerve-center. Attending its trading sessions was mandatory, if not to close deals, then at least to collect information, whether personal, such as letters, reports and rumors about one's own business activities, or public, such as prices and rates for goods, insurance, freight, exchange rates, and so forth.

In the specific case of sugar, there were other sites and organizations that facilitated the flow of information relevant to its trade. Located slightly farther away, they were a few minutes' walk from the city's medieval center. First of all, it is important to note the refineries, some of which have been identified on the detailed map of Amsterdam attached to the back cover of this book by the scholar Lodewijk Hulsman,[96] based on the indicated literature. It is also worth mentioning the island of Vlooienburg and its surroundings, where a large share of the Portuguese Jews lived and built their first synagogue, Beit Yaakov, the House of Jacob.[97] Finally, one can note the location of other institutions that would influence the sugar trade, mainly in a predatory manner, such as the Admiralty of Amsterdam, which oversaw privateering and auctioned off prizes, and the Dutch East India Company (VOC) and Dutch West India Company (WIC), which also seized and sold sugar.

Apart from directing transactions into a small area, and particularly in the case of the Bourse during a short working period of, supposedly, just a few hours a day, the use of brokers and written media also helped reduce the costs for acquiring information, increase the speed of information flow, and, moreover, improve the quality of data. We have already seen that Amsterdam's brokers played an important role in contracting freight and insurance, and in transacting merchandise, serving as witnesses, guaranteeing the fairness of operations and certifying that the parties were creditworthy. They testified before magistrates, arbitrated conflicts, and helped in proceedings before the mercantile tribunals, particularly in disputes involving transactions in which they had served as intermediaries, or with which they were more familiar.[98]

The city tried to regulate the profession and limit the number of brokers in order centralize information and avoid abuses. Even so, the number of brokers licensed by the municipal authorities exceeded 368 in 1619, and, despite the restrictions, informal and unlawful intermediaries continued to be increasingly active.[99]

Accurate, solid information was a broker's main asset. This was critical for successfully matching the desires and requirements of potential carriers and charterers, insurers and policyholders, and buyers and sellers. Brokers became increasingly specialized, familiarizing themselves with the actors involved in given markets, and becoming experts in facilitating transactions in particular goods and services.

With regard to written media, as of 1585, printed price lists[S] (price-currents) provided market prices for different products, according to their type and quality. These rates were collated from hundreds of brokers, certified by the municipal authorities, and were published on a weekly or fortnightly basis, which meant they were relatively up to date. These lists were available by subscription, and were even delivered to the home. Single copies could also be purchased for an affordable price at the Bourse. The number of items listed continued to increase, and included 350 products in 1635. White sugar from Brazil first appeared on the lists in 1609.[100]

Newspapers appeared later, sometime around 1618. Launched by the city's booming publishing market, they replaced handwritten bulletins. The latter had previously disseminated prices and news on matters that affected economics, and were sent by specialists to administrative bodies and prominent merchants who were willing to pay for them. Being mass produced, newspapers were cheaper, had much larger print runs and a more extensive reach. As a result, newspapers were also able to cover a broader range of topics relevant to mercantile circles.

R. There was a separate bourse for grain, whose building was inaugurated on the Damrak canal in 1617.

S. Jan de Vries and Ad van der Woude date the publication of the first lists to 1583, being published regularly only from 1613 onwards. According to these two authors, they were published fortnightly (every two weeks) and not weekly as claimed by Lesger, who studied the flow of information in cities (De Vries and Van der Woude, *The First Modern Economy*, p. 147; Lesger, *The Rise of the Amsterdam Market*, pp. 221, 224, 232–237).

In different ways, the new trade-related organizations adopted in Amsterdam facilitated access to an enormous quantity of information which flowed to the city from all the marketplaces to which it was linked. The large number of sources and the high frequency of incoming reports enhanced the reliability and accuracy of bits of information, which could be quickly verified and compared.[101] This is clear in the imbroglio involving the Portuguese merchant, the Dutch insurer and the English shipmaster.

The Forecourt's Arcades

There were also brokers in Porto and Lisbon, but all indications are that, instead of serving as true middlemen, their activities were far more formal and passive, aimed at authenticating transactions, particularly those involving foreigners. During most of the period examined here, the Porto city council appointed the same person to the office of broker. His, duties, however, were sometimes performed by a substitute or associates – somewhat like the notaries in modern-day Brazil. Porto probably did not yet have the critical mass to require professional brokerage services. If, on occasion, one informal broker or another acted unlawfully and there was a set of complaints about the tardiness and inadequacy of the office, the fact that an alderman argued that it was necessary to choose between either eliminating the office in its current form or reforming the institution, adding three more such officials, indicates that even though professional brokerage was advisable, it was not yet indispensable.[102] This was probably also the case in Brazil.

In effect, Porto had far fewer merchants than Amsterdam, as could be expected, and they would have numbered less than one hundred, according to Francisco Ribeiro da Silva. They might have totaled seven hundred, if one considered petty traders, retailers, grocers, fishmongers, innkeepers, stallholders and hawkers.[103] The same few people came across each other all the time in the same places. Porto did not have an organized bourse as did Amsterdam,[T] but two areas served as a meeting place for businessmen – the Adro de São Domingos (forecourt of the Monastery of Saint Dominic) and the riverside area along the Douro River.[U]

The forecourt was a covered gallery housing small shops – stalls as well as retailers. It ran along the north wall of the Dominican monastery and had a square in front. The square was named after the monastery and was the intersection for the streets on which some of the wealthiest people in the city dwelled: the Flores, Belmonte and São Domingos Bridge streets, which also had larger stores. Merchants met to transact business, chat and gossip under the forecourt's arcades, in the square or in the nearby surroundings. The monastery complex also contained a chapel of the Brotherhood of Nossa Senhora das Neves (Our Lady of the Snows), also known as the Brotherhood of Merchants to reflect its membership.

The square was also the site for seasonal fairs and was close to the junction between the Colina do Olival ("Olive Grove Hill") to the west, the riverside to the south, and the Colina da Sé ("Cathedral Hill") to the east. The Colina do Olival once housed the Jewish quarter, and New Christian merchants still lived there. It was subsequently also where the new appeals court was located. The Romanesque district was situated on the Colina da Sé, with institutions that were part of the episcopal and municipal administration. The Rua dos Mercadores ("Merchants' Street") and Pé das Aldas Street ran along the foot of the Colina da Sé, parallel to the Rio da Vila ("town stream"). Many merchants also had stores and residences on these streets.[104]

The Praça da Ribeira square, on the riverside, was also a meeting point for the business community, albeit of a far more popular nature. Surrounded by retail shops and with a daily market, it always bustled with hawkers and commoners. On one side, a doorway led to the quay while the Rua dos Mercadores (Merchants' Street) extended on the other side (northwards).[105]

Exiting the square to the west, a narrow street full of warehouses and stores, the Rua da Fonte Taurina (or Dourina), led to another square which was smaller and overlooked the quay. This was the Terreiro do Trigo ("Wheat Square") or Terreiro do Pão ("Bread Square"),[V] which was where the official weighing scales,[106] Haver do Peso, were located and where the cereal brought to the city was assessed. The Haver do Peso served a similar purpose as the Waag in Amsterdam, that is, to certify the weight of any product and to weigh merchandise subject to the *sisa*, a tax on sales and purchases, based on weight. The Royal Warehouse, that is, the customs house, where the sugar brought to the city was cleared[107] and stored, and the Casa dos Contos (Counting House), which centralized the accounting services of the royal treasury, were located on the street going up (northwards) from the Terreiro do Pão.[108]

The Counting House stood on the corner of that street and Rua Nova dos Mercadores, a thoroughfare so wide that it almost resembled a square. It was flanked by stores and warehouses, and was the site of the erstwhile mint, officially disbanded in 1607, whose building was finally converted into a barn.[W/109]

The walls, gates and posterns,[110] and the outside areas near the river[111] and the quays,[112] were observation points used to supervise the arrival and departure of ships, and the boats that ferried between ships and the quay, loading and unloading merchandise.

Apart from these well-defined sites, merchants also gathered in each other's stores,[113] offices and residences, as well as in notary offices, which numbered no more than four.[114] Sometimes, notaries did not attend to clients in their own offices, but went to the client's residence, where the other parties also converged.[115] In the sixteenth century, there was a Paço dos Tabeliães ("Notaries' Court") near the official weighing scales,[116] although all indications are that by the end of the century it no longer served this purpose.

The Four Corners

The number of merchants and trade-related professionals must have been proportional to the total number of inhabitants in Olinda and Salvador.[X] They met in certain locations in the upper and lower parts of

T. As early as 1412, merchants in Porto asked the king for a building on the Rua Nova street to serve as a bourse. The king gave his consent but the project was never implemented (Barros, "Porto: a construção de um espaço marítimo," v. 1, pp. 108–111; J. F. Afonso, "A construção de um novo centro cívico: notas para a história da Rua Nova e da zona ribeirinha do Porto no séc. XVI," offprint of *Museu 4th series 9* (2000): 42.

U. According to David G. Smith, in the mid-seventeenth century Lisbon only had some two hundred individuals involved in wholesale overseas trade (Smith, "The Mercantile Class of Portugal and Brazil," p. 15).

V. Grain was also weighed in the streets adjoining the Terreiro do Trigo (Silva, *O Porto e o seu termo*, v. 2, pp. 636–637).

W. This riverside quadrangle developed into one of the city's mercantile hubs from the fourteenth century onwards (Barros, "Porto: a construção de um espaço marítimo," v. 1, pp. 38–40).

X. Sônia A. Siqueira identified 241 merchants mentioned in the records of inquisitorial visits to Pernambuco and Bahia in 1591–1595 and 1618–1620. However, many were not contemporary, while some could have been repeated and others were never mentioned (Siqueira, *A Inquisição portuguesa e a sociedade colonial*, pp. 79–81, 340–353). David G. Smith, in turn, identified 367 merchants, petty traders and grocers living in or visiting Bahia in the first half of the seventeenth century. A list of individuals who paid taxes mentioned seventy-six wholesale merchants (Smith, "The Mercantile Class of Portugal and Brazil," pp. 280, 295–296, n. 18).

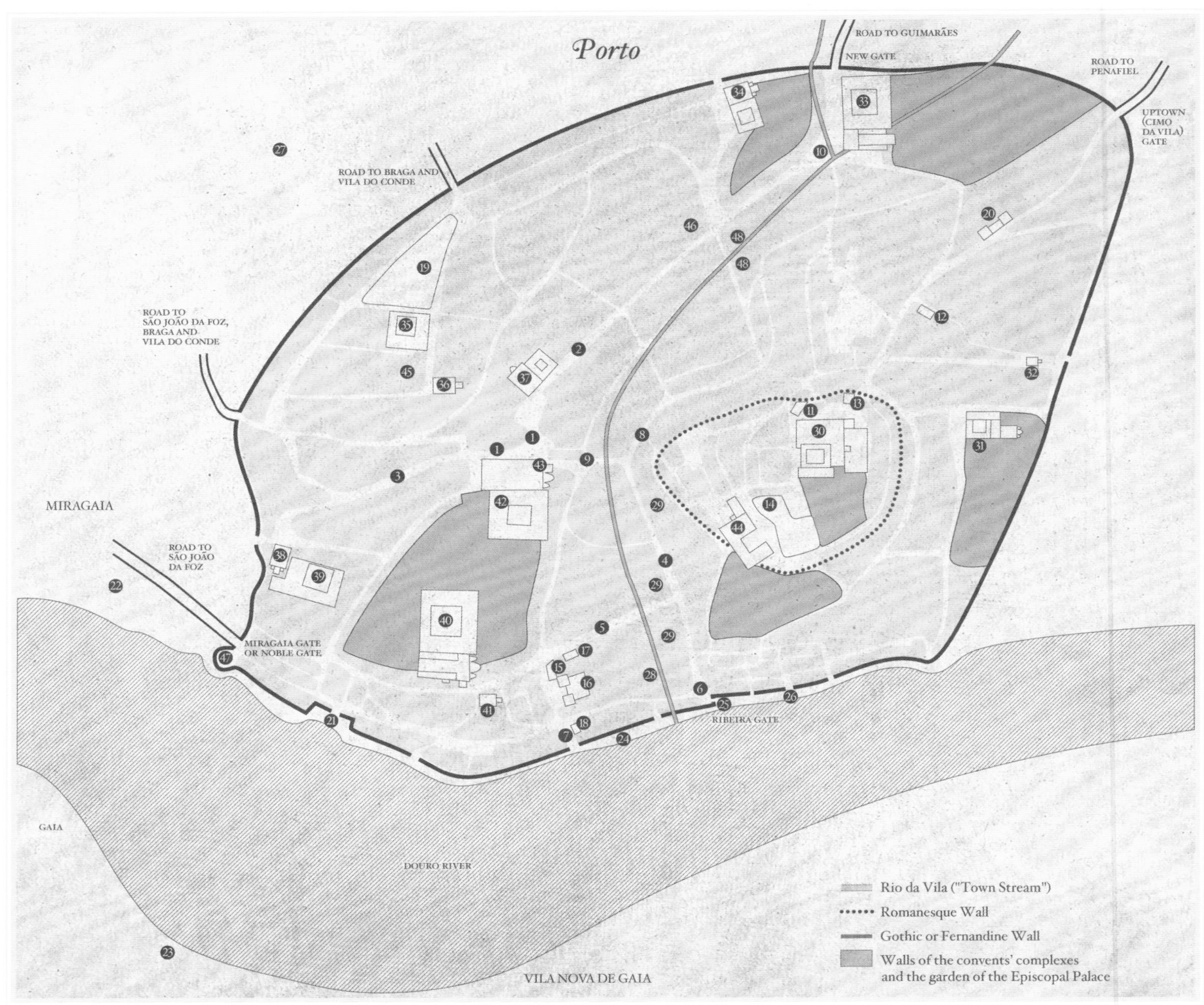

1 – Largo* de São Domingos (Forecourt) and Rua** de São Domingos (market)
2 – Rua das Flores
3 – Rua de Belmonte
4 – Rua dos Mercadores (Merchants' Street)
5 – Rua Nova
6 – Praça* da Ribeira (Riverside Square, daily market)
7 – Terreiro* do Pão ("Bread Square")
8 – Rua do Pé das Aldas (wholesale stores and retail shops)
9 – Rua da Ponte de São Domingos (São Domingos Bridge Street, wholesale stores and retail shops)
10 – Largo de São Bento (Cattle Market)
11 – City Council (Paço do Concelho)
12 – Prison Alley (Civil Prison)
13 – Prison for Clergymen
14 – Episcopal Palace
15 – Royal Treasury House (Casa dos Contos)
16 – Customs House (Armazém Real)
17 – Mint
18 – Official Weighing Scales and Notaries' Court
19 – Court of Appeals
20 – Military Governor Court (Paço do Alcaide)
21 – Shipyards of the Baths Postern (Postigo dos Banhos)
22 – Shipyards of Miragaia
23 – Shipyards of Vila Nova de Gaia
24 – Ribeira Quay
25 – Barge across the Douro and Assizor's Office
26 – Lada Quays
27 – Ropery
28 – Warehouse district
29 – Merchants' stores and tower houses
30 – Cathedral
31 – Convent of Santa Clara
32 – Chapel of Nossa Sra. do Penedo
33 – Benedictine Monastery of Ave Maria
34 – Convent of Santo Elói
35 – Benedictine Monastery of Vitória (under construction)
36 – Church of Nossa Sra. da Vitória
37 – Misericórdia Church and Chamber
38 – Church of São João de Belmonte
39 – Convent of São João Novo (under construction)
40 – Franciscan Convent
41 – Church of São Nicolau
42 – Dominican Convent
43 – Chapel of the Brotherhood of N. Sra. das Neves or of the Merchants
44 – São Lourenço College (under construction)
45 – Former Jewish Quarter
46 – Dom Lopo de Almeida Hospital (under construction)
47 – São Filipe Fort
48 – Tanneries

* *Praça*, *largo* and *terreiro* mean square in Portuguese

** *Rua* means street in Portuguese

Sources:
A Alfândega do Porto e o despacho aduaneiro (Porto: Casa do Infante, 1990); J. F. Afonso, "Manuel Luís," offprint of *Museu, 4th series*: 6 (1997); idem, "A construção de um novo centro cívico"; idem, A Rua das Flores no século XVI; idem, "A Igreja e a criação de uma paisagem urbana institucional. A envolvente da Sé do Porto no século XVI." *Douro: estudos & documentos 11*:20 (2005): 153–209"; idem, "Sobre um possível Hekhal," offprint of *Humanística e Teologia 57* (2006); idem, "A imagem tem que saltar ou o rebate dos signos. A cidade episcopal e o Porto intramuros no século XVI. Propriedade, ritual, representação e forma urbana (1499–1606)," PhD dissertation, UPC, 2008; idem, "A Praça da Ribeira no Porto," *Museu, 4th series*:17 (2008–2009): 81 ff; A. J. Morais Barros, "Porto: a construção de um espaço marítimo"; A. de Magalhães Basto, Os portuenses no Renascimento (Gaia: Pátria, 1931); idem, "Os diversos Paços do Concelho da cidade do Porto, " in *Vereaçoens, anos de 1390–1395* (Porto: CMP/GHC); J. Marques, "Património régio na cidade do Porto e seu termo nos finais do século XV (subsídios para o seu estudo)," offprint of *História*: *Revista da Faculdade de Letras da Universidade do Porto, 2nd series, 3* (1982): 73– 97; J. M. Pereira de Oliveira, *O espaço urbano do Porto. Condições naturais de desenvolvimento* (Coimbra: FLUC, 1973); C. Ruão, *Arquitectura maneirista no noroeste de Portugal. Italianismo e flamenguismo* (Coimbra: Electricidade do Norte, SA, 1996); F. R. da Silva, O Porto e o seu termo.

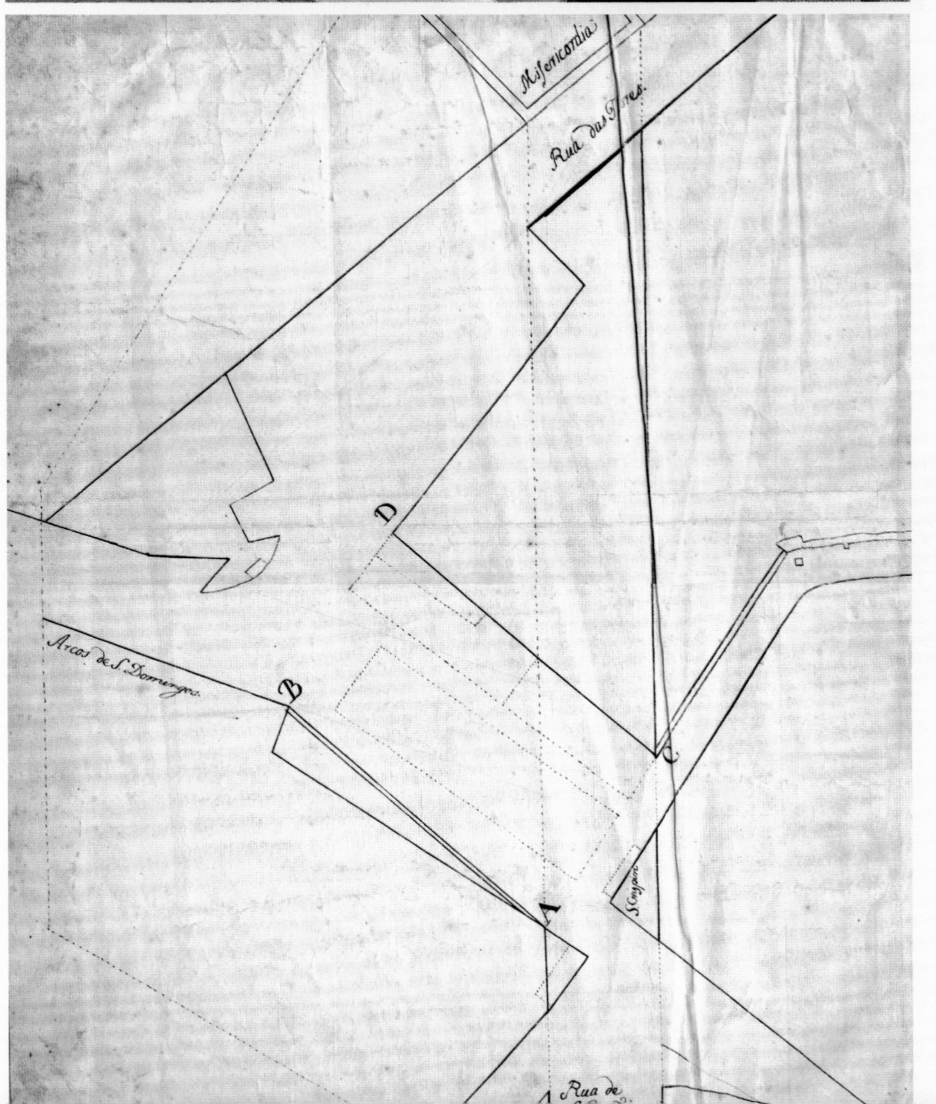

Above, The Crown Prince's House ("Casa do Infante")*: the fourteenth-century building in which the Porto customs house* (Alfândega Velha) *operated.*

Left, plan of São Domingos Square, in Porto, produced in 1799 for the proposed urban renewal of the area. The arches of São Domingos shown on the plan gave access to the forecourt's gallery.

Panoramic view of the city of Porto; *Teodoro de Sousa Maldonado* (1789).

ãs

29, Caza Antiga da Moeda
30, Hospital de S. Crispim
31, Igreja da Lapa
32, Congregados do Orat.
33, Agostinhos des calços
34, Senado.
35, Praça Nova da Ribeira

36, Senhora do Ó
37, Cathedral.
38, Paço do Bispo
39, Pelourinho
40, Patibulo
41, Caridade
42, Porta de Sima da Vª

43, Recolhimto. do Ferro
44, Igreja de S. Ildefonço
45, Convento de S. Clara
46, Porta do Sol
47, Capuchos
48, Recolhimto. das Orfas
49, Escadas dos Guindaes

50, Muro da Cidade.
51, Rio Douro
52, Estaleiro
53, Santa Marinha
54, Armazens
55, Villa Nova
56, Convento da Serr.

Godinho sc.

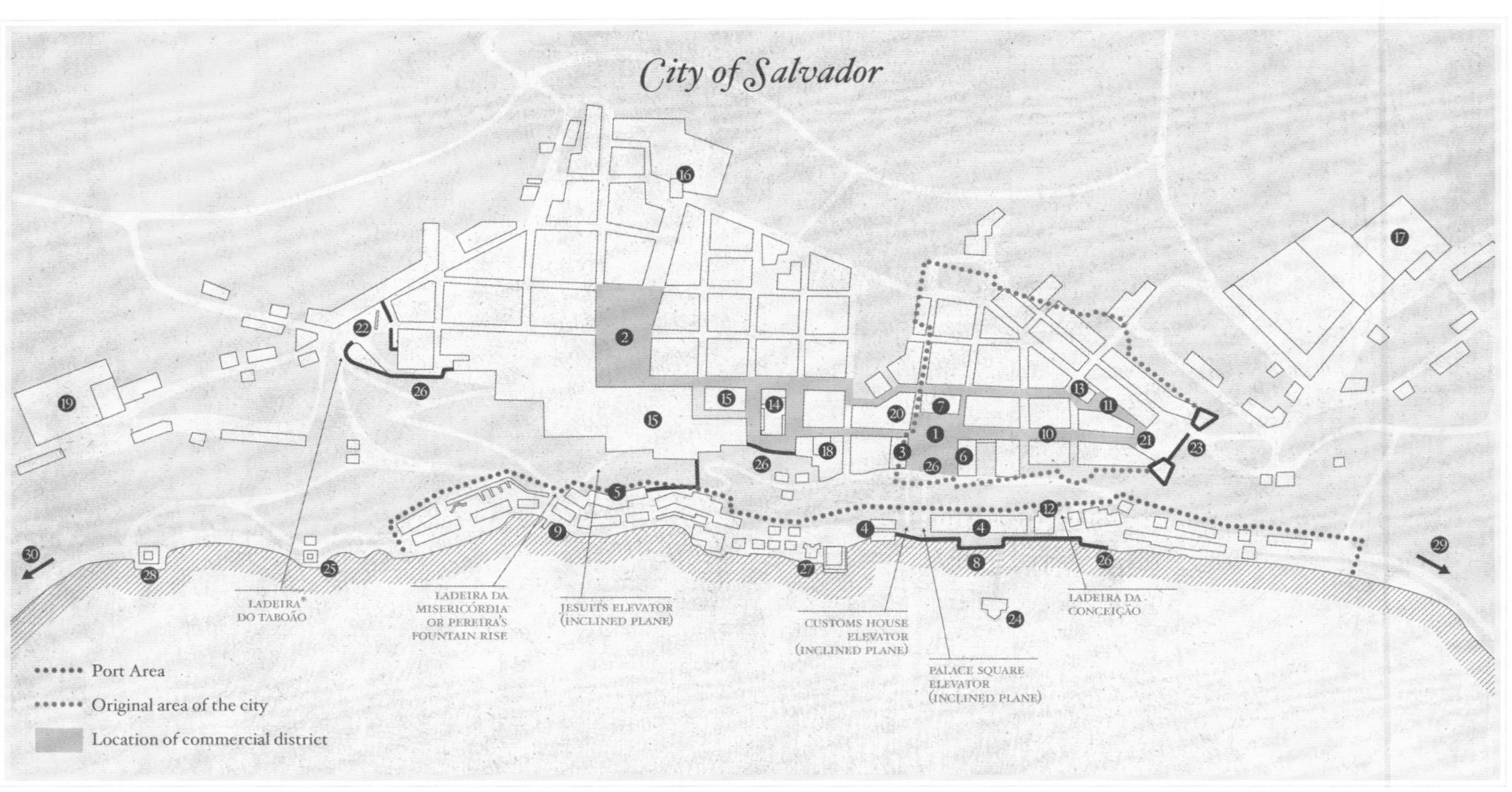

1 – Praça** do Palácio (Palace Square, now Tomé de Sousa Square)
2 – Terreiro** de Jesus
3 – Customs House and Warehouses (Later moved next to the port)
4 – Warehouses (Trapiches)
5 – Jesuits' Warehouses
6 – Governor's Palace and attached Court of Appeals
7 – City Council House and Prison
8 – Quay – general landing-place
9 – Jesuits' Quay – landing-place for seafarers
10 – Rua Direita do Palácio or Rua dos Mercadores (now Rua Chile)
11 – Largo** da Ajuda
12 – N. Sra. da Conceição Chapel
13 – Church of N. Sra. da Ajuda
14 – Cathedral (Sé do Salvador) and Episcopal Palace
15 – Jesuit Church and College (1st church)
16 – Franciscan Convent
17 – Benedictine Monastery
18 – Hospital and Church of N. Sra. da Misericórdia
19 – Church and Convent of N. Sra. do Carmo

Defense System

20 – Former Santa Luzia Gate (no longer existed)
21 – Former Santa Catarina Gate (no longer existed)
22 – Carmo Gate
23 – São Bento Gate
24 – São Marcelo Fort
25 – São Francisco Fort
26 – Defense Batteries
27 – Santo Alberto Fort
28 – Santiago Fort or Águas dos Meninos Fort
29 – Santo Antônio Fort (Barra)
30 – Monte Serrat Fort

* *Ladeira* means rise in Portuguese

** *Praça*, *largo* and *terreiro* mean square in Portuguese

Sources:
N. G. Reis, *Imagens de vilas e cidades do Brasil colonial* (São Paulo: Edusp, 2001); Universidade Federal da Bahia, *Evolução física de Salvador* (Salvador: Centro Editorial e Didático da UFBA, 1979).

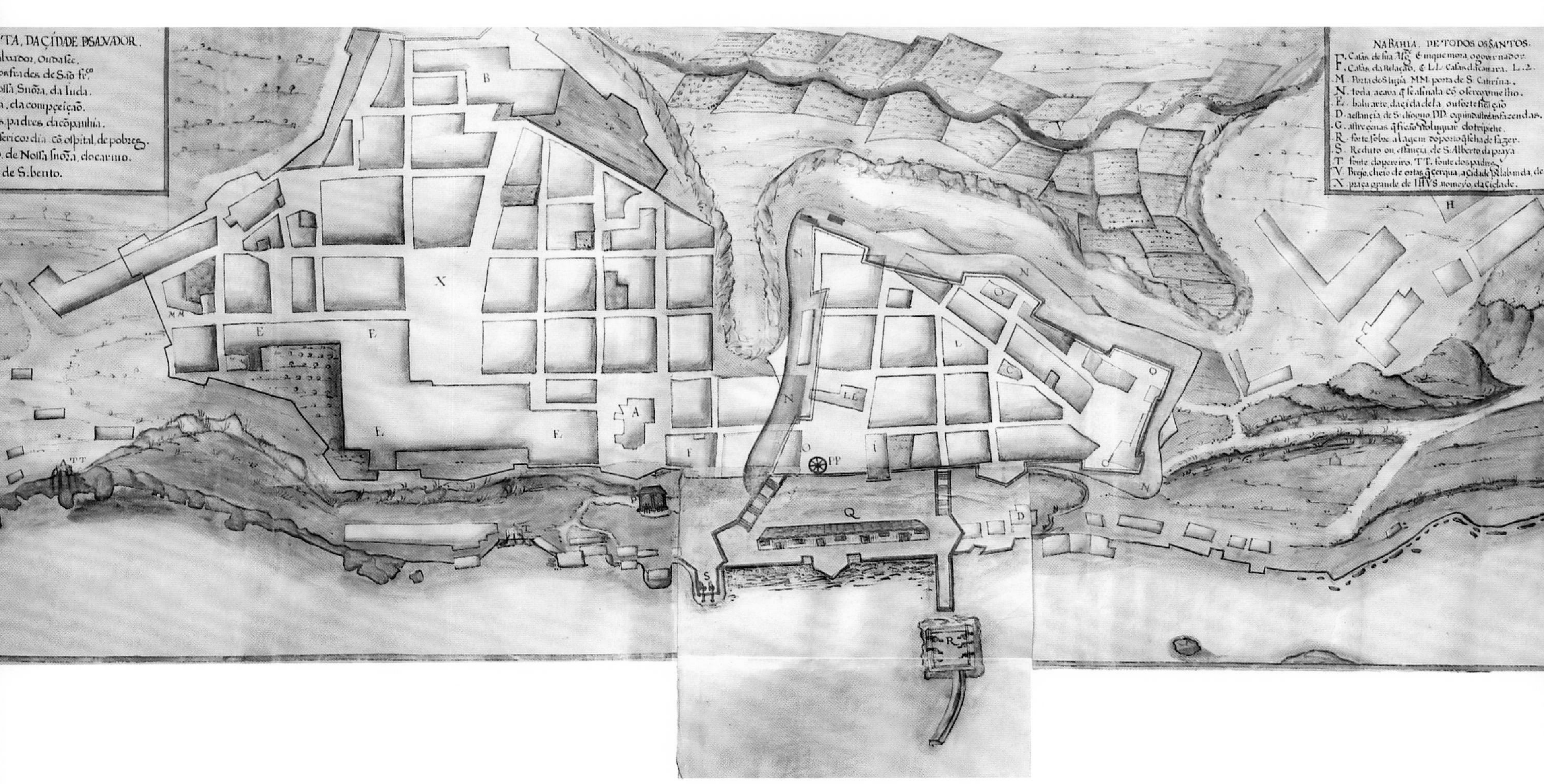

The arrangement of buildings in Salvador

In 1587, the sugar-mill owner and entrepreneur Gabriel Soares de Sousa described the square in front of the Governor- General's palace as follows:

> There is a fair square in the middle of this city, in which bulls are run on occasion, with some noble houses on the southern edge, in which the governors dwell, and the northern side has the royal treasury house, the customs house and warehouses; and the eastern flank has the city council house, prison and residential houses, owing to which it is in the shape of a square with the pillory in the middle, and its western flank is unobstructed and has a wonderful view of the sea....[119]

Opposite, above, profile of Salvador showing the height of the city in relation to sea level (ca. 1609–1616 or ca. 1638). The port and storage facilities in the Lower Town and its links with areas of the Upper Town that were also associated with trade are clearly recognizable.

Above, this page, plan of Salvador on Todos os Santos Bay, showing buildings and defense installations to be constructed; João Teixeira Albernaz, the Elder, around 1616. In the captions on the right, "F" should be "I," "DD" should be "PP" and "G" should be "Q." "O" indicates the customs house.

Stylized perspective of Olinda during the early period of the Dutch invasion, between 1630 and 1632, in an illustration published in 1644.

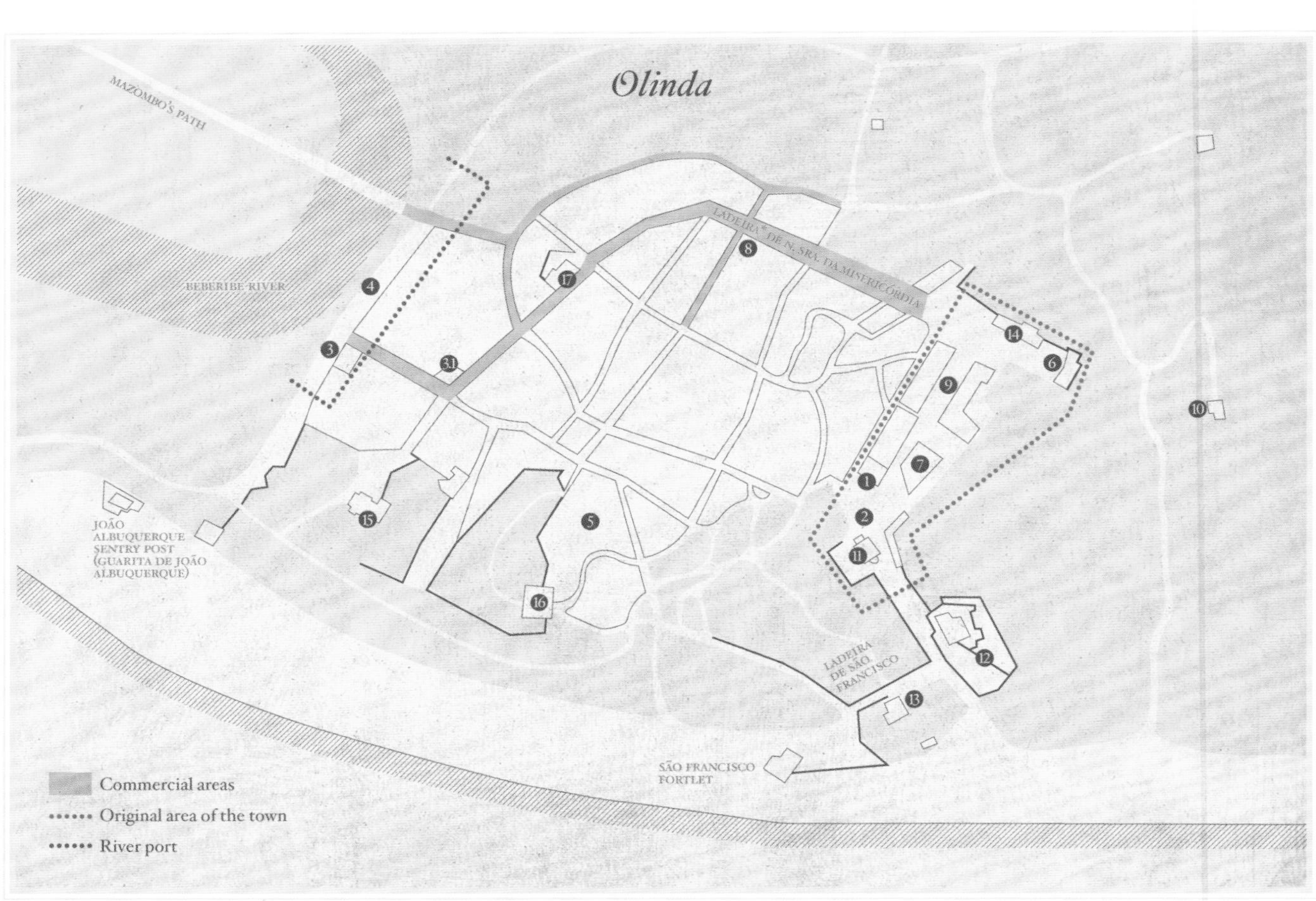

Note:
The fences around the religious houses provide a unique form of protection for the town of Olinda, forming a barrier between the sea and the inhabited area.

1 – Tower of Duarte Coelho's residence
2 – Praça da Matriz (Mother Church Square) – administrative and religious center
3 – Official Weighing Scales
 3.1 – Probable location of the customs house
4 – Varadouro – river quay
5 – Rocio Square – (where markets were held in Europe.)
6 – Largo** da Conceição
7 – Town Council House and Prison
8 – Quatro Cantos ("Four Corners")
9 – Rua*** Nova
10 – N. Sra. do Monte Chapel
11 – Salvador Mother Church
12 – Jesuit Church and College (1st church)
13 – Franciscan Convent
14 – Hospital and Church of N. Sra. da Misericórdia
15 – Benedictine Church and Monastery
16 – Church and Convent of N. Sra. do Carmo
17 – Church of São Pedro

* *Ladeira* means rise in Portuguese ** *Praça*, *largo* and *terreiro* mean square in Portuguese *** *Rua* means street in Portuguese

Source:
Reis, *Imagens de vilas e cidades do Brasil colonial.*

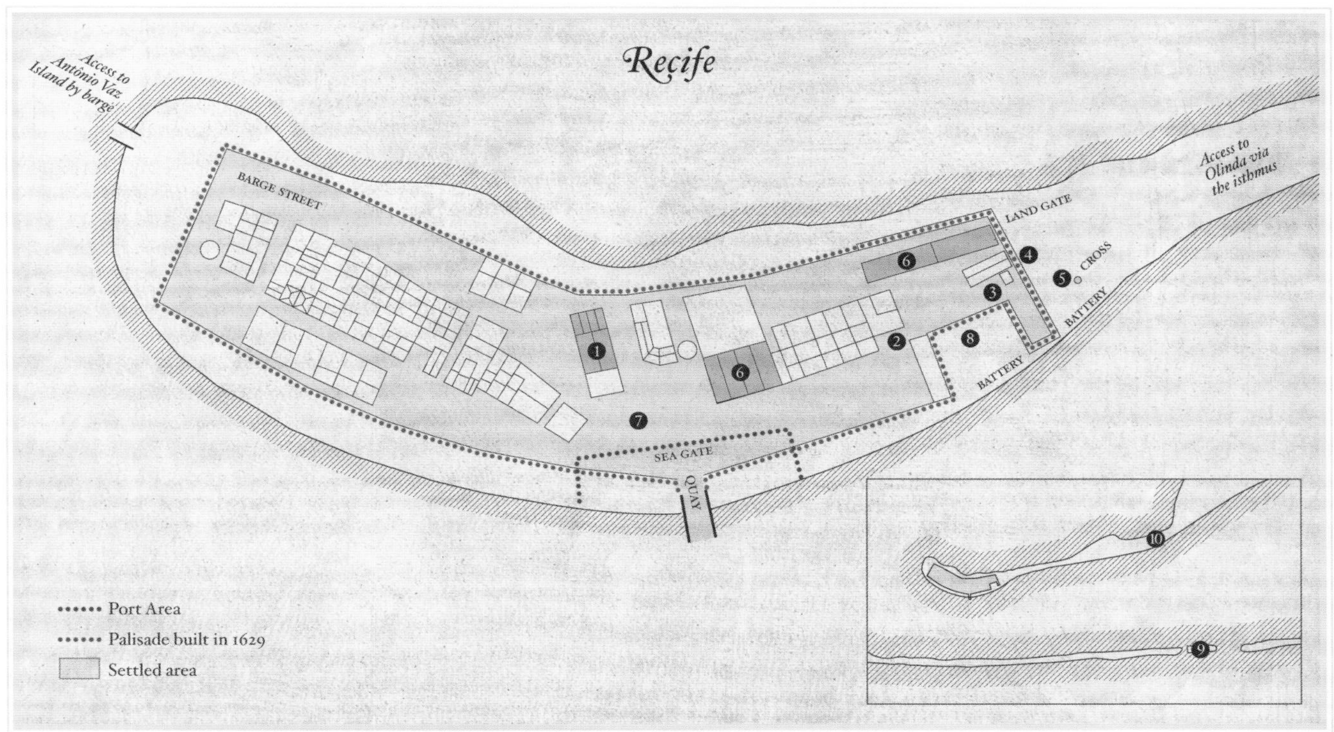

1 – Chapel and later Church of S. Frei Pedro Gonçalves, called Corpo Santo
2 – Customs House – next to the battery inside the fence (It was also located next to the old São Jorge Fort on the isthmus for some time)
3 – Probable location of the gunpowder magazine
4 – Probable location of the Guard House
5 – Cemetery
6 – Warehouses (Paços)
7 – Corpo Santo Chapel Square (Largo da Ermida do Corpo Santo)

Defense System
8 – Redoubt on the isthmus
9 – Laje Fort (Rock Fort) or Sea Fort
10 – São Jorge Fort or Old Fort

Note:
The lighter-colored buildings might not have existed during the period covered in this volume, and were drawn after later works by Dutch cartographers.

Sources:
Reis, *Imagens de vilas e cidades do Brasil colonial*; Several works by José Luiz Mota Menezes.

The port of Recife

This is how Friar Vicente do Salvador describes the port of Recife:

"...the main port of this captaincy [Pernambuco], which is the most well-known and more frequented by ships than all the other ports in Brazil; one enters through the mouth of a stone reef that is so narrow that no more than one carrack can enter at a time. Once one has entered this harbor or gone beyond the reef, there is an anchorage right there, where the large carracks are loaded, and small carracks – with one hundred tonnes or a little more – can keep afloat further. For port facilities, there is a small settlement there with some two hundred inhabitants with a parish dedicated to the Corpo Santo [Holy Body of Christ], to whom the seafarers are deeply devoted, and many shops and taverns, and the sugar depots [*passos*], which are large warehouses where the crates are stored until they are loaded onto the ships.

This settlement, which is called Recife [i.e., reef], is located at eight degrees. It is one league away from the town of Olinda, the capital of this captaincy, to which it is linked by sea and by land, because it is on the tip of a sandbar, which serves as a bridge, and the sea, which comes through the said reef entrance surrounds Recife to the east and, coming around on the other side, forms a narrow river that circles it westwards; when the tide is right, many boats and skiffs sail along this river taking wares to the town's quay [Varadouro in Olinda], where the customs house is located."[124]

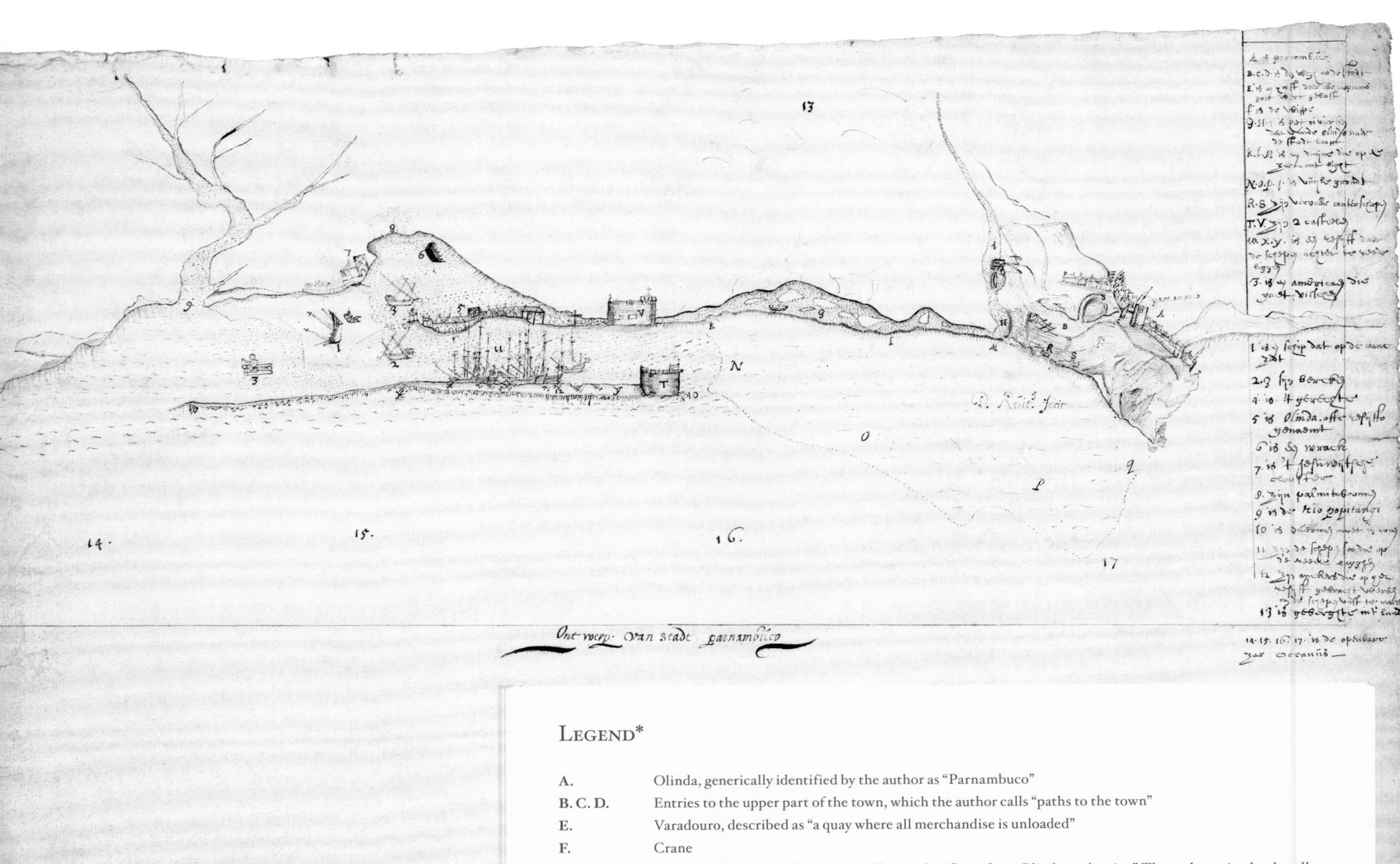

Legend*

A.	Olinda, generically identified by the author as "Parnambuco"
B. C. D.	Entries to the upper part of the town, which the author calls "paths to the town"
E.	Varadouro, described as "a quay where all merchandise is unloaded"
F.	Crane
G. H. I.	Beberibe River, described as a "small river that flows from Olinda to the city." The author mistakenly calls Recife a "city," instead of Olinda, which was then the main urban center in Pernambuco and its capital.
K. L. M.	Dunes on the coast
N. O. P. Q.	Shoals
R. S.	Counterscarps
T. V.	Two forts ("castles")
W. X. Y.	Reef behind which ships anchored
Z.	Amerindian ("American") fishing
1.	Ship stranded in a shoal
2. 3.	Barges
4.	"Courthouse"**
5.	Recife, once again confusing the town and the village, described as "Olinda, also called Recife [sic]"
6.	Shipwreck
7.	Jesuit College
8.	Palm trees
9.	Estuary of the River Afogados, which the author calls the "Popitangi River"
10.	Entrance for ships
11.	Harbor, described by the author as follows: "These are the ships, just as they are when at anchor." The Portuguese called this area the "well."
12.	Anchors taken to the reef to moor the ships
13	"Mountains," which the author claims are found in the hinterland
14. 15. 16. 17.	Open sea. Ocean
	Made by Dierick Ruiters
	Drawing of the city of Pernambuco (D. Ruiters)

* Translated from Dutch by Lodewijk Hulsman and Daniel Strum

** Curiously enough, Ruiters indicates a courthouse in Recife and not in Olinda, and even more so since by the time he visited Pernambuco in 1618, even the customs house had returned to Olinda.

Above, view of Olinda and Recife drawn by the Dutch navigator Dierick Ruiters, around 1618 or 1630.

Opposite, above, a stylized perspective of Recife in an illustration published in 1644.

On the opposite page, a view of Recife and the town of Olinda, by João Teixeira Albernaz, the Elder (ca. 1616). This portrayal emphasizes the importance of the Ribeira district next to the customs house (letter "O" in the legend).

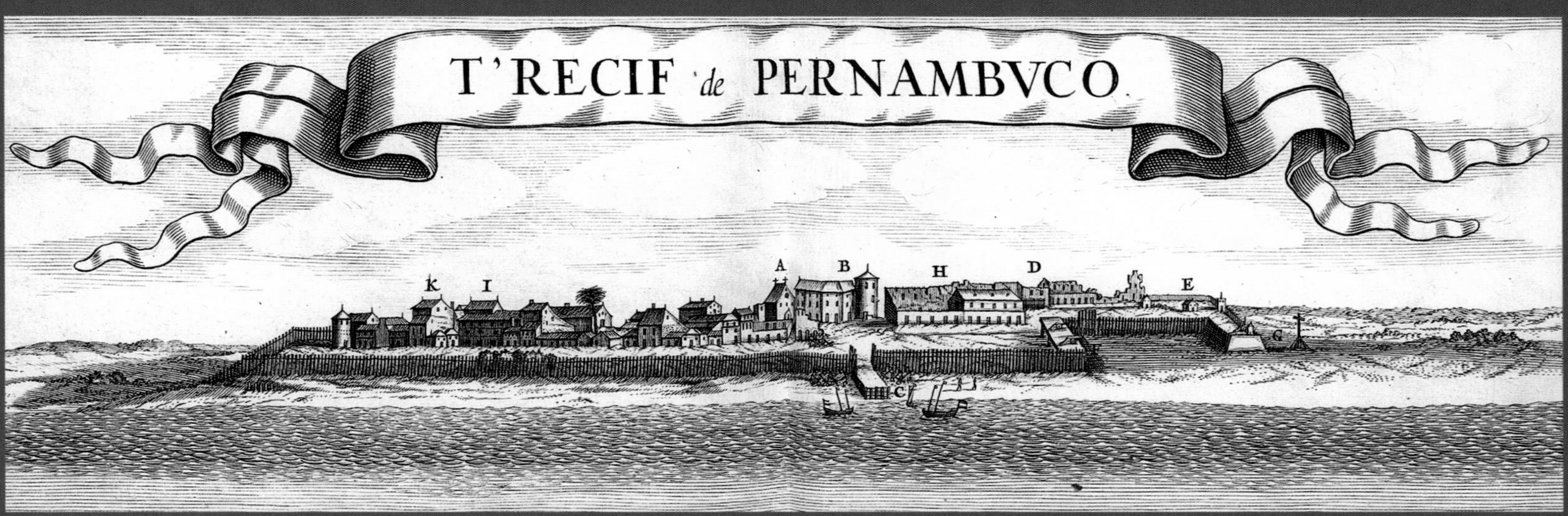
T'RECIF de PERNAMBVCO

both towns. The Upper Town in Salvador also had an official weighing scale maintained by the city council.[117] In that district, merchants established their residences and stores along its most important arteries and squares, near Brazil's main administrative and ecclesiastical buildings, and right beside the houses of the highest social echelons.[118]

Mercantile activities in Olinda also took place in the Upper Town, near the administrative and ecclesiastical institutions and the finest residences, as well as in the riverside Ribeira district. The latter linked the Upper Town and the Varadouro (quay), the anchorage for small vessels that shuttled between the town and the sugar mills, small settlements and the port of Recife. Anyone arriving at the village from the quay or along one of the trails connecting the town to Recife found the customs house slightly uphill,[Y] while the official weighing scale was on the lower side of the slope that linked the quay to the customs house.[120] Continuing along the main path and curving before the steep hill that led to the Misericórdia (the most prestigious charitable institution), one came to the "Four Corners" intersection, which served as a bourse for merchants.[121] Apart from these obligatory spots, merchants also met up at notary offices or in the houses of their peers.[122]

Merchants and other people involved in trade and shipping continuously thronged the minuscule areas which the Lower Town in Salvador and Póvoa do Recife encompassed at the time, to ship their wares in ocean-going vessels. These goods were transported in boats that took them to and from the hinterland and Olinda, in the elevators which raised them to the Upper Town in Salvador and on carts and animals which transported merchandise to Olinda, to Salvador's Upper Town or to the hinterland. Merchants stored crates of sugar in depots, known as "trapiches"[Z] in Bahia, and "passos" in Pernambuco, where they were kept until they were loaded.[AA] In the meantime, crates were also given and received in payment to and from third parties.[123]

Enhancing Correspondence

This intense flow of information within each marketplace also favored information being disseminated among overseas marketplaces. News was conveyed through correspondence and travelers who came and went, with incoming reports being retransmitted within each marketplace by fellow countrymen. Merchants used their agents, seafarers hired to transport their goods, suppliers and buyers, friends, relatives and acquaintances to obtain news from overseas. In addition, several people who lived in or traveled to various places, and with whom merchants interacted, such as lawyers, solicitors, proxies to recover debts and people transferring credit served as sources of information.[125]

As we have seen, every merchant maintained extensive correspondence with their various resident and/or traveling agents in the numerous marketplaces in which they traded.[126] In effect, correspondence and accounting were perhaps a merchant's main activities.[AB] Each ship carried bundles of letters from many senders to many addressees, and merchants – as well as others – took advantage of every departing ship to keep their correspondence up to date. Ambrósio Fernandes Brandão stated that, "In the year [15]83, when I was in the Captaincy of Pernambuco, in the town of Olinda, when a fleet was about to set sail for Portugal, I was always extremely preoccupied with the task of writing letters to be sent there."[127]

Merchants often rushed back to the same shipmaster to add addenda containing the latest news to their missives.[128] Transporting correspondence was a separate item on voyage charters, when the entire capacity of a ship was hired for a voyage, registered before Amsterdam notaries. Apart from shipmasters, traders and other travelers carried letters too.[129] The aforementioned Ambrósio described another episode in which he frantically searched for a document to send through a relative who was about to leave:

> *...a relative of mine of great consequence came to this land [Pernambuco], from Portugal, and, since he wished to return there again, I wanted to give him an important document to take with him, which I was unable to find, and in this regard I searched for it at great length through all the drawers of my office.*[130]

The gradual organization of the office of Chief-Postmaster in Portugal by the Habsburgs, included the establishment of a north-south axis, passing through Braga, Porto, Aveiro, Coimbra and Lisbon, and another axis between Lisbon and Madrid, with regular and weekly traffic. Yet its service neither encompassed the entire Portuguese territory nor became exclusive. In Porto, the office of assistant chief-postmaster was subordinated to that of the Chief-Postmaster of the Realm. Yet the former only appeared to have intervened in correspondence from overseas if there had been an outbreak of the plague at the source of the correspondence, to avoid contagion. The service was not always renowned for its diligence and speed, and various institutions based in the city of Porto had their own mail couriers. In addition, several other couriers were contracted on an ad hoc basis to transport official and private correspondence. Brazil was only included in the chief-postmaster's jurisdiction after the Restoration (when Portugal separated from the Spanish monarchy).[AC]

How often information was updated amongst marketplaces depended on the frequency of maritime traffic. As we have seen, small sailing craft were never excluded from the sugar route, and dispersed shipping (instead of fleets and convoys) even less so. These practices even remained in effect during periods when a good part of shipping was carried out by large vessels – carracks and hulks – or when they were organized into small fleets for protection.

We have also observed that seasonal difficulties were skirted, and the costs, time and risks associated with adverse seasons were always compensated by arbitrage profits through trade in goods and, no less important, by access to information. It is also clear that communications among the Dutch

Y. Initially, the customs house in Pernambuco was located on a "high and steep" site in Olinda. It was inconvenient to have to transport wares from the quay to be cleared there, since they often had to be brought down again to the foot of the hill to be loaded onto small boats or oxcarts headed for other settlements and to sugar mills. Consequently, between 1605 and 1607, the customs house was transferred to Recife. However, residents also complained about the new location, alleging that the building works undertaken in the settlement to house the customs house, or perhaps following the transfer, would jeopardize the adjoining defensive structures. As a result, a purpose-built customs house was constructed in Olinda, probably near the current city council house (For bibliography, see n. 120).

Z. The term "trapiche" ("warehouse") would also be used in Rio de Janeiro: Coaracy, *O Rio de Janeiro no século XVII*, p. 49.

AA. It is possible that the practice of keeping sugar stored near the port was more common in Pernambuco than in Bahia. In the latter, the crates were more often brought directly from the sugar mills to ocean-going ships aboard boats which traveled along the Todos os Santos Bay and the rivers which ran into this bay, without waiting in the warehouses of the Lower Town (AHU_ACL_CU_005-02, Cx.3, D.285 – 291 – [Bahia, before November 3, 1623]; Costa, *O transporte no Atlântico*, v. 1, pp. 332–333).

AB. This is what New Christians alleged in their defense before the Inquisition (IANTT, STO, IL 728, fols. 75v., 78v.-81; IL 11260, fols. 20v., 26, 123v.).

AC. Even then, the jurisdiction of the chief-postmaster in Brazil was limited, thanks to the resistance of the local powers in the colony due to its implications for secrecy, haste and costs. This was because the postal system charged postage for letters, which continued to be transported by merchant ships. The main difference was that the post office was to take care of receiving the mail bags from the shipmasters, list letters and distribute them. In Salvador, they were to be announced on a window at the Palace and distributed in the square below. The postal system was also to take care of dispatching correspondence and keep track of the departures of ships; see, M. S. Neto, "Os correios na Idade Moderna," in idem (ed.), *As comunicações na Idade Moderna* (Lisbon: Fundação Portuguesa das Comunicações, 2005), pp. 16–26; G. Ferreira, "O postilhão da América," in G. Ferreira, *Cousas e Loisas do Correio* (Lisbon: [n. n.], 1955), pp. 8, 14, 20; Silva, *O Porto e o seu termo*, v. 2, pp. 677–688).

Elegant Company Smoking and Drinking in an Inn *or* A Bordello Scene; *Jacob Duck (ca. 1635). Brothels, taverns and inns were important venues for the exchange of information among travelers. Note the map on the wall celebrating the Dutch conquest of the Brazilian Northeast.*

Woman in Blue Reading a Letter; *Johannes Vermeer (ca. 1662–1665). Here again we see a map in the background. Cartography was establishing itself as a decorative genre.*

Republic, Portugal and Brazil were never interrupted. They were maintained, directly or indirectly, overtly or covertly, with or without channeling through Portugal, using or dispensing with the involvement of neutral countries.[131] Such communication did not rely exclusively on the colonial trade, but also seized on the trade in salt, grain and Mediterranean products between the United Provinces and Portugal, which often included Spain and the Mediterranean basin.[132]

This frequent traffic enabled traveling agents to comply with their instructions to inform their principals in Portugal beforehand from Brazil regarding the details of the ships aboard which they were to consign sugar. That way, the principals could contract insurance, possibly in northern Europe, while the ships were still awaiting cargo in the colony, which usually took between forty and 120 days.[AD]

Information was also sent about shipments that had already been dispatched. Miguel Dias Santiago's nephew, for example, wrote to him from Olinda to Lisbon in June 1610, advising that, of the fifty crates of sugar that he had sent to Miguel aboard a caravel, four actually belonged to someone else. The latter was a cousin of the consignor, who also happened to be one of Miguel's nephews, whose orders Miguel should follow. The missive was possibly an erratum to a bill of lading and to the letter of advice that were sent with the shipment, in which the consignor had forgotten to mention this detail.[133] In all likelihood, he hoped that the information would arrive in time to avoid any confusion.

Addressees must also have received the same information through different channels, since shippers and drawers usually sent more than one copy of the bills of lading and bills of exchange to their consignees and drawees respectively in case one copy got lost. Bills of lading, as well as bills of exchange, were accompanied by letters of advice, providing counterparts with the details of the transaction and instructions about how to proceed.[134]

Ships not only brought letters but also crews and passengers, who described what they had seen and heard in the places they were coming from and passed through, in quays, warehouses, taverns, inns and brothels.[135]

In May 1621, a Dutchman and a Portuguese made a statement at the request of another Dutchman and another Portuguese (possibly an insurer and the insured party) before a notary public in Amsterdam. They said that they were well acquainted with a certain Domingos Gonçalves Nóbrega, living in Madeira and nicknamed "Red-Haired," due to his flaming beard. The latter had been the shipmaster of the ship *São Pedro*, which had been seized by pirates off the coast of Cape Verde during a voyage from Madeira to Bahia. The witnesses affirmed that they had eaten and drunk with him on several occasions in Madeira.[136]

If the frequency of communications depended on the intensity of traffic, speed depended on shipping technology. There were lighter and more agile sailboats as well as slower craft, while the duration of voyages could vary due to weather, currents, and to predatory activities, which were even worse than the forces of nature.[137] Even so, sailboats were the fastest way of transmitting information, and mercantile time frames operated at that pace. This was true for maturity periods for paying bills obligatory and bills of exchange, settling customs duties and realizing profits or losses. Periods for making payment on bills of exchange were stipulated according to the distances between the marketplaces.[138]

However, not all the time on a voyage was spent on the high seas. One could try to limit idle spells for ships which had already been loaded or were waiting to be unloaded in ports, streamlining loading and unloading processes. Hence, merchants often stipulated penalties to shipmasters who tarried against the charterers' orders. Likewise, merchants typically authorized them to leave without the cargo that had been contracted if the delay was liable to be excessive, and charge for the freight or lease out the freight to third parties. Occasionally, shipmasters were exempted from wasting time protesting about the shipment that was not delivered in a timely fashion. It was even possible to reduce the stopovers during an itinerary,[139] and sometimes bonuses were offered to the fastest shipmasters.[140] When the homebound journey depended on an agent, even if he was the shipmaster himself, it was possible to forbid sales with long payment terms or stipulate rigorous time frames for the return journey.

Another way to gain time was to use a vessel that was about to set sail to a destination different from the one envisaged in the letter, but which was close to it, and then take steps to have it dispatched from there through another channel, either by water or land, to the site to which it was to be sent. This could be quicker than waiting for direct transport.[141] In effect, the ports in the Atlantic Islands and in the Portuguese mainland were better informed about the sugar route as a whole. This was because these ports maintained diverse communication links both with Brazil and with northern Europe, without these two destinations being connected on a single voyage. Therefore, it was not without reason that shipmasters and supercargoes were instructed to call in at one of these ports en route to deliver and receive correspondence and instructions, and to revise plans.[142]

The end result of the information system described here is that one could not deceive many people for long. In addition, business strategies, risk management and credit analyses could be formulated, adjusted and revised according to the prevailing scenario more effectively, albeit still being far from efficient. There is no doubt that the increasing activity of pirates and corsairs tended to undermine this source of mercantile stability by breaking up communications. It is also true that information did not reach everyone involved in trade equally. One had more or fewer contacts, closer or farther away, with a greater or lesser degree of diversity. Nevertheless, whenever the geopolitical and religious context was not too hostile, both the information system and the mechanisms for compliance with norms – which largely depended on access to information – were effective enough to support the expansion of the sugar trade, with all its inherent economic, social, demographic and political dimensions.[143]

AD. The individuals who entered into the sea loans examined in the previous chapter pledged to load the proceeds within four months of their arrival in Brazil, and to inform the creditors about the ship on which they were sending the goods, so that the latter could insure the merchandise (ADP, NOT, PO2, l. 40, fols. 41v.-42v. [1615-1-28]). If this insurance really was contracted in "Flanders" – as Miguel Dias Santiago contracted from Lisbon for the shipments that his counterparts sent him from Brazil – clauses such as this reasonably presumed that the information would reach Porto and then be retransmitted from Porto to the Low Countries before the end of the four months stipulated to load the sugar. Still, we have seen that there were cases in which Dutch insurers agreed to underwrite policies for merchandise, ships and voyages about which they had little or no information (SR nos. 657, 663 n. 47. See also: Strum, "The Portuguese Jews and New Christians in the Sugar Trade," pp. 214–215; PRO, SP, 9/104, fol. 133v.). The same type of instruction was also given to the presumed supercargo Paulo Rodrigues de Aguiar, also mentioned in the previous chapter (ADP, NOT, PO2, l. 37, fols. 48–50 [1613-6-10]).

The Word

Chapter Ten

1. Brandão, *Diálogos das grandezas do Brasil*, p. 37. On this court, mainly from the social and political point of view, see: Schwartz, *Sovereignty and Society in Colonial Brazil*, passim.

2. SR nos. 375, 500, 950; Smith, "The Mercantile Class of Portugal and Brazil," pp. 370–371.

3. SR nos. 3449, 3458.

4. ADP, NOT, PO2, l. 20, fols. 237v.–239v. (1603–10–26); l. 31, fols. 20–21v. (1610-1-13); l. 38, fols. 141v.–142 (1614-6-11); l. 41, fols. 48–49 (1615-7-10); PO1, l. 140, fols. 146–146v. (1618-4-26); fols. 184v.–185v. (1618-5-19).

5. Mello, *Gente da nação*, pp. 26–27; Gonçalves, *Guerras e açúcares*, pp. 219–223.

6. SR no. 3344.

7. ADP, NOT, PO2, l. 8, fols. 134–135 (1597-7-1); 170v.–173 (1597-7-19); PO4, 1st series, l. 8, fols. 233v.–235 (02-09-1621).

8. For a more detailed discussion, see: Strum, "The Portuguese Jews and New Christians in the Sugar Trade," pp. 295–307.

9. Ibid., Appendix IV, no. 4.

10. See other cases in: SR nos. 401, 576.

11. SR nos. 114, 115.

12. SR nos. 702, 717, 720.

13. BNP, RES. 84//16 A: *Ley sobre os mercadores que quebram* (1597-03-08), p. 39. Later integrated into the *Ordenações* (*Ordenações Filipinas*, book 4, title LXXVI).

14. Ibid.

15. SR nos. 1125, 1175. *Ordenações Filipinas*, book 4, title LXXVI.

16. SR nos. 259 n. 23, 548, 551, 555, 575. S. van Leeuwen, *Commentaries on the Roman-Dutch Law* (London: Joseph Butterworth & Son, 1820), pp. 501–504.

17. Quinn and Roberds, "An Economic Explanation of the Early Bank of Amsterdam," p. 5.

18. *Ordenações Manuelinas*, book III, title XLV; *Ordenações Filipinas*, book III, title LIX.

19. Almeida, *Aritmética como descrição do real*, v. 2, pp. 365–366.

20. IANTT, STO, IL 4481, *Documentos apensos*, document n. 5, fol. 1.

21. Koen, "Duarte Fernandes," pp. 180, 187.

22. Roover, *L'évolution de la lettre de change*, pp. 99–113; Van der Wee, *The Growth of the Antwerp Market*, v. 2, pp. 348–349.

23. SR nos. 314, 2560; Malynes, *Consuetudo: vel, lex mercatoria*, passim.

24. ADP, NOT, PO2 l. 20, fols. 220v.–223v. (1603-10-15); l. 25, fols. 146v.–150 (1606-5-12); PO1, l. 133, fols. 70–72v. (1612-6-20); l. 133, fols. 77–79v. (1612-6-26); l. 133, fols. 162–163v. (1612-9-22); l. 137, fols. 131–133 (1616-3-11); l. 137, fols. 141–143v. (1616-3-22); SR no. 2604.

25. SR no. 618.

26. Strum, "The Portuguese Jews and New Christians in the Sugar Trade," pp. 288–292.

27. Gelderblom and Jonker, "Amsterdam as the Cradle of Modern Futures and Options Trading," p. 5; Van der Wee, *The Growth of the Antwerp Market*, v. 2, pp. 365–366; *Coutumes de la ville d'Anvers, dites antiquissimae* (Leuven: Katholieke Universiteit Leuven), passim.

28. J. Borges, "Provizão e regimento," pp. 60–61.

29. Ibid.

30. Ibid., pp. 56–62. For more on the Consulate, see: Smith, "The Mercantile Class of Portugal and Brazil," pp. 161–164; Costa, *O transporte no Atlântico*, v. 1, pp. 228, 266–270; Mauro, *Portugal, o Brasil e o Atlântico*, v. 1, p. 305; v. 2, pp. 201–202; Silva. *O Porto e o seu termo*, v. 1, pp. 133, 220, 466, 545–550; Almeida, *Aritmética como descrição do real*, v. 2, pp. 364–367; Moreira, *Os mercadores de Viana*, p. 126; ADP, NOT, PO2, l. 16, fols. 49–51v. (1601-4-14).

31. Charter dated July 30, 1592 in *Documentos para a história do açúcar*, p. 396.

32. Ibid., p. 398; Borges, "Provizão e regimento," pp. 44–45.

33. Ibid., pp. 47–48.

34. On the intervention by civil courts, such as royal judges [*juízes de fora*] and royal civil magistrates [*corregedores do cível*], see, for example: ADP, NOT, PO2, l. 36, fols. 101v.–102v. (1612–11–12). About the jurisdiction of the customs house magistrate and the magistrate for India, Mina and Brazil, which substituted the former in certain geographical areas and for certain issues; for jurisdiction disputes, see: Leão, *Leis extravagantes*, fols. 33v.–35v.; *Ordenações Filipinas*, book 1, title LI, LII; Almeida, *Aritmética como descrição do real*, v. 2, pp. 366–367; AGS, SSP, l. 1568, passim.

35. Go, "Marine Insurance in the Netherlands," pp. 95–117, 123; Spooner, *Risks at Sea*, p. 18. Hell, "De oude geuzen en de Opstan," pp. 290–295; Israel, *Dutch Primacy in World Trade*, p. 76; SR nos. 63, 434, 858, 1662, 1685, 1690, 1699, 1703, 1704, 1710.

36. SR nos. 212, 568, 601, 1811.

37. ADP, NOT, PO2, l. 33, fols. 116v.–118 (1611-12-7); SR nos. 212, 341.

38. ADP, NOT, PO2, l. 43, fols. 43v.–44 (1616-6-30), SR no. 341.

39. ADP, NOT, PO2, l. 33, fols. 116v.–118 (1611-12-7); l. 35, fols. 130v.–132 (1612-7-n.d.); l. 36, fols. 212–213 (1613-1-31); l. 39, fols. 96–96v. (1614-9-19): "...the said nominated arbiters can appoint a third arbiter," SR no. 1953.

40. SR no. 2038.

41. Strum, "The Portuguese Jews and New Christians in the Sugar Trade," pp. 308–313.

42. ADP, NOT, PO2, l. 33, fols. 116v.–118 (1611-12-7); IANTT, STO, IL 728, fols. 56, 164v.; SR nos. 341, 792, 871, 891, 1953, 1954.

43. ADP, NOT, PO2, l. 48, fols. 110v.–112v. (1618-3-15).

44. Go, "Marine Insurance in the Netherlands," p. 77.

45. SR no. 282.

46. ADP, NOT, PO1, l. 136, fols. 16v.–18 (1615-7-1). See also: ibid., fols. 110–112 (1615-8-18); fols. 166v.–168v. (1615-9-22); l. 138, fols. 133–135 (1617-4-12); SR no. 7.

47. Strum, "The Portuguese Jews and New Christians in the Sugar Trade," pp. 308–313.

48. Brandão, *Diálogos das grandezas do Brasil*, p. 37.

49. ADP, NOT, PO1, l. 140, fols. 1–4v. (1617-12-22). See also: PO1, l. 132, fols. 64v.–66 (1611-9-23); l. 140, fols. 28–30v. (1618-1-23); PO2, l. 20, fols. 208–210 (1603-10-6); l. 37, fols. 122–123 (1613-7-31); l. 34, fols. 13–16 (1612-1-27); fols. 133–134v. (1612-3-31).

50. PO1, l. 132, fols. 64v.–66 (1611-9-23).

51. Strum, "The Portuguese Jews and New Christians in the Sugar Trade," pp. 317–320.

52. SR no. 3472.

53. SR no. 3177.

54. SR nos. 3328, 3329.

55. Unger, *The Ship in the Medieval Economy*, p. 206; idem, *Dutch Shipbuilding before 1800*, pp. 49, 55, 59, 60.

56. SR no. 3334.

57. Granovetter, "Problems of explanation in economic sociology," pp. 38–39, 41–42.

58. For a more detailed discussion, see: Strum, "The Portuguese Jews and New Christians in the Sugar Trade," pp. 292–294. Costa suggests that a generalized mercantile morality only crystallized in the eighteenth century: Costa, "Informação e incerteza," pp. 110–111.

59. Most of the data about the impact of the both the physical and the organizational infrastructure, as well as the social fabric of the mercantile circle, in Amsterdam on the flow of information presented herein, is based on the research by Clé Lesger published in the chapter entitled "Amsterdam as a Center of Information Supply" in his book, *The Rise of the Amsterdam Market* (pp. 214–257).

60. B. Bakker, "De zichtbare stad 1578–1813," in Willem and Prak, *Geschiedenis van Amsterdam, deel II-A*, pp. 17–37; C. Lesger, "De wereld als horizon: de economie tussen 1578 en 1650," in Willem and Prak, *Geschiedenis van Amsterdam, deel II-A*, pp. 103–107; Lesger, *The Rise of the Amsterdam Market*, p. 218; Israel, *The Dutch Republic*, pp. 308–311.

61. Afonso, *A Rua das Flores no século XVI*, pp. 26–32.

62. Ibid., pp. 45–48, 50–53, 122–126.

63. Cardim, *Tratados da terra e gente do Brasil*, pp. 217, 255; Sousa, *Tratado descritivo do Brasil*, pp. 20–21, 96, 102; Moreno, *Livro que dá razão do Estado do Brasil*, pp. 40, 175 (n. 12), 176, 182–183, 182 (n. 38), 194, 203; Brandão, *Diálogos das grandezas do Brasil*, p. 33; J. Baers, *Olinda conquistada* (Recife: Secretaria de Educação e Cultura, 1977), p. 42; J. Nieuhof, *Memorável viagem marítima e terrestre ao Brasil* (São Paulo: Edusp, 1981), p. 47; Nizza da Silva, "A Sociedade," pp. 313–316; Johnson, "A indústria do açúcar," p. 278; Gândavo, *Tractado da terra do Brasil*, fols. 5, 7.

64. Mauro, *Portugal, o Brasil, e o Atlântico*, v. 1, pp. 254–265; Siqueira, "A Inquisição portuguesa e a sociedade colonial," pp. 133, 188–189, 200; Ferlini, *Terra, trabalho e poder*, pp. 220–224; Nieuhof, *Memorável viagem*, pp. 372–373; Moreno, *Livro que dá razão do Estado do Brasil*, pp. 139–140, 143, 176, 182–183; Brandão, *Diálogos das grandezas do Brasil*, pp. 8–10, 39–40, 89; Cardim, *Tratados da terra e gente do Brasil*, pp. 243, 255; Sousa, *Tratado descritivo do Brasil*, pp. 102–124; N. G. Reis, *Evolução urbana do Brasil, 1500–1720* (São Paulo: Pini, 2000), pp. 98, 100, 154, 156–157; Mello, *O nome e o sangue*, pp. 174, 182–183; Smith, "The Mercantile Class of Portugal and Brazil," pp. 76–79, 276; Mello, *Gente da nação*, p. 61; Moreno, *Livro que dá razão do Estado do Brasil*, pp. 194, 200; Oliveira, *A História do Brazil*, v. 2, fol. 136v.; Gonçalves, *Guerras e açúcares*, pp. 217–225; Siqueira, *A Inquisição portuguesa e a sociedade colonial*, p. 62; Ricupero, *A formaçao da elite colonial*, pp. 243–266, 281–319; E. C. de Mello, *Um imenso Portugal: história e historiografia* (São Paulo: Editora 34, 2002), pp. 179–220.

65. Gândavo, *Tractado da terra do Brasil*, fol. 6v.; Sousa, *Tratado descritivo do Brasil*, pp. 96–100, 102; Moreno, *Livro que dá razão do Estado do Brasil*, pp. 139–148; Oliveira, *A História do Brazil*, v. 2, fols. 145–145v.; Brandão, *Diálogos das grandezas do Brasil*, pp. 35–36, 40; Schwartz, *Sugar Plantations in the Formation of Brazilian Society*, pp. 76–78.

66. Oliveira, *A História do Brazil*, v. 2, fols. 39v.–40; see another version from the same period: Brandão, *Diálogos das grandezas do Brasil*, p. 31.

67. Moreno, *Livro que dá razão Estado do Brasil*, pp. 176–178 (n. 16); Oliveira, *A História do Brazil*, v. 2, fol. 39v.; v. Pontual and V. Milet, "Olinda: memória e esquecimento," *Revista brasileira de estudos urbanos e regionais, 5* (2002): 45–50; Gândavo, *Tractado da terra do Brasil*, fol. 6.

68. IANTT, STO, IL 728, fol. 15; Strum, "The Portuguese Jews and New Christians in the Sugar Trade," pp. 220–238.

69. Afonso, *A Rua das Flores no século XVI*, pp. 45–48, 50–53, 122–126.

70. Bakker, "De zichtbare stad 1578–1813," pp. 78–84.

71. Ibid., pp. 17–37; Lesger, "De wereld als horizon," pp. 103–107.

72. Sousa, *Tratado descritivo do Brasil*, pp. 98–100; Moreno, *Livro que dá razão do Estado do Brasil*, pp. 175–176; Cardim, *Tratados da terra e gente do Brasil*, pp. 219, 250; Brandão, *Diálogos das grandezas do Brasil*, p. 32; Reis, *Evolução urbana do Brasil*, pp. 144–146, 150, 158–159, 189.

73. See, among others: IANTT, STO, IC 1322, fol. 149v.; IC 2583, fol. 49; IC 5228, n/n (session dated 1622.12.17); IANTT, STO, IC 6987, n/n (session dated 1619.09.18).

74. IANTT, STO, IL 728, fols. 117–117v., 140–142.

75. IANTT, STO, IC 1322, fol. 150; IC 1820, fol. 15; IC 2583, fols. 38, 51v.; IC 875, 13 v.; IC 6070, fol. 55v.; IC 8461, n/n (session dated 1620.03.24); IC 9068, fol. 4v.; IC 2736, fols. 25v., 28; IL 3080 (session dated 1621.11.21); IC 5385, fol. 10.

76. IANTT, STO, IC 2583, fol. 42, 50v.

77. Silva, *O Porto e o seu termo*, v. 1, pp. 86–92; IANTT, STO, IL 3080, n/n (denunciation by Lucas Mendes), n/n (sessions dated 1621.11.19 and 1621.11.17); IC 2736, fol. 25; IC 5362, 3v.; IC 8461, n/n (session dated 1620.03.24); IC 1322, fols. 131v., 149v.; IC 12621, fol. 12v., n/n (session dated 1620.03.09); IL, 3418, fol. 23; IC 1937, n/n (session dated 1597.01.30). With regard to Amsterdam: Bakker, "De zichtbare stad 1578–1813," pp. 17, 21, 85–88. With regard to Brazil: IANTT, STO, IL 3080, n/n (session dated 1621.11.17).

78. IANTT, STO, IL 10209, n/n (testimony of Silvestre Ferros Chamorro dated 1620.2.2).

79. IANTT, STO, IC 8658 (inquiry of the articles of objection); IC 1820 (commendatory articles); IC 2200 (commendatory articles and its inquiries); IL 5390 (commendatory articles); IL 3418 (commendatory articles); IC 5304 (commendatory articles); IC 9377 (commendatory articles); IANTT, STO, IC 9068, n/n (testimony of Francisco Alvares de Soagua); IL 1400, fol. 132v.; IL 3068, fol. 19v.; IL 5390 (3as contraditas). On Brazil, see: Smith, "The Mercantile Class of Portugal and Brazil," pp. 331–333; Sousa, *Tratado descritivo do Brasil*, pp. 97, 124.

80. IANTT, STO, IC 1937, passim. With regard to Brazil, see: Cardim, *Tratados da terra e gente do Brasil*, pp. 217, 256–257; Sousa, *Tratado descritivo do Brasil*, pp. 96; Brandão, *Diálogos das grandezas do Brasil*, p. 104; L. M. Algranti, "Famílias e vida doméstica," in A. Novais (ed.), *História da vida privada no Brasil*, V. 1 (São Paulo: Companhia das Letras, 1997), pp. 113–119; *Segunda visitação do Santo Ofício às partes do Brasil*, p. 427.

81. Israel, *The Dutch Republic*, pp. 119–121.

82. Ibid., pp. 121–122, 358, 677–685; S. Schama, *The Embarrassment of Riches – An Interpretation of Dutch Culture in the Golden Age* (New York: Knopf/Random House, 1987), pp. 378, 577.

83. Algranti, "Famílias e vida doméstica," pp. 96, 152; Mello, *O nome e o sangue*, pp. 186–189; R. Vainfas, "Moralidades brasílicas: deleites sexuais e linguagem erótica na sociedade escravista," in Novais, *História da vida privada no Brasil*, v. 1, pp. 227–228; Mello, *Gente da nação*, pp. 61–64, 68–71; Siqueira, "A Inquisição portuguesa e a sociedade colonial," p. 134 n. 5; Strum, "The Portuguese Jews and New Christians in the Sugar Trade," pp. 239–243. A different view has been suggested by the Brazilian urban historian Nestor Goulart Reis, who believed that the inhabitants of the urban centers in the colony, especially the upper classes, were aloof from each other, staying within their residences: Reis, *Evolução urbana do Brasil*, pp. 133, 151.

84. Siqueira, "A Inquisição portuguesa e a sociedade colonial," pp. 134–136, 146–149, 151.

85. Israel, *The Dutch Republic*, pp. 308–311; Lesger, *The Rise of the Amsterdam Market*, p. 218.

86. Strum, "The Portuguese Jews and New Christians in the Sugar Trade," pp. 243, 302 (n. 849).

87. Lesger, *The Rise of the Amsterdam Market*, p. 151 (n. 46). See also: Barbour, *Capitalism in Amsterdam in the 17th Century*, p. 75.

88. Lesger, *The Rise of the Amsterdam Market*, p. 155; Israel, *The Dutch Republic*, pp. 345–347.

89. Lesger, *The Rise of the Amsterdam Market*, pp. 214–257; M. 'T Hart, "The Glorious City: Monumentalism and Public Space in Seventeenth-Century Amsterdam," in P. O'Brien, D. Keene and M. 'T Hart (eds.), *Urban Achievement in Early Modern Europe: Golden Ages in Antwerp, Amsterdam, and London* (Cambridge: Cambridge University Press, 2001), pp. 131–132.

90. Van Dillen, "The Bank of Amsterdam," pp. 84–92; Dehing and 'T Hart, "Linking the Fortunes," pp. 45–49; Quinn and Roberds, "An Economic Explanation of the Early Bank of Amsterdam," pp. 2–8, 21–27; Israel, *Dutch Primacy in World Trade*, pp. 77–78.

91. Lesger, *The Rise of the Amsterdam Market*, pp. 243–249; Hell, "De oude geuzen en de Opstan," pp. 290–295; Israel, *Dutch Primacy in World Trade*, p. 76.

92. Quinn and Roberds, "An Economic Explanation of the Early Bank of Amsterdam," p. 19–20.

93. Lesger, *The Rise of the Amsterdam Market*, pp. 244–245.

94. Spufford, "Access to Credit and Capital in the Commercial Centers of Europe," pp. 309–310.

95. Lesger, *The Rise of the Amsterdam Market*, pp. 222–224, 240; De Vries and Van der Woude, *The First Modern Economy*, p. 147; Israel, *Dutch Primacy in World Trade*, pp. 74–75; 'T Hart, "The Glorious City," pp. 131–132.

96. Lodewijk Hulsman assisted with research for the project that resulted in this book. He holds a PhD in history from the University of Amsterdam, where he is currently a researcher.

97. Bakker, "De zichtbare stad 1578–1813," pp. 23, 29, 31, 39; J. Zwarts, *De eerste rabbijnen en Synagogen van Amsterdam: naar archivalische bronnen* (Amsterdam: M. Hertzberger, 1929), passim.

98. SR nos. 282, 1318, 1596; Spooner, *Risks at Sea*, pp. 19, 22–23; Go, "Marine Insurance in the Netherlands," pp. 73–95, 84, 122, 154.

99. SR no. 1670; Lesger, *The Rise of the Amsterdam Market*, pp. 224–225.

100. Ibid., pp. 233, 225, 232–233.

101. Ibid., p. 221, 224, 232–237; De Vries and Van der Woude, *The First Modern Economy*, p. 149.

102. *Ordenações Manuelinas*, book 3, title XLV, Art. 17; *Ordenações Filipinas*, book 3, title LIX, Art. 19; Costa, *Informação e incerteza*, pp. 112–114; Silva, *O Porto e o seu termo*, v. 2, pp. 661–667; Barros, "Porto: a construção de um espaço marítimo," v. 1, pp. 102–105.

103. Silva, *O Porto e o seu termo*, v. 1, pp. 115–117.

104. On businessmen's meeting places, see: Strum, "The Portuguese Jews and New Christians in the Sugar Trade," pp. 243–251; Afonso, *A Rua das Flores no século XVI*, pp. 28, 31–33, 61, 77–78, 91–92, 102–105, 127–128; Silva, *O Porto e o seu termo*, v. 1, p. 87.

105. Afonso, *A Rua das Flores no século XVI*, pp. 27–28, 36; Silva, *O Porto e o seu termo*, v. 1, p. 86. On chance encounters in the Praça da Ribeira square: IANTT, STO, IC 2583, fol. 51v.

106. On the functioning of these weighing scales in the sixteenth century: Barros, "Porto: a construção de um espaço marítimo," v. 1, p. 82.

107. IANTT, STO, IL 728, fol. 164v; IC 1329, fol. 73; IC 6987, fol. 62v.; IL 3068, fols. 109–115v.; IL 11260, fol. 123v.–125; IL 3418, fol. 9.

108. ADP, NOT, PO1, l. 133, fols. 70–72v. (1612-6-20); l. 135a, fols. 66–68v.; l. 136, fols. 166v.–168v. (1615-9-22); PO2, l. 7, fols. 131–133 (1616-3-11).

109. Silva, *O Porto e o seu termo*, v. 1, p. 196; Afonso, *A Rua das Flores no século XVI*, pp. 27–28.

110. IL 3068 (session dated 1621.11.15); IC 1329, fol. 18v.; IC 5362, n/n (session dated 1618.10.23); IL 3080, n/n (session dated 1621.11.17).

111. On the area outside the Porta da Alfandega (Customs Gate): IANTT, STO, IC 8461, n/n (session dated 1620.24.03). With regard to Miragaia beach, outside the Porta de Miragaia (Gate of Miragaia), also called Porta Nova (New Gate): IL 5395, fol. 104v. With regard to the area called Areia (Sand), beyond the Porta da Ribeira (Riverside Gate): IL 12621, fols. 12–13v. Amândio J. M. Barros emphasizes encounters on the river beach during the sixteenth century: Barros, "Porto: a construção de um espaço marítimo," v. 1, p. 47.

112. IANTT, STO, IC 3068, fol. 19v.–20; IL 3418, n/n (*19th article of objection*). On the construction of the diverse quays in Porto, concluded only at the end of the sixteenth century, see: Barros, "Porto: a construção de um espaço marítimo," v. 1, pp. 56–71.

113. IANTT, STO, IC 5702, fol. 37v.; IL 3148, n/n (session dated 1621.05.19); IL 3068 n/n (sessions dated 1621.11.15 and 1621.11.16); IC 1986 n/n (session dated 1597.08.06); IC 1937, n/n (sessions dated 1596.11.02 and 1596.10.12); IL 728, fol. 211; IL 12621, fol. 17v.; IL 13018, fols. 21v.–22; IC 5702, n/n (session dated 1620.01.02).

114. ADP, NOT, *Lista dos Antigos Tabeliães da Cidade do Porto [Cópia idêntica do notário Casimiro Curado]*.

115. ADP, NOT, PO1, l. 136, fols. 4v.–5v. (1615–6–27).

116. Afonso, *A Rua das Flores no século XVI*, p. 36, n. 62.

117. AHU_ACL_CU_005–02, Cx. 3, D. 289.

118. Sousa, *Tratado descritivo do Brasil*, pp. 96–100; Schwartz, *Sugar Plantations in the Formation of Brazilian Society*, pp. 78–79; Smith, "The Mercantile Class of Portugal and Brazil," pp. 276–278; Mello, *Gente da nação,* p. 69.

119. Sousa, *Tratado descritivo do Brasil*, p. 96.

120. "Traslado do Foral de Olinda" (12 March 1537), in A. Pereira da Costa, *Anais Pernambucanos,* V. 1 (Recife: Fundarpe, 1983), p. 187; Moreno, *Livro que dá razão do Estado do Brasil*, p. 177, n. 18; B. Teensma, "Descrição da costa do Brasil na região de Pernambuco," in M. Galindo (ed.), *Viver e morrer no Brasil holandês* (Recife: Massangana, 2005), pp. 194, 212; Oliveira, *A História do Brazil*, v. 2, fols. 39v., 157v.

121. Baers, *Olinda conquistada*, pp. 39–41, 43–45, 49–50; Reis, *Evolução urbana do Brasil*, pp. 127–128, 134, 137–138, 144–145, 155, 167; Mello, *O nome e o sangue*, pp. 155–156; Teensma, "Descrição da costa do Brasil na região de Pernambuco," pp. 194, 212; Pontual and Milet, "Olinda: memória e esquecimento," pp. 45–50; Brandão, *Diálogos das grandezas do Brasil*, p. 32.

122. *Segunda visitação do Santo Ofício às partes do Brasil*, pp. 362–364, 396.

123. Sousa, *Tratado descritivo do Brasil*, pp. 96, 100, 102; Moreno, *Livro que dá razão do Estado do Brasil*, pp. 142, 176–179; Baers, *Olinda conquistada*, p. 78; Mauro, *Portugal, o Brasil e o Atlântico*, v. 1, pp. 306–307.

124. Oliveira, *A História do Brazil*, v. 2, fol. 39 v.

125. Strum, "The Portuguese Jews and New Christians in the Sugar Trade," pp. 195–197; De Vries and Van der Woude, *The First Modern Economy*, p. 149.

126. Lesger, *The Rise of the Amsterdam Market*, pp. 214, 220.

127. Brandão, *Diálogos das grandezas do Brasil*, pp. 113–114.

128. Strum, "The Portuguese Jews and New Christians in the Sugar Trade," pp. 207–213, 216.

129. IANTT, STO, IL 3418, fols. 11v.–12; Hutter, *Navegação nos séculos XVII e XVIII*, p. 139; França and Siqueira, "Introduction and Notes," p. 169; Lesger, *The Rise of the Amsterdam Market*, pp. 232, 239–240; E. R. Samuel, "Portuguese Jews in Jacobean London," *Jewish Historical Studies 18* (1953/55): 224.

130. Brandão, *Diálogos das grandezas do Brasil*, p. 114.

131. IJzerman, "Amsterdamsche bevrachtingscontraten 1591–1602," pp. 163–291; idem, *Journael van de reis naar Zuid-Amerika*, pp. 99–100; Israel, "Spain, the Spanish Embargo, and the Struggle for the Mastery of World Trade," pp. 191–192, 194–198; idem, "The Economic Contribution of the Dutch Sephardic Jewry," pp. 421, 423; idem, *Dutch Primacy in World Trade*, p. 58; Costa, *O transporte no Atlântico*, v. 1, p. 63; Vlessing, "The Portuguese-Jewish Merchant Community in Seventeenth-Century Amsterdam," pp. 238–239; Ebert, "The Trade in Brazilian Sugar," pp. 44–45, 241–244; Vasconcelos, *Do sítio de Lisboa*, p. 128.

132. Rau, *Estudos sobre a história do sal português*, pp. 147–191; Israel, *Dutch Primacy in World Trade*, pp. 7–11, 18–26, 34–37, 48–60, 86–101; Ebert, "The Trade in Brazilian Sugar," pp. 112–113, 169–170; Costa, *O transporte no Atlântico*, v. 1, pp. 115–116.

133. PRO, SP, 9/104, fol. 136.

134. SR no.1770; ADP, NOT, PO2, l. 40, fols. 41v–42v.; Malynes, *Consuetudo: vel, lex mercatoria*, pp. 134–135.

135. IANTT, STO, IL 3157, fol. 20v.; França and Siqueira, "Introduction and Notes," pp. 150–173; Siqueira, "A Inquisição portuguesa e a sociedade colonial," pp. 134–136, 146–149, 151, 192; Lesger, *The Rise of the Amsterdam Market*, pp. 215–218; Stols, "Os mercadores flamengos," p. 18.

136. SR no. 2401.

137. Costa, *O transporte no Atlântico*, v. 1, pp. 345–347.

138. Strum, "The Portuguese Jews and New Christians in the Sugar Trade," pp. 197–202; Lesger, *The Rise of the Amsterdam Market*, pp. 232, 239–240, 242–243; Malynes, *Consuetudo: vel, lex mercatoria*, pp. 99, 362–375, 392–393; Smith, "The Mercantile Class of Portugal and Brazil," p. 370.

139. ADP, NOT, PO1, 136, fols. 110–112 (1615-8-18); l. 138, fols. 133–135 (1617-4-12); PO2, l. 20, fols. 126v.–129v. (1603-8-13); l. 29, fols. 137–138v (1609-10-13); l. 36, fols. 176–178 (1613-1-4); Costa, *O transporte no Atlântico*, v. 1, pp. 329–344, 353–354.

140. SR nos. 747, 961. See also: Ebert, "The Trade in Brazilian Sugar," p. 184.

141. Strum, "The Portuguese Jews and New Christians in the Sugar Trade," p. 216.

142. SR no. 1905 n. 58; Strum, "The Portuguese Jews and New Christians in the Sugar Trade," pp. 216–218; Barros, "Porto: a construção de um espaço marítimo," v. 1, pp. 85–86; Hutter, *Navegação nos séculos XVII e XVIII*, pp. 61–63; França and Siqueira, "Introduction and Notes," pp. 260, 273–274; Costa, *O transporte no Atlântico*, v. 1, pp. 276–291. On the role stopovers played in the flow of trade-related information, see also: Lesger, *The Rise of the Amsterdam Market*, pp. 240–242.

143. See a more detailed discussion in: Strum, "The Portuguese Jews and New Christians in the Sugar Trade," pp. 187–286. See also: Stols, "Convivências e conivências luso," pp. 126–127.

Concluding Remarks

The trade in Brazilian sugar stimulated significant economic, social, demographic, environmental and geopolitical changes in the Atlantic and beyond by mobilizing a vast chain of activities which spanned oceans, climatic zones, empires and religious divides.

From the outset, the efforts made by the Crown and its agents, investors and immigrants to colonize Portuguese America sought to introduce the cultivation of sugar, which was viewed as an effective means to sustain a systematic European settlement of the territory and maintain the institutions that were to be established there. As a result of the expansion of the sugar industry, large swathes of land were deforested and an enslaved African population was transplanted while Amerindians were massacred, driven out of their land and/or compelled to work for Europeans and adopt European customs. Some Europeans were forcibly transported there, while others emigrated in exchange for incentives. The majority probably sought to escape dim prospects in their homeland, which were often worse than what they thought they would encounter in these new territories, which were still quite inhospitable. Much sweat and tears were shed to ensure that this sugar was loaded onto trading vessels, a product that would be consumed almost entirely across the ocean. It is important to keep in mind, however, that exporting sugar was never the sole motivation behind these processes.

The sugar trade was engulfed by the extensive geopolitical conflicts in which the Hispanic Monarchy, which encompassed Portugal and its domains at that time, was involved, particularly the conflict with the Dutch Republic. Sugar was a vehicle for and a source of strategic wealth that could be appropriated or compromised. The crates and vessels that transported sugar became the target of predatory attacks, while sugar-producing lands were subject to pillaging and attempts to occupy them, some of which were better orchestrated than others.

In fact, sugar exports were the colony's main source of wealth, which enabled the Luso-Brazilian population to acquire necessary and coveted European products. The sugar trade ensured not only sustenance but also some prosperity for the Atlantic Islands and Portugal, especially the northern part of the country, while at the same time invigorating the Dutch economy. Brazilian sugar generally passed through Portuguese ports, and a significant portion was then sent to the Netherlands, where some of it was refined. From there it was redistributed to final markets, mainly in northern Europe, although there were other distribution and refining centers.

This commercial flow also stimulated the marketing of other goods that accompanied sugar, and likewise promoted an entire range of activities aimed at exporting products to the South. Wares from the Atlantic Islands and the Iberian Peninsula were brought to Portuguese America, while items from the rest of Europe, especially from the northern areas of the continent, were taken to the southern regions.

The sugar trade similarly fueled the supply chains involving the products being transacted, including petty commerce, the transport sector, port activities, ship- building and tax revenues, among other industries. The expansion of the supply of Brazilian sugar also consolidated sectors of European economies closely linked to this product, such as the sugar-refining industry, high-end confectionery and popular sweet-making.

The production, refining, transport and trade in sugar opened up new avenues for investing capital from various sources, and the profits earned from activities linked to sugar were invested in other sectors and regions. Along the Atlantic and well beyond its shores, sugar traders (as well as merchants dealing in other products) offered individuals with no ties to the world of trade both investment opportunities and profits, and a range of services that might be classified as banking activities.

Merchants' activities were subject to the technological constraints of the age in terms of transport, communications, manufacturing, means of payment, credit instruments, accounting methods, and so forth. They were similarly limited by constraints imposed by theology, jurisprudence and morality with regard to the legitimacy of charging interest, extending credit, profits, and money in general. Merchants faced difficulties due to the way Roman, Germanic and local juridical traditions viewed the new trading practices. Furthermore, trading was also susceptible to the vagaries of the political and religious context, including conflagrations and persecution, trade embargos and restrictions, and privateers and pirates.

In order to overcome these challenges and ensure that their operations were more secure, effective and profitable, merchants used a range of well-established and newly developed techniques, instruments, mechanisms and institutions, both formal and informal. It is important to note here the use of insurance and the respective regulatory institutions, the private issuing of fiduciary money, indexation to imaginary units of account, a prototype of monetary authorities, derivatives, a secondary market for shares, bonds and securities, the bourse and official price lists. These institutions and instruments did not develop uniformly along the sugar routes. Owing to the dimensions and particular characteristics of this market, some institutions developed more vigorously and intensely in Amsterdam. Nevertheless, this had a ripple effect on all the marketplaces that traded directly or indirectly with and through Amsterdam.

In the same vein, merchants developed strategies in which they combined various arrangements involving overseas mercantile agency and numerous practices with regard to navigation, maritime transport and correspondence. To ensure compliance with commercial norms, they resorted to mercantile courts, to arbitration and, primarily, to mechanisms based on reputation and on economic and social incentives. Factors that were not linked to the trading world a priori also contributed towards the expansion of commerce or coevolved together with it, such as the legal system; ethnic, religious and national diasporas; urban patterns, social and leisure practices; and mechanisms for control and social pressure.

Despite the factors that conditioned trade during the age, the key issues in commercial management and operations had much in common with modern-day business activities. In their relations with overseas agents, merchants instituted and nurtured models of organizational structure and mechanisms for governance and the administration of human resources. In the area of maritime transport, they sought to optimize logistics. With regard to finance, they had to deal with accounts receivable, terms of trade, the value of currencies, interest rates, liquidity, credit and cash flow, among other pecuniary matters. In every case, they strove to ensure speed, control risks, manage information and resolve conflicts.

Finally, the expansion of sugar consumption in the West engendered lasting changes in social practices. Sugar reinvented its place by carving a niche for itself, and gave rise to a culture of sweets that pervaded society and to which we still treat ourselves to this day.

Illustration and Photo Credits

5 Bartholomeus van der Helst – *Portrait of the Merchant Daniel Bernard (1626–1714) of Amsterdam*, 1669. Painting. Museum Boijmans Van Beuningen, Rotterdam, The Netherlands. 1297. Museum Boijmans Van Beuningen, Rotterdam.

6 *Biblia en lengua Española traduzida palabra por palabra dela verdad Hebrayca por muy excelentes letrados vista y examinada por el officio dela Inquisicion.* Ferrara: con yndustria y deligencia de Abrahã Usque: a costa y despesa de Yom Tob Atias hijo de Levi Atias, 1553. Printed. Biblioteca Nacional de Portugal, Lisbon, Portugal. Reservados, RES. 412 A [title page]. © Biblioteca Nacional de Portugal.

8-9 Dirk Stoop – *Terreiro do Paço in the Seventeenth Century*, 1662. Painting. Museu da Cidade, Lisbon, Portugal. MC.PIN.261. © Museu da Cidade – Câmara Municipal de Lisboa.

14 Clara Peeters – *Still Life with Dried Fruits and Nuts, Pretzels and Alfenim*, 1611. Painting. Museo Nacional del Prado, Madrid, Spain. P01620. © Museo Nacional del Prado.

16 Cornelis Claesz. van Wieringen – *A Spanish Ship Explodes during the Battle of Gibraltar on April 25, 1607* [ca. 1621]. Painting. Rijksmuseum Amsterdam, Amsterdam, The Netherlands. SK-A-2163. Collection Rijksmuseum Amsterdam, The Netherlands.

18 Frans Post – *View of Engenho Real in Brazil* [ca. 1650–1655]. Painting. Musée du Louvre, Paris, France. Inventory no. 1724 (Image no.: 09-577593 NU). © RMN / René-Gabriel Ojéda. See 145–155.

21 *Purging House at the Jundiá Sugar Mill* [18--]. Industrial architecture (purging house). Vicência, Pernambuco, Brazil. Photography: Lia Lubambo.

24 Alexandre-François Desportes (drawer); Albert Eckout (cart.); Manufacture des Gobelins – *Les Deux Taureaux* [1661–1743]. Tapestry. Instituto Ricardo Brennand, Recife, Pernambuco, Brazil. No quota file. Acervo do Instituto Ricardo Brennand – PE – Brasil.

26-27 Joan Blaeu – [Map of the northeastern coast of Brazil from the captaincy of Rio Grande to Sergipe]. In Joan Blaeu et al., *Klencke Atlas (1660)*. Amsterdam: Joan Blaeu, 1647. Cartography (nautical chart: printed). The British Library, London, England. Maps K.A.R.(38.). © The British Library Board. Maps K.A.R. (38.).

29 Frans Post – *Sugar Mill in Brazil*, 1640. Drawing (wash). Musées Royaux des Beaux-Arts de Belgique, Brussels, Belgium. Inventory no.: 4060 / 2888. © Royal Museums of Fine Arts of Belgium, Brussels [Grafisch Buro Lefevre, Heule].

31 Tomás Hiepes – *Table with Sweets*, 1624. Painting. Private Collection.

32 *Reys-boeck van het rijcke Brasilien, Rio de la Plata ende Magallanes, Daer in te sien is de gheleghenthyet van hare Landen ende Steden haren handel ende wandel met de Vruchten ende Vrucht baerhyet der selver: Alles met Copere platen uytghebeelt. Als cock De leste reyse van der Heer van Dort, met het ver-overen vande Baeye De todos los Santos, tsamen ghestelt door / N. V. G. [Nicolas van Geelkercken (?)] Ghedruckt int Jaer onses Herren* [Dordrecht?]: Ian Canin, 1624 ["Pernambuco"]. Engraving. Koninklijke Bibliotheek, The Hague, The Netherlands. Pamphlet 3540. Den Haag, Koninklijke Bibliotheek, Pamflet 3540.

33 [Anonymous] – *Weathervane from the Amsterdam Rasphuis penitentiary, with two individuals sawing or rasping wood to obtain the scrapings used to extract dye* [16--]. Decorative arts (weathervane). Amsterdam Museum, Amsterdam, The Netherlands. Inventory no.: KA 15763. © Amsterdam Museum.

33 [Anonymous – Made in Amsterdam] – *Tobacco* [n.d.]. Decorative arts (stone tablet). Vereniging Vrienden van Amsterdamse Gevelstenen, Amsterdam, The Netherlands. No quota file (Geldersekade, 8). Foundation Friends of Amsterdam Stone Tablets (VVAG).

34 Pieter de Hooch – *Interior with Two Women Beside a Linen Chest*, 1663. Painting. Rijksmuseum Amsterdam, Amsterdam, The Netherlands. SK-C-1191. Collection Rijksmuseum Amsterdam, The Netherlands.

35 Hans Sachs (drawer); Jost Hamman (engraver) – *Eygentliche Beschreibung aller Stände auff Erden, hoher und nidriger, geistlicher und weltlicher, aller Künsten, Handwercken und Händeln. Durch d. weitberümpten / Hans Sachsen gantz fleissig beschrieben u. in teutsche Reimen gefasset.* Frankfurt am Main, 1568: ["The Oil Maker"]. Engraving. Sächsische Landesbibliothek – Staats und Universitätsbibliothek Dresden, Dresden, Germany. Lit.Germ.rec.B.2039. SLUB Dresden / Sammlungen / Lit.Germ.rec.B.2039.

35 Bernard Lens (drawer); George Vertue (engraver) – [Catching and Drying Cod: illustration from the "Codfish Map," ca. 1712]. In *The World describ'd; or, a new and correct set of maps... Each map engraved on Copper by / Herman Moll...* [London]: H. Moll, D. Midwinter, and R. Davies [1708–1720]. Engraving. The British Library, London, England. Maps C.4 TAB.17. © The British Library Board. Maps C.4 TAB.17.

36 [Anonymous – Made in Amsterdam] – *Retail Sale of Sugar Loaves* [16--]. Decorative arts (stone tablet).Vereniging Vrienden van Amsterdamse Gevelstenen, Amsterdam ,The Netherlands. No quota file (Nieuwebrugsteeg, 13). Foundation Friends of Amsterdam Stone Tablets (VVAG).

36 [Anonymous – Made in Amsterdam] – *Sewing Shop SellingNotions* [16--]. Decorative arts (stone tablet).Vereniging Vrienden van Amsterdamse Gevelstenen, Amsterdam, The Netherlands. No quota file (Rozenstraat, 13–15). Foundation Friends of Amsterdam Stone Tablets (VVAG).

36 [Anonymous – Made in Amsterdam] –*Manufacturing Paper*, 1649. Decorative arts (stone tablet). Vereniging Vrienden van Amsterdamse Gevelstenen, Amsterdam, The Netherlands. No quota file (Herengracht, 105). Foundation Friends of Amsterdam Stone Tablets (VVAG).

38 *Het Menselyk Bedryf. Vertoond, in. 100. Verbeeldingen: van: Ambachten, Konsten, Hanteeringen en Bedryven; met Versen. [...]* t'Amsterdam. / Gedaan; door; Johannes, en, Caspaares, Luiken, 1694 [A cooper at work: making casks to store wine and other liquids]. Engraving. Universiteitsbibliotheek van de Universiteit van Amsterdam, Amsterdam, The Netherlands. Bijzondere Collecties, OTM: OG 80-36, p. 40. Special Collections, University of Amsterdam, OTM: OG 80-36, p. 40.

38 *Het Menselyk Bedryf. Vertoond, in. 100. Verbeeldingen: van: Ambachten, Konsten, Hanteeringen en Bedryven; met Versen. [...]* t'Amsterdam. / Gedaan; door; Johannes, en, Caspaares, Luiken, 1694 [Copper work]. Engraving. Universiteitsbibliotheek van de Universiteit van Amsterdam, Amsterdam, The Netherlands. Bijzondere Collecties, OTM: OG 80-36, p. 29. Special Collections, University of Amsterdam, OTM: OG 80-36, p. 29.

39 [*Official price-list of several products listed on the Amsterdam Bourse*], March 3, 1636. Printed. Nederlandsch Economisch-Historisch Archief, Amsterdam, The Netherlands. Prijscouranten, AMS 1.01A-B. Collection International Institute of Social History, Amsterdam.

40 Emanuel de Witte – *Courtyard of the Amsterdam Bourse*, 1653. Painting. Museum Boijmans Van Beuningen, Rotterdam, The Netherlands. VdV 91. Museum Boijmans Van Beuningen, Rotterdam.

43 [Anonymous] – *The City of São Salvador, with Todos os Santos Bay in the Foreground* [ca. 1625]. Cartography (perspective/groundplan: printed). Mapoteca do Ministério das Relações Exteriores – Itamaraty, Rio de Janeiro, Brazil. Loose print. Mapoteca do Itamaraty.

44-45 Claes Jansz. Visscher; Hermanus Allardi Coster – [*Profile of Amsterdam*], 1611. Cartography (profile: printed). Stadsarchief Amsterdam, Amsterdam, The Netherlands. Image no.: 010094000929. © Stadsarchief Amsterdam.

47 Pedro Teixeira [Albernaz] – *La descripción de España y de las costas y puertos de sus reinos* [Map of Porto and the mouth of the Douro], 1634. Cartography (nautical chart). Österreichische Nationalbibliothek, Vienna, Austria. Cod. Min. 46 (Faks.), p. 62. ÖNB Cod. Min. 46 Faks. pag. 62.

54 Johannes Vermeer – *The Astronomer*, or *The Astrologer*, 1668. Painting. Musée du Louvre, Paris, France. RF1983-28 (Image no.: 95-014340 DE). © RMN / René-Gabriel Ojéda.

58-59 Jan Brueghel, the Elder –*Large Fish Market*, 1603. Painting. Alte Pinakothek, Munich, Germany. Inventory no.: 1889 (Image no.: 50010774). bpk | Bayerische Staatsgemäldesammlungen – Alte Pinakothek.

64 [Anonymous – Minted in Portugal] – *St. Vincent: Portuguese gold coin from the reign of King Sebastian (1557–1578)*. Numismatics (coin). Museu Numismático Português – Imprensa Nacional/ Casa da Moeda, Lisbon, Portugal. Inventory no.: 5036. Photography: Pedro Dantas dos Reis.

65 [Anonymous – Minted in Portugal] – *The"Portuguese": Portuguese gold coin from the reign of John III (1521–1557)*. Numismatics (coin). Museu do Banco de Portugal, Lisbon, Portugal. Image no.: 9001029800_A/9001029800_R. Museu do Banco de Portugal.

66-67 [João Baptista Lavanha; Luís Teixeira] – *Atlas Cosmografia* [World Map] [1597 and 1612]. Cartography (world map). Biblioteca Reale di Torino, Turin, Italy. Mscr. Vari 221, fol. 3. Su concessione del Ministero per i Beni e le Attività Culturali – Biblioteca Reale – Torino.

73 *Wapenhandelinghe van Roers Musquetten ende Spiessen Achtervolgende de Orde van Sijn Excellentie Maurits Prince van Orangie.... / Figuirlyck Uutgebeelt door Jacob de Gheyn. Met Schriftelijcke onderrechtinghe Ten dienste van alle Capiteijnen ende bevelhebbers, om hieruit hun Jonge oft onervaren soldaten de volcomen handelinge vandese wapenen te beter aentewijsen*. S Graven Hage: [n.n.], 1607 [A musketeer holding his musket]. Drawing. National Maritime Museum, Greenwich, London, England. PAD8449. © National Maritime Museum, Greenwich, London.

78-79 Alonso Sánchez Coello (studio) – *Philip II at the Banquet of the Monarchs*, 1596. Painting. Muzeum Narodowe w Warszawie, Warsaw, Poland. M.Ob.295. © Photography: Ligier Studio/Muzeum Narodowe w Warszawie.

80 [Anonymous – Minted in Portugal] – *Half-vintém: a silver coin from the reign of King Sebastian (1557–1578)*. Numismatics (coin). Museu Numismático Português – Imprensa Nacional/Casa da Moeda, Lisbon, Portugal. Inventory no.: 5068. Photography: Pedro Dantas dos Reis.

81 Dirck van Delen – *Iconoclasts in a Church*, 1630. Painting. Rijksmuseum Amsterdam, Amsterdam, The Netherlands. SK-A-4992. Purchased with the support of the BankGiro Lottery and the Funds of the Rijksmuseum.

82 [Anonymous] –*Medal used as an insignia by the Sea Beggars, the name given to the Dutch rebels who organized a naval guerrilla war using small vessels against the powerful pro-Hispanic forces*, 1574. Goldsmithing (medal). Collection Rijksmuseum Amsterdam, Amsterdam, The Netherlands. NG-VG-1-407-A and NG-VG-1-407-A-01. Collection Rijksmuseum Amsterdam, The Netherlands.

84-85 Hendrick-Cornelisz. Vroom – *Battle of Haarlemmermeer, a Naval Engagement between the Hispanic Forces and Dutch Rebels on May 26, 1573* [ca. 1621]. Painting. Collection Rijksmuseum Amsterdam, Amsterdam, The Netherlands. SK-A-602. Collection Rijksmuseum Amsterdam, The Netherlands.

86 Adriaen Thomasz. Key – *William I (1533–1584), Prince of Orange, Known as William the Silent* [ca. 1570–1584]. Painting. Rijksmuseum Amsterdam, Amsterdam, The Netherlands. SK-A-3148. Purchased with the support of the Commission for the Exhibition on William, the Silent.

88 *Patente Das Merces, Graças, E Privilegios De Qve ElRei Dom Philippe nosso senhor fez merce a estes seus Regnos. E a diante vai outra Patente das respostas das Cortes de Tomar. [...]* Lisbon: Antonio Ribeiro Impressor Del Rey Nosso Senhor. M. D. LXXXIII [1583]. Printed. Biblioteca Nacional de Portugal, Lisbon, Portugal. Reservados, RES. 64//3 A., [title page]. © Biblioteca Nacional de Portugal.

90 [Anonymous – Minted in Portugal] – *Two thousand réis with goshawk: gold coin from the period of António, Prior of Crato (1580–1583)*. Numismatics (coin). Museu Numismático Português – Imprensa Nacional/Casa da Moeda, Lisbon, Portugal. Inventory no.: 5096. Photography: Pedro Dantas dos Reis.

90 [Anonymous – Minted in Portugal] – *Sphere or two réis: copper coin from the period of António, Prior of Crato (1580–1583)*. Numismatics (coin). Museu Numismático Português – Imprensa Nacional/Casa da Moeda, Lisbon, Portugal. Inventory no.: 9521. Photography: Pedro Dantas dos Reis.

91 [Anonymous – Minted in Flanders] – *Twintigste philipsdaalder: silver coin from the reign of Philip II (1555–1598)*, 1576. Numismatics (coin). Geldmuseum, Utrecht, The Netherlands. Inventory no.: NM-11616. Geldmuseum.

93 [Anonymous – Minted in Holland] – *Leeuwendaalder: silver coin*, 1589. Numismatics (coin). Geldmuseum, Utrecht, The Netherlands. Inventory no.: 1958-0014. Geldmuseum.

94 [Anonymous – Minted in Holland] – *Leeuwendaalder: Reverse of silver coin*, 1589. Numismatics (coin). Geldmuseum, Utrecht, The Netherlands. Inventory no.: 1958-0014. Geldmuseum.

98-99 [Anonymous] – *The Milch Cow* [ca. 1580–1595]. Painting. Rijksmuseum Amsterdam, Amsterdam, The Netherlands. SK-A-2684. Collection Rijksmuseum Amsterdam, The Netherlands.

101 [Anonymous – Made in Amsterdam] – *"Beurtschip": A Dutch vessel used to transport people and small cargoes*, 1602. Decorative arts (stone tablet). Vereniging Vrienden van Amsterdamse Gevelstenen, Amsterdam, The Netherlands. No quota file. (Kromme Waal, 39). Foundation Friends of Amsterdam Stone Tablets (VVAG).

102-103 *Theatro D'El Orbe De La Tierra / De Abraham Ortello [1556–1598]. El qual antes el estremo dia de sua vida por la postrera vez ha emendado, y con nueuas Tablas y Commentarios augmentado y esclarescido.* En Anveres: En La Emprenta Plantiniana, A Costas de Ivan Baptista Vrintio, Anno M. DCII [1602] [Map: Depiction of the United Provinces (1579–1795), according to van Deventer]. Cartography (map: printed). Fundação Biblioteca Nacional, Rio de Janeiro, Brazil. CAM.05,007 Cartography (map after p. 47). Acervo da Fundação Biblioteca Nacional – Brasil.

105 [Anonymous – Made in Amsterdam] – *[Former coat of arms of the city of Amsterdam showing a* koggeschip, *a merchant vessel used in the North Sea and the Baltic]*, 1938. Decorative arts (stone tablet). Vereniging Vrienden van Amsterdamse Gevelstenen, Amsterdam, The Netherlands. No quota file. (Muntplein, 12). Foundation Friends of Amsterdam Stone Tablets (VVAG).

106 Jan Luyken (drawer and engraver) – [The exodus of Catholic magistrates and clergy from Amsterdam, shown here leaving Dam Square on May 26, 1578]. In *Oorspronck, begin, en vervolgh der Nederlandsche oorlogen, beroerten, en borgerlyke oneenigheden / door Pieter Christiaensz. Bor.* 4 dln. Amsterdam, 1679–1684. Engraving. Amsterdam Museum, Amsterdam, The Netherlands. Inventory no.: A 46609. © Amsterdam Museum.

107 Johannes a Doetecum Jr./Jan van Doetecum Jr. – *Leo Belgicus: Portrayal of the Seventeen Provinces of the Low Countries,* Rotterdam: [n.n.], 1598. Cartography (map: printed). Rijksmuseum Amsterdam, Amsterdam, The Netherlands. RP-P-OB-80.502. Collection Rijksmuseum Amsterdam, The Netherlands.

110 Diego Velazquez – *Philip III on Horseback* [1634–1635]. Painting. Museo Nacional del Prado, Madrid, Spain. P01176. © Museo Nacional del Prado.

111 Hendrik-Cornelisz. Vroom – *The Four-Masted Ship De Hollandse Tuyn, from Amsterdam, and Others Returning from Brazil under the Command of Paulus van Caerden (1569–1615 or 1616) in 1605* [May 1605–1640]. Painting. Rijksmuseum Amsterdam, Amsterdam, The Netherlands. SK-A-1361. Collection Rijksmuseum Amsterdam, The Netherlands.

112 *Het Menselyk Bedryf. Vertoond, in. 100. Verbeeldingen: van: Ambachten, Konsten, Hanteeringen en Bedryven; met Versen. [...]* t'Amsterdam. / Gedaan; door; Johannes, en, Caspaares, Luiken. 1694 [Milling and transporting grain]. Engraving. Universiteitsbibliotheek van de Universiteit van Amsterdam, Amsterdam, The Netherlands. Bijzondere Collecties, OTM: OG 80-36, p. 48. Special Collections, University of Amsterdam, OTM: OG 80-36, p. 48.

114-115 Pieter Snayers – *Siege of Ostend (1601–1604)* [16--]. Painting. Stedelijk Museum Het Prinsenhof, Delft, The Netherlands. PDS 94. Collection Museum Het Prinsenhof Delft, The Netherlands.

116 [Anonymous] – [Admiral Joris van Spilbergen's fleet attacks São Vicente in 1615]. In *Miroir Oost & West-Indical, auquel sont descriptes les deux dernieres navigations, faictes es années 1614 [...] & 1618. l'une par le renommé guerrier de mer / George de Spilbergen, par le distroict de Magellan, & ainsi tout autour de toute la terre [...] Icy sont außi adioustée deux histoires, l'une des Indes Orientales, l'autre des Indes Occidentales [...] faicte par / Jacob de Maire, lequel au costé du zud du destroict de Magellan, a descouvert un nouveau destroict [...]*. Amsterdam: Ian Iansz. [...], 1621. Engraving. Universiteitsbibliotheek Gent, Gent, Belgium. BIB.HIST.008412 (no. 2). University Library Ghent, BIB.HIST.008412 (no. 2).

118-119 Claes Jansz. Visscher [II] – [*Beheading of Johan van Oldenbarnevelt (1547–1619) on May 13, 1619*]. [n.l.]: [n.n.], 1619. Engraving. Rijksmuseum Amsterdam, Amsterdam, The Netherlands. RP-P-OB-77.320. Collection Rijksmuseum Amsterdam, The Netherlands.

120 Gerald de Jode; Cornelis de Jode – *Speculum Orbis Terrarum*. Antwerp: Deutecum Brothers, 1593 [Map of the Spanish Low Countries (1556–1581)]. Cartography (map: printed). Bayerische Staatsbibliothek, Munich, Germany. 2 Mapp. 176-75. © Bayerische Staatsbibliothek.

122 Hendrick Ambrosius Packx – *Prince Maurice of Orange (1567–1625) during the Battle of Nieuwpoort, on the Flemish Coast, in 1600* [1620–1625]. Painting. Instituut Collectie Nederland – Rijksdienst voor het Cultureel Erfgoed, Amsterdam, The Netherlands. Inventory no.: C251. Photography: Tim Koster, RCE, Rijswijk/Amsersfoort.

124 Diego Velazquez – *Portrait of Philip IV* [1626–1629]. Painting. Museo Nacional del Prado, Madrid, Spain. P01182. © Museo Nacional del Prado.

125 [Anonymous – Spanish School] – *Coach of Philip III* [15--/16--]. Transportation (coach). Museu Nacional dos Coches, Lisbon, Portugal. Inventory no.: 08922 TC (Object inventory no.: 1). © IMC / MC. Photography: Henrique Ruas, 1987.

126 *Charter granted by the States-General of the Republic of the Seven United Provinces of the Low Countries to the Dutch West India Company, creating the monopoly on shipping to the Western Hemisphere from the Cape of Good Hope to Manila in the Philippines*, June 3, 1621.Manuscript. Nationaal Archief, The Hague, The Netherlands. Topstukken Nationaal Archief / Archief van de Eerste West-Indische Compagnie (WIC), 1.05.01.01, no. 13: fol. 1 (Topstuk 11). © Nationaal Archief, Den Haag.

127 *Orbis terrarvm typvs, de integro mvltis in locis emendatvs auctore [...] Beschrijuinghe der geheeler werelt, van nieus in velen plaetsen verbetert / door Petrum Plancium. // Baptista Doetecomius Sculptor.* [Amsterdam: Laurens Jacobszoon] [1590]. Cartography (world map: printed). Universiteitsbibliotheek van de Universiteit van Amsterdam, Amsterdam, The Netherlands. Bijzondere Collecties, OTM: HB-Kaartenzaal: O.K. 112. Special Collections, University of Amsterdam, OTM: HB-Kaartenzaal: O.K. 112.

128 [Anonymous] – [Todos os Santos Bay: the fleet commanded by the Dutch admiral Pieter Pietersz. Heyn's fleet captures ships laden with sugar (1627/1656)]. In *Histoire De La Vie & Actes memorables De Frederic Henry de Nassau Prince d'Orange / Par I. Commelyn. Enrichie de Figures en taille douce & fidelement translatée du Flamand en François. Divisée en Deux Parties.* Amsterdam: Chéz la Vesve & les Heritiers de Iudocus Ianssonius, 1656. Cartography (map: printed). Instituto Ricardo Brennand, Recife – Pernambuco, Brazil. No quota file. Acervo do Instituto Ricardo Brennand – PE – Brasil.

130 Willem van Honthorst (attrib.) – *Four generations of the Princes of Orange: William I, Maurice and Frederick Henry, William II and William III* [1662–1666]. Painting. Rijksmuseum Amsterdam, Amsterdam, The Netherlands. SK-A-855. Collection Rijksmuseum Amsterdam, The Netherlands.

132-133 Diego Velazquez – *The Surrender of Breda* or *The Lances*, 1634. Painting. Museo Nacional del Prado, Madrid, Spain. P01172. © Museo Nacional del Prado.

138 *Plantes de la Martinique et de la Guadeloupe. Avec des plans et des figures de sauvages de ces pays / dessinés, coloriés et décrits par le Père Charles Plumier.* [n.l.], 1688 [Cane from India]. Engraving. Bibliothèque Nationale de France, Paris, France. JD-18-FOL, fol. 34bisv. © Bibliothèque Nationale de France.

141 [Anonymous – Made in Portugal] – *Sugarloaf mold found in an archeological site in Mata da Machada (Barreiro, 1985)* [late fifteenthth–early sixteenth century]. Equipment (sugarloaf mold). Gabinete de Arqueologia e Restauro da Câmara do Funchal (Dep. Cultura), Funchal – Madeira, Portugal. No quota file. Câmara Municipal do Funchal.

142-143 Jan van der Straet/Johannes Stradanus (drawer); Théodore Galle (engraver) – *Nova Reperta* [Stages of sugar production from sugarcane, ca. 1600]. Antwerp: Jan Galle [ca. 1620–1630]. Engraving. Université de Liège – Service des Collections Artistiques, Liège, Belgium. Legs Wittert, Inventory no.: 11784. © Collections artistiques de l'Université de Liège.

144 [Anonymous – From the Island of Madeira] – *Sugarloaf mold* [n.d.]. Equipment (sugarloaf mold). Centro de Estudos de Arqueologia Moderna e Contemporânea, Santa Cruz, Madeira, Portugal. No quota file: original from the collection of Professor Miguel Pita; part of a set recovered from archeological excavations in Jardim do Mar (southwestern Madeira) and the Palace of Consuls (Funchal). Arquivo CEAM – Centro de Estudos de Arqueologia Moderna e Contemporânea, Santa Cruz, Madeira, Portugal.

145 Theodore de Bry (engraver) [after a drawing by Jan van der Straet/Johannes Stradanus] – [The stages of sugar production at a Spanish-American sugar mill based on African slave labor]. In *Americae pars quinta nobilis & admiratione plena / Hieronymi Bezoni Mediolanensis, secundae sectionis h[istor]ia[e] Hispanorum: tum in Indos crudelitatem, Gallorumq[ue] pirataru[m] de Hispanis toties reportata spolia: [...]* Frankfurt am Main: Theodore de Bry, 1595, fig. 2. Engraving. The Library Company of Philadelphia, Philadelphia, PA, United States of America. Am 1594 Ben (b.w.) Aa599 F 61a, Part V, fig. 2. The Library Company of Philadelphia.

146 Albert Eckhout – *Mulatto Man* [ca. 1610–ca. 1666]. Painting. Nationalmuseet København, Copenhagen, Denmark. Inventory no.: N 38A5. © The National Museum of Denmark, Ethnographic Collection.

147 [Made in Morocco] – *Sugarloaf produced in Marocco using the same process known in the Atlantic in thefifteenth and sixteenth centuries* [n.d.]. Sugar (sugarloaf). Gabinete de Arqueologia e Restauro da Câmara do Funchal (Dep. Cultura), Funchal – Madeira, Portugal. No quota file. Câmara Municipal do Funchal (Museu "A Cidade do Açúcar" / Oferta do Dr. Alberto Vieira, 1995).

148 Pedro Juan de Lastanosa – *Los Veintiun Libros de los Ingenios y de las Máquinas* [Illustration: Late sixteenth-century Spanish sugar mill] [prior to 1576]. Drawing. Biblioteca Nacional de España, Madrid, Spain. Mss/3374, fol. 335v. © Biblioteca Nacional de España.

149 [Father Luís da Rocha, SJ] – [*Sketch of the Petinga sugar mill in the Recôncavo region of Bahia, which was acquired in 1742 for the Jesuit College of Santo Antão in Lisbon by Father Luís da Rocha, SJ, superior of the Conde Sugar Mill, from whose property that sugar mill had been previously detached*] [ca. 1742]. Drawing. Arquivo Nacional da Torre do Tombo, Lisbon. Portugal. Cartório dos Jesuítas, pack 12, no. 44, fol. [2] [?]. "Documento cedido pelo ANTT." Quota file: Cartório dos Jesuítas, pack 12, no. 44.

150 Pedro de Asseca [?] – [*Three-Roller Mill*], 1613. Drawing. Biblioteca da Ajuda, Lisbon, Portugal. 51-VI-54, fol. 121. Biblioteca da Ajuda.

151 *Thier Buch darinnen viel unterschiedlicher Arter der Fische vögel vierfüssigen Thiere Gewürm, Erd=und Baumfrüchte, so hin undt wieder in Brasilischen bezirck, und gebiethe, Der Westindischen Compagnie zu schauwen undt anzutreffen und daher in den Teutschen landen fremde und unbekant Alles selbst [...] bezeiget In Brasilien Unter hochlöblicher Regierung des hochgebornen Herren Johand Moritz Graffen von Nassau Gubernator Capitain, und Admiral General / von Zacharias Wagenern von Dresden* [1614–1668] [sugar mill and mill]. Drawing. Dresdner Kupferstich-Kabinett, Dresden, Germany. Inventory no.: Ca 226 a, 108. © Dresdner Kupferstich-Kabinett, Staatliche Kunstsammlugen Dresden.

151 *Thier Buch darinnen viel unterschiedlicher Arter der Fische vögel vierfüssigen Thiere Gewürm, Erd=und Baumfrüchte, so hin undt wieder in Brasilischen bezirck, und gebiethe, Der Westindischen Compagnie zu schauwen undt anzutreffen und daher in den Teutschen landen fremde und unbekant Alles selbst [...] bezeiget In Brasilien Unter hochlöblicher Regierung des hochgebornen Herren Johand Moritz Graffen von Nassau Gubernator Capitain, und Admiral General / von Zacharias Wagenern von Dresden* [1614–1668] [sugar mill and mill]. Drawing. Dresdner Kupferstich-Kabinett, Dresden, Germany. Inventory no.: Ca 226 a, 109. © Dresdner Kupferstich-Kabinett, Staatliche Kunstsammlugen Dresden.

152 [Anonymous] – *Clay sugarloaf mold from the Cordeiro Sugar Mill (Pernambuco)* [19--]. Equipment (sugarloaf mold). Museu do Homem do Nordeste, Recife – Pernambuco, Brazil. No quota file. Acervo Museu do Homem do Nordeste/Fundação Joaquim Nabuco. Recife-Pernambuco-Brasil. Photography: Lia Lubambo.

153 [Romeyn de Hooghe] – [Sugar production in a Brazilian mill]. In *Curieuse aenmerckingen der bysonderste Oost en West-Indische verwonderens-waerdige dingen; nevens die van China, Africa, en andere gewesten des werelds. Bevattende 't voornaemste van alles, wat oyt nauwkeurighs en seldsaems van deese landen, ten opsight van der selver gelegenheyd; gestalte der aerde, berghwercken, gewassen, zeeën, rivieren; seeden en Godsdiensten der menschen, &c. Is ondervonden en opgeteeckend van een seer groote meenighte der geloofwaerdighste ooghgetuygen onder meest al de natien in Europa. En uyt deselve in een bequaeme orde gebraght; oock soo met ondersoeckende als vergelijckende redenvoeringen verhandelt, / door S. de Vries. In IV. deelen.* t'Utrecht: Johannes Ribbius, boeckverkooper in de korte Jans-straet., M. DC. LXXXII [1682]. Vol. 1, post. p. 6. Engraving. John Carter Brown Library at Brown University, Providence, RI, United States of America. Accession no.: 03016 / Record no.: 03016-2 / JCB call no.: F682 V982c. Courtesy of the John Carter Brown Library at Brown University.

154-155 *Jundiá Sugar Mill: Purging House* [18--]. Industrial architecture (purging house). Vicência, Pernambuco, Brazil. Photography: Lia Lubambo.

156 Frans Post – *View of Engenho Real in Brazil* [ca. 1650–1655]. Painting. Musée du Louvre, Paris, France. Inventory no. 1724 (Image no.: 09-577593 NU). © RMN / René-Gabriel Ojéda.

158-159 Frans Post – *Brazilian Landscape with a Sugar Mill*, 1660. Painting. Statens Museum for Kunst, Copenhagen, Denmark. Inventory no.: KMSsp491. Frans Post, *Landscape in Brazil with Sugar Plantation*, 1660 – National Gallery of Denmark – © SMK Photo.

160 [Anonymous] – *Wood and iron skimmer and mug used to transfer molasses from one pan to another* [19--]. Technical utensils (skimmer and mug). Museu do Homem do Nordeste, Recife – Pernambuco, Brazil. No quota file. Donor: Ênio Pessoa Guerra. Acervo Museu do Homem do Nordeste/ Fundação Joaquim Nabuco. Recife-Pernambuco-Brasil. Photography: Lia Lubambo.

160 [Anonymous] – *Iron and copper teache from the Pau Amarelo sugar mill (Alagoas)* [19--]. Equipment (teache). Museu do Homem do Nordeste, Recife – Pernambuco, Brazil. No quota file. Donor: Irmãos Oiticica. Acervo Museu do Homem do Nordeste/Fundação Joaquim Nabuco. Recife-Pernambuco-Brasil. Photography: Lia Lubambo.

162-163 Frans Post – *Two-Wheeled, Animal-Driven Mill* [16--]. Drawing (wash). Atlas van Stolk – Museum Het Schielandshuis, Rotterdam, The Netherlands. Inventory no.: 46440. Atlas Van Stolk, Rotterdam.

167 Frans Post – *Celebration in the Countryside*, 1643/1645. Painting. Guildhall Art Gallery, London, England. Harold Samuel Collection, Inventory no.: 3753 (Image no.: 13936). © Guidhall Art Gallery, City of London.

172 *Thier Buch darinnen viel unterschiedlicher Arter der Fische vögel vierfüssigen Thiere Gewürm, Erd= und Baumfrüchte, so hin undt wieder in Brasilischen bezirck, und gebiethe, Der Westindischen Compagnie zu schauwen undt anzutreffen und daher in den Teutschen landen fremde und unbekant Alles selbst [...] bezeiget In Brasilien Unter hochlöblicher Regierung des hochgebornen Herren Johand Moritz Graffen von Nassau Gubernator Capitain, und Admiral General / von Zacharias Wagenern von Dresden* [1614–1668] ["ingenho masçiappe"]. Drawing (watercolor). Dresdner Kupferstich-Kabinett, Dresden, Germany. Inventory no.: Ca 226 a, 102. © Dresdner Kupferstich-Kabinett, Staatliche Kunstsammlugen Dresden.

182 Georg Flegel – *Still Life with Parrot* [1566–1638]. Painting. Alte Pinakothek, Munich, Germany. Inventory no.: 1622 (Image no.: 00018325). bpk | Bayerische Staatsgemäldesammlungen – Alte Pinakothek | Hermann Buresch.

184 [Anonymous – Made in Western France] – *Bestiarium. En andere teksten* [Man attacked by bees swarming from a hive] [ca. 1450]. Illumination. Museum Meermanno, The Hague, The Netherlands. MMW,10 B 25, fol. 37r. The Hague, Museum Meermanno-Westreenianum, 10 B 25, 37r.

186 [Anonymous – Made in Venice] – [Harvesting sugarcane / Sale of sugarloaves and candy sugar]. In Ububchasym de Baldach/Ibn Butlân (?–ca. 1068), *Tacuinum sanitatis in medicina*, 1490. Drawing. Österreichische Nationalbibliothek, Vienna, Austria. Codex Vindoboniensis, 2396, fol. 30v (nos. 234 and 235). ÖNB Cod. 2396 fol. 30v.

187 [Anonymous – French School] – [Man purging sugar, drinking molassess dripping from the mold and displaying white sugarloaves]. In Pedanius Dioscorides [ca. 40–90 AD], *Tractatus de Herbis* [14--]. Illumination. Biblioteca Estense Universitaria, Modena, Italy. Ms. Lat. 993 L.9.28, fol. 142. © Biblioteca Estense Universitaria.

188 Claudius Galenus (Galen; ca. 129–216 AD) –*Galeni Librorvm Prima Classis Natvram Corporis Hvmani, hoc est elementa, temperaturas, humores, structurae habitudinisq-; modos, partium anatomas, vsus, facultates & actiones, seminis deniq; foetuumq-; tractationes, complectens: Sexta Hac Nostra Editione, non parum ornamenti adepti: locis pluribus quàm in alÿs superioribus editionibus, ad graecorum librorum fidem emendatis. Locis etiam Hippocratis, quos subinde citat Galenus, in margine indicatis. Et nouis alÿs annotationibus nunc primum additis. Librorum numerum, ac diligential, versa pagina indicat.* Venetijs Apud Iuntas. M D LXXXVI [1586]. Printed. Biblioteca da Academia das Ciências de Lisboa, Lisboa, Portugal. BACL 11 735 11 [title page]. Photography: Pedro Dantas dos Reis.

188 [Anonymous] – [Commercial life of a medieval city, with an apothecary shop (right) selling sugarloaves and advertising the sale of hippocras, or mulled wine]. In Gilles de Rome [1247–1316], *Le livre du gouvernement des princes* [14--]. Miniature. Bibliothèque Nationale de France – Bibliothèque de L'Arsenal, Paris, France. ARS MS 5062, fol. 149v. © Bibliothèque Nationale de France.

189 [Master Colin] – *Pharmacy* [14--/15--]. Fresco. Castello di Issogne, Issogne – Valle d'Aosta, Italy. No quota file (Image no.: 037_442_30_4). Regione Autonoma Valle d'Aosta – Archivi dell'Assessorato istruzione e cultura – fondo Servizio catalogo e beni architettonici. Photography: Ars Una. Su concessione della Regione Autonoma Valle d'Aosta.

190 [Isidore of Seville] – [*Etymologiae De natura rerum ad Sisebutum*][Diagram showing variations of heat, cold, dryness and moisture] [12--]. Manuscript. Biblioteca Nacional de Portugal, Lisbon, Portugal. Reservados, ALC. 446, fol. [209v]. © Biblioteca Nacional de Portugal.

192 [Anonymous] – *Sugarloaf mold from archeological excavations in the Monastery of Jesus de Aveiro* [14--/15--]. Equipment (sugarloaf mold). Museu de Aveiro, Aveiro, Portugal. Inventory no.: 413/E (IFN no.: 42234 TC). © Museu de Aveiro. Photography: José Pessoa, 2010. Divisão de Documentação Fotográfica – Instituto dos Museus e da Conservação, I.P.

192 Giovannino De' Grassi – [Selling sugar by weight]. In Ububchasym de Baldach/Ibn Butlân (?–ca. 1068), *Theatrum Sanitatis* [13--]. Miniature. Biblioteca Casanatense, Rome, Italy. Ms. 4182, im. 179. Su concessione del Ministero per i Beni e le Attività Culturali. Dalla specifica dell'opera originale.

194-195 Willem Claesz. Heda – *Breakfast Table with Fruit Pie*, 1631. Painting. Gemäldegalerie Alte Meister – Staatliche Kunstsammlungen Dresden, Dresden, Germany. Inventory no.: Gal. No. 1371 (Image no.: AM-1371-PS01). © Gemäldgalerie Alte Meister, Staatliche Kunstsammlugen Dresden. Photography: Elke Estel / Hans-Peter Klut.

196 Franz Hogenberg (illustr.) – [Table decorated with animals and plants molded in sugar paste for the wedding banquet of the Duke of Jülich-Cleves-Berg and the Margravine of Baden, in 1585]. In *Beschreibung derer fürstlicher güligscher &c. Hochzeit : so im Jahr Christi tausent fünffhundert achtzig fünff, am sechszehenden Junij vnd nechstfolgenden acht Tagen, zu Düsseldorff mit grossen Freuden, fürstlichen Triumph vnd Herrligkeit gehalten worden.* Gedruckt zu Cölln: [Theodor Graminaeus], 1587. Drawing. The Getty Research Institute, Los Angeles, CA, United States of America. Image no.: grl_86-b22668_pl7.tif. The Getty Research Institute, Los Angeles (2853-048).

198 Juan van der Hamen y León – [*Still life with pottery, candied fruit, biscuits, and other comfits*], 1627. Painting. National Gallery of Art, Washington, DC, United States of America. Samuel H. Kress Collection, 1961.9.75. Juan van der Hamen y León, *Still Life with Sweets and Pottery*, Samuel H. Kress Collection. Image courtesy of the Board of Trustees, National Gallery of Art.

200 Georg Flegel – *Still Life with Fruit (dried and candied) and Comfits* [1566–1638]. Painting. Städel Museum – Städelsches Kunstinstitut, Frankfurt am Main, Germany. Image ID: 20281. © U. Edelmann – Städel Museum – ARTOTHEK: Georg Flegel, Städel Museum – Städelsches Kunstinstitut (Frankfurt am Main).

203 Osias Beert – *Still Life with Oysters, Comfits and Fruit*, 1610. Painting. Staatsgalerie Stuttgart, Stuttgart, Germany. Inventory no.: 2752. Staatsgalerie Stuttgart © Photography: Staatsgalerie Stuttgart.

205 Abraham Bosse (drawer); [Jean] le Blond (engraver) – *The Pastry Vendor* [ca. 1630]. Engraving. Museum of Fine Arts, Boston, MA, United States of America. Museum purchase with funds donated by Lia G. Poorvu, 1999.51. Photograph © 2011, Museum of Fine Arts, Boston.

208 [Anonymous] – *Glasgow Shopkeeper* [after 1790]. Painting. People's Palace, Glasgow, Scotland. 800.92.47. © Culture and Sport Glasgow (Museums), Anonymous, *Glasgow Shopkeeper*.

210-211 Abraham Bosse (drawer); [Melchior] Tavernier (ed.) – *The Pastry Shop* [ca. 1638]. Engraving. Museum of Fine Arts, Boston, MA, United States of America. Maria Antoinette Evans Fund, 30.1069.7. Photograph © 2011, Museum of Fine Arts, Boston.

212 Tomás Hiepes – *Still Life with Sweets and Dried Fruit and Nuts* [1610–1674]. Painting. Museo Nacional del Prado, Madrid, Spain. P07914. © Museo Nacional del Prado.

214 *Encyclopédie, Ou Dictionnaire Raisonné Des Sciences, Des Arts Et Des Métiers, Par Une Société De Gens De Lettres / Denis Diderot; Jean Le Rond D'Alembert (comp.) – Recuil De Planches, Sur Les Sciences, Les Arts Libéraux Et Les Arts Mechaniques. Avec Leur Explication. Deux cens soixante & neuf Planches, premiere Livraison* / [Louis-Jacques Goussier (drawer); Robert Bénard (engraver)]. A Paris, Chez Briasson, Rue Saint Jacques, à la Science. David, rue & vis-à-vis la Grille des Mathurins. Le Breton, Imprimeur ordinaire du Roy, rue de la Harpe. Durand, rue du Foin, vis-à-vis la petite Porte des Mathurins. M. DCC. LXII [1762] [Interior of a sugar refinery and ground plan]. Engraving. Bibliothèque Nationale de France, Paris, France. RES G-Z-577 (22), plate V. © Bibliothèque Nationale de France.

214 *Encyclopédie, Ou Dictionnaire Raisonné Des Sciences, Des Arts Et Des Métiers, Par Une Société De Gens De Lettres / Denis Diderot; Jean Le Rond D'Alembert (comp.) – Recuil De Planches, Sur Les Sciences, Les Arts Libéraux Et Les Arts Mechaniques. Avec Leur Explication. Deux cens soixante & neuf Planches, premiere Livraison* / [Louis-Jacques Goussier (drawer); Robert Bénard (engraver)]. A Paris, Chez Briasson, Rue Saint Jacques, à la Science. David, rue & vis-à-vis la Grille des Mathurins. Le Breton, Imprimeur ordinaire du Roy, rue de la Harpe. Durand, rue du Foin, vis-à-vis la petite Porte des Mathurins. M. DCC. LXII [1762] [Interior of a sugar refinery with details (objects and others)]. Engraving. Bibliothèque Nationale de France, Paris, France. RES G-Z-577 (22), plate VI. © Bibliothèque Nationale de France.

216 *Het Menselyk Bedryf. Vertoond, in. 100. Verbeeldingen: van: Ambachten, Konsten, Hanteeringen en Bedryven; met Versen. [...]* t'Amsterdam. / Gedaan; door; Johannes, en, Caspaares, Luiken, 1694 [Sugar refiner and refinery]. Engraving. Universiteitsbibliotheek van de Universiteit van Amsterdam, Amsterdam, The Netherlands. Bijzondere Collecties, OTM: OG 80-36, p. 45. Special Collections, University of Amsterdam, OTM: OG 80-36, p. 45.

218-219 Frans Francken, the Younger – *Banquet at the Home of Burgomaster Rockox* [ca. 1630–1635]. Painting. Alte Pinakothek, Munich, Germany. Inventory no.: 858 (Image no.: 50010619). bpk | Bayerische Staatsgemäldesammlungen – Alte Pinakothek.

220 [Anonymous – Made in London] – *Silver sugar bowl with "Chinoiserie" decorative motifs and latch* [1683–1684]. Decorative arts (sugar bowl). Victoria and Albert Museum, London, England. M.419-1927. © Victoria and Albert Museum, London (legacy Mrs. Aubrey Carter, widow of Major Carter).

221 [Anonymous – Made in Amsterdam] – *Three sugarloaves, identification plaque of homonymous sugar refinery* [17--]. Decorative arts (stone tablet). Vereniging Vrienden van Amsterdamse Gevelstenen, Amsterdam, The Netherlands. No quota file (Nieuwezijds Voorburgwal, 67). Foundation Friends of Amsterdam Stone Tablets (VVAG)

222-223 Jan Brueghel, the Elder– *Visit to the Farm* [ca. 1597]. Painting. Kunsthistorisches Museum Wien – Gemäldegalerie, Vienna, Austria. Inventory no.: GG_674. Kunsthistorisches Museum, Vienna.

226 [Anonymous] – *Apothecary sugar containers, probably from the convent of Nossa Senhora do Vencimento do Monte do Carmo, in Lisbon* [ca. 1755–1785]. Pottery (sugar container). Museu da Farmácia, Lisbon, Portugal. Inventory no.: 308. Museu da Farmácia.

229 Josefa de Ayala, or Josefa de Óbidos – *Still Life with Sweets*, 1676. Painting. Museu Municipal de Santarém, Santarém, Portugal. BMS/005005. Photography: Nuno Moreira.

231 Josefa de Ayala, or Josefa de Óbidos – *Still Life: Basket with Flowers and Various Types of Sweets* [1630–1684]. Painting. Museu Municipal de Évora, Évora, Portugal. Inventory no.: 03945 TC (Image no.: ME 1452). © IMC / MC. Photography: José Pessoa, 1999.

238 Hendrik-Cornelisz. Vroom – *Dutch Ships Attacking Spanish Galleys near the English Coast in October 1602*, 1617. Painting. Rijksmuseum Amsterdam, Amsterdam, The Netherlands. SK-A-460. Collection Rijksmuseum Amsterdam, The Netherlands.

240 [Joris Carolus] [?] – *De Groote Lichtende Ofte Vyerighe Colom Over de Zee Custen Van't Wester / Ooster / en Noorder Vaer-water. Met Privilegie, voor Achthien Jaeren.* t'Amstelredam: Jacob Aertsz. Colom, Boeckverkooper op't Water / In de Uperighe Colom, 1652. Printed. Universiteitsbibliotheek van de Universiteit van Amsterdam, Amsterdam, The Netherlands. Bijzondere Collecties, OTM: HB-Kaartenzaal: 1805 A 12 [title page]. Special Collections, University of Amsterdam, OTM: HB-Kaartenzaal: 1805 A 12 [title page].

241 *T'ghebruyck vande Zeecaerte / Gheschreven in maniere van den T'samensprake / meest ghemaeckt door / Doctroor Thomas Hood, Professor inde Schole vande Zeevaert tot Londen in Enghelandt.* Tot Amstelderam: Cornelis Claesz. Boeckvercooper opt waterint Schryff-boeck / byde oude Brugghe, 1602. Printed. Maritiem Museum Rotterdam, Rotterdam, The Netherlands. WAE4A28 [title page]. Collection Maritime Museum Rotterdam.

241 *Sailors' Registry [from Viana do Castelo]*, 1600. Manuscript. Arquivo Municipal de Viana do Castelo, Viana do Castelo, Portugal. Matrícula dos Mareantes– 1600, 949, fol. 9. AMVCT – Arquivo Municipal de Viana do Castelo: Matrícula dos Mareantes – 1600 (Quota 949).

242 *De zee-atlas ofte water-waereld: vertoonende alle de zee-kusten van het bekende deel des aerd-bodems seer dienstigh voor alle schippers en stuurlieden, mitsgaders koop-lieden om op 't kantoor gebruyckt te werden. Nieuwelijcks aldus uytgegeven. Chart of the North Sea.* Amsterdam: Hendrick Doncker [1665] [?] [Chart of the North Sea, showing the coasts of the surrounding countries, 1658]. Cartography (nautical chart: printed). Fundação Biblioteca Nacional, Rio de Janeiro, Brazil. AT.023,02,011 Cartography (4th print). Acervo da Fundação Biblioteca Nacional – Brasil.

247 Pieter Jansz. Saenredam – *Amsterdam's Former City Hall*, 1657. Painting. Rijksmusem Amsterdam, Amsterdam, The Netherlands. SK-C-1409. Collection Rijksmuseum Amsterdam, The Netherlands.

248 *Record Book of the Amsterdam College of Commissioners of Insurance for 1598 to 1621* [1622]. Manuscript. Nederlandsch Economisch-Historisch Archief, Amsterdam, The Netherlands. Bijzondere Collecties, 277, fol. 79. Collection International Institute of Social History, Amsterdam.

251 António de Holanda (attrib.) – [View of the City of Lisbon]. In *Crónica do rei D. Afonso Henriques de Duarte Galvão* [15--]. Illumination. Museu-Biblioteca Condes de Castro Guimarães, Cascais, Portugal. MCCG – 14. © Museu-Biblioteca Condes de Castro Guimarães, Câmara Municipal de Cascais. Photography: Pedro Aboim Borges.

252 *Liuro de traças de Carpintaria com todos os Modelos e medidas pera se fazerem toda a nauegação, assy d'alto bordo como de remo / traçado por Manoel Frz- official do mesmo officio*, 1616. [Caravel with 11 *rumos*]. Drawing. Biblioteca da Ajuda, Lisbon, Portugal. 52-XIV-21, fol. 108. Biblioteca da Ajuda.

253 *Liuro de traças de Carpintaria com todos os Modelos e medidas pera se fazerem toda a nauegação, assy d'alto bordo como de remo / traçado por Manoel Frz- official do mesmo officio*, 1616 [War patache]. Drawing. Biblioteca da Ajuda, Lisbon, Portugal. 52-XIV-21, fol. 111. Biblioteca da Ajuda.

254 *Liuro de traças de Carpintaria com todos os Modelos e medidas pera se fazerem toda a nauegação, assy d'alto bordo como de remo / traçado por Manoel Frz- official do mesmo officio*, 1616 [Model of a carrack]. Drawing. Biblioteca da Ajuda, Lisbon, Portugal. 52-XIV-21, fol. 71. Biblioteca da Ajuda.

255 [Pieter Bruegel, the Elder (drawer); Frans Huys (engraver)] – [*Dutch Hulk and "Boeier"*], 1565. Engraving. Museum Boijmans Van Beuningen, Rotterdam, The Netherlands. BdH 11494 (PK). Museum Boijmans Van Beuningen, Rotterdam.

255 *Libre appellat Consolat de mar. Nouament estampat e corregit. Affegits los capitol's e ordinacions dels drets del General. E del dret del pes del Senyor Rey. Ab altres coses necessaries: les quals fins al present no ere- estades estampades.* Barcelona: Dimas Ballester and Juan de Gilio, 1523. Printed. Biblioteca Nacional de Portugal, Lisbon, Portugal. Reservados, RES. 459 P [title page]. © Biblioteca Nacional de Portugal.

256 Wenzel Hollar – [*"Fluitschips"*], 1647. Engraving. Maritiem Museum Rotterdam, Rotterdam, The Netherlands. P1193-4. Collection Maritime Museum Rotterdam.

257 Reinier Nooms – [*Pinnace (the* Golden Dolphin) *and "fluit" (the* Cat)], 1650. Engraving. Nederlands Scheepvaartmuseum, Amsterdam, The Netherlands. A.0149(267). © Nederlands Scheepvaartmuseum.

257 Reinier Nooms – [*Seascape with "spiegelschip" and "fluit"*] [1640–1664]. Engraving. Fries Scheepvaartmuseum, Sneek, The Netherlands. Inventory no.: 1978-268. © Fries Scheepvaartmuseum.

258 *Icones Variarum Navium Hollandicarum Quarum Usus Maximè In Aquis Interioribus Regionis. / Notatae à famosißimo Navium Pictore Iohanne Percelles.* Amsterdam: Nicolaes I. Visscher, 1627 ["Boeier"]. Engraving. Maritiem Museum Rotterdam, Rotterdam, The Netherlands. P2341-7. Collection Maritime Museum Rotterdam.

259 Johannes Vingboons – [*View of the City of Paraiba*], 1665. Cartography (perspective). Nationaal Archief, The Hague, The Netherlands. Kaartcollectie Buitenland Leupe, 4.VELH619-83. © Nationaal Archief, Den Haag.

260 [Anonymous] – *Intaglio* (graffiti) *of a ship (possibly a xebec or a Maltese tartane) on a wall of the Church of the Visitation in Wied Qirda, Haz-Zebbug (Malta)* [n.d.]. Intaglio. Malta Maritime Museum, Vittoriosa, Malta. Inventory no.: MM 3766. Courtesy Heritage Malta (2011) – Maritime Museum Archives / National Maritime Museum Archives, Malta © 2011, Heritage Malta.

262-263 Cornelis Claesz van Wieringen – *The Dutch Fleet led by Admiral Jacob van Heemskerk Defeats Spain in the Battle of Gibraltar, on April 25, 1607* [ca. 1619]. Painting. National Maritime Museum, Greenwich – London, England. BHC0265. © National Maritime Museum, Greenwich, London, Caird Collection.

264-265 [Anonymous – Probably Made in Germany] – *Matchlock musket* [ca. 1560]. Weapon. Royal Armouries Library, Leeds, England. Inventory no.: XII.8 (Image no.: TR2001.010). © The Board of Trustees of the Armouries.

266 [João Baptista Lavanha; Luís Teixeira] – *Atlas Cosmografia* [Chart showing the western part of the Iberian Peninsula] [1597 and 1612]. Cartography (nautical chart). Biblioteca Reale di Torino, Turin, Italy. Mscr. Vari 221, fol. 7. Su concessione del Ministero per i Beni e le Attività Culturali – Biblioteca Reale – Torino.

268 [Anonymous – Made in Europe] – *Breech-Loading Iron Swivel Gun* [15--]. Weapon. Royal Armouries Library, Leeds, England. Inventory no.: XIX.3 (Image no.: A11.91). © The Board of Trustees of the Armouries.

268 *Het Menselyk Bedryf. Vertoond, in. 100. Verbeeldingen: van: Ambachten, Konsten, Hanteeringen en Bedryven; met Versen. [...]* t'Amsterdam. / Gedaan; door; Johannes, en, Caspaares, Luiken, 1694 [Cannon making]. Engraving. Universiteitsbibliotheek van de Universiteit van Amsterdam, Amsterdam, The Netherlands. Bijzondere Collecties, OTM: OG 80-36, p. 36. Special Collections, University of Amsterdam, OTM: OG 80-36, p. 36.

268 Michael Burgerhuys (maker) – *Cannon*, Middelburg, 1618. Weapon (cannon). Museu Militar de Lisboa, Lisboa, Portugal. S.13. Photography: Pedro Dantas dos Reis.

272 Paulus Moreelse – *Lieutenant-Admiral Pieter Pietersz. Heyn (1577–1629)*, 1630. Painting. Nederlands Scheepvaartmuseum, Amsterdam, The Netherlands. B.0183. © Nederlands Scheepvaartmuseum.

280 [João Baptista Lavanha; Luís Teixeira] – *Atlas Cosmografia* [Chart of part of the North Sea with the east coast of England, Northern France and The Netherlands] [1597 and 1612]. Cartography (nautical chart). Biblioteca Reale di Torino, Turin, Italy. Mscr. Vari 221, fol. 5. Su concessione del Ministero per i Beni e le Attività Culturali – Biblioteca Reale – Torino.

282 [Joris Carolus][?] *De Groote Lichtende Ofte Vyerighe Colom Over de Zee Custen Van't Wester / Ooster / en Noorder Vaer-water. Met Privilegie, voor Achthien Jaeren.* t'Amstelredam: Jacob Aertsz. Colom, Boeckverkooper op't Water / In de Uperighe Colom, 1652 [Chart showing the "Zuiderzee" (Zuyder Zee") and one of its seaways, the Vliestroom ("Vlie Stroom")]. Cartography (nautical chart: printed). Universiteitsbibliotheek van de Universiteit van Amsterdam, Amsterdam, The Netherlands. Bijzondere Collecties, OTM: 1805 A 12 (no. 37). Special Collections, University of Amsterdam, OTM: HBKaartenzaal: 1805 A 12 (no. 37).

284-285 Krystof Arciszeweski – [Map of Brazil]. In *Atlas van der Hagen* [ca. 1690]. Cartography (nautical chart: printed). Koninklijke Bibliotheek, The Hague, The Netherlands. 1049 B 11, krt. 092. Den Haag, Koninklijke Bibliotheek, 1049 B 11, krt. 092.

286 [Anonymous] – *Atlas* [Map of the Brazilian coast, from the Amazon to Rio de Janeiro] [1550–1560]. Cartography (map). National Maritime Museum, Greenwich – London, England. F1539, P/14(12r) Brazil. © National Maritime Museum, Greenwich, London.

288 *Mappas do Reino de Portugal e suas conquistas collegidos por Diogo Barbosa Machado – [Atlas das Ilhas dos Açores e Madeira]*. [n.l.: n.n.] [after 1650] [?] [Chart: portrayal depiction of the Island of Madeira]. Cartography (nautical chart: printed). Fundação Biblioteca Nacional, Rio de Janeiro, Brazil. ARC.016,09,001- 011 Cartography (map 2). Acervo da Fundação Biblioteca Nacional – Brasil.

289 [Petrus Bertius; Salomon Rogiers] – Canariae I. In *Petri Bertii Tabularum Geographicum Contractarum* [Amsterdam: Jodocus Hondius II, 1618]. Cartography (map: printed). Instituto Geográfico Nacional, Madrid, Spain. IGNC 12-D-25. Información geográfica propiedad del Instituto Geográfico Nacional.

292-293 Luís Teixeira – [*Chart of the Atlantic*] [ca. 1600]. Cartography (nautical chart). Biblioteca Nazionale Centrale di Firenze, Florence, Italy. Port. 27. With the kind permission of the Ministero per i Beni e le Attivitá Culturali della Repubblica Italiana / Biblioteca Nazionale Centrale di Firenze. Port. 27 (Firenze/BNC). This image cannot be reproduced by any means.

294 [João Teixeira Albernaz, the Elder] – *Rezão. do Estado, do Brasil no gvoverno do Norte. só.me-te. asi. como, o teve. Dõ Diogvo, de Meneses. até o annõ, de 1612* [Chart: "Terra de Santa Crvz, a que vvlgarmente, chamão Brasil."] [ca. 1616]. Cartography (nautical chart). Biblioteca Pública Municipal do Porto, Porto, Portugal. Reservados, MS 126 [5]. Belongs to the collections of the Biblioteca Pública Municipal do Porto.

298-299 *[Speculum nauticum super navigatione maris Occidentalis confectum, continens omnes oras marítimas Galliae, Hispaniae et praecipuarum partium Angliae, in diversis mappis maritimis comprehensum, uma cum usu et interpretatione earundem, accurata diligentia concinnatum: Pars Prima] / Lucam Iohannis Aurigarium* [Leiden: Frans van Raphelengen], 1586 [Nautical chart showing the Portuguese coast from the Lima River to the Mondego River]. Cartography (nautical chart: printed). Biblioteca Nacional de Portugal, Lisbon, Portugal. Cartography, C.A. 116 V. [between pages 16 and 17]. © Biblioteca Nacional de Portugal.

300 *Het Menselyk Bedryf. Vertoond, in. 100. Verbeeldingen: van: Ambachten, Konsten, Hanteeringen en Bedryven; met Versen. [...]* t'Amsterdam. / Gedaan; door; Johannes, en, Caspaares, Luiken, 1694 [Mast-making]. Engraving. Universiteitsbibliotheek van de Universiteit van Amsterdam, Amsterdam, The Netherlands. Bijzondere Collecties, OTM: OG 80-36, p. 35. Special Collections, University of Amsterdam, OTM: OG 80-36, p. 35.

300 *Het Menselyk Bedryf. Vertoond, in. 100. Verbeeldingen: van: Ambachten, Konsten, Hanteeringen en Bedryven; met Versen. [...]* t'Amsterdam. / Gedaan; door; Johannes, en, Caspaares, Luiken, 1694 [Shipyard]. Engraving. Universiteitsbibliotheek van de Universiteit van Amsterdam, Amsterdam, The Netherlands. Bijzondere Collecties, OTM: OG 80-36, p. 37. Special Collections, University of Amsterdam, OTM: OG 80-36, p. 37.

302 Wallerant Vaillant (attrib.), after Jan Lievens (?) – *Portrait of Jan Gerritsz. Bicker (1591–1653), A Merchant in Italy and the Levant, Burgomaster of Amsterdam, Married to Agneta de Graeff (1603–1656)* [1663–1664]. Painting. Amsterdam Museum, Amsterdam, The Netherlands. Inventory no.: SA 7267. © Amsterdam Museum.

304 *Liuro de traças de Carpintaria com todos os Modelos e medidas pera se fazerem toda a nauegação, assy d'alto bordo como de remo / traçado por Manoel Frz- official do mesmo officio*, 1616 [Portrait of the author]. Drawing. Biblioteca da Ajuda, Lisbon, Portugal. 52-XIV-21 [frontispiece]. Biblioteca da Ajuda.

305 Claes Jansz Visscher de Jonge – [*"Fluitschip"*], 1629. Engraving. Fries Scheepvaartmuseum, Sneek, The Netherlands. Inventory no.: 1978-273. © Fries Scheepvaartmuseum.

307 [Anonymous – Made in Amsterdam] – *Wheatfield* [n.d.]. Decorative arts (stone tablet). Vereniging Vrienden van Amsterdamse Gevelstenen, Amsterdam, The Netherlands. No quota file (Nieuwe Leliestraat, 22). Foundation Friends of Amsterdam Stone Tablets (VVAG), The Netherlands.

308 Job Adriaensz. Berckheyde – *The Baker* [ca. 1681]. Painting. Worcester Art Museum, Worcester, MA, United States of America. 1975105. Gift of Mr. and Mrs. Milton P. Higgins.

310-311 [Anonymous] – *The Ribeira Velha Market in the Early Eighteenth Century* [17--]. Tiles (panel). Museu da Cidade, Lisbon, Portugal. MC.AZU.PF.0059A. © Museu da Cidade – Câmara Municipal de Lisboa.

313 *Regimento de pilotos, e roteiro das navegaçoens da India Oriental : agora novamente emendado & acresentado co[m] o Roteiro da costa de Sofala, ate Mo[m]baça : & com os portos, & barras do Cabo de Finis taerra ate o Estreito de Gibaltar, com suas derrotas, sondas, & demonstraçoens / Pello Dezembargador Antonio de Maris Carneiro fidalguo da Caza de Sua Magestade, & seu cosmographo mor destes Reynos de Portugal.* Lisbon: Lourenço de Anvers, 1642 [The Portuguese coast from Leça to Aveiro, showing the city of Porto]. Cartography (nautical chart: printed). Biblioteca Nacional de Portugal, Lisbon, Portugal. Reservados, RES. 331//2 V. [between pages 88 and 90]. © Biblioteca Nacional de Portugal.

313 *Descripção dos Portos Maritimos do Reino de Portvgal. / Por João Teixeira Cosmografo mór de S. Mg.de Anno. 1648* [Chart: The entire Portuguese coast]. Cartography (nautical chart). Sociedade de Geografia de Lisboa, Lisbon, Portugal. Reservados A-28, fol. 1v-2. © Sociedade de Geografia de Lisboa.

314 Hadji Muhammad/Piri Reis – *Mapa-mundi* (fragment), 1513. Topkapı Sarayı Museum, Istanbul, Turkey. TSMK R.1633. Topkapi Palace Museum.

322 Pieter Bruegel, the Elder – *The Fall of Icarus* [1527/28–1569]. Painting. Musées Royaux des Beaux-Arts de Belgique, Brussels, Belgium. Inventory no.: 4030. © Royal Museums of Fine Arts of Belgium, Brussels [dig. Photography: J. Geleyns / www.roscan.be].

324 Hendrik Cornelisz. Vroom – *Dutch Pinnace Sailing near a Rocky Shore*, 1628. Painting. Nederlands Scheepvaartmuseum, Amsterdam, The Netherlands. A.1842. © Nederlands Scheepvaartmuseum.

327 *Exame das tradicoes Phariseas conferidas com á lei escrita / Por Uriel Jurista Hebreo, Com reposta a hum Semvel da Silva que faz offiçio de medico, seu falso calumniador.* Amsterdam: Paulo à Ravesteyn, anno da criaçaõ do Mundo de 5384 [1624]. Printed. Det Kongelige Bibliotek / The Royal Library, Copenhagen, Denmark. Manuscripts and Rare Books, Closed stack (Box), 91, 3120, 02255, S-1977 [title page]. Photography: Thomas Trane Petersen.

332-333 [Johannes Rem] – [*View of Amsterdam from the IJ River*] [1606]. Cartography (perspective: printed). Rijksmuseum Amsterdam, Amsterdam, The Netherlands. RP-P-1898-A-20079. Collection Rijksmuseum Amsterdam, The Netherlands.

336 [Anonymous] – *Miracle of Our Lady of Remedies for Manuel Gomes Ferraz*, 1656. Ex-voto. Dominican convent church (parish of Nossa Senhora de Monserrate), Viana do Castelo, Portugal. No quota file. Photography: Pedro Dantas dos Reis.

337 Aron Wolf Herlingen [?] (cop. and illust.) – *Seder Birkat ha-Mazon* [Prayer for ocean crossings], Deutschkreutz (Austria), 1751. Miniature. Braginsky Collection, Zurich, Switzerland. BC 217, fol. 15r. Braginsky Collection, Zurich.

338 [Anonymous] – *"Sugar-crate" furniture: closet* [16--]. Furnishings (closet). Casa-Museu Frederico de Freitas, Funchal – Madeira, Portugal. Inventory no.: 17.0145. Casa-Museu Frederico de Freitas / Photography: Roberto Pereira (DRAC).

338 Rembrandt van Rijn – *Descent from the Cross* [1606–1669]. Painting. Alte Pinakothek, Munich, Germany. Inventory no.: 395 (Image no.: 50010537). bpk | Bayerische Staatsgemäldesammlungen – Alte Pinakothek.

338 Rembrandt van Rijn – *Descent from the Cross* (verso) [1606–1669]. Painting. Alte Pinakothek, Munich, Germany. Inventory no.: 395 (Image no.: 2011-1066_395_RS). Photography: Bayerische Staatsgemälsammlugen – Alte Pinakothek, München.

339 Pieter Brueghel, the Elder (drawer); Hieronymus Cock (ed.) – *Seven Deadly Sins: Avarice* [1550/1570]. Engraving. Germanisches Nationalmuseum, Nuremberg, Germany. Inventory no.: HB 15218. Germanisches Nationalmuseum, Nürnberg.

340 Original bill of lading produced by shipmaster Diricx Cornelisz. Claes of Enkhuizen for cargo received from Luis Pereira da Silva and to be delivered to João de Leão or his proxy in Porto; Amsterdam –August 10, 1617. Manuscript/Printed. Nationaal Archief, The Hague, The Netherlands. NLHaNA- 1.01.02-12561.33.1. © Nationaal Archief, Den Haag.

342 Original private freight contract for the transportation of goods between Lisbon and Salvador with Gregório Dias Cordeiro, shipmaster of the "Santa Catarina," and (9) merchants from Lisbon; Lisbon –January 5–7, 1591. Manuscript. Arquivo Distrital de Lisboa, Lisboa, Portugal. PT-ADL-CNLSB15A/1/1/92. "Documento cedido pelo ADL." Quota: Cartório 7A, box 20, book 6.

346 António de Holanda (attrib.) – *Breviary of the countess of Bertiandos* [ca. 1515–1530]. Illumination. Biblioteca da Academia das Ciências de Lisboa, Lisboa, Portugal. Série Azul, Ms. 1813 (facsimile: Reservados 65-1, fol. 100). Photography: Pedro Dantas dos Reis.

354 Johannes Vermeer – *Woman Holding a Balance* [ca. 1664]. Painting. National Gallery of Art, Washington, DC, United States of America. Widener Collection, 1942.9.97. Johannes Vermeer, *Woman Holding a Balance*, Widener Collection. Image courtesy of the Board of Trustees, National Gallery of Art.

357 Pieter Breughel, the Elder (drawer); Pieter van der Heyden (engraver); Johannes Galle (ed.) – *The Fight of the Money-Bags and the Coffers* [post. 1570]. Engraving. Baker Library – Harvard Business School, Cambridge, MA, United States of America. Historical Collections, CF b4 xx, olvwork308229. © Bleichroeder Print Collection, Kress Collection. Baker Library Historical Collections. Harvard Business School. olvwork308229.

360 Pieter van der Heyden (engraver) (after a drawing by Pieter Brueghel, the Elder); Hieronymus Cock (ed.) – *Avarice, from the Seven Deadly Sins Series*, 1558. Engraving. The Metropolitan Museum of Art, New York, NY, United States of America. Harris Brisbane Dick Fund, 1926 (26.72.31) (Image no.: ME08901). © 2011. Image copyright, The Metropolitan Museum of Art/Art Resource/Scala, Florence.

364 *Het Menselyk Bedryf. Vertoond, in. 100. Verbeeldingen: van: Ambachten, Konsten, Hanteeringen en Bedryven; met Versen. [...]* t'Amsterdam. / Gedaan; door; Johannes, en, Caspaares, Luiken, 1694 [Sale of grain]. Engraving. Universiteitsbibliotheek van de Universiteit van Amsterdam, Amsterdam, The Netherlands. Bijzondere Collecties, OTM: OG 80-36, p. 50. Special Collections, University of Amsterdam, OTM: OG 80-36, p. 50.

366 Jonas Suyderhoeff (engraver) – [*Portrait of David Nuyts (1568–1631)*], 1631. Engraving. Stadsarchief Amsterdam, Amsterdam, The Netherlands. Image no.: 010097014560. © Stadsarchief Amsterdam.

370 Marinus van Reymerswaele – *Tax Collector and his Wife*, 1538. Painting. Alte Pinakothek, Munich, Germany. Inventory no.: 7 (Image no.: 50010428). bpk | Bayerische Staatsgemäldesammlungen – Alte Pinakothek.

371 [Anonymous – Flemish School] – *Sir Thomas Gresham* (ca. 1518–1579), 1544. Painting. Mercers' Company of the City of London, England. No quota file. The Mercers' Company.

372 *Flor Da Arismetica Necessaria, vso dos cambios, & quilatador de ouro, & prata, o mais curioso, ~q- te- sabido. ... / Composto per Affõço de Villafanhe, Guiral, & Pacheco.* Lisbon: Geraldo da Vinha, 1624 ["Table of coins of the kingdoms of Portugal, Castile, Aragon and Valencia"]. Printed. Biblioteca Nacional de Portugal, Lisbon, Portugal. S.A. 2538 P. , fol. 13v–14. © Biblioteca Nacional de Portugal.

373 [Anonymous] – *Water-powered rollers used to stretch metal into strips and mint coins simultaneously* (proof), 1620. Minting (minting roller). Museo Casa de la Moneda, Madrid, Spain. R-31. Museo Casa de la Moneda, Madrid, España.

373 [Anonymous – Made in Lisbon] – *Screw Press* (body), 1678. Minting (screw-press). Museu Arqueológico do Carmo, Lisbon, Portugal. No quota file. Photography: Pedro Dantas dos Reis.

373 [Anonymous] – *"Taschenwerk" Press* [16--] [?]. Minting (press). Germanisches Nationalmuseum, Nuremberg, Germany. Inventory no.: Z 3106. Germanisches Nationalmuseum, Nürnberg.

374 [Anonymous – Minted in Portugal (?)] – *Four cruzados: gold coin from the reign of Philip II (1580–1598)*. Numismatics (coin). Museu Numismático Português – Imprensa Nacional/Casa da Moeda, Lisbon, Portugal. Inventory no.: 5108. Photography: Pedro Dantas dos Reis.

374 [Anonymous – Minted in Portugal (?)] – *Four cruzados: gold coin from the reign of Philip III (1598–1621)*. Numismatics (coin). Museu Numismático Português – Imprensa Nacional/ Casa da Moeda, Lisbon, Portugal. Inventory no.: 5124. Photography: Pedro Dantas dos Reis.

374 [Anonymous – Minted in Portugal (?)] – *Two cruzados: gold coin from the reign of Philip II (1580–1598)*. Numismatics (coin). Museu Numismático Português – Imprensa Nacional/Casa da Moeda, Lisbon, Portugal. Inventory no.: 5109. Photography: Pedro Dantas dos Reis.

374 [Anonymous – Minted in Portugal (?)] – *Cruzado: gold coin from the reign of Philip II (1580–1598)*. Numismatics (coin). Museu Numismático Português – Imprensa Nacional/Casa da Moeda, Lisbon, Portugal. Inventory no.: 9524. Photography: Pedro Dantas dos Reis.

374 [Anonymous – Minted in Portugal] – *Five hundred réis: gold coin from the reign of King Sebastian (1557–1578)*. Numismatics (coin). Museu Numismático Português – Imprensa Nacional/Casa da Moeda, Lisbon, Portugal. Inventory no.: 13398. Photography: Pedro Dantas dos Reis.

375 [Anonymous – Minted in Portugal (?)] – *Tostão: silver coin from the reign of Philip II (1580–1598)*. Numismatics (coin). Museu Numismático Português – Imprensa Nacional/Casa da Moeda, Lisbon, Portugal. Inventory no.: 9526. Photography: Pedro Dantas dos Reis.

375 [Anonymous – Minted in Portugal (?)] – *Tostão: silver coin from the reign of Philip III (1598–1621)*. Numismatics (coin). Museu Numismático Português – Imprensa Nacional/ Casa da Moeda, Lisbon, Portugal. Inventory no.: 5130. Photography: Pedro Dantas dos Reis.

375 [Anonymous – Minted in Portugal] – *Real português dobrado: silver coin from the reign of Henry of Portugal (1578–1580)*. Numismatics (coin). Museu Numismático Português – Imprensa Nacional/ Casa da Moeda, Lisbon, Portugal. Inventory no.: 13487. Photography: Pedro Dantas dos Reis.

375 [Anonymous – Minted in Portugal (?)] – *Four vinténs: silver coin from the reign of Philip II (1580–1598)*. Numismatics (coin). Museu Numismático Português – Imprensa Nacional/Casa da Moeda, Lisbon, Portugal. Inventory no.: 5117. Photography: Pedro Dantas dos Reis.

375 [Anonymous – Minted in Portugal (?)] – *Half-tostão: silver coin from the reign of Philip II (1580–1598)*. Numismatics (coin). Museu Numismático Português – Imprensa Nacional/Casa da Moeda, Lisbon, Portugal. Inventory no.: 5116. Photography: Pedro Dantas dos Reis.

375 [Anonymous – Minted in Portugal (?)] – *Half-tostão: silver coin from the reign of Philip III (1598–1621)*. Numismatics (coin). Museu Numismático Português – Imprensa Nacional/Casa da Moeda, Lisbon, Portugal. Inventory no.: 9541. Photography: Pedro Dantas dos Reis.

375 [Anonymous – Minted in Portugal (?)] – *Two vinténs: silver coin from the reign of Philip II (1580–1598)*. Numismatics (coin). Museu Numismático Português – Imprensa Nacional/Casa da Moeda, Lisbon, Portugal. Inventory no.: 5120. Photography: Pedro Dantas dos Reis.

375 [Anonymous – Minted in Portugal (?)] – *Vintém: silver coin from the reign of Philip II (1580–1598)*. Numismatics (coin). Museu Numismático Português – Imprensa Nacional/Casa da Moeda, Lisbon, Portugal. Inventory no.: 5122. Photography: Pedro Dantas dos Reis.

375 [Anonymous – Minted in Portugal (?)] – *Vintém: silver coin from the reign of Philip III (1598–1621)*. Numismatics (coin). Museu Numismático Português – Imprensa Nacional/Casa da Moeda, Lisbon, Portugal. Inventory no.: 9549. Photography: Pedro Dantas dos Reis.

375 [Anonymous – Minted in Portugal (?)] – *Ten réis: copper coin from the reign of Philip II (1580–1598)*. Numismatics (coin). Museu Numismático Português – Imprensa Nacional/Casa da Moeda, Lisbon, Portugal. Inventory no.: 5123. Photography: Pedro Dantas dos Reis.

375 [Anonymous – Minted in Portugal] – *Fiveréis: copper coin from the reign of King Sebastian (1557–1578)*. Numismatics (coin). Museu Numismático Português – Imprensa Nacional/Casa da Moeda, Lisbon, Portugal. Inventory no.: 5073. Photography: Pedro Dantas dos Reis.

375 [Anonymous – Minted in Portugal] – *Three réis: copper coin from the reign of King Sebastian (1557–1578)*. Numismatics (coin). Museu Numismático Português – Imprensa Nacional/Casa da Moeda, Lisbon, Portugal. Inventory no.: 5075. Photography: Pedro Dantas dos Reis.

375 [Anonymous – Minted in Angra (Ilha Terceira)] – *Real: copper coin from the period of António, Prior of Crato (1580–1583)* [1582]. Numismatics (coin). Museu do Banco de Portugal, Lisbon, Portugal. Image no.: 9002370400_A/9002370400_R. Museu do Banco de Portugal.

375 [Anonymous – Minted in Portugal] – *Ceitil: copper coin from the reign of King Sebastian (1557–1578)*. Numismatics (coin). Museu Numismático Português – Imprensa Nacional/Casa da Moeda, Lisbon, Portugal. Inventory no.: 5082. Photography: Pedro Dantas dos Reis.

376 [Anonymous – Minted in Segovia (Real Ingenio)] – *Ocho escudos: Spanish gold coin*, 1614. Numismatics (coin). Amigos de la Casa de la Moneda de Segovia, Segovia, Spain. No quota file. Dr. Glenn Murray, Friends of the Segovia Mint Association / www.SegoviaMint.org / Photography: Glenn Murray.

376 [Anonymous – Minted in Segovia (Real Ingenio)] –*Cuatro escudos: Spanish gold coin*, 1608. Numismatics (coin). Amigos de la Casa de la Moneda de Segovia, Segovia, Spain. No quota file. Dr. Glenn Murray, Friends of the Segovia Mint Association / www.SegoviaMint.org / Photography: Glenn Murray.

376 [Anonymous – Minted in Segovia (Real Ingenio)] –*Dos escudos: Spanish gold coin*, 1607. Numismatics (coin). Amigos de la Casa de la Moneda de Segovia, Segovia, Spain. No quota file. Dr. Glenn Murray, Friends of the Segovia Mint Association / www.SegoviaMint.org / Photography: Glenn Murray.

376 [Anonymous – Minted in Segovia (Real Ingenio)] –*Un escudo: Spanish gold coin*, 1607. Numismatics (coin). Amigos de la Casa de la Moneda de Segovia, Segovia, Spain. No quota file. Dr. Glenn Murray, Friends of the Segovia Mint Association / www.SegoviaMint.org / Photography: Glenn Murray.

376 [Anonymous – Minted in Segovia (Real Ingenio)] –*50 reales: Spanish silver coin*, 1618. Numismatics (coin). Amigos de la Casa de la Moneda de Segovia, Segovia, Spain. No quota file. Dr. Glenn Murray, Friends of the Segovia Mint Association / www.SegoviaMint.org / Photography: Glenn Murray.

376 [Anonymous – Minted in Segovia (Real Ingenio)] –*Ocho reales: Spanish silver coin*, 1620. Numismatics (coin). Amigos de la Casa de la Moneda de Segovia, Segovia, Spain. No quota file. Dr. Glenn Murray, Friends of the Segovia Mint Association / www.SegoviaMint.org / Photography: Glenn Murray.

376 [Anonymous – Minted in Segovia (Real Ingenio)] –*Cuatro reales: Spanish silver coin*, 1621. Numismatics (coin). Amigos de la Casa de la Moneda de Segovia, Segovia, Spain. No quota file. Dr. Glenn Murray, Friends of the Segovia Mint Association / www.SegoviaMint.org / Photography: Glenn Murray.

376 [Anonymous – Minted in Segovia (Casa Vieja)] –*Cuatro reales: Spanish silver coin*, 1612. Numismatics (coin). Amigos de la Casa de la Moneda de Segovia, Segovia, Spain. No quota file. Dr. Glenn Murray, Friends of the Segovia Mint Association / www.SegoviaMint.org / Photography: Glenn Murray.

376 [Anonymous – Minted in Segovia (Real Ingenio)] –*Dos reales: Spanish silver coin*, 1608. Numismatics (coin). Amigos de la Casa de la Moneda de Segovia, Segovia, Spain. No quota file. Dr. Glenn Murray, Friends of the Segovia Mint Association / www.SegoviaMint.org / Photography: Glenn Murray.

376 [Anonymous – Minted in Segovia (Casa Vieja)] –*Dos reales: Spanish silver coin*, 1611. Numismatics (coin). Amigos de la Casa de la Moneda de Segovia, Segovia, Spain. No quota file. Dr. Glenn Murray, Friends of the Segovia Mint Association / www.SegoviaMint.org / Photography: Glenn Murray.

377 [Anonymous – Minted in Segovia (Real Ingenio)] –*Un real: Spanish silver coin*, 1608. Numismatics (coin). Amigos de la Casa de la Moneda de Segovia, Segovia, Spain. No quota file. Dr. Glenn Murray, Friends of the Segovia Mint Association / www.SegoviaMint.org / Photography: Glenn Murray.

377 [Anonymous – Minted in Segovia (Casa Vieja)] –*Un real: Spanish silver coin*, 1[612]. Numismatics (coin). Amigos de la Casa de la Moneda de Segovia, Segovia, Spain. No quota file. Dr. Glenn Murray, Friends of the Segovia Mint Association / www.SegoviaMint.org / Photography: Glenn Murray.

377 [Anonymous – Minted in Segovia (Real Ingenio)] –*Medio real: Spanish silver coin*, 162[1]. Numismatics (coin). Amigos de la Casa de la Moneda de Segovia, Segovia, Spain. No quota file. Dr. Glenn Murray, Friends of the Segovia Mint Association / www.SegoviaMint.org / Photography: Glenn Murray.

377 [Anonymous – Minted in Segovia (Casa Vieja)] – *Medio real: Spanish silver coin*, 1614 [?]. Numismatics (coin). Amigos de la Casa de la Moneda de Segovia, Segovia, Spain. No quota file. Dr. Glenn Murray, Friends of the Segovia Mint Association / www.SegoviaMint.org / Photography: Glenn Murray.

377 377 [Anonymous – Minted in Segovia (Casa Vieja)] –*Cuartillo: Spanish coin, 215 parts silver and 785 parts copper* [1566–1591]. Numismatics (coin). Amigos de la Casa de la Moneda de Segovia, Segovia, Spain. No quota file. Dr. Glenn Murray, Friends of the Segovia Mint Association / www.SegoviaMint.org / Photography: Glenn Murray.

377 [Anonymous – Minted in Segovia (Real Ingenio)] –*Ocho maravedís: Spanish copper coin*, 1618. Numismatics (coin). Amigos de la Casa de la Moneda de Segovia, Segovia, Spain. No quota file. Dr. Glenn Murray, Friends of the Segovia Mint Association / www.SegoviaMint.org / Photography: Glenn Murray.

377 [Anonymous – Minted in Segovia (Casa Vieja)] –*Ocho maravedís: Spanish copper coin*, 1619. Numismatics (coin). Amigos de la Casa de la Moneda de Segovia, Segovia, Spain. No quota file. Dr. Glenn Murray, Friends of the Segovia Mint Association / www.SegoviaMint.org / Photography: Glenn Murray.

377 [Anonymous – Minted in Segovia (Real Ingenio)] –*Cuatro maravedís: Spanish copper coin*, 1605. Numismatics (coin). Amigos de la Casa de la Moneda de Segovia, Segovia, Spain. No quota file. Dr. Glenn Murray, Friends of the Segovia Mint Association / www.SegoviaMint.org / Photography: Glenn Murray.

377 [Anonymous – Minted in Segovia (Casa Vieja)] – *Cuatro maravedís: Spanish copper coin,* 1618. Numismatics (coin). Amigos de la Casa de la Moneda de Segovia, Segovia, Spain. No quota file. Dr. Glenn Murray, Friends of the Segovia Mint Association / www.SegoviaMint.org / Photography: Glenn Murray.

377 [Anonymous – Minted in Segovia (Real Ingenio)] – *Dos maravedís: Spanish copper coin,* 1604. Numismatics (coin). Amigos de la Casa de la Moneda de Segovia, Segovia, Spain. No quota file. Dr. Glenn Murray, Friends of the Segovia Mint Association / www.SegoviaMint.org / Photography: Glenn Murray.

377 [Anonymous – Minted in Segovia (Casa Vieja)] – *Dos maravedís: Spanish copper coin,* 1602. Numismatics (coin). Amigos de la Casa de la Moneda de Segovia, Segovia, Spain. No quota file. Dr. Glenn Murray, Friends of the Segovia Mint Association / www.SegoviaMint.org / Photography: Glenn Murray.

377 [Anonymous – Minted in Segovia (Real Ingenio)] – *Un maravedí: Spanish copper coin,* 1606. Numismatics (coin). Amigos de la Casa de la Moneda de Segovia, Segovia, Spain. No quota file. Dr. Glenn Murray, Friends of the Segovia Mint Association / www.SegoviaMint.org / Photography: Glenn Murray.

378 [Anonymous – Minted in Segovia (Casa Vieja)] – *"Resello a ocho maravedís": stamp used to change the face value of a coin from four to eight maravedis,* 1603. Numismatics (stamp). Amigos de la Casa de la Moneda de Segovia, Segovia, Spain. No quota file. Dr. Glenn Murray, Friends of the Segovia Mint Association / www.SegoviaMint.org / Photography: Glenn Murray.

379 [Anonymous – Made in Guelders] – *Stuiver: silver coin,* 1580. Numismatics (coin). Geldmuseum, Utrecht, The Netherlands. Inventory no.: NM-00730. Geldmuseum.

379 [Anonymous – Made in Frisia] – *Oord: silver coin,* 1608. Numismatics (coin). Geldmuseum, Utrecht, The Netherlands. Inventory no.: 1913-0226. Geldmuseum.

379 [Anonymous – Made in Holland] – *Duit: copper coin,* 1605. Numismatics (coin). Geldmuseum, Utrecht, The Netherlands. Inventory no.: NM-03201. Geldmuseum.

379 [Anonymous – Made in Holland] – *Roosschelling: silver coin,* 1601. Numismatics (coin). Geldmuseum, Utrecht, The Netherlands. Inventory no.: NM-03192. Geldmuseum.

379 [Anonymous – Made in Holland] – *Dubbele stuiver: silver coin,* 1614. Numismatics, (coin). Geldmuseum, Utrecht, The Netherlands. Inventory no.: NM-03213. Geldmuseum.

381 [Anonymous – Made in Holland] – *Nederlandse [half] rijksdaalder: silver coin,* 1649. Numismatics (coin). Geldmuseum, Utrecht, The Netherlands. Inventory no.: NM-03287. Geldmuseum.

381 [Anonymous – Made in Holland] – *Generaliteits Leeuwendaalder: silver coin,* 1617. Numismatics (coin). Dordrechts Museum – Huis Van Gijn, Dordrecht, The Netherlands. Inventory no.: 5227. Dordrecht, Huis Van Gijn.

381 [Anonymous – Made in Holland] – *Grote gouden rijder: gold coin,* 1632. Numismatics (coin). Geldmuseum, Utrecht, The Netherlands. Inventory no.: 1921-0077. Geldmuseum.

381 [Anonymous – Made in Antwerp / Brabant] – *Patagon: silver coin from the Southern Low Countries that circulated in the Dutch Republic during the reign of Philip IV (1621–1665),* 1631. Numismatics (coin). Geldmuseum, Utrecht, The Netherlands. Inventory no.: NM-10056. Geldmuseum.

381 [Anonymous – Made in Middelburg/Zeeland] – *Daalder van 30 stuivers: silver coin,* 1602. Numismatics (coin). Geldmuseum, Utrecht, The Netherlands. Inventory no.: MA-00019. Geldmuseum.

381 Jan Jansz. Kaen – *"Muntgewicht / clemmergulden": bronze counterweight*, Amsterdam [1623-1644]. Numismatics (coin). Geldmuseum, Utrecht, The Netherlands. Inventory no.: NV-04553. Geldmuseum.

382 *Flor Da Arismetica Necessaria, vso dos cambios, & quilatador de ouro, & prata, o mais curioso, ˉq- te- sabido. ... / Composto per Affõço de Villafanhe, Guiral, & Pacheco.* Lisbon: Geraldo da Vinha, 1624 ["Table of weights and measures from the above-stated kingdoms (Portugal, Castile, Aragon, Valencia)"]. Printed. Biblioteca Nacional de Portugal, Lisbon, Portugal. S.A. 2538 P., fol. 16v.-17. © Biblioteca Nacional de Portugal.

382 [*Official prices of several products on the Amsterdam Bourse*], March 3, 1636. Printed. Nederlandsch Economisch-Historisch Archief, Amsterdam, The Netherlands. Prijscouranten, AMS 1.01A-B. Collection International Institute of Social History, Amsterdam.

384 Dirk Stoop – *Terreiro do Paço in the Seventeenth Century,* 1662. Painting. Museu da Cidade, Lisbon, Portugal. MC.PIN.261. © Museu da Cidade – Câmara Municipal de Lisboa.

386 *Het Menselyk Bedryf. Vertoond, in. 100. Verbeeldingen: van: Ambachten, Konsten, Hanteeringen en Bedryven; met Versen. [...]* t'Amsterdam. / Gedaan; door; Johannes, en, Caspaares, Luiken, 1694[Making and selling scales]. Engraving. Universiteitsbibliotheek van de Universiteit van Amsterdam, Amsterdam, The Netherlands. Bijzondere Collecties, OTM: OG 80-36, p. 27. Special Collections, University of Amsterdam, OTM: OG 80-36, p. 27.

396 Pieter Brueghel, the Younger – *The Tax Collector* or *Village Lawyer,* 1621. Painting. Museum voor Schone Kunsten Gent, Gent, Belgium. Inventory no.: 1952-G. Museum of Fine Arts Ghent © Lukas-Art in Flanders vzw.

398 *Het Menselyk Bedryf. Vertoond, in. 100. Verbeeldingen: van: Ambachten, Konsten, Hanteeringen en Bedryven; met Versen. [...]* t'Amsterdam. / Gedaan; door; Johannes, en, Caspaares, Luiken, 1694 [The Merchant]. Engraving. Universiteitsbibliotheek van de Universiteit van Amsterdam, Amsterdam, The Netherlands. Bijzondere Collecties, OTM: OG 80-36, p. 97. Special Collections, University of Amsterdam, OTM: OG 80-36, p. 97.

400 Pieter Ruttens (not.) – Authenticated copy of a bill of exchange issued in Lisbon on September 9, 1617by Richarte Vaque (drawer) instructing Manuel Homem Vieira (drawee) to pay 300 cruzados(at 115 grotento the cruzado) "at usance" to Jerónimo Dória de Andrade (payee), the same amount Francisco Dias Vila Viçosa (deliverer) handed over to the drawer, Amsterdam – November 28, 1617. Manuscript. Stadsarchief Amsterdam, Amsterdam, The Netherlands. 5075: Archief van de Notarissen ter Standplaats Amsterdam, Pieter Ruttens, l. 611A, fol. 317v. © Stadsarchief Amsterdam.

401 Afonso Vilhafane Guiral e Pacheco –*Flor Da Arismetica Necessaria, vso dos cambios, & quilatador de ouro, & prata, o mais curioso, ˉq- te- sabido... / Composto per Affõço de Villafanhe, Guiral, & Pacheco.* Lisbon: Geraldo da Vinha, 1624 ["Rule for Multiplication."]. Printed. Biblioteca Nacional de Portugal, Lisbon, Portugal. S.A. 2538 P. , fol. 28. © Biblioteca Nacional de Portugal.

402 [Anonymous – Minted in Dordrecht] – *"Rekenpenning": copper counting token used in the Rebel Provinces,* 1587. Numismatics (coin). Geldmuseum, Utrecht, The Netherlands. Inventory no.: RP-03047. Geldmuseum.

409 Pieter Claesz – *"Vanitas": Still Life with the "Spinario,"* 1628. Painting. Rijksmuseum Amsterdam, Amsterdam, The Netherlands. SK-A-3930. Collection Rijksmuseum Amsterdam, The Netherlands.

412 Rembrandt van Rijn – *Portrait of Maria Trip (1619–1683),* 1639. Painting. Rijksmuseum Amsterdam, Amsterdam, The Netherlands. SK-C-597. Collection Rijksmuseum Amsterdam, The Netherlands.

414 Jan Fransz. Bruyningh (not.) – Manuel Fernandes de Leão, a resident of The Hague, transferred a bill-obligatory to Jan Colijn in payment of merchandise purchased from him; the seller undertook all risks regarding the bill-obligatory in the presence of the notary, Nicolaas de Witte of Leiden on December 16, 1600. In Amsterdam, a second notary, Jan Fransz. Bruyningh, recognized the seal of the first; and Manuel Fernandes de Leão confirmed the transfer, recording it in his own hand in the notary's book, Amsterdam –March 31, 1601. Manuscript. Stadsarchief Amsterdam, Amsterdam, The Netherlands. 5075: Archief van de Notarissen ter Standplaats Amsterdam, Jan Fransz. Bruyningh, l. 91, fol. 128v–129. © Stadsarchief Amsterdam.

415 Printed standardized contract for the purchase and sale of shares in the Dutch West India Company (WIC). The details of the shares transacted, of the parties and of the operation itself were filled in by hand, 1629–1630. Manuscript/Printed. Stadsarchief Amsterdam, Amsterdam, The Netherlands. Image no.: 005075000002_001. © Stadsarchief Amsterdam.

416-417 Claes Jansz. Visscher – [*The Amsterdam Bourse*]. [n.l.]: [n.n.], 1612. Engraving. Stadsarchief Amsterdam, Amsterdam, The Netherlands. Inventory no.: M 82-25 (Image no.: 010097012332). © Stadsarchief Amsterdam.

420 Jan Fransz. Bruyningh (not.) – Authenticated Certified manuscript copy of an excerpt from the account book of the merchant Manuel Rodrigues Vega, recording the sale of a load of woad to Hans Staes and Hans de Verne, and corroborated by the sworn testimony of Balthasar van Nispen and Joost Brest on behalf of the seller, Amsterdam, 1597. Manuscript. Stadsarchief Amsterdam, Amsterdam, The Netherlands. 5075: Archief van de Notarissen ter Standplaats Amsterdam, Jan Fransz. Bruyningh, l. 76, fol. 222. © Stadsarchief Amsterdam.

421 Jan Fransz. Bruyningh (not.) – Payment order issued by Gaspar Dias in Lisbon to Afonso Rodrigues Cardoso in Amsterdam instructing him to pay 166 pounds Flemish after deducting the amount paid for insurance to Alberto Velecker in Amsterdam, due to a settling settlement of accounts between Dias and a certain Harman Geraldez (Herman Gerritsz.), Amsterdam, 1611. Manuscript. Stadsarchief Amsterdam, Amsterdam, The Netherlands. 5075: Archief van de Notarissen ter Standplaats Amsterdam, Jan Fransz. Bruyningh, l. 125, fol. 134v.–135 (Image no.: A14967000135). © Stadsarchief Amsterdam.

422 J. Wildens (attrib.) – *Banker* [16--] [?]. Painting. Museu Nacional de Soares dos Reis, Porto, Portugal. Inventory no.: 13732 TC (Image no.: 610 Pin CMP/ MNSR). © IMC / MC. Photography: José Pessoa, 1995.

425 Cornelis Danckertsz. de Rij (cop.) – [*Ground plan of the former City Hall of Amsterdam*], 1639. Cartography (ground plan). Stadsarchief Amsterdam, Amsterdam, The Netherlands. Inventory no.: Spl. 261-M, deel I, abf. 162 (Image no.: 010001000677). © Stadsarchief Amsterdam.

426 [Anonymous] – *Chest and cart belonging to the Wisselbank in Amsterdam, used to transport money* [16--]. Equipment (money cart) / Furnishings (chest). Amsterdam Museum, Amsterdam, The Netherlands. Inventory no.: KB 1700 / KB 1706. © Amsterdam Museum.

428 Dirck Jacobsz. (attrib.) – *Portrait of a Merchant, supposedly Egbert Gerbrantsz., and his Wife,* 1541. Painting. Amsterdam Museum, Amsterdam, The Netherlands. Inventory no.: SA 84. © Amsterdam Museum.

436 Hans Holbein, the Younger – *The Merchant Georg Gisze,* 1532. Painting. Staatliche Museen zu Berlin – Gemaldegalerie, Berlin, Germany. Inventory no.: 586 (Image no.: 00012218). bpk / Gemäldegalerie, SMB / Jörg P. Anders.

438 [Narziß Renner] [?] – [Jacob Fugger (1459–1525) in the Office of his Chief Accountant, Matthäus Schwarz (1497–ca.1574)]. In Matthäus Schwarz, *Das Schwarzsche Trachtenbuch I* [1520–1561]. Illustration (miniature). Herzog Anton Ulrich-Museum, Braunschweig, Germany. H. 27, Nor. 67a, Bild 28. Herzog Anton Ulrich-Museums Braunschweig, Kunstmuseum des Landes Niedersachsen. Fotonachweis: Museumsfotograf.

441 [Anonymous – Made in Portuguese India (Cochin)] – *Chest: Detail showing paintings inside the lid* [1601–1650]. Furnishings (chest). Museu Nacional de Arte Antiga, Lisbon, Portugal. Inventory no.: 1658 Mov (Image no.: 22168.01 TC). © IMC / MC. Photography: José Pessoa, 2000.

443 [Anonymous – Made in Portuguese India (Cochin)] – *Angelim wood and tinplate chest* [1601–1650]. Furnishing (chest). Museu Nacional de Arte Antiga, Lisbon, Portugal. Inventory no.: 1658 Mov (Image no.: 22168 TC). © IMC / MC. Photography: José Pessoa, 2000.

444 Lucas van Valckenborch; Georg Flegel (attrib.) – *Allegory of Autumn: Saleswoman Serving Distinguished Customers in the Frankfurt Weinmarkt,* 1594. Painting. Rijksbureau voor Kunsthistorische Documentatie RKD / The Netherlands Institute for Art History (Department of Old Master Paintings and Drawings), The Hague, The Netherlands. Inventory no.: 70955 (Image no.: 0000114147). Private Collection (Belgium). Photo collection RKD, The Hague.

445 [Anonymous] – [*Gonçalo Gonçalves, the Younger, and his Wife, Maria Gonçalves, in seventeenth-century dress*], 1620. Painting. Santa Casa da Misericórdia do Rio de Janeiro – Galeria de Benfeitores, Rio de Janeiro, Brazil. No quota file. Santa Casa da Misericórdia do Rio de Janeiro.

449 Georg Paul Nussbiegel (engraver) – [*The famous display of saffron and other spices in the city of Nuremberg*], 1783. Engraving. Germanisches Nationalmuseum, Nuremberg, Germany. Inventory no.: HB 2510. Germanisches Nationalmuseum, Nürnberg.

450 Juan de Pareja – *The Calling of Matthew,* 1661. Painting. Museo Nacional del Prado, Madrid, Spain. P1041. © Museo Nacional del Prado.

456 Mathias von Somer (engraver) – [*The Education of a Young Merchant*] [ca. 1650]. Engraving. Germanisches Nationalmuseum, Nuremberg, Germany. Inventory no.: HB 10922. Germanisches Nationalmuseum, Nürnberg.

457 Jacob van Ruisdael – *The Damrak in Amsterdam* [ca. 1670]. Painting. The Frick Collection, New York, NY, United States of America. 1910.1.110. © The Frick Collection.

460 *Het Menselyk Bedryf. Vertoond, in. 100. Verbeeldingen: van: Ambachten, Konsten, Hanteeringen en Bedryven; met Versen. [...]* t'Amsterdam. / Gedaan; door; Johannes, en, Caspaares, Luiken, 1694 [The Sailor]. Engraving. Universiteitsbibliotheek van de Universiteit van Amsterdam, Amsterdam, The Netherlands. Bijzondere Collecties, OTM: OG 80-36, p. 94. Special Collections, University of Amsterdam, OTM: OG 80-36, p. 94.

462 Nicolaes Maes – *The Account Keeper,* 1656. Painting. Saint Louis Art Museum, Saint Louis, MO, United States of America. 72:1950. Saint Louis Art Museum, Museum Purchase 72:1950 – *The Account Keeper*, Nicolaes Maes, 1656 (oil on canvas).

464 Giuseppe Maria Mitelli (drawer and engraver) – *Where Gold Speaks, Every Tongue is Silent,* 1678. Engraving. Baker Library – Harvard Business School, Cambridge, MA, United States of America. Historical Collections, CA i2 x, olvwork308272. © Bleichroeder Print Collection, Kress Collection. Baker Library Historical Collections. Harvard Business School. olvwork308272.

467 Bernard Picart – [*Passover Seder of the Portuguese Jews*] [n.l.: n.n.], 1725. Biblioteca Nacional de Portugal, Lisbon, Portugal. Iconography, E. 1616 P. © Biblioteca Nacional de Portugal.

470-471 Francisco Rizi – *Auto-da-Fé in Plaza Mayor, Madrid,* 1683. Painting. Museo Nacional del Prado, Madrid, Spain. P01126. © Museo Nacional del Prado.

473 [Anonymous] – [*Auto-da-Fé in Terreiro do Paço, Lisbon*] [n.l.: n.n.] [17--] [?]. Engraving. Biblioteca Nacional de Portugal, Lisbon, Portugal. Iconography, E. 4669 P. © Biblioteca Nacional de Portugal.

474 Jan Veenhuysen (drawer) – *Interior of the Portuguese Synagogue in Amsterdam* [ca. 1660]. Engraving. Joods Historisch Museum, Amsterdam, The Netherlands. Inventory no.: 01431. Collection Jewish Historical Museum, Amsterdam.

476 *Burghers of the City of Amsterdam Taking Their Oath*. In Jacobus Noordkerk, *Verhandeling over poorterschap*. [n.l.: n.n.] [ca. 1690]. Printed. Stadsarchief Amsterdam, Amsterdam, The Netherlands. Biblioteek 15030: 100499 H1004. © Stadsarchief Amsterdam.

477 [*Marriage Contract ("Ketubbah") Between David Curiel and Rachel Curiel, residents of Amsterdam*], 1617. Manuscript. The Israel Museum, Jerusalem, Israel. B. 86_0153. The Stieglitz Collection was donated to the Israel Museum, Jerusalem with the contribution of Erica and Ludwig Jesselson, New York, through the American Friends of the Israel Museum. Photo © The Israel Museum, Jerusalem by Avi Ganor.

478 Cornelis van der Voort – *Portrait of Cornelis Pietersz Hooft (1547–1626)*, 1622. Painting. Amsterdam Museum, Amsterdam, The Netherlands. Inventory no.: SB 5824. Collection Amsterdam Museum, on loan from Rijksmuseum Amsterdam.

479 Rembrandt van Rijn – *Portrait of a Man Believed to Be Dr. Ephraim Bueno (1599–1665)* [ca. 1644]. Painting. Rijksmuseum Amsterdam, Amsterdam, The Netherlands. SK-A-3982. Collection Rijksmuseum Amsterdam, The Netherlands.

488 Adriaen van Ostade – *A Lawyer in His Study*, 168[?]. Painting. Museum Boijmans van Beuningen, Rotterdam, The Netherlands. 1637. Museum Boijmans Van Beuningen, Rotterdam (legacy F. J. O. Boymans).

490 Marinus van Reymerswaele – *In the Solicitor's Office*, 1542. Painting. Alte Pinakothek, Munich, Germany. ID imagem: 1484. © Blauel/Gnamm – ARTOTHEK: Marinus van Reymerswaele, Alte Pinakothek (München).

496 *Consvetvdo, Vel Lex Mercatoria, Or The Ancient Law-Merchant. Diuided into three Parts: According To The Essentiall Parts of Trafficke. Necessarie For All Statesmen, Iudges, Magistrates, Temporall and Ciuile Lawyers, Mint-men, Merchants, Marriners, and all others negotiating in all places of the World. / By Gerard Malynes Merchant*. London: Adam Islip, 1622. Printed. Bibliothèque Nationale de France, Paris, France. F-4668 [title page]. © Bibliothèque Nationale de France.

498-499 Bartholomeus van der Helst – *The Celebration of the Peace of Münster, 1648, at the Headquarters of the Crossbowmen's Civic Guard (St George guard), Amsterdam*, 1648. Painting. Rijksmuseum Amsterdam, Amsterdam, The Netherlands. SK-C-2. On loan from the Municipality of Amsterdam.

502 *Le Parfait négociant, ou Instruction générale pour ce qui regarde le commerce de toute sorte de marchandises, tant de France que des pays estrangers ... / par le sieur Jacques Savary*. Paris: L. Billaine, 1675. Printed. Bibliothèque Nationale de France, Paris, France. RESAC V-17348 [title page]. © Bibliothèque Nationale de France.

506 [Anonymous] – [*Plan of Amsterdam*] [ca. 1612–1614]. Cartography (plant: printed). Stadsarchief Amsterdam, Amsterdam, The Netherlands. Collectie Atlas Dreesmann (Image no.: 010094008027). © Stadsarchief Amsterdam.

507 Pier Maria Baldi – [View of Porto Seen from Gaia]. In *Viaje de Cosme de Médicis por España y Portugal (1668–1669) / Lorenzo Magalotti; Pier Maria Baldi (illust.)*. Compiled with notes by Angel Sánchez Rivero and Angela Mariutti de Sánchez Rivero. Madrid: Sucesores de Rivadeneyra [1933]. Print. Biblioteca Nacional de Portugal, Lisbon, Portugal. Iconography, E.A. 326 A, no. LXIV. © Biblioteca Nacional de Portugal.

508 [João Teixeira Albernaz, the Elder] – *Rezão. do Estado, do Brasil no gvoverno do Norte. só.me-te. asi. como, o teve. Dõ Diogvo, de Meneses. até o annõ, de 1612* [Chart: "Captaincy of Itamaraca."] [ca. 1616]. Cartography (nautical chart). Biblioteca Pública Municipal do Porto, Porto, Portugal. Reservados, MS 126 [102]. Belongs to the collections of the Biblioteca Pública Municipal do Porto.

508 [João Teixeira Albernaz, the Elder] – *Rezão. do Estado, do Brasil no gvoverno do Norte. só.me-te. asi. como, o teve. Dõ Diogvo, de Meneses. até o annõ, de 1612* [Chart: "Captaincy of Pernambuco."] [ca. 1616]. Cartography (nautical chart). Biblioteca Pública Municipal do Porto, Porto, Portugal. Reservados, MS 126 [84]. Belongs to the collections of the Biblioteca Pública Municipal do Porto.

508 [João Teixeira Albernaz, the Elder] – *Rezão. do Estado, do Brasil no gvoverno do Norte. só.me-te. asi. como, o teve. Dõ Diogvo, de Meneses. até o annõ, de 1612* [Chart: "TodososSantos Bay."] [ca. 1616]. Cartography (nautical chart). Biblioteca Pública Municipal do Porto, Porto, Portugal. Reservados, MS 126 [55]. Belongs to the collections of the Biblioteca Pública Municipal do Porto.

509 Cornelis Golijath (drawer); Claes Jansz. Visscher (engraver) – [*Depiction of the coast of Pernambuco, with plans of Olinda, the City of Mauricia* (Mauritsstad) *and Recife, and views of the Palace of Vrijburg* (Fribourg), *built by Johan Maurits of Nassau-Siegen*] [Amsterdam], 1648. Cartography (map/plan/perspective: printed). Nederlands Scheepvaartmuseum, Amsterdam, The Netherlands. A.3143(03). © Nederlands Scheepvaartmuseum.

510 João Teixeira Albernaz, the Elder – *Plan of the Recovery of Bahia*, 1631. Cartography (plan). Mapoteca do Ministério das Relações Exteriores – Itamaraty, Rio de Janeiro, Brazil. a 770 a -- 1631 A – 22. Mapoteca do Itamaraty.

511 Johannes Vingboons – [*Plan of Olinda*], 1665. Cartography (plan). Nationaal Archief, The Hague, The Netherlands. Kaartcollectie Buitenland Leupe, 4.VELH619-108. © Nationaal Archief, Den Haag.

512 Jacob Vrel – *Two Women in Conversation at a Doorway* [1650–1662]. Painting. Rijksbureau voor Kunsthistorische Documentatie RKD / The Netherlands Institute for Art History (Department of Old Master Paintings and Drawings), The Hague. The Netherlands. Inventory no.: 16921 (Image no.: 0000036496). Private Collection. Photo collection RKD, The Hague.

512 Nicolaes Maes – *The Listening Housewife (The Eavesdropper)*, 1656. Painting. The Wallace Collection, London, England. P224. By permission of the Trustees of The Wallace Collection, London.

513 Bartholomeus van der Helst – *The Company of Captain Roelof Bicker and Lieutenant Jan Michielsz Blaeuw in front of the De Haan brewery at the corner of the Geldersekade and the Boomsloot (called the Lastage)*, Amsterdam, 1639. Painting. Rijksmuseum Amsterdam, Amsterdam, The Netherlands. SK-C-375. On loan from the Municipality of Amsterdam.

514 Jan Abrahamsz. Beerstraaten –*The"Paalhuis" and "Nieuwe Brug" in Amsterdam in Winter* [1640–1666]. Painting. Rijksmuseum Amsterdam, Amsterdam, The Netherlands. SK-A-20. Collection Rijksmuseum Amsterdam, The Netherlands.

514-515 Pieter van der Keere – [*Amsterdam: Seen from the River IJ River*], Amsterdam, 1618. Cartography (perspective: printed). Stadsarchief Amsterdam, Amsterdam, The Netherlands. Image no.: 10097017213. © Stadsarchief Amsterdam.

516-517 Adriaen van Nieulandt – *Dam Square in 1604 during the Procession of Lepers during Koppertjesmaandag*,1633. Painting. Amsterdam Museum, Amsterdam, The Netherlands. Inventory no.: SA 3026. © Amsterdam Museum.

518 [*Official price-list for several products on the Amsterdam Bourse*], March 3, 1636. Printed. Nederlandsch Economisch-Historisch Archief, Amsterdam, The Netherlands. Prijscouranten, AMS 1.01A-B. Collection International Institute of Social History, Amsterdam.

519 Job Adriaensz. Berckheyde – *Courtyard of the Amsterdam Bourse Building*, 1670–1690. Painting. Amsterdam Museum, Amsterdam, The Netherlands. Inventory no.: SA 3025. © Amsterdam Museum.

523 [João Eanes Melacho] – *Crown Prince's House* ("Casa do Infante")*: Former Customs House of the City of Porto* (Alfândega Velha) [13–]. Civil architecture (customs house). Arquivo Histórico Municipal do Porto, Porto, Portugal. DSC 05307. © Arquivo Histórico Municipal do Porto, 2011. Câmara Municipal do Porto | Direcção Municipal da Cultura | Departamento Municipal de Arquivos.

523 [Anonymous] – [*Porto: São Domingos Square, Biquinha Fountain, Palma Alleyand Ponte de São DomingosStreet*] [17–]. Cartography (plan). Arquivo Histórico Municipal do Porto, Porto, Portugal. Livros de Plantas, MNL, 2/A 159 (D-CDT-A3-159). © Arquivo Histórico Municipal do Porto, 2011. Câmara Municipal do Porto | Direcção Municipal da Cultura | Departamento Municipal de Arquivos.

524-525 Teodoro de Sousa Maldonado (drawer); Manuel da Silva Godinho (engraver) – [Panoramic view of the city of Porto]. In *Descripção topografica, e historica da Cidade do Porto. Que contém a sua origem, situaçaõ, e antiguidades: a magnificencia dos seus templos, mosteiros, hospitaes, ruas, praças, edificios, e fontes ... / feita por Agostinho Rebello da Costa*. Porto: Antonio Alvarez Ribeiro, 1789. Cartography (perspective: printed). Biblioteca Nacional de Portugal, Lisbon, Portugal. Reservados, RES. 2031 P. [between pages XXXII and 1]. © Biblioteca Nacional de Portugal.

526 Cristóvão Álvares (attrib.) – *Profile of Salvador, showing the height of the city in relation to sea level* [ca. 1609–1616 (alternative: ca. 1638)]. Cartography (profile). Nationaal Archief, The Hague, The Netherlands. NL-HaNA-4.VEL2167. © Nationaal Archief, Den Haag.

527 [João Teixeira Albernaz, the Elder] – *Rezão. do Estado, do Brasil no gvoverno do Norte. só.me-te. asi. como, o teve. Dõ Diogvo, de Meneses. até o annõ, de 1612* ["Plan of the City of Salvador on Todos os Santos Bay"] [ca. 1616]. Cartography (plan). Biblioteca Pública Municipal do Porto, Porto, Portugal. Reservados, MS 126 [57]. Belongs to the collections of the Biblioteca Pública Municipal do Porto.

528 [Anonymous] – [View of Olinda]. In *Historie ofte iaerlijck verhael van de verrichtinghen der geoctroyeerde West-Indische Compagnie / Johannes de Laet* / Tot Leyden: Bonaventuer ende Abraham Elsevier, 1644. Cartography (perspective: printed). Koninklijke Bibliotheek, The Hague, The Netherlands. 40 E 7 [post. p. 184]. Den Haag, Koninklijke Bibliotheek, 40 E 7, [post. p. 184]. *Publisher's note: partial reproduction.*

530 Dierick Ruiters – [*Depiction of Olinda and Recife* [ca. 1617 (alternative: ca. 1630)]. Cartography (profile). Nationaal Archief, The Hague, The Netherlands. NL-HaNA-4.VEL710. © Nationaal Archief, Den Haag.

531 [Anonymous] – [View of Recife]. In *Historie ofte iaerlijck verhael van de verrichtinghen der geoctroyeerde West-Indische Compagnie / Johannes de Laet* / Tot Leyden: Bonaventuer ende Abraham Elsevier, 1644. Cartography (perspective: printed). Koninklijke Bibliotheek, The Hague, The Netherlands. 40 E 7 [post. p. 184]. Den Haag, Koninklijke Bibliotheek, 40 E 7, [post. p. 184]. *Publisher's note: partial reproduction.*

531 [João Teixeira Albernaz, the Elder] – *Rezão. do Estado, do Brasil no gvoverno do Norte. só.me-te. asi.como, o teve. Dõ Diogvo, de Meneses. até o annõ, de 1612* ["View of Recife and the Town of Olinda"] [ca. 1616]. Cartography (perspective). Collection Biblioteca Pública Municipal do Porto, Porto, Portugal. Reservados, MS 126 [88]. Belongs to the collections of the Biblioteca Pública Municipal do Porto.

534 Jacob Duck – *Elegant Company Smoking and Drinking in an Inn* or *A Bordello Scene* [ca. 1635]. Painting. Rijksbureau voor Kunsthistorische Documentatie RKD / The Netherlands Institute for Art History (Department of Old Master Paintings and Drawings), The Hague, The Netherlands. Inventory no.: 196998 (Image no.: 0000172745). Private Collection. Photo collection RKD, The Hague.

535 Johannes Vermeer – *Woman in Blue Reading a Letter* [ca. 1662–1665]. Painting. Rijksmuseum Amsterdam, Amsterdam, The Netherlands. SK-C-251. On long-term loan from the Municipality of Amsterdam (legacy A. van der Hoop).

Appendix I

Correspondence Table

Numbers of the series of notarial records published in the scholarly journal Studia Rosethaliana* *and the issues in which they have been published.*

Nos.	*Volume*	*Number*	*Year*	*Pages*
1–6	1	1	1967	111–115
7–36	—	2	—	110–122
37–85	2	1	1968	111–126
86–119	—	2	—	257–272
120–155	3	1	1969	113–125
156–223	—	2	—	234–254
224–268	4	1	1970	115–126
269–345	—	2	—	243–261
346–422	5	1	1971	106–124
423–536	—	2	—	219–245
537–600	6	1	1972	107–122
601–671	—	2	—	229–245
672–730	7	1	1973	116–127
731–797	—	2	—	266–279
798–839	8	1	1974	138–145
840–871	—	2	—	300–307
872–931	10	1	1976	95–104
932–1081	—	2	—	212–231
1082–1190	11	1	1977	81–96
1191–1259	—	2	—	216–227
1260–1383	12	1	1978	158–179
1384–1473	13	1	1979	101–114
1474–1607	—	2	—	220–240
1608–1753	14	1	1980	79–102
1754–1821	15	1	1981	143–154
1822–1881	—	2	—	245–255
1882–2013	16	1	1982	61–84
2014–2125	—	2	—	196–218
2126–2200	17	1	1983	66–79
2201–2243	—	2	—	210–217
2244–2312	18	1	1984	61–73
2313–2393	—	2	—	159–176
2394–2448	19	1	1985	79–90
2449–2499	—	2	—	174–184
2500–2600	20	1	1986	109–130
2601–2657	21	1	1987	105–115
2658–2688	—	2	—	198–203
2689–2739	22	1	1988	58–67
2740–2775	—	2	—	189–196
2776–2815	23	1	1989	110–117
2816–2850	—	2	—	203–209
2851–2900	24	1	1990	68–77
2901–2950	—	2	—	216–225
2951–3000	25	1	1991	107–118
3001–3052	—	2	—	176–189
3053–3099	27	1 & 2	1993	171–181
3100–3149	—	2	—	204–215
3150–3199	29	1	1995	100–112
3200–3270	—	2	—	214–230
3271–3326	30	2	1996	304–318
3327–3384	31	1 & 2	1997	139–151
3385–3427	32	1	1998	82–94
3428–3452	—	2	—	210–216
3453–3498	33	1	1999	80–94
3499–3544	34	1	2000	74–88
3546–3642	35	1	2001	67–92

* "Notarial Records [Deeds] in Amsterdam relating to the Portuguese Jews in that town up to 1639," published by W. C. Pieterse and E. M. Koen. In: *Studia Rosenthaliana.*

Appendix II

Institutions that collaborated with this study

AUSTRIA

Kunsthistorisches Museum Wien
Österreichische Nationalbibliothek

BELGIUM

Collections artistiques de l'Université de Liège
Musées Royaux des Beaux-Arts de Belgique
Museum voor Schone Kunsten Gent
Universiteitsbibliotheek Ghent

BRAZIL

Fundação Biblioteca Nacional
Instituto Arqueológico, Histórico e Geográfico Pernambucano
Instituto Histórico e Geográfico Brasileiro
Instituto Ricardo Brennand
Mapoteca do Ministério das Relações Exteriores – Itamaraty
Museu Histórico Nacional
Museu do Homem do Nordeste
Museu Nacional de Belas Artes
Pinacoteca do Convento Franciscano de Santo Antônio (Igarassu, PE)
Santa Casa da Misericórdia do Rio de Janeiro

DENMARK

Det Kongelige Bibliotek – The Royal Library
Nationalmuseet København – National Museum of Denmark
Statens Museum for Kunst – National Gallery of Denmark

ENGLAND

Guildhall Art Gallery
National Maritime Museum
Royal Armouries Library
The British Library
The Mercer's Company
The National Archives
The Wallace Collection
Victoria and Albert Museum

FRANCE

Bibliothèque Nationale de France
Musée du Louvre

GERMANY

Alte Pinakothek / Bayerische Staatsgemäldesammlungen
Bayerische Staatsbibliothek
Dresdner Kupferstich-Kabinett (Staatliche Kunstsammlungen Dresden)
Gemäldegalerie Alte Meister Dresden
Germanisches Nationalmuseum
Herzog Anton Ulrich-Museum (Braunschweig)
Rosgartenmuseum Konstanz
Sächsische Landesbibliothek / Staats und Universitätsbibliothek Dresden
Staatliche Museen zu Berlin Gemäldegalerie
Staatsgalerie in der Katharinenkirche
Staatsgalerie Stuttgart

Städel Museum / Städelsches Kunstinstitut (Frankfurt am Main)
Stiftung Preußische Schlösser und Gärten Berlin-Brandenburg, Schlossmuseum Oranienburg

ISRAEL

The Israel Museum

ITALY

Biblioteca Casanatense
Biblioteca Estense Universitária
Biblioteca Nazionale Centrale di Firenze
Biblioteca Reale di Torino
Castelo de Issogne

MALTA

Malta Maritime Museum

NETHERLANDS

Amsterdam Museum
Atlas van Stolk / Museum Het Schielandshuis
Dordrechts Museum / Huis Van Gijn
Fries Scheepvaart Museum
Geldmuseum Utrecht
Gemeentearchief Rotterdam
Instituut Collectie Nederland / Rijksdienst voor het Cultureel Erfgoed
Joods Historisch Museum
Koninklijke Bibliotheek
Maritiem Museum Rotterdam
Museum Boijmans Van Beuningen
Museum Het Prinsenhof
Museum Meermanno-Westreenianum
Nationaal Archief
Nederlands Scheepvaartmuseum
Nederlandsch Economisch-Historisch Archief
Rijksbureau voor Kunsthistorische Documentatie RKD / Department of Old Master Paintings and Drawings
Rijksmuseum Amsterdam
Stadsarchief Amsterdam
Stedelijk Museum Het Prinsenhof
Universiteitsbibliotheek van de Universiteit van Amsterdam
Vereniging Vrienden van Amsterdamse Gevelstenen

POLAND

Muzeum Narodowe w Warszawie – The National Museum in Warsaw

PORTUGAL

Arquivo Distrital de Lisboa
Arquivo Distrital do Porto
Arquivo Histórico Municipal de Coimbra
Arquivo Histórico Municipal do Porto
Arquivo Histórico Ultramarino
Arquivo Municipal de Viana do Castelo
Arquivo Nacional da Torre do Tombo
Biblioteca da Academia das Ciências de Lisboa
Biblioteca da Ajuda
Biblioteca Nacional de Portugal
Biblioteca Pública Municipal do Porto
Casa-Museu Dr. Anastácio Gonçalves
Casa-Museu Frederico de Freitas (Madeira)
Centro de Estudos de Arqueologia Moderna e Contemporânea (Sta. Cruz – Madeira)
Gabinete de Arqueologia e Restauro da Câmara Municipal do Funchal (Madeira)
Igreja do Convento de São Domingos, Paróquia de N. Sra. de Monserrate (Viana do Castelo)
Museu Arqueológico do Carmo
Museu da Cidade (Lisboa)
Museu da Farmácia
Museu de Aveiro
Museu do Banco de Portugal
Museu Militar de Lisboa
Museu Municipal de Évora
Museu Municipal de Santarém
Museu Nacional de Arte Antiga
Museu Nacional de Soares dos Reis
Museu Nacional dos Coches
Museu Numismático Português (IN/CM)
Museu-Biblioteca Condes de Castro Guimarães
Palácio Nacional da Ajuda
Sociedade de Geografia de Lisboa

SCOTLAND

People's Palace (Glasgow)

SPAIN

Archivo General de Simancas
Associación Amigos de la Casa de la Moneda de Segovia
Biblioteca Nacional de España
Instituto Geográfico Nacional
Museo Casa de la Moneda
Museo Nacional del Prado
Museo Thyssen-Bornemisza

SWITZERLAND

Braginsky Collection

TURKEY

Topkapı Sarayı Müzesi – Topkapi Palace Museum

UNITED STATES OF AMERICA

Harvard Business School / The Baker Library
John Carter Brown Library at Brown University
Los Angeles County Museum of Art
Museum of Fine Arts (Boston)
National Gallery of Art
Saint Louis Art Museum
The Frick Collection
The Getty Research Institute
The Library Company of Philadelphia
The Metropolitan Museum of Art
Worcester Art Museum

Bibliography

Manuscript Sources

Archives and Collections

Arquivos Nacionais – Torre do Tombo (Lisbon)
Corpo Cronológico
Santo Ofício: Inquisição de Coimbra e Inquisição de Lisboa

Arquivo Histórico Ultramarino (Lisbon)
Conselho Ultramarino: Documentos Avulsos: Brasil – Bahia – Luísa da Fonseca
Códices (Administração Central)

Biblioteca da Ajuda (Lisbon)
Códices

Biblioteca Nacional de Portugal (Lisbon)
Biblioteca Nacional Digital
Reservados

Arquivo Distrital do Porto (Porto)
Notariais: PO1, 3ª série; PO2, série única; PO4, série única.
Cabido
Judiciais: Tribunal da Comarca do Porto, Tribunal da Relação do Porto

Arquivo Histórico Municipal do Porto (Porto)
Câmara Municipal (Actas)
Organização Antiga

Stadsarchief Amsterdam (Amsterdam)
Archief van de Notarissen ter Standplaats Amsterdam
Archief van S. Hart

Nationaal Archief (The Hague)
Staten-Generaal: Liassen e Loketkas

Gemeentearchief Rotterdam (Rotterdam)
Oud Notarieel Archief

The National Archives (London)
Public Record Office: State Paper Office

Archivo General de Simancas (Simancas)
Secretarías Provinciales: Consejo de Portugal

Bibliography

Printed Sources and Literature

A ALFÂNDEGA do Porto e o despacho aduaneiro. Exposição organizada pelo Arquivo Histórico Municipal do Porto. Porto: Casa do Infante, 1990.

ABREU E BRITO, Domingos de. *Um inquérito à vida administrativa e económica de Angola e do Brasil em fins do século XVI. Segundo o manuscrito inédito existente na Biblioteca Nacional de Lisboa*. Revised, with a preface by Alfredo de Albuquerque Felner. Coimbra: Imprensa da Universidade, 1931.

AFONSO, José Ferrão. "Manuel Luís, um contributo para a história de um mestre-pedreiro quinhentista." Offprint of: *Museu*, 4th series, no. 6, 1997.

AFONSO, José Ferrão. "A construção de um novo centro cívico: notas para a história da Rua Nova e da zona ribeirinha do Porto no séc. XVI." Offprint of: *Museu*, 4th series, no. 9, 2000.

AFONSO, José Ferrão. *A Rua das Flores no século XVI: elementos para a história urbana do Porto quinhentista*. Porto: Faup, 2000.

AFONSO, José Ferrão. "A Igreja e a criação de uma paisagem urbana institucional. A envolvente da Sé do Porto no século XVI." *Douro: estudos & documentos* 11, no. 20 (2005): 153–209.

AFONSO, José Ferrão. "Sobre um possível Hekhal: aspectos do urbanismo e arquitectura do Olival e da Vitória no Porto (sécs. XIV–XIX)." Offprint of: *Humanística e Teologia* 57 (2006).

AFONSO, José Ferrão. "A imagem tem que saltar ou o rebate dos signos. A cidade episcopal e o Porto intramuros no século XVI. Propriedade, ritual, representação e forma urbana (1499–1606)." 3 v. PhD dissertation, Universitat Politècnica de Catalunya, 2008.

AFONSO, José Ferrão. "A Praça da Ribeira no Porto: da Baixa Idade Média aos Almadas. Parte I: antes da praça." *Museu*, 4th series, no. 17 (2008–2009): 81 ff.

ALBERTO, Edite Maria da Conceição Martins. "As instituições de resgate de cativos em Portugal: sua estruturação e evolução no século XV." 2 v. Master's thesis, Universidade Nova de Lisboa, 1994.

ALBUQUERQUE, Luís de. *O tratado de Tordesilhas e as dificuldades técnicas da sua aplicação rigorosa*. Lisbon: Junta de Investigações do Ultramar, 1973.

ALBUQUERQUE, Luís de (ed.). *Portugal no mundo*. 6 v. Lisbon: Alfa, 1989.

ALBUQUERQUE, Luís de and DOMINGUES, Francisco Contente (eds.). *Dicionário de história dos descobrimentos portugueses*. 2 v. Lisbon: Círculo de Leitores, 1994.

ALENCASTRO, Luiz Felipe de. *O trato dos viventes: formação do Brasil no Atlântico Sul*. 1st ed. São Paulo: Companhia das Letras, 2000.

ALGRANTI, Leila Mezan. "Famílias e vida doméstica." In: NOVAIS, Fernando A. (ed.). *História da vida privada no Brasil*. V. 1. São Paulo: Companhia das Letras, 1997, pp. 83–154.

ALGRANTI, Leila Mezan. "Alimentação, saúde e sociabilidade: a arte de conservar e confeitar os frutos (séculos XV–XVIII)." *História: Questões & Debates: Revista do Departamento de História da UFPR*, no. 42 (2005): 33–52.

ALGRANTI, Leila Mezan. "Os doces na culinária luso-brasileira: da cozinha dos conventos à cozinha da casa 'brasileira,' séculos XVII a XIX." *Anais de história de além-mar: Revista da Faculdade de Ciências Sociais e Humanas da Universidade Nova de Lisboa* 6 (2005): 139–158.

ALLEN, Paul C. *Felipe III y la pax hispanica, 1598–1621. El fracasso de la gran estrategia*. Madrid: Alianza Editorial, 2001.

ALLOZA APARICIO, Angel. "La Junta de Almirantazgo y la lucha contra el contrabando, 1625–1643." *Espacio, Tiempo y Forma, 4th series: Historia Moderna* 16 (2003): 217–254.

ALMEIDA AMARAL, C. M. *Catálogo descritivo das moedas portuguesas*. T. 1. Lisbon: Imprensa Nacional – Casa da Moeda, 1977.

ALMEIDA, André Ferrand de. "As Misericórdias." In: MATTOSO, José (ed.). *História de Portugal*. V. 3. Lisbon: Editorial Estampa, 1997, pp. 169–176.

ALMEIDA, António Augusto Marques de. *Aritmética como descrição do real (1519–1679)*. 2 v. Lisbon: Comissão Nacional para as Comemorações dos Descobrimentos Portugueses, 1994.

ALMEIDA, António Augusto Marques de (ed.). *Dicionário histórico dos sefarditas portugueses: mercadores e gente de trato*. Lisbon: Campo da Comunicação, 2009.

ALMEIDA, Suely Cordeiro de. "Noivas de Adão e noivas de Cristo. Sedução, casamento e dotação feminina no Pernambuco colonial." *Varia História: Revista do Departamento de História da UFMG*, no. 31 (Jan. 2004): 221–241.

ANDRADE, Amélia Aguiar. "Novos espaços, antigas estratégias: o enquadramento dos espaços orientais." In: ANDRADE, Amélia Aguiar, *A construção medieval do território*. Lisbon: Livros Horizonte, 2001, pp. 117–129.

ANDRADE E SILVA, José Justino de. *Collecção chronologica da legislação portugueza*. 10 v. Lisbon: Impr. de J. J. A. Silva, 1854–1859.

ANDREWS, Kenneth R. *Elizabethan Privateering. English Privateering during the Spanish War, 1585–1603*. Cambridge: Cambridge University Press, 1964.

ANTONIL, André João. *Cultura e opulência do Brasil por suas drogas e minas*. Introduction and notes by Andrée Mansuy Diniz Silva. São Paulo: Edusp, 2007.

ANTUNES, Cátia. *Globalisation in the Early Modern Period*. Amsterdam: Aksant, 2004.

ARAGÃO, A. C. Teixeira de. *Descripção geral e historica das moedas cunhadas em nome dos reis, regentes e governadores de Portugal*. T. 2. Lisbon: Imprensa Nacional, 1877.

ARNAUT, Salvador Dias. *A arte de comer em Portugal na Idade Média*. Sintra: Colares Editora, 2000.

ARONSON, Marc and BUDHOS, Marina. *Sugar Changed the World: A Story of Magic, Spice, Slavery, Freedom and Science*. New York: Clarion Books, 2010.

ARRAIS, Raimundo Pereira Alencar. *O pântano e o riacho: a formação do espaço público no Recife do século XIX*. São Paulo: Humanitas 2004.

AYMARD, Maurice (ed.). *Dutch Capitalism and World Capitalism*. Cambridge: Cambridge University Press, 1982.

AZEVEDO, João Lúcio de (ed.). *Cartas do Padre Antonio Vieira*. V. 3. Coimbra: Imprensa da Universidade, 1928.

AZEVEDO, João Lúcio de. *Épocas de Portugal económico*. Lisbon: Clássica Editora 1988.

AZEVEDO, João Lúcio de. *História dos cristãos-novos portugueses*. Lisbon: Clássica Editora Distribuição, 1989.

BAER, Yitzhak. *A History of the Jews in Christian Spain*. 2 v. Philadelphia: Jewish Publication Society, 1992.

BAERS, João. *Olinda conquistada*. Translated by Alfredo de Carvalho. Recife: Secretaria de Educação e Cultura, 1977.

BAIÃO, António, CIDADE, Hernani and MÚRIAS, Manuel (eds.). *História da expansão portuguesa no mundo*. 3 v. Lisbon: Ática, 1937.

BAKKER, Boudewijn. "De zichtbare stad 1578–1813." In: FRIJHOFF, Willem and PRAK, Maarten, *Geschiedenis van Amsterdam, deel II-A: centrum van de wereld 1578–1650*. Amsterdam: SUN, 2004, pp. 17–102.

BARATA, Maria do Rosário Themudo. "A União Ibérica e o mundo atlântico: 1580 e o processo político português." In: VENTURA, Maria da Graça A. M. (ed.). *A União Ibérica e o mundo atlântico*. Lisbon: Edições Colibri, 1997, pp. 47–64.

BARBIERI, Rosa L. and STUMPF, Elisabeth R. T. "Origem, evolução e história das rosas cultivadas." *Revista Brasileira de Agrociência* 11, no. 4 (Jul–Sep. 2005): 267–271.

BARBOSA, Pedro Gomes. *Reconquista cristã: séculos IX–XII*. Lisbon: Ésquilo, 2008.

BARBOUR, Violet. "Dutch and English Merchant Shipping in the Seventeenth Century." *The Economic History Review* 2, no. 2 (Jan. 1930): 261–290.

BARBOUR, Violet. *Capitalism in Amsterdam in the 17th Century*. Ann Arbor: University of Michigan Press, 1963.

BARROS, Amândio Jorge Morais. "Porto: a construção de um espaço marítimo nos alvores dos tempos modernos." 2 v. PhD dissertation, Universidade do Porto, 2004.

BARROS, Amândio Jorge Morais. *Vinhos de escala e negócios das ilhas: para uma longa história das relações do Porto com os arquipélagos atlânticos no século XVI*. Porto: Grupo de Estudos História da Viticultura Duriense e do Vinho do Porto da Faculdade de Letras da Universidade do Porto, 2004.

BASTO, Artur de Magalhães. *Os portuenses no Renascimento*. Gaia: Pátria, 1931.

BASTO, Artur de Magalhães. "Os diversos paços do concelho da cidade do Porto." In: *Vereaçoens: anos de 1390–1395*. Commentary and notes by Artur de Magalhães Basto. Porto: CMP/GHC [n. d.]. (Documentos e Memórias para a História do Porto, V. 2).

BERGER, Paulo; WINZ, Antônio Pimentel and GUEDES, Max Justo. "Incursões de corsários e piratas na costa do Brasil." In: *História naval brasileira*, V. 1, T. 2. Rio de Janeiro: Serviço de Documentação Geral da Marinha, 1975, pp. 473–521.

BETHENCOURT, Francisco and CHAUDHURI, Kirti (eds.). *História da expansão portuguesa*. 5 v. Lisbon: Círculo de Leitores, 1998–1999.

BETHENCOURT, Francisco. *História das inquisições: Portugal, Espanha e Itália, séculos XV–XIX*. São Paulo: Companhia das Letras, 2000.

BETHENCOURT, Francisco. "A Inquisição." In: AZEVEDO, Carlos A. Moreira de (ed.). *História religiosa de Portugal*. V. 2. Lisbon: Círculo de Leitores, 2000, pp. 95–131.

BETHENCOURT, Francisco. "Rejeições e polémicas." In: AZEVEDO, Carlos A. Moreira de (ed.). *História religiosa de Portugal*. V. 2. Lisbon: Círculo de Leitores, 2000, pp. 45–93.

BLUTEAU, Raphael. *Vocabulario portuguez & latino*. 8 v. Coimbra: Collegio das Artes da Companhia de Jesus, 1712–1728.

BODIAN, Miriam. *Hebrews of the Portuguese Nation: Conversos and Community in Early Modern Amsterdam*. Bloomington: Indiana University Press, 1999.

BONNICHON, Philipe and FERREZ, Gilberto. "A França Antártica." In: *História naval brasileira*. V. 1, T. 2. Rio de Janeiro: Serviço de Documentação Geral da Marinha, 1975, pp. 403–471.

BONNICHON, Philipe and GUEDES, Max Justo. "A França Equinocial." In: *História naval brasileira*. V. 1, T. 2. Rio de Janeiro: Serviço de Documentação Geral da Marinha, 1975, pp. 523–586.

BORGES, José Ferreira. *Fontes, especialidade, e excellencia da administração commercial. Segundo o Código Commercial Portuguez*. Porto: Typ. Commercial Portuense, 1835.

BOUZA ÁLVAREZ, Fernando. "Portugal en la política internacional de Felipe II: por el suelo el mundo en pedazos." In: VENTURA, Maria da Graça A. M. (ed.). *A União Ibérica e o Mundo Atlântico*. Lisbon: Edições Colibri, 1997, pp. 29–46.

BOUZA ÁLVAREZ, Fernando. *Portugal no tempo dos Filipes: política, cultura, representações (1580–1668)*. Lisbon: Edições Cosmos, 2000.

BOUZA ÁLVAREZ, Fernando. *Filipe I*. Lisbon: Círculo de Leitores, 2005.

BOXER, Charles Ralph. *The Dutch in Brazil, 1624–1654*. Oxford: Clarendon Press, 1957.

BOXER, Charles Ralph. *The Dutch Seaborne Empire, 1600–1800*. New York: Knopf, 1965.

BOXER, Charles Ralph. *The Portuguese Seaborne Empire, 1415–1825*. London: Hutchinson, 1969.

BOYAJIAN, James C. *Portuguese Trade in Asia under the Habsburgs, 1580–1626*. Baltimore: Johns Hopkins University Press, 1993.

BOYAJIAN, James C. "New Christians and Jews in the Sugar Trade, 1550–1750: Two Centuries of Development of the Atlantic Economy." In: BERNARDINI, Paulo and FIERING, Norman (eds.). *The Jews and the Expansion of Europe to the West, 1450–1800*. New York: Berghahn Books, 2001, pp. 471–484.

BRAGA, Isabel M. R. Mendes Drumond. *Entre a cristandade e o islão (séculos XV–XVII): cativos e renegados nas franjas de duas sociedades em confronto*. Ceuta: Instituto de Estudios Ceutíes, 1998.

BRAGA, Isabel M. R. Mendes Drumond. "Vaidades nos conventos femininos ou das dificuldades em deixar a vida mundana (séculos XVII–XVIII)." *Revista de História da Sociedade e da Cultura* 10, t. 1 (2010): 305–322.

BRANDÃO, Ambrósio Fernandes. *Diálogos das grandezas do Brasil*. Introduced and edited by José Antônio Gonsalves de Mello, with a preface by Leonardo Dantas Silva. Recife: Editora Massangana, 1997.

BRANDÃO, João. *Grandeza e abastança de Lisboa em 1552*. Compiled and annotated by José da Felicidade Alves. Lisbon: Livros Horizonte, 1990.

BRAUDEL, Fernand. *O Mediterrâneo e o mundo mediterrânico na época de Filipe II*. 2 v. São Paulo: Martins Fontes, 1983.

BRAUDEL, Fernand. *Civilização material, economia e capitalismo*. 3 v. São Paulo: Martins Fontes, 1996.

BRITO, Pedro de. *Patriciado urbano quinhentista: as famílias dominantes do Porto (1500–1580)*. Porto: Arquivo Histórico, Câmara Municipal do Porto, 1997.

BRUIJN, J. R. "Scheepvaart en overheid omstreeks 1600." In: LESGER, Clé and NOORDEGRAAF, Leo (eds.). *Ondernemers & Bestuurders*. Amsterdam: NEHA, 1999,pp. 77–84.

BUESCU, Mircea. *História econômica do Brasil: pesquisas e análises*. Rio de Janeiro: Apec Editora S.A., 1970.

BURGON, John William. *The Life and Times of Sir Thomas Gresham, Knt., Founder of the Royal Exchange*. Published by Effingham Wilson. V. 2. London: Royal Exchange, 1839.

BURT, Ronald S. *Structural Holes: The Social Structure of Competition*. Cambridge, Mass.: Harvard University Press, 1992.

BURT, Ronald S. "Structural Holes versus Network Closure as Social Capital." In: LIN, Nan, COOK, Karen and BURT, Ronald S. (eds.). *Social Capital: Theory and Research*. New York: Aldine de Gruyter, 2001.

CAMERON, Rondo. *Concise Economic History of the World, from Paleolithic Times to the Present*. 3rd ed. New York: Oxford University Press, 1997.

CANABRAVA, Alice Piffer. *O comércio português no Rio da Prata (1580–1640)*. Belo Horizonte: Editora Itatiaia, 1984.

CARANDE, Ramón. *Carlos V y sus banqueros: la vida económica en Castilla (1516–1556)*. V. 1. Madrid: Sociedad de Estudios y Publicaciones, 1965.

CARDIM, Fernão. *Tratados da terra e gente do Brasil*. Transcription, introduction and notes by Ana Maria de Azevedo. Lisbon: Comissão Nacional para as Comemorações dos Descobrimentos Portugueses, 2000.

CAROLLO, Denise Helena Monteiro de Barros. "A política inquisitorial na restauração portuguesa e os cristãos-novos." Master's thesis, Universidade de São Paulo, 1995.

CAROLLO, Denise Helena Monteiro de Barros. "Homens de negócio cristãos-novos portugueses e a transformação do Antigo Regime." 2 v. PhD dissertation, Universidade de São Paulo, 2001.

CARVALHO, Filipe Nunes. "Da instituição das capitanias-donatárias ao estabelecimento do Governo-Geral." In: JOHNSON, Harold and SILVA, Maria Beatriz Nizza da (eds.). *Nova história da expansão portuguesa. V. 6: O Império luso-brasileiro, 1500–1620*. Lisbon: Editorial Estampa, 1992, pp. 114–136.

CARVALHO, Susana Maria Vaz. "Viana seiscentista: a visita inquisitorial de 1618." Master's thesis, Universidade do Porto, 2000.

CASTELO-BRANCO, Fernando. "A influência portuguesa na culinária japonesa." In: CARNEIRO, Roberto and MATOS, Artur Teodoro de (eds.). *O século cristão do Japão. Actas do Colóquio Comemorativo dos 450 anos de Amizade Portugal-Japão*. Lisbon: Centro de Estudos dos Povos e Culturas de Expressão Portuguesa – Instituto de História de Além-Mar, 1994, pp. 617–627.

CAVALCANTI, Vanildo Bezerra. *Recife do Corpo Santo*. Recife: Prefeitura Municipal do Recife, 1977.

CAVALCANTI, Vanildo Bezerra. *Olinda do Salvador do mundo*. Recife: ASA Pernambuco, 1986.

CECCARELLI, Giovanni. "Risky Business: Theological and Canonical Thought on Insurance from the Thirteenth to the Seventeenth Century." *Journal of Medieval and Early Modern Studies* 31, no. 3 (Fall 2001): 607–658.

CERVANTES SAAVEDRA, Miguel de. *El ingenioso hidalgo don Quijote de la Mancha*. Commentary by Diego Clemencin. Part 2, T. 5. Madrid: Oficina de D. E. Aguado, 1836.

CHAHON, Sérgio. *Os convidados para a ceia do Senhor: as missas e a vivência leiga do catolicismo na cidade do Rio de Janeiro e arredores (1750–1820)*. São Paulo: Edusp, 2008.

CHENEY, Liana de Girolami (ed.). *The Symbolism of Vanitas in the Arts, Literature, and Music: Comparative and Historical Studies* (Studies in Comparative Literature). Lewiston: Edwin Wellen Press, 1992.

COARACY, Vivaldo. *O Rio de Janeiro no século XVII*. Rio de Janeiro: Livraria José Olympio Editora, 1965.

COELHO, António Borges. *Inquisição de Évora (1533–1668)*. Lisbon: Editorial Caminho, 2002.

COINDREAU, Roger. *Les corsaires de Salé*. Preface by Henri Bosco. Paris: Société d'Éditions Géographiques, Maritimes et Coloniales, 1948.

COLEMAN, James S. "Social Capital in the Creation of Human Capital." *The American Journal of Sociology* 94: *Supplement: Organizations and Institutions: Sociological and Economic Approaches to the Analysis of Social Structure* (1988): S95–S120.

CONSIGLIERI, Carlos and ABEL, Marília. *A tradição conventual na doçaria de Lisboa*. Sintra: Colares Editora, 1999.

CONSTITUIÇOENS synodaes do Arcebispado de Braga, ordenadas no anno de 1639 pelo Illustrissimo Senhor arcebispo D. Sebastião de Matos e Noronha e mandadas imprimir a primeira vez pelo illustrissimo senhor D. João de Sousa, arcebispo e senhor de Braga, primaz das Espanhas, do Conselho de Sua Magestade, e seu Sumilher da Cortina, &c. Lisbon: Na Officina de Miguel Deslandes, 1697.

COOK, Harold J. *Matters of Exchange: Commerce, Medicine, and Science in the Dutch Golden Age*. New Haven: Yale University Press, 2007.

CORRESPONDÊNCIA do governador Dom Diogo de Meneses: 1608–1612. Anais da Fundação Biblioteca Nacional, publicados sob a administração do diretor Rodolfo Garcia, Rio de Janeiro 57 (1935): 29–81.

CORTESÃO, Jaime. *História dos descobrimentos portugueses*. 3 v. Lisbon: Círculo de Leitores, 1978–1979.

CORTESÃO, Jaime. *História da expansão portuguesa*. Lisbon: Imprensa Nacional-Casa da Moeda, 1993 (Obras Completas 4).

COSTA, João Paulo Oliveira e. *Portugal e o Japão: o século namban*. Lisbon: Imprensa Nacional-Casa da Moeda, 1993.

COSTA, Leonor Freire. "Redes interportuárias nos circuitos do açúcar brasileiro. O trajecto de Gaspar Pacheco, um banqueiro de D. João IV." In: CUNHA, Mafalda Soares da (ed.). *Do Brasil à métropole: efeitos sociais*. Évora: Universidade de Évora, 2001, pp. 15–46.

COSTA, Leonor Freire. *O transporte no Atlântico e a Companhia Geral do Comércio do Brasil (1580–1663)*. 2 v. Lisbon: Comissão Nacional para a Comemoração dos Descobrimentos Portugueses, 2002.

COSTA, Leonor Freire. "Informação e incerteza: gerindo os riscos do negócio colonial." *Ler História* 44 (2003): 103–125.

COSTA, Leonor Freire. "Merchant Groups in the Seventeenth-Century Brazilian Sugar Trade. Reappraising Old Topics with New Research Insights." *E-Journal of Portuguese History* 2, no. 1 (Summer 2004): 1–11; http://www.brown. edu/Departments/Portuguese_Brazilian_Studies/ejph/html/issue3/pdf/lfcosta.pdf

COSTA, Marisa. "Os ourives na Lisboa de Quatrocentos." In: KRUS, Luís, OLIVEIRA, Luís Felipe and FONTES, João Luís (eds.). *Lisboa Medieval – Os rostos da cidade*. Lisbon: Livros Horizonte, 2007, pp. 288–314.

COSTA, Paula Maria de Carvalho Pinto. "Ordens militares e fronteira: um desempenho militar, jurisdicional e político em tempos medievais." *História: Revista da Faculdade de Letras da Universidade do Porto*, 3rd series, 7 (2006): 79–91.

COSTA, Uriel da. *Exame das tradições farisaicas. Acrescentado com Samuel da Silva, Tratado da imortalidade da alma*. Introduction, notes and genealogical charts by Herman Prins Salomon and Isaac S. D. Sassoon. Braga: Editora APPACDM Distrital de Braga, 1995.

COUTO, Cristiana. *Arte de cozinha: alimentação e dietética em Portugal e no Brasil (séculos XVII–XIX)*. São Paulo: Editora Senac São Paulo, 2007.

COUTO, Diogo do. *Decadas da Asia, que tratam dos mares, que descobriram, armadas, que desbarataraõ, exercitos, que venceraõ, e das acçoens heroicas, e façanhas bellicas, que obraraõ os portuguezes nas conquistas do Oriente*. V. 3, década IX. Lisbon: Domingos Gonsalves, 1736.

COUTO, Diogo do. *O soldado prático*. Critical edition, preface and notes by M. Rodrigues Lapa. Lisbon: Livraria Sá da Costa, 1954.

COUTO, Jorge. "O conflito luso-francês pelo domínio do Brasil até 1580." Offprint of: *Actas dos Segundos Cursos Internacionais de Verão de Cascais, 17 A 22 de Julho de 1995* 1 (1996): 113–138.

COUTO, Jorge. *A construção do Brasil*. Lisbon: Edições Cosmos, 1997.

COUTTS, Howard and DAY, Ivan. "Sugar sculpture, porcelain and table layout 1530-1583." *Taking Shape*. Online papers and proceedings, pp. 1–22, Oct. 2008; http://www.henry-moore.org//hmi-journal/homepage/view-occasional-papers/ sugar-sculpture/intro. Accessed: 21/03/2011.

COUTUMES de la ville d'Anvers, dites antiquissimae. MONBALLYU, Jozef (ed.). Leuven: Katholieke Universiteit Leuven; http://www.kuleuven-kortrijk.be/facult/rechten/Monballyu/Rechtlagelanden/Brabantsrecht/antwerpen/antiquissimae.html.

COWELL, John. *The Interpreter: Or Booke Containing the Signification of Words*. Cambridge: John Legate, 1607.

CRUZ, António. *Os mesteres do Porto. Subsídios para a história das antigas corporações dos ofícios mecânicos*. V. 1. Porto: Edição do Sub-Secretariado de Estado das Corporações e Previdência Social, 1943.

CRUZ, Maria Augusta Lima. *D. Sebastião*. Lisbon: Círculo de Leitores, 2006.

CUNHA, Edgar Teodoro da. Índio no Brasil: imaginário em movimento." In: NOVAES, Sylvia Caiuby et al. (eds.). *Escrituras da imagem*. São Paulo: Fapesp/Edusp, 2004, pp. 101–120.

CUNHA, Mafalda Soares da (ed.). *Os espaços de um Império – estudos e catálogo*. 2 v. Lisbon: Comissão Nacional para as Comemorações dos Descobrimentos Portugueses, 1999.

D'OLIVEYRA, Nicolao. *Livro das grandezas de Lisboa. Dirigido a D. Pedro D'alcaçova, Alcayde mor das três Villas, Campo mayor, Ougella, & Idanha a nova, & Comendador das Idanhas. Com todas as Licenças necessárias*. Lisbon: por Jorge Rodriguez, 1620.

DALGADO, Sebastião Rodolfo and PIEL, Joseph M. *Glossário luso-asiático*. Part 2. Hamburg: Buske Verlag, 1921.

DAVIDS, Karel and NOORDEGRAAF, Leo (eds.). *The Dutch Economy in the Golden Age*. Amsterdam: NEHA, 1993.

DEBUS, Allen G. *Man and Nature in the Renaissance*. London: Cambridge University Press, 1978.

DEERR, Noel. *The History of Sugar*. V. 1. London: Chapman and Hall, 1949.

DEHING, Pit and 'T HART, Marjolein. "Linking the Fortunes: Currency and Banking, 1550–1800." In: 'T HART, Marjolein, JONKER, Joost and ZANDEN, Jan Luiten van (eds.). *A Financial History of the Netherlands*. Cambridge: Cambridge University Press, 1997, pp. 37–63.

DESPORTES, Françoise. "Os ofícios da alimentação." In: FLANDRIN, Jean-Louis and MONTANARI, Massimo (eds.). *História da alimentação*. Translated by Luciano Vieira Machado and Guilherme J. F. Teixeira. São Paulo: Estação Liberdade, 1998, pp. 422–436.

DIAS, João José Alves. "A moeda." In: SERRÃO, Joel and MARQUES, A. H. de Oliveira (eds.). *Nova história de Portugal*. V. 5. Lisbon: Editorial Presença, 1998, pp. 254–276.

DIFFIE, Bailey W. *Foundations of the Portuguese Empire, 1415–1580*. Minneapolis: University of Minnesota Press, 1977.

DILLEN, Johannes Gerard van. *Bronnen tot de geschiedenis van het bedrijfsleven en het gildewezen van Amsterdam*. V. 1 (1512–1611), V. 2 (1612–1632), V. 3 (1633–1672). The Hague: Martinus Nijhoff Publishers, 1929–1974 (Rijks Geschiedkundige Publicatien. Grote serie, Vv. 69, 78, 144).

DILLEN, Johannes Gerard van. "The Bank of Amsterdam." In: DILLEN, Johannes Gerard van (ed.). *History of the Principal Public Banks*. London: Routledge, 1964, pp. 79–124.

DISNEY, Anthony R. *Twilight of the Pepper Empire: Portuguese Trade in Southwest India in the Early Seventeenth Century*. Cambridge: Harvard University Press, 1978.

DOCUMENTOS para a história do açúcar. 2 v. Rio de Janeiro: Instituto do Açúcar e do Álcool, 1954.

DOLLINGER, Philippe. *The German Hansa*. Translated and edited by D. S. Ault and S. H. Steinberg. London: Macmillan, 1970.

DOMINGUES, Francisco Contente. *Os navios do mar oceano: teoria e empiria na arquitetura naval portuguesa dos séculos XVI e XVII*. Lisbon: Centro de História da Universidade de Lisboa, 2004.

DOMÍNGUEZ ORTIZ, Antonio and VINCENT, Bernard. *Historia de los moriscos*. Madrid: Alianza Editorial, 1989.

DONKIN, Robin A. *Between East and West: The Moluccas and the Traffic in Spices up to the Arrival of Europeans*. Philadelphia: American Philosophical Society, 2003.

EBERT, Christopher. "The Trade in Brazilian Sugar: Brazil, Portugal and Northwestern Europe, 1550–1630." PhD dissertation, Columbia University, New York, 2004.

EBERT, Christopher. *Between Empires: Brazilian Sugar in the Early Atlantic Economy, 1550–1630*. Leiden: Brill, 2008.

ELLIOTT, John H. *Imperial Spain, 1496–1716*. London: Edward Arnold (Publishers), 1963.

ELLIOTT, John H. *El conde-duque de Olivares, el político en una época de decadencia*. Translated by Teófilo de Lozoya, revised by Antonio Feros and the author. Barcelona: Grijalbo Mondadori, 1998.

EMMER, Peter C. "The First Global War: The Dutch versus Iberia in Asia, Africa and the New World, 1590–1609." *E-Journal of Portuguese History* 1, no. 1 (Summer 2003): 1–14; http://www.brown. edu/Departments/Portuguese_Brazilian_Studies/ejph/html/issue1/pdf/emmer.pdf

FANTOM, Glenn Stephen Murray. *El Real Ingenio de la Moneda de Segovia: fábrica industrial más antigua, avanzada y completa que se conserva de la humanidad. Razonamiento científico de la propuesta para su declaración como Patrimonio de la Humanidad.* Segovia: Cámara de Comercio e Industria de Segovia, 2008.

FARIA, Manuel Severim de. "Dos remédios para a falta de gente." In: ANTÓNIO, Sérgio, *Antologia dos economistas portugueses (século XVII)*. Compiled with preface and notes by Sérgio António. Lisbon: Livraria Sá da Costa Editora, 1974, pp. 117–163.

FERLINI, Vera Lúcia Amaral. *Terra, trabalho e poder: o mundo dos engenhos no Nordeste colonial*. Bauru: Edusc, 2003.

FERLINI, Vera Lúcia Amaral. *Açúcar e colonização*. São Paulo: Alameda, 2010.

FERNÁNDEZ-ARMESTO, Felipe. *Comida: uma história*. Rio de Janeiro: Record, 2004.

FERREIRA, Ana Maria. *Problemas marítimos entre Portugal e a França na primeira metade do século XVI*. Cascais: Patrimónia, 1995.

FERREIRA, Godofredo. "O Postilhão da América." In: FERREIRA, Godofredo (ed.). *Cousas e Loisas do Correio*. Offprint of: *Guia Oficial dos Correios, Telégrafos e Telefones*. Lisbon: [n. n.], 1955, pp. 7–34.

FLANDRIN, Jean-Louis. *Chronique de platine. Pour une gastronomie historique*. Paris: Éditions Odile Jacob, 1992.

FLANDRIN, Jean-Louis. "Tempero, cozinha e dietética nos séculos XIV, XV e XVI." In: FLANDRIN, Jean-Louis and MONTANARI, Massimo (eds.). *História da alimentação*. Translated by Luciano Vieira Machado and Guilherme J. F. Teixeira. São Paulo: Estação Liberdade, 1998, pp. 478–495.

FLANDRIN, Jean-Louis. "Preferências alimentares e arte culinária (séculos XVI–XVIII)." In: FLANDRIN, Jean-Louis and MONTANARI, Massimo (eds.). *História da alimentação*. Translated by Luciano Vieira Machado and Guilherme J. F. Teixeira. São Paulo: Estação Liberdade, 1998, pp. 640–666.

FLANDRIN, Jean-Louis. "Da dietética à gastronomia, ou a liberação da gula." In: FLANDRIN, Jean-Louis and MONTANARI, Massimo (eds.). *História da alimentação*. Translated by Luciano Vieira Machado and Guilherme J. F. Teixeira. São Paulo: Estação Liberdade, 1998, pp. 667–688.

FONSECA, Luís Adão da. "O papel de Granada no horizonte da política peninsular portuguesa em meados do século XV." In: SEGURA GRAIÑO, Cristina (ed.). *Relaciones exteriores del Reino de Granada. IV Colóquio de Historia Medieval Andaluza*. Almeria: Instituto de Estudios Almerienses, 1988, pp. 383–392.

FRANÇA, Eduardo d'Oliveira. *Portugal na época da Restauração*. São Paulo: Hucitec, 1997.

FRANÇA, Eduardo d'Oliveira and SIQUEIRA, Sônia A. "Introduction and Notes." In: *Segunda visitação do Santo Ofício às partes do Brasil pelo Inquisidor e Visitador Marcos Teixeira. Livro das Confissões e Ratificações da Bahia: 1618–1620*. Offprint of: *Anais do Museu Paulista*, t. 17, 1963.

FRANCO, José Eduardo and ASSUNÇÃO, Paulo de. *As metamorfoses de um polvo: religião e política nos regimentos da Inquisição portuguesa (séculos XVI–XIX)*. Contains the full text of records of the Portuguese Inquisition. Lisbon: Prefácio Editora, 2004.

FRANITS, Wayne. *Dutch Seventeenth-Century Genre Painting: Its Stylistic and Thematic Evolution*. New Haven, London: Yale University Press, 2004.

FREYRE, Gilberto. *Açúcar: uma sociologia do doce, com receitas de bolos e doces do Nordeste do Brasil*. São Paulo: Global, 2007.

FUENTE, Alejandro de la. "Sugar and Slavery in Early Colonial Cuba." In: SCHWARTZ, Stuart (ed.). *Tropical Babylons: Sugar and the Making of the Atlantic World, 1450–1680*. Chapel Hill: University of North Carolina Press, 2004, pp. 114–157.

FURTADO, Celso. *Formação econômica do Brasil*. São Paulo: Editora Nacional, 1989.

GAASTRA, Femme Simon and BLUSSÉ, Leonard (eds.). *Companies and Trade*. Leiden: University of Leiden Press, 1981.

GAASTRA, Femme. *The Dutch East India Company: Expansion and Decline*. Zutphen: Walburg Pers, 2003.

GALANTE, Luís Augusto Vicente. "Uma história da circulação monetária no Brasil no século XVII." PhD dissertation, Universidade de Brasília, 2009.

GALLOWAY, Jock H. *The Sugar Cane Industry: An Historical Geography from Its Origins to 1914*. Cambridge: Cambridge University Press, 1989.

GÂNDAVO, Pero de Magalhães. *Tractado da terra do Brasil no qual se contem a informação das cousas que ha nestas partes feito por P.o de Magalhaes*. Seventeenth-century manuscript; http://purl.pt/211.

GAMA, Ruy. *Engenho e tecnologia*. São Paulo: Livraria Duas Cidades, 1983.

GARCÍA-ARENAL, Mercedes and WIEGERS, Gerard. *Un hombre en tres mundos. Samuel Pallache, un judío marroquí en la Europa protestante y en la católica*. Madrid: Siglo XXI de España Editores, 2006.

GARCÍA DE PASO, José Isidoro. "The 1628 Castilian Crydown: A Test of Competing Theories of Price Level." *Hacienda Pública Española/Revista de Economía Pública* 163, no. 4 (2002): 71–91.

GARCIA, João Carlos. *O espaço medieval da reconquista no sudoeste da Península Ibérica*. Lisbon: Centro de Estudos Geográficos, 1986.

GELDER, H. Enno van. *De Nederlandse munten: geschiedenis der Nederlandse munten vanaf 500 tot heden. Muntheren, muntplaatsen, muntelsels, koerstabellen, register met alle muntnamen*. Utrecht: Het Spectrum, 1972.

GELDERBLOM, Oscar. *Zuid-Nederlandse kooplieden en de opkomst van de Amsterdamse stapelmarkt*. Hilversum: Verloren, 2000.

GELDERBLOM, Oscar and JONKER, Joost. "Amsterdam as the Cradle of Modern Futures and Options Trading, 1550–1650." *Economy and Society in the Low Countries before 1850. Working Paper Series*, 2003–2009.

GELDERBLOM, Oscar and JONKER, Joost. "Completing a Financial Revolution: The Finance of the Dutch East India Trade and the Rise of the Amsterdam Capital Market, 1595–1612." *The Journal of Economic History* 64, no. 3 (Sep. 2004): 641–672.

GERALDES, Carlos Alberto Caldeira. "Casa da Índia: um estudo de estrutura e funcionalidade (1509–1630)." Master's thesis, Universidade de Lisboa, 1997.

GEYL, Pieter. *The Revolt of the Netherlands, 1555–1609*. New York: Barnes & Noble, 1980.

GIL, Juan. *Hidalgos y samurais. España y Japón en los siglos XVI y XVII*. Madrid: Alianza Universidad, 1991.

GO, Sabine Christa. "Marine Insurance in the Netherlands, 1600–1870." PhD dissertation, Vrije Universiteit Amsterdam, 2009.

GODINHO, Vitorino Magalhães. "A evolução dos complexos histórico-geográficos." In: GODINHO, Vitorino Magalhães, *Ensaios II: sobre a história de Portugal*. 2nd ed. revised and expanded. Lisbon: Sá da Costa, 1978, pp. 15–23.

GODINHO, Vitorino Magalhães. *Os descobrimentos e a economia mundial*. 4 v. Lisbon: Editorial Presença, 1982–1983.

GOMES, Geraldo. *Engenho e arquitetura*. Recife: Editora Massangana, 2007.

GÓMEZ RIVAS, León. "El pensamiento económico en España y Holanda en el siglo XVII: la Guerra de los Treinta Años y la difusión de ideas: Hugo Grotius." *Cuadernos de Ciencias Económicas y Empresariales*, no. 37 (1999): 139–160.

GONÇALVES, Regina Célia. *Guerras e açúcares: política e economia na Capitania da Parayba – 1585–1630*. Bauru: Edusc, 2007.

GOUVEIA, David Ferreira. "Açúcar confeitado na Madeira." *Islenha: Temas Culturais das Sociedades Insulares*, no. 11 (Jul.–Dec. 1992): 35–52.

GRAIZBORD, David L. *Souls in Dispute: Converso Identities in Iberia and the Jewish Diaspora, 1580–1700*. Philadelphia: University of Pennsylvania Press, 2004.

GRANOVETTER, Mark. "Problems of Explanation in Economic Sociology." In: NOHRIA, Nitin and ECCLES, Robert G. (eds.). *Networks and Organizations*. Boston: Harvard Business School Press, 1992, pp. 25–56.

GRANOVETTER, Mark. "The Impact of Social Structures on Economic Outcomes." *Journal of Economic Perspectives* 19, no. 1 (Winter 2005): 33–50.

GREIF, Avner. "Contract Enforceability and Economic Institutions in Early Trade: The Maghribi Trader's Coalition." *The American Economic Review* 83, no. 3 (Jun. 1993): 525–548.

GREIF, Avner, MILGROM, Paul and WEINGAST, Barry R. "Coordination, Commitment and Enforcement: The Case of the Merchant Guild." *Journal of Political Economy* 102, no. 3 (Aug. 1994): 745–776.

GROTIUS, Hugo. *The Rights of War and Peace Including the Law of Nature and of Nations (1625)*. Translated from the original Latin of Grotius with notes and illustrations from political and legal writers by A. C. Campbell, with an introduction by David J. Hill. New York: M. Walter Dunne, 1901.

GROTIUS, Hugo. *Commentary on the Law of Prize and Booty*. Edited and introduced by Martine Julia van Ittersum. Indianapolis: Liberty Fund, 2006.

GUEDES, Max Justo. "As guerras holandesas no mar." In: *História naval brasileira*. V. 2, T. 1 A. Rio de Janeiro: Serviço de Documentação Geral da Marinha, 1990, pp. 7–422.

GUIDOTTI, P. E. and RODRIGUEZ, C. A. "Dollarization in Latin America – Gresham Law in Reverse." *International Monetary Fund Staff Papers*, no. 39 (1992): 518–544.

HAMILTON, Earl Jefferson. *American Treasure and the Price Revolution in Spain, 1501–1650*. New York: Octagon Books, 1965.

HARRELD, Donald J. "Atlantic Sugar and Antwerp's Trade with Germany in the Sixteenth Century." *Journal of Early Modern History*, no. 7 (2003): 148–163.

HAZLETT, Alexander Dean. "The Nau of the Livro Nautico: Reconstructing a Sixteenth-Century Indiaman from Texts." PhD dissertation, Texas A&M University, 2007.

HEIJER, Henk den. *De geschiedenis van de WIC*. Zutphen: Walburg Pers, 2002.

HELL, Maarten. "De oude geuzen en de Opstand: politiek en lokaal bestuur in tijd van oorlog en expansie 1578–1650." In: FRIJHOFF, Willem and PRAK, Maarten. *Geschiedenis van Amsterdam, deel II-A: centrum van de wereld 1578–1650*. Amsterdam: SUN, 2004, pp. 241–298.

HERCULANO, Alexandre. *História da origem e estabelecimento da Inquisição em Portugal*. 2nd. ed., 3 v. Lisbon: Imprensa Nacional, 1864–1872.

HESPANHA, António Manuel. "Os áustrias em Portugal – Balanço historiográfico." *Lusotopie*. Leiden: Centre d'Étude d'Afrique Noir/CNRS – Brill, 1998, pp. 145–155.

HIRSCHMAN, Albert O. "A Generalized Linkage Approach to Development with Special Reference to Staples." In: HIRSCHMAN, Albert O., *Essays in Trespassing: Economics to Politics and Beyond*. Cambridge: Cambridge University Press, 1981, pp. 59–97.

HOCHSTRASSER, Julie Berger. *Still Life and Trade in the Dutch Golden Age*. New Haven: Yale University Press, 2007.

HOSOKAWA, Antonieta Buriti de Souza. "O tratado da cozinha portuguesa – códice I.E. 33: aspectos culturais e linguísticos." PhD dissertation, Universidade de São Paulo, 2006.

HOUAISS, Antônio and VILLAR, Mauro de Salles. *Dicionário Houaiss da língua portuguesa*. Rio de Janeiro: Objetiva, 2001.

HUERTA DE SOTO, Jesús. "La teoría bancaria en la Escuela de Salamanca." In: HUERTA DE SOTO, Jesús, *Nuevos estudios de economía política*. Madrid: Unión Editorial, 2002, pp. 73–99.

HUNT, Endwin S. and MURRAY, James M. *A History of Business in Medieval Europe, 1200–1550*. Cambridge: Cambridge University Press, 1999.

HUTTER, Lucy Maffei. *Navegação nos séculos XVII e XVIII. Rumo: Brasil*. São Paulo: Edusp, 2005.

HUUSSEN JR., Arend H. "The Legal Position of the Jews in the Dutch Republic c. 1590–1796." In: ISRAEL, Jonathan Irvine and SALVERDA, R. (eds.). *Dutch Jewry: Its History and Secular Culture (1500–2000)*. Leiden: Brill, 2002, pp. 25–41.

HUUSSEN JR., Arend H. "The Legal Position of the Sephardi Jews in Holland, Circa 1600." In: MICHMAN, Jozeph (ed.). *Dutch Jewish History*. V. 3. Jerusalem: The Institute for Research on Dutch Jewry, 1993, pp. 19–41.

HYMAN, Philip and HYMAN, Mary. "Os livros de cozinha na França entre os séculos XV e XIX." In: FLANDRIN, Jean-Louis and MONTANARI, Massimo (eds.), *História da alimentação*. Translated by Luciano Vieira Machado and Guilherme J. F. Teixeira. São Paulo: Estação Liberdade, 1998, pp. 625–639.

IGLESIA GARCÍA, Jesús de la. "Martín de Azpilcueta y su 'Comentario resolutorio de cambios.'" *Información Comercial Española* 789 (Dec. 2000–Jan. 2001): 77–84.

"INVENTÁRIOS e contas da casa de D. Denis (1278–1282)." Compiled by Anselmo Braamcamp Freire. *Arquivo Histórico Português*. Lisbon: 1916, v. 10, pp. 41–59.

IJZERMAN, J. W. (ed.). *Journael van de reis naar Zuid-Amerika (1598–1601) door Hendrik Ottsen*. The Hague: Martinus Nijhoff Publishers, 1918.

IJZERMAN, J. W. "Amsterdamsche bevrachtingscontracten 1591–1602, 1. de vaart op Spanje en Portugal. *Economisch-Historisch Jaarboek*, no. 17 (1931): 163–291.

ISRAEL, Jonathan Irvine. *Dutch Primacy in World Trade, 1585–1740*. Oxford: Clarendon Press, 1989.

SRAEL, Jonathan Irvine. "Spain, the Spanish Embargo, and the Struggle for the Mastery of World Trade, 1585–1660." In: ISRAEL, Jonathan Irvine, *Empires and Entrepots – The Dutch, the Spanish Monarchy and the Jews, 1585–1713*. London: Hambledon Press, 1990, pp. 190–212.

ISRAEL, Jonathan Irvine. "Manuel Lopez Pereira of Amsterdam, Antwerp and Madrid: Jew, New Christian, and Adviser of the Conde-Duque de Olivares." In: ISRAEL, Jonathan Irvine. *Empires and Entrepots – the Dutch, the Spanish Monarchy and the Jews, 1585–1713*. London: Hambledon Press, 1990, pp. 247–264.

ISRAEL, Jonathan Irvine. "Spain and the Dutch Sephardim, 1609–1660." In: ISRAEL, Jonathan Irvine. *Empires and Entrepots – the Dutch, the Spanish Monarchy and the Jews, 1585–1713*. London: Hambledon Press, 1990, pp. 355–415.

ISRAEL, Jonathan Irvine. "The Economic Contribution of the Dutch Sephardic Jewry to Holland's Golden Age, 1595–1713." In: ISRAEL, Jonathan Irvine. *Empires and Entrepots – the Dutch, the Spanish Monarchy and the Jews, 1585–1713*. London: Hambledon Press, 1990, pp. 417–445.

ISRAEL, Jonathan Irvine. *The Dutch Republic. Its Rise, Greatness and Fall, 1477–1806*. Oxford: Clarendon Press, 1995.

ISRAEL, Jonathan Irvine. "The Sephardi Contribution to Economic Life and Colonization in Europe and the New World (16th–18th Centuries)." In: BEINART, Haim (ed.). *The Sephardi Legacy*. Jerusalem: Magnes Press, 1992, v. 2, pp. 365–398.

ISRAEL, Jonathan Irvine. *La República holandesa y el mundo hispánico, 1606–1661*. Madrid: Editora Nerea, 1997.

ISRAEL, Jonathan Irvine. "Diasporas Jewish and Non-Jewish and World Maritime Empires." In: MCCABE, Ina Baghdiantz, HARLAFTIS, Gelina and MINOGLOU, I anna Pepelas (eds.). *Diaspora Entrepreneurial Networks: Four Centuries of History*. Oxford: Berg, 2005, pp. 3–26.

JOHNSON, Harold. "Das feitorias às capitanias." In: JOHNSON, Harold and SILVA, Maria Beatriz Nizza da (eds.). *Nova história da expansão portuguesa. V. 6: O Império luso-brasileiro, 1500–1620*. Lisbon: Editorial Estampa, 1992, pp. 207–239.

JOHNSON, Harold. "A indústria do açúcar, 1570–1630." In: JOHNSON, Harold and SILVA, Maria Beatriz Nizza da (eds.). *Nova história da expansão portuguesa. V. 6: O Império luso-brasileiro, 1500–1620*. Lisbon: Editorial Estampa, 1992, pp. 240–302.

KAHR, Madlyn Millner. *Dutch Painting in the Seventeenth Century*. 2nd ed. Boulder: Westview Press, 1993.

KAMEN, Henry. *Philip of Spain*. New Haven: Yale University Press, 1998.

KAPLAN, Yosef. "The Social Functions of the Herem in the Portuguese Jewish Community of Amsterdam in the Seventeenth Century." In: MICHMAN, Jozeph (ed.). *Dutch Jewish History*. V. 1. Jerusalem: The Institute for Research on Dutch Jewry, 1984, pp. 111–155.

KAPLAN, Yosef. "The Travels of Portuguese Jews from Amsterdam to the 'Lands of Idolatry.'" In: KAPLAN, Yosef (ed.). *Jews and Conversos*. Jerusalem: World Union of Jewish Studies, Magnes Press, 1985, pp. 197–224.

KAPLAN, Yosef. "The Portuguese Community in Seventeenth-Century Amsterdam and the Ashkenazi World." In: MICHMAN, Jozeph (ed.). *Dutch Jewish History*. V. 2. Jerusalem: The Institute for Research on Dutch Jewry, 1986, pp. 23–45.

KAPLAN, Yosef. "The Portuguese Community of Amsterdam in the 17th Century: Between Tradition and Change." In: HAIM, Abraham (ed.). *Society and Community. Proceedings of the Second International Congress for Research of the Sephardi and Oriental Jewish Heritage*. Jerusalem: Misgav Yerushalayim, 1991, pp. 141–171.

KAPLAN, Yosef. "The Intellectual Ferment in the Spanish-Portuguese Community of Seventeenth-Century Amsterdam." In: BEINART, Haim (ed.). *The Sephardi Legacy*. V. 2. Jerusalem: Magnes Press, Hebrew University, 1992, pp. 288–314.

KAPLAN, Yosef. "Deviance and Excommunication in the Eighteenth Century: A Chapter in the Social History of the Sephardi Community of Amsterdam." In: MICHMAN, Jozeph (ed.). *Dutch Jewish History*. V. 3. Jerusalem: The Institute for Research on Dutch Jewry, 1993, pp. 103–115.

KAPLAN, Yosef. "Wayward New Christians and Stubborn New Jews: The Shaping of a Jewish Identity." In: GARTNER, Lloyd and STOW, Kenneth (eds.). *Jewish History – The Robert Cohen Memorial Volume*. Haifa: Haifa University Press, 1994, v. 8, nos. 1–2, pp. 27–41.

KAPLAN, Yosef. "The Self-Definition of the Sephardic Jews of Western Europe and their Relation to the Alien and Stranger." In: GAMPEL, Benjamin R. (ed.). *Crisis and Creativity in the Sephardic World – 1391–1648*. New York: Columbia University Press, 1997, pp. 121–145.

KAPLAN, Yosef. "An Alternative Path to Modernity." In: KAPLAN, Yosef. *An Alternative Path to Modernity: The Sephardi Diaspora in Western Europe*. Leiden: Brill, 2000, pp. 1–28.

KAPLAN, Yosef. "Jewish Amsterdam's Impact on Modern Jewish History." In: GRAETZ, Michael (ed.). *Shöpferische Momente des europäischen Judentums in der frühen Neuzeit*. Heidelberg: Universitätsverlag C. Winter, 2000, pp.19–62.

KEBLUSEK, Marika. *Boeken in de hofstad: Haagse boekcultuur in de Gouden Eeew*. Hilversum: Verloren, 1997.

KEDAR, Benjamin Z. *Merchants in Crisis: Genoese and Venetian Men of Affairs and the Fourteenth Century Depression*. New Haven: Yale University Press, 1976.

KELLENBENZ, Hermann. "Der Brasilienhandel der Hamburger 'Portugiesen' zu Ende des 16. und in der ersten Hälfte des 17 Jahrhunderts." *Portugiesische Forschungen der Görres-Gesellschaft, Aufsätze zur Portugiesischen Kulturgeschichte*, no. 1, pp. 316–34, 1960.

KLAUS, Sabine K. and LIBIN, Laurence. "A Symposium on the Respectability of the Square Piano." *American Musical Instrument Society Newsletter* 32, no. 1 (Spring 2003): 5–6.

KLEIN, Peter. "The Use of Wood in Rembrandt's Workshop. Wood Identification and Dendrochronological Analyses." In: DOEL, Marieke Van den et al. (eds.). *The Learned Eye: Regarding Art, Theory and the Artist's Reputation. Essays for Ernst van de Wetering*. Amsterdam: Amsterdam University Press, 2005, pp. 28–37.

KOEN, E. M. "Duarte Fernandes, koopman van de Portugese natie te Amsterdam." *Studia Rosenthaliana* 2, no. 2 (1968): 178–193.

LACERDA, Silvestre. "A tanoaria: a arte e a técnica." In: ALVES, Jorge F. (ed.). *A indústria portuense em perspectiva histórica – Actas do Colóquio*. Porto: Faculdade de Letras da Universidade do Porto, 1998, pp. 381–393.

LACH, Donald Frederick and KLEY, Edwin J. van. *Asia in the Making of Europe*. Chicago: University of Chicago Press, 1994.

LAMPING, A. J. *Johannes Polyander, een dienaar van Kerk en Universiteit*. Leiden: Brill, 1980.

LANGHANS, Franz-Paul. *As corporações dos ofícios mecânicos. Subsídios para a sua história*. With an essay by Marcello Caetano. Lisbon: Imprensa Nacional de Lisboa, 1943–1946.

LARIOUX, Bruno. "Cozinhas medievais (séculos XIV e XV)." In: FLANDRIN, Jean-Louis and MONTANARI, Massimo (eds.). *História da alimentação*. Translated by Luciano Vieira Machado and Guilherme J. F. Teixeira. São Paulo: Estação Liberdade, 1998 447–465.

LAUDAN, Rachel. "A Kind of Chemistry." *Petits Propos Culinaires*, no. 62 (1999): 8–22.

LAUDAN, Rachel. "Birth of the Modern Diet." *Scientific American*. Exclusive Online Issue, no. 11 (Jan. 2004): 11–16; http://www.rachellaudan. com/wp-content/uploads/2007/08/birth_of_the_modern_diet.pdf. Accessed: 10/09/2010.

LAVAL, Francisco Pyrard de. *Viagem de Francisco Pyrard de Laval, contendo a notícia de sua navegação às Índias Orientais, Ilhas de Maldiva, Maluco e ao Brasil, e os diferentes casos que lhe aconteceram na mesma viagem nos dez anos que andou nestes países (1601 a 1611)*. Portuguese translation revised and annotated by J. H. da Cunha Rivara, edition revised and updated by A. de Magalhães Basto. Porto: Livraria Civilização, 1944.

LEÃO, Gaspar de. *Desengano de perdidos*. Introduction by Eugénio Asensio. Coimbra: Universidade de Coimbra, 1958.

LEÃO, Duarte Nunez de. *Descripção do Reino de Portugal*. Lisbon: Jorge Rodriguez, 1610.

LEÃO, Duarte Nunez de. *Leis extravagantes collegidas e relatadas pelo licenciado Dvarte Nunes do Liam per mandado do muito alto & muito poderoso rei Dom Sebastiam Nosso Senhor*. Lisbon: Antonio Gonçalvez, 1569.

LEEUWEN, Simon van. *Commentaries on the Roman-Dutch Law*. London: Joseph Butterworth & Son, 1820.

LEITE, José Roberto Teixeira. Viajantes do imaginário: a América vista da Europa, séc. XV–XVII. *Revista USP*, no. 30 (Jun.–Aug. 1996): 32–45.

LEMPS, Alain Huetz. "As bebidas coloniais e a rápida expansão do açúcar." In: FLANDRIN, Jean-Louis and MONTANARI, Massimo (eds.). *História da alimentação*. Translated by Luciano Vieira Machado and Guilherme J. F. Teixeira. São Paulo: Estação Liberdade, 1998, pp. 611–624.

LESGER, Clé and NOORDEGRAAF, Leo (eds.). *Entrepreneurs and Entrepreneurship in Early Modern Times – Merchant and Industrialist within the Orbit of the Dutch Staple Market – Hollandse Historische Reeks*. V. 24. The Hague: Stichting Hollandse Historische Reeks, 1996.

LESGER, Clé. "De wereld als horizon: de economie tussen 1578 en 1650." In: FRIJHOFF, Willem and PRAK, Maarten. *Geschiedenis van Amsterdam, deel II-A: centrum van de wereld 1578–1650*. Amsterdam: SUN, 2004, pp. 103–187.

LESGER, Clé. *The Rise of the Amsterdam Market and Information Exchange: Merchants, Commercial Expansion and Change in the Spatial Economy of the Low Countries c. 1550–1630*. Translated by J. C. Grayson. Aldershot: Ashgate, 2006.

LIMA, Fernando Carlos G. de Cerqueira. "Uma análise crítica da literatura sobre a oferta e circulação de moeda metálica no Brasil nos séculos XVI e XVII." *Estudos Econômicos* 35, no. 1 (2005): 169–201.

LIMA, Fernando Carlos G. Cerqueira. "Sugar and Metals as Commodity Money in Colonial Brazil." *Economic History Society Annual Conference*, University of Durham, March 26–28, 2010.

LIPINER, Elias. *Os baptizados em pé. Estudos acerca da origem e da luta dos cristãos-novos em Portugal*. Lisbon: Vega, 1998.

LIPPMANN, Edmund O. Von. *História do açúcar*. V. 2. Rio de Janeiro: Instituto do Açúcar e do Álcool, 1942.

LISBOA, Dom Marcos de, *Constituições synodaes do bispado do Porto*. Coimbra: 1585.

LIVERMORE, Harold. "A marinha mercante holandesa no comércio do Brasil." *Revista Portuguesa de História* 5 (1951): 493–498.

LIVRO da visitação do Santo Ofício da Inquisição ao Estado do Grão-Pará (1763–1769). Original document, introduction by J. R. Amaral Lapa. Petrópolis: Vozes, 1978.

LIVRO primeiro do governo do Brasil (1607–1633). Edited by João Paulo Salvado, Susana Münch

Miranda, Luís Pinheiro. Transcription by João Carlos Oliveira. Lisbon: Comissão Nacional para as Comemorações dos Descobrimentos Portugueses, 2001.

LOPES, Fernão. *Crónica de D. Fernando*. Introduction by Salvador Dias Arnaut. Porto: Livraria Civilização-Editora, 1966.

LOPES, Fernão. *Crónica de D. João I*. V. 1. Introduction by Humberto Baquero Moreno, preface by António Sérgio. Porto: Livraria Civilização-Editora, 1983.

LOPEZ, Robert S. and RAYMOND, Irving W. "Introduction and Notes." In: *Medieval Trade in the Mediterranean World*. New York: Columbia University Press, 2001.

LUNSFORD, Virginia West. *Piracy and Privateering in the Golden Age Netherlands*. New York: Palgrave MacMillan, 2005.

LUZZATO, Gino. "Les banques publiques de Venise (siècles XVI–XVIII)." In: DILLEN, Johannes Gerard van (ed.). *History of the Principal Public Banks*. London: Routledge, 1964, pp. 39–78.

MACEDO, Jorge Borges de. "História diplomática portuguesa: constantes e linhas de força." *Revista Nação e Defesa* 1 (1987).

MAGALHÃES, Joaquim Romero. *O Algarve económico, 1600–1773*. Lisbon: Editorial Estampa, 1993.

MAGALHÃES, Joaquim Romero. "A estrutura das trocas." In: MATTOSO, José (ed.). *História de Portugal*. Lisbon: Editorial Estampa, 1997. V. 3, pp. 283–316.

MALYNES, Gerard. *Consuetudo: vel, lex mercatoria*. London: Adam Islip, 1622.

MARCHANT, Alexander. *Do escambo à escravidão: as relações econômicas entre portugueses e índios na colonização do Brasil (1500–1580)*. São Paulo: Companhia Editora Nacional, 1980.

MARNOCO E SOUZA, José Ferreira. *Das letras, livranças e cheques*. 2 v. Coimbra: França Amado, 1905–1906.

MARQUES, A. H. de Oliveira. *A sociedade medieval portuguesa*. 3rd ed. Lisbon: Livraria Sá da Costa, 1974, pp. 131–150.

MARQUES, A. H. de Oliveira. *História de Portugal*. V. 2. Lisbon: Palas Editores, 1983.

MARQUES, A. H. de Oliveira. "Técnicas artesanais – fabrico de moeda." In: SERRÃO, Joel and MARQUES, A. H. de Oliveira (eds.). *Nova história de Portugal*. V. 5. Lisbon: Editorial Presença, 1998, pp. 63–64.

MARQUES, A. H. de Oliveira (ed.). *História dos portugueses no Extremo Oriente*. 6 v. Lisbon: Fundação Oriente, 1998–2003.

MARQUES, A. H. de Oliveira and DIAS, João José Alves. *Atlas histórico de Portugal e do ultramar Português*. Lisbon: Centro de Estudos Históricos-Universidade Nova de Lisboa, 2003.

MARQUES, José. "Património régio na cidade do Porto e seu termo nos finais do século XV (subsídios para o seu estudo)." Offprint of: *História: Revista da Faculdade de Letras da Universidade do Porto*, 2nd series, 3: *Actas do Colóquio o Porto na Época Moderna* (1982): 73– 97.

MATTOSO, José (ed.). *História de Portugal*. Vv. 2–3. Lisbon: Editorial Estampa, 1992–1993.

MATTOSO, José. *Identificação de um país. Ensaios sobre as origens de Portugal. 1096–1325*. V. 1. Lisbon: Editorial Estampa, 1995.

MAURO, Frédéric. "Le Brésil au XVIIe siècle: documents inédits relatifs à l'Atlantique Portugais." Offprint of: *Brasília* 11 (1961): 127–285.

MAURO, Frédéric. *Portugal, o Brasil e o Atlântico, 1570–1670*. 2 v. Lisbon: Editorial Estampa, 1989.

MEA, Elvira Cunha de Azevedo. "A Igreja em reforma." In: SERRÃO, Joel and MARQUES, A. H. de Oliveira (eds.). *Nova história de Portugal*. V. 5. Lisbon: Editorial Presença, 1998, pp. 413–446.

MEA, Elvira Cunha de Azevedo. "A rotura das comunidades cristãs novas do litoral – século XVII." In: *O litoral em perspectiva histórica (sécs. XVI–XVIII): actas*. Porto: Faculdade de Letras da Universidade do Porto, 2002, pp. 263–273.

MEA, Elvira Cunha de Azevedo. "Os portuenses perante o Santo Ofício – século XVI." In: *I Congresso sobre a Diocese do Porto. Tempos e Lugares de Memória: Homenagem a D. Domingos de Pinho Brandão*. V. 2. Porto: Faculdade de Letras da Universidade do Porto, 2002, pp. 415–430.

MEDIEVAL Trade in the Mediterranean World. Illustrative documents translated with introduction and notes by Robert S. Lopez and Irving W. Raymond. New York: Columbia University Press, 1955.

MELÉ, Domènec. "Early Business Ethics in Spain: The Salamanca School (1526–1614)." *Journal of Business Ethics* 22, no. 3 (1999): 175–189.

MELLO, Evaldo Cabral de. *Olinda restaurada: guerra e açúcar no Nordeste, 1630–1654*. Rio de Janeiro: Topbooks, 1998.

MELLO, Evaldo Cabral de. *O nome e o sangue: uma parábola familiar no Pernambuco colonial*. Rio de Janeiro: Topbooks, 2000.

MELLO, Evaldo Cabral de. *Um imenso Portugal: historia e historiografia*. São Paulo: Editora 34, 2002.

MELLO, Evaldo Cabral de. *O Brasil holandês (1630–1654)*. São Paulo: Penguin Classics, 2010.

MELLO, José Antônio Gonsalves de. *Tempo dos flamengos: influência da ocupação holandesa na vida e na cultura do norte do Brasil*. Recife: Editora Massangana, 1987.

MELLO, José Antônio Gonsalves de. "Introduction and Notes." In: MELLO, José Antônio Gonsalves de. "Os livros das saídas das urcas do porto do Recife." *Revista do Instituto Arqueológico, Histórico e Geográfico Pernambucano*, 1993, pp. 33-34.

MELLO, José Antônio Gonsalves de. "Os livros das saídas das urcas do porto do Recife." *Revista do Instituto Arqueológico, Histórico e Geográfico Pernambucano* (1993).

MELLO, José Antônio Gonsalves de. *Gente da nação*. Recife: Editora Massangana, 1996.

MENDES, Claudinei Magno Magre. "A coroa portuguesa e a colonização do Brasil. Aspectos da atuação do Estado na constituição da colônia." *História: Revista do Departamento de História da Unesp* 16 (1997): 233–253.

MENESES, Avelino de Freitas de. "A moeda." In: SERRÃO, Joel and MARQUES, A. H. de Oliveira (eds.), *Nova história de Portugal*. V. 7. Lisbon: Editorial Presença, 2001, pp. 355–363.

MENEZES, José Luiz Mota (ed.). *Atlas histórico e cartográfico do Recife*. Recife: Fundação Joaquim Nabuco/Editora Massangana, 1985.

MERÊA, Paulo. "A solução tradicional da colonização do Brasil." In: DIAS, Carlos Malheiro (ed.). *História da colonização portuguesa do Brasil. Edição Monumental comemorativa do primeiro centenário da Independência do Brasil*. V. 3. Porto: Litografia Nacional, 1924.

MICHMAN, Jozeph (ed.). *Dutch Jewish History*. Vv. 1, 3. Jerusalem: The Institute for Research on Dutch Jewry, 1993.

MINTZ, Sidney Wilfred. *Sweetness and Power. The Place of Sugar in Modern History*. New York: Viking Penguin, 1985.

MONTEIRO, Nuno Gonçalo. "Elites locais e mobilidade social em Portugal nos finais do Antigo Regime." *Análise Social: Revista do Instituto de Ciências Sociais da Universidade de Lisboa* 32, no. 141 (1997): 335–368.

MONTEIRO, Nuno Gonçalo. As conjunturas políticas: Olivares e a Guerra dos Trinta Anos (1618–1648). In: RAMOS, Rui (ed.). *História de Portugal*. 4th ed. Lisbon: Esfera dos Livros, 2010, pp. 286–294.

MORAIS SILVA, António de. *Diccionario da língua portugueza recopilado dos vocabulários impressos até agora, e nesta segunda edição novamente emendado, e muito accrescentado, por Antonio de Moraes Silva, natural do Rio de Janeiro. Oferecido ao Muito Alto e Muito Poderoso, Príncipe Regente N. Senhor*. T. 1. Lisbon: Typographia Lacerdina, 1813.

MORAIS SILVA, António de. *Novo dicionário compacto da língua portuguesa*. 5 v. Lisbon: Editorial Confluência, 1961.

MOREIRA, Manuel António Fernandes. *Os mercadores de Viana e o comércio do açúcar brasileiro no século XVII*. Viana do Castelo: Câmara Municipal de Viana do Castelo, 1990.

MOREIRA, Manuel António Fernandes. "O porto de Viana do Castelo na época dos Descobrimentos, abordagem das fontes." In: *O litoral em perspectiva histórica (sécs. XVI–XVIII): actas*. Porto: Faculdade de Letras da Universidade do Porto, 2002, pp. 41–46.

MORENO, Diogo de Campos. *Livro que dá razão do Estado do Brasil – 1612*. Critical edition with introduction and notes by Helio Vianna. Recife: Comissão organizadora e executiva das comemorações do tricentenário da Restauração Pernambucana (Arquivo Público Estadual), 1955.

MORGAN, Kenneth. *Bristol and the Atlantic Trade in the Eighteenth Century*. Cambridge: Cambridge University Press, 1993.

MOSCHANDREAS, Maria. *Business Economics*. 2nd ed. London: Business Press, 1994.

MUÑOZ DE JUANA, Rodrigo. "Scholastic Morality and the Birth of Economics: The Thought of Martín de Azpilcueta." *Journal of Markets & Morality* 4, no. 1 (Spring 2001): 14–42.

NARDI, Jean Baptiste. *O fumo brasileiro no período colonial: lavoura, comércio e administração*. São Paulo: Editora Brasiliense, 1996.

NETO, Margarida Sobral. "Os correios na Idade Moderna." In: NETO, Margarida Sobral (ed.). *As comunicações na Idade Moderna*. Lisbon: Fundação Portuguesa das Comunicações, 2005, pp. 15–74.

NEWITT, Malyn D. D. *A History of Portuguese Overseas Expansion, 1400–1668*. New York: Routledge, 2005.

NIEUHOF, Joan. *Memorável viagem marítima e terrestre ao Brasil*. Translated by Moacir J. Vasconcelos. Introduction and notes by José Honório Rodrigues. São Paulo: Edusp, 1981.

NIZZA DA SILVA, Maria Beatriz. A população. In: JOHNSON, Harold and SILVA, Maria Beatriz Nizza da (eds.). *Nova história da expansão portuguesa. V. 6: O Império luso-brasileiro, 1500–1620*. Lisbon: Editorial Estampa, 1992, pp. 303–329.

NIZZA DA SILVA, Maria Beatriz. A sociedade. In: JOHNSON, Harold and SILVA, Maria Beatriz Nizza da (eds.). *Nova história da expansão portuguesa. V. 6: O Império luso-brasileiro, 1500–1620*. Lisbon: Editorial Estampa, 1992, pp. 403–478.

NOVAIS, Fernando A. (ed.). *História da vida privada no Brasil*. V. 1. São Paulo: Companhia das Letras, 1997.

NOVINSKY, Anita. *Cristãos novos na Bahia*. São Paulo: Perspectiva, 1972.

NUSTELING, Hubert P. H. "The Jews in the Republic of the United Provinces: Origin, Numbers and Dispersion." In: ISRAEL, Jonathan and SALVERDA, Reinier (eds.), *Dutch Jewry: Its History and Secular Culture (1500–2000)*. Leiden: Brill, 2002, pp. 43–62.

"TRASLADO do Foral de Olinda (12 March 1537)." In: COSTA, F. A. Pereira da. *Anais pernambucanos*. V. 1. Recife: Fundarpe, 1983, p. 187.

OLIVAL, Fernanda. *As ordens militares e o estado moderno. Honra, mercê e venalidade em Portugal (1641–1789)*. Lisbon: Estar Editora, 2001.

OLIVAL, Fernanda. "Mercado de hábitos e serviços em Portugal (séculos XVII–XVIII)." *Análise Social: Revista do Instituto de Ciências Sociais da Universidade de Lisboa* 38, no. 168 (2003): 743–769.

OLIVAL, Fernanda. "Juristas e mercadores à conquista das honras: quatro processos de nobilitação quinhentistas." *Revista de História Económica e Social*, 2nd series, 4 (2004): 151–182

OLIVAL, Fernanda. "Rigor e interesses: os estatutos de limpeza de sangue em Portugal." *Cadernos de Estudos Sefarditas* 4 (2004): 151–182.

OLIVAL, Fernanda. "Structural Changes within the 16th-Century Portuguese Military Orders." *E-Journal of Portuguese History* 2, no. 2 (Winter 2004): 1–20; http://www.brown. edu/Departments/Portuguese_Brazilian_Studies/ejph/html/issue4/pdf/folival.pdf

OLIVAL, Fernanda. *D. Filipe II*. Lisbon: Círculo de Leitores, 2006.

OLIVEIRA, António de. *Poder e oposição política em Portugal no período filipino, 1580–1640*. Lisbon: Difel, 1990.

OLIVEIRA, António de. *D. Filipe III*. Lisbon: Círculo de Leitores, 2008.

OLIVEIRA, Cristóvão Rodrigues de. *Lisboa em 1551. Sumário em que brevemente se contêm algumas coisas assim eclesiásticas como seculares que há na cidade de Lisboa (1551)*. Introduction and notes by José da Felicidade Alves. Lisbon: Livros Horizonte, 1987.

OLIVEIRA, Eduardo Freire de. *Elementos para a história do município de Lisboa*. 17 v. Lisbon: Tipographia Universal, 1882–1911.

OLIVEIRA, J. M. Pereira de. *O espaço urbano do Porto. Condições naturais de desenvolvimento*. 2 v. Coimbra: Instituto de Alta Cultura/Centro de Estudos Geográficos Anexo à Faculdade de Letras da Universidade de Coimbra, 1973.

OLIVEIRA, Maria Lêda. *A história do Brazil de Frei Vicente do Salvador: história e política no Império Português do século XVII*. 2 v. Rio de Janeiro & São Paulo: Odebrecht, Versal, 2008.

ORDENAÇÕES do Senhor Rei D. Afonso V. 5 v. Coimbra: Real Imprensa da Universidade, 1792.

ORDENAÇÕES Filipinas. 5 v. and juridical apparatus compiled by Cândido Mendes de Almeida Lisbon: Fundação Calouste Gulbenkian, 1985.

ORDENAÇÕES Manuelinas. 5 v. Lisbon: Fundação Calouste Gulbenkian, 1984.

OXFORD English Dictionary. Oxford: Oxford University Press, 2011;

http://www.oed.com.

PARKER, Geoffrey. *The Dutch Revolt*. Ithaca: Cornell University Press, 1977.

PARKER, Geoffrey. *The Grand Strategy of Philip II*. New Haven: Yale University Press, 1998.

PEDREIRA, Jorge M. "Costs and Financial Trends in the Portuguese Empire, 1415–1822." In: BETHENCOURT, Francisco and CURTO, Diogo Ramada (eds.). *Portuguese Oceanic Expansion, 1400–1800*. Cambridge: Cambridge University Press, 2007, pp. 49–87.

PEREIRA, Ana Margarida. *A Inquisição no Brasil. Aspectos da sua actuação nas capitanias do Sul (de meados do séc. XVI ao início do séc. XVIII)*. Coimbra: Fluc, 2006 (Colecção Estudos, no. 61).

PEREIRA, Franklin. *Ofícios do couro na Lisboa medieval*. Prefácio de Cláudio Torres. Lisbon: Prefácio, 2008.

PEREIRA, Isaías da Rosa. *Documentos para a história da Inquisição em Portugal*. Porto: Arquivo Histórico Dominicano Português, 1984.

PETERSON, T. Sarah. *Acquired Taste: The French Origins of Modern Cooking*. New York: Cornell University Press, 1994.

PHILLIPS, Carla Rahn. *Six Galleons for the King of Spain: Imperial Defense in the Early Seventeenth Century*. Baltimore: Johns Hopkins University Press, 1986.

PHILLIPS JR., William D. Sugar in Iberia. In: SCHWARTZ, Stuart (ed.), *Tropical Babylons: Sugar and the Making of the Atlantic World, 1450–1680*. Chapel Hill: UNC Press, 2004, pp. 27–41.

PIETERSE, W. C. and KOEN, E. M. (eds.). "Notarial Records [Deeds] in Amsterdam Relating to the Portuguese Jews in That Town up to 1639." *Studia Rosenthaliana* 1–35 (1967–2001).

POELWIJK, Arjan. *In dienste vant suyckerbacken: De Amsterdamse suikernijverheid en haar ondernemers, 1580–1630*. Hilversum: Verloren, 2003.

POHL, Hans. "Die Zuckereinfuhr nach Antwerpen durch Portugiesische Kaufleute während des 80jährigen Krieges." *Jahrbuch für Geschichte von Staat, Wirtschaft und Gesellschaft Lateinamerikas*, no. 4 (1967): 348–373.

POHL, Hans. *Die Portugiesen in Antwerpen (1567–1648)*. Wiesbaden: Steiner, 1977.

POLÓNIA, Amélia. "Vila do Conde: um porto nortenho na expansão ultramarina quinhentista." PhD dissertation, Universidade do Porto, 3 v., 1999.

POLÓNIA, Amélia. "Mestres e pilotos das carreiras ultramarinas (1596–1648)." Offprint of: *História: Revista da Faculdade de Letras da Universidade do Porto*, 2nd series, 12 (1995): 271–354.

POLÓNIA, Amélia. "Os náuticos das carreiras ultramarinas." *Oceanos – Navios e navegações, Portugal e o mar*. Lisbon, Comissão Nacional para as Comemorações dos Descobrimentos Portugueses, no. 38 (Apr.–Jun. 1999): 113–128.

POLÓNIA, Amélia. *D. Henrique*. Lisbon: Círculo de Leitores, 2005.

PONTUAL, Virgínia and MILET, Vera. "Olinda: memória e esquecimento." *Revista brasileira de estudos urbanos e regionais* 5 (2002): 39–57.

POSTHUMUS, Nicolaas Wilhelmus. *Nederlandsche prijsgeschiedenis*. V. 1. Leiden: Brill, 1943.

PRADO JR., Caio. *História econômica do Brasil*. São Paulo: Editora Brasiliense, 1978.

PRAK, Maarten. *The Dutch Republic in the Seventeenth Century. The Golden Age*. Translated by Diane Webb. Cambridge: Cambridge University Press, 2005.

PRIMEIRA visitação do Santo Officio às partes do Brasil: confissões da Bahia 1591–1592, with a preface by J. Capistrano de Abreu. Rio de Janeiro: F. Briguet, 1935.

PRIMEIRA visitação do Santo Officio às partes do Brasil: denunciações da Bahia, 1591–1593. São Paulo: Editora Paulo Prado, 1925.

PRIMEIRA visitação do Santo Ofício às partes do Brasil: denunciações e confissões de Pernambuco: 1593–1595. Introduction by José Antônio Gonsalves de Mello. Recife: Fundarpe; Diretoria de Assuntos Culturais, 1984.

PRIORE, Mary Lucy Murray Del. Retrato da América quando jovem: imagens e representações sobre o novo continente entre os séculos XVI e XVII. *Estudos Históricos* 5, no. 9 (1992): 3–13.

"PROVISÃO e regimento do consulado portuguez." In: BORGES, J.F. *Fontes, especialidade, e excellencia da administração commercial. Segundo o Código Commercial Portuguez*. Porto: Typ. Commercial Portuense, 1835.

PRYOR, John H. "Commenda: The Operation of the Contract in Long-Distance Commerce at Marseilles during the Thirteenth Century." *Journal of European Economic History* 13, no. 2 (1984): 397–440.

QUINN, Stephen and ROBERDS, William. "An Economic Explanation of the Early Bank of Amsterdam, Debasement, Bills of Exchange, and the Emergence of the First Central Bank." *Federal Reserve Bank of Atlanta. Working Paper Series*, no. 13 (Sep. 2006): 1–48.

RAMOS, Rui (ed.). *História de Portugal*. 4th ed. Lisbon: Esfera dos Livros, 2010.

RAU, Virgínia and SILVA, Maria Fernanda Gomes da. *Os manuscritos do Arquivo da Casa de Cadaval respeitantes ao Brasil*. V. 1. Coimbra: Imprensa da Universidade, 1956.

RAU, Virgínia. *O açúcar de S. Tomé no segundo quartel do século XVI*. Lisbon: Centro de Estudos de Marinha, 1971.

RAU, Virgínia. *Estudos sobre a história do sal português*. Lisbon: Editorial Presença, 1984.

RAU, Virgínia. "Aspectos do pensamento económico português durante o século XVI." In: RAU, Virgínia, *Estudos sobre história económica e social do Antigo Regime*. Introduction by João Manuel Garcia (ed.). Lisbon: Editorial Presença, 1984, pp. 83–129.

REESSE, J. J. *De suikerhandel van Amsterdam van het begin der 17de eeuw tot 1813: een b drage tot de handelsgeschiedenis des vaderlands*. Haarlem: J. L. E. I. Kleynenberg, 1908.

"REGIMENTO de 17 de dezembro de 1548 do governador geral do Brasil." In: *Documentos para a história do açúcar*. V. 1. Rio de Janeiro: Instituto do Açúcar e do Álcool, 1954, pp. 45–62.

REIS, Nestor Goulart. *Evolução urbana do Brasil, 1500–1720*. São Paulo: Pini, 2000.

REIS, Nestor Goulart. *Imagens de vilas e cidades do Brasil Colonial*. São Paulo: Edusp, 2001.

RESENDE, Garcia de. *Crónica de D. João II e miscelânea*. Introduction by Joaquim Veríssimo Serrão. Lisbon: Imprensa Nacional-Casa da Moeda, 1973.

RESENDE, Garcia de. *Cancioneiro geral*. Compiled with preface and notes by Álvaro J. da Costa Pimpão and Aida Fernanda Dias. Coimbra: Centro de Estudos Românicos (Instituto de Alta Cultura), 1973.

RÉVAH, Israël Salvador. "Pour l'histoire des nouveaux-chrétiens portugais: la rélation généalogique d'I. de M. Aboab." *Boletim Internacional de Bibliografia Luso-Brasileira* 2, no. 1 (1961): 276–312.

RÉVAH, Israël Salvador. *Uriel da Costa et les marranes de Porto*. Cours au Collège de France 1966–1972. Édition presentée et annotée par Carsten L. Wilke. Paris: Centre Culturel Calouste Gulbenkian, 2004.

RICHSHOFFER, Ambrosius. *Diário de um soldado da Companhia das Índias Ocidentais: 1629–1632*. São Paulo: Instituição Brasileira de Difusão Cultural, 1978.

RICO, Francisco. "Resolutorio de cambios de Lázaro de Tormes (hacia 1552)." *Dicenda: Cuadernos de Filología Hispánica* 7 (1987): 117–131.

RICUPERO, Rodrigo. *A formação da elite colonial: Brasil, c.1530–c.1630*. São Paulo: Alameda, 2009.

ROBERTS, Benjamin. *Sex and Drugs Before the Rock 'n' Roll. Youth Culture and Masculinity in Holland's Golden Age*. Amsterdam: Amsterdam University Press (in press).

RODRIGUES, Domingos. *Arte de cozinha*. Sintra: Colares Editora, 1995.

RODRIGUES, Teresa Ferreira. "As estruturas populacionais." In: MATTOSO, José (ed.). *História de Portugal*. V. 3. Lisbon: Editorial Estampa, 1997, pp. 179–217.

RODRÍGUEZ MOREL, Genaro. "The Sugar Economy of Española in the Sixteenth Century." In: SCHWARTZ, Stuart (ed.). *Tropical Babylons: Sugar and the Making of the Atlantic World, 1450–1680*. Chapel Hill: University of North Carolina Press, 2004, pp. 85–114.

ROOVER, Raymond Adrien de. "What is Dry Exchange? A Contribution to the Study of English Mercantilism." *Journal of Political Economy* 52, no. 2 (1944): 250–266.

ROOVER, Raymond Adrien de. *Gresham on Foreign Exchange*. Cambridge: Harvard University Press, 1949.

ROOVER, Raymond Adrien de. *L'évolution de la lettre de change*. Paris: Librairie Armand Collin, 1953.

ROOVER, Raymond de. "The Organization of Trade." In: POSTAN, M. M., RICH, E. E. and MILLER, Edward (eds.). *The Cambridge Economic History of Europe*. V. 3. Cambridge: Cambridge University Press, 1963, pp. 42–118.

ROOVER, Raymond de. "New Interpretations of the History of Banking." In: KIRSHNER, Julius (ed.). *Business, Banking and Economic Thought in Late Medieval and Early Modern Europe. Selected Studies of Raymond de Roover*. Chicago: University of Chicago Press, 1974, pp. 200–238.

ROOVER, Raymond de. "Gerard de Malynes as an Economic Writer: From Scholasticism to Mercantilism." In: KIRSHNER, Julius (ed.). *Business, Banking and Economic Thought in Late Medieval and Early Modern Europe. Selected Studies of Raymond de Roover*. Chicago: University of Chicago Press, 1974, pp. 346–66.

RUÃO, Carlos. *Arquitectura maneirista no noroeste de Portugal. Italianismo e flamenguismo*. Coimbra: Electricidade do Norte, SA, 1996.

RUSSELL-WOOD, A. J. R. *Fidalgos and Philanthropists: The Santa Casa da Misericórdia of Bahia, 1550–1755*. Berkeley: University of California Press, 1968.

SALDANHA, António Vasconcelos de. *As capitanias do Brasil. Antecedentes, desenvolvimento e extinção de um fenómeno atlântico*. Lisbon: Comissão Nacional para as Comemorações dos Descobrimentos Portugueses, 2001.

SALOMON, Herman Prins (ed.). "The 'De Pinto' Manuscript. A 17th-Century Marrano Family History." *Studia Rosenthaliana* 9, no. 1 (1975): 1–62.

SALOMON, Herman Prins. *Portrait of a New Christian. Fernão Álvares Melo 1569–1632*. Paris: Fundação Calouste Gulbenkian, 1982.

SALOMON, Herman Prins. *Os primeiros portugueses de Amesterdão: documentos do Arquivo Nacional da Torre do Tombo, 1595–1606*. Braga: [n. n.], 1983.

SALOMON, Herman Prins and SASSOON, Isaac S. D. "Introduction." In: SARAIVA, António José. *The Marrano Factory: The Portuguese Inquisition and Its New Christians*. Leiden: Brill, 2001, pp. IX–XIV, 231–341

SALVADOR, Vicente do. *História do Brasil, 1500–1627*. Revised by Capistrano de Abreu, Rodolfo Garcia and Friar Venâncio Willeke. Introduction by Aureliano Leite. Belo Horizonte: Editora Itatiaia; São Paulo: Edusp, 1982.

SAMUEL, Edgar R. "Portuguese Jews in Jacobean London." *Jewish Historical Studies* 18 (1953–1955): 171–230.

SANTIAGO FERNÁNDEZ, Javier de. "El documento monetal del vellón en el reinado de Felipe II: su ordenación y trascendencia." *Revista General de Información y Documentación* 11, no. 2 (2001): 117–140.

SANTOS FILHO, Lycurgo de Castro. *História geral da medicina brasileira*. V. 1. São Paulo: Edusp, 1991.

SARAIVA, António José. *The Marrano Factory: The Portuguese Inquisition and Its New Christians*. Translated, revised and supplemented by Herman Prins Salomon and Isaac S. D. Sassoon. Leiden: Brill, 2001.

SARAMAGO, Alfredo, "Prefácio." In: RODRIGUES, Domingos. *Arte de cozinha*. Sintra: Colares Editora, 1995, pp. 9–29.

SARAMAGO, Alfredo. *Para a história da doçaria conventual portuguesa*. Lisbon: CTT Correios, 2000.

SCHAMA, Simon. *The Embarrassment of Riches – An Interpretation of Dutch Culture in the Golden Age*. New York: Knopf/Random House, 1987.

SCHAUB, Jean-Frédéric. *Portugal na Monarquia Hispânica (1580–1640)*. Lisbon: Livros Horizonte, 2001.

SCHAUB, Jean-Frédéric. *Le Portugal au temps du comte-duc d'Olivares (1621–1640). Le conflit de juridictions comme exercice de la politique*. Madrid: Casa de Velázquez, 2001.

SCHWARTZ, Stuart B. *Sovereignty and Society in Colonial Brazil. The High Court of Bahia and its Judges, 1609–1751*. Berkeley: University of California Press, 1973.

SCHWARTZ, Stuart B. *Sugar Plantations in the Formation of Brazilian Society: Bahia, 1550–1835*. Cambridge: Cambridge University Press, 1985.

SCHWARTZ, Stuart B. "A Commonwealth within Itself. The Early Brazilian Sugar Industry, 1550–1670." In: SCHWARTZ, Stuart (ed.). *Tropical Babylons. Sugar and the Making of the Atlantic World, 1450–1680*. Chapel Hill: University of North Carolina Press, 2004, pp. 158–200.

SEGUNDA visitação do Santo Ofício às partes do Brasil pelo Inquisidor e Visitador Marcos Teixeira. Livro das Confissões e Ratificações da Bahia: 1618–1620. Introduction and notes by Eduardo d'Oliveira França and Sônia A. Siqueira. Offprint of: *Anais do Museu Paulista*, t. 17, 1963.

SEQUEIRA, G. de Matos. *Depois do terramoto. Subsídios para a história dos bairros ocidentais de Lisboa*. V. 3. Lisbon: Academia das Ciências de Lisboa, 1967 (original ed. 1922).

SERRÃO, Joaquim Veríssimo. *História de Portugal*. V. 4. Lisbon: Editorial Verbo, 1978.

SERRÃO, Joaquim Veríssimo. *O tempo dos Filipes em Portugal e no Brasil: 1580–1668. Estudos históricos*. Lisbon: Colibri, 1994.

SERRÃO, Joel and MARQUES, A. H. de Oliveira (eds.). *Nova história da expansão portuguesa*. 11 v. Lisbon: Editorial Estampa, 1986–2001.

SERRÃO, Joel and MARQUES, A. H. de Oliveira (eds.). *Nova história de Portugal*. Vv. 2–3. Lisbon: Editorial Presença, 1993–1996.

SHILLINGTON, Violet Mary and CHAPMAN, Annie Beatrice Wallis. *The Commercial Relations of England and Portugal*. New York: Burt Franklin, 1970.

SILVA, Andrée Mansuy Diniz. "Introduction and Notes." In: ANTONIL, André João. *Cultura e opulência do Brasil por suas drogas e minas*. São Paulo: Edusp, 2007.

SILVA, Francisco Ribeiro da. "Pirataria e corso sobre o Porto (aspectos seiscentistas)." Offprint of: *História: Revista da Faculdade de Letras da Universidade do Porto* 2 (1979): 1–27.

SILVA, Francisco Ribeiro da. "O corso inglês e as populações do litoral lusitano (1580–1640)." Offprint of: *Actas do Colóquio 'Santos Graça' de Etnografia Marítima. V. 3: Povoamento e administração*, Póvoa de Varzim, Câmara Municipal da Póvoa de Varzim (1985): 311–336.

SILVA, Francisco Ribeiro da. *O Porto e o seu termo (1580–1640): os homens, as instituições e o poder*. 2 v. Porto: Arquivo Histórico – Câmara Municipal do Porto, 1988.

SILVA, J. Gentil da. *Stratégie dês affaires à Lisbonne entre 1595 et 1607. Lettres marchandes dês Rodrigues d'Evora et Veiga*. Paris: Librarie Armand Colin, 1956.

SILVA, Isabel Morgado de Sousa e. "A Igreja e a Ordem de Cristo no primeiro quartel do séc. XVI: a criação das comendas novas." In: *Estudos em homenagem ao professor doutor José Marques*. V. 2. Porto: Flup, 2006, pp. 249–261.

SILVA, Luiz Augusto Rebello da. *História de Portugal nos séculos XVII e XVIII*. V. 3. Lisbon: Imprensa Nacional, 1867.

SIMONSEN, Roberto Cochrane. *História econômica do Brasil, 1500–1820*. São Paulo: Editora Nacional, 1978.

SIQUEIRA, Sônia A. *A Inquisição portuguesa e a sociedade colonial*. São Paulo: Editora Ática, 1978 (Ensaios, V. 56).

SIQUEIRA, Sônia A. "A Inquisição portuguesa e a sociedade colonial – Ação do Santo Ofício na Bahia e Pernambuco na época das visitações." Professorial dissertation, Universidade de São Paulo, 1994.

SLUITER, Engel. "Dutch-Spanish Rivalry in the Caribbean Area, 1594–1609." *The Hispanic American Historical Review* 28, no. 2 (May 1948): 165–96.

SLUITER, Engel. "Os holandeses no Brasil antes de 1621." *Revista do Instituto Arqueológico, Histórico e Geográfico Pernambucano* 46 (1967): 187–207.

SMITH, David Grant. "The Mercantile class of Portugal and Brazil in the Seventeenth Century: A Socio-Economic Study of the Merchants of Lisbon and Bahia, 1620–1690." PhD dissertation, University of Texas, Austin, 1979.

SMITH, David Grant. "Old Christian Merchants and the Foundation of the Brazil Company, 1649." *The Hispanic American Historical Review* 54, no. 2 (May 1974): 233–259.

SMITH, Woodruff D. *Consumption and the Making of Respectability, 1600–1800*. London: Routledge, 2002.

SOLIS, Duarte Gomes. *Discursos sobre los comercios de las dos Indias: donde se tratan matérias importantes de estado y guerra*. Lisbon: n. n., 1622.

SOLIS, Duarte Gomes. *Alegación en favor de la Compañia de la India Oriental: comercios ultramarinos, que de nuevo se instituyó en el reyno de Portugal*. Compiled with a preface by Moses Bensabat Amzalak. Lisbon: Editorial Império, 1955.

SOUSA, Gabriel Soares de. *Tratado descritivo do Brasil em 1587*. Edited by Francisco Adolfo de Varnhagen and revised by Leonardo Dantas Silva. Recife: Editora Massangana, 2000.

SOUSA, Francisco Clode. *Obras de referência dos museus da Madeira*. Introduction to the exhibition at Museu de Arte Sacra do Funchal and at Palácio Nacional da Ajuda, 2008; http://www.paroquiatomasaquino.com/cms2/docs/encontros_culturais/MuseusMadeira.pdf. Accessed: 28/11/2011.

SOUZA, Bernardino José. *O pau-brasil na história nacional*. With a chapter by Arthur Neiva and commentary by Oliveira Viana. Illustrated edition with 10 plates and one color illustration. São Paulo: Companhia Editora Nacional, 1939.

SOYER, François. *The Persecution of the Jews and Muslims of Portugal: King Manuel I and the End of Religious Tolerance (1496–7)*. Leiden: Brill, 2007.

SPOONER, Frank C. *Risks at Sea: Amsterdam Insurance and Maritime Europe, 1766–1780*. Cambridge: Cambridge University Press, 1983.

SPUFFORD, Peter. "Access to Credit and Capital in the Commercial Centers of Europe." In: DAVIS, Karl and LUCASSEN, Jan (eds.). *A Miracle Mirrored: The Dutch Republic in European Perspective*. Cambridge: Cambridge University Press, 1995, pp. 303–337.

STOLS, Eddy. *De Spaanse Brabanders of de Handelsbetrekkingen der Zuidelijke Nederlanden met de Iberische Wereld, 1598–1648*. Brussels: Paleis der Academién, 1971.

STOLS, Eddy. "Os mercadores flamengos em Portugal e no Brasil antes das conquistas holandesas." Offprint of: *Anais de História* 5 (1973): 9–53.

STOLS, Eddy. "The Southern Netherlands and the Foundation of the Dutch East and West Indies Companies." *Acta Historiae Neerlandicae, Studies on the History of the Netherlands* 9 (1976): 30–47

STOLS, Eddy. "Dutch and Flemish Victims of the Inquisition in Brazil." In: LECHNER, Jan (ed.). *Essays on Cultural Identity in Colonial Latin America*. Leiden: TBC, 1988, pp. 43–62.

STOLS, Eddy. "Convivências e conivências luso-flamengas na rota do açúcar brasileiro." *Ler História*, no. 32 (1997): 119–147.

STOLS, Eddy. "The Expansion of the Sugar Market in Western Europe." In: SCHWARTZ, Stuart (ed.). *Tropical Babylons: Sugar and the Making of the Atlantic World, 1450–1680*. Chapel Hill: University of North Carolina Press, 2004, pp. 237–288.

STOLS, Eddy. "Aparências, imagens e metamorfoses dos africanos na pintura e na escultura flamenga e holandesa (sécs. XV a XVII)." In: FURTADO, Júnia Ferreira (ed.). *Sons, formas, cores e movimentos na modernidade atlântica: Europa, América e África*. V. 1. São Paulo: Annablume, 2008, pp. 229–275.

STRUM, Daniel. "The Portuguese Jews and New Christians in the Sugar Trade: Managing Business Overseas – Kinship and Ethnicity Revisited (Amsterdam, Porto and Brazil, 1595–1618)." PhD dissertation, The Hebrew University of Jerusalem, 2009.

SUBRAHMANYAM, Sanjay. *O império asiático português, 1500–1700. Uma história política e económica*. Lisbon: Difel, 1995.

SUSSMAN, Nathan. "Debasements, Royal Revenues, and Inflation in France during the Hundred Years' War, 1415–1422." *The Journal of Economic History* 53, no. 1 (1993): 44–70.

SUSSMAN, Nathan. "Missing Bullion or Missing Documents: A Revision and Reappraisal of French Minting Statistics: 1385–1415." *The Journal of European Economic History* 19, no. 1 (1990): 147–162.

SWETSCHINSKI, Daniel Maurice. "The Portuguese Jewish Merchants of Seventeenth-Century Amsterdam: A Social Profile." PhD dissertation, Brandeis University, Waltham, 1979.

SWETSCHINSKI, Daniel Maurice. "Kinship and Commerce – The Foundations of Portuguese Jewish Life in 17th-Century Holland." *Studia Rosenthaliana* 13, no. 2 (1997): 52–74.

SWETSCHINSKI, Daniel M. "Conflict and Opportunity in 'Europe's other Sea': The Adventure of Caribbean Jewish Settlement." *American Jewish History* 72, no. 2 (1982): 212–240.

SWETSCHINSKI, Daniel Maurice. *Reluctant Cosmopolitans – The Portuguese Jews of Seventeenth-Century Amsterdam*. London: The Littman Library of Jewish Civilization, 2000.

SWETSCHINSKI, Daniel Maurice. "From the Middle Ages to the Golden Age, 1516–1621." In: BLOOM, J. C. H., FUCKS-MANSFELD, R. G. and SCHÖFFER, I. (eds.). *The History of the Jews in the Netherlands*. Translated by A. J. Pomerans and E. Pomerans. Oxford: The Littman Library of Jewish Civilization, 2002, pp. 44–84.

'T HART, Marjolein, JONKER, Joost and ZANDEN, Jan Luiten Van (eds.). *A Financial History of the Netherlands*. Cambridge: Cambridge University Press, 1997.

'T HART, Marjolein. "The Glorious City: Monumentalism and Public Space in Seventeenth-Century Amsterdam." In: O'BRIEN, Patrick, KEENE, Derek and 'T HART, Marjolein (eds.). *Urban Achievement in Early Modern Europe: Golden Ages in Antwerp, Amsterdam, and London*. Cambridge: Cambridge University Press, 2001, pp. 128–150.

TANNAHILL, Reay. *Food in History*. New York: Crown, 1989.

TAVARES, Maria José Pimenta Ferro. *Os judeus em Portugal no século XV*. Lisbon: Universidade Nova de Lisboa, 1982–1984.

TAVARES, Maria José Pimenta Ferro. "A moeda de D. João II aos Filipes (1481–1640)." In: SARAIVA, José Hermano (ed.). *História de Portugal*. V. 4. Lisbon: Editorial Verbo, 1983, pp. 273–289.

TAVARES, Maria José Pimenta Ferro. *Pobreza e morte em Portugal na Idade Média*. Lisbon: Presença, 1989.

TAVARES, Paulino Mota. *Mesa, doces e amores no séc. XVII português*. Preface by Maria José Azevedo Santos. Sintra: Colares Editora, 1999.

TAWNEY, R. H. "Dr. Thomas Wilson." In: WILSON, Thomas, *A Discourse upon Usury by Way of*

Dialogue and Orations, for the Better Variety and More Delight of All Those that Shall Read this Treatise (1572). London: G. Bell & Sons, 1925.

TEENSMA, Benjamin. "Descrição da costa do Brasil na região de Pernambuco." In: GALINDO, Marco (ed.). *Viver e morrer no Brasil holandês*. Recife: Massangana, 2005, pp. 187–223.

TEIXEIRA, Dante Luiz Martins. "A alegoria dos continentes de Jan van Kessel o Velho (1626–1679): uma visão seiscentista da fauna dos quatro cantos do mundo." In: FERRÃO, Cristina and SOARES, José Paulo Monteiro (eds.). *Brasil holandês*. V. 1. 1st ed. Petrópolis: Index, 2002, pp. 1–143.

TENENTI, Alberto. *Naufrages, corsaires et assurance maritimes à Venise, 1592–1609*. Paris: S.E.V.P.E.N, 1959.

THOMAZ, Luís Filipe and ALVES, Jorge Santos. "Da cruzada ao Quinto Império." In: BETHENCOURT, Francisco and CURTO, Diogo Ramada (eds.). *A memória da nação*. Lisbon: Livraria Sá da Costa Editora, 1991, pp. 81–164.

THOMAZ, Luís Filipe. *De Ceuta a Timor*. Lisbon: Difel, 1994.

TINHORÃO, José Ramos. *As festas no Brasil colonial*. São Paulo: Editora 34, 2000.

TRASLADO autentico de todos os privilégios concedidos pelos Reys destes Reynos, & Senhorios de Portugal aos Officiaes, & Familiares do Santo Officio da Inquisição. Lisbon: Miguel Manescal, 1691.

TRILLO SAN JOSÉ, Carmen. "Los aranceles de la ciudad de Granada al final de la Edad Media." *Arqueología y Territorio Medieval: Revista de arqueología del área de historia medieval*, no. 3 (1996): 253–272.

TUCCI CARNEIRO, Maria Luiza. *Preconceito racial: Portugal e Brasil-Colônia*. São Paulo: Editora Brasiliense, 1983.

UCHA, José Martin et al. "Apicum: gênese dos campos arenosos e degradação dos manguezais em dois municípios baianos." *E.T.C. – Educação, Tecnologia e Cultura: Revista do Centro Federal de Educação Tecnológica da Bahia* 3, no. 2 (2004): 26–27.

UITTERDIJK, J. Nanninga. *Een Kamper handelshuis te Lissabon, 1572–1594, handelscorrespondentie, rekeningen en bescheiden*. Zwolle: De erven J. J. Tijl, 1904.

UNGER, Richard W. *Dutch Shipbuilding before 1800: Ships and Guilds*. Amsterdam: Van Gorcum, 1978.

UNGER, Richard W. *The Ship in the Medieval Economy, 600–1600*. Montreal: McGill-Queen's University Press, 1980.

UNIVERSIDADE FEDERAL DA BAHIA. *Evolução física de Salvador*. Salvador: Centro de Estudos da Arquitetura na Bahia/Centro Editorial e Didático da UFBA, 1979.

VAINFAS, Ronaldo. "Moralidades brasílicas: deleites sexuais e linguagem erótica na sociedade escravista." In: NOVAIS, *História da vida privada no Brasil*. V. 1. São Paulo: Companhia das Letras, 1997, pp. 221–273.

VALLADARES, Rafael. *A conquista de Lisboa: violência militar e comunidade política em Portugal, 1578–1583*. Alfragide: Texto Editora, 2010.

VARNHAGEN, Francisco Adolfo de. *História geral do Brasil*. T. 1. 5th complete ed. São Paulo: Edições Melhoramentos, 1956.

VARNHAGEN, Francisco Adolfo de. *História geral do Brasil*. T. 2. 4th complete ed. São Paulo: Edições Melhoramentos, 1948.

VASCONCELOS, Luís Mendes de. *Do sítio de Lisboa, diálogos (1608)*. Edited and annotated by José da Felicidade Alves. Lisbon: Livros Horizonte, 1990.

VAZ, J. Ferraro. *Livro das moedas de Portugal – Preçário*. Braga: Livraria Cruz, 1972.

VELEZ, Manuela Sobral Blanco. "As linhas marítimo-comerciais portuguesas no Oriente (séc. XVI–meados do séc. XVII)." In: ALBUQUERQUE, Luís de and GUERREIRO, Inácio (eds.). *II Seminário internacional de história indo-portuguesa: actas*. Lisbon: Instituto de Investigação Científica Tropical, 1985, pp. 73–99.

VEEN, Ernest van. "VOC Strategies in the Far East (1605–1640)." *Bulletin of Portuguese/Japanese Studies* 3 (Dec. 2001): 85–105.

VIEIRA, Alberto. "Sugar Islands: the Sugar Economy of Madeira and the Canaries, 1450–1650." In: SCHWARTZ, Stuart (ed.). *Tropical Babylons: Sugar and the Making of the Atlantic World, 1450–1680*. Chapel Hill: University of North Carolina Press, 2004, pp. 42–84.

VIEIRA, Alberto. *Açúcares, meles e aguardente no quotidiano Madeirense*. Funchal: CEHA Biblioteca Digital, 2004; http://www.madeira-edu.pt/Portals/31/CEHA/bdigital/avieira/doces.pdf. Accessed: 30/09/2010.

VIEIRA, Alberto. *A caixa de açúcar na Madeira*. Funchal: CEHA Biblioteca Digital, 2009; http://www.madeira-edu.pt/Portals/31/CEHA/bdigital/hsugar-caixa.pdf. Accessed: 28/11/2011.

VITERBO, Francisco Marques de Sousa. "Artes industriaes e industrias portuguezas. A indústria Sacharina (Primeira série)." Offprint of: *O Instituto: Revista científica e literária* 55 (1908).

VITERBO, Fr. Joaquim de Santa Rosa de. *Elucidario das palavras, termos e frases que em Portugal antigamente se usaram e que hoje regularmente se ignoram*. T. 1. Lisbon: A. J. Fernandes Lopes, 1865.

VLESSING, Odette. "New Light on the Earliest History of Amsterdam Portuguese Jews." In: MICHMAN, Jozeph (ed.). *Dutch Jewish History*. V. 3. Jerusalem: The Institute for Research on Dutch Jewry, 1993, pp. 43–73.

VLESSING, Odette. "The Portuguese-Jewish Merchant Community in Seventeenth-Century Amsterdam." In: LESGER, Clé and NOORDEGRAAF, Leo (eds.). *Entrepreneurs and Entrepreneurship in Early Modern Times – Merchant and Industrialist within the Orbit of the Dutch Staple Market – Hollandse Historische Reeks*. V. 24. The Hague: Stichting Hollandse Historische Reeks, 1996, pp. 223–243.

VLESSING, Odette. "Thomas Nunes Pina." In: BETHLEHEM, J., HIEGENTLICH, F. and HOOGEWOUD, F. J. (eds.). *Gids voor onderzoek naar de geshiedenis van de joden in Nederland*. Amsterdam: Schiphouwer en Brinkman, 2000, pp. 115–125.

VLESSING, Odette. "De Portugezen in de Gouden Eeuw II." *Habinjan /De opbouw: Orgaan van de Portugees-Israëlietische gemeente te Amsterdam* 44, no. 1 (Sep. 1992): 16–24.

VRIES, Jan de. *A economia da Europa numa época de crise (1600–1750)*. Lisbon: Publicações Dom Quixote, 1983.

VRIES, Jan de. *The Industrious Revolution: Consumer Behavior and the Household Economy, 1650 to the Present*. New York: Cambridge University Press, 2008.

VRIES, Jan de and WOUDE, A. van der. *The First Modern Economy – Success, Failure, and Perseverance of the Dutch Economy, 1500–1815*. Cambridge: Cambridge University Press, 1997.

WALLERSTEIN, Immanuel. *El moderno sistema mundial. La agricultura capitalista y los Orígenes de la economía-mundo europea en el siglo XVI*. V. 1. Madrid: Siglo XXI Editores, 1991.

WEE, Herman van der. *The Growth of the Antwerp Market and the European Economy (Fourteenth–Sixteenth Centuries)*. 2 v. The Hague: Martinus Nijhoff Publishers, 1963.

WEE, Herman van der. "The Influence of Banking and the Rise of Capitalism in North-West Europe." In: THEICHOVA, A., HENTENRYK, G. K. and ZIEGLER, D. (eds.). *Banking, Trade and Industry: Europe, America and Asia from the Thirteenth to the Twentieth Century*. Cambridge: Cambridge University Press, 1997, pp. 173–188.

WEIMANN, Gabriel. "On the Importance of Marginality: One More Step into the Two-Step Flow of Communication." *The American Sociological Review* 47, no. 6 (Dec. 1982): 764–773.

WILSON, Thomas. *A Discourse upon Usury by Way of Dialogue and Orations, for the Better Variety and More Delight of All Those that Shall Read this Treatise (1572)*. Historical introduction by R. H. Tawney. London: G. Bell & Sons, Ltd, 1925.

WINKELMAN, P. H. *Bronnen voor de geschiedenis van de Nederlandse oostzeehandel in de zeventinde eeuw Deel II, Amsterdamse bevrachtingscontracten van notaris Jan Franssen Bruyningh 1593–1600* (R.G.P. grote serie CLXI, 's-Gravenhage). Leiden: Martinus Nijhoff, 1977.

WOLTERS, Willem G. "Managing Multiple Currencies with Units of Account: Netherlands India 1600–1800." Paper contributed to the XVI International Economic History Congress of the International Economic History Association, Helsinki, Finland, August 21–25, 2006, pp. 1–31; http://www.helsinki.fi/iehc2006/papers2/Wolters.pdf

YUN CASALILLA, Bartolomé. *Marte contra Minerva: el precio del Imperio Español, c. 1450–1600*. Barcelona: Crítica, 2004.

ZWARTS, Jacob. *De eerste rabbijnen en synagogen van Amsterdam: naar archivalische bronnen*. Amsterdam: M. Hertzberger, 1929.